LIBRARY OF SECOND TEMPLE STUDIES

101

formerly the Journal for the Study of the Pseudepigrapha Supplement Series

Editor
Lester L. Grabbe

Founding Editor
James H. Charlesworth

Editorial Board
Randall D. Chesnutt, Jan Willem van Henten, Judith M. Lieu,
Steven Mason, James R. Mueller, Loren T. Stuckenbruck,
James C. VanderKam

Themes and Texts, Exodus and Beyond

Essays in Honour of Larry J. Perkins

Edited by

Robert J. V. Hiebert
Trinity Western University

Don Dongshin Chang
Northwest Seminary and College at the Associated Canadian
Theological Schools of Trinity Western University

Jonathan Numada
Northwest Seminary and College at the Associated Canadian
Theological Schools of Trinity Western University

Kyung S. Baek
Trinity Western University

LONDON • NEW YORK • OXFORD • NEW DELHI • SYDNEY

A Tribute to Larry J. Perkins

With Contributions by Scholars of the Septuagint and Related Literature:

Martin G. Abegg Jr. • Kyung S. Baek • Dirk Büchner • Karlena Cagnoli
Don Dongshin Chang • Stephen Anthony Cummins • Craig A. Evans
Marie J. Fortin • Robert J. V. Hiebert • Joel Korytko • Wolfgang Kraus
Jean Maurais • Jonathan Numada • Albert Pietersma • Daniela Scialabba
James M. Scott • Emanuel Tov • Christine Waring

T&T CLARK

Bloomsbury Publishing Plc, 50 Bedford Square, London, WC1B 3DP, UK
Bloomsbury Publishing Inc, 1385 Broadway, New York, NY 10018, USA
Bloomsbury Publishing Ireland, 29 Earlsfort Terrace, Dublin 2, D02 AY28, Ireland

BLOOMSBURY, T&T CLARK and the T&T Clark logo
are trademarks of Bloomsbury Publishing Plc

First published in Great Britain 2024
This paperback edition published 2025

Copyright © Robert J. V. Hiebert, Jonathan Numada, Don Dongshin Chang, Kyung S. Baek
and contributors, 2024

Robert J. V. Hiebert, Jonathan Numada, Don Dongshin Chang, Kyung S. Baek have asserted their right
under the Copyright, Designs and Patents Act, 1988, to be identified as editors of this work.

All rights reserved. No part of this publication may be: i) reproduced or transmitted in
any form, electronic or mechanical, including photocopying, recording or by means of any
information storage or retrieval system without prior permission in writing from the publishers;
or ii) used or reproduced in any way for the training, development or operation of artificial
intelligence (AI) technologies, including generative AI technologies. The rights holders expressly
reserve this publication from the text and data mining exception as per Article 4(3) of the
Digital Single Market Directive (EU) 2019/790.

Bloomsbury Publishing Plc does not have any control over, or responsibility for, any third-party websites
referred to or in this book. All internet addresses given in this book were correct at the time of going to
press. The author and publisher regret any inconvenience caused if addresses have changed or sites have
ceased to exist, but can accept no responsibility for any such changes.

A catalogue record for this book is available from the British Library.

Library of Congress Cataloging-in-Publication Data
Names: Hiebert, Robert J. V. (Robert James Victor), editor.
Title: Themes and texts, Exodus and beyond : essays in honour of Larry J. Perkins /
edited by Robert J. V. Hiebert, Trinity Western University, Don Dongshin Chang, Northwest Seminary and
College at the Associated Canadian Theological Schools of Trinity Western University, Jonathan Numada,
Northwest Seminary and College at the Associated Canadian Theological Schools of Trinity Western
University, Kyung S. Baek, Trinity Western University.
Description: London ; New York : T&T Clark, 2024. |
Series: The library of second temple studies | Includes bibliographical references and index. |
Summary: "Examines the book of Exodus across four topics: (1) The Septuagint, (2) Exodus in the
Septuagint, (3) Exodus in Second Temple Jewish Literature, and (3) Exodus in the New Testament and
Christianity"-- Provided by publisher.
Identifiers: LCCN 2023028494 | ISBN 9780567705488 (hb) | ISBN 9780567705525
(pb) | ISBN 9780567705518 (ebook) | ISBN 9780567705495 (epdf)
Subjects: LCSH: Bible. Exodus--Criticism, interpretation, etc. | Bible.
Exodus--Examinations, questions, etc. | Jewish religious literature--History and criticism. |
Bible. Exodus. Greek--Versions--Septuagint. | Bible. Exodus--Relation to the New
Testament. | Bible. New Testament--Relation to Exodus. | Perkins, Larry J. (Larry James), 1948-
Classification: LCC BS1245.52 .T47 2024 | DDC 222/.1206--dc23/eng/20230814
LC record available at https://lccn.loc.gov/2023028494

ISBN:	HB:	978-0-5677-0548-8
	PB:	978-0-5677-0552-5
	ePDF:	978-0-5677-0549-5
	eBook:	978-0-5677-0551-8

Series: Library of Second Temple Studies, volume 101

Typeset by Trans.form.ed SAS

For product safety related questions contact productsafety@bloomsbury.com.

To find out more about our authors and books visit www.bloomsbury.com
and sign up for our newsletters.

Contents

List of Contributors ix
List of Figures xv

INTRODUCTION
Robert J. V. Hiebert, Don Dongshin Chang, Jonathan Numada,
and Kyung S. Baek 1

PART I:
THE SEPTUAGINT

Chapter 1
Emanuel Tov
The Number of Text Branches of the Scripture Text 11

Chapter 2
Dirk Büchner
Namer, Curser, Blasphemer: Leviticus 24:10–16 according to the Septuagint
and the Targums 22

Chapter 3
Christine Waring
Flying Sickles Sound Scarier:
The Role of Harvest as Judgment Metaphor in the LXX as a Foundation
for the Translation of מְגִלָּה as Δρέπανος in Zechariah 5:1–4 41

Chapter 4
Albert Pietersma
From the Exodus to the Exile:
A Commentary on the Greek Text-As-Produced Psalm 80 52

PART II:
EXODUS IN THE SEPTUAGINT

Chapter 5
ROBERT J. V. HIEBERT
In and Out of Egypt: Genesis as Prelude to the Exodus Story ... 71

Chapter 6
KARLENA M. CAGNOLI
The Tree of the Sacred Text: Reflections on Greek Exodus
in Dialogue with Antoine Berman ... 89

Chapter 7
JOEL F. KORYTKO
Slaves to the Septuagint: Applying Greek Legal Terminology
for Slaves to Exodus 21:7 ... 104

Chapter 8
JEAN MAURAIS
From Exodus to Deuteronomy? A Study on Interdependence
in the Greek Pentateuch ... 121

Chapter 8
DON DONGSHIN CHANG
The Sojourner in Exodus and Beyond:
Theological Conceptualization of *Gēr* in the Old Testament ... 143

PART III:
EXODUS IN THE SECOND TEMPLE JEWISH LITERATURE

Chapter 9
MARTIN G. ABEGG, JR.
The Text of Exodus in the Qumran Corpus ... 159

Chapter 10
JONATHAN NUMADA
Prayer and Peace in 3 Maccabees 2:2–20:
Trusting Precedent for Deliverance or Uttering Threats
against the King? ... 174

PART IV:
EXODUS IN THE NEW TESTAMENT AND CHRISTIANITY

Chapter 11
CRAIG A. EVANS
Mark's Incipit in Early Amulets and the Question of Its Original Reading   189

Chapter 12
MARIE J. FORTIN
Combined Themes of a Composite Citation:
Exodus and Wilderness in Mark 1:1–3   216

Chapter 13
JAMES M. SCOTT
Jesus' Performative Utterances and the Construction
of the Future Anterior   233

Chapter 14
KYUNG S. BAEK
Matthew's Rewriting and Mosaic Discourse   249

Chapter 15
STEPHEN ANTHONY CUMMINS
Deliverance into the Coming Kingdom of God:
Exodus Motifs in 1 Thessalonians   266

Chapter 17
WOLFGANG KRAUS
On the Reception of Exodus 24 and 25 in the Epistle to the Hebrews   279

Chapter 17
DANIELA SCIALABBA
Exodus and *egressio*:
Observations on Biblical Terminology in the Latin Language   298

Bibliography of Larry J. Perkins   311

Index of References   330
Index of Authors   353

Contributors

Martin G. Abegg, Jr., PhD (Hebrew Union) is Emeritus Professor at Trinity Western University. He is coauthor of *The Dead Sea Scrolls Bible* (Harper, 1999), *The Dead Sea Scrolls: A New Translation* (Harper, 2005), and general editor of *The Dead Sea Scrolls Editions* (Brill, 2021–). His research interests are the Dead Sea Scrolls and texts and versions of the Hebrew Bible.

Kyung S. Baek, PhD (Manchester) teaches at Trinity Western University and other theological institutions. In addition, he is the Director for the Dead Sea Scrolls Institute at Trinity Western University and Director of Biblical and Theological Studies at Pacific Life Bible College. He is coauthor of *Leviticus at Qumran: Text and Interpretation* (Brill, 2017), as well as a coeditor of *Reading the Bible in Ancient Traditions and Modern Editions: Studies in Memory of Peter W. Flint* (SBL, 2017), *The War Scroll, War and Peace in the Dead Sea Scrolls and Related Literature* (Brill, 2016), and *Celebrating the Dead Sea Scrolls: A Canadian Collection* (SBL, 2011). His research interests are the Dead Sea Scrolls, the Gospels, the New Testament's use of the Old Testament, and biblical interpretation.

Dirk L. Büchner, DLitt (Stellenbosch) is Professor at Trinity Western University. He is a fellow of the John William Wevers Institute of Septuagint Studies and treasurer of the International Organization for Septuagint and Cognate Studies. He is working on the *Leuitikon* volume of the SBL Commentary on the Septuagint and has edited a volume of collected essays by contributors to the series, entitled *The SBL Commentary on the Septuagint, an Introduction* (SBL, 2017). His areas of teaching and research are Hebrew Bible, Septuagint lexicography, Aramaic studies, Hebrew grammar, and religion and science.

Karlena M. Cagnoli, MA (Trinity Western University) is a graduate student specializing in LXX Studies at the Associated Canadian Theological Schools of Trinity Western University. This article "The Tree of the Sacred Text" is her first publication. She is currently in the final stages of her thesis ("'Trials of the Foreign': An Investigation of the Septuagint of Genesis 49:1–12"). Her research interests include the Greek Pentateuch, the Book of the Twelve in the Septuagint, Second Temple Judaism, and Translation Studies and its potential application to ancient Jewish/Christian scripture and Islamic texts. A native of Vancouver, B.C., she now lives in Italy where she teaches Biblical Hebrew, Biblical Greek, biblical interpretation, and studies in the Gospels.

Don Dongshin Chang, PhD (Manchester) is Associate Professor at Northwest Seminary and College at the Associated Canadian Theological Schools of Trinity Western University. He is a Research Associate in the Dead Sea Scrolls Institute and a fellow of John William Wevers Institute for Septuagint Studies. He is the author of *Phinehas, the Sons of Zadok, and Melchizedek: Priestly Covenant in Late Second Temple Texts* (T&T Clark, 2016) and has contributed to *The War Scroll, War and Peace in the Dead Sea Scrolls and Related Literature* (Brill, 2016) and *T&T Clark Encyclopedia of Second Temple Judaism*. Currently, he is co-authoring *1 Maccabees: A Handbook on the Greek Text* (BHLXX) and *1 Maccabees* (SBLCS). His research interests focus on 1 Maccabees, Priestly Covenant, Sojourner in the Old Testament, the Septuagin, and the New Testament, and biblical interpretation.

Stephen Anthony Cummins, DPhil (Oxford) is Professor at Trinity Western University. He is coeditor of *Acts of Interpretation; Scripture, Theology, and Culture* (Eerdmans, 2018) and has authored many articles: "Scripture, Theology, and Culture: Considerations and Contributions" (Eerdmans, 2018); "Newness of Life: Gospel, Church, and the Common Good in Romans 12–13" (Fortress, 2018); "Paul, Exile, and the Economy of God" (InterVarsity Press, 2017); "Torah, Jesus, and the Kingdom of God in the Gospel of Mark" (Eerdmans, 2016); "John the Baptist" (InterVarsity Press, 2013); "Divine Life and Corporate Christology: God, Messiah Jesus, and the Covenant Community in Paul" (Eerdmans, 2007); and "Integrated Scripture, Embedded Empire: the Ironic Interplay of 'King' Herod, John and Jesus in Mark 6.1-44" (T&T Clark, 2006). His main research interests focus on Jesus and the Gospels, Paul, and the theological interpretation of Scripture.

Craig A. Evans, PhD (Claremont), DHabil (Budapest), is the John Bisagno Distinguished Professor of Christian Origins at Houston Christian University. He is the author of numerous publications including *Jesus and His Contemporaries* (Brill, 1995), *Mark* (Thomas Nelson, 2001), *Jesus and the Ossuaries* (Baylor, 2003), *Matthew* (Cambridge, 2012), and *Jesus and the Manuscripts* (Hendrickson, 2020). He is also editor of *The Encyclopedia of the Historical Jesus* (Routledge, 2008). Evans has appeared in many documentaries and news programs on the historical Jesus and Christian origins and has lectured at Cambridge, Oxford, Yale, and other universities and museums. His main interests focus on Jesus, the Gospels, the Dead Sea Scrolls, and archaeology.

Marie-Josée Fortin, PhD cand. (Union School of Theology) is an affiliated professor at Northwest Seminary. She has published "La neurologie au service de la théologie et l'odeur d'un sacrifice" (forthcoming), "Hide or Seek: Perseverance in the Composite Citations of Hebrews 10:37-38," in *Reading Hebrews and 1 Peter from Global Perspectives* (LNTS, forthcoming), and articles in *La Revue Théologique de SEMBEQ* (2020–present). Her main research interests focus on the composition of biblical narrative texts, New Testament's use of the Old Testament, Jewish and

Greco-Roman rhetoric and culture, hermeneutics, and the relation between neurology and theology. She is currently undergoing a comparative study of composite citations in narrative and epistolary texts as part of her PhD studies.

Robert J. V. Hiebert, PhD (Toronto) is the Director of the John William Wevers Institute for Septuagint Studies and Professor at the Associated Canadian Theological Schools of Trinity Western University. He also serves as the President of the International Organization for Septuagint and Cognate Studies and as Joint-Editor-in-Chief of the Society of Biblical Literature Commentary on the Septuagint (SBLCS) series. He is the author of *The "Syrohexaplaric" Psalter* (Scholars Press, 1989) and numerous papers, essays, and book chapters in the area of Septuagint and cognate studies. He is the editor of *"Translation Is Required": The Septuagint in Retrospect and Prospect* (SBL, 2010) and *The Old Greek Psalter: Studies in Honour of Albert Pietersma* (Sheffield Academic Press, 2001). Currently, he is preparing the critical edition of Greek 4 Maccabees for the Göttingen Septuaginta series and a commentary on Septuagint Genesis for the SBLCS series. His research focuses primarily on the books of Genesis, Psalms, and 4 Maccabees.

Joel Korytko, DPhil (Oxford) teaches at Trinity Western University. He is a Fellow of the John William Wevers Institute for Septuagint Studies. In addition to developing curriculum, he works as an academic mentor in competency based theological education at Northwest Seminary and College. He is the coauthor of *The Society of Biblical Literature Commentary on the Septuagint: Exodus* (SBL Press, forthcoming), and the author of an upcoming monograph on the Septuagint version of Exodus. His article "The Death Penalty in OG Exodus in Light of Graeco-Egyptian Legal Formulations" won the Wevers Prize in Septuagint Studies in 2020. His research focuses on the Septuagint, New Testament's use of the Old Testament, and the Hebrew Bible.

Wolfgang Kraus, DrTheol DHabil (Erlangen/Nuremberg) is Professor Emeritus of New Testament Studies with a chair at the University of the Saarland. In addition, he is Research Associate at the University of Pretoria and the Institut für Septuaginta und Biblische Textforschung at the Kirchliche Hochschule Wuppertal. He is also Co-Director at the Institut für christlich-jüdische Studien und Beziehungen, Augustana-Hochschule Neuendettelsau. He is Co-Editor-in-chief of *Septuaginta Deutsch* and of *Handbuch zur Septuaginta/Handbook of the Septuagint*. He coedited *"...mehr als Steine. Synagogen-Gedenkband Bayern"* (5 vols.) and is author of *Das Volk Gottes. Zur Grundlegung der Ekklesiologie bei Paulus*. His research interests focus on the New Testament in the context of ancient Judaism, Septuagint and its reception, and Jewish-Christian dialogue.

Jean Maurais, PhD (McGill) is Vice-Dean and Professor of Old Testament at the Faculté de Théologie Évangélique at Acadia University in Montreal, Canada. He is also an adjunct professor at Trinity Western University and fellow of the John William

Wevers Institute for Septuagint Studies. He is the author of *Characterizing Old Greek Deuteronomy as an Ancient Translation* (Brill, 2022). His research interests include the Septuagint, the books of Deuteronomy and Jeremiah, translation theory, as well as Hebrew Bible textual criticism.

Jonathan Numada, PhD (McMaster Divinity) is Academic Dean and Assistant Professor at Northwest Seminary and College at the Associated Canadian Theological Schools of Trinity Western University, and Research Fellow at the John William Wevers Institute for Septuagint Studies. His research and publications focus on the areas of Gospel studies, Septuagint, and Hellenistic Judaism.

Albert Pietersma, PhD (Toronto) is Professor Emeritus of Septuagint and Hellenistic Greek at the University of Toronto. He is the joint editor, with Benjamin G. Wright, of *A New English Translation of the Septuagint*.

Daniela Scialabba, PhD (Strasbourg) is Associate Professor at the Pontifical Biblical Institute of Rome and Scientific Coordinator of the *Historical and Theological Lexicon of the Septuagint* and researcher at FSCIRE. She was a researcher and teacher (ANR project, "Pluritext") at the Faculty of Catholic Theology of the University of Strasbourg. Since 2012, she has been a member of the editorial board of the *Historical and Theological Lexicon of the Septuagint* (Mohr Siebeck). In addition, she collaborates in several international projects on the study of the Septuagint. Her research concerns the Old Testament and Hebrew literature in Greek. She has published *Creation and Salvation: Models of Relationship between the God of Israel and the Nations in the Book of Jonah, in Psalm 33 (MT and LXX) and in the Novel 'Joseph and Aseneth'* (Mohr Siebeck, 2019), which received the Prize "Alberigo 2018" of the European Academy of Religion (FSCIRE, Bologna). In addition, she is a member of the executive committee of the International Organization for Septuagint and Cognate Studies (IOSCS) and of the scientific editorial board of the international series Septuagint and Cognate Studies (SCS).

James M. Scott, DrTheol (Tübingen) is Professor at Trinity Western University. He is the author of *Bacchius Judaeus: A Denarius Commemorating Pompey's victory over Judea* (Vandenhoeck & Ruprecht, 2015), *On Earth as in Heaven: The Restoration of Sacred Space and Sacred Time in the* Book of Jubilees (Brill, 2004), *Geography in Early Judaism and Christianity: The Book of Jubilees* (Cambridge, 2002), *2 Corinthians* (Hendrickson, 1998), *Paul and the Nations: The Old Testament and Jewish Background of Paul's Mission to the Nations with Special Reference to the Destination of Galatians* (Mohr-Siebeck, 1995), and *Adoption as Sons of God: An Exegetical Investigation into the Background of UIOQESIA in the Pauline Corpus* (Mohr-Siebeck, 1992). He has edited *Restoration: Old Testament, Jewish, and Christian Conceptions* (Brill, 2001) and *Exile: Old Testament, Jewish, and Christian Conceptions* (Brill, 1997).

Emanuel Tov, PhD (Hebrew University) is J. L. Magnes Professor Emeritus of Bible at the Hebrew University. He has published many monographs on the textual criticism of the Hebrew Bible, the Septuagint, and the Qumran scrolls. His latest book is *Textual Criticism of the Hebrew Bible*, revised and expanded fourth edition (Fortress, 2022). He was the Editor-in-Chief of the Dead Sea Scrolls publication project and of the annual *Textus* (1984–90; 2017–22).

Christine Waring is currently a graduate student in the biblical studies program at the Associated Canadian Theological Schools of Trinity Western University. Her primary focus is on New Testament studies.

Figures

12.1.	The beginning of Mark in Codex Vaticanus (B)	190
12.2.	The beginning of Mark in miniscule 33 (the "queen of the miniscules")	190
12.3.	The beginning of Mark in Codex Koridethi (Θ)	191
12.4.	The beginning of Mark in Codex 28	191
12.5.	The beginning of Mark in Codex Sinaiticus (א)	192
12.6.	The beginning of Mark in Codex Sangallensis (n)	193
12.7.	The beginning of Mark in Peshitta Yohanna MS C	194
12.8.	The beginning of Mark in an illustrated Coptic ms	194
12.9.	The beginning of Mark in *Novum Instrumentum omne* (1516). Courtesy of the Dunham Bible Museum, Houston Baptist University	195
12.10.	P.Oxy. LXXVI 5073. Courtesy of the Egypt Exploration Society and Imaging Papyri Project, Oxford	200

Introduction

Robert J. V. Hiebert, Don Dongshin Chang, Jonathan Numada, and Kyung S. Baek

The present volume is edited by members associated with the John William Wevers Institute for Septuagint Studies and the Associated Canadian Theological Schools, both located on the campus of Trinity Western University in Langley, BC, Canada. This monograph includes contributions from an international team of scholars who specialize in Septuagint studies, many of whom are well-known in their fields. As members of the Wevers Institute, we are delighted to present this collection of essays written in tribute to the career and scholarship of Dr. Larry J. Perkins.

Larry J. Perkins is Emeritus Professor of Biblical Studies and President Emeritus at Northwest Seminary and College in Langley, British Columbia, Canada. His educational resume includes a Bachelor of Arts (Honours) in Classical Studies from the University of British Columbia, a Bachelor of Arts in Theology from Oxford University, a Master of Arts in Near Eastern Studies from the University of Toronto, and another Master of Arts from Oxford University, a PhD in Septuagint Studies from the University of Toronto, and a Master of Education in Higher Education Administration from the University of British Columbia. The diversity of his educational pursuits reflects a breadth in research interests in the areas of Septuagint, Hebrew Bible, New Testament, and Theology more generally.

On first impression, one might think that Larry's major contribution to theological education lies in the field of academic administration. This impression would be understandable, given that he was the Academic Dean of Northwest for 19 years (1980–1999). It was during this period that Larry and the Northwest team were instrumental in establishing a consortium of seminaries that came to be known as the Associated Canadian Theological Schools of Trinity Western University (ACTS of TWU). Larry also served as the president of Northwest for a further 11 years from 2000 to 2011, while concurrently taking on the duties of Academic Dean of ACTS from 1996 to 2004. Although he "retired" from full-time teaching in 2015, Larry has remained active in both academic and ecclesial service. He has served as the co-founder and director of Northwest Seminary and College's Korean Master of Arts, Master of Divinity, and Doctor of Ministry in Global Christian Leadership programs that were launched in 2015. Larry also—as a "retired" faculty member—supported the development of Northwest's competency-based theological education programs, a contribution now widely recognized as a major innovation in seminary training. As an emeritus professor he continues to teach and mentor graduate theses in programs at ACTS, Northwest, and TWU's Religious Studies department.

Larry's record of scholarship is as impressive as his career in academic leadership. He is a founding member of TWU's Septuagint Institute, established in 2005, and later renamed the John William Wevers Institute for Septuagint Studies in 2011, one of the few research institutes in the world dedicated to the study of the Septuagint. As of August 2022, Larry has written or edited four books and translated the book of Exodus for the *New English Translation of the Septuagint* (NETS). He has also published forty-one peer-reviewed articles and book chapters, seventeen book reviews in peer-reviewed journals, contributed three entries to the *Anchor Bible Dictionary*, and presented twenty-five papers at conferences of the International Organization for Septuagint and Cognate Studies, the Society of Biblical Literature, and the Canadian Society of Biblical Studies. In addition, he has written 119 posts on his personal website, most of which are academic treatments of topics in biblical studies. Among his continuing research endeavours is a commentary on the Septuagint of Exodus that will appear in the Society of Biblical Literature Commentary on the Septuagint series.

As can be seen by the contributions to this volume by scholars such as Martin G. Abegg, Jr., Dirk Büchner, Stephen Anthony Cummins, Craig A. Evans, Robert J. V. Hiebert, Wolfgang Kraus, Albert Pietersma, and Emanuel Tov, Larry is a respected member of his generation of Septuagint and New Testament specialists. Furthermore, Larry has been instrumental in the development of a younger generation of scholars and graduate students, having supervised fifteen master's theses during his career and either taught as students or directly supported the careers of many other young and emerging scholars. Some of these have contributed essays to this volume, namely Don Dongshin Chang, Marie J. Fortin, Joel Korytko, Jean Maurais, Jonathan Numada, and Christine Waring. Others with whom Larry has worked in theological education—be they scholarly colleagues or former students—include the likes of Donald A. Carson, Stanley E. Porter, Brian Rapske, and Steven Runge.

Larry is best known as a scholar for his work on the Septuagint text of Exodus, but he has also published in the area of New Testament studies, particularly the Gospel of Mark. The essays in the present volume are arranged according to a canonical and chronological sequence that reflects these interests.

The contributions in Part I of this volume, entitled "The Septuagint," deal with issues that are important in the field of Septuagint studies such as textual criticism and translation technique. Emanuel Tov's essay entitled "The Number of Text Branches of the Scripture Text" is the first one in this section. In his chapter, Tov examines questions concerning the existence of text families that testify to the emergence of the Hebrew Bible, normally classified according to the broad categories of Masoretic Text (MT), Samaritan Pentateuch, and the Septuagint. However, Tov maintains that this approach to seeking the "original text" of Scripture may be overly selective and not truly representative of the origins of the Hebrew Bible. He argues that the Septuagint provides evidence that, in some cases, the earliest form of Scripture may have been quite different from the MT. The three major textual traditions of which scholars often speak today exhibit both significant agreements and substantial differences. Tov contends that this makes speaking of a "unified textual tradition" highly problematic.

Dirk Büchner examines the relationship between interpretation and translation in his chapter "Namer, Curser, Blasphemer: Leviticus 24:10–16 according to the Septuagint and the Targums." Büchner chooses this passage because it is a rare example of instructions being prefaced by a narrative. While the Targums and Midrash take interpretive liberties with the text to draw connections to the crime of blasphemy, Büchner argues that the Greek text still attempts to remain faithful to difficult nuances present in the Hebrew. This is despite the fact that the Greek makes some interpretive adjustments and changes to the storyline to make it more understandable for its readers.

In her essay, "Flying Sickles Sound Scarier: The Role of Harvest as Judgment Metaphor in the LXX as a Foundation for the Translation of מְגִלָּה as δρέπανος in Zechariah 5:1–4," Christine Waring engages the question of Septuagint translation technique in the Greek rendering of the Hebrew term. She argues that, while earlier proposals that suggest the existence of different consonantal texts underlying the MT and the *Vorlage* of the LXX have some merit, a stronger case can be made for the influence of the use of the harvest metaphor in the broader literary context of Zechariah 5. When viewed in the light of metaphors for judgment current in the Greek culture and literature of the time, one can understand how this equivalence came about.

Albert Pietersma's contribution concludes the first section with his essay entitled "From Exodus to the Exile: A Commentary on the Greek Text-as-Produced Psalm 80." Pietersma operates within the frame of reference of the so-called interlinear paradigm in his examination of the translation technique of LXX Psalm 80. He contends that the potential for linguistic interference by the Semitic source text on the translation product did not impede the translator's ability to use Greek idiom. When one accounts for the twin variables of the idiomatic use of Greek and interference from the source text, one can get a clear sense of the form of the text with which the translator was working. Pietersma offers a close linguistic commentary on Psalm 80 and in the process argues that, since the translator's goal was to produce a faithful "formal" translation (for lack of better terminology), the Greek text as we have it today, as well as ensuing commentary on Psalm 80 throughout its reception history, suggest that there may have been different text forms of Psalm 80 in circulation, the Old Greek giving testimony to just one of these.

Part II of this volume includes contributions on the theme of "Exodus in the Septuagint." The scholars contributing to this section investigate intertextual links between the book of Exodus and other parts of the Septuagint, such as Genesis, Leviticus, and Deuteronomy, and translation issues pertaining to God's identity and some of the laws found in Exodus. These essays provide useful background for our understanding of how the translators made sense of their Hebrew source texts to create translations that were understandable and meaningful for their readers.

Robert J. V. Hiebert contributes the first chapter to this section in his essay "In and Out of Egypt: Genesis as Prelude to the Exodus Story." Hiebert observes that the canonical function of the book of Genesis as the introduction to the Hebrew Bible as a whole and the Pentateuch in particular positioned the Old Greek version of Genesis to serve as a resource for translating other parts of the LXX. Hiebert demonstrates how this is something that is particularly noticeable in places where there are thematic and philological resonances involving Genesis and other parts of the canon.

In "The Tree of the Sacred Text: Reflections on Greek Exodus in Dialogue with Antoine Berman," Karlena M. Cagnoli argues that French translation theorist Antoine Berman's approach to "literal translations" provides a useful tool for evaluating translation technique in the Septuagint. This is because he views language as a holistic system of signifiers rather than purely as a text, which allows for a translation to be seen as a literary work in its own right. Cagnoli applies this paradigm to examples from the Greek text of Exodus, arguing that, while the Exodus translators demonstrate creativity in their rendering of the Hebrew text, they are not seeking to produce an independent work but to provide a faithful witness to the source text.

Joel Korytko's contribution to this volume entitled "Slaves to the Septuagint: Applying Greek Legal Terminology for Slaves to Exodus 21:7" reexamines earlier explanations for the Greek Exodus translator's rendering of אמה and העבדים as οἰκέτις and αἱ δοῦλαι. Korytko traces how these renderings are influenced by Greco-Egyptian legal considerations as attested in the legal sources found among the documentary papyri, rather than in biblical or rabbinic traditions. This suggests that the translators were not merely seeking to render Hebrew into Greek, but to provide a sense of these laws that would have been relevant for readers at the time.

In "From Exodus to Deuteronomy? A Study on Interdependence in the Greek Pentateuch," Jean Maurais investigates the connections between the Greek texts of these two books. In response to John Lee's proposal that translators of the different parts of the Pentateuch worked simultaneously and collaborated in their work, Maurais examines the intertextual connections that can be detected. Based upon his analysis, he argues that the translator of Greek Deuteronomy relied on a text that was already in existence. While the data available is not without points of ambiguity, Maurais concludes from the evidence that the translator of Deuteronomy was dependent on the text of Old Greek Exodus to deal with certain translational challenges.

Don Dongshin Chang's essay "The Sojourner in Exodus and Beyond: Theological Conceptualization of *gēr* in the Old Testament" examines the role of foreigners or immigrants in Israelite society and during the exile. Chang argues that the ideal reflected in the book of Exodus, as well as in the Deuteronomistic history, was for *gērîm* to be included as members of the community, and to be granted rights of land inheritance and full participation as covenant members (Deut 26:11). Ezekiel later supports and explicates the teachings of the Torah by envisioning that *gērîm* too would one day have an inheritance in the land alongside ethnic Israelites. This points to the fact that the identity of the covenant people as envisioned by the book of Exodus is broader than is sometimes understood.

The two essays of Part III explore the significance of Exodus for understanding Second Temple Jewish literature. The of Martin G. Abegg Jr. and Jonathan Numada explore how Exodus was received in the Qumran literature and 3 Maccabees. Abegg's essay, "The Text of Exodus in the Qumran Corpus," consists of a series of discrete studies that demonstrate the truth of the axiom that "details matter" by showing that a large collection of minute details may have significant interpretive implications. He draws upon his text-critical work on the Dead Sea Scrolls to provide insight into the development of the Hebrew language in matters of orthography, morphology, the Hebrew verb system, the employment of the *tetragrammaton*, exegetical traditions concerning the half-shekel tax, and the interpretive tendencies found in paraphrastic revisions of the Pentateuch at Qumran. Abegg demonstrates that these various revisions reveal a tendency on the part of the scribes at Qumran to make changes to Scripture if they thought that it would help to clarify its meaning or support a theological position.

In his essay entitled "Prayer and Peace in 3 Maccabees 2:2-20: Trusting Precedent for Deliverance or Uttering Threats against the King?," Numada analyzes the prayer of Simon in the previously mentioned passage in the light of social-scientific criticism. He observes that the writer of 3 Maccabees seemingly does everything he can to polemicize the sins of Philopator against Jews in Palestine and Egypt so that his infamy surpasses even that of the Pharaoh of the exodus, to judge by the rhetoric employed. However, while the rhetoric and polemic found in 3 Maccabees suggest that there was a great deal of antagonism between Egyptian Jews and their Greek rulers, Numada argues that the goal of the author was to prevent violent conflict in the future by presenting prayer as an outlet for Jews who had strong passions concerning their identity. Ultimately, the author of 3 Maccabees agrees with other writers, such as the one responsible for the *Letter of Aristeas*, that the preferred future of his readers was to be found in a kind of "non-exodus" in which the audience would find its inheritance in Egypt.

Part IV, which contains the final collection of essays, focuses on New Testament studies, the emergence of Christianity, and Mark's Gospel. In his essay entitled "Mark's Incipit in Early Amulets and the Question of Its Original Reading," Craig A. Evans argues for the originality of the long version of Mark 1:1 in which Jesus is identified as "the Son of God." Evans surveys a broad range of textual evidence, in particular that found in amulets from late antiquity, to show that there was a tendency to shorten and abbreviate the Gospel incipits. Evans thus disagrees with those who regard the phrase υἱοῦ (τοῦ) θεοῦ in Mark 1:1 to be a later scribal addition or an interpretive gloss, and considers it to be an important phrase included by the author to assist in the reader's interpretation of this Gospel.

Marie Fortin's essay, "Combined Themes of a Composite Citation: Exodus and Wilderness in Mark 1:1–3," constitutes an analysis of how the author of the Gospel of Mark uses the Jewish Scriptures to emphasize the book's unique message. Fortin pursues an intertextual study that examines how the citations of Exodus 20:23, Malachi 3:1, and Isaiah 40:3 interact with the themes present in the Markan context. She contends that the composite nature of Mark 1:1–3 is not a manipulation of the surface-level meanings of these passages but is the result of careful exegetical and theological reflection on the part of Mark's author. She argues that one important function of these citations in Mark is to introduce the motif of "the way," and bring to remembrance in the mind of the reader the related themes and lessons that can be found in their original contexts.

James M. Scott's contribution entitled "Jesus' Performative Utterances and the Construction of the Future Anterior" addresses the question as to why Jesus' proclamation of God's Kingdom in Mark's Gospel resulted in the emergence of a movement that continued to grow despite his crucifixion as a royal pretender. Scott employs speech-act theory to argue that Jesus' kingdom came into being through its being announced, and that this prefigurative vision of an anticipated kingdom that was both past and future in its orientation presented a challenge to power structures that could not be extinguished through violence.

In "Matthew's Rewriting and Mosaic Discourse," Kyung S. Baek explores the interaction and continuity between the Gospel of Matthew and Second Temple Mosaic Discourse. While the influence of Torah traditions on the structure of Matthew's Gospel is well known, Baek investigates Matthew's portrayal of Jesus as a re-presentation of Moses at Sinai, who brings the Torah to its readers. Building on the work of Hindy Najman and George J. Brookes, Baek argues that Matthewengages with Mosaic Discourse so as to convey a sense of authority, authenticity, immediacy, and continuity with Second Temple Judaism in his Gospel.

In his essay entitled "Deliverance into the Coming Kingdom of God: Exodus Motifs in 1 Thessalonians," Stephen Anthony Cummins traces several points of resonance with the book of Exodus in 1 Thessalonians. His survey demonstrates that these can take the form of typological correspondences, shared imagery, and general themes. Cummins notes that these occur at several levels, relating to elements such as the Thessalonians' deliverance from idolatry through their acceptance of the gospel, Paul's relationship to the church at Thessalonica, the identity of the Thessalonian Christians as a covenant people, and their eschatological destiny within God's plan for creation. Cummins observes that Paul draws upon these theological and linguistic resources that have their origins in the book of Exodus for his understanding of both his own mission as well as the Thessalonians' vocation, showing that the influence of Exodus upon the New Testament can occur at very subtle and nuanced levels.

Wolfgang Kraus' contribution entitled "On the Reception of Exodus 24 and 25 in the Epistle to the Hebrews" examines the reception of the Septuagint text of Exodus 24:8 and 25:39–40 in Hebrews 8 and 9. Kraus maintains that the use of these texts, in dialogue with other interpretive and theological traditions, serves the broader Christological argument of Hebrews 7:1–10:18 that presents Jesus as the high priest for a new cultic order. Hebrews uses the paradigm of cultic theology to reframe Christological kerygma to argue that believers can start to participate in an eschatological perfection in the present time, even while they await its full realization in the future.

Finally, Daniela Scialabba concludes this volume with her essay entitled "Exodus and *egressio*: Observations on Biblical Terminology in the Latin Language." Scialabba investigates the use and reception of the Latin term for *exodus* and its role in the Latin religious lexicon. In particular, she traces the implications of it being a loan word from Greek, exploring how this term came to be employed, especially considering other Latin equivalents that did not cease to be used. This influences readers in their reception of the book of Exodus and its account of the migration of the Israelites out of Egypt, showing us that the word "exodus" in the Latin language came to symbolize a narrative rather than merely a verbal action.

The editors express their gratitude to the contributors for the breadth and depth of the scholarship reflected in the essays of the present volume. This international group of scholars represents a broad range of disciplines and methodologies in many areas of current research on the Bible and the Septuagint, including textual criticism, philology, linguistics, social-scientific criticism, biblical-theological analysis, and reception history. While diverse in the approaches that they use, they are united in demonstrating that the Septuagint in general, and the book of Greek Exodus in particular, played a significant role in the development of Judeo-Christian traditions, and that Septuagint research will continue to play a vital role in the future of biblical studies. It is our hope that these essays constitute a fitting tribute to Larry J. Perkins, our friend, colleague, and mentor. Larry, we celebrate your career, and we express our heartfelt thanks to you for your commitment to your students, to theological education, and to biblical scholarship.

Sola Deo Gloria!

PART I
THE SEPTUAGINT

Chapter 1

The Number of Text Branches of the Scripture Text

Emanuel Tov

1. Text branches of the Hebrew Bible

Scholars have a certain perception of the text of the Hebrew Bible; usually they presume that the Scripture books started off as an early text, also named the "original text," or a series of early texts. This is a topic of great importance for scholarship even though there are no firm answers to the difficult questions surrounding the enigma of the early text. Several theories have been launched regarding the early text and the development of the Hebrew Bible.[1] These theories always start from an abstract theoretical point of departure, trying to integrate the scant evidence into a theoretical framework.

However, it may be better not to start with theories, but with the texts themselves. The result is not necessarily more objective because of the fragmentary state of the evidence, but the point of departure is more realistic. The description then starts with a group of textual witnesses of the Hebrew Bible that have been preserved from ancient times and that form the basis for continued thinking about the early text.[2] This group of witnesses has grown in the last century thanks to the discoveries in the Judean Desert. These witnesses do not reflect the earliest stage of the Scripture text, and may even be remote from it, yet scholars do point out what their place is in the reconstructed development of the biblical text. That development is usually depicted as a tree with the early (original) text at the top with branches representing

---

[1] For a good description, see Shemaryahu Talmon, "The Old Testament Text," in *The Cambridge History of the Bible,* ed. Peter R. Ackroyd and Christopher F. Evans (Cambridge: Cambridge University Press, 1970), I:159–99.

[2] See my analysis of the early text of the Bible in Emanuel Tov, *Textual Criticism of the Hebrew Bible,* 4th edition, revised and expanded (Minneapolis: Fortress Press, 2022), 338–48 (henceforth: *TCHB*[4]).

developments subsequent to the early text. Scholars rightly wonder how to define a text branch, how many branches there are, and how the relation between them should be depicted. Abstract as they may be, these are important questions for the understanding of textual relations.

Some of these questions have been posed in the past. Regarding the number of text branches, throughout the last two centuries the traditional answer has been that there were three text branches in the Torah (presented as the tripartite division: the Masoretic Text [MT], Samaritan Pentateuch [SP], and the Septuagint [LXX]), and two or three in the other books.[3] These descriptions were based on a preconceived idea that there ought to be a tripartite division of the evidence as in the case of the internal divisions of the texts of the New Testament[4] and of the Septuagint.[5] However, we suggest that there can be any number of branches of the Scripture text, created and preserved without any pattern.[6]

How does one determine whether a textual witness (ancient translation or ancient text such as the Judean Desert texts) or a group of witnesses reflect(s) a separate text branch? The determination of what comprises a text branch depends on the subjective recognition of special features, mainly in literary content, but also in textual peculiarities (e.g., harmonizations in the Torah). Smaller scale deviations are included in "twigs" that emerge from the branches. In principle, the number of these branches is endless, as suggested elsewhere,[7] but in practice not many are known. However, it should be remembered that only a small percentage of the evidence that was circulating in the last centuries BCE is known to us.[8]

In the next paragraphs the potential text branches are listed, summarized in §5.

2. Texts included in the Masoretic Text

The texts included in MT form the basis of the description of all the other texts. Each book in MT forms a text branch separate from the other texts until proven otherwise.

---

[3] See Tov, *TCHB*[4].
[4] Eldon Jay Epp, *Perspectives on New Testament Textual Criticism: Collected Essays, 1962–2004*, NovTSup 116 (Leiden: Brill, 2005), 59–100 (66).
[5] The view that the manuscript evidence of the LXX is based on three branches, Lucian, Hesychius, and Origen goes back to a statement of Jerome, *Praefatio in Librum Paralipomenon*, ed. J. P. Migne, *PL* xxviii (Paris, 1846), 1324–25; see Sidney Jellicoe, *The Septuagint and Modern Study* (Oxford: Clarendon, 1968), 134–71.
[6] The descriptions and detailed stemmata (genealogical trees) for each of the Scripture books in the comprehensive handbook of Armin Lange come closest to such a conception: *Handbuch der Textfunde vom Toten Meer, I: Die Handschriften biblischer Bücher von Qumran und den anderen Fundorten* (Tübingen: Mohr Siebeck, 2009). For details, see §6.
[7] Emanuel Tov, "A Modern Textual Outlook Based on the Qumran Scrolls," *HUCA* 53 (1982): 11–27.
[8] The distinction between branches, to be recorded in Table 1.3, and "twigs" remains problematic. For example, the SP group (the pre-Samaritan scrolls and SP) forms a branch, while some of the Reworked Pentateuch texts (4QRP[a,b] and 4QRP[c,d]) are recorded as twigs emanating from that branch. See Emanuel Tov, "The Development of the Text of the Torah in Two Major Text Blocks," in idem, *Textual Developments, Collected Essays, Volume 4* (Leiden: Brill, 2019), 237–56. Their context exegesis is substantial, but they are based on the text of the SP group, and therefore are recorded in a subordinate position in the tentative stemma of the Torah in the study mentioned in the previous note.

In those other few cases listed in §5, there are no substantial differences between MT and the other text sources.

3. The Septuagint as the source of major deviations from MT

Next to the MT, the LXX, to which Larry J. Perkins devoted many important studies, is the most significant textual witness. Some will claim that the LXX is more significant, as it often reflects a text that is older than its counterpart in MT.[9] Indeed, the LXX reflects more ancient extra-masoretic material than all the Qumran scrolls taken together (compare Table 1.1 with Table 1.2). The MT and the LXX often differ in details that pertain to the developmental stages of Hebrew Scripture.[10]

These differences are not surprising, since in antiquity many divergent copies of Hebrew Scripture were in circulation. Some of these internal differences are minor, while others involve a verse, a whole paragraph, chapter, or even book. All these copies contain "Scripture."

When turning to the background of these differences, the assumption is unavoidable that the Hebrew scrolls used for the Greek translation were valuable and sometimes more ancient than the proto-MT. Otherwise they would not have contained so much data that scholars consider relevant to the textual and literary development of the biblical books.

The special character of the source of the LXX seems to be related to either one of two factors or to a combination thereof: (1) the idiosyncratic Hebrew scrolls used for the Greek translation were *not* embraced by the circles that fostered the proto-MT; and (2) the relatively early date of the translation enterprise (285–150 BCE), involving still earlier Hebrew scrolls, that explains the existence of vestiges of earlier literary stages of the biblical books in the LXX. However, only a combination of the two factors explains that ancient scrolls, such as probably used for the Greek translation, still circulated in the third and second centuries BCE, when some of the MT-like texts already existed, such as 4QJer^a, which is dated around 200 BCE. In the reality of the third and second centuries BCE, it was probably not unusual that scrolls other than those of the Masoretic tradition were chosen as the base for the translation.

When ascribing the idiosyncratic character of the Hebrew scrolls underlying the LXX to their early date, we find some support for this approach in the Qumran documents: two early Qumran scrolls (200–150 BCE) likewise reflect redactional features different from MT (4QJer^{b,d}). See §3.

A summary of the significant textual and literary features of the LXX differing from MT involves the details included in Table 1.1,[11] recording both features that may have antedated the proto-MT and features that may have come afterwards. The data in the summarizing Table 1.3 are based mainly on the literary features.

---

[9] Tov, *TCHB*^{4}, 231–32 (Table 1.1).

[10] However, it needs to be remembered that the text of the LXX needs to be retroverted into Hebrew before it can be used profitably in the textual criticism of the Hebrew Bible.

[11] Revised from Tov, *TCHB*^{4}, 231–32.

Table 1.1. Textual and literary features of the Septuagint books[1]

Book in LXX	Literary elements earlier than proto-MT	Textual elements earlier than proto-MT	Literary elements later than proto-MT	Textual elements later than proto-MT
Genesis			chronology	harm.
Exodus			Exodus 35–40	exeg. harm.
Leviticus				harm.
Numbers				harm.
Deuteronomy				harm.
Joshua	lit. elements			
Judges				
1–2 Samuel	lit. elements	MT: errors, changed theophoric names		
1 Kings			rewr. comp.	
2 Kings			chronology	
Isaiah				
Jeremiah	lit. elements			
Ezekiel	lit. elements			
Minor Prophets				
Psalms	few lit. elements			
Proverbs	lit. elements			exeg.
Ruth				
Song				
Lamentations				
Ecclesiastes				
Esther			rewr. comp.	
Esther A-Text			rewr. comp.	
Daniel			rewr. comp.	
Ezra-Nehemiah	lit. elements in LXX-Neh 11			
1–2 Chronicles	few lit. elements			

4. Qumran scrolls

In the following books, the Qumran scrolls reflect significant literary variants when compared with MT (see Table 1.2). In Joshua and Canticles, the Qumran fragments reflect text branches separate from proto-MT and the LXX. In Jeremiah, the fragments go together with the LXX, and in 1–2 Samuel they are sometimes joined with the LXX and at other times they form a separate branch.[2]

---

[1] The following abbreviations are used: harm. (= harmonization), lit. (= literary), exeg. (= exegesis), and rewr. comp. (= rewritten composition). Highlighted units: relation unclear.
[2] For further details, see Tables 1.1 and 1.3.

Table 1.2. Literary deviations from MT in the Qumran scrolls

	Scroll agreeing with LXX	Scroll deviating from other sources
Joshua		4QJosh[a] [3]
1–2 Samuel	4QSam[a] [4]	
1 Samuel 2		4QSam[a] [5]
1 Samuel	4QSam[b] [6]	
Jeremiah	4QJer[b] [7]	
Jeremiah	4QJer[d] [8]	
Canticles		4QCant[a] [9]

5. The Samaritan Pentateuch and the pre-Samaritan texts

The editorial interventions by the SP group (pre-Samaritan Qumran scrolls[10] and SP) in a text like the proto-MT render the text of that group into a new literary edition of the biblical text when compared with the other texts. The most characteristic readings of the SP group were created by substantial editorial manipulations of the manuscript on which it was based.[22] In its literary and textual features, the SP group reflects a separate branch, sharing a common origin with the LXX.

6. Number and nature of the text branches

Summarizing the characterizations of the preceding paragraphs, we are seemingly faced with only three text branches in the Torah: MT, SP, and the LXX, but such an approach would present a formalistic and simplistic presentation of the evidence based on the procedures of previous research. For example, it is unclear whether the LXX and SP in the Torah differ sufficiently enough to be counted as two separate entities. In the following discussion the argument is advanced that they belong to the same text block. In the post-Pentateuchal books, the situation is more complicated since these texts sometimes represent the same text branch. This approach represents a novel understanding of the text branches.

---

[3] See Emanuel Tov, "The Literary Development of the Book of Joshua as Reflected in the Masoretic Text, the LXX, and 4QJosh[a]," in idem, *Textual Criticism of the Hebrew Bible, Qumran, Septuagint: Collected Essays, Volume 3*, VTSup 167 (Leiden: Brill, 2015), 132–53.

[4] See Jason K. Driesbach, *4QSamuel[a] and the Text of Samuel*, VTSup 171 (Leiden: Brill, 2016), 100, 130, 145, 179, 264, 280.

[5] See Tov, *TCHB*[4], 140–44, and Driesbach, 4QSamuel[a], 284–86, 321–29.

[6] Thus Frank M. Cross, Donald W. Parry, and Richard Saley, "51. 4QSam[a]," in Frank M. Cross, Donald W. Parry, Richard Saley and Eugene Ulrich, *Qumran Cave 4.XII: 1–2 Samuel*, DJD XVII (Oxford: Clarendon, 2005), 222–23, confirmed by my own analysis.

[7] See Tov, *TCHB*[4], 234–36.

[8] See Tov, *TCHB*[4], 234–36.

[9] See Emanuel Tov, "106. 4QCant[a-c]," in Eugene Ulrich et al., *Qumran Cave 4.XI: Psalms to Chronicles*, DJD XVI (Oxford: Clarendon, 2000), 195–219.

[10] These are Qumran scrolls that are very similar to SP, one of which presumably served as its basis.

[22] See Tov, *TCHB*[4], 174–78.

In our search for the number of the text branches of Hebrew Scripture, we should constantly be reminded that only some of the evidence from the last pre-Christian centuries is known to us. Thus, all summaries compiled today are based on currently known evidence as well as on our interpretation. For example, the LXX of Job is much shorter than MT, but scholars usually ascribe the difference in length to the translator. Accordingly, despite the differences between the two, the MT and LXX of Job probably reflect the same text branch.

Table 1.3 summarizes the number of the text branches in the Scripture books based on a subjective understanding of the relation between the text sources. Each column records the texts representing a certain text branch included in a single text and, in two cases, in two texts (column 4: MT–LXX; column 7: Qumran–LXX). The listing of the Qumran scrolls reflects our understanding of the essence of a scroll. Thus, 4QJosh^a and 4QCant^{a,b} are recorded as reflecting literary traditions additional to MT and the LXX, explained as either ancient text traditions or exegetical versions subsequent to proto-MT–LXX.[23] 4QSam^a sometimes reflects a third source next to MT and the LXX.[24] 4QRP^{a,b} are recorded as "twigs" that branched off from the SP group with which they were closely connected,[25] and not as two independent text branches.

Taking into consideration that scholars espouse different opinions about the textual sources, the chart of the textual relations in Table 1.3 differs from that depicted by others.[26] The differences between the text branches and their number were caused by the vicissitudes of the textual transmission and the choices made by the translators who used scrolls of different textual character in different books.[27]

---

[23] See nn. 13 and 19.
[24] See n. 15.
[25] See Tov, "Development of the Text."
[26] Several of the stemmata to be mentioned in the following are based on theoretical *a priori* assumptions. The stemma in Ronald S. Hendel, *Steps to a New Edition of the Hebrew Bible*, Text-Critical Studies 10 (Atlanta: SBL Press, 2016), 198, distinguishes between two text blocks in Exodus (MT versus LXX-SP). Rudolf Kittel, *Über die Notwendigkeit und Möglichkeit einer neuen Ausgabe der hebräischen Bibel. Studien und Erwägungen, Studien und Erwägungen* (Leipzig: Edelmann, 1901), 43–47 distinguishes between two recensions, LXX and MT that go back to one common text. Likewise, the diagram of Frederik E. Deist, *Towards the Text of the Old Testament*, 2nd ed. (Pretoria: D.R. Church Booksellers, 1981), 235, reckons with the MT and LXX traditions. On the other hand, other stemmata are based on a three-pronged manuscript tradition (MT, SP, LXX): the local texts theory of William F. Albright, "New Light on Early Recensions of the Hebrew Bible," *BASOR* 140 (1955): 27–33, and Frank M. Cross, "The Evolution of a Theory of Local Texts," in *Qumran and the History of the Biblical Text*, ed. Frank M. Cross and Shemaryahu Talmon (Cambridge, MA: Harvard University Press, 1975), 306–20. This theory is also depicted in the stemma of Ernst Sellin and Georg Fohrer, *Einleitung in das Alte Testament*, 11th ed. (Heidelberg: Quelle & Meyer, 1969), 567, that arranges the texts into MT type, LXX type, and LXX type; Talmon, "The Old Testament Text," in *The Cambridge History of the Bible*, 1:195; and Ralph W. Klein, *Textual Criticism of the Old Testament: The Septuagint after Qumran* (Philadelphia: Fortress Press, 1974), 70–71. Lange, *Handbuch*, presents very detailed stemmata of books reflecting two, three or four different branches: two in Joshua, Samuel–Kings, Isaiah, Jeremiah, Minor Prophets, Psalms, Ecclesiastes; three in the Torah, Judges, Ezekiel, Ruth, Canticles, and Lamentations; four in Daniel (see pp. 173, 199–519). Benjamin Ziemer, "A Stemma for Deuteronomy," in Michael Langlois, ed., *The Dead Sea Scrolls and the Samaritan Pentateuch*, CBET 94 (Leuven: Peeters, 2019), 127–97 (191), presents three witnesses of Deuteronomy (MT, SP, LXX) based on a thorough analysis.
[27] The footnotes refer to discussions of the textual character of the books, especially the latest ones.

1 *The Number of Text Branches of the Scripture Text* 17

Table 1.3. Number of the text branches in the Scripture books

1	2	3	4	5	6	7
	MT	SP	MT–LXX	LXX	Qumran	Qumran–LXX
Torah[1]	x	x		x		
Joshua[2]	x			x	4QJosh[a]	
Judges[3]			x			
1–2 Samuel[4]	x					4QSam[a]
1 Samuel 2[5]	x				4QSam[a]	
1 Samuel[6]	x					4QSam[b]
1–2 Kings[7]	x			x		
Isaiah[8]			x			
Jeremiah[9]	x					4QJer[b,d]
Ezekiel[10]	x			x		
Minor Prophets[11]	x			x		
Psalms[12]			x			
Proverbs[13]	x			x		
Job[14]			x?			

[1] See n. 8. The witnesses of the Torah are *sui generis*: the SP group (SP and the pre-Samaritan scrolls) forms one branch together with related scrolls, the LXX forms another one, and together they form one tradition block. See n. 8. They are recorded here as three branches based on two tradition blocks.
[2] See n. 13.
[3] There are no substantial differences between the textual witnesses. See Hans Ausloos, "13.1 Textual History of Judges," *THB*, vol. 1B, *Pentateuch, Former and Latter Prophets* (Leiden: Brill, 2017), 277–80. The short text of 4QJudg[a] in Judg 6:7–10 probably reflects a textual mishap (homoioteleuton), and not a pre-Deuteronomistic scroll. See the discussion in Tov, *TCHB⁴*, 313.
[4] See n. 14.
[5] See n. 15.
[6] See n. 16.
[7] See Tov, *TCHB⁴*, 306–309.
[8] There are no substantial differences between the textual witnesses. See Arie van der Kooij, "6.1.2.2.2 and 6.3 Septuagint," in *THB*, vol. 1B, 463, 489–92.
[9] See n. 17.
[10] See William A. Tooman, "8.1 Textual History of Ezekiel," in *THB*, vol. 1B, 559–69; Johan Lust, "8.3 Septuagint," in *THB*, vol. 1B, 581–85.
[11] See Christopher J. Fresch, "9.1 Textual History of the Minor Prophets," in *THB*, vol. 1B, 589–600; W. Edward Glenny, "9.3. Septuagint," in *THB*, vol. 1B, 614–22.
[12] There are no substantial differences between the textual witnesses since the LXX translation is very close to MT and the much deviating Qumran scrolls probably reflect liturgical copies. See Emanuel Tov, "The Aid of the LXX in Establishing the Original Text of the Psalter" (forthcoming).
[13] See Michael V. Fox, *Proverbs: An Eclectic Edition with Introduction and Textual Commentary*, The Hebrew Bible: A Critical Edition, 1 (Atlanta: SBL Press, 2015), 36–61; Emanuel Tov, "Recensional Differences between the Masoretic Text and the Septuagint of Proverbs," in idem, *The Greek and Hebrew Bible: Collected Essays on the Septuagint*, VTSup 72 (Leiden: Brill, 1999), 419–31.
[14] There are no substantial differences between the textual witnesses since the much shorter text of LXX-Job was probably based on a Hebrew text like MT. See Maria Gorea, "The Book of Job," in Alison G. Salvesen and Timothy Michael Law, *Oxford Handbook of the Septuagint* (Oxford: University Press, 2021), 369–83 (371); Claude E. Cox, "Job," in James K. Aitken, ed., *The T&T Companion to the Septuagint* (London: Bloomsbury, 2015), 385–400 (393).

Canticles[15]		x	4QCant[a,b]
Ruth[16]		x	
Ecclesiastes[17]		x	
Lamentations[18]		x	
Esther[19]	x		x
Daniel[20]	x		x
Ezra–Nehemiah[21]	x		x
Chronicles[22]	x		x

(Table 1.3 continued)

On the basis of Table 1.3, we witness a unified textual tradition in the MT and LXX, not challenged by Qumran fragments, in the following books: Judges, Isaiah, Psalms, Job?, Ruth, Ecclesiastes, and Lamentations. This unified tradition should not be equated with the early (original) text of these books, but it is not impossible that sometimes this was the case. In all these instances, no text branches are known that involve literary (editorial) developments, while all of them evince some textual variation, including scribal developments, such as two Isaiah scrolls written in the Qumran scribal practice style (1QIsa^a, 4QIsa^c).

In several other books, the MT and the LXX display a two-pronged tradition: 1–2 Kings, Ezekiel, Minor Prophets, Proverbs, Esther, Daniel, Ezra–Nehemiah, Chronicles.

In other books, the two-pronged tradition involves a combination of texts: MT and the combined text of a Qumran scroll and the LXX (4QSam^a, 4QSam^b, 4QJer^{b,d}), the combined text of MT–LXX and a Qumran scroll (4QCant^{a,b}).

In Joshua, three different text traditions are known (MT, LXX, 4QJosh^a). Likewise, in the Torah, the witnesses are divided into three text branches deriving from two earlier text blocks, MT, and the other witnesses.[23]

---

[15] The LXX is close to MT. See Bénédicte Lemmelijn, "14.1 Textual History of Canticles," in *THB*, vol. 1C, *Writings* (Leiden: Brill, 2017), 321–26 and note 19.

[16] There are no substantial differences between the textual witnesses. See Melanie Köhlmoos, "13.1 Textual History of Ruth," in *THB*, vol. 1C, 303–305 (304).

[17] There are no substantial differences between the textual witnesses. See Michael V. Fox, "15.1 Textual History of Qohelet," in *THB*, vol. 1C, 339–44 (340): "The book is in the view of the present writer, basically a textual unity that has reached us in a form that is probably close to the original. This does not exclude the possibility of minor changes, including additions, in the Hebrew transmission."

[18] The LXX and MT reflect the same text, while 4QLam reflects a few independent readings, not enough for rendering it into a separate source. See Gideon Kotzé, "16.1 Textual History of Lamenetations," in *THB*, vol. 1C, 357–60, and Rolf Schäfer, "16.2.2 Masoretic Texts and Ancient Texts Close to MT," in *THB*, vol. 1C, 362–73.

[19] The LXX translation includes several exegetical additions. See Emanuel Tov, "Three Strange Books of the LXX: 1 Kings, Esther, and Daniel Compared with Similar Rewritten Compositions from Qumran and Elsewhere," in idem, *Hebrew Bible, Greek Bible, and Qumran: Collected Essays*, TSAJ 121 (Tübingen: Mohr Siebeck, 2008), 283–305.

[20] This translation includes several late exegetical additions. See the study mentioned in n. 47.

[21] See Zipora Talshir, "19.3.1 Septuagint," in *THB*, vol. 1C, 615–20.

[22] See Gary N. Knoppers, "20.3.1 Septuagint," in *THB*, vol. 1C, 670–76.

[23] See the study mentioned in n. 8.

It is difficult to know whether there is a logic behind the different text patterns in the various Scripture books. The LXX books display different patterns since in some cases they side with MT while in other ones they represent different literary features.[24] Possibly the fragmentary nature of the evidence provides a misleading picture. For example, literary features that resembled those of LXX-Jeremiah[25] may have existed also for other prophetic books. Or possibly the LXX translators who were active in a certain milieu or period only had access to scrolls of a specific nature.[26]

One thing is clear, there is no evidence for a tripartite tradition of the textual evidence that was axiomatic for those scholars who look to MT, SP, and the LXX as the main representatives of the Scripture text. We therefore reckon with one, two, or three different branches in the Scripture books, while in principle their number is endless. It seems that the factor of coincidence (§6) may have determined the number of the surviving text branches.

7. Coincidence as a determining factor

Coincidence is a determining factor in the analysis of all ancient literatures that have been preserved fragmentarily. Among other things, the factor of coincidence may have determined how many text branches have survived.[54] Possibly at one time there existed more branches that have been lost in the meantime. What we now name a "unified textual tradition" may not have been unified in the past since the number of text branches may have been larger than depicted in Table 1.3.

Bibliography

Albright, William F. "New Light on Early Recensions of the Hebrew Bible." *BASOR* 140 (1955): 27–33.

Ausloos, Hans. "13.1 Textual History of Judges." Pages 277–80 in *Textual History of the Bible, The Hebrew Bible*, vol. 1B: *Pentateuch, Former and Latter Prophets*. Edited by Armin Lange and Emanuel Tov. Leiden: Brill, 2017.

Cox, Claude E. "Job." Pages 385–400 in *The T&T Companion to the Septuagint*. Edited by James K. Aitken. London: Bloomsbury, 2015.

---

[24] See Table 1.1.
[25] See Table 1.2 and Tov, *TCHB*⁴, 286–94.
[26] Remarkably some of the LXX translations that form a tradition block with MT (col. 4) belong to the *kaige*-Theodotion tradition (Canticles, Ruth, Lamentations), while Psalms and Ecclesiastes were close to that tradition. All these translations may be considered relatively late. We may expand this hypothesis into a general thought that the unified character of the textual witnesses (Judges, Isaiah, Psalms, Job?, Ruth, Ecclesiastes, and Lamentations) may reflect the lateness of their textual traditions. On the other hand, the late books of Daniel and Esther are characterized by the late Additions in the LXX based on Hebrew texts that deviate much from MT.
[54] For examples, see Emanuel Tov, "The Coincidental Textual Nature of the Collections of Ancient Scriptures," in idem, *Textual Criticism of the Hebrew Bible, Qumran, Septuagint*, 20–35. See further Alan Millard, "Only Fragments from the Past: The Role of Accident in Our Knowledge of the Ancient Near East," in *Writing and Ancient Near Eastern Society: Papers in Honour of Alan R. Millard*, ed. P. Bienkowski et al. (London: T&T Clark, 2005), 301–19.

Cross, Frank M., Donald W. Parry, and Richard Saley. "51. 4QSamᵃ." Pages 222–23 in *Qumran Cave 4.XII: 1-2 Samuel*. DJD XVII. Edited by Frank M. Cross, Donald W. Parry, and Richard, Saley, and Eugene Ulrich. Oxford: Clarendon, 2005.

Cross, Frank M. "The Evolution of a Theory of Local Texts." Pages 306–20 in *Qumran and the History of the Biblical Text*. Edited by Frank M. Cross and Shemaryahu Talmon. Cambridge, MA: Harvard University Press, 1975.

Deist, Frederik E. *Towards the Text of the Old Testament*. 2nd ed. Pretoria: D. R. Church Booksellers, 1981.

Driesbach, Jason K. *4QSamuelᵃ and the Text of Samuel*. VTSup 171. Leiden: Brill, 2016.

Epp, Eldon Jay. *Perspectives on New Testament Textual Criticism: Collected Essays. 1962-2004*. NovTSup 116. Leiden: Brill, 2005.

Fresch, Christopher J. "9.1 Textual History of the Minor Prophets." Pages 589–600 in *Textual History of the Bible, The Hebrew Bible*, vol. 1B: *Pentateuch, Former and Latter Prophets*. Edited by Armin Lange and Emanuel Tov. Leiden: Brill, 2017.

Fox, Michael V. "15.1 Textual History of Qohelet." Pages 10–15 in *Textual History of the Bible, The Hebrew Bible*, vol. 1C: *Writings*. Edited by Armin Lange and Emanuel Tov. Leiden: Brill, 2017.

Fox, Michael V. *Proverbs: An Eclectic Edition with Introduction and Textual Commentary*. The Hebrew Bible: A Critical Edition, 1. Atlanta: SBL Press, 2015.

Glenny, W. Edward. "9.3. Septuagint." Pages 614–22 in *Textual History of the Bible, The Hebrew Bible*, vol. 1B: *Pentateuch, Former and Latter Prophets*. Edited by Armin Lange and Emanuel Tov. Leiden: Brill, 2017.

Gorea, Maria. "The Book of Job." Pages 369–83 in *Oxford Handbook of the Septuagint*. Edited by Alison G. Salvesen and Timothy Michael Law. Oxford: University Press, 2021.

Hendel, Ronald S. *Steps to a New Edition of the Hebrew Bible*. Text-Critical Studies 10. Atlanta: SBL Press, 2016.

Jerome, *Praefatio in Librum Paralipomenon*. Edited by J. P. Migne. PL xxviii. Paris, 1846.

Jellicoe, Sidney. *The Septuagint and Modern Study*. Oxford: Clarendon, 1968.

Kittel, Rudolf. *Über die Notwendigkeit und Möglichkeit einer neuen Ausgabe der hebräischen Bibel. Studien und Erwägungen*. Leipzig: Edelmann, 1901.

Klein, Ralph W. *Textual Criticism of the Old Testament: The Septuagint after Qumran*. Philadelphia: Fortress Press, 1974.

Knoppers, Gary N. "20.3.1 Septuagint." Pages 670–76 in *Textual History of the Bible, The Hebrew Bible*, vol. 1C: *Writings*. Edited by Armin Lange and Emanuel Tov. Leiden: Brill, 2017.

Köhlmoos, Melanie. "13.1 Textual History of Ruth." Pages 303–305 in *Textual History of the Bible, The Hebrew Bible*, vol. 1C: *Writings*. Edited by Armin Lange and Emanuel Tov. Leiden: Brill, 2017.

Kotzé, Gideon. "16.1 Textual History of Lamentations." Pages 357–60 in *Textual History of the Bible, The Hebrew Bible*, vol. 1C: *Writings*. Edited by Armin Lange and Emanuel Tov. Leiden: Brill, 2017.

Lange, Armin. *Handbuch der Textfunde vom Toten Meer. I: Die Handschriften biblischer Bücher von Qumran und den anderen Fundorten*. Tübingen: Mohr Siebeck, 2009.

Lemmelijn, Bénédicte. "14.1 Textual History of Canticles." Pages 321–26 in *Textual History of the Bible, The Hebrew Bible*, vol. 1C: *Writings*. Edited by Armin Lange and Emanuel Tov. Leiden: Brill, 2017.

Millard, Alan. "Only Fragments from the Past: The Role of Accident in Our Knowledge of the Ancient Near East." Pages 301–19 in *Writing and Ancient Near Eastern Society: Papers in Honour of Alan R. Millard*. Edited by P. Bienkowski et al. London: T&T Clark, 2005.

Schäfer, Rolf. "16.2.2 Masoretic Texts and Ancient Texts Close to MT." Pages 362–73 in *Textual History of the Bible, The Hebrew Bible*, vol. 1C: *Writings*. Edited by Armin Lange and Emanuel Tov. Leiden: Brill, 2017.

Sellin, Ernst, and Georg Fohrer. *Einleitung in das Alte Testament*. 11th ed. Heidelberg: Quelle & Meyer, 1969.

Talmon, Shemaryahu. "The Old Testament Text." Pages 159–99 in vol. 1 of *The Cambridge History of the Bible*. Edited by Peter R. Ackroyd and Christopher F. Evans. Cambridge: Cambridge University Press, 1970.

Talshir, Zipora. "19.3.1 Septuagint." Pages 615–20 in *Textual History of the Bible, The Hebrew Bible*, vol. 1C: *Writings*. Edited by Armin Lange and Emanuel Tov. Leiden: Brill, 2017.

Tooman, William A. "8.1 Textual History of Ezekiel." Pages 559–69 in *Textual History of the Bible, The Hebrew Bible*, vol. 1B: *Pentateuch, Former and Latter Prophets*. Edited by Armin Lange and Emanuel Tov. Leiden: Brill, 2017.

Tov, Emanuel. "A Modern Textual Outlook Based on the Qumran Scrolls." *HUCA* 53 (1982): 11–27.

Tov, Emanuel. "Recensional Differences between the Masoretic Text and the Septuagint of Proverbs." Pages 419–31 in *The Greek and Hebrew Bible: Collected Essays on the Septuagint*. VTSup 72. Leiden: Brill, 1999.

Tov, Emanuel. *Textual Criticism of the Hebrew Bible*. 4th ed, revised and expanded. Minneapolis: Fortress Press, 2012.

Tov, Emanuel. "The Coincidental Textual Nature of the Collections of Ancient Scriptures." Pages 30–35 in *Textual Criticism of the Hebrew Bible, Qumran, Septuagint: Collected Essays. Volume 3*. VTSup 167. Leiden: Brill, 2015.

Tov, Emanuel. "The Literary Development of the Book of Joshua as Reflected in the Masoretic Text, the LXX, and 4QJosh[a]." Pages 132–53 in *Textual Criticism of the Hebrew Bible, Qumran, Septuagint: Collected Essays. Volume 3*. VTSup 167. Leiden: Brill, 2015.

Tov, Emanuel. "Three Strange Books of the LXX: 1 Kings, Esther, and Daniel Compared with Similar Rewritten Compositions from Qumran and Elsewhere." Pages 283–305 in *Hebrew Bible, Greek Bible, and Qumran: Collected Essays*. TSAJ 121. Tübingen: Mohr Siebeck, 2008.

Ziemer, Benjamin. "A Stemma for Deuteronomy." Pages 127–97 in *The Dead Sea Scrolls and the Samaritan Pentateuch*. Edited by Michael Langlois. CBET 94. Leuven: Peeters, 2019.

Chapter 2

Namer, Curser, Blasphemer:
Leviticus 24:10–16 according to the Septuagint and the Targums*

Dirk Büchner

1. Introduction

The Hebrew narrative in Leviticus 24 about the son of an Egyptian father and Israelite mother who was executed for blasphemy is quite sparing in detail, providing a number of opportunities for the earliest translators who rendered it into Greek and Aramaic to make interpretive decisions. It happens to be one of two episodes in the book of Leviticus in which there is a brief narrative serving as preface to a set of instructions, the other found at the beginning of ch. 10. In this essay, I will present the preliminary work towards commenting on the Old Greek of this chapter for the Leviticus volume in the Society of Biblical Literature Commentary on the Septuagint series (SBLCS). The intention of this study is not to engage in any great depth with the Hebrew text and its meaning, but rather to comment on the way the Septuagint translator (hereafter G) and occasionally the targumists respond to the vocabulary and syntax of their Hebrew original. Accordingly, Greek words and phrases will be cited and given careful attention. It will be shown that the Septuagint version of this narrative, though adhering closely to the items of the source text, makes some adjustment to the Hebrew storyline, especially with respect to the person of Moses. Nevertheless, the Septuagint does not simplify or dismiss difficulties presented by the Hebrew. By contrast, the Targums and Midrash go to some lengths to conflate the offender's actions to that of blasphemy and remove complexities present in the accompanying legal instruction.

---

* It is an honour and a pleasure to dedicate this essay to my friend, valued colleague and fellow Pentateuch commentator Larry Perkins. I look up to him for advice and support, especially on matters of grammar and syntax. He has always provided an immediate and wise response to my questions.

2 Namer, Curser, Blasphemer

Here now follows a verse-by-verse commentary. The readings that appear are in order, MT, followed by the Göttingen Septuagint text, followed by the English translation of NETS.[1]

Verses 10-11

ויצא בן אשה ישראלית והוא בן איש מצרי בתוך בני ישראל וינצו במחנה בן
הישראלית ואיש הישראלי
ויקב בן האשה הישראלית את השם ויקלל ויביאו אתו אל משה ושם אמו שלמית בת
דברי למטה דן

Καὶ ἐξῆλθεν υἱὸς γυναικὸς Ἰσραηλίτιδος, καὶ οὗτος ἦν υἱὸς Αἰγυπτίου, ἐν τοῖς υἱοῖς Ισραηλ· καὶ ἐμαχέσαντο ἐν τῇ παρεμβολῇ ὁ ἐκ τῆς Ἰσραηλίτιδος καὶ ὁ ἄνθρωπος ὁ Ἰσραηλίτης·
καὶ ἐπονομάσας ὁ υἱὸς τῆς γυναικὸς τῆς Ἰσραηλίτιδος τὸ ὄνομα κατηράσατο, καὶ ἤγαγον αὐτὸν πρὸς Μωυσῆν· καὶ τὸ ὄνομα τῆς μητρὸς αὐτοῦ Σαλωμὶθ θυγάτηρ Δαβρὶ ἐκ τῆς φυλῆς Δάν.

NETS: And a son of an Israelite woman (and he was the son of an Egyptian) came out among the sons of Israel, and the Israelite woman's son and the Israelite person began fighting in the camp.
And the Israelite woman's son called down a curse while naming the Name. And they brought him to Moyses—now his mother's name was Salomith, daughter of Dabri, of the tribe of Dan—

Comment

υἱὸς Αἰγυπτίου. The translator resists literally rendering the Hebrew element "man."

ἐν τοῖς υἱοῖς Ισραηλ. Hebrew בתוך is most often rendered by the full expression ἐν + μέσῳ, except when the Hebrew lexeme has a locational sense, as it is here as well as in Gen 9:21, of Noah being drunk within his tent (compare Gen 18:24; Exod 2:5). Here then, the second element is missing in Greek and neither is it present in any Septuagint mss. It is nevertheless impossible to visualize the locational idea expressed by the wording, but suggestions are given by various translators: Vahrenhorst (mitten unter = NETS among), Harlé and Pralon (au milieu) and Wevers (motion towards).[2]

ὁ ἄνθρωπος ὁ Ἰσραηλίτης. The unusual Hebrew construction is discussed in GKC §126 r.[3] It may be that G correctly assumes the first word also to be definite, but

---

[1] John William Wevers, *Leviticus, Septuaginta: Vetus Testamentum Graecum Auctaritate Academiae Scientiarum Gottingensis editum II, 2* (Göttingen: Vandenhoeck & Ruprecht, 1986); Dirk Büchner, "Leuitikon," in Albert Pietersma and Benjamin G. Wright III, eds., *A New English Translation of the Septuagint* (New York: Oxford University Press, 2007), 82–106.
[2] Martin Vahrenhorst, "Leuitikon," in *Septuaginta Deutsch, Erläuterungen und Kommentar I: Genesis bis Makkabäer*, ed. Martin Karrer and Wolfgang Kraus (Stuttgart: Deutsche Bibelgesellschaft, 2011), 420; Paul Harlé and Didier Pralon, *Le Lévitique*, La Bible d'Alexandrie 3 (Paris: Cerf, 1988), 195; and John William Wevers, *Notes on the Greek Text of Leviticus*, SCS 44 (Atlanta: Scholars Press, 1991), 393.
[3] Accessed through BibleWorks 7.

under normal circumstances the Greek article does not appear for things not yet encountered in the narrative. For this reason, it is likely that G has before him a text in which the Hebrew article appears, and this is indeed attested at Qumran.[4]

ἐμαχέσαντο. For the ingressive aspect of the middle, see Smyth §1924.[5] The verb can also mean in general, to quarrel, which perhaps allows the episode to be a battle of words rather than a fistfight.

ἐπονομάσας. This Greek verb means to call someone by a name or to pronounce a name (LSJ).[6] Hebrew ויקב can be taken in a variety of meanings, and these are set out one by one in *b. Sanh.* 56a with clever exposition and proof-texting: curse, perforate, name expressly (see also the entries in Jastrow, 930 for Hebrew נקב).[7]

κατηράσατο. In this apodosis is seen one of the few times where G, while rendering a Hebrew paratactic construction by circumstantial participle followed by indicative, does not spoil it with an intrusive καί. The verb καταράομαι is common in Genesis, rendering both curse verbs ארר and קלל. It is not employed by Exodus, who renders קלל by κακολογέω as does G Leviticus outside of this chapter. Here, however, he maintains Genesis' choice of καταράομαι, which is naturally found in absolute usage for the action of calling down curses, but typically it takes an indirect object in the dative. Neither the Targums nor G add an object for the verb, though it is tempting to take τὸ ὄνομα preceding it as object in the light of v. 15's prohibition.

ἐπονομάσας…τὸ ὄνομα κατηράσατο. Is there interpretive value in the grammatical subordination of the first verb? Wevers and Vahrenhorst agree that the action of naming (the participle) is muted by G who regards the crime only complete with the action of calling down the curse (indicative).[8] Larry Perkins, in a personal communication, suggested that the action expressed by the participle is the specific crime committed and the main verb expresses the consequences or implications of that action, hence "by naming/because he named…he cursed." The Targums go to some trouble to portray the action as a single act of naming and by implication blaspheming. Onk and PsJ have for the second verb רגז Aphel with the meaning of provoke (the Lord) to anger, synonymous with blaspheme and Neof has the technical term for blaspheme, חרף.[9] The Talmud wrestles with the same problem and solves it by concluding that the two verbs refer to one and the same action: ויקב ויקלל למימרא הוא קללה דנוקב *Vayyiqov vayy'qallel*: that is to say, *noqev* means to curse (*Sanh.* 56a.12, my translation).[10]

A second question pertaining to the interpretive value of the Septuagint is whether or not there is an exegetically motivated meaning shift to be found in the Septuagint from "curse" to "name." If G read the first verb as deriving from קבב or נקב with the meaning of "curse," it would appear that, based upon a developing tradition that the Name is not to be pronounced, he made an interpretive alteration that changed the

---

[4] 4QLev[b] and 11QpaleoLev[a]. See Wevers, *Notes*, 393 n. 16.
[5] Accessed via Perseus.
[6] Accessed via Perseus.
[7] Aramaic sources and reference works are accessed through the Comprehensive Aramaic Lexicon Project (hereafter CAL, http://cal.huc.edu).
[8] Wevers, *Notes*, 393; Vahrenhorst, "Leviticus," 420.
[9] See the entries in CAL with links to the lexica of Jastrow and Levy.
[10] Talmudic and Midrashic sources are accessed through Sefaria.org.

action.¹¹ An alternative explanation is that the translator read the verb נקב (also occurring in v. 16), in the sense of pronounce (so NJB, NEB, JPS) and simply rendered it with the appropriate Greek verb.¹² This is what we notice also in the Aramaic versions here and at v. 16, all of which render נקב by the root פרש Pa., meaning to express clearly or pronounce. Notice, however, that PsJ inserts a negative colouring וחרף (and blasphemed), and so does N with בגדפין (in blasphemy). These additions reframe the action: to pronounce means to blaspheme, also stated by *m. Sanhedrin* 7.5 המגדף אינו חיב עד שיפרש השם *the blasphemer is not liable for punishment until he pronounces the Name*. Sifra's explanation is identical: he did not curse with an epithet (בכינוי); he cursed by means of the explicitly pronounced name (שם המפורש) he heard at Sinai.¹³ It would appear that the Septuagint builds up to a single action: the crime of blasphemy took the form of a curse in which the Name was pronounced. It must be taken into consideration, however, that in the verses that follow, the Septuagint demonstrates a different approach to the Targums, in that it maintains a distinction between the individual of the narrative who curses, and the potential wrongdoer of the case law who might name the Name (v. 16).

Verse 12

ויניחהו במשמר לפרש להם על פי יהוה פ

καὶ ἀπέθεντο αὐτὸν εἰς φυλακὴν διακρῖναι αὐτὸν διὰ προστάγματος κυρίου.

NETS: and they put him away in custody to decide about him by the ordinance of the Lord.

Comment

ἀπέθεντο. In the first half of the verse, the Hebrew is faithfully rendered but there is no reason not to assume that Moses is included in the subject of the verb. G does not elaborate on what constitutes the group referred to in the plural. The Targums expand at length but focus on Moses as the decision-maker.

ἀπέθεντο...διακρῖναι. G is generally content to render Hebrew infinitives with Greek infinitives, and the result is not the best usage but neither is it nonsensical. The actions of putting and deciding seems a bit too distant for a genuine consecutive infinitive and

---

[11] An idea made popular by Abraham Geiger, *Ursprung und Uebersetzung der Bibel in ihrer Abhängigkeit von der inneren Entwicklung des Judentums* (Breslau: Heinauer, 1857), 274. See Wevers, *Notes*, 393, Vahrenhorst, "Leviticus," 412, and compare Martin Rösel, "Theologie der griechischen Bibel: zur Wiedergabe der Gottesaussagen im LXX-Pentateuch," *VT* 48, no. 1 (1998): 57, and Martin Rösel, "Exkurs: Übersetzung und Gebrauch des Gottesnamens," in *Septuaginta Deutsch, Erläuterungen und Kommentare I: Genesis bis Makkabäer* (ed. Martin Karrer and Wolfgang Kraus; Stuttgart: Deutsche Bibelgesellschaft, 2011), 414; for the developing tradition, see Geiger, *Ursprung*, 263–79.

[12] See Jacob Weingreen, "The Case of the Blasphemer (Leviticus XXIV, 10ff.)," *VT* 22, no. 1 (1972): 118–19, and Jacob Milgrom, *Leviticus 23–27*, AB 3B (New York: Doubleday, 2001), 2108; also Harlé and Pralon, *Le Lévitique*, 195.

[13] Sifra, *Emor* 14.2–3, see CAL פרש with link to Jastrow, 1242.

contemporary Koine would have employed ἵνα plus subjunctive. Though it is more common in the Documentary Sources (DS) for ἀπάγω to be associated with detaining a wrongdoer, ἀποτίθημι is attested too, as it is in P.Eleph. 12: γεγράφαμεν Πλειστάρχωι τῶι φυλακίτηι περὶ τῶν παροινησάντων σε ἀποθέσθαι αὐτοὺς εἰς τὴν φυλακήν we wrote to Pleistarchos the guard about the drunkards, for you to put them in prison. Similar wording is found also in P.Gurob 10.[14]

φυλακὴν. The article on the Hebrew noun could be an indicator of nothing more than a place of confinement in general. In the DS the Greek word is mostly indefinite, for instance in P.Cair.Zen. 1 59044: ἐπειδὴ ἐκεῖνος μέν ἐστιν ἐν φυλακῆι. In Ptolemaic Egypt the local village policeman, komophylakites, or an oikonomos could arrest and put someone in prison. Those held (κατέχω) in prison feel oppressed and unfairly treated (καταδυναστεύω) and are typically mistreated there in order to exact money owed, and the danger of prisoners perishing (καταφθείρω) was always present. Bauschatz provides an overview of the terminology and points out that many allegations of unfair treatment were unfounded or exaggerated.[15]

διακρῖναι αὐτὸν. The Hebrew expression לפרש להם "should be made clear to them" (NRSV) is difficult. Milgrom presents possible meanings of the Qal and is content to suggest "render a verdict," though indicating that a Piel would be more fitting.[16] HAL has "give a clear decision" and BDB "to declare distinctly to them."[17] It is best understood as an impersonal expression as the English versions have it. Syr reads "to be explained" and the Targums, amid expansions, have the passive "to be made clear." Milgrom views the intention of the Hebrew storyline as that of presenting a set of laws by way of a narrative in which Moses and those in council with him are uncertain of what to do.[18] The OG, on the other hand, makes quite a different point. The prepositional phrase of the Hebrew "to them" becomes a direct object "him," thereby redirecting attention from the indecision of the council to an action performed upon the accused himself. Vahrenhorst suggests that an outcome had already been reached.[19]

It is difficult to explain the use of διακρίνω in the active followed by an accusative of the person. If one were to judge by the flow of the narrative, it means "to make a decision with respect to him" (Wevers)[20] "de le juger" (BA),[21] "ihn abzuurteilen" (Vahrenhorst),[22] "pass judgement on [him], subject [him] to a thorough examination" (Muraoka),[23] all of which nicely fit the context. To be sure, the verb is freely encountered in the DS and Classical Literature (hereafter CL) in the semantic domain of legal judgment, meaning "receive a hearing" or "have a case heard" or "go to trial," tidily fitting the present circumstance if the individual under suspicion is in a holding cell

---

[14] Documentary papyri are accessed through papyri.info.
[15] John F. Bauschatz, "The Strong Arm of the Law? Police Corruption in Ptolemaic Egypt," *The Classical Journal* 103 (2007): 22–25.
[16] Milgrom, *Leviticus*, 2111.
[17] Accessed via Bible Works 7.
[18] Milgrom, *Leviticus*, 2102–106.
[19] Vahrenhorst, "Leviticus," 412.
[20] Wevers, *Notes*, 394.
[21] BA, 195.
[22] Vahrenhorst, "Leviticus," 420.
[23] Takamitsu Muraoka, *A Greek-English Lexicon of the Septuagint* (Louvain: Peeters, 2009), 152.

until a verdict can be reached by some process. However, when conveying that idea, the verb always appears in the passive and, when not used absolutely, is accompanied by prepositional clauses or the dative, as the following examples will illustrate (translations are my own unless otherwise indicated). The first two have πρός clauses referring to the one bringing the complaint: P.Mich. I 39 (mid-third century): ἀπόδος οὖν αὐτῶι τὴν ἀντιγραφὴν καὶ ἀπόστειλον πρὸς ἡμᾶς, ἵνα διακριθῆι πρὸς αὐτόν, *deliver the indictment then to him and send him to us in order to have the issue decided on the charge of his accuser* (πρὸς αὐτόν) (tr. APIS, adapted); P.Col. 4 88 (mid-third century) ὅπως παραγενόμενοι διακριθῶμεν πρὸς σέ, *in order that we, being present, may have our case judged in relation to you* (tr. APIS, adapted). To this may be added P.Mich. 1 98 and P.Sorb. 3 107 for identical usage. In the next examples the defendants appear in the dative: P.Tebt. 3.772 (mid-third century): ἐάν σοι φαίνηται, συνεδρεύσας Ἀσκληπιάδει… ὅπως διακριθῶ τοῖς κυρίοις τῶν κτημάτων, "you will therefore do well, if it please you, to join in session Asklepiades…so that my case against the owners of the vineyards may be heard";[24] UPZ 1 71 (late second century): διὸ καὶ ἡγούμενος δεῖν ἐπ' ἄλλου μὲν μηθενὸς αὐτῶι διακριθῆναι, ἐπὶ σοῦ δ' αὐτοῦ γέγραφά σοι, *therefore, since I am of the opinion that I should not enter into dispute with him before anyone else but you yourself, I wrote to you.* Analogous is P.Cair.Zen 2 59140 (mid-third century) ἀλλ' εἴ τι Κριτίας ἐνκαλεῖ, ἑτοιμός εἰμι αὐτῶι διακριθῆναι, *but if Kritias accuses at all, I am ready to take him to trial*; and P.Sorb. 3. 103 (late third century): εἰ δὲ μή, ἀπόστειλον ὅπως ἐπὶ τοῦ καθήκοντος κριτηρίου διακριθῶσιν, *but if not, send him that they may go to trial at the appropriate court.*

Classical usage is similar:[25] Plato *Laws* 937b, πρὶν τὴν δίκην διακεκρίσθαι, *before the verdict is settled* (accusative as subject of the infinitive in indirect speech); Xen. *Hist. Hell.* 5.2.10, εἰ δέ τι ἀμφίλογον πρὸς ἀλλήλους γίγνοιτο, δίκῃ διακριθῆναι, "and if any dispute should arise in any case between these purchasers and the exiles, it was to be settled by legal process."[26]

The verb does occur in the active, but once again followed by prepositional clauses or absolutely, to indicate the separation or distinguishing of alternative positions: BGU 6 1465 of third century Elephantine: ἐμμενῶ ἐν οἷς Ὀννῶφρις καὶ Ἰμούτης ἢν διακρίνωσιν περὶ ὧν ἐγκαλῶ Ἄνδρωνι καὶ οὗτος ἐμοί, *I abide by whatever decision is reached by Onnofris and Imoutes concerning the matters of which I accuse Andron and he me.* Absolute usage is more common in the Classical sources: Xen. *An.* 6.1.22, διαπορουμένῳ δὲ αὐτῷ διακρῖναι ἔδοξε κράτιστον εἶναι τοῖς θεοῖς ἀνακοινῶσαι, *in a quandary to arrive at a decision, he thought it best to consult the gods*; Xen. *Hist. Mem.* 1.1.9, ἃ τοῖς ἀνθρώποις ἔδωκαν οἱ θεοὶ μαθοῦσι διακρίνειν, *the things the gods gave men to settle in their minds by studying*; Plato *Laws* 847b, τὰ κοινὰ δικαστήρια διακρινόντων κατὰ νόμον, *the public courts shall decide as the law directs*; Arist. *Equit.* 749, ἵν' εἰδῇς ὁπότερος νῷν ἐστί σοι εὐνούστερος, διάκρινον, "make up your mind that you may know

---

[24] Roger S. Bagnall, and Peter Derow, eds., *The Hellenistic Period. Historical Sources in Translation. New Edition* (Maiden, MA: Blackwell, 2004), 162.
[25] Classical sources are accessed through *Thesaurus Linguae Graecae* under license from Norma Marion Alloway Library, Trinity Western University. Abbreviations follow the convention of LSJ.
[26] Carleton L. Brownson, *Xenophon. Hellenica, Books I-V. With an English Translation*, LCL 89 (Cambridge, MA: Harvard University Press, 1961), 33.

which one of us two is more well-disposed toward you"; and in Aristoph, *Wasps*, 764, Philocleon says: τοῦτο δὲ Ἅιδης διακρινεῖ πρότερον ἢ 'γὼ πείσομαι, *but Hades will decide before this* (τοῦτο) *happens to me*.

There are nevertheless examples in CL of the verb followed by an accusative of the thing, denoting multiple options between which to decide or differentiate: Hdt. 1.11, ἱκέτευε μή μιν ἀναγκαίη ἐνδέειν διακρῖναι τοιαύτην αἵρεσιν, *he pleaded not to be forcefully bound to decide upon the choice* [that is, of either killing someone or dying]; Hdt. 1.172, τοῦτο γὰρ οὐκ ἔχω ἀτρεκέως διακρῖναι, *I cannot clearly distinguish* [viz. which of the two languages influenced the other]; Hdt. 1.100, τάς τε δίκας γράφοντες ἔσω παρ' ἐκεῖνον ἐσπέμπεσκον, καὶ ἐκεῖνος διακρίνων τὰς ἐσφερομένας ἐκπέμπεσκε, "they would write down their pleas and send them in to him and passing judgement, he would send out the matters brought in." The verb abounds in Plato, wherever a decision is required between opposing positions (*Rep*. 2.348a-b, 376b and *Laws* 834a). Aristotle is fond of it in the sense of "distinguish" or "separate": *Nic. Eth*. 1119a, τὰ λοιπὰ ζῷα διακρίνει τὰ βρώματα, *the lower animals make a distinction with respect to food*; *Rhet*. 1375b, ὥσπερ ἀργυρογνώμων ὁ κριτής ἐστιν, ὅπως διακρίνῃ τὸ κίβδηλον δίκαιον καὶ τὸ ἀληθές, *the judge is like an assayer of silver, [duty bound] to distinguish adulterated justice from true justice*. In each of these, the objects of the verb in the accusative are plural referring to options that are abstract by nature. When, exceptionally, the accusative of the person follows the verb it is again in the plural and understood in the meaning of separate or distinguish: Plato *Hipp. Min*. 364c, referring to what most distinguishes Achilles and Odysseus, τί ἔλεγες περὶ τούτοιν τοῖν ἀνδροῖν; πῶς διέκρινες αὐτούς; *what did you say about these two men? How did you distinguish them one from the other*?

In summary, the evidence of the verb's function in non-translational contexts provides no support for taking αὐτόν as an accusative of respect "about him" naturally following the verb in its absolute sense of "pass judgment" or "come to a decision" or "make a judgment in a case." If the translator is to be given his due, he appears to have refrained from utilizing any ready-made solutions. He passed up the opportunities handed him of firstly rendering the Hebrew impersonal verb by a passive and, secondly, of supplying for the Hebrew prepositional clause a Greek prepositional clause or dative. He clearly did not wish to convey the meaning "to make a decision about him," or "give him a hearing." Instead, he employed the accusative following the active of διακρίνω for which any of the following are suitable meanings: "separate," "divide," "set aside," "distinguish from someone else." These meanings happen to overlap wholly with those of Aram. פרש Peal which may have been in view as he read the verb in MT. Whatever it is that drove his decision, he succeeds in bringing the offender into sharper relief, set apart or distinguished by a divine decree (see p. 31). Moses and those around him do not buy time to come to a decision, they already know what is to be done.

Incidentally, there are some ways in which the blasphemer was distinguished from another offender, legally speaking. Expansions on this verse in the Targums and Sifra *Emor* 14 draw comparisons between him and the wood-gatherer of Num 15:34 who was also witnessed committing sacrilege, put into custody awaiting a decision; he too was given a guilty verdict by the Lord and executed. However, unlike the wood-gatherer, the blasphemer was half-Israelite, and the witnesses of his misdeed did not merely observe it, but heard the Name being pronounced. Hearing such an oath placed an obligation on the witnesses (Lev 5) and necessitated the hand-laying rite to clear them from pollution.[27]

διὰ προστάγματος κυρίου. The expression על פי יהוה suggests a decision reached only by oracular means. It is rendered by διὰ προστάγματος κυρίου here and seven times in Numbers (either Numbers follows Leuitikon or it is the other way around). The response in Greek is quite different from the original, which leads the modern reader to infer some interpretive motives. A noun in the genitive with διά can be taken either as the instrument or the phrase as a whole may indicate the manner of the action. Not only that, but there are a range of possibilities for what may be understood by πρόσταγμα. It is one of three cases in Leuitikon where πρόσταγμα is said to be "of κύριος" and the only time in the book in which πρόσταγμα is found in a prepositional phrase, that is, given a role or function by which a matter could be settled. This is in stark contrast to the word's more common appearance as divine ordinance laid down either to keep or to transgress. The translator must have had some current usage in mind that was appropriate to his train of thought.

Prepositional phrases with πρόσταγμα outside the Septuagint provide an ample stock of comparative material. From it will emerge some possibilities of how to understand the word when it is deployed as a means of settling tricky legal situations or as determining the way such situations were to be handled. We limit our selection to texts from the third century unless indicated otherwise, and for the sake of convenience πρόσταγμα will be rendered into English by "ordinance" throughout. From the data it appears that there are three functional categories one might identify for this word: royal ordinances, *ad hoc* ordinances, and ordinances in the divine command formula. First and highest on the list, πρόσταγμα is an ordinance "of the king," that is, a standing order in general circulation that has the power to determine how things are to be done. Royal ordinances are familiar to those needing them to support a legal argument or to make a decision. In and of themselves they have instrumental power or effect, according to which persons arrange and direct their actions.

A search of prepositional phrases in which the noun is preceded by διά yielded only two cases. The first is P.Amh. 2. 33: προστεταχότων τῶν προγόνων ὑμῶν διὰ τοῦ ὑποκειμένου προστάγματος τοὺς προσπορευομένους συνηγόρους πρὸς τὰς προσοδικὰς κρίσεις ἐπὶ βλάβῃ τῶν προσόδων πρᾶξαι εἰς τὸ βασιλικὸν διπλοῦν τὸ ἐπιδέκατον καὶ τούτοις μηκέτι ἐξεῖναι συνηγορᾶσαι, "although your ancestors have ordained by the decree appended that advocates who take up fiscal cases to the detriment of the revenues shall be made to pay to the Crown the ten per cent caution-money doubled and shall not be allowed to act as advocates any longer."[28] The other is SB 16 12519 (2nd) containing a royal ordinance that no one is to buy or sell property belonging to a temple, with a warning to anyone who might transgress the things stipulated by the ordinance (τῶν διηγορευμένων διὰ τοῦ προστάγματος παραπράξῃ).

---

[27] See Milgrom, *Leviticus*, 2113.
[28] A. S. Hunt and C. C. Edgar, *Select Papyri. Official Documents. Petitions and Applications*, LCL 282 (Cambridge, MA: Harvard University Press, 1934), 247.

Three further examples suggest instrumentality. In P.Mich. 1 57 Lysanias berates Theophilos for absconding from a trial in which he would have been acquitted. Nevertheless, he is encouraged to return, having furnished himself with προστάγματα which will enable him to get the better of his adversaries: ἀκηκόαμεν δὲ καὶ δυνατόν σε πορίσαι προστάγματα εἰς τὸ τιμωρηθῆναι αὐτούς, *we have heard that you are able to procure προστάγματα in order to take vengeance on them*. Next, P.Petr. 2 38 R (b) brings report of individuals who sell oil at a higher price than has been stipulated in or by the regulation: πλείονος τιμῆς τῆς ἐν τῶι προστάγματι διασεσαφημένης. A final example of instrumentality is the prepositional phrase in P.Zen.Pestm. 49, from Eukles to Apollonios informing him of a letter about a taxable talent: τήν τε (sc. ἐπιστολήν) περὶ τοῦ ταλάντου ὅπως περιέληι ἐκ τοῦ προστάγματος τοῦ γραφέντος Πύθωνι..., *the [letter] about the talent, that he strike it [from his assessment] in keeping with the ordinance* [Jouguet, 'selon l'ordonnance'[29]] *directed in writing to Python...* Jouguet comments that the ordinance could have emanated from the king or from a *dioiketes*.[30] A text that explains nicely the role of a royal πρόσταγμα in a given situation, as well as revealing the relationship between πρόσταγμα and διάγραμμα is SB 18 13256 in which Poseidonios accuses two *chrematistai* of unfairly obstructing his petitions to the king. In line 6 he informs Artemon the *epistates*, that he has submitted to them justificatory documents including a πρόσταγμα τοῦ βασιλέως. In fact, he holds up the πρόσταγμα in support of his case as a counter to the general civil ordinance (τό ἐπὶ πάντων διάγραμμα) cited by his opponents. In a portion of the text he later crosses out, Poseidonios recounts what happened to a certain Archebios attempting to make an appeal similar to his own: by the king's ordinance and the general ordinance, Archebios was condemned and imprisoned after writing a complaint: κατὰ τὸ πρόσταγμα τοῦ βασιλέως καὶ τὸ διάγραμμα κατακέκριται Ἀρχήβιος...ἐντεύξεις γράφων καὶ νῦν ἐστιν ἐν τῶι δεσμωτηρίωι.[31]

Having considered examples where the impression is given of the royal προστάγματα themselves having instrumental value, there are formulae occurring in contexts similar to our present verse, in which procedural activities are conducted in accordance with known royal προστάγματα, in other words more suggestive of manner than instrumentality. In P.Cair.Zen. 1 59021, Demetrios alerts Apollonios about difficulties encountered in reminting foreign metal into Ptolemaic currency as he was accustomed to do, κατὰ τὸ πρόσταγμα ὃ κελεύει ἡμᾶς λαμβάνειν καὶ κατεργάζεσθαι, *by the regulation that orders [him] to receive and remint*. The petition in ZPE 152.191 requires Philon, who failed to pay taxes, be fined as ordinance demanded: πραχθῆναι... τὸ κατὰ πρόσταγμα ἐπίτιμον. In P.Cair.Zen. 5 59832 Zenon fears ὑπὸ τὸ πρόσταγμα γενέσθαι falling foul of an ordinance as a result of being unable to pay off debt.

UPZ 1 112 lists stipulations for tax farming, according to which each farmer is to act as best they can in an ethical manner κατὰ τοὺς νόμους καὶ τὰ διαγράμματα καὶ τὰ προστάγματα καὶ τὰ διορθώμεθα τὰ ὑφ' ἡμῶν διατασσόμενα ἐφ' ἑκάστης ὠνῆς, "in accordance with the laws, ordinances, ordinances amendments promulgated [by

---

[29] Pierre Jouguet, "Petit Supplément aux Archives de Zénon," *Cinquantenaire de l'École pratique des hautes études* (Paris: Éduard Champion, 1921), 221.
[30] Jouguet, "Archives," 223.
[31] Herwig Maehler, "Eine neue ptolemäische Enteuxis," *ArchPF* 33 (1987): 23–31.

the king] for each contract" (tr. Lewis).³² A number of texts, such as UPZ 1 116 and P.Petr. 3 72, are records of owners registering property as required by legal procedure: ἀπογράφομαι κατὰ τὸ ἐκτεθὲν πρόσταγμα τὴν ὑπάρχουσάν μοι οἰκίαν καὶ αὐλη, *I register in accordance with the regulation set down, my house and courtyard*. P.Enteux. 12 instructs an official to ensure that a stipulation about living space be fairly applied: παράδειξον αὐτοῖς τὰ μέρη κατὰ τὸ πρόσταγμα, *allot them their portions according to the regulation*. Here one might add the petition in which the miller Thasias reports to Petesouchos the village scribe the damage the former incurred after individuals invaded her workplace, disabling her milling equipment and arresting her daughter. She requests κατὰ τὸ πρόσταγμα ἐπελθεῖν σε ἐπὶ τὸ ἐργαστήριον ὅπως εἰδὼς, *that in accordance with the procedure [he] make a visit and inspect her premises*.

If we read the clause in Lev 24:12 in the light of royal ordinances, we could think of it in the following ways:

1. Moses and his council were guided by a divine ordinance, given, in the way ordinances were understood to be given, on the initiative of the regent.
2. Moses' actions were in conformity with the requirements of the divine ordinance known to him.

Here the point could be made that, in the Septuagint's version, Moses and his council were already acting by divine decree given them, not awaiting it, as suggested by the Hebrew. Or, since this event was unprecedented, it means that the way they proceeded was as divine ordinance would have demanded.

Either or both of these being valid, Moses' standing is elevated. He is the knowledgeable lawgiver and judge not lacking in understanding of correct procedure. It should be noted, however, that in all but one of the cited passages the article appears with the noun, indicating known or specific προστάγματα relating to each sphere of concern. But the article is missing in Lev 24:12, leading us to consider other alternatives.

The second option is to understand πρόσταγμα as a one-time new directive solicited from higher authority governing a specific need arising from an unknown cause. Only upon the issuance of such a command could a specific matter be settled. We notice that, in the majority of such cases, πρόσταγμα is indefinite. We begin with ad hoc directives that may be solicited from the king. In PSI 5 502 Panakestor, anticipating Apollonios' displeasure (evident later in the same document), asks Zenon to remind Apollonios to ask the king for προστάγματα, as he said he would: σπούδασον μνησθῆναι αὐτῶι ἵνα τὰ προστάγματα λάβηι παρὰ τοῦ βασιλέως καθάπερ ὡμολόγησεν ἡμῖν.³³ P.Mich. 1 71 tells of a strategos who wrote a πρόσταγμα ordering a debt-collector to exact funds owing to the writer of the complaint. Since the debt-collector ignored the instruction, the complainant asks the king to order (προστάξαι) another strategos to write (a presumably more strongly worded πρόσταγμα) to the debt-collector to

---

³² Naphtali Lewis, *Greeks in Ptolemaic Egypt: Case Studies in the Social History of the Hellenistic World*, Classics in Papyrology 2 (Oakville, CT: American Society of Papyrologists, 2001), 19.

³³ John White, *Light from Ancient Letters* (Philadelphia: Fortress Press, 1986), 42, translates "in order that the king receive the instructions," which adds another dimension to the current argument.

exact what is owed κατὰ τὸ διάγραμμα (general regulations) in order for the wronged party not to suffer injustice. In P.Eleph.DAIK 1, we read of an individual sent off for hard labour, having posed as someone's legal representative without having obtained a πρόσταγμα, either from the king or from the chrematistai (οὐ λαβὼν πρόσταγμα παρὰ τοῦ βασιλέως οὐδὲ παρὰ χρηματιστῶν).

Such προστάγματα were also solicited from lesser officials in order for a course of action to proceed or for a situation to be remedied. PSI 5 539 is a complaint about a certain Phanias who is obstructing the delivery of wine to a sanctuary where Phemennas is the priest. The latter requests an official to write to Phanias to release the wine, since without a πρόσταγμα, he will keep holding on to it and the temple will be in difficulties: δέομαι οὖν σου γράψαι Φανίαι ἀφεῖναι τὸν οἶνον...τοῖς ἐν τῶι τόπωι ἀφῆκεν ἄνευ προστάγματός σου...με οὐθενὸς καθυστερεῖν. Where a πρόσταγμα is written for a specific case is evident in P.Col. 3 12, in which Attinas requests that his brother be paid on time, κατὰ τὸ γεγραμμένον αὐτῶι πρόσταγμα πρὸς Ἀπολλόδωρον τὸν οἰκονόμον, *in agreement with the ordinance written in his behalf to Apollodoros the oikonomos*. In P.Cair.Zen. 2 59236, Neoptolemos petitions the *dioiketes* to provide him with a πρόσταγμα to submit to the relevant palace officials for them to reassess the taxes payable on his father's vineyard: δέομαι οὖν σου, εἴ σοι δοκεῖ, ἐπισκέψασθαι περὶ τούτων, καὶ...δοῦναί μοι πρόσταγμα πρὸς Ἑρμόλαον καὶ Πετοσῖριν ὅπως ἂν ἐκ τριῶν ἐτῶν τὴν ἐπιγραφὴν καὶ τῶι πατρὶ ποιήσωνται. The court session hearing the case of Dositheos against Herakleia recounted in P.Gurob 2 becomes constituted κατὰ τὸ... γραφὲν αὐτῶι πρόσταγμα οὗ ἐστιν ἀντίγραφον τόδε *upon the authority of a written copy of the πρόσταγμα issued by Aristomachos, strategos of the Arsinoite nome, for that purpose*. A final example is P.Hib. 1 34, whose wording is not unlike Lev 24:12. Antigonos relates that ἐμοῦ γὰρ ἀπαγαγόντος Καλλίδρομον...εἰς τὸ ἐν Σινάρυ δεσμωτήριον κατὰ πρόσταγμα Δωρίωνος τοῦ ἐπιστάτου, *[he] had imprisoned Kallidromos (the donkey-thief) by order of Dorion the epistates*.[34]

If we read the clause in Lev 24:12 with these texts as background, it could be understood in the following way: in the absence of a standing directive for a misdeed of this nature, Moses obtained in the moment a πρόσταγμα from κύριος appropriate to his unique conundrum. Moses acted by a πρόσταγμα and isolated the wrongdoer. This is certainly the most attractive option. It is similar in kind to the rendering provided by Onk and PsJ for the words על פי יהוה found in the Hebrew, that is, על גזירת מימרא דייי, "by the decision of the Divine Memra."

The third option brings us back to the notion of manner. It is to read the prepositional phrase as similar in function to a formula κατὰ πρόσταγμα τοῦ θεοῦ occurring in dozens of contemporary texts and inscriptions. The so-called divine command formula or divine imperative is well-treated in recent literature.[35] The manner in

---

[34] For comment, see Bauschatz, "Strong Arm," 29.

[35] Gil Renberg, "Dreams and Other Divine Communications from the Isiac Gods in the Greek and Latin Epigraphical Record," in *Individuals and Materials in the Greco-Roman Cults of Isis (SET) Agents, Images, and Practices*, ed. Valentino Gasparini and Richard Veymiers; Religions in the Graeco-Roman World 187 (Leiden: Brill, 2018), 649–71; Eleni Fassa, "Divine Commands, Authority, and Cult: Imperative Dedications to the Egyptian Gods," *Opuscula. Annual of the Swedish Institutes at Athens and Rome (OpAthRom)* 9 (2016): 59–70.

which the formula is employed in letters and dedicatory inscriptions is not unlike the expression in Lev 24:12 since, in both instances, πρόσταγμα is indefinite, preceded by a preposition and followed by a divine epithet in the genitive. In both, a directive revealed on the initiative of a deity provides the explanation for a human act of dedication or obedience. Incidentally, the divine command formula is most often associated with Sarapis, the patron deity of the Ptolemaic dynasty and of Alexandria itself. From the DS, three texts are noteworthy. The first is a letter written by a certain Zoilos to Apollonios the finance minister (P.Cair.Zen. 59034). Zoilos cleverly builds an argument requesting the funds for a Sarapide shrine to be built. He begins by relating how Sarapis had repeatedly instructed him (χρηματίζειν) through dreams to make provision for the building and punished him with illness for requesting to be relieved of the responsibility. Amplifying his rhetoric, he frames the instruction as a divine command, τὸ ὑφ' αὐτοῦ προστασσόμενον, and ultimately presents his request as nothing less than a set of divine orders to be obeyed if Apollonios is to remain in Sarapis' good books: καλῶς οὖν ἔχει, Ἀπολλώνιε, ἐπακολουθῆσαί σε τοῖς ὑπὸ τοῦ θεοῦ προστάγμασιν, ὅπως ἂν εὐίλατός σοι ὑπάρχων ὁ Σάραπις. A second example is UPZ 1 20 in which the sisters Taues and Taous, wronged by their own relatives, appeal to the king's generosity. Their food allowance inside the Sarapieion was dwindling despite their late father's friend Ptolemaios having come to their aid. His help, according to them, was not a decision motivated by familial loyalty but following divine orders (οὐ κατὰ προγονικὴν αἵρεσιν…κατὰ πρόσταγμα δὲ τοῦ θεοῦ). A third is the letter (P.Cair. Zen. 3 59426) in which Dromon asks Zenon to order one of his associates to buy some Attic honey. He needs it for his eyes, says Dromon, but adds that his need (or Zenon's provision) would be in line with divine mandate: χρείαν γὰρ ἔχω πρὸς τοὺς ὀφθαλμοὺς κατὰ πρόσταγμα τοῦ θεοῦ.

The same formula is common to the Inscriptional Literature (hereafter IL), found on a number of monuments recording acts of devotion. Three examples among dozens are worth citing, the first of which is the Delian Chronicle (IG XI,4 1299). The priest Apollonios makes it known very early on that he produced the inscription κατὰ πρόσταγμα τοῦ θεοῦ, explaining a few lines later that the god instructed him on several occasions through dreams (ἐχρημάτισεν κατὰ τὸν ὕπνον). The second is an inscription appearing on the offering receptacle of Sarapieion A at Delos (IG XI,4 1247). Ktesias, who erected the receptacle, dedicates it to Sarapis, Isis and Anubis, also mentioning that he did so κατὰ πρόσταγμα τοῦ θεοῦ. A final example, this time hailing from Memphis, is a dream-interpreter's sign to passers-by advertising his divinely sanctioned gifts (Saqqara, third century Memphis Bernand IsMetr 112). It reads ἐνύπνια κρίνω τοῦ θεοῦ πρόσταγμα ἔχων, "I judge dreams, having the mandate of the god."[36]

If the divine command formula emphasizes the command itself and diminishes the effect of the individual's initiative (so Fassa),[37] it would fit Lev 24:12 where the translator is aware of this understanding of πρόσταγμα to indicate the sole initiative of κύριος who, in the course of the event, issues an order to Moses to obey, which

---

[36] Gil Renberg, "Incubation at Saqqâra," *Proceedings of the 25th International Congress of Papyrology Ann Arbor 2007*, ed. Traianos Gagos; American Studies in Papyrology Special Edition (Ann Arbor: American Society of Papyrologists, 2010), 651.

[37] Fassa, "Divine Commands," 60–61.

he duly does. However, the formula may be more ambiguous, denoting a broader range of experience and human initiative.[38] Zoilos clearly trades on Apollonios' sense of duty and piety.[39] The sisters in the Serapieion may be prompting the king to act with a benevolence commensurate with Apollonios' devotion to Sarapis. Though Dromon's request may tell us about Sarapis' reputation for revealing medical advice through dreams (so White),[40] there may be an equally plausible connection between the way Dromon politely approaches the request and his appeal to Zenon's religious sensitivity. It is likely that in the IL, wherever the divine command formula occurs, the religious encounter as a whole, from instruction to application, is interpreted as, or becomes in the eyes of the beholder, a mode of action by divine mandate. Though Renberg does not take the argument quite that far, he recognizes that it is the writer's decision to refer to the encounter.[41] In other words, underscoring one's actions in this way elevates one's own credibility. In the dedicatory inscriptions, the divine command formula is an expression of proper devotional action befitting a pious worshiper rather than specifically evoking the actual command of the god. Formal considerations are also important. The noun is without exception indefinite, whereas known or specified προστάγματα are always definite.

Bringing this to bear on Lev 24:12 means that G as narrator elevates Moses' credentials by presenting him as one who acts not on a specific command but in pious devotion "by divine mandate." A contrast is found earlier in 10:1 where Aaron's sons bring the πῦρ ἀλλότριον ὃ οὐ προσέταξεν κύριος, which is to say "strange fire as the Lord would not have had it," and the only time in the Pentateuch that κύριος is the subject of the cognate verb προστάσσω.

Whether or not we can ever be sure of the translator's reasons for selecting this wording, it seems clear that he wants to present a side of Moses not seen in the Hebrew. In Hebrew the focus is on Moses and his entourage, indecisive, awaiting an oracular decision. In the Septuagint the focus is on their judicious decision, guided by a divine πρόσταγμα, or acting as divine protocol would have demanded.

Verses 13–14

וידבר יהוה אל משה לאמר
הוצא את המקלל אל מחוץ למחנה וסמכו כל השמעים את ידיהם על ראשו ורגמו אתו כל העדה

Καὶ ἐλάλησεν κύριος πρὸς Μωυσῆν λέγων
Ἐξάγαγε τὸν καταρασάμενον ἔξω τῆς παρεμβολῆς, καὶ ἐπιθήσουσιν πάντες οἱ ἀκούσαντες τὰς χεῖρας αὐτῶν ἐπὶ τὴν κεφαλὴν αὐτοῦ, καὶ λιθοβολήσουσιν αὐτὸν πᾶσα ἡ συναγωγή.

---

[38] Renberg, "Dreams," 666.
[39] Gil Renberg and William Bubelis, "The Epistolatory Rhetoric of Zoilos of Aspendos and the Early Cult of Sarapis: Re-reading P.Cair.Zen. 1 59034," ZPE 177 (2011): 179.
[40] White, *Ancient Letters*, 25.
[41] Renberg, "Dreams," 660.

NETS: And the Lord said to Moyses, saying, "Take the one who called down the curse outside the camp, and all who heard shall lay their hands on his head, and the whole congregation shall stone him."

Comment

ἐλάλησεν. G makes no effort to suggest that the divine ordinance specific to the offense begins at this point. The Lord now simply speaks, as he does in the rest of the book. It is nevertheless of interest that, at the end of the episode in v. 23, the people do as the Lord ordered Moses (καθὰ συνέταξεν κύριος).

τὸν καταρασάμενον. G follows the Hebrew wording. In v. 14 there is perfect equivalence from Hebrew to Greek (even to the inclusion of possessive pronouns on parts of the body) and careful reflection of word order. This may illustrate the respect held for the divine words present in the original. It also serves to illustrate how effortlessly Greek word order and syntax can coincide with Hebrew word order and syntax. By contrast, the Targums do not have "the one who cursed" but "the one who blasphemed" in an effort to prevent this action being disassociated from those of v. 11 (Onk, PsJ רגז Af.; N חרף Pa.).

λιθοβολήσουσιν αὐτὸν πᾶσα ἡ συναγωγή. The prescribed sentence for the one who called down the curse is carried out in v. 23. Regular casuistic law now continues, directed to the Israelite people as a whole.

Verses 15–16

ואל בני ישראל תדבר לאמר איש איש כי יקלל אלהיו ונשא חטאו
ונקב שם יהוה מות יומת רגום ירגמו בו כל העדה כגר כאזרח בנקבו שם יומת

καὶ τοῖς υἱοῖς Ισραηλ λάλησον καὶ ἐρεῖς πρὸς αὐτούς Ἄνθρωπος ἄνθρωπος ἐὰν
καταράσηται θεόν, ἁμαρτίαν λήμψεται·
ὀνομάζων δὲ τὸ ὄνομα κυρίου θανάτῳ θανατούσθω· λίθοις λιθοβολείτω αὐτὸν
πᾶσα συναγωγὴ Ἰσραήλ· ἐάν τε προσήλυτος ἐάν τε αὐτόχθων, ἐν τῷ ὀνομάσαι
αὐτὸν τὸ ὄνομα κυρίου τελευτάτω.

NETS: "And speak to the sons of Israel, and you shall say to them, 'If a person, a person should curse God, he shall assume guilt. Whoever names the name of the Lord—by death let him be put to death; let the whole congregation of Israel stone him with stones. Whether a guest or a native, when he names the name of the Lord, let him die.'"

Comment

Narratologically, vv. 15–16 constitute an aesthetically pleasing response to v. 11 in both Hebrew and Greek since the same two verbs, cursing and naming, appear this time in reverse order. Here the more serious penalty is connected to the action of naming. In comparison with the strict one-to-one equivalence of the previous verse, there are now some variations of expression in the Greek.

v. 15

καὶ τοῖς υἱοῖς Ισραηλ λάλησον. This clause illustrates how G avoids wooden rendering. Instead of rendering the preposition, he employs the dative, and the imperative instead of the literalistic imperatival future. The same approach is seen at 9:3.

καὶ ἐρεῖς πρὸς αὐτούς. Either G had before him ואמרת אליהם (compare Syr) or he wished to provide greater emphasis (than would have λέγων) on the fact that the sons of Israel were the ones being addressed on the subject matter of cursing God and naming the Name.

ἐὰν καταράσηται θεόν. The Hebrew vocabulary of this verse is identical with the wording of Exod 22:27. In the Greek of that passage קלל is softened to κακολογέω and אלהים rendered in the plural by θεούς. The prohibition of cursing God appearing at this point in the present context has puzzled ancient and modern interpreters, since it appears to be a separate injunction, unrelated to the actions of v. 11, in which God was not explicitly cursed. In an effort to bring them into alignment, the Targums rewrite the offense in v. 15 as blaspheme before God (Onk), blaspheme and belittle the substitute name of God (PsJ; also *b. Sanh.* 56a 15), and pronounce in blasphemy the name of God (N). G makes no similar move to blend the actions into a single one, but renders the Hebrew faithfully at this point.

θεόν. It may be that, by the use of indefinite θεός without possessive pronoun, G may have alluded to a pseudonym for the Tetragrammaton, since its precise Hebrew equivalent אלהים would count as a substitute name or epithet.[42]

ἁμαρτίαν λήμψεται. G has a preference for the indefinite noun, even when it is definite in Hebrew (19:8 and 20:17). Of syntactical interest is that the Hebrew apodotic vav is ignored, producing a natural Greek apodosis. There is the chance that, by reversing the Hebrew word order, G places emphasis on the effect of insulting the divine. That is to say, it is sin-guilt that will be incurred in this instance. The assumption of sin automatically requiring recompense is in both Hebrew and Greek thinking a matter between the offender and the deity. What this verse in Greek then means is that anyone cursing the God of the Israelites (even by epithet) would have him to deal with.

v. 16

ὀνομάζων. That G renders נקב in this way is in alignment with his understanding of the verb's meaning in v. 11. All the Aramaic versions follow suit, although PsJ and N clarify by adding that it was done with blasphemous intent, as they do above. The idea of blasphemy as by-product is not something G wishes to press.

δέ. The adversative δέ is significant, also reflected in PsJ (ברם). Its effect is to create a distinction between the two offenses of cursing God and naming the Name, as well as their modes of punishment. The act of cursing God (v. 15) attracts sin-guilt and is a matter to be settled between God and the offender. But naming the name of the Lord (v. 16) deserves public execution and only at this point is there explicit and repeated

---

[42] See Milgrom, *Leviticus*, 2115.

reference to death. When the Name is uttered, it is a witnessed act. The offender is to be publicly tried and executed by human agency.[43] Such a distinction makes sense because other offenses in which sin-guilt is assumed do not automatically carry the death penalty unless it is so stipulated (see 19:8 and 22:9).

τὸ ὄνομα κυρίου. The full expression in Greek occurs twice in the verse. At first שם יהוה is faithfully rendered, as it is in the Targums. The presence of indefinite שם at the end of the verse seems not to be a case of haplography since it invited all kinds of clarification. G harmonizes to שם יהוה, Onk has "the name," PsJ "blasphemes the specific name" (יחריף שמא דמיהד), N "the name of his God," and Syr "my name."

θανάτῳ θανατούσθω...τελευτάτω. The verbs for dying used by G follow a broad pattern. When accounting for מות Hophal in the formula מות יומת (the serious offenses in ch. 20) he prefers the passive of θανατόω. For מות Hiphil he employs ἀποκτείνω and for מות Qal, ἀποθνῄσκω and active τελευτάω. The latter is found referring to a corpse in 21:11 as befits its natural usage in CL of someone who has died. More interestingly, it refers to Aaron's sons who died by divine hand in 16:1 for sacrilege. Korytko, in a study of verbs in the semantic domain of capital punishment, finds that, in CL, τελευτάω may refer to someone who died as a result of receiving the death sentence, but is never found as a technical term in any prescriptions for death by execution.[44] Its use in 16:1 is therefore natural, but here it is unusual. An attempt at explanation begins by noticing that G reads not יומת but ימות, the consequence of involuntary sacrilege to be avoided in 16:2 and 13. Why does he not render ἀποθανεῖται here as he does there? Perhaps due to the gravity of the present offense, the verb he selects is the one previously employed for the death of Aaron's sons.

λίθοις λιθοβολείτω. While the verb רגם is unique to Lev and Num, this is the only instance of the intensive with infinitive absolute. G defaults to his usual representation of the expression when אבן is present. It is rhetorically skillful because, like the Hebrew, his formula has the same element repeated.

At this point, it is worth setting side by side the complete Greek and Aramaic storylines. The Septuagint presents the following narrative:

> The son of the Israelite woman, while naming the Name, called down a curse; and [the imprecation having been witnessed,] he was brought to Moses (v. 11). In accordance with divine ordinance, he was detained in prison so as to separate him or distinguish him [from others like him] (v. 12). Kyrios then spoke (v. 13): Take the one who cursed outside the camp. Those who heard must lay hands on him and the whole community must pelt him with stones (v. 14). [Thus far we have the specific instructions relating to this individual, which are carried out in v. 23.] Now the entire congregation is instructed: In the case of someone who curses God, sin and its consequence

---

[43] Milgrom, *Leviticus*, 2118; Erhard Gerstenberger, *Das dritte Buch Mose / Leviticus*, ATD 6 (Göttingen: Vandenhoeck & Ruprecht, 1993), 364.
[44] Joel Korytko, "Death of the Covenant Code: Evaluating the Translation of Laws with Capital Punishment in Old Greek Exodus 21.1–23.19 in Light of Graeco-Egyptian Law" (PhD diss., University of Oxford, 2022), 53.

is what they will attract, but anyone who pronounces the Name of Kyrios is to be executed by stoning. Having pronounced the Name, that person is to die. (vv. 15–16)

The same narrative according to the Targums runs as follows:[45]

> The son of the Israelite woman blasphemously named the Name and angered God by the blasphemy; and [these words having been witnessed,] he was brought to Moses (v. 11). [Setting aside the lengthy expansions] They bound him in prison until [the verdict] should be made clear by a decision of the Memra of Adonay (v. 12). Adonay then spoke (v. 13): Take the one who blasphemed outside the camp. Those who heard must lay hands on him and the whole community must pelt him with stones (v. 14). Anyone who blasphemes before his God, even by using a substitute name, assumes guilt, and/but one who blasphemously pronounces the Name of Adonay is to be executed by stoning. At the very moment he names the Specific Name, he must be killed (vv. 15–16).

The Targums produce a seamless narrative in which all the actions of the Hebrew original are adjusted to fit a single action of naming the Name in blasphemy. What ought to be done to the blasphemer is revealed by divine decision. There is to be the single penalty of public execution.

The Septuagint makes explicit the act of naming the Name and presents a Moses who does not vacillate but acts according to, or directed by, a divine precept to isolate the wrongdoer. The Lord speaks a set of instructions that make a distinction between the two actions of pronouncing and cursing, for which there appear to be separate courses of action. The real person in the narrative who cursed is to be taken outside the camp, have hands placed on him, and stoned. The assumed subject of the casuistic law who curses "God" is liable to guilt and its consequences. But one who names the name of Kyrios is to be executed by stoning. In naming the Name of Kyrios, he is to die.

The direction taken by the Septuagint is not too distant from the Hebrew except for a few subtle points. No notion is entertained of Moses being in need of direction or uncertain of what to do. The divine ordinance is not something Moses awaits; it is what directs his actions. Nevertheless, the act of naming the Name as severe transgression cannot be said to be an innovation of the Septuagint translator. It would be more accurate to say that the translator goes along with a tradition that read נקב as "pronounce," which allows him to bring this misdeed to the forefront by contrasting it with the act of cursing God. As Milgrom reminds us, this is an episode in which law comes by way of a narrative.[46] Overtly, the Egyptian-Israelite transgressor of the narrative (both in Hebrew and in Greek) was executed as the one who cursed. But the

---

[45] A note: as far as can be gathered from the lexica, the following verbal forms all refer to the act of blasphemy: רגז Aphel, חרף Pael and גדיפין plural noun.
[46] Milgrom, *Leviticus*, 2102–106.

potential wrongdoer who pronounces the Name, that is, anyone in the congregation of the sons of Israel, is situated in the lawgiving and would die as one who pronounces (בנקבו / ἐν τῷ ὀνομάσαι αὐτὸν). That aspect is presented a little more forcefully by the Septuagint. But by flattening the Hebrew vocabulary into a single misdeed of blasphemy, the Targums relinquish much that is offered us by the Hebrew composition and its Greek translation.

Bibliography

Bagnall, Roger S., and Derow, Peter eds. *The Hellenistic Period: Historical Sources in Translation. New Edition*. Maiden, MA: Blackwell, 2004.

Bauschatz, John F. "The Strong Arm of the Law? Police Corruption in Ptolemaic Egypt." *The Classical Journal* 103 (2007).

Büchner, Dirk. "Leuitikon." *A New English Translation of the Septuagint*. Edited by Albert Pietersma and Benjamin G. Wright III. New York: Oxford University Press, 2007.

Brownson, Carleton L. *Xenophon. Hellenica. Books I–V. With an English Translation*. LCL 89. Cambridge, MA: Harvard University Press, 1961.

Fassa, Eleni. "Divine commands, authority, and cult: Imperative dedications to the Egyptian gods." *Opuscula. Annual of the Swedish Institutes at Athens and Rome (OpAthRom)* 9. 2016.

Geiger, Abraham. *Ursprung und Uebersetzung der Bibel in ihrer Abhängigkeit von der inneren Entwicklung des Judentums*. Breslau: Heinauer, 1857.

Gerstenberger, Erhard. *Das dritte Buch Mose / Leviticus*. ATD 6. Göttingen: Vandenhoeck & Ruprecht, 1993.

Harlé, Paul and Didier Pralon. *Le Lévitique*. La Bible d'Alexandrie 3. Paris: Cerf, 1988.

Hunt, A. S., and C. C. Edgar. *Select Papyri. Official Documents. Petitions and Applications*. LCL 282. Cambridge, MA: Harvard University Press, 1934.

Jouguet, Pierre. "Petit Supplément aux Archives de Zénon." *Cinquantenaire de l'École pratique des hautes études*. Paris: Éduard Champion, 1921.

Korytko, Joel. "Death of the Covenant Code: Evaluating the Translation of Laws with Capital Punishment in Old Greek Exodus 21.1–23.19 in Light of Graeco-Egyptian Law." PhD diss., University of Oxford, 2022.

Lewis, Naphtali. *Greeks in Ptolemaic Egypt: Case Studies in the Social History of the Hellenistic World*. Classics in Papyrology 2. Oakville, CT: American Society of Papyrologists, 2001.

Maehler, Herwig. "Eine neue ptolemäische Enteuxis." *ArchPF* 33 (1987).

Milgrom, Jacob. *Leviticus 23–27*. AB 3B. New York: Doubleday, 2001.

Muraoka, Takamitsu. *A Greek–English Lexicon of the Septuagint*. Louvain: Peeters, 2009.

Renberg, Gil and William Bubelis. "The Epistolatory Rhetoric of Zoilos of Aspendos and the Early Cult of Sarapis: Re-reading P.Cair.Zen. 1 59034." *ZPE* 177 (2011).

Renberg, Gil. "Dreams and Other Divine Communications from the Isiac Gods in the Greek and Latin Epigraphical Record." *Individuals and Materials in the Greco-Roman Cults of Isis (SET) Agents, Images, and Practices*. Edited by Valentino Gasparini and Richard Veymiers. Religions in the Graeco-Roman World 187. Leiden: Brill, 2018.

Renberg, Gil. "Incubation at Saqqâra." *Proceedings of the 25th International Congress of Papyrology Ann Arbor 2007*. Edited by Traianos Gagos. American Studies in Papyrology Special Edition. Ann Arbor: American Society of Papyrologists, 2010.

Rösel, Martin. "Exkurs: Übersetzung und Gebrauch des Gottesnamens." *Septuaginta Deutsch. Erläuterungen und Kommentare I: Genesis bis Makkabäer*. Edited by Martin Karrer and Wolfgang Kraus. Stuttgart: Deutsche Bibelgesellschaft, 2011.

Rösel, Martin. "Theologie der griechischen Bibel: zur Wiedergabe der Gottesaussagen im LXX-Pentateuch." *VT* 48, no. 1 (1998): 49–62.

Vahrenhorst, Martin. "Leuitikon." *Septuaginta Deutsch, Erläuterungen und Kommentare I: Genesis bis Makkabäer*. Edited by Martin Karrer and Wolfgang Kraus. Stuttgart: Deutsche Bibelgesellschaft, 2011.

Weingreen, Jacob. "The Case of the Blasphemer. Leviticus XXIV, 10ff." *VT* 22, no. 1 (1972).

Wevers, John William. *Notes on the Greek Text of Leviticus*. SCS 44. Atlanta: Scholars Press, 1991.

Wevers, John William. *Leviticus. Septuaginta: Vetus Testamentum Graecum Auctaritate Academiae Scientiarum Gottingensis editum II, 2*. Göttingen: Vandenhoeck & Ruprecht, 1986.

White, John. *Light from Ancient Letters*. Philadelphia: Fortress Press, 1986.

Chapter 3

Flying Sickles Sound Scarier: The Role of Harvest as Judgment Metaphor in the LXX as a Foundation for the Translation of מְגִלָּה as Δρέπανος in Zechariah 5:1–4*

Christine Waring

In Zech 5:14, there is an interesting deviation between the MT and the LXX.[1] When one compares the New Revised Standard Version and the New English Translation of the Septuagint,[2] one will see shifts in word order, expansion, verb tenses and verb forms, but the focus of the present study is the deviation in the judgement metaphors present in the text. The MT word מְגִלָּה (scroll) has become δρέπανος (sickle) in the LXX. This study will attempt to determine how these changes originated. Are they, for instance, examples of homophony, different patterns of Hebrew vocalization or divergences in the consonantal textual tradition, aspects of the translator's technique, misunderstandings of the original Hebrew text, or theologically motivated deviations from the original text? George E. Howard, the translator of the Twelve Prophets for

---

* In 2018, I had the pleasure of taking an Exposition of Exodus class with Professor Larry Perkins. I remember Professor Perkins explaining how the culture of the LXX translators could have shaped the differences in how the Tabernacle is characterized in the MT from "the tent of meeting" to "the tent of witness" in the LXX. His knowledge of the textual traditions found within the MT and LXX opened a whole new world of wonder. As I have furthered my studies, the richness of questions that can be asked about biblical interpretation and manuscript tradition has inspired me to dig deeper. This paper is an attempt to engage with the questions that have become available to me through Larry Perkins' passion and knowledge. I want to thank the editorial committee for inviting me to contribute to this *Festschrift* in honour of Larry Perkins' 75th birthday.

[1] I will be using the text with the recognition that it is a part of the *Kaige* recension. My purpose is to investigate how that community group translated and/or revised the text rather than focusing on determining the context of the Old Greek (older texts of the LXX).

[2] When the LXX is translated into English I will be using the New English Translation of the Septuagint as it was specifically translated to compare with the New Revised Standard Version which follows the MT. Unless mentioned, all English translations of the biblical text will be from the NRSV.

NETS, suggests that the difference from scroll to sickle "is traceable to a different consonantal text."[3] While I do not disagree with Howard's statement, I believe that a re-examination of this case and an explanation regarding how it came about will be helpful because understanding the process by which a change has occurred in the text informs us not only of the values and culture of the receivers of the text, but also of how the text itself was shaped by culture.

This essay will look at the specific factors that led to the differentiation between the MT and the LXX in Zechariah. I will argue that 1) the variations in reading the Hebrew text at the time of translation as a result of different vocalizations, 2) the lack of contextual markers in the text, and 3) the use of the *harvest as judgment* metaphor in the passage and in other sources led either the copyists of the Hebrew text or the LXX translators mistakenly to parse מגלה as a feminine noun and to correct it to מגל. This will be made clear in a short discussion of different Hebrew vocalizations of the consonantal text by surveying the various contexts in the MT where מְגִלָּה is found and identifying the translational equivalents in the LXX to see if there is a pattern of interpreting מְגִלָּה as מַגָּל. It will also be important to focus on the translation technique of the LXX Minor Prophets corpus because, as W. Edward Glenny explains, these books "have been traditionally understood to be one collection."[4] The second part of this paper will look at whether the shift from מְגִלָּה to מַגָּל to δρέπανος could have been influenced by a cultural understanding of judgement within the biblical text and other sources.

As my focus is on the judgement metaphor shift in Zechariah 5, I will trace the appearance of δρέπανος throughout the LXX and analyze the Hebrew terms that are used to translate it, looking for examples of homophony (similar sounding words) and different Hebrew vocalizations. Next, I will track the use of מְגִלָּה in the MT and compare its occurrences in parallel passages from the LXX to determine patterns of translation. Thereafter, I will analyze how δρέπανος is used within the context of these passages to determine whether the translators of the LXX or the scribes who transmitted the Hebrew text had cultural reasons for deviating from מְגִלָּה. While it may seem as though I am engaging in reconstructing the Hebrew text from which the LXX was translated rather than engaging with the LXX itself, I believe this process will result in a better understanding of the Greek OT.[5] As the purpose of this essay is to determine the reason for the difference between the MT and the LXX of Zech 5:1–4, this approach will demonstrate that the translators of the LXX often used the same Greek term to translate multiple Hebrew terms. It will also allow us to determine whether there is a pattern of translation based upon the connotations

---

[3] George E. Howard, "The Twelve Prophets: to the Reader," in *New English Translation of the Septuagint* (New York: Oxford University Press, 2009), 779.

[4] W. Edward Glenny, *Hosea: A Commentary Based on Hosea in Codex Vaticanus,* Septuagint Commentary Series (Boston: Brill, 2013), 2. See also Jennifer M. Dines, *The Septuagint*, ed. Michael A. Knibb (New York: T&T Clark, 2004), 121. She states that most scholarship suggests that the LXX Minor Prophets were all translated by one translator. This stance is also that of Howard. See Howard, "The Twelve Prophets," 781.

[5] I believe that the variation is possibly related to cultural metaphors surrounding judgement. Accordingly, I will not investigate whether the deviation came from a Hebrew textual tradition or from the translators of the LXX.

3 Flying Sickles Sound Scarier   43

of a word as opposed to its denotations. This will be helpful as I believe the shift in the MT and LXX Zech 5:1–4 is the result of producing a translation based upon the connotations of a word, something akin to dynamic equivalency, rather than using a formal equivalent.

Before dealing with specific texts in the LXX and MT, I believe that it is important to analyze the Hebrew terms that are translated as δρέπανος in order to determine whether the differences between in the MT and LXX could possibly be the result of differences in consonant division, homophony, or a different vocalization of the Hebrew text.

In Zechariah 5, both occurrences of מְגִלָּה (scroll) precede the term עָפָה (flying), which agrees in the gender, number, and state/definiteness with מְגִלָּה, implying that עָפָה is modifying or describing the head noun. It is not likely that those reading the Hebrew text would err in dividing the consonants, as the ה ending would have been an obvious indicator to the translators as it is marking the noun and the participle as feminine. Even if the ה is mistaken for a ת or a ח, the full range of translation options available to the translators/scribes for either מְגִלָּה or עָפָה are not reflected in the LXX.[6]

When looking for differences in the vocalization of the Hebrew text, we see that the term δρέπανος is used twelve times in the LXX to translate six Hebrew terms. I have created Table 3.1 to assess the pronunciation of these terms.

Table 3.1. The pronunciation of the Hebrew terms translated as δρέπανος in the LXX

MT	Transliteration	NRSV	Used
מַזְמֵרָה	măz·mē·rā(h)	Pruning hook	4
מַחֲרֵשָׁה	mă·ḥărē·šā(h)	Iron plowshare	1
מַגָּל	măg·gāl	Sickle	2
חֶרְמֵשׁ	ḥĕr·mēš	Sickle	2
דָּרְבָן	dār·bān	Goading Stick	1
מְגִלָּה	məgil·lā(h)	Scroll	2

As can be seen, none of the terms are similar enough to be regarded as homophonous. Even מַגָּל, the term that is most like מְגִלָּה, has a different number of syllables, although it would be only missing the ה from מְגִלָּה. However, while the pronunciation of מְגִלָּה and מַגָּל are quite different, vowel signs were not present in Hebrew when LXX Zechariah was translated,[7] as they were introduced by the Masoretes much later (between 600–1000 C.E.).[8] Rather, the vocalization traditions were handed down orally when LXX Zechariah was translated. This means that מגלה could have been vocalized in different ways, resulting in uncertainty on the part of the translators of the Hebrew

---

[6] The potential spelling mistakes based on an addition from the preceding word for עָפָה is תְּעָפָה, "gloom," and for מְגִלָּה is תְּמוֹל, "yesterday." These terms are not reflected in the LXX or in any major manuscript traditions.
[7] Scholarship places LXX Zechariah between the first century BCE. See Dines, *The Septuagint*, 50.
[8] Bruce K. Waltke and Michael Patrick O'Connor, *An Introduction to Biblical Hebrew Syntax* (Winona Lake, IN: Eisenbrauns, 1990), 21.

text. I believe this is one of the factors that account for the differences between the MT and LXX in Zechariah 5.

Another factor is the lack of contextual markers within Zechariah 5. The term מְגִלָּה occurs twenty-two times in the MT: fourteen in Jeremiah 36, four in Ezekiel 2:9–3:3, twice in Zech 5:1–2, once in Ps 40:8, and once in Ezra 6:2. The only time מְגִלָּה is ever translated as δρέπανος is in Zechariah. In Jeremiah 36, Ezekiel 2, Psalm 40, and Ezra/2 Esd 6:2, מְגִלָּה is translated as either βίβλος (book), κεφαλίς, or κεφαλὶς βιβλίου (lit. head of the book). These translational choices are supported within the texts themselves as there are also repeated terms in those passages such as כתב ("write"),[9] ספר ("inscription/writing"),[10] פרשׂ ("stretched out"),[11] and קרא ("read")[12] which function as contextual clues that would help the LXX translator make the appropriate choice or prompt the Hebrew scribe to copy it correctly. However, these types of contextual markers are missing in MT Zechariah 5. One could argue that the measurements in v. 2 provide the necessary contextual clues for the rendering of *scroll* rather than *sickle*, but the general orientation of length and width could also apply to the blade and handle of a sickle. Without other contextual clues, these measurements are not helpful in determining the proper vocalization of מגלה. This could have led the translators of the LXX to conclude that it is a masculine noun and to drop the ה.

Another factor can be seen when looking at how δρέπανος is used to translate other Hebrew words, as can be seen in the examples in Table 3.2:

Table 3.2. References of the Hebrew terms translated as δρέπανος in the LXX

MT	NRSV	References
מַזְמֵרָה	Pruning hook	Isa 2:4; 18:5; Mic 4:3; Joel 3:10
מַחֲרֵשָׁה	Iron plowshare	1 Kgdms 13:20
מַגָּל	Sickle	Joel 3:13; Jer 50:16
חֶרְמֵשׁ	Sickle	Deut 16:9; 23:24
דָּרְבָן	Goading Stick	1 Kgdms 13:21
מְגִלָּה	Scroll	Zech 5:1-2

Some of these examples can be translated literally as the term refers to a specific object. An example is found in 1 Kgdms 13:20–21 where the referent of מַחֲרֵשָׁה (δρέπανος) is a direct formal equivalent. The context of the passage refers to the Israelites going down to Philistia to have their iron plowshares sharpened. The translator uses a formal equivalent denoted by the word.

Δρέπανος is also used figuratively in three distinct contexts. In the first context, δρέπανος is used to express a shift from wartime to peacetime or vice versa with the phrases, "and they shall beat their daggers into plows and their spears into *pruning hooks* [δρέπανα], and no more shall nation take up dagger against nation, neither shall they learn to wage war anymore" (Isa 2:4b NETS; emphasis added) and "Beat your

---

[9] See Jer 36:2, 4, 6, 18; Ezek 2:10; Ps 40:8.
[10] See Jer 36:2, 4, 8, 13, 32; Ezek 2:9; Ps 40:8.
[11] See Ezek 2:10.
[12] See Jer 36:4, 6, 8–10, 13–15.

plows into swords and your *sickles* [τὰ δρέπανα] into barbed lances" (Joel 3:10 NETS; emphasis added). In each of these texts, a tool used for one purpose is transformed into a tool for another. A spear is turned into a pruning hook because there is peace and a sickle is turned into a barbed lance because of war. The term δρέπανος is used poetically in these contexts to express a shift from a time of peace to a time of war.

The second example of how δρέπανος is used figuratively is as a reference to the harvest, more specifically either the harvest season or the harvesting of grain. The text, "You shall count for yourself seven complete weeks; when you have started the *sickle* [δρέπανον] on the standing grain, you shall begin to count seven weeks" (Deut 16:9 NETS; emphasis added). The context of this passage uses the sickle to refer to the harvest season. This term is also used to contrast gleaning from harvesting: "Now if you go into your neighbor's standing grain, then you shall collect ears with your hand, and you shall not cast a *sickle* [δρέπανον] on your neighbor's standing grain" (Deut 23:24 NETS; emphasis added).

The third example uses δρέπανος metaphorically and refers to divine judgement. This use is also found in Isa 18:5 and Joel 3:13.[13] The term that is translated as δρέπανος in Isa 18:5 is מַזְמֵרָה and while this is a different Hebrew term than is translated as such in Zech 5:1, it is used within the context of judgement which constitutes this as an appropriate passage in which to engage. The pericope in Isa 18:1–7 is an oracle concerning "the land of whirring wings that is beyond the rivers of Cush" (18:1).[14] There is some controversy on the details of who is under judgement in Isaiah 18[15] but there is no controversy over how the imagery in 18:5–6 is functioning.[16] Here is the passage as translated in the NETS:

> Before **the harvest** [τοῦ θερισμοῦ], when the blossom has been completed and the unripe grape blossoms—a grape-bearing blossom—then he will **take away** [ἀφελεῖ] the little clusters with **pruning hooks** [τοῖς δρεπάνοις] and **take away** [ἀφελεῖ] the small branches and **cut them off** [κατακόψει] and leave them together to the birds of heaven and to the beasts of the earth. And the birds of heaven will be gathered over **them** [ἐπ' αὐτοὺς], and all the beasts of the earth will come upon **him** [αὐτὸν] (Isa 18:5–6 NETS, emphasis added).

The removal of the clusters and small branches that occurs here takes place "before the harvest…" The terms ἀφαιρέω ("take away") and ἀποκόπτω ("cut off") reflect

---

[13] There are a number of other times where harvest is used as a judgement metaphor in the Old Testaament but I am only engaging with these as they use the term δρέπανος in the parallel passages in the LXX.

[14] For a discussion on the different translations of v. 1 see John N. Oswalt, *The Book of Isaiah: Chapters 1–39*, The New International Commentary on the Old Testament, ed. R. K. Harrison and Robert L. Hubbard, Jr. (Grand Rapids: Eerdmans, 1986), 359-60; Hans Wildberger, *Isaiah 13–27*, A Continental Commentary, trans. Thomas H. Trapp (Minneapolis: Fortress Press, 1991), 212–17.

[15] I believe that Ethiopia is a likely candidate. See Wildberger, *Isaiah 13–27*, 221–22. For an alternative view see J. Alec Motyer, *Isaiah: An Introduction and Commentary*, Tyndale Old Testament Commentaries 20 (Downers Grove, IL: InterVarsity Press, 1999), 153–54; Oswalt, *Isaiah 1–39*, 361.

[16] See Robert Jamieson, A. R. Fausset, and David Brown, *Commentary Critical and Explanatory on the Whole Bible*, vol. 1 (Oak Harbor, WA: Logos Research Systems, 1997), 450; Oswalt, *Isaiah*, 361–62; Wildberger, *Isaiah 13–27*, 221.

the Hebrew terms כרת ("cuts off"), תזז ("clears"), and סור ("removes") in the parallel passage. Hans Wildberger, in his commentary of Isaiah, explains this imagery:

> This particular activity was done in order to remove young shoots that were not going to produce fruit, as well as some leaves… The tendrils that have been torn from the vines are the Ethiopians who have fallen in battle, upon whom the vultures will descend.[17]

This destructive act of pruning leads the reader to v. 6 where "the birds of heaven will be gathered over *them* and all the beasts of the earth will come upon *him*…" The pronouns reference those who have been "cut off" and "taken away" and they are further punished as the imagery here indicates being feasted on by scavengers.

Wildberger also notes that "Isaiah uses terminology that is employed in the imagery known to us from the curse formulas of the Assyrian treaties, 'May Ninurta, leader of the gods, fell you with his fierce arrow, and fill the plain with your corpses, *give your flesh to eagles and vultures to feed upon*.'"[18]

The use of Assyrian Treaty curses in connection with the term δρέπανος suggests that this use of metaphor connects with how it is functioning in Zechariah 5, as in v. 3, the flying sickle is called ἡ ἀρά (the curse). While the connection to "curse" between Isa 18:1–7 and Zech 5:1–4 is not explicit, it reveals that the use of sickle in Zechariah 5 is used in a similar context.

The next use of δρέπανος is found in a pericope in LXX Joel 3:1–16 and it is translated from מַגָּל. The pericope in Joel 3 focuses on the Lord's judgement of the nations. It begins with a section of prose (vv. 1–8) and ends with a poem (9–16). The prose begins with a summary of God's restoration of Israel, the judgement of the nations, and the charges brought against them (vv. 1–3). Verse 4 introduces the first oracle of judgement against Tyre and Sidon and the charges summarized in v. 3 are expanded and specified in vv. 5–6. The language around judgment in this section revolves around "payment" and "returning payment." God's judgment is that what Judah and Jerusalem suffered would happen to Tyre and Sidon as well. They would be removed from their land.

The poetic section calls the nations to war (vv. 9–12) at the "Valley of Jehoshaphat" (v. 12). It is likely that this name is not of an actual location but is used to create a judgement scene as *Jehoshaphat* can be literally translated as "God judges."[19] The nations are called to war, and this war is against Tyre, Sidon, and the nations surrounding Judah:

---

[17] Wildberger, *Isaiah 13–27*, 221.

[18] Wildberger, *Isaiah 13–27*, 222 (emphasis added). See D. J. Wiseman, "The Vassal-Treaties of Esarhaddon," *Iraq* 10, no. 1 (1958), 62 (ll. 425–27). See also Figure 135 in Othmar Keel, *The Symbolism of the Biblical World: Ancient Near Eastern Iconography and the Book of Psalms* (Winona Lake, IN: Eisenbrauns, 1997), 104.

[19] See Graham S. Ogden and Richard R. Deutsch, *Joel & Malachi: A Promise of Hope—A Call to Obedience*, International Theological Commentary (Grand Rapids, MI: Eerdmans, 1999), 41; David Prior, *The Message of Joel, Micah & Habakkuk*, The Bible Speaks Today, ed. J. A. Motyer (Downers Grove: InterVarsity Press, 1999), 82; Richard James Coggins, *Joel and Amos*, The New Century Bible Commentary (Sheffield: Sheffield Academic Press, 2000), 53.

> Let all the nations rouse themselves
> > and come up to the valley of Iosaphat,
> For there I will sit to pass judgement
> > on all the nations round about,
>
> Send forth sickles [δρέπανα], because the harvest has come.
> > Go in, tread, for the winepress is full.
> The vats overflow because their wickedness is full. (Joel 3:12–13 NETS)

LXX Joel 3:11b lacks "Bring down your warriors, O LORD" (NRSV) and there is some controversy on how it should be interpreted,[20] but regardless, the command in Joel 3:13 LXX is to destroy the gathered nations. A metaphor of harvest is used in this command. Sickles are sent out to harvest and the imperative πατεῖτε (tread) builds off and expands this imagery.[21] This same imagery of "treading" (πατεῖν) is used more explicitly in Isaiah:

> Why are your robes red, and your garments like theirs who tread the wine press? I have trodden the wine press alone… I trod them in my anger and trampled them in my wrath; the juice spattered on my garments, and stained all my robes… I trampled down peoples in my anger, I crushed them in my wrath, and I poured out their lifeblood on the earth. (Isa 63:1–6 NRSV)

As can be seen in its use in Isaiah, this imagery in Joel pictures the overflowing of blood from the destruction of the nations.

Despite the controversy of Joel 3:11, the overall imagery found within Joel 3:13 is one of intense destruction. The use of δρέπανος within this type of context would again reinforce the choice of the LXX translators, or possibly scribes working with the Hebrew, to change מגלה to מגל in Zechariah 5.

The Pentateuch LXX was written for a community of Greek speakers presumably in Egypt[22] to replace the reading of the Hebrew text during the public reading of scripture.[23] It is not clear how the book of the Twelve in the LXX was used by this community, but Jennifer M. Dines postulates:

> [W]hat suddenly stimulated interest in [the Twelve] around the mid-second century BCE? An answer may lie in the very different historical situation. The third century had been a relatively stable time, but the second century was marked by power struggles between the Ptolemies and Seleucids

---

[20] See Prior, *Joel, Micah & Habakkuk*, 93; Ogden, *Joel & Malachi*, 45; Coggins, *Joel and Amos*, 59.
[21] See David A. Hubbard, *Joel and Amos: An Introduction and Commentary*, Tyndale Old Testament Commentaries 25 (Downers Grove, IL: InterVarsity Press, 1989), 83.
[22] See James K. Aitken, "The Septuagint and Egyptian Translation Methods," in *XV Congress of the International Organization for Septuagint and Cognate Studies, Munich 2013*, ed. M. Maiser and M. van der Meer (Atlanta, GA: SBL Press, 2016), 293. See also Nina L. Collins, *The Library of Alexandria and the Bible in Greek*, VTSup 82 (Leiden: Brill, 2000), 7.
[23] See Staffan Olofsson, *Translation Technique and Theological Exegesis: Collected Essays on the Septuagint Version* (Winona Lake, IN: Eisenbrauns, 2009), 6.

and, for Jews, by the Maccabean Revolt and its consequences. It was a time of turmoil, uncertainty, conflicting loyalties, both within and without Judaism... Perhaps a need was felt for the old prophet to speak to a new generation, and this led to their rediscovery, their updating and, in Greek-speaking Judaism, their translation.[24]

Evidence for a Greek-speaking Jewish community in Ptolemaic Alexandria as the recipients for the Pentateuch LXX can found in the *Letter of Aristeas* and the Greek *Prologue* to the Sirach.[25] The translation of the Book of the Twelve in the LXX potentially would have been used to address issues within diaspora communities, and this may have influenced their understanding of their sacred text and how best to translate it.[26] From a cultural standpoint, both the translators and the audience of the LXX could have been aware that the idea of harvest served as a judgment metaphor not only within the context of the OT, but also in the surrounding culture.[27]

Within Greek mythology, in the Hesiodic succession myth the god Kronos castrates his father Ouranos on the request of his mother:

> But huge Earth groaned within from the strain, and she devised an evil trick. Quickly making a gray unconquerable substance, she fashioned a *huge sickle* [μέγα δρέπανον], and she spoke to her dear children. She said, encouragingly, but sorrowing in her own heart: "My children, begotten by a mad father, if you are willing to listen to me, let us take vengeance for your father's wicked outrage. For he first devised unseemly deeds." So she spoke, but fear seized them all, nor did any of them speak. Then, taking courage, the crooked-counseling Kronos answered his excellent mother: "Mother, I will undertake this deed... So he spoke, and vast Earth rejoiced greatly in her heart. She took Kronos and hid him in an ambush. She placed the *saw-toothed sickle* [ἅρπην καρχαρόδοντα] in his hands. She laid out the whole plot. Great Sky came, dragging night, and he lay all over Earth, wanting to make love, and he was spread out all over her. Then the child reached out from his ambush with his left hand, and with his right hand he held the *huge sickle, long and saw-toothed* [μακρὴν καρχαρόδοντα], and furiously he cut off his father's genitals, and he threw them away, to fall backwards. (Hes. *Theog.* 147–179)

The great sickle in the Greek is introduced as the μέγα δρέπανον in line 160 and is then referred to in line 175 as ἅρπην καρχαρόδοντα, "the jagged sickle." Barry B. Powell, in his introduction to his translation of *The Poems of Hesiod,* argues that it was written

---

[24] Dines, *Septuagint*, 50.
[25] See Anna Passoni Dell'Acqua, "Translating as a Means of Interpreting: The Septuagint and Translation in Ptolemaic Egypt," *Die Septuaginta–Texte, Theologien, Einflüsse* (2010): 322–39.
[26] See Dell'Acqua, "Translating as Means of Interpreting," 325.
[27] We cannot assume that the original audience was aware of Greek and Egyptian mythology. However, these cultural influences provide some examples of how the sickle was used as a symbol in the target audience's host culture.

approximately between the eighth to ninth century BCE,[28] significantly before the translation of LXX Zechariah. However, Kronos was not a major deity in the Greek pantheon and there is a lack of art and other archeological evidence that the Hesiodic poems were as widespread as Homer.[29] The use of a sickle in battle is also found in Lycurgus' *Against Leocrates*:

> And such was the nobility, gentlemen, of those kings of old that they preferred to die for the safety of their subjects rather than to purchase life by the adoption of another country. That at least is true of Codrus, who, they say, told the Athenians to note the time of his death and, taking a beggar's clothes to deceive the enemy, slipped out by the gates and began to collect firewood in front of the town. When two men from the camp approached him and inquired about the conditions in the city he killed one of them with a blow of his *sickle* [τῷ δρεπάνῳ]. (Lycurgus, *Against Leocrates*, line 86)

There is also reference to a use of a sickle in the Hercules myth: "Look! Come see, the son of Zeus is killing the Lernean Hydra with a golden *sickle* (χρυσέαις ἅρπαις); my dear, look at it" (Euripides, *Ion*. 190). A Greek vase from 525 BCE (Malibu 83.AE.346) also portrays the defeat of Hydra with a sickle. These examples continue to demonstrate that the use of δρέπανος would have been consistent with the cultural understanding of the term and could be used within the context of Zech 5:1–4.

As was mentioned earlier, there is evidence that the LXX was written for Greek-speaking Jews in Alexandria and therefore would have been translated by someone within that community. While it is impossible to prove that the translators of the LXX had read *The Poems of Hesiod*, *Ion*, or *Against Leocrates*,[30] they were in an urban area that was a leading center of Greek literature and culture that had one of the largest libraries in the world.[31]

As has been shown, the LXX translators have no set pattern of translating מְגִלָּה as מַגָּל elsewhere from the Hebrew text, so the deviation between the MT and LXX in Zechariah 5 can be explained by (1) looking at the lack of contextual markers, and (2) the variability of the reading of Hebrew text at the time of translation. This

---

[28] Hesiod, *The Poems of Hesiod: Theogony, Works and Days, and The Shield of Herakles*, trans. Barry B. Powell (Oakland: University of California Press, 2017), 2.

[29] There is some commentary on *Theogony* by "the founder of the Stoics, Zeno of Citium (IV-2 B.C.) and edited by Zenodotos of Ephesos (III-1 B.C.) and Aristophanes of Byzantium (II-1 B.C.)." See George Sarton, *Ancient Science Through the Golden Age of Greece* (New York: Dover Publications, 1952), 153. For an example of the Kronos myth in the fourth century CE, see Jan N. Bremmer and Andrew Erskine, eds., *The Gods of Ancient Greece: Identities and Transformations* (Edinburgh: Edinburgh University Press, 2011), 401–402. This could suggest a wider knowledge of Kronos, but it could also be a resurgence in the Kronos myth. The Kronos myth has a rather complicated history as the myth did not originate in Greece but in the Succession Myth in the ancient Near East. For an overview see Jan N. Bremmer, "The Ancient Near East," in *The Oxford Handbook of Ancient Greek Religion*, ed, Esther Eidinow and Julia Kindt (Oxford: Oxford University Press, 2015), 605–35.

[30] There are only two fragments of *Theogony* found in Egypt before 1 CE: TM 60164, which dates to 300–201 BCE, and P. Ryl. 1 54, which dates to 25 BCE–25 CE. There are also no fragments of *Ion* or *Against Leocrates* before 1 CE.

[31] For a brief history of the Library of Alexandria see George Hinge and Jens A. Krasilnikoff, *Alexandria: A Cultural and Religious Melting Pot* (Aarhus: Aarhus University Press, 2009), 80–82.

variability expressed itself through different vocalizations because of the lack of vowel signs.

In Zechariah 5:1–4 the prophet has a vision of judgement "that goes out over the face of the whole land [against] everyone who steals… and everyone who swears falsely" (v. 3). The repetition and expansion present in v. 4 emphasizes the complete destruction of those the LORD of hosts deems wanting. There are contextual clues in Zech 5:1–4 which could have helped the translators identify the original term as מְגִלָּה, such as the allusion to "curse" and "everyone who steals…and everyone who swears falsely…" (v. 3) in Deut 29:21 and Exodus 11–12.[32] The shift from scroll to sickle suggests that the translators of the LXX, or the scribes who produced the text they were working from, were either unaware of these allusions or believed that their community would better understand the text by changing the term.

The copyists of the MT and the translators of the LXX were concerned with passing on their sacred text to the next generation in a way that they would readily understand. Because of this, they would on occasion update antiquated spelling or correct terms they believed had erroneously entered the text.[33] This well-known practice suggests that "correcting" the grammatical gender of a noun would have been permissible within their theological framework. The idea that the text needed correcting would have been reinforced because of how δρέπανος was used in judgement texts in the LXX and the use of *harvest* as a metaphor for *judgment*, not only within the biblical text but potentially because of its use in Greek mythology. The shift of imagery from מְגִלָּה to מַגָּל suggests the scribes and translators of LXX Zechariah believed the change would bring clarity to the meaning of the text in their communities.

Bibliography

Aitken, James K. "The Septuagint and Egyptian Translation Methods." Pages 269–93 in *XV Congress of the International Organization for Septuagint and Cognate Studies, Munich 2013*. Edited by M. Maiser and M. van der Meer. Atlanta, GA: SBL Press, 2016.

Ausloo, H., J. Cook, F. García Martínez, B. Lemmelijn, and M. Vervenne, eds. *Translating a Translation: The LXX and its Modern Translations in the Context of Early Judaism*. Leuven: Uitgeverij Peeters, 2008.

Bremmer, Jan N., and Andrew Erskine, eds. *The Gods of Ancient Greece: Identities and Transformations*. Edinburgh: Edinburgh University Press, 2011.

Coggins, Richard James. *Joel and Amos*. The New Century Bible Commentary. Sheffield: Sheffield Academic Press, 2000.

Collins, Nina L. *The Library of Alexandria and the Bible in Greek*. VTSup 82. Leiden: Brill, 2000.

Dines, Jennifer M. *The Septuagint*. Edited by Michael A. Knibb. New York: T&T Clark, 2004.

Euripides. "Ion." *The Complete Greek Drama*. Edited by Whitney J. Oates and Eugene O'Neill, Jr. Translated by Robert Potter. New York: Random House, 1938.

---

[32] For an explanation of those allusions see Michael R. Stead, *The Intertextuality of Zechariah 1–8* (New York: T&T Clark, 2009), 193–96.

[33] See Waltke and O'Connor, *An Introduction to Biblical Hebrew Syntax*, 12, 17.

Futato, Mark David. *Beginning Biblical Hebrew*. Winona Lake, IN: Eisenbrauns, 2003.
Glenny, W. Edward. *Hosea: A Commentary Based on Hosea in Codex Vaticanus*. Septuagint Commentary Series. Boston, MA: Brill, 2013.
Hesiod. *The Poems of Hesiod: Theogony, Works and Days, and The Shield of Herakles*. Translated by Barry B. Powell. Oakland, CA: University of California Press, 2017.
Hinge, George, and Jens A. Krasilnikoff. *Alexandria: A Cultural and Religious Melting Pot*. Aarus: Aarus University Press, 2009.
Hubbard, David A. *Joel and Amos: An Introduction and Commentary*. Tyndale Old Testament Commentaries 25. Downers Grove, IL: InterVarsity Press, 1989.
Howard, George E. "The Twelve Prophets: To the Reader." Pages 777–822 in *New English Translation of the Septuagint and the Other Greek Translations Traditionally Included under That Title*. Edited by Albert Pietersma and Bengamin G. Wright. New York: Oxford University Press, 2009.
Jamieson, Robert, A. R. Fauseet, and David Brown. *Commentary Critical and Explanatory on the Whole Bible*. Oak Harbor: Logos Research Systems, 1997.
Keel, Othmar. *The Symbolism of the Biblical World: Ancient Near Eastern Iconography and the Book of Psalms*. Translated by Timothy J. Hallett. Winona Lake, IN: Eisenbrauns, 1997.
Lycurgus. "Against Leocrates." In *Minor Attic Orators*. Translated by J. O. Burtt. Cambridge, MA: Harvard University Press, 1962.
Motyer, J. Alec. *Isaiah: An Introduction and Commentary*. Tyndale Old Testament Commentaries 20. Downers Grove, IL: InterVarsity Press, 1999.
Ogden, Graham S., and Richard R. Deutsch. *Joel & Malachi: A Promise of Hope—A Call to Obedience*. International Theological Commentary. Grand Rapids, MI: Eerdmans, 1999.
Olofsson, Staffan. *Translation Technique and Theological Exegesis: Collected Essays on the Septuagint Version*. Winona Lake, IN: Eisenbrauns, 2009.
Oswalt, John N. *The Book of Isaiah: Chapters 1–39*. The New International Commentary on the Old Testament. Edited by R. K. Harrison and Robert L. Hubbard, Jr. Grand Rapids, MI: Eerdmans, 1986.
Peters, Melvin K. H., ed. *XIII Congress of the International Organization for Septuagint and Cognate Studies Ljubljana, 2007*. Atlanta, GA: SBL, 2008.
Prior, David. *The Message of Joel Micah & Habakkuk*. Edited by J. A. Motyer. Downers Grove, IL: InterVarsity Press, 1999.
Sarton, George. *Ancient Science Through the Golden Age of Greece*. New York: Dover Publications, 1952.
Stead, Michael R. *The Intertextuality of Zechariah 1–8*. New York: T&T Clark, 2009.
Waltke, Bruce K., and Michael Patrick O'Connor. *An Introduction to Biblical Hebrew Syntax*. Winona Lake, IN: Eisenbrauns, 1990.
Watts, John D. *Isaiah 1–33*. WBC 24. Waco, TX: Word Books Publisher, 1985.
Wildberger, Hans. *Isaiah 13–27*. Translated by Thomas H. Trapp. Minneapolis, MN: Fortress Press, 1991.
Wisemen, D. J. "The Vassal-Treaties of Esarhaddon." *Iraq* 20, no 1 (1958): i–99.

Chapter 4

From the Exodus to the Exile:
A Commentary on the Greek Text-As-Produced Psalm 80*

Albert Pietersma

1. Introduction

As is well known, for the historical study of literature it is axiomatic to make a distinction between, on the one hand, the event of production, and on the other, its history of reception. In the case of the so-called Septuagint, its event of production occurred incrementally from the third century BCE to the last century BCE, with its history of reception stretching from before the common era to the present, including the New Testament, re-conceptualized as the New Covenant superseding the Old Covenant. Accordingly, the object of research of the present commentary is the text-as-produced in distinction from the text-as-received; moreover, it is the text-as-produced both in terms of text-form and text-semantics. To conceptualize the verbal makeup of the text-as-produced, I shall have recourse to the so-called interlinear paradigm that undergirds both NETS and SBLCS, according to which the leading characteristic of the translation is its isomorphism to the Hebrew source text. To construe the interlinear paradigm as a straitjacket that excludes conventional use of the Greek language from the LXX is not only absurd linguistically but borders on deliberate distortion of both the paradigm as a heuristic tool and the constituent structure of the translated LXX.

Almost forty years ago John Lee had occasion to write:

---

* It gives me great pleasure to honor Larry Perkins, a former student and University of Toronto graduate with a PhD in Septuagint Studies.

It is beyond question that the majority of the books of the LXX exhibit, to a
greater or lesser extent, features that are abnormal for Greek and must be due
to the influence of a Semitic language. On this there is general agreement.[1]

If Lee is right, how then is it possible for anyone to deny that linguistic interference from a Semitic language belongs to the constituent structure of the translated Septuagint? Moreover, if Lee is right, how is it possible for anyone to deny that linguistic interference must be the baseline of the corpus, given that it is a foreign element in a Greek document? As noted, the fact that linguistic interference belongs to the constituent structure of the LXX in no way calls into question the theme of Lee's book, namely, that translators time and again preferred Greek idiom to a "translationese" variety of the language. But this too belongs to the constituent structure of the Septuagint-as-produced. Surely, the issue here is not one of *either/or* but one of *both/and*!

2. Outline

Psalm 80 begins with presumed cultic paraphernalia based on etymology, including an individual to whom the text is said to pertain (v. 1). Israel is summoned to prepare with song and the music of many instruments for the festival of the new moon in accordance with divine decree—placed as a witness in Ioseph when he left Egypt, where he encountered a foreign language upon arrival (vv. 2–6). God, says he, (presumably) freed Israel from slavery in Egypt. When Israel called on him he rescued and shielded him, and tested him at a water of dispute. God testifies against Israel and admonishes his people not to worship foreign gods because he himself is Israel's god who led Israel out of Egypt, despite which Israel paid no attention (vv. 7–12). So, he sent them off into exile to follow the practices of their heart. A divine contrary-to-fact lament precedes a prediction about the (apparent) doom of God's enemies (vv. 13–16). The psalm ends on a positive note, recalling that God nourished Israel with the very best (v. 17).

3. Commentary

Psalm 80:1

למנצח || על הגתית || לאסף

Εἰς τὸ τέλος, ὑπὲρ τῶν ληνῶν· τῷ Ασαφ.

Regarding completion. Over the wine vats. Pertaining to Asaph.

Εἰς τὸ τέλος. Although this phrase occurs 55 times in the Old Greek Psalter and was added secondarily on a number of occasions, G's intended meaning remains obscure. The reason for this is no doubt that its origin in the Psalter is occasioned by

---

[1] J. A. L. Lee, *A Lexical Study of the Septuagint Version of the Pentateuch*, SCS 14 (Chico, CA: Scholars Press, 1983), 11–12.

a perceived etymological association in the Hebrew source text. Since לנצח ("forever") is regularly translated, idiomatically, by εἰς τέλος ("completely") in the body of individual psalms (18×), and since G has analyzed למנצח in the superscripts as deriving from the same root (√נצח), a similar link is forged in the Greek, with a matching number of morphemes in the corresponding pairs. In the superscripts, τέλος may carry its common meaning. That, here and elsewhere in Psalms, it was of eschatological import, as Rösel has argued,[2] may well be true for the text-as-received, though scarcely for the text-as-produced.[3] So, with specific reference to Ps 43:1, Didymus the Blind comments that τέλος is frequently mentioned, "because the end (τὸ ἔσχατον) is something longed for, for the sake of which all other things occur." Not inconceivably, εἰς τὸ τέλος constitutes minimal exposition of the source text at the phrasal level wherever it happens to occur, with a potential for wider application in the psalm's reception history.[4]

ὑπὲρ τῶν ληνῶν. Like the preceding phrase, this too is a mechanical rendering of its counterpart, occurring also in the superscripts of 8:1 and 83:1. Whatever the meaning of Hebrew הגתית, G analyzed it as the plural of גת ("wine-press"?) with the article preposed. BDB parses the Hebrew as an adjectival form of √גי, a root of uncertain meaning. As a result, modern translations of the Hebrew gloss the phrase by "The Gittith," and if the phrase ὑπὲρ τῶν ληνῶν was meant to flag the tune of a well-known vintage song to which Psalms 8, 80, and 83 were to be sung, G did not understand it so. Instead, G did here what he did regularly in the superscripts, namely, to render prepositions according to a common equivalent and to translate unfamiliar expressions etymologically. While it cannot be claimed that all instances of Hebrew על are rendered by Greek ὑπέρ, it is nonetheless of some interest that, whereas the source text in superscripts structurally similar to that of Psalm 80 typically uses על, though some other prepositions as well, G uses ὑπέρ + the genitive exclusively. It may further be noted that at Ps 8:1, Theodotion and Aquila render the same phrase as ὑπὲρ τῆς γετθίτιδος, therefore, an inflected transcription but scarcely understood as a tune to be imitated. Since ληνός can refer to a vat in which grapes are pressed or trodden, and since the putative Hebrew counterpart can have that meaning as well, there is good reason to posit "wine-press" or "wine-vat" as its meaning in the three superscripts. It deserves noting, however, that both within and without the LXX ληνός can also denote a trough used for other purposes, such as, watering troughs for sheep (cf. Gen 30:38, 41). Eusebius, in his commentary on Psalms,[5] connects ὑπὲρ τῶν ληνῶν with εἰς τὸ τέλος and makes them into a prophecy about the ingathering of believers into the churches throughout the world (125.46).

---

[2] Martin Rösel, "Die Psalmüberschriften des Septuaginta-Psalters," in *Der Septuaginta-Psalter: Sprachliche und theologische Aspekte*, ed. Erich Zenger, HBS 32 (Freiburg: Herder, 2001), 125–48 (138).
[3] Frank-Lothar Hossfeld and Erich Zenger, *Psalms 2: A Commentary on Psalms 51–100*, trans. Linda M. Maloney, Hermeneia (Minneapolis: Fortress Press, 2005), 326.
[4] See further Jannes Smith, "God, Judges, Snakes, and Sinners: A Commentary on the Old Greek Text of Psalm 57," in *The SBL Commentary on the Septuagint: An Introduction*, ed. Dirk Büchner (Atlanta: SBL Press, 2017), 241–56 (243).
[5] Eusebius of Caesarea, *Commentaria in Psalmos*, PG 23 (Paris: Migne, 1857).

τῷ Ασαφ. This phrase occurs twelve times in Psalms (49:1; 72:1–82:1) and might best be analyzed on the analogy of τῷ Δαυιδ versus τοῦ Δαυιδ, as argued by Didymus the Blind at Ps 24:1. That this phrase serves to indicate Davidic authorship, whatever its Hebrew counterpart may be thought to mean, is most unlikely. In spite of the recognized intimate bond between Dauid and the Psalms, Greek exegetical tradition did not construe it as a *nota auctoris*, and neither did the translator himself. Thus, Didymus the Blind in a comment on Ps 24:1 writes:

εἰς τὸν Δαυὶδ ὁ ψαλμὸς λέγεται· ἄλλο γάρ ἐστιν τοῦ Δαυὶδ εἶναι καὶ ἄλλο τῷ Δαυίδ. τοῦ Δαυὶδ λέγεται, ὅτ<α>ν ᾖ{ν} αὐτὸς αὐτὸν πεποιηκὼς ἢ ψάλλων. αὐτῷ δὲ λέγεται, ὅταν εἰς αὐτὸν φέρηται[6] ("the psalm is said to be regarding Dauid. For 'of Dauid' and 'to Dauid' mean different things; 'of Dauid' is used when he himself composed it or played it, whereas 'to him' is used when it pertains to him.")

A similar point is made by G himself when he labels the closing psalm (151) as εἰς Δαυίδ ("regarding Dauid") but also ἰδιόγραφος, i.e., "written by Dauid himself," in contrast to the psalms that precede. Interestingly, Didymus' criterion for authorship, namely, composition or performance, are uniquely combined in Psalm 151, since the first-person account of Dauid's early life includes in v. 3 a direct reference to his performing on the harp: "My hands made an instrument; / my fingers tuned a harp" (NETS). Didymus' other conclusion, however, namely, that the dative indicated that the psalm in question "pertained to Dauid," apparently left ample room for typological and messianic interpretation, as is clear from his own commentary on Psalms. Eusebius (224.20–21), commenting on the same superscription, opted for a more theological explanation when he noted that the words of the psalm were composed through the Holy Spirit for Dauid (τῷ Δαυίδ), which explains why the rest of the interpreters (παρὰ τοῖς λοιποῖς ἑρμηνευταῖς) read τοῦ Δαυίδ (224.21–22). Effectively, therefore, τῷ Δαυίδ and τοῦ Δαυίδ amounted to the same thing! The latter is the standard rendering of Aquila, Symmachus, and Theodotion.

[ψαλμός]. Although MT lacks מזמור, according to *BHS* some Hebrew MSS add it, as (reputedly) does the Greek. The Greek side, however, is textually more diverse than the Hebrew. First off, many MSS transpose τῷ Ασαφ / ψαλμός, including Sinaiticus though not Vaticanus, although the two are commonly thought to be textual congeners. Secondly, P.Bodmer XXIV (Ra 2110), the Gallican Psalter, and nine MSS of the so-called *L* recension (i.e., the Byzantine text) omit ψαλμός. Given the fact that ψαλμός was prone to be added in transmission history, it more than likely is not Old Greek.

---

[6] Didymus the Blind, *Commentarii in Psalmos 22–26.10*, in *Didymos der Blinde, Psalmenkommentar (Tura-Papyrus). Teil II: Kommentar zu Psalm 22–26,10*, ed. Michael Gronewald, Papyrologische Texte und Abhandlungen 4 (Bonn: Habelt, 1968), 74.10-11.

Psalm 80:2

הרנינו לאלהים עוזנו ‖ הריעו לאלהי יעקב

Ἀγαλλιᾶσθε τῷ θεῷ τῷ βοηθῷ ἡμῶν,

ἀλαλάξατε τῷ θεῷ Ιακωβ

Rejoice in God our helper;
shout for joy to the God of Iakob

τῷ βοηθῷ ἡμῶν. Like MT, G read here a form of עז (עזז), "strength, might." Although its most common equivalent in Psalms is δύναμις and cognates (22×), on three occasions he opted for βοηθός (27:7; 58:18; 80:2) and once for βοήθεια (61:8). All four are divine epithets.

Psalm 80:3

שאו זמרה ותנו תף ‖ כנור נעים עם נבל

λάβετε ψαλμὸν καὶ δότε τύμπανον,

ψαλτήριον τερπνὸν μετὰ κιθάρας·

Raise a melody, and sound a drum,
delightful harp with lyre.

ψαλμόν. The formation of this term (active verbal noun) as well as its use in Classical Greek indicates that ψαλμός referred to the activity of making music on a stringed instrument and by extension to the sound so produced, rather than to a composition of set form, whether instrumental or vocal. Its earliest attestation is in a fragment of Phrynichus (sixth century BCE). As is clear from its cognates, ψάλλω ("to pluck"), ψάλτης ("harper"), ψαλτήριον ("harp" or "psalter"), as well as from later Septuagintal formations (1–2 Supplements, 1 Esdras, Sirach) ψαλτῳδός ("harp-singer"), ψαλτῳδέω ("to sing to a harp"), the primary reference of ψαλ- was to instrumental in distinction from vocal music, in other words, to playing rather than to singing, even though in ψαλτῳδ- the two are combined. These forms are the more interesting for existing temple practice—real or imagined—since the ψαλτ-component has no explicit warrant in the Hebrew. Within the Psalter they are reminiscent of ψαλμὸς ᾠδῆς / ᾠδὴ ψαλμοῦ in Ps 29:1 and elsewhere, a combination explained by Eusebius (417.32) as singing to a harp. Although later Greek knows a variety of forms based on ψαλμός, for example, ψαλτῳδία ("psalm-singing") and ψαλμῳδός ("psalmist"), with reference to the biblical psalms as songs to be sung, these do not make their appearance in the LXX, except secondarily. That ψαλμός continued to have its instrumental sense in post-Classical Greek is clear from a passage such as Amos 5:23, which speaks of ψαλμὸς ὀργάνων, the "psalming," that is, "plucking/strumming" of instruments. The same is true for 1 Rgns 16:18 where Dauid is said to be expert at playing music, and likely as well 2 Rgns 23:1. Other references like Iob 21:12; 30:31; Pss 70:22; 80:3; 97:5; Zach 6:14; Esa 66:20; Lam 3:14; 5:14 are less explicit but favor an instrumental sense, the more since in several of these passages ψαλμός glosses Hebrew instrumental terms: עוגב ("flute") in both Iob passages, נבל ("harp/lute/guitar") in Ps 70:22—a term elsewhere in Psalms translated by ψαλτήριον (and in 107:3 by κιθάρα, "lyre")—and more ambiguously נגינה ("music/song") in Lam 3:14 and 5:14. Least clearly instrumental are Idt 16:1; 3 Makk 6:35; Pss 146:1; 151:1; Pss Sol 3:2; 15:3. In light of this, it would seem appropriate to suggest that, in the LXX, ψαλμός carries a basically instrumental sense, unless proven otherwise, a conclusion supported by *GELS*. All of this is not to say that some occurrences cannot be construed as being vocal in emphasis. Reception history, therefore, had enough to build on. It bears noting further that in Josephus both ψαλμός (cf. 12.323.4) and ψάλλω (cf. 12.349.2) have an instrumental sense, while Philo avoids both and uses ὕμνος and ὑμνέω (cf. 2.82.4) instead. Even ψαλτήριον he uses only twice when citing Ioubal's (Jubal's) invention in Gen 4:21. In Ps 80:3, NETS has opted for (musical) melody on the strength of the primarily instrumental sense of ψαλμός. Admittedly, the Hebrew counterpart to ψαλμός in v. 3a is not מזמור, its standard equivalent in Psalms, but זמרה, "melody, song," which straddles instrumental and vocal music.

δότε τύμπανον. This mode of expression for playing a drum is unique in the LXX, and a pre- LXX *TLG* search gives the same results. It would seem, therefore, that, while נתן תף is a viable mode of expression in Hebrew, it is questionable that δότε τύμπανον is the same in Greek.[7] Although *GELS* s.v. δίδωμι has 23 sub-entries, Ps 80:3 is conspicuous by its absence, despite the fact that it is a unique usage in the LXX. Similarly, LEH fails to mention Ps 80:3.

τύμπανον. The Greek τύμπανον, according to West,[8] was not a kettledrum (contra LSJ and *Accordance*), that is, a drum with a skin stretched over a hollow brass or copper hemisphere, but rather a shallow frame of 30–50 cm in diameter, covered with skin probably front and back, though only one side was struck. Held upright in the left hand, it was struck with the fingertips or knuckles of the right hand. In Psalms, and elsewhere in the LXX, it is a translation of Hebrew תף, variously rendered as "frame drum," "tambourine," or "timbrel." Both the τύμπανον and the תף were typically played by women.

ψαλτήριον. This instrument, dubbed "plucking instrument" by West emerged as the ordinary generic word for the harp.[9] Thrice in the Psalter (32:2; 91:4; 143:9) it is mentioned as a ten-stringed instrument, which may well have been its standard number, in distinction from the lyre with seven or eight strings. As West notes,[10] stringed instruments were played by plucking with the fingers, striking with a plectrum or a combination of both. In terms of Hebrew equivalent, it is most often paired with Hebrew נבל but also at times with כנור. So, for example, in Psalms, six times it translates נבל (32:2; 56:9; 94:1; 107:3; 143:9; 150:3) and three times it renders כנור (48:5; 80:3; 149:3).

---

[7] Cf. Henry St. John Thackeray, *A Grammar of the Old Testament in Greek* (Cambridge: Cambridge University Press, 1909), 39; and J. A. L. Lee, *A Lexical Study of the Septuagint Version of the Pentateuch*, SCS 14 (Chico, CA: Scholars Press, 1983), 11.
[8] Martin L. West, *Ancient Greek Music* (Oxford: Clarendon Press, 1992), 124.
[9] West, *Ancient Greek Music*, 74.
[10] West, *Ancient Greek Music*, 48.

κιθάρας. The Greek κιθάρα or lyre is almost consistently matched with Hebrew כנור, the only exceptions being Gen 4:21 where, apparently, ψαλτήριον renders כנור and κιθάρα translates עוגב, "flute," and Ps 80:3 seemingly reversed the standard matchup. Though the lyre typically had seven or eight strings, West notes examples with only five or three.[11]

Psalm 80:4–5

תקעו בחדש שופר ‖ בכסה ליום חגנו
כי חק לישראל הוא ‖ משפט לאלהי יעקב

4 σαλπίσατε ἐν νεομηνίᾳ σάλπιγγι,
ἐν εὐσήμῳ ἡμέρᾳ ἑορτῆς ἡμῶν·
5 ὅτι πρόσταγμα τῷ Ισραηλ ἐστὶν
καὶ κρίμα τῷ θεῷ Ιακωβ.

4 Trumpet with a trumpet at new moon,
at a high day of our feast,
5 because it is an ordinance for Israel
and a judgment belonging to the God of Iakob.

ἐν νεομηνίᾳ. Whereas MT simply uses the adjective חדש, "new," to connote the festival, G opts for its technical designation. Most often in the LXX it is contracted to νουμηνία. Commentators on the Hebrew text commonly assign Ps 81(80) to the autumnal festival of Tabernacles.[12] As for the Greek psalm—it only speaks explicitly about the festival of the new moon. For pentateuchal references to the festival, see Exod 40:2, 17 and Num 10:10; 29:6.

σαλπίσατε—σάλπιγγι. The term σάλπιγξ, perhaps surprisingly, translates both lexemes in Psalms that have the sense of trumpet or horn, namely, שופר and חצצרה. In the remainder of the LXX, it translates all five of the lexemes which have the same semantic component, namely, also: יובל, קרן, and תקוע. Accordingly, although Tate may well be correct that the Hebrew trumpet of 80:4 was made of the horn of an animal, usually a ram's horn, that is less assured of the Greek σάλπιγξ.[13] As for the cognate construction in this verse, the earliest instance is Num 10:8, but in Num 10:10 with direct reference to the festival of the new moon. From Num 10:8 onward, however, it occurs in the book of Iesous as well as beyond. Interestingly, according to *TLG*, the cognate construction, with or without the preposition ἐν, is peculiar to the LXX, and the verbal form is sparingly attested prior to the LXX. As is clear from Ps 97:6, a Greek trumpet could be made of beaten (ἐλατός) metal or horn (κεράτινος). In 2 Suppl 15:14,

---

[11] West, *Ancient Greek Music*, 49.
[12] So, for example, D. F. Baethgen, *Handkommentar zum Alten Testament: Die Psalmen* (Göttingen: Vandenhoeck & Ruprecht, 1892); C. A. Briggs and E. G. Briggs, *Psalms II*, ICC (Edinburgh: T&T Clark, 1906–1907), 211 (Passover or Tabernacles); Hans-Joachim Kraus, *Psalms 60–150: A Continental Commentary*, trans. Hilton C. Oswald (Minneapolis: Fortress Press, 1993), 148; Marvin E. Tate, *Psalms 51–100*, WBC 20 (Dallas, TX: Word Books, Publisher, 1990), 318; and Artur Weiser, *The Psalms: A Commentary*, trans. Herbert Hartwell, OTL (Philadelphia: Westminster John Knox, 1962), 553.
[13] Marvin E. Tate, *Psalms 51–100*, WBC 20 (Dallas, TX: Word Books, 1990), 318.

trumpets and trumpets made of horn are mentioned in sequence, seemingly referencing trumpets made of two different materials. Moreover, Sir 50:16 notes explicitly the beaten metal variety. Numbers 10:2 speaks specifically of two beaten silver trumpets to summon the Israelites to break camp on their desert journey. Since, as West notes, the Greek metal σάλπιγξ was generally made of bronze with a bone mouthpiece, the two silver trumpets of Num 10:2 were likely of special importance and prestige. In terms of function—so West continues—the trumpet was not used for musical purposes but, instead, to give signals for battle and ritual and ceremonial occasions, as was, of course, the case in the Hebrew Bible (cf., e.g., Num 10:2).[14] Finally, whereas the Hebrew of v. 4b reads "at the full moon on the day of our feast," G uses here ἐν εὐσήμῳ ἡμέρᾳ, "on a day of good signs/ signals etc.," possibly in recognition of the function and purpose of the trumpet. The word εὔσημος occurs only here in the LXX, although the adverb is found in Dan LXX 2:19 for zero Aramaic.

ὅτι—Ιακωβ. The wording of both texts is relatively straight forward, apart from the added conjunction καί, which is uncontested. All Hebrew–Greek matches are common occurrences in Psalms. Also of some interest is that 2110 inserts an article in the dative before Ιακωβ, which lays no serious claim to being original.

Psalm 80:6

עדות ביהוסף שמו || בצאתו על ארץ מצרים || שפת לא ידעתי אשמע

μαρτύριον ἐν τῷ Ιωσηφ ἔθετο αὐτὸν
ἐν τῷ ἐξελθεῖν αὐτὸν ἐκ γῆς Αἰγύπτου·
γλῶσσαν, ἣν οὐκ ἔγνω, ἤκουσεν·

A testimony in Ioseph he made him,
when he went out from the land of Egypt.
A tongue he heard, which he did not know;

Ιωσηφ. While the unique spelling of Joseph's name in MT may be intentional, as de Boer, *pace* Tate,[15] believes, G evidently ignored it.

αὐτόν. Whereas in MT the masc. sg. suffix of שמו must refer to חק ("statute") or משפט ("judgment") in v. 5a or b, the masculine pronoun of the Greek can only be a mistake in gender, that is, masculine in place of neuter—something scarcely unique in the Greek Psalter (26:4[bis]; 31:6; 73:18; 108:27; 117:23; 118:50; 131:6). Though NETS suggests that the reference may possibly be to Israel or Iakob in the preceding verse, on second thought, it is almost certainly an incorrect explanation of the phenomenon. Interestingly, Pap. Bodmer XXIV (Ra 2110) reads αὐτό to agree with μαρτύριον. It omits, however, ἐν τῷ 2°, and in general terms the scribe of 2110 made a variety of plain mistakes. Moreover, since עדות is a feminine noun, the correction must be inner-Greek.

---

[14] Tate, *Psalms 51–100*, 118.
[15] P. A. H. de Boer, "Psalm 81:6a: Observations on Translation and Meaning of One Hebrew Line," in W. B. Barrick and J. R. Spencer, eds., *In the Shelter of Elyon: Essays on Ancient Palestinian Life and Literature in Honor of G. W. Ahlström*, JSOTSup 31 (Sheffield: JSOT Press, 1984), 75–77. Cf. Tate, *Psalms 51–100*, 319.

ἐκ γῆς Αἰγύπτου. MT's counterpart for ἐκ is על, which can only mean that the exodus *from* Egypt, as the Greek would have it, is instead a move *against* Egypt, as Kraus, Tate and Weiser construe MT.[16] To cite Tate as an example: "when he (the God of Jacob) went out against the land of Egypt" (cf. Exod 11:4: the death of the firstborn). There is little doubt about what the Greek means, namely, that it was Ioseph who came forth from the land of Egypt (cf. Gen 50:24–25).

γλῶσσαν, ἣν οὐκ ἔγνω, ἤκουσεν. Tate (319) helpfully delineates three views on the interpretation of the Hebrew text of v. 6c: (1) it refers to the Israelites, oppressed by the Egyptians, a people who spoke a foreign language; (2) it refers to the voice of God, unfamiliar to Israel-in-Egypt; (3) it refers to Yahweh's voice, speaking through a prophet the message contained in vv. 7–17. In terms of Tate's three-fold delineation, it is difficult to see how the Greek can fit into any one of them. If Ioseph is the subject of Greek 80:6b, as Tate (319) rightly concludes, it is highly improbable not to make him the subject of the next stich as well. In that case, G is not only responsible for assigning 6b to Ioseph rather than to Ioseph's god but 6c as well, indicating that he did not know the language when he was first brought to Egypt. Both Kraus and Tate want to link 6c with 11c.[17] While this may make the Hebrew text more cohesive, the linking finds no support in the Greek, which makes do with the text at hand within narrow confines. Furthermore, the segment about Ioseph acts as a patent disruption in the narrative flow of the psalm.

Psalm 80:7

הסירותי מסבל שכמו || כפיו מדוד תעברנה

ἀπέστησεν ἀπὸ ἄρσεων τὸν νῶτον αὐτοῦ,
αἱ χεῖρες αὐτοῦ ἐν τῷ κοφίνῳ ἐδούλευσαν.

he removed his back from burdens;
his hands slaved at the basket.

ἀπέστησεν. Hebrew סור, "to turn aside," is translated either by ἀφίστημι (6×) or ἐκκλίνω (7×). Moreover, whereas the Hebrew verb is first person sg., the Greek verb is third person sg. In both cases, however, God may well be the subject, creating a rather difficult sequence of actors, since 7b must refer to Israel in slavery (but see the following discussion). The same happens in 6c, and for the same reason.

τὸν νῶτον αὐτοῦ. Uniquely in the LXX, the Hebrew "shoulder" (שכמו) is here paired with the Greek "back," which seems to suggest that the burden was thought of as being carried on a person's back rather than on his shoulder.

αἱ χεῖρες αὐτοῦ ἐν τῷ κοφίνῳ ἐδούλευσαν. The Greek reads תעבדנה in place of MT's תעברנה, therefore, an interchange of *daleth* and *resh*. If Flashar is correct in thinking that it was G who emended his source text from מדוד to בדוד, it may well be that the interchange of *daleth* and *resh* predated the LXX, and was thus part of

---

[16] Kraus, *Psalms 60–150*; Tate, *Psalms 51–100*; Weiser, *The Psalms: A Commentary*.
[17] Kraus, *Psalms 60–150*, 147, and Tate, *Psalms 51–100*, 320.

G's parent text.[18] MT's עבר, "to pass over," is commonly rendered here by "were freed," so, for example, by Kraus, Tate and Weiser. Thus, while in MT the hands of the Israelites were freed from bondage, in the Greek they were enslaved to bondage.

κοφίνῳ. This word occurs only here and in JudgB 6:19. According to LSJ, in later times this word was used especially by Jews, but no concrete evidence for this claim is being provided.

Psalm 80:8

בצרה קראת ואחלצך || אענך בסתר רעם || אבחנך על מי מריבה סלה

Ἐν θλίψει ἐπεκαλέσω με, καὶ ἐρρυσάμην σε·
ἐπήκουσά σου ἐν ἀποκρύφῳ καταιγίδος,
ἐδοκίμασά σε ἐπὶ ὕδατος ἀντιλογίας.

διάψαλμα

In affliction you called upon me, and I rescued you;
I hearkened to you in a secret spot of a tempest;
I tested you at a water of dispute.

Interlude on strings

ἐπεκαλέσω με. In Psalms, Hebrew קרא I, "to invoke, cry out," is translated most often by either ἐπικαλέομαι (28×) or κράζω (κέκραξα) (22×). When קרא I has a suffix, G typically renders it by ἐπικαλέομαι and a direct object, but when it takes אל as a complement, he renders it by κράζω (κέκραξα) and πρός. Here קרא I lacks a complement and G opts for ἐπικαλέομαι, to which he adds a direct object without warrant from the source text, as he does in four instances elsewhere (55:10; 101:3; 137:3; 146:9). No doubt G's motivation for doing what he did was a question of isomorphism with his source text.

ἐπήκουσα. As Cox has shown, Hebrew ענה ("to answer") is always translated in Psalms by either ἐπακούω or εἰσακούω when God is the grammatical subject. While Barr has argued that ἐπακούω can indeed mean "to answer" and while it is true that ענה and -ακούω can have a certain semantic overlap, seeing that already in Classical Greek ὑπακούω regularly means "to answer/counter," it is nonetheless of interest that G employs ἀποκρίνομαι when God is not perceived to be the subject (87:1; 101:24; 118:42). As a result, Cox is justified in seeing an interpretive shift in Psalms from a god who answers to a god who heeds or listens (cf. MM, §1873). Of interest is that the verb is in the past tense, despite Hebrew *yiqtol*, hence descriptive of what happened in the past.

ἐν ἀποκρύφῳ καταιγίδος. Hebrew רעם is commonly rendered as "thunder" or a "thundercloud." G here uniquely paired it with καταιγίς, a "tempest," a "squall" and even a "hurricane," a word G uses ten times in Psalms for five Hebrew lexemes, five times for סער, "tempest/storm-wind." Why he preferred a tempest to a thundercloud

---

[18] Martin Flashar, "Exegetische Studien zum Septuagintapsalter," *ZAW* 32 (1912): 81–116, 161–89, 241–68 (113 n. 1).

is difficult to know. What is relatively certain is that the genitive of καταιγίδος might best be read as an objective genitive, whether or not G intended it so, that is, a secret spot *for/against* a tempest.

ἐπὶ ὕδατος ἀντιλογίας. Both here and in Ps 105:32 G followed Greek Num 20:13 in translating the place name Meribah, a name with which he may not have been familiar. In Exod 17:7 Massah and Meribah are translated by Πειρασμός ("Testing") and Λοιδόρησις ("Raillery"). Of interest is, nevertheless, that three times G used ἀντιλογία to translate ריב, "strife, dispute" (17:44; 30:21; 54:10).

ἐδοκίμασά σε. Although Kraus proposes to read MT in the light of Exod 17:7; Num 20:13; Ps 105:32, namely, that Israel tested its god, in Ps 80:8 the roles are clearly reversed in the Hebrew and the Greek. In other words, it was God, says he, who put Israel to the test.[19]

διάψαλμα. The meaning and function of its Hebrew counterpart (סלה) were apparently as unfamiliar to G as they are to modern commentators. The Greek term, however, is reasonably transparent, since it is derived from διαψάλλω, an intensive form of ψάλλω.[20] In literal terms, it would therefore have to mean something like "plucked/ played through," as a result of which it is commonly glossed as "musical interlude" (e.g., LSJ, *GELS*). Muraoka sensibly describes it as occurring "between two contiguous passages of a poem." Since the musical interlude, by virtue of the Greek root ψάλ-, can be further specified as an interlude on a stringed instrument, NETS has added this further specification. Although the word is common in Psalms, it also appears in Hab 3:3, 9, 13 in both the OG and the so-called Venetus text but apparently never in extra-biblical Greek apart from dependent literature. In all likelihood, then, it is a neologism in Psalms (so Munnich). If that is indeed the case, G shows here a surprising level of creativity, since the link he forges between ψάλλω/ψαλμός and διάψαλμα finds no support in his parent text. In formal terms it was evidently thought to signal a pause in the singing while the music continued, and as such would have had a questionable role to play at the end of an entire piece. Presumably for that reason it was not placed by G at the close of Psalms, 3:9; 23:10 and 45:12, even though in all three instances MT features סלה. As interlude it makes reasonable sense after v. 5, the introduction of an eight-verse divine oracle. The perceived function of διάψαλμα was evidently like that of a διαύλιον in drama, an interlude played on the flute (αὐλός) between choruses (cf. Keil-Delitzsch) (see also μεσαύλιον). Interestingly, a scholion to Aristophanes, *Frogs* (TLG 5014.012) notes: "someone blows a διαύλιον, so called just like the διάψαλμα" (διαύλιον προσαυλεί τις. ὥσπερ τὸ διάψαλμα λέγεται, οὕτω καὶ τοῦτο). It is thus likely that if G was the first to use διάψαλμα he patterned it after (δια)ψάλλω/ψαλμός, prompted by the flute interlude of Greek drama.

---

[19] Kraus, *Psalms 60–150*, 81.
[20] Olivier Munnich, "Etude lexicographique du Psautier des Septante" (PhD diss., Université de Paris-Sorbonne, 1982), 72–75.

Psalm 80:9

שמע עמי ואעידה בך ‖ ישראל אם תשמע לי

ἄκουσον, λαός μου, καὶ διαμαρτύρομαί σοι·
Ισραηλ, ἐὰν ἀκούσῃς μου,

Hear, O my people, and I am testifying against you;
O Israel, if you would hear me!

διαμαρτύρομαι. MT reads here a modal form, namely, a *yiqtol* Hiphil cohortative, but G opts for a present indicative. In other words, the warning is in progress.

Psalm 80:10

לא יהיה בך אל זר ‖ ולא תשתחוה לאל נכר

οὐκ ἔσται ἐν σοὶ θεὸς πρόσφατος,
οὐδὲ προσκυνήσεις θεῷ ἀλλοτρίῳ·

There shall be no recent god among you,
nor shall you do obeisance to a foreign god.

πρόσφατος. Given that on three occasions in Psalms ἀλλότριος, "strange, foreign," is used to translate Hebrew זר, "strange" (43:21; 53:5; 108:11), the first one in reference to a god, G opts here uniquely for πρόσφατος. The reason is, no doubt, to avoid using ἀλλότριος in consecutive stichs, seeing that ἀλλότριος is a standard equivalent for נכר (6×). Though πρόσφατος occurs only here in the Psalter, both it and its cognate adverb occur nine times elsewhere in the LXX and are relatively popular in Greek literature generally.

προσκυνήσεις. This lexeme is the overwhelming default for the Histaphal of שחה, or, alternatively, the Hithpalel of חוה, "to bow, worship," well-nigh throughout the LXX. The term may or may not connote divine worship whether it has a complement in the accusative or the dative. Typically the dative reflects the preposition ל in the source text.

Psalm 80:11

אנכי יהוה אלהיך ‖ המעלך מארץ מצרים ‖ הרחב פיך ואמלאהו

ἐγὼ γάρ εἰμι κύριος ὁ θεός σου
ὁ ἀναγαγών σε ἐκ γῆς Αἰγύπτου·
πλάτυνον τὸ στόμα σου, καὶ πληρώσω αὐτό.

For I am the Lord your God,
who brought you up out of the land of Egypt.
Open wide your mouth, and I will fill it.

γάρ. Given that this particle is attested by all witnesses, it may well be Old Greek, even though it is without explicit warrant in the source text. As it is, 11a is causally linked to 10a and b, that is to say, Israel shall have no other gods, *for* the Lord is his god and to that end has brought Israel out of Egypt. According to Tate, the Hebrew of 11a is read by some as, "I, Yahweh, am your God." Quite clearly, this is not how G read his source text. Cf. Exod 20:5.[21]

πλάτυνον—αὐτό. Although, as Tate notes,[22] the Hebrew counterpart of this line is often placed after 6c,[23] it again finds no support in the Greek.

Psalm 80:12

ולא שמע עמי לקולי || וישראל לא אבה לי

καὶ οὐκ ἤκουσεν ὁ λαός μου τῆς φωνῆς μου,
καὶ Ισραηλ οὐ προσέσχεν μοι·

And my people did not hear my voice;
and Israel paid no attention to me.

οὐ προσέσχεν. The Hebrew equivalent, namely, אבה לא, "not to be willing," is a relatively popular phrase in MT, beginning with the Pentateuch. Its standard Greek translation is "negative" + ἐθέλω or βούλομαι. Only in our present verse, being the sole occurrence of the phrase in Psalms, is οὐ προσέσχεν being used. Its effect and perhaps its raison d'être as well is that, rather than being an act of refusal or rebellion, it is portrayed as an act of inattention and being self-absorbed, and thus may conceivably anticipate v. 13.

Psalm 80:13

ואשלחהו בשרירות לבם || ילכו במועצותיהם

καὶ ἐξαπέστειλα αὐτοὺς κατὰ τὰ ἐπιτηδεύματα τῶν καρδιῶν αὐτῶν,
πορεύσονται ἐν τοῖς ἐπιτηδεύμασιν αὐτῶν.

And I sent them away in accordance with the practices of their hearts;
they shall walk in their practices.

καὶ ἐξαπέστειλα. In light of the fact that the two *qatal* verbs are rendered by aorist indicatives in v. 12, it is perhaps no surprise that the *weyiqtol* is made to follow suit. More of a surprise, however, is that the *yiqtol* in 13b yielded a future indicative, as it admittedly often does. It thus becomes a prediction, rather than being a historical fact like 13a. Yet, of greatest interest in this verse is the semantics of the initial verb. While G routinely translates שלח I by ἐξαποστέλλω (19×), ἀποστέλλω (8×) and ἐκτείνω

---

[21] Tate, *Psalms 51–100*, 320.
[22] Tate, *Psalms 51–100*, 320.
[23] So Kraus, *Psalms 60–150*, 147.

(4×)—without differentiating between Qal and Piel—the Piel in 80:13 is glossed in BDB by "to give over," as a result of which commentators on the Hebrew translate accordingly (see *HALOT* as well). So, whereas, according to the Hebrew, God gave the Israelites over to their own stubborn hearts (cf. NRSV), in the Greek he sent them away, it would seem, into exile to continue their practice. To what extent G translated with deliberation we may never know.

αὐτούς. Given that *BHS* cites some evidence for a plural suffix, it may be that G had a parent text different from MT.

κατὰ τὰ ἐπιτηδεύματα—ἐπιτηδεύμασιν. Nine times G made use of ἐπιτήδευμα, seven of which render a form of עלל, "deed." The Hebrew counterparts in 12a and b are respectively שרירות, "stubbornness," and מועצות, "counsels," both uniquely paired with ἐπιτήδευμα in the entire LXX.

Psalm 80:14–15

לו עמי שמע לי ‖ ישראל בדרכי יהלכו
כמעט אויביהם אכניע ‖ ועל צריהם אשיב ידי

14 εἰ ὁ λαός μου ἤκουσέν μου,
Ισραηλ ταῖς ὁδοῖς μου εἰ ἐπορεύθη,
15 ἐν τῷ μηδενὶ ἂν τοὺς ἐχθροὺς αὐτῶν ἐταπείνωσα
καὶ ἐπὶ τοὺς θλίβοντας αὐτοὺς ἐπέβαλον τὴν χεῖρά μου.

14 If my people had heard me,
if Israel had walked by my ways,
15 in no time I would have humbled their enemies,
and on those that afflict them I would have put my hand."

εἰ—ἐπέβαλον (v. 15). Although the Hebrew of vv. 14 to 15 is typically construed as a wish by reading שמע not as a predicate participle but as *yiqtol* (cf. dittography of preceding י), G read it as a so-called past contrary-to-fact condition, with a double protasis as well as a double apodosis. Needless to say, the condition's truth value is closed, that is, what is being posited cannot become true.

ταῖς ὁδοῖς—εἰ. Of some interest is not only that 2110 preposes εἰ ἐν before ταῖς and then omits εἰ later in the stich, but that the same reading is attested by La^G Aug(ustine) Ga(llican Psalter). La^R places εἰ at the head of 14b. To be noted as well is the preposition of ב in MT. The likely source of this correction is Origen's Hexapla. Lastly, several manuscripts of the Byzantine text (*L*) omit εἰ altogether, in agreement with MT.

Psalm 80:16

משנאי יהוה יכחשו לו ‖ ויהי עתם לעולם

οἱ ἐχθροὶ κυρίου ἐψεύσαντο αὐτῷ,
καὶ ἔσται ὁ καιρὸς αὐτῶν εἰς τὸν αἰῶνα.

The enemies of the Lord lied to him,
and their season will be forever.

οἱ ἐχθροὶ κυρίου. Although in Psalms, the most common Hebrew counterpart of Greek ἐχθρός is איב, "enemy" (circa 70 ×), in four instances G pairs it with שנא, "hater" (9:14; 40:8; 80:16; 117:7). Since κυρίου here translates the tetragrammaton, it is, as usual, anarthrous, although isomorphism often triggers an article.

ἐψεύσαντο αὐτῷ. What precisely the Hebrew of 16aβ and b means is unclear, and since G does little, if anything, more than replace his source text with default equivalents, he unfortunately is of no help to decode the source text. G takes כחש to mean "to deceive" or "to lie," a sense attributed to it four out of five times (17:45; 58:13; 65:3; 80:16). Perhaps the biggest problem in both texts is the referent of αὐτῷ and לו. According to Kraus, the Hebrew pronominal must refer back to "Israel" in v. 14b.[24] The referent of αὐτῷ is more ambiguous still, for the simple reason that G mimics the Hebrew and the nearest singular referent is κυρίου. Thus, it is difficult not to read the Greek as: the Lord's enemies lied to him (i.e., the Lord).

καὶ ἔσται ὁ καιρὸς αὐτῶν εἰς τὸν αἰῶνα. G's use of defaults continues. This much would seem to be clear, namely, that αὐτῶν refers to "the enemies of the Lord." What lies in store for them is quite another matter. On the face of it, the line might well predict eternal bliss, even though the immediate context scarcely supports it. Greek καιρός translates עת sixteen times, and three more are rendered by εὐκαιρία. In none of these, however, does καιρός *per se* mean "crisis" or "danger."

Psalm 80:17

ויאכילהו מחלב חטה ‖ ומצור דבש אשביעך

καὶ ἐψώμισεν αὐτοὺς ἐκ στέατος πυροῦ
καὶ ἐκ πέτρας μέλι ἐχόρτασεν αὐτούς.

And he fed them with wheat's fat,
and from a rock he satisfied them with honey.

ἐψώμισεν—ἐχόρτασεν. The two instances of Hiphil (w)yiqtol in 17a and b gives MT a modal nuance. G, on the other hand, did not read them as modal but instead rendered them as aorist indicatives. Moreover, the third masc. sg. suffix of the initial verb and the second masc. sg. suffix of the second one are both rendered by αὐτούς. In the latter case, however, G may well have had a parent text different from MT (cf. *BHS*). To be noted further is that, whereas the Hebrew of v. 17a has a third masc. sg. subject, 17b has a first common sg. subject. It therefore seems as though G did some leveling of his source text, possibly under the influence of the third person reference of v. 16. There is, moreover, no doubt that in both stichs God is the subject.

ἐκ στέατος πυροῦ. Tate (321) is no doubt correct that the idea is that of "fine wheat flour," or, as the Kraus translation renders the phrase, "the marrow of wheat." The question here is, of course, whether "wheat's fat" is conventional usage or even an acceptable Greek mode of expression. As for Psalms, we find it only in 80:17 and 147:3, both times as a direct translation of the source text. One might further add Deut

---

[24] So Kraus, *Psalms 60–150*, 146.

32:14, which speaks of "with fat of kidneys of wheat." Lastly, one might cite Hos 7:4 where στέαρ translates בצק, "dough," and is thus thought to mean "dough." Though in conventional Greek usage, στέαρ meaning "dough" is indeed attested, neither Ps 80:17 nor Ps 147:3 would seem to be about "dough."

ἐκ πέτρας μέλι. Cf. Deut 32:13.

4. Summary

Judging from the number of corrections made or recommended by commentators on the Hebrew text of this psalm, its history of transmission must not have been particularly felicitous. Furthermore, given that a translation of formal correspondence/equivalence tends to preserve the transmitted text in its mode of production, it is typically of little help restoring the source text. See, for example, discussions on verses 1, 6abc, 13a, and 16ab. All of this is *not* to say that the Greek Psalter lacks conventional use of language and even literary nuggets, but it *is* to suggest where the baseline must lie, as well as the burden of proof.

Bibliography

Ausloos, Hans. "למנצח in the Psalm Headings and Its Equivalent in LXX." Pages 131–39 in *XII Congress of the International Organization for Septuagint and Cognate Studies: Leiden 2004*. Edited by Melvin K. H. Peters. SCS 54. Atlanta: Society of Biblical Literature, 2006

Austermann, Frank. *Von der Tora zum Nomos: Untersuchungen zur Übersetzungsweise und Interpretation im Septuaginta-Psalter*. MSU 27. Göttingen: Vandenhoeck & Ruprecht, 2003.

Baethgen, D. F. *Handkommentar zum Alten Testament: Die Psalmen*. Göttingen: Vandenhoeck & Ruprecht, 1892.

Barr, J. "The Meaning of Ἐπακούω and Cognates in the LXX." *JTS* 31 (1980): 67–72.

Boer, P. A. H. de. "Psalm 81:6a: Observations on Translation and Meaning of One Hebrew Line." Pages 67–80 in *The Shelter of Elyon*. Edited by W. B. Barrick and J. R. Spencer. JSOTSup 31. Sheffield: JSOT Press, 1984.

Boyd-Taylor, Cameron. "The Classification of Literalism in Ancient Hebrew–Greek Translation." Pages 131–52 in *Die Sprache der Septuaginta, LXX. H 3*. Edited by Eberhard Bons and Jan Joosten. Gütersloh: Güterloher Verlaghaus, 2015.

Briggs, C. A., and E. G. Briggs. *Psalms II*. ICC. Edinburgh: T&T Clark, 1906–1907.

Cox, Claude. "Εἰσακούω and Ἐπακούω in the Greek Psalter." *Bib* 62 (1981): 251–58.

Didymus the Blind, *Commentarii in Psalmos 22–26.10*, in *Didymos der Blinde, Psalmenkommentar (Tura-Papyrus)*. Teil II: *Kommentar zu Psalm 22–26,10*. Edited by Michael Gronewald. Papyrologische Texte und Abhandlungen 4. Bonn: Habelt, 1968.

Eusebius of Caesarea. *Commentaria in Psalmos*. PG 23. Paris: Migne, 1857.

Flashar, Martin. 1912. "Exegetische Studien zum Septuagintapsalter." *ZAW* 32 (1912): 81–116, 161–89, 241–68.

Flavius Josephus. *Jewish Antiquities*. Vol. V: Books 12-13. Translated by R. Marcus. LCL 365. Cambridge, MA: Harvard University Press, 1943.

Hossfeld, Frank-Lothar, and Erich Zenger. *Psalms 2: A Commentary on Psalms 51–100*. Translated by Linda M. Maloney. Hermeneia. Minneapolis: Fortress Press, 2005.

Kasser, Rodolphe, and Michel Testuz. *Papyrus Bodmer XXIV: Psaumes XVII—CXVIII*. Cologny-Genève: Bibliothèque Bodmer, 1967 (= Rahlfs 2110).

Keil, C. F., and F. Delitzsch. *Biblical Commentary on the Old Testament*. Edinburgh: T&T Clark, 1857.

Kraus, Hans-Joachim. *Psalms 60–150: A Continental Commentary*. Translated by Hilton C. Oswald. Minneapolis: Fortress Press, 1993.

Lee, J. A. L. *A Lexical Study of the Septuagint Version of the Pentateuch*. SCS 14. Chico, CA: Scholars Press, 1983.

Moulton J. H., and G. Milligan. *The Vocabulary of the Greek Testament Illustrated from the Papyri and other Non-literary Sources*. London: Hodder & Stoughton, 1914–29.

Munnich, Olivier. "Etude lexicographique du Psautier des Septante." PhD diss., Université de Paris-Sorbonne, 1982.

Philo Judaeus. *On the Creation. Allegorical Interpretation of Genesis 2 and 3*. Translated by F. H. Colson and G. H. Whitaker. LCL 226. Cambridge, MA: Harvard University Press, 1929.

Pietersma, Albert. "David in the Greek Psalms." Pages 11–22 in *A Question of Methodology: Albert Pietersma Collected Essays on the Septuagint*. Edited by Cameron Boyd-Taylor. Leuven et al: Peeters, 2013 (1980).

Rahlfs, Alfred. *Psalmi cum Odis. Septuaginta: Vetus Testamentum Graecum Auctoritate Academiae Litterarum Gottingensis editum X*. Göttingen: Vandenhoeck & Ruprecht, 1967 (1931).

Rösel, Martin. "Die Psalmüberschriften des Septuaginta-Psalters." Pages 125–48 in *Der Septuaginta-Psalter: Sprachliche und theologische Aspekte*. Edited by Erich Zenger. HBS 32. Freiburg: Herder, 2001.

Sailhamer, John H. *The Translational Technique of the Greek Septuagint for the Hebrew Verbs and Participles in Psalms 3–41*. SIBG 2. New York: Peter Lang, 1991.

Smith, Jannes. "God, Judges, Snakes, and Sinners: A Commentary on the Old Greek Text of Psalm 57." Pages 241–56 in *The SBL Commentary on the Septuagint: An Introduction*. Edited by Dirk Büchner: Atlanta: SBL Press, 2017.

Tate, Marvin E. *Psalms 51–100*. WBC 20. Dallas, TX: Word Books, Publisher, 1990.

Thackeray, Henry St. John. *A Grammar of the Old Testament in Greek*. Cambridge: Cambridge University Press, 1909.

Weiser, Artur. *The Psalms: A Commentary*. Translated by Herbert Hartwell. OTL. Philadelphia: Westminster John Knox, 1962.

West, Martin L. *Ancient Greek Music*. Oxford: Clarendon Press, 1992.

PART II

EXODUS IN THE SEPTUAGINT

Chapter 5

In and Out of Egypt:
Genesis as Prelude to the Exodus Story*

Robert J. V. Hiebert

1. Introduction

The book of Genesis serves as an introduction to the biblical metanarrative, and more specifically to the Pentateuch within that larger corpus. In the first eleven chapters of Genesis, which contain the Bible's version of primeval history, the reader encounters stories about the creation of the cosmos, the origins of all life including humankind, and the consequences of human attempts to usurp the divine prerogatives. Then in chs. 11–50, the narrative pace slows to focus on the lives of Abram, the ancestor of both the Israelite and Ishmaelite peoples, and three generations of his descendants, featuring Isaac, Jacob, and Jacob's sons, with the spotlight settling on Joseph, who rises to prominence among his brothers when he assumes a leading role in the administration of the unnamed Egyptian pharaoh of the time. In the remaining books of the Pentateuch, the narrative pace slows even more, centering on the story of the Israelite people during the lifetime of their great leader and emancipator, Moses.

It will become evident to any reader of these accounts that Egypt and the sojourn of Abram's descendants there, along with their migration from the territory of that ancient Near Eastern superpower, constitute a significant part of the overarching metanarrative. In fact, it would not be an exaggeration to say that Israel's experience with and in Egypt turns out to be a prominent theme throughout both the Hebrew Bible/Jewish Scriptures and the New Testament.

---

* I am very pleased to be able to contribute this essay to a volume that celebrates the life and career of my friend and distinguished colleague, Larry Perkins.

The present essay involves an investigation of some of the philological and thematic resonances in the stories found in the Pentateuch that have to do with Israel's connections with Egypt. The focus is on the Hebrew and Old Greek (OG) versions of those narratives. Specific texts in Genesis 12, 13, and 15 will serve as the points of departure for considering these resonances. It would be in order, however, to begin with a brief overview of relevant passages before embarking upon a more detailed investigation of this subject.

The first mention of Egypt (מִצְרַיִם) in the Hebrew Bible occurs in Gen 10:6, 13, where the referent is, in fact, one of the sons of Ham and a grandson of Noah. The Greek translator, however, does not here use the counterparts that are employed elsewhere in the book for מִצְרַיִם, when referring to Egypt (Αἴγυπτος), or for מִצְרִי or מִצְרִים, when reference is being made to Egyptian(s) (Αἰγύπτιος/Αἰγυπτία/Αἰγύπτιοι: see 12:14; 16:1; 39:1), but he opts instead for a transcription of the Hebrew name, Μεσραίμ (Mesraim). The typical kinds of references to Egypt/Egyptians in Genesis begin with the first of three scenarios that are associated with famine. In 12:10–13:1, it is famine that motivates Abram, Sarai, and Lot to go down to Egypt and reside there for a time. Abram's connection with Egypt is also reinforced through Hagar, the Egyptian slave-girl שִׁפְחָה מִצְרִית / παιδίσκη Αἰγυπτία, whom Sarai gives to him as a wife when she is unable to bear children, and by whom he has a son named Ishmael (16:1–6, 15). Hagar later sees to it that Ishmael gets a wife from the land of Egypt (21:21). In 26:1–3, where mention is made of another famine, Isaac is instructed by Yahweh not to go down to Egypt but to continue to reside in the Promised Land. Then, beginning in 41:53, the reader encounters a series of episodes that take place against the backdrop of a third famine that occurs בְּכָל־הָאָרֶץ, "throughout the world" / ἐν πάσῃ τῇ γῇ, "in all the earth" (41:57), but that because of the stockpiling of stores of grain in Egypt in years of plenty due to the foresight and wise planning of Joseph, who comes to be installed by Pharaoh as second in command over all the land of Egypt (41:43), כָּל־הָאָרֶץ, "all the world" / πᾶσαι αἱ χῶραι, "all the countries," come(s) to Egypt to buy food (41:57). Included among those who take this journey for food are the brothers of Joseph, who has preceded them there as a slave (עֶבֶד / παῖς, 39:17, 19), sold by those same brothers out of jealousy because of the preferential treatment he has received from his and their father, Jacob, to Ishmaelite or Midianite traders who, in turn, sell him in Egypt to Potiphar, one of Pharaoh's officials (37:23–28, 36). Joseph's rise to prominence through a series of providential turns of events entails his being given charge of the welfare of the nation of Egypt during years of both plenty and famine (39:1–6, 19–23; 41:17–45). The brothers do not recognize him when they arrive in Egypt, and they prostrate themselves (חָוָה Hishtaphel) before him / do obeisance (προσκυνέω) to him (42:6), which reminds Joseph of the dreams he has had previously about them bowing down to him (37:5–11). In response to his gruff demeanour when they first meet him in Egypt and his charge that they are spies (מְרַגְּלִים / κατάσκοποι, 42:9, 14), they refer to themselves as his servants (עֲבָדִים / παῖδες, 42:10). On a subsequent occasion, Judah even characterizes them all as Joseph's domestics (οἰκέται, 44:16), for which the MT's counterpart is עֲבָדִים, as has been the case for παῖδες. Ironically, it turns out that Joseph ends up making slaves of (הֶעֱבִיד...לַעֲבָדִים) / subjugating as slaves (κατεδουλώσατο...εἰς παῖδας) the Egyptians (47:21)[1] rather than members of his own family. Although Egypt becomes a place for Jacob and his family to sojourn safely during Joseph's tenure as a high official in Egypt, the desire of both Jacob and Joseph as they look ahead to their eventual deaths is that their final resting places not be in Egypt but in the Promised Land (47:29–30; 50:25). Joseph anticipates that God will eventually bring them up (עָלָה Hiphil / ἀνάγω) out of Egypt to the land that he promised on oath to Abraham, Isaac, and Jacob (50:24). All of this, of course, has been anticipated in the covenant that Yahweh makes with Abram while the latter is in the Promised Land, a covenant in which Yahweh promises that, following the sojourn of Abram's offspring as aliens and slaves in a land that is not their own (15:13), in the fourth generation "they shall come out" (יָצָא / ἐξέρχομαι) and "they shall come back here" (יָשׁוּבוּ הֵנָּה) / "they shall be brought back here" (ἀποστραφήσονται ὧδε) (15:14, 16).

2. Famine and relocation

A logical place to begin the consideration of this topic, then, is in Genesis 12, where Abram himself journeys to the land of Egypt because of a famine that has taken hold in Canaan.

Genesis 12:10

MT: וַיְהִי רָעָב בָּאָרֶץ וַיֵּרֶד אַבְרָם מִצְרַיְמָה לָגוּר שָׁם כִּי־כָבֵד הָרָעָב בָּאָרֶץ

NRSV: Now there was a famine in the land. So Abram went down to Egypt to reside there as an alien, for the famine was severe in the land.

LXX: Καὶ ἐγένετο λιμὸς ἐπὶ τῆς γῆς, καὶ κατέβη Ἀβρὰμ εἰς Αἴγυπτον παροικῆσαι ἐκεῖ, ὅτι ἐνίσχυσεν ὁ λιμὸς ἐπὶ τῆς γῆς.

NETS: And a famine occurred upon the land, and Abram went down to Egypt to reside there as an alien, for the famine prevailed upon the land.

The Septuagint translator (G) renders the noun רָעָב, which occurs first here in Genesis, as the lexeme λιμός 23 times in total in the book.[2] This is the case in the two subsequent accounts in this book that involve famines (chs. 26 and 41–47). Furthermore, in the story of the Israelites after they have left Egypt and are in the wilderness where they recall how in Egypt they sat "at the cauldrons of meat" (ἐπὶ τῶν λεβήτων τῶν κρεῶν) / "by the fleshpots" (עַל־סִיר הַבָּשָׂר) and had plenty to eat, their complaint against Moses and Aaron is that they have brought them out into "this wilderness"

---

[1] The Hebrew *Vorlage* of the OG here was undoubtedly הֶעֱבִיד...לַעֲבָדִים (cf. the Samaritan Pentateuch), rather than the MT's הֶעֱבִיר...לֶעָרִים, "He removed [them] to the cities."

[2] Genesis 12:10(2×); 26:1(2×); 41:27, 30(2×), 31, 36(2×), 50, 54(2×), 56, 57; 42:5; 43:1; 45:6, 11; 47:4, 13(2×), 20.

(τὴν ἔρημον ταύτην / הַמִּדְבָּר הַזֶּה) to kill them "by famine" (ἐν λιμῷ) / "with hunger" (בְּרָעָב) (Exod 16:3). Subsequently, included in the litany of curses in Deuteronomy 28 that are pronounced on those who will violate the covenantal commandments in the Promised Land is λιμός, "famine" / רָעָב, "hunger" (v. 48).

G's equivalent for יָרַד Qal in 23 of its 25 occurrences in Genesis is, as in the present case, καταβαίνω.[3] This equivalence obtains in the two other accounts of descent into Egypt during the two famines mentioned (chs. 26 and 42–46). The Greek counterpart to גּוּר Qal is παροικέω a total of nine times, a term that denotes living as a πάροικος, namely a "temporary resident" or "resident alien."[4] This rendering occurs as well in connection with the episodes involving the two famines described later in the book (26:3; 47:4). In Num 20:15, where the Egyptian sojourn is recounted, the counterpart to παροικέω is יָשַׁב. In Deut 26:5, however, where a creedal formulation is associated with an offering of firstfruits at the sanctuary, the Greek version of the liturgy begins: Συρίαν ἀπέβαλεν ὁ πατήρ μου καὶ κατέβη [וַיֵּרֶד] εἰς Αἴγυπτον, καὶ παρῴκησεν [וַיָּגָר] ἐκεῖ ἐν ἀριθμῷ βραχεῖ, "My ancestor abandoned Syria and went down into Egypt and sojourned there, few in number." The substantival cognate to παροικέω does occur in Genesis in the passage that talks about Abram hearing while in a trance (ἔκστασις) that his "offspring shall be alien (πάροικος / גֵּר) in a land not its own, and they shall enslave them and maltreat them and humble them for four hundred years" (Gen 15:12, 13). In the book of Exodus, the reader is informed that, when Moses names his firstborn son Gersam (Γηρσάμ) / Gershom (גֵּרְשֹׁם), he says, "Because I am a resident alien [πάροικος / גֵּר] in a foreign land" (2:22; cf. 18:3). In a subsequent statement that harks back to Israel's sojourn in Egypt, the following prohibition is made: "You shall not abhor an Egyptian, because you were a resident alien [πάροικος / גֵּר] in his land" (Deut 23:7[8]). This contrasts somewhat with the barring of entry to the assembly (ἐκκλησία / קָהָל) of the Lord / Yahweh to various kinds of people such as a "castrated male" (θλαδίας / פְּצוּעַ־דַּכָּא, "one whose testicles are crushed"), "one made a eunuch" (ἀποκεκομμένος / כְּרוּת שָׁפְכָה, "whose penis is cut off"), "[o]ne from a prostitute" (ἐκ πόρνης / מַמְזֵר "born of an illicit union"), an "Ammanite" (Ἀμμανίτης / עַמּוֹנִי "Ammonite"), or a "Moabite" (Μωαβίτης / מוֹאָבִי) (Deut 23:1[2]–3[4]).

3. Enslavement in Egypt

Israelite subservience to the Egyptians is anticipated already in the story of Abram, and the terminology employed in Pentateuchal descriptions of that state of affairs is noteworthy.

---

[3] Genesis 11:5, 7; 12:10; 15:11; 18:21; 24:16, 45; 26:2; 28:12; 37:35; 38:1; 42:2, 3, 38(1°); 43:4, 15, 20 (Hebrew infinitive absolute plus cognate finite form construction is rendered simply by a single finite form of καταβαίνω); 44:23, 26(2×); 45:9; 46:3, 4. The exception to the יָרַד Qal / καταβαίνω equivalence involves πορεύομαι in 43:5.

[4] Genesis 12:10; 19:9; 20:1; 21:23, 34; 26:3; 32:4(5); 35:27; 45:7. John A. L. Lee, *A Lexical Study of the Septuagint Version of the Pentateuch*, SBLSCS 14 (Chico: Scholars Press, 1983), 60–61.

Genesis 15:13

MT: וַיֹּאמֶר לְאַבְרָם יָדֹעַ תֵּדַע כִּי־גֵר יִהְיֶה זַרְעֲךָ בְּאֶרֶץ לֹא לָהֶם וַעֲבָדוּם וְעִנּוּ אֹתָם אַרְבַּע מֵאוֹת שָׁנָה

NRSV: Then the LORD said to Abram, "Know this for certain, that your offspring shall be aliens in a land that is not theirs, and shall be slaves there, and they shall be oppressed for four hundred years.

LXX: καὶ ἐρρέθη πρὸς Ἀβράμ Γινώσκων γνώσῃ ὅτι πάροικον ἔσται τὸ σπέρμα σου ἐν γῇ οὐκ ἰδίᾳ, καὶ δουλώσουσιν αὐτοὺς καὶ κακώσουσιν αὐτοὺς καὶ ταπεινώσουσιν αὐτοὺς τετρακόσια ἔτη.

NETS: And it was said to Abram, "Knowledgeably you shall know that your offspring shall be alien in a land not its own, and they shall enslave them and maltreat them and humble them for four hundred years.

G renders the verbs עָבַד Qal and עָנָה Piel as δουλόω and ταπεινόω, respectively. This is the only place in the Pentateuch where δουλόω occurs, though the Greek translator of Lev. 26:13 opts for its noun cognate δοῦλος, "slave" (LSJ)—also rarely employed in the Pentateuch—when rendering עֶבֶד to describe the status of Abram's descendants, the Israelites in Egypt in the time of Moses.[5] In the book of Genesis, the most common equivalent by far for the Hebrew noun עֶבֶד is παῖς, "servant, slave" (LSJ), including instances in which Abraham (18:3) and Jacob (32:10[11]) each refer to themselves as God's παῖς, Joseph is called a παῖς by Potiphar's wife (39:17, 19) and Pharaoh's chief cupbearer (41:12), and Joseph's brothers call themselves Joseph's παῖδες (42:10, 11, 13).[6] In 44:33, however, Judah refers to himself as both Joseph's παῖς and his οἰκέτης, "domestic" (MGS), and in 44:16 likewise he says that he and his brothers are both Joseph's παῖδες and his οἰκέται, while in 50:18 the brothers as a group call themselves Joseph's οἰκέται.[7] In 50:17, Joseph's brothers refer to themselves as עַבְדֵי אֱלֹהֵי אָבִיךָ, "the servants of the God of your father," and G here employs the term θεράπων, "attendant" (MGS, LSJ), to render עֶבֶד.[8] In the book of Exodus, this equivalence occurs almost

---

[5] The עֶבֶד / δοῦλος equivalence appears once elsewhere in the Pentateuch in reference to the Israelite people as a whole (Deut 32:36). Otherwise, the δουλ- root is found just three other times in the Mosaic corpus, each one having to do with the regulation of slavery in the context of the Israelite community: עֲבָדִים / δοῦλαι (Exod 21:7); עֶבֶד / δοῦλος (Lev 25:44); אָמָה / δούλη (Lev 25:44).

[6] Of the 88 occurrences of עֶבֶד in the book of Genesis, G's equivalent is παῖς 80 times: 9:25, 26, 27; 12:16; 14:15; 18:3, 5; 19:2, 19; 20:8, 14; 21:25; 24:2, 5, 9, 10, 14, 17, 34, 35, 52, 53, 59, 61, 65(2×), 66; 26:15, 19, 25, 32; 30:43; 32:5, 6, 11, 17(2×), 19, 21; 33:5, 14; 39:17, 19; 40:20(2×); 41:10, 12, 37, 38; 42:10, 11, 13; 43:18, 28; 44:7, 9(2×), 10, 16, 17, 18(2×), 19, 21, 23, 24, 27, 30, 31(2×), 32, 33; 46:34; 47:3, 4(2×), 19, 25; 50:2, 7.

[7] In Gen 9:25, Noah's curse upon Canaan is: עֶבֶד עֲבָדִים יִהְיֶה לְאֶחָיו, "lowest of slaves shall he be to his brothers" / παῖς οἰκέτης ἔσται τοῖς ἀδελφοῖς αὐτοῦ, "a slave, a domestic, shall he be to his brothers." In Gen 27:37, Isaac tells Esau that he has relegated all of Jacob's brothers to the status of his οἰκέται.

[8] Benjamin Wright suggests that, although the idea of being a "slave of God…does not seem to have ready sources in Hellenistic literature," it is "prevalent…in the Greek magical papyri." He mentions by way of example the words of a supplicant to the god Sarapis in a fourth-century CE text: "I am your slave [δοῦλος] and petitioner and have hymned your valid and holy name" (*PGM* XIII.637–638 in Karl Preisendanz, *Papyri Graecae Magicae: Die griechischen Zauberpapyri* II [Leipzig/Berlin: B. G. Teubner, 1931], 116; Hanz Dieter Betz, ed., *The Greek Magical Papyri in Translation* [Chicago:

exclusively in relation to Pharaoh's attendants,[9] though in 4:10 and 14:31 it appears in descriptions of Moses *vis-à-vis* his relationship with Yahweh/God.[10] In ch. 5, those Israelites who have been assigned supervisory roles over their compatriots in their brick-making task refer to themselves as Pharaoh's עֲבָדִים, which G renders both as οἰκέται (5:15, 16) and as παῖδες (5:16).[11]

This kind of semantic differentiation by the Greek translators of Genesis and Exodus when rendering עֲבָדִים is indicative of the distinctions that were made in the Greek-speaking world with respect to people who were in subservient relationships of one sort or another. Benjamin Wright comments:

> In contrast to Hebrew, which had one principal word for male servants/slaves [עֶבֶד] and two for female servants/slaves [אָמָה, שִׁפְחָה], Greek had quite a number. Each of these had important distinctions in the classical period, but evidently during the Hellenistic period, the several different terms for slaves began to be used more often as synonyms, the older distinctions being generally abandoned. The place where this synonymity is most noticeable is in the papyri, most of which come from Egypt... In the Hellenistic and Roman periods, these words can be found maintaining their usual distinctions with relative frequency, but all can be used of slaves in general and do not have to retain the earlier classical differentiation.[12]

The University of Chicago Press, 1986], 183 n. 84, 187). Wright goes on to say that, since "most of these papyri date from well after the first century CE…such use may have come to these magical texts via Jewish or Christian sources. It would seem, then, that this idea is unique to Jews, an idea that they drew from their scriptural traditions and their self conception as a nation of people who are 'servants of God,' as opposed to servants of human rulers" (Benjamin G. Wright, "*'Ebed/Doulos*: Terms and Social Status in the Meeting of Hebrew Biblical and Hellenistic Roman Culture," *Semeia* 83/84 [1998]: 83–111 (108–109); see also Benjamin G. Wright, "Δοῦλος and Παῖς as Translations of עבד: Lexical Equivalences and Conceptual Transformations," in *IX Congress of the International Organization for Septuagint and Cognate Studies, Cambridge, 1995*, ed. Bernard A. Taylor, SBLSCS 45 [Atlanta: Scholars Press, 1997], 263–77).

[9] Exodus 5:21; 7:10(2°), 20, 28(8:3), 29(8:4); 8:5(9), 7(11), 17(21), 20(24), 25(29), 27(31); 9:14, 20, 30, 34; 10:1, 6, 7; 11:3; 12:30; 14:5. In the following cases there is no MT counterpart to θεράπων: Exod 7:9, 10(1°); 9:8. Joel Korytko observes that θεραπεία, a cognate of θεράπων, was a term used "for the royal household guard in Alexandria" during the Ptolemaic period ("The 'Law of the Land' in the Land of Lagides: A Comparative Analysis of Exodus 21.1–32" [Master of Theological Studies thesis, Associated Canadian Theological Schools of Trinity Western University, 2018], 29; and see, for example, Polybius, *The Histories* 4.87.5; 15.25.17 [second century BCE]; Diodorus Siculus, *Library of History* 31.17c [first century BCE]). The term παῖδες is also used by the Lord as cited by Moses regarding Pharaoh's officials in Exod 11:8.

[10] In Exod 33:11, θεράπων is the counterpart to מְשָׁרֵת, the term used to describe Joshua as the assistant to Moses.

[11] Korytko suggests that, in Exod 5:10–16, G may be distinguishing between the Israelites in general as Pharaoh's οἰκέται, who are required to make the same quantity of bricks while having to find straw themselves as they did previously when they had been provided with straw, and their Israelite supervisors who, he posits, call themselves παῖδες in v. 16 when complaining to Pharaoh about having been beaten by the Egyptian taskmasters because the daily quota of bricks is not being met ("The 'Law of the Land,'" 29–30). It is possible to construe G's employment of different terms this way, though the fact that the Israelite supervisors ask Pharaoh "Why are you acting like this to your domestics [τοῖς σοῖς οἰκέταις]?" in 5:15 immediately following the description of their beating in v. 14 makes it at least as likely that they are referring both to their own ill treatment and to the increased work load of the Israelite brick makers, who are also called οἰκέται in v. 16.

[12] Wright, "*'Ebed/Doulos*," 89.

Wright distinguishes the previously mentioned Greek terms in the following ways: δοῦλος is "a general word for slave"; παῖς is "a less general and more familiar word"; οἰκέτης is a term for "a domestic or household slave"; and θεράπων is a designation for a "personal attendant."[13] Yet he maintains that Second Temple period Jewish writers use "words for slaves as they know them to be used in their contemporary socio-cultural environment, that is, that the main terms for slaves can be roughly synonymous even though in individual uses some distinction of function might be intended."[14] Furthermore, he observes that the greater frequency with which δοῦλος— largely absent in the Pentateuch[15]—appears in the later books of the Septuagint "where all the major terms for slaves serve broadly as synonyms," and the increasing interchangeability of those terms in the Septuagint corpus as a whole, are consistent with what is "evidenced in the koine of the period."[16] He regards a contributing factor to this variability of usage to be what Joseph Mélèze-Modrzejewski refers to as two sets of vocabulary in legal parlance in Ptolemaic and Roman Egypt: "un vocabulaire quotidien, familial, qui apparaît notamment danse les lettres privées" and "une terminologie officielle qui apparaît dans les actes publics, en particulier les requêtes qui sont soumises aux autorités, ou dans des actes privés."[17] Wright states that it is in the everyday vocabulary of private correspondence that the synonymous use of terms occurs most frequently and that "both the Greek biblical translations and other Second Temple Jewish works use those terms that appear most frequently in the papyri as synonyms."[18]

G's choice of δουλόω as the counterpart to עָבַד Qal in Gen 15:13 represents something of a semantic shift, not to mention a change in the verb–subject–direct object dynamic. To be specific, the Hebrew lexeme in the Qal stem here means "to serve someone as a slave" (*HALOT*) and the subject of this verb is Abram's offspring while

---

[13] Wright, "*'Ebed/Doulos*," 89.

[14] Wright, "*'Ebed/Doulos*," 107.

[15] Wright is not sure what to make of the infrequent appearance of δοῦλος in the Pentateuch. He opines variously that perhaps the "translators considered the term derogatory or insulting in a way that the others were not"; or that "the use of this particular term was not thought to be appropriate for slaves who would have been used primarily in the household while other terms would" be appropriate, though he acknowledges that "the few cases of *doulos* that do occur in the Septuagint proper serve to blur this distinction"; or that "the terms other than *doulos* connote a greater familiarity between slave and master" (Wright, "*'Ebed/Doulos*," 93, 97, 108). Korytko comments on the oddity of the infrequent appearance of δοῦλος in the Pentateuch inasmuch as he considers it to be "the most generic term for a slave in Ptolemaic Egypt," though elsewhere he suggests that the evidence from both Ptolemaic sources and Septuagint Exodus indicates that παῖς is a generic term for slave, applicable to someone "who would be involved in *both* agricultural labor and potentially household duties." Thus, for example, παῖς and παιδίσκη may be paired in literary and documentary sources with δουλ- and οικετ- forms to distinguish those engaged in "agricultural work or menial labor" from those involved in "household-only" tasks, respectively ("The 'Law of the Land,'" 31, 33–34, 63–64).

[16] Wright, "*'Ebed/Doulos*," 108.

[17] Joseph Mélèze-Modrzejewski's comments come in a response to a colloquium presentation by Jean A. Straus entitled "La terminologie de l'esclavage dans les papyrus grecs d'époque romaine trouvés en Égypte," *Actes du colloque 1973 sur l'esclavage, Besançon 2-3 mai 1973*, Annales littéraires de l'Université de Besançon 182 (Paris: Les belles lettres, 1976), 333–50 (347). See Wright, "*'Ebed/Doulos*," 89–90.

[18] Wright, "*'Ebed/Doulos*," 90.

its object is the people of this foreign land that is not named but which is of course Egypt, whereas the Greek verb means "to enslave" (LSJ, MGS) and the subject is the inhabitants of that land while the object is Abram's offspring. The עָנָה Piel/Hithpael / ταπεινόω equivalence is usual in Genesis,[19] except for Gen 16:6 where G's counterpart to עָנָה Piel is κακόω. In this context, the עָנָה Piel / κακόω equivalence signifies the harsh treatment of Hagar the Egyptian by Sarai, while in Gen 16:9 the עָנָה Hithpael / ταπεινόω equivalence denotes Hagar's submission to Sarai. Elsewhere in the Pentateuch when the Egyptian subjection of the Israelites is referred to, the עָנָה Piel / ταπεινόω equivalence occurs in Exod 1:12 and Deut 26:6, while the עָנָה Piel / κακόω equivalence appears in Exod 1:11. As for καὶ κακώσουσιν αὐτούς in Gen 15:13, there is no counterpart in the MT, though John Wevers suggests plausibly that this clause is a doublet on וְעִנּוּ אֹתָם.[20] In Deut 26:6, the רָעַע Hiphil / κακόω equivalence is also employed to describe how the Egyptians treated the Israelites.

The length of the period of Israelite enslavement in an unnamed foreign land is anticipated in Gen 15:13 to be 400 years, whereas in 15:16 it is stated that Abram's descendants will return to Canaan "in the fourth generation." Exodus 12:40 says that the time of the Israelite sojourn in Egypt was 430 years. The difference in these numbers can be explained either in terms of the 400 years applying specifically to the period of harsh treatment of the Israelites when a new king "who did not know Joseph" ascended the throne (Exod 1:8) and the 430 years including the time of their favourable treatment during the governorship of Joseph, or this numerical discrepancy, along with the mention of the return to Canaan in the fourth generation, can be regarded as imprecise approximations.

4. Egypt's trials

Israelite and Egyptian proximity as recounted both in Genesis and elsewhere in the Pentateuch impacts negatively not only the Israelites but also the Egyptians.

Genesis 12:17

MT: וַיְנַגַּע יְהוָה אֶת־פַּרְעֹה נְגָעִים גְּדֹלִים וְאֶת־בֵּיתוֹ עַל־דְּבַר שָׂרַי אֵשֶׁת אַבְרָם

NRSV: But the LORD afflicted Pharaoh and his house with great plagues because of Sarai, Abram's wife.

LXX: καὶ ἤτασεν ὁ θεὸς τὸν Φαραὼ ἐτασμοῖς μεγάλοις καὶ πονηροῖς καὶ τὸν οἶκον αὐτοῦ περὶ Σάρας τῆς γυναικὸς Ἀβράμ.

NETS: And God tried Pharao and his house with great and grievous trials because of Sara, Abram's wife.

---

[19] Genesis 15:13; 16:9; 31:50; 34:2.
[20] John William Wevers, *Notes on the Greek Text of Genesis*, SBLSCS 35 (Atlanta: Scholars Press, 1993), 211.

5 *In and Out of Egypt* 79

G renders נגע Piel as the lexeme ἐτάζω, and the cognate noun נֶגַע as ἐτασμός.²¹ These are the only occurrences of those equivalences in Genesis. Wevers observes that this verb plus cognate noun expression was not emulated by later Greek translators.²² Indeed, there is no other occurrence of ἐτασμός in a part of the Septuagint corpus for which a Semitic *Vorlage* has survived.²³

The verb ἐτάζω appears already in the writings of Plato.²⁴ The earliest attested occurrence of ἐτασμός, apart from its appearance in LXX Gen 12:17, is in an arguably contemporaneous letter that was found in Herakleopolis and is dated May 27, 268 BCE, from someone named Lykomedes addressed to a certain Hippodamos, in reference to τὸν ἐτασμὸν τῶν κατηγορουμένων, "the investigation of charges."²⁵ This would constitute evidence that the term was by then in common use and thus the suggestion in LEH that ἐτασμός might be a neologism in the Septuagint turns out not to be the case.²⁶

It is noteworthy that the deity is identified as ὁ θεός in Gen 12:17 whereas the MT attests the tetragrammaton.²⁷ In the book of Exodus, the one occurrence of the noun נֶגַע is rendered as πληγή, "plague" (11:1), and πληγή is also the equivalent for נֶגֶף, "plague," in this book (12:13). In both cases, the situation of course involves a different Pharaoh than the one with whom Abram had dealings, and what is being referred to are the dramatic events that occur in the contest between specifically Yahweh / the Lord and the Egyptian monarch regarding which of those two rulers the Israelites will ultimately serve.²⁸

Apart from the word πληγή, there is a range of terms used to characterize the arsenal that Yahweh/the Lord employs to manifest his sovereignty to the Egyptians and to wrest the people of Israel in Moses' day from Pharaoh's oppressive grasp in order to enable them to begin their journey to the land that has been promised to them and their ancestors before them. The most common of these is σημεῖον, "sign," which

---

²¹ Elsewhere in the book of Genesis, the Greek counterparts to the verb נגע are ἅπτω, "touch" (3:3; 20:6; 26:11; 32:26[25], 33[32]), βδελύσσομαι, "loathe" (26:29), and ἀφικνέομαι, "reach" (28:12), verbs that express the different senses in which Hebrew word can be used.

²² Wevers, *Notes on the Greek Text of Genesis*, 172. The counterparts to ἐτάζω include דָּרַשׁ, "search," "investigate" (1 Suppl/1 Chron 28:9; 1 Esd 9:16/Ezra 10:16); בָּהַן, "search," "test" (1 Suppl/1 Chr 29:17; Pss 7:10[9]; 138[139]:23); בָּקַשׁ, "investigate" (Esth 2:23); חָקַר, "search out," "test," "examine" (Iob/Job 32:11; Ier/Jer 17:10; Lam 3:40); שָׁוָה, "pay back" (Iob/Job 372:3); and פָּקַד, "prescribe" (Iob/Job 36:23).

²³ Idt. 8:27 and 2 Makk. 7:37 are the only other places in the OG version in which ἐτασμός is found.

²⁴ "The two words for year, ἐνιαυτός and ἔτος, are really one. For that which brings to light within itself the plants and animals, each in its turn, and examines [ἐξετάζον] them, is called by some ἐνιαυτός, because of its activity within itself [ἐν ἑαυτῷ], and by others ἔτος, because it examines [ἐτάζει]... The whole phrase is 'that which examines within itself [τὸ ἐν αὐτῷ ἐτάζον],' and this one phrase is divided in speech so that the two words ἐνιαυτός and ἔτος are formed from one phrase" (Plato, *Cratylus* 410d [Fowler, LCL]).

²⁵ P.Sorb. 1.9 = Trismegistos 2936, line 2r.

²⁶ Johan Lust, Erik Eynikel, and Katrin Hauspie, *A Greek–English Lexicon of the Septuagint*, 2nd ed. (Stuttgart: Deutsche Bibelgesellschaft, 2003), "ἐτασμός."

²⁷ Wevers observes that a "C b t variant text does substitute κυριος and equals MT, whereas a 961 O text has the double divine name" (Wevers, *Notes on the Greek Text of Genesis*, 172).

²⁸ In the book of Exodus, the verb נגע in its various stems is rendered as προσπίπτω, "fall" (4:25), θιγγάνω "touch" (12:22; 19:12[1°]), and ἅπτω, "touch" (19:12[2°], 13; 29:37; 30:29).

typically renders אוֹת,[29] and the next most frequently occurring one is τέρας, "wonder," which the Greek translator uses as the counterpart to מוֹפֵת.[30] These Greek and Hebrew terms frequently appear in the plural and are in fact often paired (e.g., Exod 7:3). Furthermore, instances of apparent harmonization are to be found in contexts where both Greek terms occur when the only Hebrew counterpart in the MT is either the singular or plural form of מוֹפֵת.[31] This pair of equivalences is also joined in the book of Deuteronomy by another one—πειρασμός/πειρασμοί / מַסּוֹת/מַסָּה "trial(s)"—to form a triad of terms used to describe the mighty acts of Israel's God in Egypt.[32] Additional ways of expressing these events in the book of Exodus include the following: θαυμάσια / נִפְלָאוֹת, "wonders" (3:20); κρίσις μεγάλη, "great judgment" / שְׁפָטִים גְּדֹלִים, "mighty acts of judgment" (6:6); ἐκδίκησις μεγάλη, "great vengeance" / שְׁפָטִים גְּדֹלִים, "great acts of judgment" (7:4); συναντήματα, "encounters" / מַגֵּפֹת, "plagues" (9:14); and the phrase ποιήσω τὴν ἐκδίκησιν, "I will execute vengeance" / אֶעֱשֶׂה שְׁפָטִים, "I will execute judgments (12:12).

5. Departing from Egypt

The descriptions of various departures from Egypt in the Pentateuch involve certain similarities in language and attendant circumstances.

Genesis 12:18

MT: וַיִּקְרָא פַרְעֹה לְאַבְרָם וַיֹּאמֶר מַה־זֹּאת עָשִׂיתָ לִּי לָמָּה לֹא־הִגַּדְתָּ לִּי כִּי אִשְׁתְּךָ הִוא

NRSV: So Pharaoh called Abram, and said, "What is this you have done to me? Why did you not tell me that she was your wife?

LXX: καλέσας δὲ Φαραὼ τὸν Ἀβρὰμ εἶπεν Τί τοῦτο ἐποίησάς μοι, ὅτι οὐκ ἀπήγγειλάς μοι ὅτι γυνή σού ἐστιν;

NETS: Now when Pharao had called Abram he said, "What is this you have done to me, that you did not tell me that she is your wife?

G employs the circumstantial participle καλέσας to subordinate the first clause of the MT to the second one[33] and utilizes δέ to signify the change of subject to Pharaoh. The inclusion of τοῦτο as the counterpart to זֹאת gives rise to a Hebraism. Only in this verse in Genesis is ὅτι on its own G's counterpart to לָמָּה,[34] with the result that the MT's two questions are here reconfigured as a single one. This first ὅτι in the present verse thus introduces the explanation of what Pharaoh says Abram has done, or more accurately,

---

[29] Exodus 3:12; 4:8(2×), 9, 17, 28, 30; 8:23; 10:1, 2; 12:13.
[30] Exodus 4:21; 7:9; 11:9, 10.
[31] Exodus 7:9; 11:9, 10.
[32] Deuteronomy 4:34; 7:19; 29:3(2×).
[33] Herbert W. Smyth, *Greek Grammar*, rev. Gordon M. Messing (Cambridge, MA: Harvard University Press, 1956), §2054.
[34] In Gen 18:13 and 44:4 the counterpart is τί ὅτι.

what he has failed to do. The employment of the Greek copula verb to render the Hebrew pronoun, the subject in this verbless clause, constitutes an acceptable translation that conveys the meaning of the source text.[35]

Genesis 12:19

MT: לָמָה אָמַרְתָּ אֲחֹתִי הִוא וָאֶקַּח אֹתָהּ לִי לְאִשָּׁה וְעַתָּה הִנֵּה אִשְׁתְּךָ קַח וָלֵךְ

NRSV: Why did you say, 'She is my sister,' so that I took her for my wife? Now then, here is your wife, take her, and be gone."

LXX: ἵνα τί εἶπας ὅτι Ἀδελφή μού ἐστιν; καὶ ἔλαβον αὐτὴν ἐμαυτῷ εἰς γυναῖκα. καὶ νῦν ἰδοὺ ἡ γυνή σου ἐναντίον σου· λαβὼν ἀπότρεχε.

NETS: Why did you say, 'She is my sister'? And I took her to myself for a wife. And now here is your wife before you; take her; be gone."[36]

Unlike the לָמָה / ὅτι equivalence found in the preceding verse, the most commonly attested counterpart to that Hebrew interrogative form in Genesis is the phrase ἵνα τί that appears in the present verse.[37] The presence of ὅτι in this verse serves to introduce the direct speech of Pharaoh, which is without a counterpart here in the MT. The rendering of the verbless clause אֲחֹתִי הִוא as Ἀδελφή μού ἐστιν replicates the strategy employed in the previous verse where γυνή σού ἐστιν is the counterpart to אִשְׁתְּךָ הִוא. The prepositional phrase ἐναντίον σου that follows ἡ γυνή σου has no counterpart in the MT. But the declaration in Gen 24:51 by Laban and Bethuel to Abraham's servant, "Look, Rebekah is before you," הִנֵּה־רִבְקָה לְפָנֶיךָ / ἰδοὺ Ρεβέκκα ἐνώπιόν σου, reveals that לְפָנֶיךָ would be the expected Hebrew equivalent for the prepositional phrase, whether the preposition is ἐνώπιον, as is the case in 24:51, or ἐναντίον as in 12:19. The aptness of the comparison between these two verses is confirmed by what follows the deictic statement in both cases: קַח וָלֵךְ, "take her, and be gone" (12:19); "take her and go" (24:51) / λαβὼν ἀπότρεχε, "take her; be gone" (12:19); "take her, go" (24:51).[38] Once again, as in 12:19, a Hebrew paratactic construction is rendered by means of a circumstantial participle followed by a finite verb that is not preceded by the conjunction καί. Furthermore, G renders הָלַךְ Qal as ἀποτρέχω in Genesis only in 12:19 and in 24:51. The only other place in this book where the לָקַח plus הָלַךְ sequence occurs (קְחוּ וָלֵכוּ), the circumstantial participle plus imperative combination is found in the words of Joseph to his brothers, λαβόντες ἀπέλθατε, "go off, taking [the purchase of

---

[35] Wevers, *Notes on the Greek Text of Genesis*, 173; Bruce K. Waltke and Michael P. O'Connor, *An Introduction to Biblical Hebrew Syntax* (Winona Lake: Eisenbrauns, 1990), §§4.5c, 8.4.1a. See also Gordon J. Wenham, *Genesis 1–15*, WBC 1 (Waco: Word Books, 1987), 284–85, especially his comments in notes 12.a-a, 18.c-c, and 19.a-a.

[36] NETS has "take her; hurry off" for λαβὼν ἀπότρεχε, but as John Lee points out, by the third century BCE, ἀποτρέχω "it is commonly found in the sense of 'depart', 'leave', without any suggestion of running or even haste" (*A Lexical Study*, 125).

[37] The 14 other occurrences are found in Gen 4:6(2×); 24:31; 25:22, 32; 27:46; 29:25; 31:27(26), 30; 32:30; 33:15; 42:1; 44:7; 47:15.

[38] In Gen 24:51, NETS has "take her, leave quickly" for λαβὼν ἀπότρεχε.

your household's grain allowance]" (42:33). Elsewhere in the Pentateuch, this same Hebrew verbal sequence—וּלְכוּ...קְחוּ—is found in Pharaoh's words to Moses and Aaron following the tenth plague in his demand that the Israelites leave Egypt, and it is rendered by G as ἀναλαβόντες πορεύεσθε, "Take [both your sheep and cattle], and get going" (Exod 12:32).[39]

In other places where the Israelites' departure from Egypt under the leadership of Moses and Aaron is the focus of consideration, there are additional ways of describing that process and the rationale for it to take place. These pertain, first, to statements about Pharaoh sending away (שָׁלַח / ἐξαποστέλλω) the Israelites so that they may "sacrifice" (זָבַח / θύω) to Yahweh / the Lord (Exod 8:4[8]) or "serve" (עָבַד / λατρεύω) him (Exod 10:3, 7). Second, a number of passages feature Pharaoh's command for the Israelites to "go" (הָלַךְ / ἔρχομαι) and "sacrifice" (זָבַח / θύω) to their God (8:21[25]), or to "go" (הָלַךְ / πορεύομαι [Exod 10:8], βαδίζω [Exod 10:24; 12:31]) and "serve" (עָבַד / λατρεύω) him. Exodus 12:31 also contains Pharaoh's command: קוּמוּ צֵאוּ, "Rise up, go away" / Ἀνάστητε καὶ ἐξέλθατε, "Arise, and go out."

As indicated previously, in several passages describing the exodus of the Israelites from Egypt in the time of Moses, the matter of who will be allowed to depart comes up in the exchanges between Pharaoh and Moses. In Exod 10:9, Moses says: בִּנְעָרֵינוּ וּבִזְקֵנֵינוּ נֵלֵךְ בְּבָנֵינוּ וּבִבְנוֹתֵנוּ בְּצֹאנֵנוּ וּבִבְקָרֵנוּ נֵלֵךְ, "We will go with our young and our old; we will go with our sons and daughters and with our flocks and herds" / Σὺν τοῖς νεανίσκοις καὶ πρεσβυτέροις πορευσόμεθα, σὺν τοῖς υἱοῖς καὶ θυγατράσιν καὶ προβάτοις καὶ βουσὶν ἡμῶν, "With the young and old men we will go, with our sons and daughters and sheep and cattle." Pharaoh then raises the prospect of them wanting to include their טַף, "little ones" / τὴν ἀποσκευήν, "chattels" (v. 10) and then insists that only הַגְּבָרִים / οἱ ἄνδρες, "men," will be allowed to go on this journey to serve (עָבַד / λατρεύω) their God (Exod 10:3, 7). In Exod 10:24, Pharaoh insists that the Israelite cattle must stay but that the טַף, "children" / ἡ ἀποσκευή, "chattels," may go along. Moses counters this by asserting that they will need their animals for זְבָחִים וְעֹלוֹת, "sacrifices and burnt offerings" / ὁλοκαυτώματα καὶ θυσίας, "whole burnt offerings and sacrifices," in order to serve (עָבַד / λατρεύω) their God (vv. 25–26). In Exod 12:32 after the tenth plague involving the death of the firstborn, Pharaoh grants the Israelites permission to take their livestock in his haste to be rid of them.

This kind of entourage coming out of Egypt seems to be anticipated in the portrayal of Abram's departure from Egypt with great wealth in "livestock" (מִקְנֶה / κτήνη), "silver" (כֶּסֶף / ἀργύριον), and "gold" (זָהָב / χρυσίον) (Gen 13:1–2). The Israelite exodus is also foreshadowed in Genesis 15 in the context of the covenant that Yahweh / the LORD establishes with Abram. There he is promised that his descendants "shall come out with great possessions," יֵצְאוּ בִּרְכֻשׁ גָּדוֹל / "shall come out here with much baggage," ἐξελεύσονται ὧδε μετὰ ἀποσκευῆς πολλῆς (v. 14). Note that, in this case,

---

[39] A different kind of collocation of the two Hebrew verbs is found in Deut 20, pertaining to a different kind of situation—namely, explanation of the protocols for Israelites preparing for war—and involving the combination of λαμβάνω plus πορεύομαι in prescribing what should occur in the case of a man who has become "engaged to a woman but has not yet taken her [וְלֹא לְקָחָהּ / καὶ οὐκ ἔλαβεν αὐτήν]...: Let him go [יֵלֵךְ / πορευέσθω] and return to his house" (20:7).

ἀποσκευή, "baggage," is the counterpart to רְכוּשׁ, "possessions," rather than to טַף, "little ones" (Exod 10:10) or "children" (Exod 10:24). In the time of Moses, in addition to the Israelites being allowed by Pharaoh to leave with their "flocks" (צֹאן) and "herds" (בָּקָר) / "sheep" (πρόβατα) and "cattle" (βόες) (Exod 12:32), they "plunder" (נָצַל Piel / σκυλεύω) the Egyptians (12:36), asking for and receiving from them כְּלֵי־כֶסֶף וּכְלֵי זָהָב וּשְׂמָלֹת, "jewelry of silver and gold, and...clothing" / σκεύη ἀργυρᾶ καὶ χρυσᾶ καὶ ἱματισμόν, "silver and gold articles and clothing" (12:35).

The exodus from Egypt under Moses' leadership is prefigured as well in the descriptions of arrangements concerning the final resting places for both Jacob and Joseph (Gen 50). Abram goes up (עָלָה / ἀναβαίνω) from Egypt along with Sarai and Lot (13:1). Some two generations later, Jacob exacts from Joseph the promise that he will see to it that his father is buried in the ancestral tomb in Canaan. When Pharaoh is made aware that Joseph is thus obligated, he grants him permission to do so. Here the verb sequence pertaining to Joseph's action is עָלָה Qal + קָבַר / ἀναβαίνω + θάπτω: אֶעֱלֶה־נָּא וְאֶקְבְּרָה אֶת־אָבִי...עֲלֵה וּקְבֹר אֶת־אָבִיךָ, "[L]et me go up, so that I may bury my father... Go up, and bury your father" / ἀναβὰς θάψω τὸν πατέρα μου... Ἀνάβηθι, θάψον τὸν πατέρα σου "I will go up and bury my father... Go up; bury your father" (Gen 50:5, 6).[40]

Some noteworthy aspects of the story of Jacob's death and burial reflect the cultural realities, theological interests, and intertextual connections that are part and parcel of the crafting of this narrative in both its Hebrew *Vorlage* and Greek translation as well as its linkage with other stories that have been discussed. For example, the description of the funeral cortège that accompanies Jacob's body from Egypt to Canaan for burial includes not only all the household of Joseph and his brothers (Gen 50:8) but also an impressive contingent comprised of כָּל־עַבְדֵי פַרְעֹה זִקְנֵי בֵיתוֹ וְכֹל זִקְנֵי אֶרֶץ־מִצְרָיִם, "all the servants of Pharaoh, the elders of his household, and all the elders of the land of Egypt" / πάντες οἱ παῖδες Φαραὼ καὶ οἱ πρεσβύτεροι τοῦ οἴκου αὐτοῦ καὶ πάντες οἱ πρεσβύτεροι γῆς Αἰγύπτου, "all the servants of Pharao and the elders of his house and all the elders of the land of Egypt" (Gen 50:7). This latter detail may resonate to some degree with the mention of the men (אֲנָשִׁים / ἀνδράσιν) to whom Pharaoh gives orders concerning Abram to "set him on the way" / "join in escorting him" (שָׁלַח Piel / συμπροπέμπω) out of Egypt, along with his wife and the rest of his entourage (Gen 12:20). Furthermore, the description of the preparation of Jacob's body reflects both an awareness, especially in the Hebrew text, of the customs practised in Egypt, and a certain reticence, particularly in the Greek text, in associating too closely what was done with Jacob's body in such practices. Thus the Hebrew author states that Jacob's body was embalmed (חָנַט)—a procedure that was typically performed for pharaohs, the nobility, and other officials, but only occasionally for common people.[41] G, on the other hand, rather than rendering that term with an equivalent like ταριχεύω, "mummify, embalm" (MGS), or σκελετεύω, "embalm" (MGS), that has to do with preserving the body, opts for ἐνταφιάζω, "prepare for burial" (MGS, LSJ)—a practice that might well include

---

[40] Abram, for his part, receives the promise after his return from his sojourn in Egypt that he will be "buried [תִּקָּבֵר / ταφείς] in a good old age" (Gen 15:15).
[41] Richard N. Jones, "Embalming," *AYBD* 2:490–96 (491–92).

wrapping the body in an ἐντάφιον, "funerary sheet, burial shroud" (MGS). This move may have been due to the translator's desire to downplay a connection with the rites associated with embalming in Egypt, which was a religious act performed by priests in the service of Anubis, the god of the dead, to ensure that the individual's life could continue in the hereafter and that his/her ba (similar to the concept of the soul or spirit) could recognize the body when returning to it.[42] It is curious that the Hebrew text states that "physicians [רֹפְאִים] embalmed Israel" (50:2), given the fact that, in Egypt, physicians were distinguished from embalmers and comprised another class of priests, namely those devoted to Sekhmet, the goddess of healing.[43] Apart from the theological implications associated with embalming, perhaps the fact that embalmers and physicians would engage in some of the same procedures in handling a body, such as making incisions, led the Hebrew author to eschew any such distinction in professional terminology. G, however, attributes the work of preparing Jacob's body to ἐνταφιασταί, "undertakers" (LSJ) or "buriers" (MGS), a term that, like ἐνταφιάζω, is cognate to ἐντάφιον, which is attested in texts as early as the sixth-fifth century BCE.[44] The mention of forty days for the process of embalming the body and of seventy days for the mourning period seems to be generally compatible with what is known from texts that describe these rites.[45]

In Joseph's case, prior to his death he informs his brothers that God will bring them up (עָלָה Hiphil / ἀνάγω) from Egypt to the land he promised to their ancestors, and he makes them swear that they will then also carry up (עָלָה Hiphil / συναναφέρω) his bones with them (Gen 50:24, 25). The words of Joseph's charge to the Israelites,

---

[42] Jones, "Embalming," 493.
[43] Jones, "Embalming," 493.
[44] E.g., the lyric poet Simonides: ἐντάφιον δὲ τοιοῦτον εὐρὼς οὔθ' ὁ πανδαμάτωρ ἀμαυρώσει χρόνος, "Such a funeral-gift [or 'shroud'] neither mould nor all-conquering time shall destroy" (Simonides, Fragments 531.4–5 [Campbell, LCL]). See also Isocrates (fifth–fourth century BCE): καλόν ἐστιν ἐντάφιον ἡ τυραννίς, "royalty is a glorious shroud" (Isocrates, Archidamus (Or. 6) 45 [Norlin, LCL]). The earliest attested occurrence of the verb ἐνταφιάζω appears to be in LXX Gen 50:2. The noun ἐνταφιαστής is found in late third- or early second-century BCE papyri from Tanis in the Fayum region of Egypt: e.g., Μαχάται ἐπιστάτηι Τάνεως παρ' Ὀνν[ώφριος] ἐνταφιαστοῦ, "To Machatas the overseer of Tanis from Onn[ophris] the undertaker/burier" (P.Köln 15.594, lines 1–2); [π]αρὰ Ἀμεννεῦτος τοῦ Ὡρ[ο]υ ἐνταφιαστοῦ ἐκ κώμης Τάνεως τοῦ Ἀρσινοίτου ν[ομο]ῦ, "[f]rom Amenneus the son of Hor[o]s, the undertaker/burier from the village of Tanis of the Arsinoite n[om] e" (P.Tarich 3 a, lines 1–2). See Charikleia Armoni, Das Archiv der Taricheuten Amenneus und Onnophris aus Tanis (P.Tarich), Papyrologica Coloniensia 37 (Paderborn: Ferdinand Schöningh, 2013); Peter van Minnen, review of Das Archiv der Taricheuten Amenneus und Onnophris aus Tanis (P.Tarich), by Charikleia Armoni, BASP 51 (2014): 245–48; Marja Vierros, review of Das Archiv der Taricheuten Amenneus und Onnophris aus Tanis (P.Tarich), by Charikleia Armoni, Bryn Mawr Classical Review 2015.02.52 (https://bmcr.brynmawr.edu/2015/2015.02.52/); Robert W. Daniel, "Petition concerning Kittens," in Thomas Backhuys, Charikleia Armoni et al., Kölner Papyri (P. Köln) Band 15, Sonderreihe der Abhandlungen Papyrologica Coloniensia 7/15 (Paderborn: Ferdinand Schöningh, 2017), 1–11.
[45] Jones, "Embalming," 493; Gordon J. Wenham, Genesis 16–50, WBC 2 (Grand Rapids: Zondervan, 2000), 488; Sofie Schiødt, "Medical Science in Ancient Egypt: A Translation and Interpretation of Papyrus Louvre-Carlsberg (pLouvre E 32847 + pCarlsberg 917)," PhD Thesis, University of Copenhagen, 2021; Faculty of Humanities, University of Copenhagen, "Ancient Egyptian manual reveals new details about mummification" (https://phys.org/news/2021-02-ancient-egyptian-manual-reveals-mummification.html); Jozef Vergote, Joseph en Égypte: Genèse chap. 37–50, à la lumière des études égyptologiques récentes, Orientalia et biblica lovaniensia 3 (Louvain: Publications Universitaires, 1959), 197–200; Herodotus, The Persian Wars 2.86–88.

including this latter equivalence, are recalled in Exod 13:19 where it is said that Moses took Joseph's bones with him at the time of the exodus. Joseph is said to have lived 110 years (Gen 50:22, 26), which corresponds to what was considered to be the ideal life span in ancient Egypt.[46] In his case, the Hebrew text says that "he was embalmed [חָנַט] and placed in a coffin [אָרוֹן] in Egypt" (50:26), the only time that a coffin is mentioned in the Old Testament.[47] The Greek counterpart to אָרוֹן is the semantically equivalent term σορός, whereas the choice of θάπτω to render חָנַט is an interesting one inasmuch as θάπτω is the usual equivalent for קָבַר "bury" (*DCH*, BDB) in Genesis.[48] Glossing θάπτω as "bury" would create a potential tautology in regard to a sequence consisting of Joseph's burial followed by his body being placed in a coffin. As is evident from how this term can be used in non-translation Greek texts, however, it can have to do with performing funeral rites of various sorts associated with interment:

αὐτοῦ οἱ καὶ σῆμα τετεύξεται, οὐδέ τί μιν χρεὼ ἔσται τυμβοχόης, ὅτε μιν θάπτωσιν Ἀχαιοί.

Here too will his sepulcher be prepared, nor will he have need of a heaped-up mound when the Achaeans perform his funeral rites.[49]

ἐννῆμαρ μέν κ' αὐτὸν ἐνὶ μεγάροις γοάοιμεν, τῇ δεκάτῃ δέ κε θάπτοιμεν δαινῦτό τε λαός, ἑνδεκάτῃ δέ κε τύμβον ἐπ' αὐτῷ ποιήσαιμεν, τῇ δὲ δυωδεκάτῃ πολεμίξομεν, εἴ περ ἀνάγκη.

For nine days we will wail for him in our halls, and on the tenth we will make his funeral, and the people will feast, and on the eleventh we will heap a mound over him, and on the twelfth we will do battle, if we must.[50]

οὕτω πετηνῶν τόνδ' ὑπ' οἰωνῶν δοκεῖ ταφέντ' ἀτίμως τοὐπιτίμιον λαβεῖν, καὶ μήθ' ὁμαρτεῖν τυμβοχόα χειρώματα μήτ' ὀξυμόλποις προσσέβειν οἰμώγμασιν, ἄτιμον εἶναι δ' ἐκφορᾶς φίλων ὕπο.

So it is decided that he should get his due reward by receiving a dishonourable funeral from the flying birds; that he should neither lie under a laboriously raised burial-mound nor be dignified with high-pitched musical wailings; and that he should not have the honour of a funeral procession from his family.[51]

---

[46] Wenham, *Genesis 16–50*, 490; Vergote, *Joseph en Égypte*, 200–201.
[47] Wenham, *Genesis 16–50*, 491.
[48] Gen 15:15; 23:4, 6(2×), 8, 11, 13, 15, 19; 25:9, 10; 35:19, 29; 47:29, 30; 49:29, 31(3×); 50:5(2×), 6, 7, 13, 14. The only other occurrence of θάπτω in Genesis has no Hebrew counterpart (50:12). קָבַר is rendered by something else than θάπτω just once in Genesis, i.e., κατορύσσω "bury" (NETS) in 48:7. On two other occasions, קָבַר has no Greek counterpart (35:8, 50:14[2°]).
[49] Homer, *Iliad* 21.322–323 (Murray, rev. Wyatt, LCL).
[50] Homer, *Iliad* 24.664–667 (Murray, rev. Wyatt, LCL).
[51] Aeschylus, *Seven against Thebes* 1020–1024 (Sommerstein, LCL).

6. Into the Negeb/wilderness

The descriptions of the route taken by both Abram and his descendants after they have left Egypt exhibit similarities.

Genesis 13:1

MT: וַיַּעַל אַבְרָם מִמִּצְרַיִם הוּא וְאִשְׁתּוֹ וְכָל־אֲשֶׁר־לוֹ וְלוֹט עִמּוֹ הַנֶּגְבָּה

NRSV: So Abram went up from Egypt, he and his wife, and all that he had, and Lot with him, into the Negeb.

LXX: Ἀνέβη δὲ Ἀβρὰμ ἐξ Αἰγύπτου, αὐτὸς καὶ ἡ γυνὴ αὐτοῦ καὶ πάντα τὰ αὐτοῦ καὶ Λὼτ μετ' αὐτοῦ, εἰς τὴν ἔρημον.

NETS: Then Abram went up from Egypt, he and his wife and all that was his and Lot with him, into the wilderness.

Occurring first in 12:9, נֶגֶב is translated as ἔρημος to designate a location, namely, the "dry south country"[52] in the land of Canaan, as is the case also in Gen 13:1, 3. The Hebrew term נֶגֶב, "Negeb," in these contexts typically applies to the northernmost of the several wildernesses that are mentioned in the Hebrew Bible, which include, in more or less descending order moving southward, Zin, Paran, and Sinai.[53] Thereafter in this book,[54] it is rendered as λίψ, which indicates a direction instead of a location, namely, southwest. Wevers notes that the נֶגֶב / ἔρημος equivalence appears elsewhere in the Septuagint.[55] In regard to the cases in Num 13:17(18), 22(23), which are part of the narrative about the sending of men on a reconnaissance mission to spy out (תּוּר / κατασκέπτομαι) the Promised Land,[56] whereas there is little doubt that the Hebrew wording refers specifically to the Negeb region, the Greek wording seems to indicate that a broader range of territory is in view. The scene for this episode is set in Num 12:16(13:1) where it is said that the Israelites have encamped in the wilderness of Paran. Moses' set of instructions to the spies begins with the words, עֲלוּ זֶה בַּנֶּגֶב, "Go up there into the Negeb" (13:17[18]), which is followed by the report of what the spies did in response, וַיַּעֲלוּ בַנֶּגֶב, "They went up into the Negeb" (13:22[23]). The Greek counterparts to these instructions, however, are, Ἀνάβητε ταύτῃ τῇ ἐρήμῳ, "Go up by this wilderness" (13:18[17]), and καὶ ἀνέβησαν κατὰ τὴν ἔρημον, "And they went up by the wilderness" (13:23[22]). The Greek phrasing in each case suggests the route that the spies

---

[52] Steven A. Rosen, "Negeb," *AYBD* 4:1061–64 (1061).
[53] Anson F. Rainey and R. Stephen Notley, *The Sacred Bridge: Carta's Atlas of the Biblical World* (Jerusalem: Carta, 2006, 2014), 120; David R. Seely, "Zin, Wilderness of," *AYBD* 6:1095–96; Jeffries M. Hamilton, "Paran," *AYBD* 5:162.
[54] Genesis 13:14; 20:1; 24:62; 28:14.
[55] Numbers 13:17(18), 22(23); 21:1; Deut 34:3; Josh 15:21; Isa 21:1, and 30:6. Wevers, *Notes on the Greek Text of Genesis*, 168.
[56] Joseph accuses his brothers of coming to Egypt as spies (Gen 42:9, 14), where the terminology is מְרַגְּלִים/κατάσκοποι. In Num 13, although a different Hebrew verbal root, תּוּר, is employed, the Greek counterpart, κατασκέπτομαι, is the verbal cognate to κατάσκοποι.

take through what is envisaged to be a generalized wilderness area rather than one of the destination points implied by the Hebrew phrase בַּנֶּגֶב, "into the Negeb." Admittedly, that wilderness is differentiated by references to the wilderness of Paran where the Israelites were camped, as noted previously (see also 13:26[27]), and to the wilderness of צִן, "Zin" / Σίν, "Sin," which was part of the territory that was spied out (13:21[22]). In the remaining cases of the נֶגֶב / ἔρημος equivalence, however, no such differentiation is evident in the Septuagint.

7. Conclusion

The preceding investigation of certain Pentateuchal texts that tell of the peregrinations of the Israelite ancestors and their descendants has served to highlight the connections between Israel and Egypt that feature rather prominently in those narratives. The philological and thematic resonances of these connections can be traced in the Hebrew and Old Greek versions of the narratives though, as has been shown, both versions at times link the relevant texts in distinctive ways.

Bibliography

Aeschylus. *Persians. Seven against Thebes. Suppliants. Prometheus Bound.* Edited and translated by Alan H. Sommerstein. LCL 145. Cambridge, MA: Harvard University Press, 2009.

Armoni, Charikleia. *Das Archiv der Taricheuten Amenneus und Onnophris aus Tanis (P.Tarich).* Papyrologica Coloniensia 37. Paderborn: Ferdinand Schöningh, 2013.

AYBD = The Anchor Yale Bible Dictionary. Edited by David Noel Freedman. 6 vols. New York: Doubleday, 1992.

Betz, Hanz Dieter, ed. *The Greek Magical Papyri in Translation.* Chicago: The University of Chicago Press, 1986.

Daniel, Robert W. "Petition concerning Kittens." Pages 1–11 in *Kölner Papyri (P. Köln) Band 15.* Edited by Thomas Backhuys, Charikleia Armoni et al. Sonderreihe der Abhandlungen Papyrologica Coloniensia 7/15. Paderborn: Ferdinand Schöningh, 2017.

Diodorus Siculus. *Library of History, Volume XI: Fragments of Books 21–32.* Translated by Francis R. Walton. LCL 409. Cambridge, MA: Harvard University Press, 1957.

Faculty of Humanities. University of Copenhagen, "Ancient Egyptian manual reveals new details about mummification" (https://phys.org/news/2021-02-ancient-egyptian-manual-reveals-mummification.html).

Herodotus. *The Persian Wars, Volume I: Books 1–2.* Translated by A. D. Godley. LCL 117. Cambridge, MA: Harvard University Press, 1920.

Homer. *Iliad, Volume II: Books 13–24.* Translated by A. T. Murray. Revised by William F. Wyatt. LCL 171. Cambridge, MA: Harvard University Press, 1925.

Isocrates. *To Demonicus. To Nicocles. Nicocles or the Cyprians. Panegyricus. To Philip. Archidamus.* Translated by George Norlin. LCL 209. Cambridge, MA: Harvard University Press, 1928.

Korytko, Joel. "The 'Law of the Land' in the Land of Lagides: A Comparative Analysis of Exodus 21.1–32." Master of Theological Studies thesis, Associated Canadian Theological Schools of Trinity Western University, 2018.

Lee, John A. L. *A Lexical Study of the Septuagint Version of the Pentateuch*. SBLSCS 14. Chico: Scholars Press, 1983.

Lust, Johan, Erik Eynikel, and Katrin Hauspie. *A Greek–English Lexicon of the Septuagint*. 2nd ed. Stuttgart: Deutsche Bibelgesellschaft, 2003.

Plato. *Cratylus. Parmenides. Greater Hippias. Lesser Hippias*. Translated by Harold North Fowler. LCL 167. Cambridge, MA: Harvard University Press, 1926.

Polybius. *The Histories, Volume II: Books 3–4*. Translated by W. R. Paton. Revised by F. W. Walbank, Christian Habicht. LCL 137. Cambridge, MA: Harvard University Press, 2010.

Polybius. *The Histories, Volume IV: Books 9–15*. Translated by W. R. Paton. Revised by F. W. Walbank, and Christian Habicht. LCL 159. Cambridge, MA: Harvard University Press, 2011.

Preisendanz, Karl. *Papyri Graecae Magicae: Die griechischen Zauberpapyri* II. Leipzig/Berlin: B. G. Teubner, 1931.

Rainey, Anson F., and R. Stephen Notley. *The Sacred Bridge: Carta's Atlas of the Biblical World*. Jerusalem: Carta, 2006, 2014.

Schiødt, Sofie. "Medical Science in Ancient Egypt: A Translation and Interpretation of Papyrus Louvre-Carlsberg (pLouvre E 32847 + pCarlsberg 917)." PhD thesis, University of Copenhagen, 2021.

Smyth, Herbert W. *Greek Grammar*. Revised by Gordon M. Messing. Cambridge, MA: Harvard University Press, 1956.

Stesichorus, Ibycus, Simonides. *Greek Lyric, Volume III: Stesichorus, Ibycus, Simonides, and Others*. Edited and translated by David A. Campbell. LCL 476. Cambridge, MA: Harvard University Press, 1991.

Straus, Jean A. "La terminologie de l'esclavage dans les papyrus grecs d'époque romaine trouvés en Égypte." Pages 333–50 in *Actes du colloque 1973 sur l'esclavage, Besançon 2–3 mai 1973*. Annales littéraires de l'Université de Besançon 182. Paris: Les belles lettres, 1976.

van Minnen, Peter. Review of *Das Archiv der Taricheuten Amenneus und Onnophris aus Tanis (P.Tarich)*, by Charikleia Armoni. BASP 51 (2014): 245–48.

Vergote, Jozef. *Joseph en Égypte: Genèse chap. 37–50, à la lumière des études égyptologiques récentes*. Orientalia et biblica lovaniensia 3. Louvain: Publications Universitaires, 1959.

Vierros, Marja. Review of *Das Archiv der Taricheuten Amenneus und Onnophris aus Tanis (P.Tarich)*, by Charikleia Armoni. *Bryn Mawr Classical Review* 2015.02.52 (https://bmcr.brynmawr.edu/2015/2015.02.52/).

Waltke, Bruce K., and Michael P. O'Connor. *An Introduction to Biblical Hebrew Syntax*. Winona Lake: Eisenbrauns, 1990.

Wenham, Gordon J. *Genesis 1–15*. WBC 1. Waco: Word Books, 1987.

Wenham, Gordon J. *Genesis 16–50*. WBC 2. Grand Rapids: Zondervan, 2000.

Wevers, John William. *Notes on the Greek Text of Genesis*. SBLSCS 35. Atlanta: Scholars Press, 1993.

Wright, Benjamin G. "Δοῦλος and Παῖς as Translations of עבד: Lexical Equivalences and Conceptual Transformations." Pages 263–77 in *IX Congress of the International Organization for Septuagint and Cognate Studies, Cambridge, 1995*. Edited by Bernard A. Taylor. SBLSCS 45. Atlanta: Scholars Press, 1997.

Wright, Benjamin G. "'*Ebed/Doulos*: Terms and Social Status in the Meeting of Hebrew Biblical and Hellenistic Roman Culture." *Semeia* 83/84 (1998): 83–111.

Chapter 6

The Tree of the Sacred Text:
Reflections on Greek Exodus in Dialogue with Antoine Berman[*]

Karlena M. Cagnoli

1. Introduction

In recent decades, Septuagint scholars have turned to the field of Translation Studies[1] to gain fresh perspectives concerning the relationship between the translated texts of the Septuagint corpus and their Semitic source texts. Translation theorists, philosophers, and historians offer a treasure trove of insights that has been largely unexplored in Septuagint Studies. The present essay converses with the ideas of Antoine Berman, an influential French translation theorist of the late twentieth century,[2] with the aim of demonstrating how Berman's theory of literal translation is constructive for understanding translation phenomena which occur in the Septuagint. A few key concepts expounded in Berman's writings are first presented and then followed by reflective commentary on extracts from Greek Exodus.

---

[*] It is a wonderful privilege to join fellow-students of Larry Perkins, along with his colleagues around the world, in honouring him with a contribution to this *Festschrift* on the occasion of his seventy-fifth birthday. Professor Perkins has been a wonderful source of inspiration and encouragement to me over the years in regard to what it means to be a Christian scholar and teacher. He continues to be a most gracious and patient host of the biweekly Greek reading series historically known as "Greek for Breakfast."
[1] Fairly recent examples include Albert Pietersma, Benjamin Wright, and Cameron Boyd-Taylor, who evince dependence on the work of Gideon Toury (see Albert Pietersma, *A Question of Methodology: Collected Essays on the Septuagint,* ed. Cameron Boyd-Taylor [Leuven: Peeters, 2013], 143–378, and Cameron Boyd-Taylor, *Reading Between the Lines: The Interlinear Paradigm for Septuagint Studies,* BTS 8 [Leuven: Peeters, 2011]), and Theo van der Louw, who explores translation universals (Theo van der Louw, *Transformations in the Septuagint: Towards an Interaction of Septuagint Studies and Translation Studies* [Leuven: Peeters, 2007]).
[2] Antoine Berman (1942–1991) was also a philosopher, translator, and translation historian. After his untimely death, many of Berman's writings were published posthumously by his wife, Isabelle Berman. These publications are primarily compilations of his lecture notes.

1.1. Berman's concept of literal translation

Berman's concept of literal translation is somewhat different from any traditional definition of the term. Theo van der Louw, for example, defines literal translation as occurring when a source text lexeme is translated by a target language counterpart that has a shared lexical meaning or when syntactical structures in the source text are replicated with formal correspondents.[3] In this definition, there is the notion of one-to-one correspondence in conceptualizing literality as a translation technique or method.[4] James Barr, in his seminal volume entitled *The Typology of Literalism in Ancient Biblical Translations*, seeks to analyze and define "different kinds of literality, diverse levels of literal connection, and various kinds of departure from the literal."[5] Barr also presupposes that literality is a method.[6] Conversely, Berman conceives literalism (or literal translation) as "work on the letter (*lettre*),"[7] and this is categorically *not* a method.[8]

The *lettre* of the original literary work (i.e., the source text) is its being-in-language and consists of more than its semantic content, syntax, or meaning. It is the essence of the literary work as a totality and includes elements such as its form, language, linguistic patterns, rhythms, discursive order, the quality and quantity of its signifiers, and its networks of signification.[9]

---

[3] According to van der Louw, "in practice, only relatively short sentences allow for literal translation. The longer the sentence, the more likely it has to be adapted to the T[arget] L[anguage] syntax" (van der Louw, *Transformations*, 64).

[4] Van der Louw employs the term "transformation" in his study, which is synonymous with "translation technique" or "translation method" (*Transformations*, 382).

[5] James Barr, *The Typology of Literalism in Ancient Biblical Translations*, MSU 15 (Göttingen: Vandenhoeck & Ruprecht, 1979), 281. Barr proposes linguistic criteria (e.g., "division into elements or segments"; "quantitative addition or subtraction of elements"; "consistency or non-consistency in the rendering"; "the accuracy and level of semantic information") that could be useful for classifying a translation according to one of six modes of literality or, alternatively, as a more "free" translation.

[6] Barr, *The Typology of Literalism*, 281, 283, 307, 320, and 325.

[7] In fact, Berman's "unquestioned assumption of [his] own activity as a translator [was] that translating was first and foremost and its essence 'work on the letter'" (Antoine Berman, Isabelle Berman, and Valentina Sommella, *The Age of Translation: A Commentary on Walter Benjamin's "The Task of the Translator,"* trans. Chantal Wright [London: Taylor & Francis, 2018], 20).

[8] According to Berman, "each text poses specific 'problems' of translatability—which is why there can be no method in this field" (Berman, Berman, and Sommella, *The Age of Translation*, 68). Elsewhere he writes that "we can formulate 'regulatory principles' for the translation of the letter but these principles are not methodical. Between the space devoted to principles and the act of translating there is an obscure elective space where subjectivity and the unconscious intervene" (42).

[9] Concerning these networks of signification, Berman writes that every literary work "contains a hidden dimension, an 'underlying' text, where certain signifiers correspond and link up, forming all sorts of networks beneath the 'surface' of the text itself... It is this *subtext* that carries the network of word-obsessions. These underlying chains constitute one aspect of the rhythm and signifying process of the text. After long intervals certain words may recur, certain kinds of substantives that constitute a particular network, whether through their resemblance or their aim, their 'aspect'" (Antoine Berman, "Translation and the Trials of the Foreign," in *The Translation Studies Reader*, ed. and trans. Lawrence Venuti [London/New York: Routledge, 2000], 292). There may be no specific value in the signifiers in themselves. Rather, what "*makes sense* is their linkage, which in fact signals a most important dimension of the work" (Berman, "Translation and the Trials," 293). Italicized and hyphenated words are idiosyncrasies of Berman's writing style and manner of expression.

"In a text composed in its mother tongue," says Berman, "the relationship of form and content, of the signifier to the signified is one of absolute unity"[10] in which "each signifier in the text is both indissolubly tied to all other signifiers and to its own diachronic historical aspect."[11] The *lettre* of the text therefore exists as a fixed entity: "The text is its language. We might call this the *Innigkeit*[12] of the text and its language, which is infinite. The text is, from the beginning, so intimately connected to its language that no changes in its 'tone' and 'meaning' can ever affect its being, no more than changes in the language itself, which are never external to it."[13] However, "translation does not work like this."[14] The process of translation will inevitably affect these signifiers and their networks. Consequently, "the relationship between form and content is looser (because the same thing can be translated in several different ways); the relationship of the signifier to other signifiers has also become random…and the signifier's link to its own diachrony is undone."[15]

1.2. Translation and commentary

Berman considers translation and commentary to be very similar in that they both involve "work on the *lettre*."[16] The two tasks are "inseparable, to the point that it is impossible to say that one 'precedes' the other."[17] Says Berman, "commentary occupies a space-in-between translation and original and is thus situated as close as possible to what is being *said* in the original text."[18] As such, Berman makes a distinction between work on the *lettre* of the original text and its translation(s). The *lettre* of the source text, as defined in §1.1, is its essence and totality as an (original) literary work, its being-in-language.[19] In contrast, the being-in-language of the translated text has its origins in the *lettre* of the original work. The relationship between the signifiers, form, and content is looser than if it had been original. Unlike the fixed *lettre* of its source text, the translated text(s) undergoes a process of (re-)translation. This ongoing process may occur, for example, with the translator's own (re)-engagement with the text as a translator/reader, with other translators/readers who are familiar with the languages of both the source and target texts, or with new translations of

---

[10] Berman, Berman, and Sommella, *The Age of Translation*, 70.
[11] Berman, Berman, and Sommella, *The Age of Translation*, 125.
[12] German for "intimacy."
[13] Berman, Berman, and Sommella, *The Age of Translation*, 123–24.
[14] Berman, Berman, and Sommella, *The Age of Translation*, 125.
[15] Berman, Berman, and Sommella, *The Age of Translation*, 125.
[16] Berman, Berman, and Sommella, *The Age of Translation*, 20.
[17] Berman, Berman, and Sommella, *The Age of Translation*, 76.
[18] Berman, Berman, and Sommella, *The Age of Translation*, 76.
[19] Citing Tamara Kamenszain's description of the Talmudists' task of commentary in which for them "the Torah and Hebrew coincide word for word" (Tamara Kamenszain, *El texto silencioso* [Mexico City: Universidad Nacional Autónoma de México, 1983], 87), Berman sees a second "possible definition of commentary: the attention paid to the being-in-language(s) of the work" (Antoine Berman, "Criticism, Commentary and Translation: Reflections based on Benjamin and Blanchot," trans. Luise von Flotow, in *Translation Studies: Critical Concepts in Linguistics*, ed. Mona Baker [London: Routledge, 2009], 1:99). In this type of commentary, says Berman, "so attentive is commentary to this being-in-language(s) that it can only be the commentary of an original" (1:99).

the source text. Consequently, the *lettre* (or being-in-language) of the translation is "unfixed" and, therefore, in terms of commentary on its *lettre* apart from its source text,[20] "untrustworthy."[21] In this regard, Berman quotes the philosopher Walter Benjamin: "[C]ommentary and translation are to the text what style and mimesis are to nature: the same phenomenon observed from different viewpoints. On the tree of the sacred text they are merely the eternal rustling of the leaves, on the tree of the profane, the timely falling of the fruit."[22] A sacred text, says Berman, "knows neither fame nor decline and…commentary and translation are perpetually inscribed within it as part of its most intimate life."[23] Translation is a manifestation of the original, as its transplant in new soil, which gives the sacred text a sort of new life or rebirth.[24] On the other hand, translation is an echo or sometimes only a fragment of the *lettre* of the original text ("the tree of the sacred text").

If one accepts Berman's evaluation of a translation's *lettre* as "unfixed" or "untrustworthy" in having a being-in-language that is external to itself (that is, it is derived from a source text), this has implications for one's methodological approach to commentary and exegesis of a translated text of the Septuagint, such as Greek Exodus. In the last several decades, Septuagintalists have debated whether the translated texts were produced as independent texts in their own right or whether these translations were derived from and therefore dependent on the form and content of their respective Semitic source texts. As a proponent of the latter view, Cameron Boyd-Taylor contends that:

> the fundamental nature of the Septuagint as a translation is one of derivation and dependence upon its parent. This still seemed a reasonable way of characterizing its relationship to the source text, and raised an interesting question, what if the place occupied by the Greek translation in the target culture was such that its formal dependence upon the Hebrew text constituted an integral part of its meaning… On the assumption of interlinearity, the Septuagint *qua* translation would have originally lacked the status of an independent text within the target culture. Rather it would have formed the Greek half of a virtual Greek-Hebrew diglot.[25]

On the other hand, Natalio Fernández Marcos is representative of Septuagint scholars who argue for the fundamental autonomy of the Septuagint. He affirms that:

---

[20] According to Berman, apart from comparison with its source text, "commentary on a translated text (which is commonplace) can only be a movement through meaning, whereas by its very nature, commentary is *commentary-on-the-letter*" (Berman, Berman, and Sommella, *The Age of Translation*, 28).

[21] Berman, Berman, and Sommella, *The Age of Translation*, 28.

[22] Walter Benjamin, "Die Aufgabe des Übersetzers [1923]," in *Gesammelte Schriften*, ed. Rolf Tiedemann and Hermann Schweppenhäuser (Frankfurt: Suhrkamp Verlag, 1991), 92, quoted in Berman, Berman, and Sommella, *The Age of Translation*, 27–28.

[23] Berman, Berman, and Sommella, *The Age of Translation*, 92. Conversely, a profane text thrives on its fame and, when it is ripe for translation, it bears its autumn fruit.

[24] Berman, Berman, and Sommella, *The Age of Translation*, 92.

[25] Boyd-Taylor, *Reading Between the Lines*, 5.

the LXX translation originated and circulated as an independent literary work, understandable within the Greek linguistic system without recourse to the Hebrew (or 'the necessity of having an eye to the Hebrew'). The Septuagint was not a Targum, it replaced the original Hebrew in the liturgy as well as in education of the Hellenistic Jews. Consequently, the arbiter of meaning cannot be the Hebrew but instead, the context.[26]

In a similar vein, Martin Rösel makes the intriguing claim that "most translators wanted to produce original writings that—intentionally or not—incorporated their own understanding of the biblical material."[27] To be sure, translators are writers and translation is both a science and an art that involves some measure of linguistic skill and creativity. Yet, if one's aim is an original writing that intentionally incorporates interpretation of biblical material, choosing to do so in the form of a translation, according to Berman, would be virtually unachievable:

> [A]nalysis and interpretation are characterized by reaching beyond the letter [*lettre*] to the meaning. It would be impossible to make this the basis of translation, which consists precisely of not *reaching beyond* the letter [*lettre*], but, instead, *carrying* it from the shore of one language to the other. This is where the question gets even more complex. Because translation *also* carries meaning across… If the reconstitution of meaning is what counts in the relationship with a literary work, then there is no question: translation is one of the most deficient ways of reconstituting *Bedeutung*.[28] Because the transfer of meaning that it enacts is incomplete, and distortional.[29]

---

[26] Natalio Fernández Marcos, "Reactions to the Panel on Modern Translations," in *X Congress of the International Organization for Septuagint and Cognate Studies, Oslo, 1998*, SBLSCS 51, ed. Bernard A. Taylor (Atlanta: Society of Biblical Literature, 2001), 235–36, quoted in Cameron Boyd-Taylor, *Reading Between the Lines*, 14. The implications of Berman's assertion that a commentary of a translation detached from its source text can *only* be a movement through meaning rather than a commentary on its being-in-language (its *lettre*) are evident in Fernández Marcos' claim that "the arbiter of meaning [when approaching the translation as an independent text] cannot be the Hebrew but instead the context."

[27] Martin Rösel, *Tradition and Innovation: English and German Studies on the Septuagint*, SBLSCS 70 (Atlanta: SBL Press, 2018), 14. On the other hand, Rösel claims that the Greek translators' "aim was not to rewrite the Bible or to comment on it, but to produce an authoritative Greek version that was suitable for the needs of Jewish groups in the Hellenistic world. Because they were aware that they were translating and producing not an ordinary text but Scripture, they obviously felt restricted in how they could treat this text… Even if cast in a new language, they will still be able to speak directly into the new situation and provide confidence in the God of Israel and his just government of the whole world. Thus scriptural interpretation in the LXX is not an end in and of itself or an academic exegetical game" (81). However, he goes on to say, "Instead, it manifests the ways in which the translators and their community understood Scripture and *how they thought it should be understood*" (emphasis mine).

[28] *Bedeutung* is German for "importance, meaning, significance."

[29] Berman, "Criticism, Commentary and Translation," 106. In addition, as previously stated, the sometimes-violent process of translation can result in the unintentional creation of new signifiers and networks of signification with some degree of randomness and disruption to the diachrony of signifiers.

Needless to say, if a translation project of this nature *were* to be attempted, almost certainly, the source text would need to be accessible for oral/written commentary to complete what was incomplete or distorted in the translation.[30] For translators who would wish to create an "original writing," it seems evident that a Targum (as an example of a commentary genre) would be a better option than translation.

No one can deny that, at a certain point, Septuagint translations gained status as texts in their own right. However, to what extent would it be possible for translators "to produce original writings" within the confines of a translation? Chantal Wright suggests that there are (modern) translators who have begun to experiment with "ways in which the translator takes responsibility for the letter [*lettre*] of the translation, instituting new signifying networks, that merit analysis."[31] Even so, would such a complex (and rather modern) enterprise have entered the minds of ancient translators and/or been achievable? In light of these complex issues and Berman's concept of literal translation, we now turn to reflection on examples from Greek Exodus.

2. The "eternal rustling of the leaves" in Greek Exodus

The "eternal rustling of the leaves" can be detected in Greek Exodus. Early in the translation, it is readily apparent that this is a translation of a Semitic *Vorlage*. This source text originated in oral tradition and took shape over time. Once written down in Hebrew script, the text was reworked through the years in scribal copying and editing. Scribes from earlier periods often took the liberty of omitting or adding elements, "sometimes on a small scale, but often substantially."[32] Evidence found at Qumran suggests, however, that "this freedom was not sanctioned" in proto-Masoretic texts, although there was always "unconscious creation of scribal mistakes."[33] It is not known when the concept of careful reproduction of an exemplar came into being, although, according to Emanuel Tov, "one could say that it was conceived together with the creation of MT, but the *Vorlage* of the LXX was probably also a precise text."[34] Comparative analysis of the Masoretic Text (MT) with Greek Exodus have led scholars to conclude that the translator's *Vorlage* closely resembled the consonantal MT and thus the MT is the baseline of the present study.[35] In turn, the text of Greek

---

[30] In saying that the source text would need to be accessible, this does not necessarily suggest a physical text in written form. The source text can also be present in the form of oral transmission (e.g. scribes or members of the community who have knowledge of the source text; oral reading / oral commentary of the source text in the community and so forth).

[31] "Both [Leonardo] Venuti's foreignizing translation (2008) and Clive Stott's translation-as-experiential writing (2012a, 2012b)" are cited as examples. Chantal Wright, Translator's Introduction to *The Age of Translation*, by Berman, Berman, and Sommella, 26.

[32] Emanuel Tov, *Scribal Practices and Approaches Reflected in the Texts Found in the Judean Desert*, STDJ 54 (Leiden: Brill, 2004), 23.

[33] Tov, *Scribal Practices*, 23.

[34] In any case, "except for the proto-Masoretic (proto-rabbinic) family, evidenced from 250 BCE onwards," most scribes "often considered themselves also to be petty collaborators in the creation of the books" (Tov, *Scribal Practices*, 23).

[35] It is, of course, acknowledged that anyone with the goal of engaging in "serious literary research cannot do so without making a detailed prior study of the textual material available with respect

Exodus (hereafter *Exod*),³⁶ like all of the translations in the Septuagint corpus, has a complex transmission history of its own. It is therefore difficult to discern, when there are additions or omissions or other variations compared to the MT, whether these differences can be explained as deriving from a *Vorlage* other than the MT, as originating with the translator himself,³⁷ or as later alterations by subsequent scribes of the Hebrew/Greek texts. Discerning the different layers of transmission history is one of the challenges in the critical study of such an ancient text.

Exod has been characterized as generally "an accurate, relatively free translation in good Koine Greek"³⁸ and "a word-for-word rendering" which produces Greek that "is often stilted," but nonetheless generally "conveys the sense of the Hebrew text well."³⁹ Quantitative representation of the Hebrew text is frequently evident in the translation and the word order of the source text is often carefully followed. "Isomorphism" and "interlinearity"⁴⁰ have been used as terms to describe how the translator (G) of *Exod* produced his text.⁴¹ Nonetheless, even within the first few lines of *Exod*, it becomes apparent that, overall, this is no "translation-as-calque (or translation-as-copy)" which is defined by Berman as "the naïve production of (or attempt at reproducing) a *tangible* resemblance."⁴² In fact, G has sometimes been successful in creating a somewhat literary Greek style. In the opening verses, for example, instead of rendering the Hebrew *vav* conjunction with καί, a rendering which would be more stereotypical, G has translated *vav*, at various points, with the postpositive conjunction δέ (e.g. 1:5, 6, 7[2×], 8, 9, 12, 16, 17, 18, 19, 20, 22).⁴³ This would be a small, yet significant, example

---

to the passage in question" (Bénédicte Lemmelijn, *A Plague of Texts? A Text-Critical Study of the So-Called 'Plagues Narrative' in Exodus 7:14–11:10* [Leiden: Brill, 2009], 4).

³⁶ The Old Greek text, which, in this essay, is John William Wevers' Göttingen critical edition: *Septuaginta: Vetus Testamentum Graecum Auctoritate Academiae Scientiarum Gottingensis editum II, 1: Exodus*, ed. John William Wevers, adiuvante U. Quast (Göttingen: Vandenhoeck & Ruprecht, 1991).

³⁷ The reference to one translator does not preclude the possibility that more than one translator was involved in the task of translating the book of Exodus. See, for example, John William Wevers, *Notes on the Greek Text of Exodus*, SBLSCS 30 (Atlanta: Scholars Press, 1990), xiv; and Martha Lynn Wade, *Consistency of Translation Techniques in the Tabernacle Accounts of Exodus in the Old Greek*, SBLSCS 49 (Atlanta: SBL, 2003).

³⁸ Wade, *Consistency of Translation Techniques*, 2.

³⁹ Larry Perkins, "Exodus to the Reader," in *A New English Translation of the Septuagint*, ed. Albert Pietersma and Benjamin G. Wright (Oxford: Oxford University Press, 2007), 43.

⁴⁰ Perkins, "Exodus to the Reader," 43. More recently, Perkins has qualified that the translator "focuses primarily on producing a Greek text that is readable, sensible and somewhat contextualized for Greek speakers who cannot reference the Hebrew text. Communicating the meaning of the Hebrew text as he discerned it has priority over literal, isomorphic renderings that reflect Hebrew syntax or specific features. Word order is an exception in that his Greek translation usually shows serial fidelity with the MT's word order" (Larry Perkins, "Renderings of Paronymous Infinitive Constructions in OG Exodus and Implications for Defining the Character of the Translation," *HTS* [South Africa], 78, no. 1 [2022]: 8. Incidentally, Perkins' definition of the term "literal" would be identical to van der Louw's definition which defines literal translation as a translation technique.

⁴¹ In this regard, it is striking that Goethe is quoted by Berman as saying, "A translation which attempts to identify itself with the original in the end comes close to an interlinear version and greatly enhances our understanding of the original; this in turn leads us, compels us as it were, to the source text" (Antoine Berman, *The Experience of the Foreign: Culture and Translation in Romantic Germany*, trans. S. Heyvaert [New York: State University of New York Press, 1992]), 59.

⁴² Berman, Berman, and Sommella, *The Age of Translation*, 117.

⁴³ G's translation choice is in keeping with Herbert Smyth's classification of the copulative δέ, which "marks transition, and is the ordinary particle used in connecting successive clauses or sentences

of Berman's claim that a translator's choice can express the potentiality of the being-in-language of its source text. Thus, G had a concern for a logical ordering of thought with its conceptual cadences and implicit punctuation. John Lee cites Exod 2:8 as an example in which, rather than translating ותאמר in accordance with a common pattern (e.g. καὶ εἶπεν or, alternatively, εἶπεν δέ = ותאמר), G "has done something more subtle: he has used ἡ δέ to introduce 'topicalization'" in which case the known information (i.e. the topic = ἡ θυγάτηρ Φαραώ) is given less prominence and the new information (i.e. the comment = ἡ δὲ εἶπεν...Πορεύου) is given more prominence.[44] While the Hebrew also shows topicalization, G has chosen an appropriate Greek idiom to make this topicalization explicit.[45] Departing somewhat from the *lettre* of his *Vorlage*, G adds the logical linker οὖν ("therefore, thus") in Exod 1:10, indicating again, his interest in shaping the logical flow of the narrative.

The fact that the Pentateuch translators "produced a mixture of natural and unnatural Greek, a Greek text with a Hebraic flavour," John Lee considers to be "a matter of *style*, not language."[46] However, such variations may be explained, in part, as the attempt to develop potentialities of correspondence between the two languages of Hebrew and Greek during the process of translation. For Berman, developing these potentialities "is the task of translation *which thereby proceeds towards the discovery of the 'kinship' of languages.*"[47] This "kinship" of languages, according to Benjamin, is *überhistorische*[48] and "rests on the fact that in each language taken as a whole, one and indeed the same thing is meant; this is however unattainable by any single language, but rather is attainable only through the totality of their complementary intentions: pure language."[49] In his work on the *lettre*, G has exploited the translatability of the Hebrew text and its potential for what is immanently present in its *lettre* to be rendered into Greek. In Exod 1, there are three different Greek counterparts for Hebrew עם (ἔθνος (1:9); γένος (1:9); λαός (1:20, 22). Verse 9, in particular, is sensitively rendered with G marking a distinction between the nation (ἔθνος) of Egypt and the race (γένος) of Israel. G has thus introduced a whole new gamut of different signifiers, yet these signifiers are immanent in the *lettre* of the Hebrew text in view of the fact that "people" is a general category that encompasses "nation" and "race." The language is sometimes colourful and expressive with, for example, the translator's judicious choice

which add something new or different, but not opposed, to what precedes" (Herbert Smyth, *Greek Grammar* [Cambridge, MA: Harvard University Press, 1956], §2836; Steven E. Runge, *Discourse Grammar of the Greek New Testament: A Practical Introduction for Teaching and Exegesis* [Peabody, MA: Hendrickson, 2010], §2.3).

[44] John A. L. Lee, *The Greek of the Pentateuch: Grinfield Lectures on the Septuagint 2011–2012* (Oxford: Oxford University Press, 2018), 36–37.
[45] Lee, *The Greek of the Pentateuch*, 39.
[46] Lee, *The Greek of the Pentateuch*, 269. As such, the Pentateuch translators' "method of rendering did involve some conscious choice and effort in each case, so as to steer a course between the extremes of totally unnatural and totally natural Greek" (268).
[47] Lee, *The Greek of the Pentateuch* 189–90.
[48] Berman explains that Benjamin is referring to a distinctive, "sopra-historical" (*überhistorische*) kinship that is not based on resemblance nor on a common origin (e.g. Latin and the languages of French, Italian, and Spanish) (Lee, *The Greek of the Pentateuch*, 127).
[49] Walter Benjamin, "Die Aufgabe des Übersetzers [1923]," in *Gesammelte Schriften,* ed. Rolf Tiedemann and Hermann Schweppenhäuser (Frankfurt: Suhrkamp Verlag, 1991), 13, quoted in Berman, Berman, and Sommella, *The Age of Translation,* 128.

of κατασοφίζομαι as a counterpart for the Hithpael of חכם in Exod 1:10, describing Pharaoh's devious conniving to subdue and dominate the Israelites. G has chosen different verbs to render root ענה II in 1:11 (למען ענתו בסבלתם = ἵνα κακώσωσιν αὐτούς) and 1:12 (וכאשר יענו אתו = καθότι δὲ αὐτοὺς ἐταπείνουν). There is also semantic differentiation in regard to the verb חיה: 1:16 (וחיה = περιποιεῖσθε), 17–18, 22 (חיה = ζωογονέω), and in 1:19 (כי חיות = τίκτουσιν γάρ). In 1:14, Wevers observes that "the unusual choice of the rare compound κατοδυνᾶν 'cause hurt, pain' to render the root מרר Piel may have been stylistically determined, i.e. a succession of κατα compounds: κατεδυνάσευον, κατωδύνων and κατεδουλοῦντο."[50] With all of these choices, it seems as if G, indeed, has worked on the *lettre* of his translation, striving to develop potentialities immanent in the *lettre* of his *Vorlage* and searching to discover a kinship between the languages of Hebrew and Greek. The translation, now transplanted in Greek soil, has experienced a rebirth and, in its unique way, manifests the "eternal rustling of the leaves" of its sacred tree, its Hebrew parent text.

Despite evidence of some natural literary features in *Exod*, there are points where the being-in-language (the *lettre*) of its source text seems to have loosened in the Greek translation to the point of becoming somewhat undone. In this sense, the echo of the source text resonates with less clarity. For example, Exod 1:7a reads: οἱ δὲ υἱοὶ Ισραηλ ηὐξήθησαν καὶ ἐπληθύνθησαν καὶ χυδαῖοι ἐγένοντο καὶ κατίσχυον σφόδρα σφόδρα.[51] A series of four coordinate verbal constructions begins with two aorist verbs, which are the standard counterparts for Qal פרה and רבה in Genesis.[52] Here, the order of the Greek verbs with respect to the MT is slightly different, with the counterpart of רבה preceding the rarer verb שרץ. The latter is rendered periphrastically with an aorist copula verb and its predicate (χυδαῖος). The usual meaning of χυδαῖος ("common," NETS), as noted by Graham Davies, "hardly fits the context."[53] Finally, an imperfect verb, which is significantly less frequent in the Pentateuch than the aorist,[54] suddenly appears after the string of aorists. The imperfect κατίσχυον was later "levelled by the popular tradition to an aorist form κατίσχυσαν under the influence of the coordinate aorists."[55] The final clause of the verse, ἐπλήθυνεν δὲ ἡ γῆ αὐτούς, which is rendered in NETS as "[n]ow the land kept multiplying them," seems quite awkward on a literary level and does not, at first blush, make much sense. This is likely the reason why, in the literary tradition, manuscripts 53' attest to an attempt "to improve the sense by their επληθυνθη αυτοις" and, as noted by Wevers, the Hebrew source text was "more exactly

---

[50] John William Wevers, *Notes on the Greek Text*, 7.
[51] "But the sons of Israel increased and multiplied and became common and were growing very, very strong" (NETS).
[52] E.g., Gen 1:22, 28; 8:17; 9:1, 7; 35:11.
[53] Graham I. Davies, in *Commentary on Exodus 1–10*, vol. 1 of *A Critical and Exegetical Commentary on Exodus 1–18*, ICC (London: T&T Clark, 2019), 164. Davies suggests that "probably, like the adverb χύδην, it has the sense of 'overflowing, widespread' here (see the excellent note of BAlex [La Bible d'Alexandrie], pp. 74–75), which fits this occurrence of שרץ well." For Wevers, G has interpreted the verb שרץ metaphorically (Wevers, *Notes on the Greek Text*, 3). NETS has translated the Greek term χυδαῖος according to the principle that "Greek words in the LXX normally mean what they meant in the Greek of that period" (NETS, xvii).
[54] Trevor V. Evans, *Verbal Syntax in the Greek Pentateuch: Natural Greek Usage and Hebrew Interference* (Oxford: Oxford University Press, 2001), 202.
[55] Wevers, *Notes on the Greek Text*, 3.

rendered [with respect to the MT] by Aq[uila] and Sym[machus] with καὶ ἐπληρώθη ἡ γῆ ἀπ' αὐτῶν."[56] G was also capable of rendering these constructions, yet did not. Thus, (re-)translations carried out by figures such as Aquila, Symmachus, and Theodotion attest to the "unfixed" nature of the *lettre* of a translation, as Berman has described.

At times, the semantic richness of the Hebrew text is diminished in *Exod*. For example, G's choice of δόξα and its cognates to render various Hebrew lexemes has resulted in semantic levelling.[57] Perkins creates a compelling case that G may have been "seeking to emphasize the concept of Yahweh's glory in his translation,"[58] adding that "such a hypothesis requires us to assume that the translator gave attention to motifs within discourse units and even over several discourse units."[59] Could this be a case in which G has intentionally originated new networks of signification? This is a fascinating possibility. If one eliminates the twelve occurrences of כבד (a standard counterpart to δόξα) from the 33 instances in which δόξα appears, one is left with 21, of which roughly half occur in Moyses' Song (Exod 15). In essence, G has attempted to bring out the poetic dimension of his source text's *lettre* in his translational work. This likely led to his innovative use of what Deborah Levine Gera has described as a δόξα *leitmotif*, a resounding repetition which permitted G to stay reasonably close to the meaning of his *Vorlage* while simultaneously connecting Moyses' Song to a common theme.[60] It is in Moyses' Song, Perkins points out, that the δόξα motif begins to occur and after that to reoccur with some frequency.[61] Evidently, G did not initiate his translation project with the δόξα motif as a signifying network, yet the theological theme of Yahweh's glory which emerged through the process of translating the Song seems to have stayed with the translator, likely influencing some of his later translation choices (e.g. Exod 33:19 [δόξα = טוב];[62] 34:29, 30, 35 [δοξάζω = קרן][63]).

---

[56] Wevers, *Notes on the Greek Text*, 3.
[57] For a complete list of the Hebrew counterparts for δόξα and its cognates, see Larry Perkins, "'Glory' in Greek Exodus: Lexical Choice in Translation and Its Reflection in Secondary Translations," in *"Translation is Required": The Septuagint in Retrospect and Prospect*, ed. Robert J. V. Hiebert (Atlanta: SBL, 2010), 89–90.
[58] Perkins, "'Glory' in Greek Exodus," 103.
[59] Perkins, "'Glory' in Greek Exodus," 103.
[60] Deborah Levine Gera, "Translating Hebrew Poetry into Greek Poetry: The Case of Exodus 15." *BIOSCS* 40 (2007), 118–19. It is striking, as Perkins has noted, that the verbs ἐνδοξάζομαι and παραδοξάζω appear for the first time in *Exod*, suggesting that G enriched his translation with new Greek words derived from δόξα (Perkins, "'Glory' in Greek Exodus," 90). Levine Gera also observes that, besides other poetic elements, G's use of the prefix κατά "repeatedly lends a similar sound to a series of disparate verbs" (Levine Gera, "Translating Hebrew Poetry," 116).
[61] Perkins, "'Glory' in Greek Exodus," 88.
[62] The translator has interpreted "all the good attributes of Yahweh' as his glory" (Perkins, "'Glory' in Greek Exodus," 99). Untranslatability (see the following discussion) may have also contributed to G's decision to employ δόξα for טוב since, in the translator's mind, the particularity and uniqueness of Yahweh's attributes could not be reduced to "good." Irreducibility is often an impetus for commentary. This fragment of commentary into what the translator might have intended (which could be considered synonymous with "interpretation") is still "the eternal rustling of the leaves" of its sacred tree and can only be perceived by analyzing the being-in-language of the Greek text in light of its Hebrew *lettre*, as both Perkins and Levine Gera have done.
[63] According to Perkins, "the emphasis of the translator was on the actual state of Moses' countenance, arising from his encounters with Yahweh, and the impact this was having on the Israelites.... Yahweh's radiant glory shining in Moses' countenance is a visible demonstration of Yahweh's presence" (Perkins, "'Glory' in Greek Exodus," 97).

There are indications that, at times, there was a real struggle between G and the *lettre* of his *Vorlage* during the translation process. The backdrop for some of this struggle was untranslatability. According to Berman, untranslatability occurs when a text expresses a particular meaning, "a meaning that one might define as the text's drive to particularity (uniqueness) and an assertion of its fullness (or self-sufficiency)."[64] For Berman, "untranslatability is one of the ways in which the text asserts itself as an inaccessible and untouchable reality."[65] When faced with this "untouchable reality," Berman argues that translation can give way to commentary.[66] Commentary, that space-in-between translation and original, may provide a glimpse into the translator's interpretation of what he thinks is being said in the source text (which can be different from its semantic meaning). Moyses hid his face from God, not because he was afraid to look at God (as in the MT) since no one can see God and live, but rather because "he was being reverent to look down before God" (Exod 3:6b, NETS). The Lord himself did not meet Moyses with the intention of killing him (MT), but instead it was an *angel* of the Lord (4:24, NETS). The seventy elders did not see the God of Israel (MT), but rather "they saw the place, there where the God of Israel stood" (24:10, NETS).

Untranslatability is often encountered in the domain of figurative language. In *Exod*, the "otherness" of the Israelite deity was something that G seemed concerned to protect, as is exemplified in Exod 15:3:

Exodus 15:3

[67]יהוה איש מלחמה יהוה שמו

κύριος συντρίβων πολέμους, κύριος ὄνομα αὐτῷ.[68]

Despite the MT reading of איש מלחמה, some scholars have proposed that גבור במלחמה in the Samaritan Pentateuch and Peshitta suggests that G read גבור as שובר, rendering his translation as συντρίβων πολέμους, although this is uncertain.[69] The Hebrew letters *gimel* and *shin* are not typically confused in scribal practice and the *vav* appearing between the last two root letters of גבור would have had to be read between the first two letters of שובר. Alternatively, G may have viewed the undesirable reading of איש as some type of scribal error. With his knowledge of scribal practices, he sought to explain the presumed corruption. One such explanation could lie in שוא root 2,[70] which occurs

---

[64] Berman, Berman, and Sommella, *The Age of Translation*, 79–80.
[65] In terms of Berman's "untranslatability," perhaps there is no greater "inaccessible and untouchable reality" in the Hebrew sacred writings than the divine name. In the Greek Scriptures, translation of the Tetragrammaton emerged from orality. The translation of the divine name with the epithet κύριος reflects the *qere* of the Hebrew text (that is, the vowel pointing of the אדני) rather than the *kethibh* (the reading reflected by the consonants) (Berman, Berman, and Sommella, *The Age of Translation*, 20).
[66] Berman, Berman, and Sommella, *The Age of Translation*, 73.
[67] "The LORD is a warrior; the LORD is his name."
[68] "The Lord, when he shatters wars, the Lord is his name."
[69] See Emanuel Tov, *Textual Criticism of the Hebrew Bible*, 3rd ed., revised and expanded (Minneapolis: Fortress Press, 2012), 86. גִּבּוֹר (transcription of the Samaritan Pentateuch and Peshitta, BHS is written as גיבור in Tov's text.
[70] Cognates of the Hebrew verb denote "devastation," "ruin," or "desolation" and include שׁוֹאָה (BDB, s.v. "II. שׁוֹא," and "שָׁאָה," "שׁוֹאָה"; e.g. Isa 10:3; cf. Isa 47:11; Zeph 1:15; Job 30:14) and שׁוֹאָה (BDB, s.v.

only once in the Hebrew Bible at Ps 35:17 in the phrase השיבה נפשי משאיהם ("Rescue me from their ravages," NRSV).[71] BDB suggests that שוא is a parallel form of the root שאה, a term that denotes "make a din or crash, crash into ruins."[72] This meaning is certainly in line with the meaning of Greek συντρίβω ("shatter, shiver to atoms," "shatter, crush"),[73] which appears as the participle συντρίβων in Exod 15:3. If this Greek participle was replicating a Hebrew participle, the Qal participle of the verb שוא would be שא.[74] Turning again to איש מלחמה, G construed the "corruption" as metathesis of the letters *alef* and *shin*, appearing in some form of the verb שוא (or שאה), in which case, at some point, the internal vowel letter *vav* would have been mistakenly read as a *yod*[75] to produce the "corrupted" reading איש. Whether the Hebrew *Vorlage* read גבור מלחמה or איש מלחמה, συντρίβων πολέμους was the translator's striving to produce a literal translation of his source text.[76]

Concerning G's treatment of idioms, the literal rendering καὶ ἤνεγκαν ἕκαστος ὧν ἔφερεν αὐτῶν ἡ καρδία ("and they brought, every one of those whose heart carried them," Exod 35:21)[77] evokes the being-in-language of the Hebrew idiom נשאו לבו, creating a somewhat more compelling metaphorical image in the Greek translation than the arguably less vivid [πάντας τοὺς] ἑκουσίως βουλομένους ("all who freely desired," Exod 36:2) or even the combination of literal and free [καὶ πᾶσαι αἱ γυναῖκες, αἷς] ἔδοξεν τῇ διανοίᾳ αὐτῶν ("and all the women to whose mind it seemed good," Exod 35:26). These three different renderings of the idiom within a short span exhibit the translator's creative discovery of potentialities of kinship between Hebrew and Greek. Berman's assertion that a translation's being-in-language is unfixed can also be seen. The translator can still be found engaging with his source text, retranslating the Hebrew idiom anew.

3. Conclusion

More research and analysis of Berman's theory of translation remains to be done, including detailed critical analysis of his assumptions about the nature of language and translation. Nonetheless, in this paper, there has been an attempt to explore briefly how

---

"מְשׁוֹאָה, מְשֹׁאָה"; Zeph 1:15; Job 30:3; 38:27; Ps 74:3).
[71] The translator of the Greek Psalter renders the Hebrew text of Ps 35[34]:17 as ἀποκατάστησον τὴν ψυχήν μου ἀπὸ τῆς κακουργίας αὐτῶν ("Rescue me from their ravages," NETS).
[72] "שׁוֹא," and "שָׁאָה," BDB, 996 and 980.
[73] LSJ, "συντρίβω," 1728–29.
[74] Similarly, if it were the root שאה, the participle would be שאה.
[75] Interchange between *vav* and *yod* was quite common in biblical manuscripts (Tov, *Textual Criticism*, 227–28).
[76] Despite the suggestion by some scholars that *Exod* portrays God as a peacemaker, Perkins convincingly refutes this claim through careful examination of the context and analysis of the translation technique of Exodus. For a full list of scholars who hold this opinion and a critical analysis of the argument, see Larry Perkins, "'The Lord is a Warrior'—'The Lord Who Shatters Wars': Exod 15:3 and Jdt 9:7; 16.2," *BIOSCS* 40 (2007): 121–38 (121 n. 2).
[77] The English renderings in this paragraph are extracted from Jan Joosten, "Translating the Untranslatable: Septuagint Rendering of Hebrew Idioms," in *"Translation is Required": The Septuagint in Retrospect and Prospect*, ed. Robert J.V. Hiebert, SBLSCS 56 (Atlanta: Society of Biblical Literature, 2010), 64–65.

Berman's concept of literal translation can be profitable for investigating translation processes in a Septuagint text. Berman borrows Benjamin's metaphor of "the eternal rustling of the leaves" of the sacred tree to describe the relationship between the *lettre* of the source text and its (re-)translation(s) and commentary. Bermanian thought and textual analysis of *Exod* suggests that the being-in-language of *Exod*, in its totality, was not conceived of as original writing, contra Rösel and Fernández Marcos. Instead, its being-in-language was and always will be "the eternal rustling" of its Hebrew source. One may certainly read and interpret *Exod* independently of its source text, making context the arbiter of meaning. Doing so, however, means laying aside *Exod*'s essence, its very being-in-language. Such readings permit literary interpretation but preclude critical exegesis. As Berman rightly argues, commentary of a translation, independent of its source, can "only be a movement through meaning."[78] He warns commentators that the *lettre* of the translated text is unfixed and will not always be trustworthy. Due to this very fact, Albert Pietersma, Benjamin Wright, and Cameron Boyd-Taylor have proposed the interlinear paradigm as a heuristic tool for Septuagint exegesis and research. Their "working hypothesis of linguistic interlinearity"[79] as a paradigm for Septuagint research might be construed to be too narrow a baseline,[80] even if Septuagint translators have, at times, produced what would be, in Berman's words, a "translation-as-copy" (e.g. linguistic interlinearity). In contrast, the metaphor of the sacred tree extends the two-dimensional (vertical and horizontal) aspects of the interlinear paradigm to encompass the entire, multi-dimensional, and complex being-in-language (*lettre*) of the source text and its manifestation in subsequent translations and commentary.

If a translator's (and commentator's) task is work on the *lettre*, as Berman argues it is, this work will move beyond interlinearity. The translator of *Exod* has often done just that. G has drawn out what was immanent in the *lettre* of its Hebrew source, exploiting its potential for fulfilment and expression in the inherently more inflected and lexically richer classical Greek language. In other instances, G has shown a reluctance to translate his Hebrew source, confronting its untranslatability and finding alternatives, including commentary, to render his *Vorlage*. Aspects of the "unfixed" state of *Exod* include the phenomenon of randomness or instability among signifiers and its reception history, which includes subsequent (re-)translations (e.g., Aquila; Symmachus; Theodotion) and revisional/scribal activity, within the Greek Septuagint tradition.

---

[78] Berman, Berman, and Sommella, *The Age of Translation*, 28.
[79] Pietersma, *A Question of Methodology*, 376.
[80] To be fair, if one recasts the "virtual Greek–Hebrew diglot" (Boyd-Taylor, *Reading Between the Lines*, 5) as the ideal of a fully realized Greek version of every aspect of the Hebrew *lettre* (being-in-language) (and, to be sure, fully realizing the *lettre* of one language into a different language is an impossible ideal, even in Berman's view [e.g. Berman, Berman, and Sommella, *The Age of Translation*, 41]), then the interlinear paradigm would even more clearly be understood as purely a metaphor (rather than, as is sometimes mistakenly assumed, a specific translation method). The fact that it is "virtual" means that it is metaphorical. Framed in this way, the interlinear paradigm/metaphor would then come closer to what is expressed by the metaphor of the sacred tree and its eternal rustling leaves (translation and commentary).

Bibliography

Barr, James. *The Typology of Literalism in Ancient Biblical Translations*. MSU 15. Göttingen: Vandenhoeck & Ruprecht, 1979.

Benjamin, Walter. "Die Aufgabe des Übersetzers [1923]." *Gesammelte Schriften*. Edited by Rolf Tiedemann and Hermann Schweppenhäuser. Frankfurt: Suhrkamp Verlag, 1991.

Berman, Antoine. "Criticism, Commentary and Translation: Reflections based on Benjamin and Blanchot." (Translated by Luise von Flotow.) Pages 92–113 in Vol. 1 of *Translation Studies: Critical Concepts in Linguistics*. Edited by Mona Baker. London: Routledge, 2009.

Berman, Antoine. *The Experience of the Foreign: Culture and Translation in Romantic Germany*. Translated by S. Heyvaert. New York: State University of New York Press, 1992.

Berman, Antoine. "Translation and the Trials of the Foreign." Pages 284–97 in *The Translation Studies Reader*. Edited and translated by Lawrence Venuti. London/New York: Routledge, 2000.

Berman, Antoine, Isabelle Berman and Valentina Sommella. *The Age of Translation: A Commentary on Walter Benjamin's "The Task of the Translator."* Translated by Chantal Wright. London: Taylor & Francis, 2018.

Boyd-Taylor, Cameron. *Reading Between the Lines: The Interlinear Paradigm for Septuagint Studies*. BTS 8. Leuven: Peeters, 2011.

Davies, Graham I. *Commentary on Exodus 1–10*. Vol. 1 of *A Critical and Exegetical Commentary on Exodus 1–18*. ICC. London: T&T Clark, 2019.

Evans, Trevor V. *Verbal Syntax in the Greek Pentateuch: Natural Greek Usage and Hebrew Interference*. Oxford: Oxford University Press, 2001.

Fernández Marcos, Natalio. "Reactions to the Panel on Modern Translations." Pages 233–40 in *X Congress of the International Organization for Septuagint and Cognate Studies, Oslo, 1998*. Edited by Bernard A. Taylor. SBLSCS 51. Atlanta: Society of Biblical Literature, 2001.

Joosten, Jan. "Translating the Untranslatable: Septuagint Rendering of Hebrew Idioms." Pages 59–70 in *"Translation is Required": The Septuagint in Retrospect and Prospect*. Edited by Robert J. V. Hiebert. SBLSCS 56. Atlanta: Society of Biblical Literature, 2010.

Kamenszain, Tamara. *El texto silencioso*. Mexico City: Universidad Nacional Autónoma de México, 1983.

Lee, John A. L. *The Greek of the Pentateuch: Grinfield Lectures on the Septuagint 2011–2012*. Oxford: Oxford University Press, 2018.

Lemmelijn, Bénédicte. *A Plague of Texts? A Text-Critical Study of the So-Called 'Plagues Narrative' in Exodus 7:14–11:10*. Leiden: Brill, 2009.

Levine Gera, Deborah. "Translating Hebrew Poetry into Greek Poetry: The Case of Exodus 15." *BIOSCS* 40 (2007): 107–20.

Louw, Theo van der. *Transformations in the Septuagint: Towards an Interaction of Septuagint Studies and Translation Studies*. Leuven: Peeters, 2007.

Perkins, Larry. "Exodus to the Reader." Pages 43–51 in *A New English Translation of the Septuagint*. Edited by Albert Pietersma and Benjamin G. Wright. Oxford: Oxford University Press, 2007.

Perkins, Larry. "'Glory' in Greek Exodus: Lexical Choice in Translation and Its Reflection in Secondary Translations." Pages 87–106 in *"Translation is Required": The Septuagint in Retrospect and Prospect*. Edited by Robert J. V. Hiebert. SBLSCS 56. Atlanta: Society of Biblical Literature, 2010.

Perkins, Larry. "The Lord is a Warrior"—"The Lord Who Shatters Wars": Exod 15:3 and Jdt 9:7; 16.2." *BIOSCS* 40 (2007): 121–38.

Perkins, Larry. "Renderings of Paronymous Infinitive Constructions in OG Exodus and Implications for Defining the Character of the Translation," *HTS* [South Africa], 78, no. 1 [2022]: 1–8.

Pietersma, Albert. *A Question of Methodology: Collected Essays on the Septuagint*. Edited by Cameron Boyd-Taylor. Leuven: Peeters, 2013.

Rösel, Martin. *Tradition and Innovation: English and German Studies on the Septuagint*. SBLSCS 70. Atlanta: SBL Press, 2018.

Runge, Steven E. *Discourse Grammar of the Greek New Testament: A Practical Introduction for Teaching and Exegesis*. Peabody, MA: Hendrickson, 2010.

Septuaginta: Vetus Testamentum Graecum Auctoritate Academiae Scientiarum Gottingensis editum II, 1: Exodus. Edited by John William Wevers with the assistance of U. Quast. Göttingen: Vandenhoeck & Ruprecht, 1991.

Smyth, Herbert. *Greek Grammar*. Cambridge, MA: Harvard University Press, 1956.

Tov, Emanuel. *Scribal Practices and Approaches Reflected in the Texts Found in the Judean Desert*. STDJ 54. Leiden: Brill, 2004.

Tov, Emanuel. *Textual Criticism of the Hebrew Bible*. 3rd ed., revised and expanded. Minneapolis: Fortress Press, 2012.

Wade, Martha Lynn. *Consistency of Translation Techniques in the Tabernacle Accounts of Exodus in the Old Greek*. SBLSCS 49. Atlanta: Society of Biblical Literature, 2003.

Wevers, John William. *Notes on the Greek Text of Exodus*. SBLSCS 30. Atlanta: Scholars Press, 1990.

Wright, Chantal. Translator's Introduction to Antoine Berman, Isabelle Berman and Valentina Sommella. *The Age of Translation: A Commentary on Walter Benjamin's "The Task of the Translator."* Translated by Chantal Wright. London: Taylor & Francis, 2018.

Chapter 7

Slaves to the Septuagint:
Applying Greek Legal Terminology for Slaves to Exodus 21:7

Joel F. Korytko

1. Introduction

Learning to question and challenge assumptions is difficult for a new scholar. As a young, entry-level researcher, I observed the exegetical precision and keen intuitions of Larry Perkins that helped me form my own sense of scholarly curiosity. Under his tutelage I learned that sometimes, along with analytical observation, interpreting a text is also an intuitive process. When previous explanations have not been satisfactory there is warrant for a re-evaluation of the data. This present essay, in the spirit of Perkins' mentoring, suggests that such a re-examination is necessary in the case of Septuagint Exod 21:7.

Exodus 21:7[1]

וכי ימכר איש את בתו לאמה לא תצא כצאת העבדים

Ἐὰν δέ τις ἀποδῶται τὴν ἑαυτοῦ θυγατέρα οἰκέτιν, οὐκ ἀπελεύσεται ὥσπερ ἀποτρέχουσιν αἱ δοῦλαι.

The *crux interpretum* of this verse is how to explain the terms employed for slavery (אמה = οἰκέτις; העבדים = αἱ δοῦλαι), and the rendering of the Hebrew masculine term for slaves (העבדים) with a Greek feminine counterpart (αἱ δοῦλαι).[2]

---

[1] Hebrew and Greek biblical texts employed in this essay are those of *BHS*, the Göttingen edition of the LXX, and where texts are lacking in the Göttingen series, Rahlfs' edition.
[2] Aquila, Theodotion, and Symmachus all depart from the rendering αἱ δοῦλαι (see Kevin G. O'Connell, *The Theodotionic Revision of the Book of Exodus: A Contribution to the Study of the Early History of the Transmission of the Old Testament in Greek*, HSM 3 [Cambridge, MA: Harvard University, 1972], 24–25). Only Aquila attests a rendering of לאמה, which becomes εἰς οἰκέτιν (24).

2. Previous interpretations of Exodus 21:7

In the past, others have attempted to explain the variegated terminology for slaves on the basis of rabbinic sources.³ In general, these interpretive approaches have posited that the two terms, οἰκέτις and αἱ δοῦλαι, represent Israelite and non-Israelite female slaves, respectively. Recently, rabbinic influence on the text has been rejected by Jan Joosten in favour of viewing the LXX text as reflecting interpretive conclusions that stem from the Second Temple period and the translator's own exegetical inclinations.⁴ This is due, in part, to the tenuous nature of reading the much later rabbinic materials back into this period, which has been increasingly recognized as methodologically difficult to sustain.⁵ Joosten instead views the terminology in 21:7 as reflecting an interpretation that seeks to harmonize Exod 21:2–11 with the roughly parallel legal materials in Deut 15:12–18. Given the latter text's explicit allowance for male and female slaves to go free in the seventh year, and Deuteronomy's lack of a parallel to Exod 21:7–11, it is supposed that Exod⁶ has rendered his *Vorlage* in a way that still permits both male and female slaves to go free. The translation harmonizes the two legal traditions. This is done by introducing the category of "concubine"— distinct from other kinds of slaves—and suggesting that this is an appropriate gloss for οἰκέτις:

> As to the word οἰκέτις, *in Greek lexicography* it is usually viewed simply as the feminine of οἰκέτης ("household slave"). The Septuagint data indicate a different usage, however. *In the Greek version*, the feminine equivalent of οἰκέτης is θεράπαινα… We may conclude that *in the language of the Septuagint*, this specific word defines the girl as a concubine.⁷

---

³ E.g., Zecharia Frankel, *Ueber den Einfluss der Palästinensischen Exegese auf diealexandrinische Hermeneutik* (Leipzig: J. A. Barth, 1851), 91; Abraham Geiger, *Urschrift und Uebersetzungen der Bibel in ihrer Abhängigkeitvon der inneren Entwicklung des Judentums*, 2nd ed. (Frankfurt am Main: Verlag Madda, 1928), 187–88; Geza Vermes, "Bible and Midrash: Early Old Testament Exegesis," in *Cambridge History of the Bible*, vol. 1, ed. Peter Ackroyd and Christopher F. Evans (Cambridge: Cambridge University Press, 1970), 199–231. Alain Le Boulluec and Pierre Sandevoir seem to affirm this approach (*La Bible d'Alexandrie: L'Exode* [Paris: Cerf, 1989], 216). It has also been suggested that the translator's *Vorlage* read אמות instead of עבדים (so William Henry Covici Propp, *Exodus 19–40: A New Translation with Introduction and Commentary* [New York: Doubleday, 2006], 118–19). This suggestion—which seems unconvincing as will become apparent in the present essay—has not played a significant role in the literature and will not be pursued here.

⁴ Jan Joosten, "Legal Hermeneutics and the Tradition Underlying the Septuagint," in *XV Congress of the International Organization for Septuagint and Cognate Studies: Munich, 2013*, ed. Wolfgang Kraus, Michaël N. van der Meer, and Martin Meiser, SBLSCS 64 (Atlanta: Society of Biblical Literature, 2016), 555–64.

⁵ Joosten, "Legal Hermeneutics," 554–55.

⁶ This designation will be used to refer to either the Greek translation of Exodus or its translator.

⁷ Joosten, "Legal Hermeneutics," 556–57, italics added. Le Boulluec and Sandevoir, referring also to Lev 19:20, comment as well on the sexual contexts in which οἰκέτις appears (*L'Exode*, 216). They do not use the word "concubine," but such an inference could be made. John A. L. Lee seems to gloss οἰκέτις as "household slave." (*A Lexical Study of the Septuagint Version of the Pentateuch*, SBLSCS 14 [Chico, California: Scholars Press, 1983], 33). Similarly, the rendering in NETS is "domestic slave."

Here we can see that, in order to establish his conclusion about οἰκέτις, Joosten distinguishes between the extra-biblical Greek lexicographical definitions of οἰκέτις and Septuagintal usage.

The present study attempts to demonstrate that this distinction is likely unnecessary when the literary and documentary texts are reconsidered. The Septuagintal occurrences of οἰκέτις may not necessitate a special category in this case. Joosten also concedes, "Admittedly, one problem remains. Why the female slaves are referred to with the word δοῦλαι while the male slave is called παῖς has not been explained."[8] A potential answer to this lexicographic conundrum may emerge from papyrological legal sources, which could provide a Graeco-Egyptian legal interpretive framework for understanding the use of this terminology in the Septuagint.[9] It is necessary, therefore, to evaluate the relevant data for both οἰκέτις and δούλη.

3. Defining οἰκέτις and δούλη

3.1. Defining οἰκέτις

It is perhaps not surprising for the claim to be made that אמה in Exod 21:7 refers to concubines. This has been suggested previously by various scholars.[10] The question at hand is whether there is extra-biblical justification to define οἰκέτις in this way.

The main terms for slaves in the period preceding the Septuagint translation are δοῦλος, οἰκέτης, θεράπων, and ἀνδράποδον.[11] According to William Westermann, the "[i]ncontrovertible designations for slaves" are δοῦλος, ἀνδράποδον (with cognates), and σῶμα—though this latter term is usually accompanied by qualifiers to make the

---

[8] Joosten, "Legal Hermeneutics," 557.
[9] I have suggested recently that there is an correlation between Ptolemaic law and the laws of the Greek Covenant Code: Joel F. Korytko, "The 'Law of the Land' in the Land of the Lagids: A Comparative Analysis of Exodus 21.1–32" (M.A. thesis, Trinity Western University, 2018); idem, "Death of the Covenant Code: Evaluating the Translation of Laws with Capital Punishment in Old Greek Exodus 21.1–23.19 in Light of Graeco-Egyptian Law" (DPhil diss., The University of Oxford, 2022); idem, "The Death Penalty in OG Exodus in Light of Graeco-Egyptian Legal Formulations," *JSCS* 54 (2021): 75–92. See also Jelle Verburg, "The Septuagint and Legal Traditions" (DPhil diss., The University of Oxford, 2021). It should be made clear that my claims in "The 'Law of the Land'" about οἰκέτις in Exod 21:7 are to be discounted in light of the present study. The same should be said for οἰκέτης/θεράπαινα in 21:26–27, since they are based on the same faulty argument. Unfortunately, I made a mistake similar to that of A. L. Pavlovskaja in supposing that οἰκέτης (and by extension οἰκέτις) pertains to a special category of slave in Ptolemaic Egypt ("Die Sklaverei im hellenistischen Ägypten," *Die Sklaverei in hellenistischen Staaten im 3.–1. Jh. v. Chr.* [ed. T. V. Blavatskaja, E. S. Golubcova, and A. I. Pavlovskaja; Wiesbaden: Steiner, 1972, translated from Russian], 185–99). A more accurate reading of Exod 21:26–27 and its terms for slavery will be explored in the upcoming Society of Biblical Literature Commentary on the Septuagint volume on Exodus.
[10] Cornelis Houtman, *Exodus*. Vol. 3: *Chapters 20–40*, Historical Commentary on the Old Testament (Leuven: Peeters, 2000), 3:123, 127; Le Boulluec and Sandevoir (acknowledging Henri Cazelles, *Études sur le code d'alliance* [Paris: Letouzey et Ané, 1946], 47) state that the term might be equivalent to a second-tier wife of some sort (*L'Exode*, 216).
[11] Fritz Gschnitzer, "Studien zur griechischen Terminologie der Sklaverei. 1: Grundzüge des vorhellenistischen Sprachgebrauchs," in *Abhandlungen der Geistes- und Sozialwissenschaftlichen Klasse, Jahrgang 1963, Heft 9–15* (Mainz: Akademie der Wissenschaften und der Literatur, 1964), 1284–310 (1285).

restricted status clear.¹² These are the primary designations used in law.¹³ He goes on to state, "Caution must be used in the translation of the numerous words such as *oiketēs, therapōn, pais, paidarion*, which fundamentally have another significance than 'slave' but are often, though loosely, employed by the ancient writers with that meaning."¹⁴ Caution is indeed warranted in the present discussion since οἰκέτις is not included in the preceding list of terms. In fact, the evidence from various ancient sources shows that οἰκέτις is not the standard feminine counterpart to οἰκέτης.¹⁵ The pre-hellenistic data confirm that θεράπαινα is, despite its etymological distinctiveness, the semantic feminine counterpart to οἰκέτης.¹⁶ Their combination in Exod 21:26–27 thus matches pre-hellenistic stock pairings and should not be considered particularly Septuagintal.¹⁷ οἰκέτις, despite the fact that it is morphologically a feminine counterpart to οἰκέτης, must then be evaluated on its own. It is fascinating to observe that every single occurrence of οἰκέτις for which there is adequate context relates either to marriage, procreation, or concubine relationships with respect to female slaves. As far as I am aware, this has not been noted by classicists or in lexicographic entries.¹⁸ Proceeding in a chronological fashion, we will begin with the literary texts outside of the LXX and then move to the documentary sources.¹⁹ This is a simple task, since there are not many attestations of οἰκέτις. Some will be less helpful in this lexicographic endeavor, but the overall portrait that emerges aligns with what is found in the Septuagint.²⁰

---

¹² William Linn Westermann, *The Slave Systems of Greek and Roman Antiquity*, Memoirs of the American Philosophical Society 40 (Philadelphia: American Philosophical Society, 1955), 5.
¹³ Westermann, *The Slave Systems*, 5.
¹⁴ Westermann, *The Slave Systems*, 5.
¹⁵ "In den Plural οἰκέται sind die Sklavinnen natürlich oft genug eingeschlossen; sollen sie gesondert bezeichnet werden, dann behilft man sich, wo οἰκέτις fehlt, mit θεράπαινα, dem regelrechten Fem. zu θεράπων. ,Diener und Dienerinnen' heißt also im Attischen gewöhnlich οἰκέται καὶ θεράπαιναι. Der Ausdruck θεράπων…hatte eben weitgehend dieselbe Bedeutung angenommen wie οἰκέτης, so verschieden auch die beiden Wörter ihrem Ursprung nach waren" (Gschnitzer, "Studien," 1303).
¹⁶ One assumes that Gschnitzer (cited in previous footnote) intends, by his remark "wo οἰκέτις fehlt," to indicate that οἰκέτις does not occur with οἰκέτης. These terms do not appear as counterparts in the relevant literary texts.
¹⁷ This seems to be implied in Joosten, "Legal Hermeneutics," 556–57.
¹⁸ E.g., LSJ, οἰκέτις I., "fem. of οἰκέτης" and II. "housewife." The new Cambridge lexicon (CGL) glosses in similar fashion to LSJ: "female servant or slave…; housewife (confined to the home)" (Faculty of Classics, University of Cambridge, and James Diggle, *The Cambridge Greek Lexicon*, 2 vols. [Cambridge: Cambridge University Press, 2021], 990). Gschnitzer, "Studien," does not further define the term.
¹⁹ Translations of literary texts come from the database at https://www.loebclassics.com. Documentary source translations are my own unless otherwise stated. This study includes literary texts up until Galen (second century CE).
²⁰ Not included in this study is the phrase ἐφέστιον οἰκέτιν in Sophocles, *Fragments*, 866, 1. Harold Cherniss and W. C. Helmbold translate ἐφέστιος as "the hearth" in Plutarch, *Moralia, Volume XII: Concerning the Face Which Appears in the Orb of the Moon. On the Principle of Cold. Whether Fire or Water Is More Useful. Whether Land or Sea Animals Are Cleverer. Beasts Are Rational. On the Eating of Flesh*, LCL 406 (Cambridge, MA: Harvard University Press, 1957), 323. It is uncertain how to interpret οἰκέτις here. Perhaps an appalling analogy is being drawn between the debased, pleasure-seeking treatment of animals by men and the debased, pleasure-seeking sexual ravaging of a fireside οἰκέτις. It may be that ἐφέστιον οἰκέτιν is the complementary accusative of τιθασὸν χῆνα and περιστεράν governed by διασπῶντες ("A tame goose and a dove, as a fireside οἰκέτις…pulled different ways").

3.1.1. οἰκέτις *in the literary texts*

Euripides, *Electra* 104-110

ἢ γάρ τις ἀροτὴρ ἤ τις οἰκέτις γυνὴ φανήσεται νῶιν, ἥντιν' ἱστορήσομεν εἰ τούσδε ναίει σύγγονος τόπους ἐμή. ἀλλ' εἰσορῶ γὰρ τήνδε πρόσπολόν τινα πηγαῖον ἄχθος ἐν κεκαρμένωι κάραι φέρουσαν, ἑζώμεσθα κἀκπυθώμεθα δούλης γυναικός

For either some plowman or serving maid will come in our sight, from whom we may ask if my sister lives in this place. But now that I see this maidservant, bearing a weight of water on her shorn head, let us sit down, and inquire of this slave girl.

In the section of the play by Euripides that precedes this quotation, Orestes has arrived to save his sister Electra and to exact retribution on their mother for murdering their father. Electra, a royal, has been married off to a peasant instead of to a noble. Orestes has just made mention of this sister and of the fact that she has been forced to marry (ll. 98–99). Immediately thereafter, οἰκέτις is the term chosen to refer to a female slave. This example provides the weakest connection between οἰκέτις and concubinage from the literary texts, but there could still be a thematic connection. The pejorative implication on the protagonist's part would be that the slave women here in Argos, like his sister, were those who were consigned to unwanted marriages. There may also be a connection between the demeaned status as a result of the marriage of a royal to a peasant and the mention of an οἰκέτις, who, it is being argued, was a concubine of sorts—implying someone of demeaned pseudo-marital status. In the rest of Euripides' works, δούλη is the term typically employed for female slaves (52×).[21] οἰκέτις appears only here in a context that involves a forced marriage resulting in a lowly marital status.

Hippocrates, *Airs, Waters, Places* XXI.18-21

ὑπὸ τούτων τῶν ἀναγκέων οὐ πολύγονόν ἐστι τὸ γένος τὸ Σκυθικόν. μέγα δὲ τεκμήριον αἱ οἰκέτιδες ποιέουσιν· οὐ γὰρ φθάνουσι παρὰ ἄνδρα ἀφικνεύμεναι καὶ ἐν γαστρὶ ἴσχουσιν διὰ τὴν ταλαιπωρίην καὶ ἰσχνότητα τῆς σαρκός

These are the causes which make the Scythian race unfertile. A clear proof is afforded by their slave-girls. These, because of their activity and leanness of body, no sooner go to a man than they are with child.

Hippocrates' corpus contains a large number of the attestations of οἰκέτις. Unfortunately, many of the occurrences do not provide any significant context other than the revelation that Hippocrates has visited this or that οἰκέτις.[22] The text cited is

---

[21] θεράπαινα is found a few times.
[22] Texts that will not be discussed for this reason are Hippocrates, *Epidemics* 4.1.9, 32, 33; 5.1.19; 7.1.112. Note that other terms for female slaves are used in *Epidemics*, so οἰκέτις should not

particularly insightful. Hippocrates chooses οἰκέτις when making a generalization about the Scythians. He associates these οἰκέτιδες with the expectation of procreation. That Hippocrates prefers οἰκέτις in this context might be an indication that the term applies to Scythian slave women who were openly sexually active, ostensibly with their masters. These births seem to be described as somewhat public, which could indicate that we are not here dealing with undesired children from extemporaneous and clandestine advances of a master. These are the slave women at whom all can look for evidence of Hippocrates' claim. The slave women who are publicly birthing their masters' children are labelled οἰκέτιδες, which might indicate a definition akin to "concubines."

Hippocrates, *Epidemics* **2.4.5**

Ἡ Στυμάργεω οἰκέτις ᾗ οὐδὲ αἷμα ἐγένετο ὡς ἔτεκε θυγατέρα, ἀπέστραπτο τὸ στόμα, καὶ ἐς ἰσχίον καὶ σκέλος ὀδύνη

The house servant of Stymarges, who did not even bleed when she bore a daughter, had the mouth of her womb retroverted.

This οἰκέτις is associated with childbearing.

Hippocrates, *Epidemics* **4.1.38**

Τῇ οἰκέτιδι, ἣν νεώνητον ἐοῦσαν κατεῖδον

The newly purchased servant girl whom I saw...

Hippocrates says that this οἰκέτις had not menstruated for seven years, which could work against the idea that the lexeme refers to a slave used for concubinage/childbearing purposes. However, it does say she was healed and then did menstruate. It is possible that Hippocrates was tasked with helping her so she could take on this responsibility.

Theocritus, *Idyll* **18.38–42**

ὦ καλά, ὦ χαρίεσσα κόρα, τὺ μὲν οἰκέτις ἤδη. ἄμμες δ' ἐς δρόμον ἦρι καὶ ἐς λειμώνια φύλλα ἑρψεῦμες στεφάνως δρεψεύμεναι ἁδὺ πνέοντας, πολλὰ τεοῦς, Ἑλένα, μεμναμέναι ὡς γαλαθηναὶ ἄρνες γειναμένας ὄιος μαστὸν ποθέοισαι

Beautiful and gracious girl, now you are a housewife. But we shall go early tomorrow to the running course and the flower meadows to gather fragrant garlands, and we shall have many thoughts of you, Helen, as suckling lambs miss the udder of the ewe that bore them.

necessarily be considered simply an automatic choice for a slave. See δούλη in *Epidemics* 5.1.35, 41, 6.7.1; θεράπαινα in 5.1.85. It is uncertain if this latter term was a designation for anyone other than a "female slave." It could signify a free servant.

This is a traditional song (*epithalamium*) sung at the wedding door of a newly married couple. Here the song is for mythological Helen and Menelaus, idyllic figures in ancient Greek history. LSJ and CGL gloss οἰκέτις in only this text as "housewife."[23] This is a possible translation, but it is also plausible that Helen is here called οἰκέτις for a specific reason, as a part of the humor of the song. In context, she is in bed with Menelaus on their wedding day, but he has fallen asleep (cf. ll. 9–15). This is intentionally comedic[24] and seems to point to a marriage not yet consummated. She is, in a sense, an illegitimate wife at this point, even though she is in bed with her husband! For the singers to label her as an οἰκέτις at this juncture could be a comedic way of framing her current predicament. Note that her present status of οἰκέτις is contrasted by means of μέν/δέ and ἤδη/ἦρι with what her status will be on the next day: τὺ μὲν οἰκέτις ἤδη. ἄμμες δ' ἐς δρόμον ἦρι, "now you are a[n] οἰκέτις. But we shall go early tomorrow to the running course…" The pejorative use of οἰκέτις seems to be a way of conveying the idea that today she is in the demeaned position of a married virgin.[25] The next day, on the other hand, will be a different story. οἰκέτις might then be used as a playfully creative and roundabout way of saying "married / not married" or "illegitimately married." This metaphorical use would align with its general use elsewhere if it does indeed refer to a slave who is in an open, procreative relationship with a master but is not his legal wife.

Callimachus, *Aetia*, fr. 65

Αὐτομά[της] εὐναὲς ἐπών[υμον, ἀλ]λ' ἀπὸ σ[εῖ]ο λούονται λοχίην οἰκέτιν

FAIR-FLOWING (water), called after Automate, but from you they draw water for washing a slave who has given birth

This reference to a bathing pool is likely a place for a purification rite.[26] Other similar Argive bathing rituals relate to (legal) marriage.[27] Perhaps the contrastive ἀλ]λ' points to the possibility that the οἰκέτις is the expected bather because of her illegitimacy, but the text is too fragmentary to be certain of anything other than associating οἰκέτις with childbirth.

Philo, *On Mating with the Preliminary Studies* XXVII, 151–152

ἀδικοῦμαι καὶ παρασπονδοῦμαι τό γε ἐφ' ὑμῖν ὁμολογίας παραβαίνουσιν. ἀφ' οὗ γὰρ ἐνεκολπίσασθε τὰ προπαιδεύματα, τῆς ἐμῆς θεραπαινίδος τὰ ἔγγονα, τὴν μὲν ὡς γαμετὴν ἐξετιμήσατε, ἐμὲ δὲ οὕτως ἀπεστράφητε, ὡς μηδὲ πώποτε

---

[23] LSJ denotation II, and CGL 990, respectively.
[24] *Theocritus, Moschus, Bion*, trans. Neil Hopkinson, LCL 28 (Cambridge, MA: Harvard University Press, 2015), 261 n. 3.
[25] The previous lines allude to her virginity through Artemis and Athena (l. 36; cf. *Theocritus* [trans. Hopkinson], 265 n. 14).
[26] Deborah Steiner, *The Idea of the Chorus in Greek Culture: Choral Constructions in the Poetry, Art and Social Practices of the Archaic and Early Classical Period* (Cambridge: Cambridge University Press, 2021), 289 n. 67.
[27] Steiner, *The Idea of the Chorus in Greek Culture*, 289–90.

ἐς ταὐτὸν ἐλθόντες. ἀλλ᾽ ἴσως ἐγὼ μὲν ταῦτα περὶ ὑμῶν ὑπείληφα, ἐκ τῆς φανερᾶς πρὸς τὴν οἰκέτιν ὁμιλίας τὴν ἄδηλον πρὸς ἐμὲ αὐτὴν ἀλλοτρίωσιν τεκμαιρομένη

> I am wronged and betrayed, in so far as you have broken faith with me. For ever since you took to your arms the lower forms of training, the children of my handmaid, you have given her all the honour of the wedded wife, and turned from me as though we had never come together. And yet perhaps, in thinking this of you, I may be but inferring from your open company with her my servant a less certain matter, your alienation from me.

Philo is personifying philosophy in this dialogue. In the metaphorical context, the οἰκέτις has children with the husband/lord (i.e., "the children of my handmaid"). There is also an *assumed and public* sexual relationship here between the master and the οἰκέτις (i.e., "your open company with her my servant"). Additionally, particular focus is given to the rightful status of the "the wedded wife," which points to her rights as the legal wife as opposed to those of the οἰκέτις (i.e., "you have given her all the honour of the wedded wife"). This text seems to be describing the tension between a lawful wife and an illegitimate wife. It is solely here, in this very specific context, that Philo uses the term οἰκέτις. This can be compared to his use of other terms for slaves elsewhere (δούλη [12×]; παιδίσκη [16×]; θεράπαινα [8×]; δοῦλος [159×]; οἰκέτης [54×]). Philo only chooses to use the term οἰκέτις in a context having to do with a slave in an open sexual relationship with her master and in contrast to the master's relationship with his legal wife.

Finally, Galen (second century CE) utilizes οἰκέτις on two occasions.[28] Both texts are corrupted due to scribal activity in wording that has been altered in order to prevent Hippocrates (the physician discussed by Galen) from mentioning that his female relation condoned prostitution.[29] Despite this textual corruption, it is interesting that scribes altered the text to read οἰκέτις *in contexts referring to frequent sexual liaisons*, alluding to the sexual connotations associated with this term.

3.1.2. οἰκέτις *in the documentary sources*

It is unfortunate that extant papyri yield no references to οἰκέτις. However, inscriptions are replete with attestations. It is also here that οἰκέτις can be connected to the terminology of Greek law. Most references are found in manumission records. What is helpful about these epigraphic materials is that they contain rote formulations. There is not really any discernible literary flare or embellishment. At the same time, because of the specific subject matter (manumission), brevity, and terseness of these inscriptions, any procreative or pseudo-connubial connections with οἰκέτις are not

---

[28] According to TLG, *De semine libri ii*, vol. 4, p. 525, l. 9 and *De foetuum formatione libellus*, vol. 4, p. 654, l. 4. οἰκέτις is used synonymously with θεράπαινα in *De praenotione ad Posthumum*, vol. 14, p. 632, l. 2, but no further details are available as this character in the story is tertiary.

[29] Tyler Mayo, "Research and Experiment in Early Greek Thought" (PhD diss., University of Michhigan, 2019), 93.

discernible. What is apparent, however, is that οἰκέτις is distinguished from δούλη. This suggests that the former was considered to be the designation for a particular category of slave. Consider the following example, which is representative:

ArchEph (1924) 166,405,A. 7–20 (131 BCE?)[30]

[Ἀ]ρίστ[ω][ν Ἀ]λεξ[ά][ν]δρο[υ][ἀφ]ῆκ[εν] [ἐλ]ευ[θ]έ[ρα]ν [τ]ὴ[ν] [ἑα]υ[τοῦ ο][ἰκ]έτ[ιδα] [Ζ]ων[αρί][δ]α Ἀσ[κ]ληπι[ά]δο[υ κ]ατ[ὰ] τὸ[ν] [ν]ό[μ]ο[ν]

Ariston of Alexander has released as an emancipated person his slave girl, Zonarid of Asclepios, according to the law.

This inscription demonstrates what is the stock legal language throughout the available records. The typical verb for emancipation is used (ἀφίημι), along with a predicated form of ἐλεύθερος (here via a double accusative). Those releasing the slaves are named. Note, however, that ll. 45–46 describe another emancipation, with the slave labelled a δούλη: τὴ[ν αὐτῶν] [δ]ού[λ]ην. It could be argued that this is an arbitrarily chosen synonymous term. Such a conclusion is less tenable in light of other inscriptions.

Another emancipation record, from the same location and approximate date as the previous inscription, uses οἰκέτης for emancipated male slaves three times (ll. 4, 10, 20) and οἰκέτις once.[31] In another section it refers to another emancipated female slave as a δούλη (l. 12). If the scribe were aiming to use synonymous terms here, it might be expected that οἰκέτης would have been switched with δοῦλος or the like. This is not the case. Synonymous renderings become even harder to establish when other records from the same time and place are in view. We can compare the texts previously mentioned with ArchEph (1924) 155,401 (133 BCE), a manumission list from basically the same time and place, in which only δούλη appears (6×). Similarly, in ArchEph (1924) 155,403 (125 BCE) only δούλη occurs (2×); in ArchEph (1924) 155,400 (late first century BCE) only δούλη is employed (4×); in ArchEph (1924) 188,418a (50 BCE) only δούλη is used (5×); and in IG IX,2 1282 (50 BCE) only δούλη is found (4×). It seems, based on the lack of synonymous renderings elsewhere in these inscriptions (and in any of the literary texts for that matter), that οἰκέτις was not directly equivalent to δούλη.[32] It is a term that is singled out in the manumission records.[33]

Finally, one poetic inscription also associates οἰκέτις with childbearing:

---

[30] See also, e.g., ArchEph (1945–1947) 110,59,V. 29–30 (20–18 BCE) (cf. ArchEph [1917] 1,303,C. 10–11 [late first century BCE / early first century CE]): Ζωσίμην τὴν ἑαυτῶν οἰκέτιδα γεγονυῖαν εὐάρεστον ἀφῆκαν ἐλευθέραν δωρεάν, "They released freely as an emancipated person Zosime their slave girl, having been pleasing [to them];" SEG 26:689. 2–5 (150–100 BCE): Φι]λουμένην τὴν ἑα[υτοῦ οἰκέτιδα καὶ τὸ αὐ]τῆς παιδάριον...[.......... ἀφῆ]κεν ἀπελευθέρ[ους, "He released as emancipated persons his slave girl Philomene and her child."

[31] ArchEph (1924) 166,404,D. 30–31 (131–129 BCE). Cf. ll. 30–31: ἀ[φῆ]καν τ[ὴν ἑαυτῶν οἰκέτιν Δη] μαι[ν]έταν Ὠφ[ε][λ]ίωνος ἐλε[υθέραν, "They released as an emancipated person their slave girl, Dameneta of Ophelion."

[32] δούλη would be a less specific term, under which οἰκέτις could be subsumed. One could call an οἰκέτις a δούλη should concubinage not be in view.

[33] See also σῶμα γυναικεῖον/γυναικός, which is repeated without significant variation in other manumission records (cf. Westermann, *The Slave Systems*, 5).

IMT Kyz Kapu Dağ 1727 (4 BCE)

Φαῖνε, Θόαν, Βάκχοιο φυτὸν τόδε· ματέρα γάρ σουρύσῃ τοῦ θανάτου, οἰκέτιν Ὑψιπύλαν

Thoas, show her this, Bacchus' plant, for you will save from death your mother, the slave Hypsipyle

In Greek myth, Hypsipyle was sold as a slave to Lycurgus, king of Nemea. She became his son's nursemaid. Thoas was her son born during her time as a slave. The use of οἰκέτις here is connected to her childbearing (of Thoas) as a slave before she was freed.

Besides these texts, there are a series of undated inscriptions that leave the responsibility of burial to various οἰκέτιδες (TAM III,1 276, 429, 483, 490, 743).[34]

3.1.3. Conclusion regarding οἰκέτις in the literary and documentary texts

The literary and documentary sources suggest that οἰκέτις is not a term for "female slave," "domestic slave," or even "housewife," but rather that it is a designation for a female slave who is used openly for procreative purposes as a sort of concubine.[35] Whether or not οἰκέτις is directly analogous to a concubine (παλλακίς) is difficult to determine. What can be said with some confidence is that it is not only in the Septuagint that the term οἰκέτις is associated with a role akin to that of a "concubine." For this reason, to claim "a different usage" than that evinced in the classical sources, namely that in the Septuagint "this specific word defines the girl as a concubine"[36] would be to fail to take into account the contexts in which οἰκέτις appears throughout the rest of the Greek record. οἰκέτις as a female slave used for procreation (i.e., a "concubine") is what the literary record suggests, and the documentary sources suggests that οἰκέτις was likely a specific sub-category of a female slave.[37] There is no special Septuagintal definition at play here.

It is now possible to look at the other uses of οἰκέτις in the LXX corpus and to see how the extra-biblical resources affirm its use therein.

3.1.4. Other uses of οἰκέτις in the LXX

There are two other uses of οἰκέτις in the corpus. These are found in Lev 19:20 and Prov 30:23. The latter text is quite terse, but the procreative connotation of οἰκέτις makes the aphorism stand out. In Prov 30:21, the sage declares, "Through three things the earth is shaken and the fourth it is not able to bear." One such situation involves οἰκέτις ἐὰν ἐκβάλῃ τὴν ἑαυτῆς κυρίαν, an "οἰκέτις if she throws out her mistress." This is a relatively straightforward representation of the Hebrew (ושפחה כי־תירש גברתה). The choice of

---

[34] Cf. also IG IX,2 1257. 1–3 (undated).
[35] This would be in contrast to a female slave who is used as a sexual object without any public recognition of this act. Such abuse was a common part of Greek slavery.
[36] Joosten, "Legal Hermeneutics," 556–57.
[37] It is not being suggested that οἰκέτις connoted a different status with respect to the free/slave distinction.

οἰκέτις for שפחה ("maidservant/slave") is a translation that perhaps reflects the subtext of the Hebrew, that is, that the slave girl, *through her favoured sexual status*, replaces the legal wife and thus has her ostracised from the family.

Leviticus 19:20 also focuses on relations between a man and a שפחה to whom he has either laid claim or is betrothed, or for whom he has in some way spoken.[38] The interpretive crux lies with שפחה נחרפת לאיש, "a maidservant acquired for a man." The translator renders this phrase as οἰκέτις διαπεφυλαγμένη ἀνθρώπῳ, "an οἰκέτις closely guarded for a man." The nature of the guarding here is not altogether clear. It may be that the slave is being saved for a man and has not had relations with him yet.[39] It may also be that this οἰκέτις is reserved for procreative acts *only with this one man*. She is thus to remain in sexual fidelity to her master, since she is a slave who is specifically designated for such activity. This position brings the possibility of bearing children. Should she be sexually active with another, this could endanger both the family planning and stability of the household through unwanted and biologically unrelated children. The "close guarding" here might be more in line with this reasoning than pointing to some sort of chastity. The translator seems to have introduced οἰκέτις into a context in which sleeping with a slave would be most problematic, that is, when she was sexually bound to her master.[40]

Before Exod 21:7 can be discussed with its renderings of οἰκέτις and αἱ δοῦλαι, it is necessary first to deal with the latter term.

3.2 δούλη in Graeco-Egyptian law

3.2.1. δούλη in typical Greek law

δοῦλος and δούλη are some of the most common terms in Greek legal speech for "slave."[41] In the time prior to Greek Exodus, this designation seems to have used for a slave who lived in the household of a master.[42] In the pre-hellenistic authors, δοῦλος/δούλη, in contrast to other terms for slaves, are often used to focus on the legal status of the slave (i.e., free/unfree).[43] Greek law codes prior to the time of the creation of the Greek Pentateuch and during the Ptolemaic period utilize these designations to refer to slaves, with the only real focus being, as expected, on their subject status.[44] This definition of δούλη would then have a generic sense, and could be what is referred to in Exod 21:7. This will be explored in §4.

---

[38] See *HALOT*, 1621.
[39] Joosten claims that οἰκέτις signifies "a female slave…who has been designated to a man but has not yet had sexual relations with him" ("Legal Hermeneutics," 557).
[40] Based on these observations, further exploration of this law in Greek Leviticus as it relates to the legal and social culture concerning slaves in Ptolemaic Egypt would probably be fruitful.
[41] Westermann, *The Slave Systems*, 5.
[42] Westermann, *The Slave Systems*, 12. If this is correct, it would make it difficult to claim that domesticity was a point of differentiation between οἰκέτις and αἱ δοῦλαι in Exod 21:7.
[43] Gschnitzer, "Studien," 1299–300, 1302, 1306.
[44] Pre-hellenistic: see, e.g., SEG 26:72 (375 BCE) ἐὰν δὲ δόλος ἦι ὁ πωλῶν ἢ δόλη, ὑπ<α>ρχέτω…; FD III 1:294, col. 1. 12 (425–375 BCE); Ptolemaic: P.Hal. 1.188–189 (259 BCE) with ἐὰν δὲ ὁ δ[οῦλος ἢ ἡ] δούλη…, l. 196 with[See preceding] ἐὰν ὁ δοῦλος ἢ ἡ δούλη…; P.Lille 1 29,1. 29 (third century BCE) with[see preceding] ὑπὸ δούλου ἢ δούλης.

3.2.2. One possible Graeco-Egyptian legal use of δούλη

There is another sense that δούλη could take on—one that is admittedly speculative. It would explain why αἱ δοῦλαι appears in Exod 21:7 instead of αἱ παιδίσκαι or the like.[45] Some preliminary considerations are in order.

In previous scholarship it has been debated whether παιδίσκη refers in a strict sense to slaves in Ptolemaic Egypt.[46] More recently, Roger Bagnall comments, "It seems clear today, as Scholl says…, that Rostovtzeff was correct in taking the term *paidiskē* to mean slave girl…"[47] The claim here is that παιδίσκη was a term for a slave and not for a free servant. If we take this conclusion for granted, then this sense of δούλη may be found in one, or perhaps two, legal texts that are worth mentioning.

P.Petr. (2) 1 13 (238 BCE) is a will drawn up by one Peisias, the testator. In the document he bequeaths various possessions, including slaves.[48] The point of focus for our present purposes is the phrase παιδίσκην δ[ο]ύλην (line 1.11). That δούλην modifies παιδίσκη is odd, since we would assume that παιδίσκη itself is an adequate designation for a slave.[49] δούλην would appear to be redundant. Furthermore, the rest of the references to the παῖς and παιδίσκη who are bequeathed in this will have no such modifiers (ll. 1.8–10). That they are all cited as possessions of Peisias makes it indisputably clear that we are here talking about slaves. So, what then is the function of δούλην? I have not found an answer to that question in the secondary sources.[50]

---

[45] This hypothesis would solve the dilemma previously noted: "Why the female slaves are referred to with the word δοῦλαι while the male slave is called παῖς has not been explained" (Joosten, "Legal Hermeneutics," 557).

[46] E.g., William Linn Westermann, *Upon Slavery in Ptolemaic Egypt* (New York: Columbia University Press, 1929), 56.

[47] Roger S. Bagnall, *Everyday Writing in the Graeco-Roman East* (Berkeley/Los Angeles: University of California Press, 2011), 59. Bagnall here refers to the debate on the use of the term in the Zenon papyri, which are the most contested texts.

[48] The relevant section reads as follows: ἐὰν [δέ] τι ἀνθρώπινον πάσχω, καταλείπω [τὰ ὑπάρχοντά] μοι τὰ [ἐν Ἀ]λεξανδρείαι Πισικράτει τῶι υἱῶι μ[ο]υ τ[ῶ]ι ἐκ Νικ[οῦ]ς, συν[οικ]ίαν καὶ τὰ ὑπάρχοντά μοι ἐκεῖ σκεύη πάντα καὶ παῖ[δα]ς Διονύσιον καὶ Εὔτυχον Σύρους καὶ παιδίσκην Ἀβίσιλαν [κ]αὶ ταύτης θυγατέρα Εἰρήνην Σύρας, Ἀξιοθέαι δὲ Ἱππ[ίου] Λυκίδι τῆι ἐμαυτοῦ γυναικὶ παιδίσκην δ[ο]ύλην Σύρα[ν] Λιβύσειον καὶ τὴν οἰκίαν τὴν ὑπάρχουσάν μοι [ἐν κ]ώμηι Βουβάστωι τοῦ Ἀρσινοίτου, "But if I suffer the mortal fate, I bequeath my possessions in Alexandria to Pisikrates, my son from Niko: a tenement house and all the furniture belonging to me there and my Syrian slaves Dionysios and Eutychos and my female slave Absila and her daughter Eirene, both of them from Syria. To Exiothea, daughter of Hippias, from Lycia, my wife, (I bequeath) a Syrian slave-girl Libyseion and the house belonging to me in the village of Boubastos in the Arsinoite nome" (translation by Roger S. Bagnall and Peter Derow, *The Hellenistic Period: Historical Sources in Translation* [New York: John Wiley & Sons, 2008], 242).

[49] This phrase was part of the reason that led Westermann to conclude that παιδίσκη did not mean "slave" in and of itself (*Upon Slavery*, 56).

[50] Reinhold Scholl, *Corpus der ptolemäischen Sklaventexte*, 3 vols. (Stuttgart: F. Steiner, 1990), 1.220–21, only comments on whether the text should be read as δουλικήν (*Corpus der ptolemäischen Sklaventexte*, 3 vols. [Stuttgart: F. Steiner, 1990], 1:220–21). This does not alleviate the problem of redundancy). J. A. Straus does not mention the tautological nature of δούλη in these texts and groups them into categories, though the status of the παιδίσκη is unclear. He also acknowledges that a situation having to do with a purchase makes it clear that slavery is involved ("La terminologie grecque de l'esclavage dans les papyrus de l'Égypte lagide et romaine," in *Actes du colloque 1973 sur l'esclavage. Besançon 2–3 mai 1973* [Besançon: Presses Universitaires de Franche-Comté, 1976], 333–50 [389] [cf. 385]). One supposes that the act of giving a slave as a possession should also be

Unless we are to assume a tautology on the part of the scribe here—which would be surprising in a document that would undoubtedly have been reviewed for accuracy—then δούλην must function as some kind of qualifier for the term παιδίσκη, "slave." It may be that the term δούλη indicates a specific role for a female slave. Note that, in this papyrus, Libyseion is the δούλη-slave who is bequeathed to Peisias' free wife Exiothea. Peisias is codifying in his will that Libyseion will remain a δούλη-slave after his death. What could this mean? Is it possible that it signifies that Libsyeion is to remain a slave who is forbidden to have sexual relations? If so, she would not be able to interfere with Exiothea in regard to any financial or other matters involving children or family after Peisias' death. It might be argued that this all seems too speculative. However, there is another fragmentary text that mirrors what is seen in P.Petr. (2) 1 13.

P.Giss. 1 2 (173 BCE) is a marriage contract.[51] In it, the bride specifies that, as part of her dowry, a slave will come into the husband's household with the bride. Line 13 describes this slave as a παιδίσκην δο[ύλην αὐτῆς] ἧι ὄνομα Στολίς, "a δούλη-slave whose name is Stolis." It is unfortunate that δο[ύλην must be reconstructed, but given the size of the lacunae, it fits the space and is what is suggested by the editors of the papyrus. Once again, there is no reason to include δούλη here to indicate a slave status. That is abundantly clear because Stolis is included as a possession to be given along with other components of the dowry. δούλη again seems to be tautologous. Yet it is interesting that the contract stipulates that no concubines are allowed for the man in the future (l. 20). This slave girl coming with the bride will not be allowed to be a sexual partner at a later time. Could it be that δούλη is here meant formally and contractually to delimit the sexual activity of this incoming slave with her new master? Perhaps δούλη is included so that it will not be possible for the man to claim that the incoming female slave is an exception to the contractual obligation concerning concubines.

Despite the inconclusive nature of the texts, both P.Petr. (2) 1 13 and P.Giss. 1 2 exhibit attributive uses of δούλη that might intimate something about the procreative availability of a female slave to her master. It could be a term that was used in specific contexts in which the sexual services of a slave needed to be specified contractually, as would likely be the case in most life scenarios. Whatever the case, it cannot be denied

---

regarded as belonging to the category of a purchase and could clear up the ambiguity of the situation depicted in P.Petr. (2) 1 13. Bagnall and Derow translate δούλη as "slave-girl" (*The Hellenistic Period*, 242).

[51] The relevant section reads as follows: ἐξέδοτο ἑαυτὴν Ὀλυ[μ]πιὰς Διονυσίου Μα[κ]έτα μετὰ κυρίου τοῦ ἑαυτῆς πατρὸς Διονυσίου Μακεδόνος τῆς δευτέρας ἱππαρχίας ἑκατονταρούρου Ἀνταίωι Ἀθηναίωι τῶν Κινέου τῆς δευτέρ[α]ς ἱππαρχίας ἑκαντοντ[α]ρούρωι [εἶναι] γυναῖκα γαμετὴν φερνήν π[ρ]οσφερομένην εἰς χ[αλκοῦ] λόγον τάλαντα ἐνενήκοντα πέντε καὶ παιδίσκην δο[ύλην αὐτῆς] ἧι ὄνομα Στολὶς καὶ τὸ ταύτης παιδίον ὑποτίτθιον ἧι ὄνομα Α[...] χαλκοῦ ταλάντοις πέντε ὥστ᾽ εἶναι τὰ πάντα χαλκοῦ τάλαν[τα ἑκατόν], "Es gab sich Olympias, Tochter des Dionysios, Makedonierin, mit dem Rechtsbeistand, ihrem Vater Dionysios, Makedone, von der zweiten Hipparchie, Hundertarurenbesitzer, dem Antaios, Athener, einem der Leute des Kineas, von der zweiten Hipparchie, Hundertarurenbesitzer, als Ehefrau hin, als Mitgift und ihre Sklavin...mit Namen Stolis und deren Säugling mit Namen A[ ]in Kupfer fünf Talente, insgesamt in Kupfer Talente [einhundert]" (Scholl, *Corpus*, vol. 1, 223–24).

that δούλη appears attributively in these oddly 'tautological' situations, and *only in contexts that pertain to free wives, their husbands, and their relationships to particular female slaves.*

Now, at last, we can turn to Exod 21:7 and draw some conclusions.

4. Exodus 21:7 and the employment of οἰκέτις and αἱ δοῦλαι

Since οἰκέτις has been identified as a term for a slave who is somewhat akin to a "concubine," Exod's rendering becomes more comprehensible. The father in 21:7 is not simply giving his daughter as a "domestic slave,"[52] but rather as a slave who will be available for sexual relations with her master. This aspect of the relationship is probably already made explicit in the Hebrew of v. 10, where the master must not deprive the slave of ענתה, "her [right of] sexual intercourse."[53] It may be, then, that the Hebrew text's focus on procreative acts led the translator to render אמה as οἰκέτις in v. 7. It may also have seemed inappropriate in Graeco-Egyptian culture to employ a generic term for a slave like παιδίσκη as the counterpart to אמה in v. 7. The law in vv. 7–11 might, then, be understood to imply the likelihood of sexual relations between masters and all female slaves. We have already seen that Greek marriage contracts could specify a rule of non-concubinage. Thus a biblical law that may have been open to such an interpretation could have been negatively received in Graeco-Egyptian culture where faithfulness to a legal wife could, in some measure, be contractually stipulated.

We come now to the heretofore unsatisfactorily explained translation choice of αἱ δοῦλαι. That Exodus chooses to render the masculine term העבדים with a feminine one represents an interpretive maneuver that I have labelled "superficial semantic fidelity," which is evident throughout the Greek Covenant Code.[54] By this I mean that Exodus will often employ a Greek term that shares some kind of semantic overlap with its Hebrew counterpart (e.g., αἱ δοῦλαι and העבדים in 21:7) although the actual meaning in the Greek text will be substantially different (here αἱ δοῦλαι refers only to female slaves and not to the male slaves of vv. 2–6[55]). Two interpretive options emerge for αἱ δοῦλαι from the present study. First, if the typically attested use of δούλη is meant here, then 21:7 should read, "Now if someone sells his own daughter as a concubine, she shall not be manumitted[56] in the same way as the (rest of the) female slaves." On this reading, it must be assumed that αἱ δοῦλαι generally refers to all other female slaves, with perhaps a focus on their legal status. The problem with regard to this reading is the fact that there is no obvious reason why Exodus

---

[52] So NETS.
[53] The meaning of this term is debated. See *HALOT*, 855. Exod renders this with τὴν ὁμιλίαν αὐτῆς, which seems to correspond to understanding the Hebrew to mean "her [right of] sexual intercourse."
[54] See Korytko, "Death of the Covenant Code."
[55] Cf. Houtman, *Exodus*, vol. 3, 127, regarding vv. 2–6 referring only to male manumission, which is then alluded to in 21:7 with the mention of העבדים.
[56] Regarding Exodus here using Greek legal terminology for manumission, see Lee, *A Lexical Study*, 127–28.

would focus on legal status here involving αἱ δοῦλαι and yet would do so nowhere else.⁵⁷ αἱ παιδίσκαι would have been completely suitable terminology if female slaves in a generic sense were in the translator's mind. That choice of terminology would also maintain Exodus' usual pattern of translation equivalencies. As for the second interpretive option, if αἱ δοῦλαι is interpreted in the light of its usage in papyrological texts discussed, then this verse could be translated, "Now if someone sells his own daughter as a concubine, she shall not be manumitted in the same way as the non-concubinates (female slaves)."⁵⁸ This rendering is innovative in that it occurs only in contexts having to do with concubinage. It also solves the problem of the first translation since δούλη in its generic sense would already include οἰκέτις as a subcategory of slave within its semantic range (which necessitates the translation "the [rest of the] female slaves"). Instead, οἰκέτις and this adjectival δούλη would be antonyms that symmetrically represent the totality of female slaves, namely, the concubinate and the non-concubinate.

Finally, another comment is in order about the change from העבדים to αἱ δοῦλαι. Why did the Greek translator render the Hebrew masculine term for slaves with a feminine one? Previous answers to this question have been noted in this chapter. Here it is proposed that this change could reflect a desire on the part of the translator to align his rendering of the source text with Graeco-Egyptian legal standards as seems to be evidenced elsewhere in the Covenant Code.⁵⁹ Classical Greek law maintained equity for males and females in regard to slavery legislation.⁶⁰ This is indicated by the fact that Greek law codes use predominantly masculine terms, but the laws are applied to both males and females.⁶¹ Law codes in Ptolemaic Egypt even include clauses in which penalties involving beating and torture are the same for both males and females!⁶² It may be that, had Exod opted for a masculine equivalent to העבדים, then the law in 21:7 could have implied that male slaves were accorded rights of manumission after six years that females did not enjoy.⁶³ This incongruence with Graeco-Egyptian standards would be avoided by employing the feminine term.⁶⁴

---

⁵⁷ Moreover, others have noted the reticence of the early translators to use the δοῦλος/δούλη when speaking of slaves (e.g., Suzanne Daniel, *Recherches sur le vocabulaire du culte dans la Septante* [Paris: Klincksieck, 1966], 103 and n. 38; Benjamin G. Wright, "Δοῦλος and Παῖς as Translations of עבד: Lexical Equivalences and Conceptual Transformations," in *IX Congress of the International Organization for Septuagint and Cognate Studies, Cambridge, 1995*, ed. Bernard A. Taylor, SBLSCS 45 [Atlanta: Scholars Press, 1997], 263–77 [270]). Why was this hesitancy abandoned here? If αἱ δοῦλαι is read as a substantival adjective in this speculative sense of "non-concubinate," then it could be that we are not here dealing with a case of the typically unwelcome nominal δοῦλος/δούλη.

⁵⁸ This translation assumes that δοῦλαι is a substantival adjective.

⁵⁹ See Korytko, "Death of the Covenant Code." Elsewhere in the law of 21:7–12, Exod seems to draw on the stock terminology for contractual female marital provisions in 21:11 with τὰ δέοντα καὶ τὸν ἱματισμόν (Korytko, "The 'Law of the Land,'" 77–78).

⁶⁰ Such equal treatment can be discerned in the statement by Westermann: "So far as known [sic], the laws of the Greek city-states placed no restrictions upon the use to which male or female slaves might be put by the owner" (*The Slave Systems*, 12).

⁶¹ Male and female slaves can both be mentioned, but this is not at all necessary (see n. 44).

⁶² See P.Hal. 1. 188–189, 196–197 (259 BCE).

⁶³ This may be what the Hebrew actually means (cf. n. 55).

⁶⁴ Such an explanation does not rule out the possibility that Exod modifies the law in order to accommodate it to what is found elsewhere in the Pentateuch (so Joosten, "Legal Hermeneutics," 555–57).

5. Slaves to the Septuagint

By re-evaluating the primary source data, it has become plausible to suggest that, in the sources outside of the LXX, οἰκέτις is in fact a designation for a woman whose status is somewhat like that of a concubine. Likewise, the legal documentary papyri provide a potential explanation for the employment of both δούλη and οἰκέτις in Exod 21:7. Similarly, Graeco-Egyptian legal influence on the translator could account for the change from masculine העבדים to feminine αἱ δοῦλαι.

The present study has attempted to show that doing rigorous spade work in texts contemporaneous with, but outside of, the biblical corpus in its relevant early versions is incumbent upon those who toil in the field of Septuagint studies. Traditional "Septuagintal" lexicographic definitions cannot be assumed to be adequate, and primary source data and genre-specific analysis should be included in all such investigations. It is possible that the Septuagint may even end up being the launching point for contributions to other disciplines. This study is intended as a case-in-point. Septuagint scholarship need not be enslaved to the biblical corpus.[65]

Bibliography

Bagnall, Roger S. *Everyday Writing in the Graeco-Roman East*. Berkeley/Los Angeles: University of California Press, 2011.

Bagnall, Roger S., and Peter Derow. *The Hellenistic Period: Historical Sources in Translation*. New York: John Wiley & Sons, 2008.

Cazelles, Henri. *Études sur le code d'alliance*. Paris: Letouzey et Ané, 1946.

Daniel, Suzanne. *Recherches sur le vocabulaire du culte dans la Septante*. Paris: Klincksieck, 1966.

Faculty of Classics, University of Cambridge, and James Diggle. *The Cambridge Greek Lexicon*. 2 vols. Cambridge: Cambridge University Press, 2021.

Frankel, Zacharias. *Ueber den Einfluss der palästinischen Exegese auf die alexandrinische Hermeneutik*. Leipzig: J. A. Barth, 1851.

Geiger, Abraham. *Urschrift und Uebersetzungen der Bibel in ihrer Abhängigkeitvon der inneren Entwicklung des Judentums*. 2nd ed. Frankfurt am Main: Verlag Madda, 1928.

Gschnitzer, Fritz. "Studien zur griechischen Terminologie der Sklaverei. 1: Grundzüge des vorhellenistischen Sprachgebrauchs." Pages 1283–310 in *Abhandlungen der Geistes und sozialwissenschaftlichen Klasse, Jahrgang 1963, Heft 9–15*. Mainz: Akademie der Wissenschaften und der Literatur, 1964.

Houtman, Cornelis. *Exodus*. Vol. 3: *Chapters 20–40*. Historical Commentary on the Old Testament. Leuven: Peeters, 2000.

Joosten, Jan. "Legal Hermeneutics and the Tradition Underlying the Septuagint." Pages 555–64 in *XV Congress of the International Organization for Septuagint and Cognate Studies: Munich, 2013*. Edited by Wolfgang Kraus, Michaël N. van der Meer, and Martin Meiser. SBLSCS 64. Atlanta: Society of Biblical Literature, 2016.

A study of parallel laws in the Pentateuch and other potential interpretive moves in Exodus is a desideratum. If Exodus does not do this elsewhere, perhaps the Graeco-Egyptian legal paradigm should be prioritized.

[65] Special thanks are extended to Steel Lane for his editorial suggestions regarding the present essay.

Koehler, Ludwig, et al. *The Hebrew and Aramaic Lexicon of the Old Testament*. Leiden: Brill, 1994–2000.

Korytko, Joel F. "Death of the Covenant Code: Evaluating the Translation of Laws with Capital Punishment in Old Greek Exodus 21.1–23.19 in Light of Graeco-Egyptian Law." DPhil diss., The University of Oxford, 2022.

Korytko, Joel F. "The Death Penalty in OG Exodus in Light of Graeco-Egyptian Legal Formulations." *JSCS* 54 (2021): 75–92.

Korytko, Joel F. "The 'Law of the Land' in the Land of the Lagids: A Comparative Analysis of Exodus 21.1–32." M.A. thesis, Trinity Western University, 2018.

Le Boulluec, Alain, and Pierre Sandevoir. *La Bible d'Alexandrie: L'Exode*. Paris: Cerf, 1989.

Lee, John A. L. *A Lexical Study of the Septuagint Version of the Pentateuch*. SBLSCS 14. Chico: Scholars Press, 1983.

Mayo, Tyler. "Research and Experiment in Early Greek Thought." PhD diss., University of Michigan, 2019.

O'Connell, Kevin G. *The Theodotionic Revision of the Book of Exodus: A Contribution to the Study of the Early History of the Transmission of the Old Testament in Greek*. HSM 3. Cambridge, MA: Harvard University Press, 1972.

Pavlovskaja, A. L. "Die Sklaverei im hellenistischen Ägypten." Pages 185–99 in *Die Sklaverei in hellenistischen Staaten im 3.–1. Jh. v. Chr.* Edited by T. V. Blavatskaja, E. S. Golubcova, and A. I. Pavlovskaja. Wiesbaden: Steiner, 1972. Translated from Russian.

Plutarch. *Moralia. Volume XII: Concerning the Face Which Appears in the Orb of the Moon. On the Principle of Cold. Whether Fire or Water Is More Useful. Whether Land or Sea Animals Are Cleverer. Beasts Are Rational. On the Eating of Flesh*. Translated by Harold Cherniss and W. C. Helmbold. LCL 406. Cambridge, MA: Harvard University Press, 1957.

Propp, William Henry Covici. *Exodus 19–40: A New Translation with Introduction and Commentary*. New York: Doubleday, 2006.

Scholl, Reinhold. *Corpus der ptolemäischen Sklaventexte*. Vol. 1. 3 vols. Stuttgart: F. Steiner, 1990.

Steiner, Deborah. *The Idea of the Chorus in Greek Culture: Choral Constructions in the Poetry, Art and Social Practices of the Archaic and Early Classical Period*. Cambridge: Cambridge University Press, 2021.

Straus, J. A. "La terminologie grecque de l'esclavage dans les papyrus de l'Égypte lagide et romaine." Pages 333–50 in *Actes du colloque 1973 sur l'esclavage. Besançon 2–3 mai 1973*. Besançon: Presses Universitaires de Franche-Comté, 1976.

Theocritus, Moschus, Bion. Translated by Neil Hopkinson. LCL 28. Cambridge, MA: Harvard University Press, 2015.

Vermes, Geza. "Bible and Midrash: Early Old Testament Exegesis." Pages 199–231 in vol. 1 of *Cambridge History of the Bible*. Edited by Peter Ackroyd and Christopher F. Evans. Cambridge: Cambridge University Press, 1970.

Westermann, William Linn. *The Slave Systems of Greek and Roman Antiquity*. Memoirs of the American Philosophical Society 40. Philadelphia: American Philosophical Society, 1955.

Westermann, William Linn. *Upon Slavery in Ptolemaic Egypt*. New York: Columbia University Press, 1929.

Wright, Benjamin G. "Δοῦλος and Παῖς as Translations of עבד: Lexical Equivalences and Conceptual Transformations." Pages 263–77 in *IX Congress of the International Organization for Septuagint and Cognate Studies, Cambridge, 1995*. SBLSCS 45. Edited by Bernard A. Taylor. Atlanta: Scholars Press, 1997.

Chapter 8

From Exodus to Deuteronomy? A Study on Interdependence in the Greek Pentateuch

Jean Maurais

1. Introduction

It is a pleasure to dedicate this essay to Larry Perkins who was a valued mentor as I was taking my first steps in the world of Septuagint studies. His generosity and intellectual rigor were formative influences in my own life and scholarship. The topic at hand touches on issues that he addresses in his work on Greek Exodus.[1] For the purposes of this paper, I will examine the issue of interdependence (or intertextuality) in the Greek Pentateuch, focusing on the claim that the Deuteronomy translator borrowed from Greek Exodus. The context of this inquiry is the common assumption that the translations of the Greek Pentateuch were produced by different translators in the canonical order: Genesis first, followed by Exodus, Leviticus, and so on.[2] This consensus is mostly conjectural, given the paucity of historical evidence, and perhaps

---

[1] Larry Perkins, "Greek Exodus and Greek Isaiah: Detection and Implications of Interdependence in Translation," *BIOSCS* 42 (2009): 18–33. References to the Greek Pentateuch or the Greek version of one of its components (e.g., Deuteronomy) in this paper denote its initial translation, which is tentatively dated to the first half of the third century BCE. Unless stated otherwise, the Greek texts are cited from Wevers' major critical editions of Exodus and Deuteronomy, while the Hebrew has been reproduced from *BHS*.

[2] See, for example, the conclusion in Martin Rösel, *Übersetzung als Vollendung der Auslegung: Studien zur Genesis-Septuaginta*, BZAW 223 (Berlin: de Gruyter, 1994), 257. Cf. Emanuel Tov, "The Septuagint Translation of Genesis as the First Scripture Translation," in *In the Footsteps of Sherlock Holmes: Studies in the Biblical Text in Honour of Anneli Aejmelaeus*, ed. Kristin De Troyer, T. Michael Law, and Marketta Liljeström, CBET 72 (Leuven: Peeters, 2014), 47–64. An argument in favor of different translators based on lexical considerations was presented long ago by Friedrich Baumgärtel in "Zur Entstehung der Pentateuchseptuaginta," in *Beiträge zur Entstehungsgeschichte der Septuaginta*, ed. Johannes Herrmann and Friedrich Baumgärtel, BWAT NF 5 (Stuttgart: Kohlhammer, 1923), 53–62. The most complete study on this topic at present is that of Hayeon Kim, *Multiple Authorship of the Septuagint Pentateuch: The Original Translators of the Pentateuch,*

reflects an anachronistic view of the ways in which the Pentateuch was conceived and employed during this period.³

John A. L. Lee recently moved the discussion forward by arguing at length that the five books of the Pentateuch were translated simultaneously and that their translators collaborated.⁴ This scenario would explain, among other things, the large number of neologisms that are employed in similar contexts in each book of the Pentateuch. Their originality makes it unlikely that they would have been created independently by different individuals.⁵ Moreover, these new terms or expressions translate entire semantic fields, implying that some kind of word list or glossary was employed to ensure that specific Hebrew terms were matched to the appropriate Greek equivalent.⁶ In Lee's mind, the only possible explanation is that the translators collaborated and worked from a common word list.⁷

Though Lee's suggestion is insightful and intriguing in many respects, the chronological aspect of this theory—that the translators worked simultaneously—runs contrary to another set of observations. Other scholars have argued that individual books of the Greek Pentateuch assume familiarity with other translations of this corpus. For example, Cornelius den Hertog contends that some of the terminology employed in Greek Deuteronomy is borrowed from Greek Exodus. He cites Deut 15:17, the law of the release of slaves, where the rather generic term נתן is employed to denote the piercing of the slave's ear against the doorpost. This term is translated somewhat surprisingly by the use of a very specific Greek equivalent, τρυπάω ("to bore through"). This Greek term is also the one found in the parallel law of Exod 21:6, where it is a closer match to the Hebrew רצע ("to pierce through"). The Deuteronomy

---

Multiple Authorship of the Septuagint Pentateuch, STHB 4 (Leiden: Brill, 2020). Kim concludes that each book of the Pentateuch was translated by a distinct individual. However, Theo van der Louw argues that Greek Genesis and the first part of Greek Exodus were produced by the same translator. See Theo A. W. van der Louw, "The Unity of LXX Genesis and Exodus," *VT* 70, no. 2 (2020): 270–84. That the translations were produced sequentially is often simply assumed. See, for example, Melvin K. H. Peters, "To the Reader of Deuteronomion," in *A New English Translation of the Septuagint*, ed. Albert Pietersma and Benjamin G. Wright (Oxford: Oxford University Press, 2009), 141.

³ James Barr questioned the frequent assumption concerning the priority of Genesis ("Did the Greek Pentateuch Really Serve as a Dictionary for the Translation of the Later Books?" in *Hamlet on a Hill: Semitic and Greek Studies Presented to Professor T. Muraoka on the Occasion of His Sixty-Fifth Birthday*, ed. Martin F. J. Baasten and Wido Th. Van Peursen [Leuven: Peeters, 2003], 538–40).

⁴ John A. L. Lee, *The Greek of the Pentateuch: Grinfield Lectures on the Septuagint 2011–2012* (Oxford: Oxford University Press, 2018), 173–209.

⁵ Lee, *Greek of the Pentateuch*, 185.

⁶ Others have suggested that similar lists could have existed prior to the translation. See Cécile Dogniez and Marguerite Harl, *Le Deutéronome*, La Bible d'Alexandrie 5 (Paris: Cerf, 1992), 63; Anneli Aejmelaeus, "The Septuagint and Oral Translation," in *XIV Congress of the IOSCS, Helsinki 2010*, ed. Melvin K. H. Peters, SCS 59 (Atlanta: Society of Biblical Literature, 2013), 8–12. Lee argues that most were created in the course of translation. See Lee, *Greek of the Pentateuch*, 199–202. The existence of a word list is not a novel idea (203 n. 76), but Lee's discussion presents the most sustained argument in its favor. A similar argument has also been put forward in the context of the book of Samuel in Sarah Yardney, "The Use of Glossaries by the Translators of the Septuagint," *Textus* 28 (2019): 157–77.

⁷ Lee further argues that the existence of a written list is the only way for translators to remember all the mappings of a particular semantic field. However, some well-known terms undoubtedly had Greek equivalents before the translation effort was initiated. Moreover, the translators also had freedom to choose a different term at times depending on several factors. The list was only a guide. See Lee, *Greek of the Pentateuch*, 201–204.

translator seems to have consulted and borrowed from the Exodus passage when translating 15:17.[8] Of particular interest in this example is the fact that the verb רצע in the Exodus passage is a *hapax legomenon*. The Hebrew term, therefore, cannot be the point of contact between these laws. Moreover, the noun מרצע is also found in both texts and translated using a technical term, ὀπήτιον. These are the only occurrences of these nouns (both Hebrew and Greek) in the Pentateuch. It seems plausible, therefore, that the presence of difficult (or ambiguous) technical terms in the Hebrew text of Deuteronomy and the existence of a parallel passage in Exodus prompted the Deuteronomy translator to consult Exodus in its Greek version for help.

Other potential occurrences of such interdependencies can be posited, but this type of inquiry is fraught with difficulties.[9] In the context of this paper, I will limit myself to the relationship between Exodus and Deuteronomy, though the same should be done (and in some cases has been attempted) for the other books as well.[10] Should a number of borrowings be identified with some degree of plausibility, it would provide a strong indication that these translations were produced sequentially and would signify which of the two came first.

2. Criteria for assessing interdependency

Studies on intertextuality in the Septuagint, especially with a view to determining whether specific translators were aware of other translations, have been many.[11] The

---

[8] Cornelius G. den Hertog, Michael Labahn, and Thomas Pola, "Deuteronomion," in vol. 1 of *Septuaginta Deutsch: Erläuterungen und Kommentare zum griechischen Alten Testament. Genesis bis Makkabäer*, ed. Wolfgang Kraus and Martin Karrer (Stuttgart: Deutsche Bibelgesellschaft, 2011), 529.

[9] John Wevers identifies several instances where the Deuteronomy translator apparently borrowed from the Greek versions of Exodus, Leviticus, and Numbers. These are discussed in John W. Wevers, "The LXX Translator of Deuteronomy," in *IX Congress of the International Organization for Septuagint and Cognate Studies*, ed. Bernard A. Taylor, SCS 45 (Atlanta: Scholars Press, 1997), 68–69. On the other hand, Zacharias Frankel argues that the Deuteronomy translator did not demonstrate awareness of the other translations (*Ueber den Einfluss der palästinischen Exegese auf die alexandrinische Hermeneutik* [Leipzig: Barth, 1851], 207–209).

[10] Cornelius G. den Hertog's study on the relationship between Leviticus, Numbers, and Deuteronomy may constitute a good starting point, though I find many of his examples unconvincing ("Erwägungen zur relativen Chronologie der Bücher Levitikus und Deuteronomium innerhalb der Pentateuchübersetzung," in *Im Brennpunkt: die Septuaginta. Band 2: Studien zur Entstehung und Bedeutung der griechischen Bibel*, ed. Siegfried Kreuzer and Jürgen Peter Lesch, BWANT 161 [Stuttgart: Kohlhammer, 2004], 216–28). For a criticism of den Hertog's approach, see Martin Rösel, "Von der Tora zum Nomos—Perspektiven der Forschung am griechischen Pentateuch," in *Einleitung in die Septuaginta*, ed. Siegfried Kreuzer, LXX.H 1 (Gütersloh: Gütersloher Verlagshaus, 2016), 102–104. Of note is Dorival's study on intertextuality in Greek Numbers. Though the list he provides contains intertextual connections that are made with a remote Hebrew or Greek text, those that appear to depend on a prior Greek translation rely on Genesis, Exodus, and Leviticus. The only instance in which a connection to Deuteronomy can be identified (Num 27:12–14 to Deut 32:49–51) does not require reference to Greek Deuteronomy, since the interdependence can be established based on the Hebrew text. See Gilles Dorival, "Les phénomènes d'intertextualité dans le livre grec des Nombres," in *Kata tous O' "Selon les Septante": Trente études sur la Bible grecque des Septante*, ed. Gilles Dorival and Olivier Munnich (Paris: Cerf, 1995), 253–85.

[11] See the bibliography in Myrto Theocharous, *Lexical Dependence and Intertextual Allusion in the Septuagint of the Twelve Prophets: Studies in Hosea, Amos and Micah*, LHBOTS 570 (London: Bloomsbury T&T Clark, 2012), 6–7 nn. 25 and 26.

starting point for such inquiries is a Greek rendering which is difficult to explain in light of its translator's usual practice.¹² Jennifer Dines offers the following criteria (here relayed by Myrto Theocharous):

1. A resemblance between two texts must not be explicable as independent renderings of similar *Vorlagen*.
2. It must not be the outcome of each translator's normal translation practice.¹³
3. One rendering must fit its presumed Hebrew equivalent, and thus its context, more appropriately than the other, so that dependence is plausible in one direction.¹⁴

This example fits these criteria quite well. However, it would not be possible to assess dependence solely on the basis of the noun מרצע and its equivalent ὀπήτιον. Since the lexical match is found in both texts, it would be impossible to determine which translator might have relied on the other (if there was, in fact, reliance, one way or another), however rare the term. This type of evidence would only be admissible once we have established dependency and chronological sequence on other grounds.

Perkins also argues that the identification of interdependence is more convincing when the context of each occurrence is properly accounted for and some thematic coherence can be observed.¹⁵ For this reason, my inquiry will proceed using passages in Exodus and Deuteronomy that deal with similar material. This is, in any case, where the majority of such borrowings have been identified.

3. Analysis

In the following sections, I will investigate eleven instances of ostensible interdependence that have been offered as examples of borrowing from Greek Exodus by the Deuteronomy translator. As will become apparent, some of these texts were especially prone to scribal activity and assimilation. The context of these possible intertextual connections is therefore significant and must be examined before presuming interdependence.¹⁶

---

¹² As Theocharous states, quoting Barr, these are of the most convincing type. See Theocharous, *Lexical Dependence and Intertextual Allusion*, 8; Barr, "Did the Greek Pentateuch Really Serve as a Dictionary for the Translation of the Later Books?" 541.

¹³ Though this may seem to raise the bar too high, the translator's frequent use of various lexemes makes such interdependencies impossible to differentiate from mere coincidence with any degree of certainty. See Cécile Dogniez, "L'intertextualité dans la LXX de Zacharie 9–14," in *Interpreting Translation: Studies on the LXX and Ezekiel in Honour of Johan Lust*, ed. Florentino García Martínez and Marc Vervenne, BETL 192 (Leuven: Peeters, 2005), 89. Kim demonstrates that most of the shared vocabulary of the Greek Pentateuch translations are "natural equivalents," and therefore of little use for the task at hand (*Multiple Authorship of the Septuagint Pentateuch*, 19).

¹⁴ Theocharous, *Lexical Dependence and Intertextual Allusion*, 21. Theocharous quotes an unpublished paper by Jennifer Dines, "The Twelve Among the Prophets" (presented in a Grinfield Lecture on the Septuagint, Oxford, March 1, 2007), 5. I have omitted Dines' fourth point concerning apparent interdependencies not being "traceable to a passage in the Pentateuch used independently by each translator" since it is not pertinent to this study.

¹⁵ Perkins, "Greek Exodus and Greek Isaiah," 29.

¹⁶ I have not included in this study the many instances in which a harmonizing plus in the Greek text of Deuteronomy is also found in the Samaritan Pentateuch (Smr). In all probability, such pluses were

3.1. Deuteronomy 7:22b and Exodus 23:29

The first type of apparent borrowing is observed in a significant plus found in Deut 7:22b. After stating that the Canaanites will not disappear quickly before the Israelites, the MT of Deuteronomy provides a single reason in the final clause while the Greek translation provides two:

Exod 23:29	לא אגרשנו מפניך בשנה אחת פן תהיה הארץ שממה ורבה עליך חית השדה	οὐκ ἐκβαλῶ αὐτοὺς ἐν ἐνιαυτῷ ἑνί, ἵνα μὴ γένηται ἡ γῆ ἔρημος καὶ πολλὰ γένηται ἐπὶ σὲ τὰ θηρία τῆς γῆς·
Deut 7:22b	לא תוכל כלתם מהר פן תרבה עליך חית השדה	οὐ δυνήσῃ ἐξαναλῶσαι αὐτοὺς τὸ τάχος, ἵνα μὴ γένηται ἡ γῆ ἔρημος καὶ πληθυνθῇ ἐπὶ σὲ τὰ θηρία τὰ ἄγρια.

The extant Hebrew witnesses of Deuteronomy do not attest to such a plus and the phrase γένηται ἡ γῆ ἔρημος καί is *sub obelus* in hexaplaric witnesses.[17] Another noteworthy feature is that, while the Greek plus is identical to its Exodus counterpart, the second part of this final clause is translated differently in Exodus and Deuteronomy, specifically with respect to the rendering of the verb רבה and the noun שדה. Thus, if the Deuteronomy translator copied the final clause from Greek Exodus, he limited himself to the first part and provided his own translation of the second part. The final clause is introduced by ἵνα μή, which is not the most frequent equivalent for פן in Deuteronomy, though it is employed on occasion.[18] However, the remainder of the final clause corresponds to what the Deuteronomy translator would produce from the Hebrew text. Though such significant pluses are rarely introduced by the Deuteronomy translator, John Wevers' suggestion can be entertained here.[19] The conclusion reached in such cases will depend on how one views the possibility of the translator inserting such significant pluses in light of his overall technique. I personally remain skeptical but will categorize this one as a possibility.

---

already present in the translator's *Vorlage* and do not represent instances of borrowing at the level of the Greek text. For a list of these occurrences and an argument along those lines, see Emanuel Tov, "Textual Harmonizations in the Ancient Texts of Deuteronomy," in *Mishneh Toda: Studies in Deuteronomy and Its Cultural Environment in Honor of Jeffrey H. Tigay*, ed. Nili S. Fox, David A. Glatt-Gilad, and Michael J. Williams (Winona Lake, IN: Eisenbrauns, 2009), 15–28 (23–24, 27). On the relationship between these textual families, see Emanuel Tov, "From Popular Jewish LXX-SP Texts to Separate Sectarian Texts: Insights from the Dead Sea Scrolls," in *The Samaritan Pentateuch and the Dead Sea Scrolls*, ed. Michaël Langlois, CBET 94 (Leuven: Peeters, 2019), 19–40, esp. 23; Emanuel Tov, "The Shared Tradition of the Septuagint and the Samaritan Pentateuch," in vol. 4 of *Textual Developments: Collected Essays*, VTSup 181 (Leiden: Brill, 2019), 357–72; Benjamin Ziemer, "A Stemma for Deuteronomy," in *The Dead Sea Scrolls and the Samaritan Pentateuch*, ed. Michaël Langlois, CBET 94 (Leuven: Peeters, 2019), 127–97.

[17] The plus is widely attested in the Greek textual history. According to Wevers' critical edition, it is only omitted in the Arabische Übersetzung (Paris, Bibl. Nat., Arab 9) and in Barh 228 (Barhebraeus' Scholia on the Old Testament—thirteenth century CE).

[18] Four out of twenty-eight instances: 7:22; 19:6; 22:9, and 32:27. In 32:27, the two occurrences of the פן particle are translated by ἵνα μή and μή, respectively.

[19] On the different approaches to attributing such pluses to the translator or his *Vorlage*, see Jean Maurais, "The Quest for LXX Deuteronomy's Translator: On the Use of Translation Technique in Ascertaining the Translator's *Vorlage*," in *Die Septuaginta—Themen, Manuskripte, Wirkungen: 7. Internationale Fachtagung veranstaltet von Septuaginta Deutsch (LXX.D), Wuppertal 19. –22. Juli 2018*, ed. Eberhard Bons et al., WUNT 444 (Tübingen: Mohr Siebeck, 2020), 186–203.

3.2. Deuteronomy 9:12 and Exodus 32:7

In his study of Deut 9:12, a passage recalling the golden calf episode, Wevers contends that the Deuteronomy translator was almost certainly acquainted with the Greek Exodus parallel account since his translation mimics that of Exod 32:7 in two different ways.[20] This is first argued on the basis of the phrase ἐκ γῆς Αἰγύπτου (highlighted) which does not fully correspond to MT's ממצרים. Instead, it matches Greek Exodus where the MT reads מארץ מצרים:

Exod 32:7	לך רד כי שחת עמך אשר העלית מארץ מצרים	Βάδιζε κατάβηθι τὸ τάχος ἐντεῦθεν· ἠνόμησεν γὰρ ὁ λαός σου, οὓς ἐξήγαγες ἐκ γῆς Αἰγύπτου·
Deut 9:12a	קום רד מהר מזה כי שחת עמך אשר הוצאת ממצרים	Ἀνάστηθι κατάβηθι τὸ τάχος ἐντεῦθεν, ὅτι ἠνόμησεν ὁ λαός σου, οὓς ἐξήγαγες ἐκ γῆς Αἰγύπτου·

However, Carmel McCarthy's survey of similar expressions throughout Deuteronomy highlights several inconsistencies that are not limited to this passage. The Greek counterpart to MT's shorter form of מצרים (employed with several prepositions) is preceded by γῆ in 1:30; 4:45, 46; 6:21a; 9:12, 26; 16:12; 24:18, and 25:17.[21] McCarthy surmises that there appears to have been "a certain amount of fluidity" concerning this formula "when it is the land of Egypt that is in question (rather than its king, army or diseases)."[22] Though the Samaritan Pentateuch (Smr) agrees only once with Greek Deuteronomy in the context of these longer readings, the impetus towards consistency in such oft-repeated phrases is perhaps best understood as taking place at the level of the translator's source text.[23] This being the case, both Greek Exodus and Greek Deuteronomy would have rendered the same *Vorlage* independently. But even if one assumes that the longer reading found in Greek Deuteronomy was produced during the translation process, its frequent occurrence throughout the book undermines the possibility that it was done under the influence of Exod 32:7.

Wevers goes on to argue that the translation of the Piel of שחת by ἀνομέω in the same verse is influenced by the similar rendering in the Exodus account.[24] Here, the translator's normal translation practice has not been sufficiently considered (see guideline in §2). Whenever the translator interprets the Hebrew verb in the sense of

---

[20] See John W. Wevers, *Notes on the Greek Text of Deuteronomy*, SCS 39 (Atlanta: Scholars Press, 1995), 163.

[21] "Regarding the formula ארץ מצרים, the M and the G agree in seventeen occurrences (1:27; 5:6, 15; 6:12; 8:14; 10:19; 11:10; 13:6, 11; 15:15; 16:3b; 20:1; 24:22; 29:1, 15, 24; 34:11), and, for the shorter formula מצרים, they agree ten times (4:20, 34, 37; 6:22; 11:3; 16:1, 6; 23:5; 24:9; 26:8). Only twice (9:7; 16:3a) does the *Vorlage* of M feature the longer form against G's shorter form." See Carmel McCarthy, *Deuteronomy*, Biblia Hebraica Quinta 5 (Stuttgart: Deutsche Bibelgesellschaft, 2007), 52*–53*.

[22] McCarthy, *Deuteronomy*, 52*.

[23] See McCarthy for a description of the variants of this phrase in the ancient versions, which most likely speak to divergent Hebrew source texts, in McCarthy, *Deuteronomy*, 53*. Wevers appears to attribute this variant to the translator, while the LXX.D *Kommentar* does not specify. See Wevers, *Notes on the Greek Text of Deuteronomy*, 103, 124; den Hertog, Labahn, and Pola, "Deuteronomion," 552.

[24] See the discussion in Wevers, *Notes on the Greek Text of Deuteronomy*, 163–64.

moral corruption (five out of ten instances in Deuteronomy), he translates it using ἀνομέω (twice from the Piel form, three times from the Hiphil). The similar rendering in Exodus is probably, therefore, no more than a coincidence.[25]

Wevers also passes over a more significant similarity between these two Greek texts. The phrase τὸ τάχος ἐντεῦθεν is present in Greek Exodus but does not correspond to anything in the MT. Rather, the corresponding Hebrew phrase is found in MT Deuteronomy: מהר מזה. In his comments on the Exodus text, Wevers surmises that the Exodus translator's *Vorlage* must have read מהר מזה.[26] Though this judgment is not supported by any manuscript evidence, such an insertion from Deuteronomy into Exodus is characteristic of the type of assimilation performed in pre-Samaritan texts. As is well known, segments of reported speeches in Deuteronomy that have no equivalent in Exodus are inserted there to provide the necessary precedent.[27] In this particular case, Smr does not attest to this insertion in Exod 32:7, but the plus fits this pattern.

3.3. Deuteronomy 9:13 and Exodus 33:3, 5

Another possible occurrence of interdependence is found in the next verse, Deut 9:13, and the connection with Exodus may be operative on more than one level. The expression עם קשה ערף is rendered using λαὸς σκληροτράχηλος. As Wevers notes, it replicates a similar rendering found twice in Exodus 33 (33:3, 5), a passage that parallels the Deuteronomy account.[28] On the face of it, this is a clever rendering that communicates the meaning of the Hebrew idiom. It could very well be that the Exodus rendering influenced the Deuteronomy translator.[29] But the reverse might be true as well. Two other features of this verse deserve attention in relation to Greek Exodus:

---

[25] A similar case could be made for the verb ἐξάγω which is found in both accounts but matched to different Hebrew terms (עלה and יצא). However, a closer look at the usual equivalents in both Greek Exodus and Deuteronomy shows that this equivalence is regularly used in each book so that it becomes more probable that each translator achieved this outcome independently. Moreover, since the Deuteronomy translator is familiar with the verse's vocabulary, one would wonder why he would want to mimic Greek Exodus for one or two expressions while translating the rest differently according to his own practice.

[26] John W. Wevers, *Notes on the Greek Text of Exodus*, SCS 30 (Atlanta: Scholars Press, 1990), 521.

[27] Michael Segal argues that many of the pluses found in pre-Samaritan texts that are apparently taken from Deuteronomy and inserted into earlier books can be understood as attempts "to provide a 'source' for the…'quotations' in the final book of the Pentateuch" ("The Text of the Hebrew Bible in Light of the Dead Sea Scrolls," *Materia giudaica* 12, nos. 1–2 [2007]: 16–17). This feature of the pre-Samaritan tradition has been observed in several recent studies including those of Emanuel Tov, *Textual Criticism of the Hebrew Bible* (Philadelphia: Fortress Press, 2012), 80–82; Jonathan Ben-Dov, "Text Duplications between Higher and Lower Criticism: Num 20–21 and Deut 2–3," in *The Dead Sea Scrolls and the Samaritan Pentateuch*, ed. Michaël Langlois, CBET 94 (Leuven: Peeters, 2019), 217–42; Molly M. Zahn, *Rethinking Rewritten Scripture: Composition and Exegesis in the 4QReworked Pentateuch Manuscripts* (Leiden: Brill, 2011), 143–56.

[28] Wevers, *Notes on the Greek Text of Deuteronomy*, 164.

[29] Contra Peter Schwagmeier who appears to catalog this instance as an indication of dependency by Greek Exodus on Greek Deuteronomy ("Exodos/Exodus," in *Introduction to the Septuagint*, ed. Siegfried Kreuzer, trans. David A. Brenner and Peter Altman [Waco, TX: Baylor University Press, 2019], 101). In Deuteronomy, this rendering is encountered for the first time at 9:6 where it translates the same Hebrew idiom.

(1) Wevers argues that the plus highlighted in the following—stating that the Israelites were twice identified as stiff-necked—demonstrates that the Deuteronomy translator was aware of the Exodus 33 narrative. The plus does not involve direct borrowing, but it is rather a commentary on the Exodus passage where Israel is twice labeled as such.

| Deut 9:13 | ויאמר יהוה אלי לאמר ראיתי את העם הזה והנה עם קשה ערף הוא | καὶ εἶπεν κύριος πρός με Λελάληκα πρὸς σὲ ἅπαξ καὶ δὶς λέγων Ἑώρακα τὸν λαὸν τοῦτον, καὶ ἰδοὺ λαὸς σκληροτράχηλός ἐστιν· |

Wevers' reference to the Greek expression suggests that he sees the connection as happening at the level of the Greek text.[30] Yet, the nature of the reference is such that it cannot be used as an argument for dependency on Greek Exodus. The Deuteronomy translator could very well be referring to, and commenting on, the narrative in its Hebrew form. (2) There are in fact four instances of the expression identifying Israel as stiff-necked in the broader Exodus 32–34 narrative in its MT form, three if we posit that the translator consulted its Greek version (33:3, 5, 34:9).[31] Even if the expression ἅπαξ καὶ δίς is construed to imply several instances, it seems difficult to infer what exactly the Deuteronomy translator had in mind, should the plus be attributed to him. I categorize this example as unlikely since a borrowing from Greek Exodus is not necessary for such a connection to be made.

3.4. Deuteronomy 9:27 and Exodus 32:13

The next potential instance of intertextual influence is rather intriguing in that several factors complicate the picture. In 9:27, Moses recalls his plea to YHWH after witnessing Israel's unfaithfulness.

| Exod 32:13a | זכר לאברהם ליצחק ולישראל עבדיך אשר נשבעת להם בך | μνησθεὶς Ἀβραὰμ καὶ Ἰσαὰκ καὶ Ἰακὼβ τῶν σῶν οἰκετῶν, οἷς ὤμοσας κατὰ σεαυτοῦ |
| Deut 9:27a | זכר לעבדיך לאברהם ליצחק וליעקב | μνήσθητι Ἀβραὰμ καὶ Ἰσαὰκ καὶ Ἰακὼβ τῶν θεραπόντων σου, οἷς ὤμοσας κατὰ σεαυτοῦ· |

---

[30] Wevers, *Notes on the Greek Text of Deuteronomy*, 164. The phrase occurs a few times in the Septuagint corpus, but its presence in Deut 9:13 cannot be taken as a case of direct borrowing from these contexts (1 Rgns 17:39; 2 Esd 23:20; 1 Makk 3:30). See also McCarthy, *Deuteronomy*, 77*.

[31] The MT version of Deut 9:13 is found in MT Exod 32:9 in nearly identical form (the direct object is אל משה instead of אלי because of the context). However, Greek Exodus omits it entirely. In his discussion of this omission, Wevers sees no reason to attribute the omission to the translator's *Vorlage* since there is no evidence for a shorter parent text and "no palaeographic factors which would make such an omission accidental" (*Notes on the Greek Text of Exodus*, 523). He suggests it was intentionally omitted by the translator to "increase the dramatic effect of the narrative." Its omission from Greek Exodus nevertheless raises the possibility that MT might represent an expanded text in this case, not unlike the probable insertion of מהר מזה from Deut 9:12 to Exod 32:7 discussed in §3.2. For an argument along these lines, see Ben-Dov, "Text Duplications," 223–24.

The relative clause at the end of Deut 9:27a could represent an instance of borrowing from Greek Exodus.³² Greek Deuteronomy also appears to follow the word order found in the Exodus passage.³³ However, careful analysis reveals differences in lexical choice and verbal form. For example, עבד is rendered as οἰκέτης in Exodus, while the Deuteronomy translator employs this term in other contexts and prefers θεράπων here.³⁴ These translational variations strongly suggest that the differences with MT Deuteronomy in the first part of this passage are manifestations of a variant source text and are not cases in which borrowing from Greek Exodus has occurred. That the Deuteronomy translator would, in this context, borrow οἷς ὤμοσας κατὰ σεαυτοῦ from Greek Exodus while ignoring these differences is possible. Nevertheless, it seems more likely that his *Vorlage* was assimilated to the Exodus parallel prior to translation.³⁵ The Hebrew phrase is not found in this form elsewhere in Deuteronomy, but its components are part of a recurring Deuteronomic phrase ("which he/YHWH swore to") and its Greek rendering is consistent with what its translator would have done.³⁶

3.5. Deuteronomy 16:7 and Exodus 12:8–9

Another example frequently cited in this context is Deut 16:7. Its legislation is said to reconcile the command to roast (and prohibition to boil) the meat of the Passover sacrifice found in Exod 12:8–9 and the command to boil it in the MT of Deut 16:7.³⁷ The combination of "you will boil and roast" observed in Greek Deuteronomy would seem to lessen the difficulty.³⁸

| Exod 12:9 | אל תאכלו ממנו נא ובשל מבשל במים
כי אם צלי אש ראשו על כרעיו ועל קרבו | οὐκ ἔδεσθε ἀπ' αὐτῶν ὠμὸν οὐδὲ ἡψημένον ἐν ὕδατι, ἀλλ' ἢ ὀπτὰ πυρί, κεφαλὴν σὺν τοῖς ποσὶν καὶ τοῖς ἐνδοσθίοις. |

---

[32] As suggested in Dogniez and Harl, *Le Deutéronome*, 179; Tov, "Textual Harmonizations in the Ancient Texts of Deuteronomy," 22.
[33] Greek Exodus reflects a small difference (יעקב vs. ישראל) that is more in line with MT Deuteronomy, though the presence of יעקב in Smr of Exod 32:13 suggests that the Exodus translator simply had a different *Vorlage* here, one that was perhaps influenced by the Deuteronomy parallel.
[34] In Greek Deuteronomy, οἰκέτης is preferred (six of eight instances) to describe the Israelites' situation in Egypt (5:15; 6:21; 15:15; 16:12; 24:18; 24:22). In the 15:17 passage discussed in this chapter, it describes the slave who commits to his master for life, while 34:5 applies the term (rather exceptionally) to Moses as a servant of YHWH. Otherwise, θεράπων designates Moses in 3:24, the fathers in 9:27, and Pharaoh's attendants in 29:1 and 34:11.
[35] Verses 26 and 29 also attest to several variants between the LXX and the MT which have to do with the omission or addition of the phrases ἐκ γῆς Αἰγύπτου and ἐν τῇ ἰσχύι σου τῇ μεγάλῃ. Since these occur frequently in Deuteronomy and relate more closely to internal standardization, I will not discuss them here. See Wevers, *Notes on the Greek Text of Deuteronomy*, 172–74.
[36] McCarthy, *Deuteronomy*, 49*–50*. The phrase is omitted in A*, G, and οἱ λοιποί, "the others." See Wevers, *Notes on the Greek Text of Deuteronomy*, 173.
[37] Anneli Aejmelaeus, "Die Septuaginta des Deuteronomiums," in *On the Trail of the Septuagint Translators: Collected Essays*, CBET 50 (Leuven: Peeters, 2007), 157–80 (175).
[38] See the discussion in Wevers, *Notes on the Greek Text of Deuteronomy*, 269; McCarthy, *Deuteronomy*, 100*; den Hertog, Labahn, and Pola, "Deuteronomion," 568. Wevers suggests that this may reflect the way the Passover meal was prepared in the translator's context.

Deut 16:7	ובשלת ואכלת במקום אשר יבחר יהוה אלהיך בו	καὶ ἑψήσεις καὶ ὀπτήσεις
	ופנית בבקר והלכת לאהליך	καὶ φάγῃ ἐν τῷ τόπῳ, ᾧ ἂν ἐκλέξηται κύριος ὁ θεός σου αὐτόν, καὶ ἀποστραφήσῃ τὸ πρωὶ καὶ ἀπελεύσῃ εἰς τοὺς οἴκους σου.

The verb ἕψω is found in both passages, though employed in conflicting ways.[39] Exodus prohibits the eating of meat ἡψημένον ἐν ὕδατι, while Deuteronomy prescribes it (ἑψήσεις). If borrowing did occur, presumably the inspiration for the Deuteronomy plus of καὶ ὀπτήσεις is the qualifier ὀπτὰ πυρί found in Exod 12:8 and 9. This plus would then be an attempt to smooth out the tension and would demonstrate awareness of the Exodus prescription. It is not unlike a similar collocation in 2 Chr 35:13 ("to boil/cook by fire"), which is understood by many to be a way of connecting contradictory traditions by placing them side-by-side.[40] It is worth pondering, however, whether this connection required knowledge of Greek Exodus. The most obvious connection between the two passages in Greek is ὀπτὰ πυρί and ὀπτάω, but this is not a case of direct borrowing. The underlying צלי אש ("roasted by/in fire") in Exod 12:8-9 occurs only there in the Pentateuch, but the verb צלה ("to roast") is only found in a similar context in 1 Sam 2:15. Evidently, the Hebrew root was not unknown to the Exodus translator and probably the same was true of the Deuteronomy translator since the verb ὀπτάω is frequently used in Greek to denote the roasting of meat by fire. It constitutes a natural choice here and does not require knowledge of Greek Exodus.

Another possibility, of course, is that there was a conflation of variants. In the very next verse, we have what seems to be a double translation:

Deut 16:8a	ששת ימים תאכל מצות וביום השביעי עצרת	ἓξ ἡμέρας φάγῃ ἄζυμα, καὶ τῇ ἡμέρᾳ τῇ
	ליהוה אלהיך	ἑβδόμῃ ἐξόδιον, ἑορτὴ κυρίῳ τῷ θεῷ σου

In this passage, Smr has substituted חג for עצרת, likely under the influence of a similar phrase in Exod 13:6.[41] Wevers argues that LXX (i.e., the translator) combined both. Nevertheless, ἑορτή consistently renders חג in Greek Deuteronomy, which raises the possibility that the translator had both variants in his source text.[42] By analogy, it

---

[39] The similar rendering of the Hebrew בשל in both passages suggests that the translators were not aware of the possibility that בשל could perhaps be used in the more general sense of "cooking," thus not necessarily presenting a contradiction (as in 2 Chr 35:18). See the observations in S. R. Driver, *A Critical and Exegetical Commentary on Deuteronomy* (Edinburgh: T&T Clark, 1902), 193-94. Bernard M. Levinson argues that the Hebrew text of Deuteronomy is a conscious revision of the Exodus legislation (*Deuteronomy and the Hermeneutics of Legal Innovation* [Oxford: Oxford University Press, 1997], 73).

[40] See the discussion in Eckart Otto, *Deuteronomium 12-34. Erster Teilband: 12,1-23,15*, HThKAT (Freiburg: Herder, 2016), 1381; Eckart Otto, "Rechtshermeneutik in der Hebräischen Bibel: Die innerbiblischen Ursprünge halachischer Bibelauslegung," *ZABR* 5 (1999): 90-92.

[41] McCarthy, *Deuteronomy*, 100*.

[42] A similar observation could be made in Deut 32:19 where what seems to be a double translation actually renders two attested variants of a single verb.

is possible to envision that the Deuteronomy translator also had both verbs in his Hebrew text of v. 7: ובשלת ("and you will boil"), וצלית ("and you will roast").

I would categorize this instance as inconclusive. The plus could be present in the translator's Hebrew text or motivated by his knowledge of the Exodus prescription in its Hebrew form.

3.6. Deuteronomy 16:8 and Exodus 12:16

The next phrase in Deut 16:8 goes on to prescribe the type of activity that can take place on the seventh day of the festival. Greek Deuteronomy's rendering is longer than the MT counterpart, integrating an exception clause: "You shall do no work on it except that which shall be done for life" (NETS). The plus is almost identical to the parallel passage in Exod 12:16. Wevers argues that this represents another instance of harmonization achieved by borrowing from Greek Exodus.[43] Emanuel Tov also leans in this direction, especially since the Greek and Hebrew texts differ slightly in the Exodus passage. The term ποιηθήσεται in the phrase πλὴν ὅσα ποιηθήσεται πάσῃ ψυχῇ seems out of place as a rendering of יאכל.[44]

Exod 12:16b   כל מלאכה לא יעשה בהם אך אשר יאכל לכל   πᾶν ἔργον λατρευτὸν οὐ ποιηθήσεται ἐν
              נפש הוא לבדו יעשה לכם   αὐταῖς, πλὴν ὅσα ποιηθήσεται πάσῃ
                                                       ψυχῇ, τοῦτο μόνον ποιηθήσεται ὑμῖν.
Deut 16:8b   לא תעשה מלאכה   οὐ ποιήσεις ἐν αὐτῇ πᾶν ἔργον <u>πλὴν ὅσα
                                                       ποιηθήσεται ψυχῇ</u>.

Looking at Deut 16:8b, one notices that the prohibition in the first part of this phrase is similar to that of the one in Exodus, but its constituents are ordered differently in both Hebrew and Greek. One begins in the active voice and the other in the passive.[45] Moreover, MT Deut 16:8b only contains לא תעשה מלאכה, while the Greek text adds ἐν αὐτῇ πᾶν as well as the exception clause. It is worth noting, however, that other Hebrew witnesses attest to the reading found in the Greek text:

MT	Smr	4Q30 (4QDeut^c)	LXX
לא	לא	לא	οὐ
תעשה	תעשה	תעשה	ποιήσεις
		בו	ἐν αὐτῇ
	כל	כל	πᾶν
מלאכה	מלאכה	מלאכה	ἔργον
	עבדה		

---

[43] Wevers, *Notes on the Greek Text of Deuteronomy*, 269; Wevers, "The LXX Translator of Deuteronomy," 69. Wevers states that the translator borrowed the full πλὴν ὅσα ποιηθήσεται πάσῃ ψυχῇ, but in fact πάσῃ is omitted in Deut 16:8.

[44] Tov, "Textual Harmonizations in the Ancient Texts of Deuteronomy," 27 n. 22.

[45] The pronominal phrase is also in the singular instead of the plural to fit the context.

That Smr reflects influence from the Exodus passage can perhaps be inferred from the plus of עבדה.⁴⁶ This tendency is not limited to Smr since 4Q30 contains the exact wording of Greek Deuteronomy's presumed *Vorlage*, perhaps also exhibiting dependence on the MT version of Exod 12:16. This evidence could be taken to imply that the rest of the phrase probably existed in the Deuteronomy translator's *Vorlage* as well. In light of the extant Hebrew witnesses, there is no reason to think that the Deuteronomy translator consulted Greek Exodus for this phrase. In fact, the rendering in Greek Exodus is quite different, not only with respect to word order and voice, but also because it contains a plus relative to Deut 16:8b—namely, λατρευτόν.

Aejmalaeus vacillates between the two options, especially since the end of Exod 12:16 (τοῦτο μόνον ποιηθήσεται ὑμῖν = הוא לבדו יעשה לכם) is not incorporated into Deuteronomy, resulting in a Greek phrase that appears incomplete in comparison to its Hebrew counterpart. But since the Greek wording in Deuteronomy mimics the translation of Exodus, she suggests that there was probably no underlying Hebrew here and that the plus was borrowed from Greek Exodus.⁴⁷

Pluses such as this one are difficult to adjudicate. I tend to side with Eckart Otto here, who states that the variants attested in 4Q30 point to considerable assimilating activity at the level of the Hebrew text and probably in the translator's *Vorlage* as well.⁴⁸ Also a consideration is the fact that the plus is not identical to the Greek Exodus version as it omits the πᾶν (= כל), thus producing a different meaning.⁴⁹

3.7. Deuteronomy 21:14 / 24:7 and Exodus 21:8 / 12:16(17^LXX)

In Deut 24:7 and 21:14, the translator appears to render the Hithpael of עמר (a rare usage) with Greek terms that are also found in parallel passages from Exodus. The Deuteronomy and Exodus texts share a common theme: In Exodus 21:8, a husband/master cannot sell a slave woman to a foreigner, should she displease him. That would be dealing treacherously with her. The verb בגד ("to deal treacherously") is translated using a good Greek equivalent, ἀθετέω.⁵⁰

---

⁴⁶ Based on the witness of Smr in Deut 16:8, it seems reasonable to infer that the phrase כל מלאכת עבדה was probably in the *Vorlage* of the Exodus translator, who renders the expression by πᾶν ἔργον λατρευτόν.

⁴⁷ Aejmalaeus, "Die Septuaginta des Deuteronomiums," 174. She adds: "Die Übersetzer arbeitet hier als Schriftgelehrter und trägt Sorge dafür, dass die Bestimmungen über den Feiertag eindeutig sind und dass die eine Ausnahme vom Arbeitsverbot gelten darf. Für diese Lösung spricht auch, dass ψυχή an der Dtn-Stelle die Bedeutung 'für das Leben' zu haben scheint; לכל נפש heist in Ex 12:16 'für Jeden'. Die Bestimmung über das Passahlamm ist ein analoger Fall…dem Charakter des Dtn als 'Gesetzeswiederholung' entsprechend wird die Bestimmung in Einklang gebracht mit dem Gesetz in Ex. An den beiden letztgenannten Stellen geht es um Einzelheiten, die für die Praxis der Gemeinde wichtig waren. Der Blickwinkel des Übersetzers ist eindeutig religiös" ("Die Septuaginta des Deuteronomiums," 174–75).

⁴⁸ Otto, *Deuteronomium 12–34. Erster Teilband: 12,1–23,15*, 1681.

⁴⁹ Compare the NETS translation of each for reference.

⁵⁰ This is the only occurrence of the Hebrew verb in the Pentateuch, but its many occurrences in Isaiah and Jeremiah are frequently translated using ἀθετέω. Cf. Dogniez and Harl, *Le Deutéronome*, 245.

Exod 21:8	אם רעה בעיני אדניה אשר לא יעדה והפדה לעם נכרי לא ימשל למכרה בבגדו בה	ἐὰν μὴ εὐαρεστήσῃ τῷ κυρίῳ αὐτῆς ἣν αὑτῷ καθωμολογήσατο, ἀπολυτρώσει αὐτήν· ἔθνει δὲ ἀλλοτρίῳ οὐ κύριός ἐστιν πωλεῖν αὐτήν, ὅτι **ἠθέτησεν** ἐν αὐτῇ.
Deut 21:14	והיה אם לא חפצת בה ושלחתה לנפשה ומכר לא תמכרנה בכסף לא תתעמר בה תחת אשר עניתה	καὶ ἔσται ἐὰν μὴ θέλῃς αὐτήν, ἐξαποστελεῖς αὐτὴν ἐλευθέραν, καὶ πράσει οὐ πραθήσεται ἀργυρίου· οὐκ **ἀθετήσεις** αὐτήν, διότι ἐταπείνωσας αὐτήν.

A similar case is presented in Deut 21:14, here concerning a wife acquired as prisoner of war. If the husband is not pleased with her, he may not sell her. The Hebrew text then has the Hithpael of עמר, with the probable sense of (not) "trading (in commerce)."[51] Anneli Aejmelaeus suggests that the Deuteronomy translator was not familiar with this verb, looked to Greek Exodus for help, and borrowed the term ἀθετέω.[52] This scenario is similar to that of the slave law of Deut 15:17 discussed in the introduction. The term ἀθετέω is only found here in Greek Deuteronomy, so that the rendering is difficult to evaluate from the perspective of translation technique. But this scenario seems plausible as it meets the requirements stated at the outset: ἀθετέω seems a better match to the Hebrew term and context found in the Exodus parallel (see guideline #3).

The second (and only other) occurrence of the Hithpael of עמר is found in Deut 24:7. Here the law deals with kidnapping and the verb describes what the kidnapper may attempt to do with the victim (e.g., to trade the kidnapped person).

Exod 21:16(17^LXX)	וגנב איש ומכרו ונמצא בידו מות יומת	Ὃς ἂν κλέψῃ τίς τινα τῶν υἱῶν Ἰσραήλ, καὶ **καταδυναστεύσας** αὐτὸν ἀποδῶται, καὶ εὑρεθῇ ἐν αὐτῷ, θανάτῳ τελευτάτω.
Deut 24:7	כי ימצא איש גנב נפש מאחיו מבני ישראל והתעמר בו ומכרו ומת הגנב ההוא ובערת הרע מקרבך	Ἐὰν δὲ ἁλῷ ἄνθρωπος κλέπτων ψυχὴν ἐκ τῶν ἀδελφῶν αὐτοῦ τῶν υἱῶν Ἰσραήλ, καὶ **καταδυναστεύσας** αὐτὸν ἀποδῶται, ἀποθανεῖται ὁ κλέπτης ἐκεῖνος· καὶ ἐξαρεῖς τὸν πονηρὸν ἐξ ὑμῶν αὐτῶν.

Here also, the Greek verb is the same as the one found in the parallel Exodus law. One complicating factor is the absence of the words מבני ישראל והתעמר בו in the MT of Exod 21:16. This material is found only in its Greek version. Wevers and Aejmelaeus both posit that the phrase must have been present in the Exodus source

---

[51] It may be etymologically related to the Ugaritic ġmr(m). See *HALOT*, s.v. "עמר."

[52] Aejmelaeus, "Die Septuaginta des Deuteronomiums," 160. As McCarthy remarks, the passage was difficult for translators, as is attested by the Vulgate (*Deuteronomy*, 110*–11*). The Peshitta and Targumim apparently recognize its meaning, however, interpreting it as "trading." Wevers observes that the Vulgate may have based its translation on the LXX in this instance (*Notes on the Greek Text of Deuteronomy*, 341).

text.⁵³ This seems to be a reasonable assumption based on what has been observed so far.⁵⁴ Since the *Vorlage* of both translations would have been the same, it is difficult to assess the direction of borrowing. However, in light of the previous instance of borrowing for the same verb, it seems probable that καταδυναστεύω was borrowed from Greek Exodus as was the case with ἀθετέω in Deut 21:14.⁵⁵

Cases such as this align with Aejmelaeus' observation that the Deuteronomy translator's use of previous Greek translations is often motivated by difficulties in his source text.⁵⁶ This becomes an important factor when considering whether a particular instance of interdependence should be attributed to the translator.

3.8. The Decalogue (Deuteronomy 5 and Exodus 20)

I now turn to the Decalogue where several such instances of borrowing from Greek Exodus have been reported. These have been saved for last since the textual situation in these verses is particularly complex and extensive assimilation is attested in both directions. The first point that needs to be made is that achieving identical wording in both Greek texts (as it is often the case in MT) was clearly not an objective of the Deuteronomy translator.⁵⁷ This can be demonstrated from the first of the ten words. As Aejmelaeus points out, the texts of Exod 20:3 and Deut 5:7 are identical in their MT form. However, they are translated differently in Greek Exodus and Deuteronomy:⁵⁸

Exod 20:3 MT Deut 5:7 MT	לא יהיה לך אלהים אחרים על פני
Exod 20:3 LXX	οὐκ ἔσονταί σοι θεοὶ ἕτεροι πλὴν ἐμοῦ.
Deut 5:7 LXX	οὐκ ἔσονταί σοι θεοὶ ἕτεροι πρὸ προσώπου μου.

Though the translators resort to different strategies in keeping with their general approaches to rendering their books, it seems reasonable to posit that the Exodus and Deuteronomy renderings stem from the same Hebrew *Vorlage*.⁵⁹

---

53 Its presence in the Greek Exodus *Vorlage* may have been part of an effort to harmonize both laws. See Wevers, *Notes on the Greek Text of Exodus*, 330–31; Aejmelaeus, "Die Septuaginta des Deuteronomiums," 160.
54 Note, however, that den Hertog, Labahn, and Pola posit that the phrase in LXX Exod 21:17 did not have a Hebrew equivalent and was inserted from Greek Deuteronomy ("Deuteronomion," 580).
55 See the similar conclusion in Otto, *Deuteronomium 12–34. Erster Teilband: 12,1–23,15*, 1280.
56 This may not be the only motivation since the translator may also refer to these as sources for his interpretations, but it appears to be an important one. Aejmelaeus says, "Theoretisch wäre es möglich, dass die fünf Übersetzer sich gleichzeitig an die Arbeit gemacht haben. In Wirklichkeit aber war es anders. Der Übersetzer von Dtn scheint die anderen Bücher schon in griechischer Form zu kennen und benutzt sie als Hilfe an schwierigen Stellen, aber auch als Quelle seiner Interpretationnen und nimmt gelegentlich Bezug auf relevante Stellen." In the context of the Decalogue, she adds: "Der Übersetzer nimmt zwar nicht überall Bezug auf andere Schriftstellen...aber bei schwierigen Stellen sucht er Hilfe von Parallelstellen" ("Die Septuaginta des Deuteronomiums," 160–61).
57 See the comments to this effect in Innocent Himbaza, *Le Décalogue et l'histoire du texte: Études des formes textuelles du Décalogue et leurs implications dans l'histoire du texte de l'Ancien Testament*, OBO 207 (Göttingen: Vandenhoeck & Ruprecht, 2004), 181–83.
58 Aejmelaeus, "Die Septuaginta des Deuteronomiums," 161.
59 See Alain Le Boulluec and Pierre Sandevoir, *L'Exode*, La Bible d'Alexandrie 2 (Paris: Cerf, 1989), 205. There are no attested variants for this verse except for 1Q13 (1QPhyl), which begins with כי לא.

8 From Exodus to Deuteronomy?

Three verses later, in Deut 5:10, we find the affirmation that YHWH's mercy extends to a thousand generations of those who keep his commands (מצותו).[60] According to Wevers, the translator employs πρόσταγμα instead of the usual ἐντολή to render מצוה, mirroring Greek Exodus. This is the only instance of πρόσταγμα as equivalent of מצוה out of 39 instances in Deuteronomy and it happens to match the Exodus rendering. It would represent another indication that the Deuteronomy translator borrowed from Greek Exodus.[61]

Exod 20:6	ועשה חסד לאלפים לאהבי ולשמרי מצותי	καὶ ποιῶν ἔλεος εἰς χιλιάδας τοῖς ἀγαπῶσίν με καὶ τοῖς φυλάσσουσιν τὰ προστάγματά μου.
Deut 5:10	ועשה חסד לאלפים לאהבי ולשמרי מצותו	καὶ ποιῶν ἔλεος εἰς χιλιάδας τοῖς ἀγαπῶσίν με καὶ τοῖς φυλάσσουσιν τὰ προστάγματά μου.

While this is a valid point from the perspective of translation technique, a similar observation can be made concerning Greek Exodus. There, πρόσταγμα also renders מצוה in the Decalogue, but ἐντολή is employed for the remaining three instances of מצוה. The Greek πρόσταγμα is also found elsewhere in both books, usually as the equivalent of Hebrew חק.[62] The use of πρόσταγμα is therefore unusual in both contexts, undermining our ability to determine which translator might have borrowed from the other. The word πρόσταγμα has a specific nuance in the Hellenistic period, designating a royal ordinance, the will of the king.[63] In some contexts, it also refers to divine ordinances or oracles revealed in a dream. The former is an apt rendering in this context, and it seems a strange coincidence that both translators would have arrived at this rendering independently.[64] Nevertheless, it is difficult to establish dependency one way or another based on this one feature.

The last possible occurrence examined in this study is found the final verse of the Decalogue.[65] Wevers argues that the text of Greek Deuteronomy has been borrowed

---

[60] The first-person pronoun μου represents the Qere in the MT, but the pronoun is also attested in Smr and 4Q41 (4QDeut^n).
[61] Wevers, *Notes on the Greek Text of Deuteronomy*, 101; Larry Perkins, "Deuteronomy," in *The T&T Clark Companion to the Septuagint*, ed. James K. Aitken (London: Bloomsbury, 2015), 73.
[62] Of 21 instances of חק in Deuteronomy, two are rendered by πρόσταγμα (11:32; 12:1). The use of πρόσταγμα in these two contexts could be explained by the fact that these verses act as a bridge between the paraenetic section that precedes and the legal material that follows.
[63] Joachim Schaper, "Exodos," in vol. 1 of *Septuaginta Deutsch: Erläuterungen und Kommentare zum griechischen Alten Testament. Genesis bis Makkabäer*, ed. Wolfgang Kraus and Martin Karrer (Stuttgart: Deutsche Bibelgesellschaft, 2011), 300.
[64] In effect, πρόσταγμα qualifies this legal material. In Ptolemaic Egypt, the προστάγματα are royal decrees constituting the will of the king-legislator. For an extended discussion on this topic, see Joseph Mélèze Modrzejewski, "Tora et *nomos*: comment la Tora est devenue une 'loi civique' pour les Juifs d'Égypte," in *Un peuple de philosophes. Aux origines de la condition juive* (Paris: Fayard, 2011), 197; Anna Passoni Dell'Acqua, "La terminologia dei reati nei προστάγματα dei Tolemei e nella versione dei LXX," in vol. 2 of *Proceedings of the XVIII International Congress of Papyrology: Athens, 25–31 May 1986*, ed. Vasileios G. Mandēlaras (Athens: Greek Papyrological Society, 1988), 335–50; Hélène Cadell, "Vocabulaire de la législation ptolémaïque: problème du sens de *dikaioma* dans le Pentateuque," in *Kata tous O' "Selon les Septante": Trente études sur la Bible grecque des Septante*, ed. Gilles Dorival and Olivier Munnich (Paris: Cerf, 1995), 208–209.
[65] Smr includes an additional command.

from Greek Exodus, yet does not specify what exactly he has in mind.⁶⁶ He goes on to state in his *Notes* on Exodus and Deuteronomy that the Greek rendering of Exod 20:17 is on the whole much closer to MT Deut 5:21.⁶⁷ Differences between the Greek texts and their respective MT equivalents are underlined here and would, on the whole, support this assertion:

Exod 20:17	לא תחמד בית רעך לא תחמד אשת רעך ועבדו ואמתו ושורו וחמרו וכל אשר לרעך	οὐκ ἐπιθυμήσεις τὴν <u>γυναῖκα</u> τοῦ πλησίον σου. οὐκ **ἐπιθυμήσεις** τὴν <u>οἰκίαν</u> τοῦ πλησίον σου <u>οὔτε τὸν ἀγρὸν αὐτοῦ</u> οὔτε τὸν παῖδα αὐτοῦ οὔτε τὴν παιδίσκην αὐτοῦ οὔτε τοῦ βοὸς αὐτοῦ οὔτε τοῦ ὑποζυγίου αὐτοῦ οὔτε παντὸς κτήνους αὐτοῦ οὔτε ὅσα τῷ πλησίον σού ἐστιν.
Deut 5:21	ולא תחמד אשת רעך ולא תתאוה בית רעך שדהו ועבדו ואמתו שורו וחמרו וכל אשר לרעך	οὐκ ἐπιθυμήσεις τὴν γυναῖκα τοῦ πλησίον σου. οὐκ **ἐπιθυμήσεις** τὴν οἰκίαν τοῦ πλησίον σου οὔτε τὸν ἀγρὸν αὐτοῦ οὔτε τὸν παῖδα αὐτοῦ οὔτε τὴν παιδίσκην αὐτοῦ οὔτε τοῦ βοὸς αὐτοῦ οὔτε τοῦ ὑποζυγίου αὐτοῦ οὔτε παντὸς κτήνους αὐτοῦ οὔτε ὅσα τῷ πλησίον σού ἐστιν.

The textual situation is complex, so I will limit myself to two features that are more immediately relevant to the inquiry at hand:

1. The first is the rendering of ἐπιθυμήσεις for MT's תתאוה in the second prohibition (highlighted). The use of this verb constitutes one of the differences between MT Deuteronomy and MT Exodus since the latter has תחמד in this position. The repetition of ἐπιθυμήσεις in Greek Deuteronomy could signal borrowing from Greek Exodus. But it could also be a matter of translation technique since both Hebrew terms are synonymous. The three occurrences of the Hebrew verbal root אוה in Deuteronomy are all rendered using ἐπιθυμέω.⁶⁸ On this basis alone, I would have to label this case as inconclusive. But when one considers the Hebrew witnesses for this verse, both Smr and 4Q41 (4QDeutⁿ) employ תחמד for the second prohibition.⁶⁹ It is also possible, then, that Greek Deuteronomy's *Vorlage* contained תחמד. In the end, it is nearly

---

⁶⁶ Wevers, "The LXX Translator of Deuteronomy," 68. I will not discuss the apparent omission of conjunctions in this context.

⁶⁷ Wevers, *Notes on the Greek Text of Exodus*, 314; Wevers, *Notes on the Greek Text of Deuteronomy*, 104.

⁶⁸ The other two occurrences of אוה are found in 12:20 and 14:26. In these two places, the verb is found in the Piel form, whereas the Hithpael is attested in the Decalogue (5:21). In the context of the Decalogue, Le Boulluec and Sandevoir argue that ἐπιθυμήσεις is perhaps the better match for תתאוה (*L'Exode*, 210–11).

⁶⁹ As McCarthy points out, "Smr has assimilated the whole verse to Exod 20:17, whereas it is only this verb (תתאוה) that 4QDeutⁿ, 4QPhylʲ, and XQPhyl³ have assimilated." However, the Nash Papyrus follows Deuteronomy in reproducing תתאוה. See McCarthy, *Deuteronomy*, 69*.

impossible to decide between these two options.⁷⁰ For the purposes of this study, however, this rendering offers no basis for positing a borrowing from Greek Exodus.

2. The list of people, animals, and possessions that make up most of the verse contains a plus in relation to MT, that of the cattle (οὔτε παντὸς κτήνους αὐτοῦ). Since the plus is not found in the MT of either Exod 20:17 or Deut 5:21 (or any other Hebrew witnesses), it is impossible for us to infer borrowing from one or the other. The plus is reminiscent of the similar list found in Deut 5:14, the Sabbath commandment, where the list of animals ends similarly (ובהמתך = καὶ πᾶν κτῆνός σου). That the plus in 5:21 was inspired by this phrase is likely. Nevertheless, since ובהמתך is attested in both the MT and Greek version of Deut 5:14, as well as the MT and Greek version of the Exodus parallel, it remains unhelpful for this inquiry.

Should interdependency be posited between Greek Exodus and Greek Deuteronomy, the ordering of this list rather points in the opposite direction.⁷¹ It might be counted as a significant piece of counterevidence against the thesis pursued here, but the situation is more complex as Innocent Himbaza shows in his major study of these texts.⁷² Examples of potential borrowing in both directions abound. More to the point, Tov's study of the Nash Papyrus presents a synopsis of all extant Hebrew and Greek witnesses of the Decalogue (including MT, LXX, and the Nash Papyrus).⁷³ What immediately strikes the eye is that, for each Greek variant, a Hebrew equivalent can be found in one or more witnesses. The sole exception is the phrase οὔτε παντὸς κτήνους αὐτοῦ just discussed in the context of 5:21. It may instead represent a case of borrowing within the same book. The textual landscape of the Decalogue makes it difficult to argue for a translator borrowing from the Greek text of the other book. A more likely explanation is that provided by Himbaza: since the *Vorlagen* of both Greek Exodus and Greek Deuteronomy show many affinities with other harmonizing texts, the assimilating activity probably took place at that level.⁷⁴

---

⁷⁰ See Himbaza, *Le Décalogue et l'histoire du texte*, 156.
⁷¹ As frequently suggested in Le Boulluec and Sandevoir, *L'Exode*.
⁷² See n. 57. Indeed, the textual history of the Decalogue presents significant issues that would deserve a more extensive discussion than has been possible for the few examples dealt with here.
⁷³ Emanuel Tov, "The Papyrus Nash and the Septuagint," in *A Necessary Task: Essays on Textual Criticism of the Old Testament in Memory of Stephen Pisano*, ed. Dionisio Candido and Leonardo Pessoa de Silva Pinto, AnBibSt 14 (Rome: G & B Press, 2020), 33–50.
⁷⁴ Himbaza, *Le Décalogue et l'histoire du texte*, 164–65, 232–34. See also Tov, "The Papyrus Nash and the Septuagint," 39. Another possible explanation is that portions of these books—particularly those that might have been in use in a liturgical setting—were already translated into Greek and incorporated into the translation of Greek Deuteronomy when the entirety of the book was done. See Cornelius G. den Hertog, "Joden, christenen en hun Schrift: een bundel opstellen aangeboden bij het afscheid van C. J. den Heyer," available online at https://ub16.uni-tuebingen.de/Record/1624325130/; den Hertog, Labahn, and Pola, "Deuteronomion," 530. However, the grounds for positing a different translator for these portions (the Decalogue, the *Shema*) are not as solid as appear at first glance. See Tov, "The Papyrus Nash and the Septuagint," 33, 45–46; Aejmelaeus, "Die Septuaginta des Deuteronomiums," 179.

4. Conclusion

The evidence adduced for the claim that the Deuteronomy translator knew the Greek version of other Pentateuchal books (here Exodus) is not as unambiguous as is sometimes claimed. Nevertheless, there are some indications of possible borrowing from Greek Exodus. I have summarized in Table 8.1 the conclusions drawn from each instance surveyed so far.

Table 8.1

	Inconclusive	Unlikely	Possible	Probable
Deut 7:22b // Exod 23:29			×	
Deut 9:12 // Exod 32:7		×		
Deut 9:13 // Exod 33:3, 5		×		
Deut 9:27 // Exod 32:13		×		
Deut 15:17 // Exod 21:6				×
Deut 16:7 // Exod 12:8–9	×			
Deut 16:8 // Exod 12:16		×		
Deut 21:14 // Exod 21:8				×
Deut 24:7 // Exod 12:16(17^{LXX})				×
Deut 5:10 // Exod 20:6	×			
Deut 5:21 // Exod 20:17	×			

The most probable instances are those in which the borrowing is restricted to small changes, principally at the level of the word. These are triggered by a difficulty (usually linguistic in nature) and are not the result of harmonization of speeches or laws. In fact, the latter does not appear to be a significant concern when looking at the whole. This needs to be taken into consideration in evaluating individual possibilities.

The fact that most of the suggested cases of possible borrowing stem from the same cluster of texts is also telling. As known from other sources, there was considerable copying and editorial activity during the Second Temple period focusing on specific sections such as the Decalogue and Mosaic speeches. This situation complicates the type of investigation conducted in this study. Since the Deuteronomy translator highly valued the quantitative reproduction of his source text (the Deut 5:7 passage being an example)—sometimes resorting to creative solutions to satisfy this norm—I tend to view large-scale additions (clauses or more) as something that most probably stems from his *Vorlage*. This is especially true when their character is such that they reflect the translator's usual translation practice.[75] The instance that I have labeled as a possibility is one concerning which there is less certainty with respect to translation technique. Others might disagree since it

---

[75] In other words, when the Greek represents a style that is calqued on the Hebrew source. See the comments to this effect in Anneli Aejmelaeus, "What Can We Know about the Hebrew *Vorlage* of the Septuagint?" in *On the Trail of the Septuagint Translators: Collected Essays*, CBET 50 (Leuven: Peeters, 2007), 81.

is also possible that the translator contributed more extensively to such editorial activities. But in the "hot spots" just mentioned, I suggest that prudence is the best course of action.

So where does this leave us with Lee's thesis concerning collaboration and simultaneous translation projects? The simultaneity of the translation projects seems ruled out, but the existence of a glossary is still possible. However, the cases of probable borrowing discussed suggest that, for the terms and passages in question, no glossary was necessary. Knowledge of the existence of a parallel passage (a speech or a law), and the ability to consult it in its Greek version, would have been sufficient. Though Tov deals with editing at the level of the Hebrew text, his conclusion to his study on harmonization is relevant in this context: "The person(s) who added the harmonizing additions in the various sources was (were) very well acquainted with the context, as well as with parallel descriptions in other chapters…he was (they were) also well aware of the parallels between Deuteronomy and the preceding books."[76] Thus, however we imagine the mechanics of such borrowings, these findings suggest that, as with the scribes described by Tov, the Deuteronomy translator was quite familiar with the contents of the Pentateuch. Moreover, he employed a *Vorlage* that was already assimilated in several places to its Exodus counterpart.[77] The present paper has not exhausted all possible instances of this phenomenon, but more research into potential borrowing between pentateuchal translations will undoubtedly refine our understanding of their relationship and the related textual developments.

Bibliography

Aejmelaeus, Anneli. "The Septuagint and Oral Translation." Pages 8–12 in *XIV Congress of the IOSCS, Helsinki 2010*. Edited by Melvin K. H. Peters. SCS 59. Atlanta: Society of Biblical Literature, 2013.

Aejmelaeus, Anneli. "Die Septuaginta des Deuteronomiums." Pages 157–80 in *On the Trail of the Septuagint Translators: Collected Essays*. CBET 50. Leuven: Peeters, 2007.

Aejmelaeus, Anneli. "What Can We Know about the Hebrew *Vorlage* of the Septuagint?" Pages 71–106 in *On the Trail of the Septuagint Translators: Collected Essays*. CBET 50. Leuven: Peeters, 2007.

Barr, James. "Did the Greek Pentateuch Really Serve as a Dictionary for the Translation of the Later Books?" Pages 523–43 in *Hamlet on a Hill: Semitic and Greek Studies Presented to Professor T. Muraoka on the Occasion of His Sixty-Fifth Birthday*. Edited by Martin F. J. Baasten and Wido Th. Van Peursen. Leuven: Peeters, 2003.

Baumgärtel, Friedrich. "Zur Entstehung der Pentateuchseptuaginta." Pages 53–62 in *Beiträge zur Entstehungsgeschichte der Septuaginta*. Edited by Johannes Herrmann and Friedrich Baumgärtel. BWAT NF 5. Stuttgart: Kohlhammer, 1923.

---

[76] Tov, "Textual Harmonizations in the Ancient Texts of Deuteronomy," 28.

[77] Though this is a very interesting question, I am not concerned here with the precise means of access to Greek Exodus, whether it should be attributed to memory or easy access to a manuscript. For a discussion of this issue, see Theocharous, *Lexical Dependence and Intertextual Allusion in the Septuagint of the Twelve Prophets*, 8.

Ben-Dov, Jonathan. "Text Duplications between Higher and Lower Criticism: Num 20–21 and Deut 2–3." Pages 217–42 in *The Dead Sea Scrolls and the Samaritan Pentateuch*. Edited by Michaël Langlois. CBET 94. Leuven: Peeters, 2019.

Boulluec, Alain Le, and Pierre Sandevoir. *L'Exode*. La Bible d'Alexandrie 2. Paris: Cerf. 1989.

Cadell, Hélène. "Vocabulaire de la législation ptolémaïque: problème du sens de *dikaioma* dans le Pentateuque." Pages 207–21 in *Kata tous O' "Selon les Septante": Trente études sur la Bible grecque des Septante*. Edited by Gilles Dorival and Olivier Munnich. Paris: Cerf, 1995.

Dell'Acqua, Anna Passoni. "La terminologia dei reati nei προστάγματα dei Tolemei e nella versione dei LXX." Pages 335–50 in Vol. 2 of *Proceedings of the XVIII International Congress of Papyrology: Athens. 25–31 May 1986*. Edited by Vasileios G. Mandēlaras. Athens: Greek Papyrological Society, 1988.

den Hertog, Cornelius G., Michael Labahn, and Thomas Pola. "Deuteronomion." Pages 523–601 in Vol. 1 of *Septuaginta Deutsch: Erläuterungen und Kommentare zum griechischen Alten Testament. Genesis bis Makkabäer*. Edited by Wolfgang Kraus and Martin Karrer. Stuttgart: Deutsche Bibelgesellschaft, 2011.

den Hertog, Cornelius G. "Erwägungen zur relativen Chronologie der Bücher Levitikus und Deuteronomium innerhalb der Pentateuchübersetzung." Pages 216–28 in *Im Brennpunkt: die Septuaginta. Band 2: Studien zur Entstehung und Bedeutung der griechischen Bibel*. Edited by Siegfried Kreuzer und Jürgen Peter Lesch. BWANT 161. Stuttgart: Kohlhammer, 2004.

den Hertog, Cornelius G. "Joden, christenen en hun Schrift: een bundel opstellen aangeboden bij het afscheid van C. J. den Heyer." See https://ub16.uni-tuebingen.de/Record/1624325130/.

Dines, Jennifer. "The Twelve Among the Prophets." Presented as the Grinfield Lecture on the Septuagint, Oxford. March 1, 2007.

Dogniez, Cécile. "L'intertextualité dans la LXX de Zacharie 9–14." Pages 81–96 in *Interpreting Translation: Studies on the LXX and Ezekiel in Honour of Johan Lust*. Edited by Florentino García Martínez and Marc Vervenne. BETL 192. Leuven: Peeters, 2005.

Dogniez, Cécile., and Marguerite Harl. *Le Deutéronome*. La Bible d'Alexandrie 5. Paris: Cerf, 1992.

Dorival, Gilles. "Les phénomènes d'intertextualité dans le livre grec des Nombres." Pages 253–85 in *Kata tous O' "Selon les Septante": Trente études sur la Bible grecque des Septante*. Edited by Gilles Dorival and Olivier Munnich. Paris: Cerf, 1995.

Driver, S. R. *A Critical and Exegetical Commentary on Deuteronomy*. Edinburgh: T&T Clark. 1902.

Frankel, Zacharias. *Ueber den Einfluss der palästinschen Exegese auf die alexandrinische Hermeneutik*. Leipzig: Barth, 1851.

Himbaza, Innocent. *Le Décalogue et l'histoire du texte: Études des formes textuelles du Décalogue et leurs implications dans l'histoire du texte de l'Ancien Testament*. OBO 207. Göttingen: Vandenhoeck & Ruprecht, 2004.

Kim, Hayeon. *Multiple Authorship of the Septuagint Pentateuch: The Original Translators of the Pentateuch, Multiple Authorship of the Septuagint Pentateuch*. STHB 4. Leiden: Brill, 2020.

Lee, John A. L. *The Greek of the Pentateuch: Grinfield Lectures on the Septuagint 2011–2012*. Oxford: Oxford University Press, 2018.

Levinson, Bernard M. *Deuteronomy and the Hermeneutics of Legal Innovation.* Oxford: Oxford University Press, 1997.

Maurais, Jean. "The Quest for LXX Deuteronomy's Translator: On the Use of Translation Technique in Ascertaining the Translator's *Vorlage.*" Pages 186–203 in *Die Septuaginta—Themen, Manuskripte, Wirkungen: 7. Internationale Fachtagung veranstaltet von Septuaginta Deutsch (LXX.D). Wuppertal 19.–22. Juli 2018.* Edited by Eberhard Bons et al. WUNT 444. Tübingen: Mohr Siebeck, 2020.

McCarthy, Carmel. *Deuteronomy.* Biblia Hebraica Quinta 5. Stuttgart: Deutsche Bibelgesellschaft, 2007.

Modrzejewski, Joseph Mélèze. "Tora et *nomos*: comment la Tora est devenue une 'loi civique' pour les Juifs d'Égypte." Pages 193–216 in *Un peuple de philosophes. Aux origines de la condition juive.* Paris: Fayard, 2011.

Otto, Eckart. "Rechtshermeneutik in der Hebräischen Bibel: Die innerbiblischen Ursprünge halachischer Bibelauslegung." *ZABR* 5 (1999): 75–98.

Otto, Eckart. *Deuteronomium 12–34. Erster Teilband: 12,1–23,15.* HThKAT. Freiburg: Herder. 2016.

Perkins, Larry. "Greek Exodus and Greek Isaiah: Detection and Implications of Interdependence in Translation." *BIOSCS* 42 (2009): 18–33.

Peters, Melvin K. H. "To the Reader of Deuteronomion." Pages 141–46 in *A New English Translation of the Septuagint.* Edited by Albert Pietersma and Benjamin G. Wright. Oxford: Oxford University Press, 2009.

Rösel, Martin. "Von der Tora zum Nomos—Perspektiven der Forschung am griechischen Pentateuch." Pages 97–106 in *Einleitung in die Septuaginta.* Edited by Siegfried Kreuzer. LXX.H 1. Gütersloh: Gütersloher Verlagshaus, 2016.

Rösel, Martin. *Übersetzung als Vollendung der Auslegung: Studien zur Genesis-Septuaginta.* BZAW 223. Berlin: de Gruyter, 1994.

Schaper, Joachim. "Exodos." Pages 258–324 in Vol. 1 of *Septuaginta Deutsch: Erläuterungen und Kommentare zum griechischen Alten Testament. Genesis bis Makkabäer.* Edited by Wolfgang Kraus and Martin Karrer. Stuttgart: Deutsche Bibelgesellschaft, 2011.

Schwagmeier, Peter. "Exodos/Exodus." Pages 89–105 in *Introduction to the Septuagint.* Edited by Siegfried Kreuzer. Translated by David A. Brenner and Peter Altman. Waco, TX: Baylor University Press, 2019.

Segal, Michael. "The Text of the Hebrew Bible in Light of the Dead Sea Scrolls." *Materia giudaica* 12.1–2 (2007): 5–20.

Theocharous, Myrto. *Lexical Dependence and Intertextual Allusion in the Septuagint of the Twelve Prophets: Studies in Hosea, Amos and Micah.* LHBOTS 570. London: Bloomsbury T&T Clark, 2012.

Tov, Emanuel. "From Popular Jewish LXX-SP Texts to Separate Sectarian Texts: Insights from the Dead Sea Scrolls." Pages 19–40 in *The Samaritan Pentateuch and the Dead Sea Scrolls.* Edited by Michaël Langlois. CBET 94. Leuven: Peeters, 2019.

Tov, Emanuel. "Textual Harmonizations in the Ancient Texts of Deuteronomy." Pages 15–28 in *Mishneh Toda: Studies in Deuteronomy and Its Cultural Environment in Honor of Jeffrey H. Tigay.* Edited by Nili S. Fox, David A. Glatt-Gilad, and Michael J. Williams. Winona Lake, IN: Eisenbrauns, 2009.

Tov, Emanuel. "The Papyrus Nash and the Septuagint." Pages 33–50 in *A Necessary Task: Essays on Textual Criticism of the Old Testament in Memory of Stephen Pisano.* Edited by Dionisio Candido and Leonardo Pessoa de Silva Pinto. AnBibSt 14. Rome: G & B Press, 2020.

Tov, Emanuel. "The Septuagint Translation of Genesis as the First Scripture Translation." Pages 47–64 in *In the Footsteps of Sherlock Holmes: Studies in the Biblical Text in Honour of Anneli Aejmelaeus*. Edited by Kristin De Troyer, T. Michael Law, and Marketta Liljeström. CBET 72. Leuven: Peeters, 2014.

Tov, Emanuel. "The Shared Tradition of the Septuagint and the Samaritan Pentateuch." Pages 357–72 in Vol. 4 of *Textual Developments: Collected Essays*. VTSup 181. Leiden: Brill, 2019.

Tov, Emanuel. *Textual Criticism of the Hebrew Bible*. Philadelphia: Fortress Press, 2012.

van der Louw, Theo A. W. "The Unity of LXX Genesis and Exodus." *VT* 70, no. 2 (2020): 270–84.

Wevers, John W. "The LXX Translator of Deuteronomy." Pages 57–89 in *IX Congress of the International Organization for Septuagint and Cognate Studies*. Edited by Bernard A. Taylor. SCS 45. Atlanta: Scholars Press, 1997.

Wevers, John W. *Notes on the Greek Text of Deuteronomy*. SCS 39. Atlanta: Scholars Press, 1995.

Wevers, John W. *Notes on the Greek Text of Exodus*. SCS 30. Atlanta: Scholars Press, 1990.

Yardney, Sarah. "The Use of Glossaries by the Translators of the Septuagint." *Textus* 28 (2019): 157–77.

Zahn, Molly M. *Rethinking Rewritten Scripture: Composition and Exegesis in the 4QReworked Pentateuch Manuscripts*. Leiden: Brill, 2011.

Ziemer, Benjamin. "A Stemma for Deuteronomy." Pages 127–97 in *The Dead Sea Scrolls and the Samaritan Pentateuch*. Edited by Michaël Langlois. CBET 94. Leuven: Peeters, 2019.

Chapter 9

The Sojourner in Exodus and Beyond: Theological Conceptualization of *Gēr* in the Old Testament*

Don Dongshin Chang

1. Introduction

The term *gēr* has been supposed to have a trajectory of development in its meaning(s) in the Old Testament/Hebrew Bible from resident alien to convert to Judaism.[1] Since P. Benzinger analyzed the term *gēr* under the separate divisions of the Book of the Covenant (Exod 20:22–23:33), Deuteronomy, and the Priestly sources, the distinctions among the usages of the term in different texts were recognized and have been studied accordingly.[2] Socio-historical studies on the term have suggested various social groups

---

* It is a great privilege and joy to dedicate this essay to a *Festschrift* that honours my leader, mentor, colleague, and supporter, Dr. Larry J. Perkins, for his lifelong scholarship and service for the seminary education and the church. This is a revised version of a paper presented in a Bible and Theology session at the annual conference of the Evangelical Missiological Society in Dallas Texas, September 15–17, 2017. Some content and the tone of the present paper may reflect the original context. Hebrew *gēr* is a significant but often misunderstood concept in the field of missiology. In an article entitled "Theological Basis of a Sojourner," Dong Kwang Ra attempts to establish the *NaGuNeh* theology by arguing for the missiological meaning of the term *NaGuNeh* from the Bible based upon reading *gēr* from a traveler perspective. Dong Kwang Ra, "Theological Basis of a Sojourner," *KJCS* 20 (2001): 187–209. This odd approach is due to the mistranslation of *gēr* in English and Korean versions. See Joong-Ho Chong, "A Study on Ger in Ancient Israelite Society," *KJSS* 23 (2004): 511–13.

[1] Diether Kellermann, "גור gûr," *TDOT* 2:439–49; John R. Spencer, "Sojourner," *AYBD* 6:103–104. Carmen Palmer provides a brief summary of the history of the study of *gēr* in the Old Testament in her, *Converts in the Dead Sea Scrolls: The Gēr and Mutable Ethnicity*, STDJ 126 (Leiden: Brill, 2018), 10–16.

[2] P. Benzinger, "Fremdlinge bei den Habräern," *RE* 6 (1899): 262–65. T. Meek also recognized the term is used differently in different sources: in the J and E source, it means "immigrant"; the Covenant code and Deuteronomy use the term as "resident alien"; in the P source and Holiness Code, it can be rendered as "proselyte." See T. Meek, "The Translation of GER in the Hexateuch and its Bearing on the Documentary Hypothesis," *JBL* 49 (1930): 172–80.

in Israelite history as referents of the term.³ Douglas and Rendtorff identified them as the remnants of Northern Israel.⁴ Krauss related them to the Gentile females who were ordered to be separated from their families by Ezra but remained and converted to Judaism in the post-exilic period.⁵ However, sociological identification has not been able to single out a widely accepted group of people as the referent of the term.⁶ Other controversial scholarly discussions about the term ger focus on its meaning as 'convert',⁷ which is considered to have developed during the late Second Temple period.⁸

Despite the complex development of the meaning of the term, there seems to be a coherent orientation of the meaning of *gēr* in the Old Testament/Hebrew Bible.⁹ The present study reviews the process of theological conceptualization of the term *gēr* in its 93 instances in the Old Testament.¹⁰ Theologically, the land-allotment as inheritance under the covenantal context seems a key element in the conceptualization in Deuteronomy and the Deuteronomistic history.¹¹ Furthermore, the key idea seems to be recognized and is re-oriented in Ezekiel's oracle of the restored or eschatological temple and the Land. Based on this framework, the present study attempts to plot a trajectory of the theological conceptualization of the term *gēr* using the framework of "orientation–disorientation–reorientation"¹² with a particular interest in the theological identities of the term as representing an "in-group" and "out-group" of the people of God.

---

3   Socio-historically, the term may be a reference to a particular group of people who moved in and dwelled among the Israelites or to their social status in the Israelite/Jewish community. For the *gēr* as "the waves of immigrants coming from the northern kingdom after the fall of Samaria in 721 BC," see B. Broshi, "The Expansion of Jerusalem in the Reigns of Hezekiah and Manasseh," *IEJ* 24 (1974): 21–26; for the *gēr* as "Israelites who remained in the land and joined the community of the returnees," see Christiana van Houten, *The Alien in Israelite Law*, JSOTSup 107 (Sheffield: Sheffield Academic Press, 1991), 156; and for the *gēr* as "the members of the Samaritan leading classes," see J. G. Vink, *The Date and Origin of the Priestly Code in the Old Testament*, OtSt 15 (Leiden: Brill, 1969), 48. Christoph Bultmann investigates the term from the perspective of social status in *Der Fremde im antiken Juda*, FRLANT 153 (Göttingen: Vandenhoeck & Ruprecht, 1992).
4   Rolf Rendtorff, "The *gēr* in the Priestly Laws of the Pentateuch," in *Ethnicity and the Bible*, ed. Mark G. Brett (Leiden: Brill, 2002), 77–87, esp. 86. Kyung-Taek Ha argues that the *gēr* in the Deuteronomic triad "*gēr*–orphan–widow" in Deuteronomy is a technical term as a reference to the refugees from the northern kingdom after the fall of Samaria. He further argues that the special usage of the term is reflected in the Deuteronomistic histories (Josh 8:33, 35; 2 Sam 1:13). See Kyung-Taek Ha, "Understanding the Multicultural Society," *KPJT* 39 (2010): 70–71.
5   Stuart Krauss, "The Word 'ger' in the Bible and Its Implications," *JBQ* 34 (2006): 264–70.
6   A diachronic study on the identities of *gēr* has been made by Christiana van Hooten who concludes that "the legal status of the alien has changed dramatically over time." See van Houten, *The Alien in Israelite Law*, 164.
7   Matthew Thiessen's study against W. C. Allen is an example. Matthew Thiessen, "Revisiting the προσήλυτος in 'the LXX,'" *JBL* 132 (2013): 333–50.
8   Conversion to Judaism is largely considered a Hellenistic idea. Shaye J. D. Cohen, "Crossing the Boundary and Becoming a Jew," *HTR* 82 (1989): 25.
9   So Mark A. Awabdy, *Immigrants and Innovative Law: Deuteronomy's Theological and Social Vision of the* גר, FAT 2/67 (Tübingen: Mohr Siebeck, 2014).
10 68 instances are attested in the Pentateuch. Among them only two instances are found in Genesis. The remainder are in Exodus (12×), Leviticus (21×), Numbers (11×), and Deuteronomy (22×).
11 In this sense, this study suggests a theological answer to Spencer's riddle of the identity of Levites who are said to "sojourn" but are not "sojourners." Spencer, "Sojourner," 6:103–104.
12 The framing sequence of "orientation," "dis-orientation," and "re-orientation" is borrowed from Walter Brueggemann who uses it to classify the Psalms in his *The Message of the Psalms: A Theological Commentary* (Minneapolis, MN: Fortress Press, 1984).

2. Orientation of *gēr*: sojourner in Exodus

2.1. *gēr* as non-Israelite identity

Generally, the term *gēr* refers to a group of (or groups of) people who are ethnically non-Israelites (or foreigners) but living among Israelites.[13] One of the first impressions of the concept is that *gēr* is an "out-group" among Israelites. The term *gēr* (sojourner) appears several times paired with the term, אֶזְרָח (*'ezraḥ*), which means "native-born," as its opposite (Exod 12:19; Lev 16:29; 18:26; 24:16, 22; Josh 8:33). Also, the people who were defined as *gēr* have a vulnerable status in Israelite society, so they need to be taken care of with other vulnerable people such as widows and orphans, receiving charitable support. The Deuteronomic triad of "*gēr*–orphan–widow" is a well-known set from Deuteronomy (especially in the law code of Deut 12–26) and the Prophets.

The low-key, out-group image of *gēr* works in Exod 2:21–27, where the *gēr* is considered underprivileged along with the widow and the orphan (אַלְמָנָה וְיָתוֹם; Exod 22:21–23) who are supposed not to be mistreated or oppressed among the Israelites. However, conceptually, the passage places the *gēr* into the "in-group" instead of leaving it an "out-group." The passage follows the Decalogue in Exodus 20, and it is mentioned in part of the covenant-making process of Exodus 19 to 24. The covenant-making process in Exodus 19–24 asserts a relational definition of who the Israelites are as a whole to Yahweh. So, the Decalogue (Exod 20) and the following laws in Exodus 21–23 are the covenantal stipulations or contract policies which are subordinate to the overall contract or covenant. Therefore, although the existence of the term *gēr* implies a distinction of the designated group from the rest, the idea that the *gēr* is an underprivileged group of people along with the orphan and the widow indicates that the *gēr* stays theologically under the overall covenantal framework which recognizes a single group of people in relation to God.[14]

2.2. *gēr* as Israelites' identity

The sympathetic perspective of the *gēr* is based on the Israelites' self-identity as *gēr*. Abraham identifies himself as a *gēr* in his conversation with the Hittites when Abraham wants to buy a grave site for his wife Sarah (Gen 23:4).[15] In the Midianite

---

[13] Jeffrey H. Tigay, *Deuteronomy*, The JPS Torah Commentary (Philadelphia, PA: The Jewish Publication Society, 1996), 12. Jose E. Ramírez Kidd begins his study on this term by commenting how this concept was challenged by two alternative theories: (1) immigrants from the northern kingdom since 721 BCE and (2) internal social differentiation in Juda by Bultmann. See Jose E. Ramírez Kidd, *Alterity and Identity in Israel: The* גר *in the Old Testament*, BZAW 283 (Berlin: Walter de Gruyter, 1999), 5–6. Sarna defines the *gēr* as "a foreign-born permanent resident whose status was intermediate between the native-born citizen (*ezraḥ*) and the foreigner temporarily residing outside his community (*nokhri*)." See Nahum M. Sarna, *Exodus*, The JPS Torah Commentary (Philadelphia, PA: The Jewish Publication Society, 1991), 137.

[14] Concerning this, it is worth noting that LXX translates the term *ger* into προσήλυτος, "proselyte" in majority of the instances (63 times). See Ha, "Understanding the Multicultural Society," 69. See also van Houten, *The Alien in Israelite Law*, 179–83. Generally, προσήλυτος is considered as a late Second Temple-period term.

[15] In Gen 23, Abraham's self-identification as *gēr* is closely related to land possession. Abraham's conversation with the Hittites is all about buying a piece of land (a den) for Sarah's grave. The passage seems to be more than simply buying a piece of a graveyard. The purpose of Gen 23 is

wilderness, Moses names his son Gersom because he becomes a *gēr* in a foreign land (Exod 2:22). In Psalm 39, the psalmist (David according to the superscription) identifies himself as a *gēr* like his ancestors (Ps 39:12).

The laws given to the Israelites to help the *gēr* in Exod 22:21 are justified based on the Israelites' own experience. In the covenantal stipulations of ethics (Exod 22:15–31), the Israelites are prohibited from taking advantage of the widow or orphan (Exod 22:22; v. 21 in MT). Oppression of the *gēr* is also prohibited because Israelites were *gērim* in the land of Egypt (Exod 22:21). The passage continues to give a warning; when the *gēr*, widow, and orphan are mistreated and cry out to God, God will listen to them. The warning reminds the audience of Exod 2:23–25, where God hears the Israelites' own cry for help in their slavery in Egypt and remembers his covenant with Abraham. A same petition is found in Exod 23:9, "you shall not oppress a *gēr*. You know the heart of a *gēr*, for you were *gērim* in the land of Egypt." This command is written in the context of a lawsuit (Exod 23:6–9). The passage strongly encourages Israelites to practice justice towards the *gēr* and not to oppress them because the Israelites know the heart (or soul) of the *gēr* (אֶת־נֶפֶשׁ הַגֵּר) due to their own experience in Egypt (23:9).[16] Ramírez Kidd explains the Israelites' self-identification as *gērim* as follows:

> The majority of references to the *gēr* in the Old Testament are late, the experience of the exile made Israel aware of "how it feels to be a *gēr*" (Exod 23:9). After the exile the *gēr* became a mirror of their own story. The attitude towards the *gēr* in the Old Testament reveals, therefore, Israel's understanding of its own identity. That is why the command to love the *gēr* is founded in Israel's own experience (Deut 10, 19).[17]

In David's prayer in 1 Chr 29:10–19, David identifies the Israelites as the *gērim* before God as their ancestors (v. 15). The prayer is about David's preparation for the Temple construction. It is worth noting that the statements immediately surrounding the verse (v. 15: David's identification of Israel as *gērim*) are very similar to each other by testifying that all the abundance (of the materials) prepared for the construction belong to God (vv. 14 and 16). The immediate literary structure suggests that the Israelites' identity as *gērim* before God is based on the confession that everything that they have acquired belongs to him. A similar idea is found in the concept of the year of *Jubilee*, especially in relation to the possession of the Land (Lev 25:23).

---

to argue the Israelite claim to the land of Canaan as a legitimate land holder (Bruce K. Waltke, *Genesis: A Commentary* [Grand Rapids, MI: Zondervan, 2001], 315–16; Gordon Wenham, *Genesis 16–50*, WBC 2 [Dallas, TX: Word Books, 1994], 128, 130–31). In other words, buying land, is theologically the most important theme in this chapter. Therefore, Abraham's self-identification as *gēr* is not simply notice that he is from a foreign land but more significantly that he does not possess land among the Hittites. This understanding of Gen 23 sheds light on the further discussion of the concept of *gēr* in the present study because holding land as inheritance seems to be one of the key elements in the conceptualization of *gēr* in the Old Testament. Further discussion will occur on this point in the following section.

[16] See also Lev 19:34.
[17] Ramírez Kidd, *Alterity and Identity in Israel*, 132.

2.3. Covenant and land: key theological elements of the conceptualization of *gēr*

A brief overview of the term *gēr* shows two perspectives on the word in the Old Testament: (1) the *gēr* in Israel and (2) Israel as *gēr*.[18] Theologically, Israel's self-identity as *gēr* becomes the basis for the Israelites' attitude toward the *gēr* among them. However, even "the *gēr* in Israel" does not place the *gēr* in the "out-group" of Israel. Deuteronomy and the Deuteronomistic history prescribe the covenantal understanding of the *gēr*. Deuteronomy 31 and Joshua 8 make this overtly clear in their description of the procedure of the covenant-making ceremony. After giving his final sermon (Deut 29–30), Moses envisages how the Israelites will perform the covenant renewal by reading the laws on the feast of tabernacles in every seventh year in Canaan (Deut 31:9–13). In v. 12, Moses commands the Levites and the elders of Israel to assemble the people (הַקְהֵל אֶת־הָעָם; v. 12a) for the regular hearing of the law. The following list shows who constitute the people. The *gēr* is to be counted as part of the people with men, women, and the little ones: הָאֲנָשִׁים וְהַנָּשִׁים וְהַטַּף וְגֵרְךָ אֲשֶׁר בִּשְׁעָרֶיךָ ("men, women, and children, and your *gēr* who are in your town"; v. 1a).

Joshua 8 describes the actualization of Deuteronomy 31. After the capture of Ai, Joshua built an altar on Mt. Ebal and performed blessings and curses. Half of the Israelites stood in front of Mt. Gerizim and the other half stood in front of Mt. Ebal, as prescribed in Deuteronomy 29. In Josh 8:33, all Israel (וְכָל־יִשְׂרָאֵל) with their elders and officers and their judges (וּזְקֵנָיו וְשֹׁטְרִים וְשֹׁפְטָיו; Josh 8:33a) are ordered to stand at the opposite sides of the ark. The following phrase, כַּגֵּר כָּאֶזְרָח ("as *gēr* as the native-born" or "alien as well as citizen" [NRSV]; v. 33a) emphasizes no discrimination between the *gēr* and the native-born as parts of וְכָל־יִשְׂרָאֵל ("all Israel"; 8:33a).

The *gēr* takes part in the blessings and curses performed as a part of Israel.[19]

The participation of the *gēr* in the covenantal ceremony sheds light on an understanding of many cultic regulations in Exodus and Leviticus, where the *gēr* holds very similar responsibilities and rights to the native Israelite. A law of festival diet, according to which Israelites must eat unleavened bread, applies to both the natives of the land (בְּאֶזְרַח הָאָרֶץ) and the *gēr* (גֵּר) without discrimination (Exod 12:19). The regulations for the day of atonement are to be observed by the native (הָאֶזְרָח) and the *gēr* (וְהַגֵּר; Lev 16:29) without distinction. In Lev 17:8–9, it is regulated that a person, either from the house of Israel (מִבֵּית יִשְׂרָאֵל) or from the *gēr*, who offers a burnt offering or a sacrifice but does not bring the offering to the entrance of the tent of meeting (tabernacle), should be cut off from his people (וְנִכְרַת הָאִישׁ הַהוּא מֵעַמָּיו). This verse presupposes that the *gēr* is already part of the community who might well be cut off from the people. The *gēr* is also included in the regulation

---

[18] For a detailed classifications of the various usage of the concept of *gēr* based on this perspective, consult Ramírez Kidd, *Alterity and Identity in Israel*, 130–33.

[19] The reference to the native born (אֶזְרָח; Josh 8:33) possibly carries the post-exilic perspective of this passage, because not many Israelites were born in the land (אֶזְרָח) at the time of Joshua. For this anachronistic view, Woudstra argues that the distinction between the *'ezraḥ* and the *gēr* is a distinction between ethnic backgrounds (those native to Israel and those who were not) rather than territorial (or spatial) distinction. See Marten H. Woudstra, *The Book of Joshua*, NICOT (Grand Rapids, MI: Eerdmans, 1981), 149.

for the vows (לְכָל־נִדְרֵיהֶם) or freewill offerings (לְכָל־נִדְבוֹתָם) with the house of Israel (אִישׁ מִבֵּית יִשְׂרָאֵל; Lev 22:18–19). The *gēr* as well as the native (הָאֶזְרָח) are prohibited from doing what Egyptians or Canaanites do (Lev 18:26). The practice of child sacrifice to Molech was strongly prohibited for both the sons of Israel (אִישׁ מִבְּנֵי יִשְׂרָאֵל) and the *gēr* (Lev 20:2). A *gēr* (כַּגֵּר) faces the same penalty (stoning to death) as the native (כָּאֶזְרָח) when he blasphemes Yahweh's name (Lev 24:16). Other cultic regulations are to be applied to the native and the *gēr* without discrimination. Reading these verses, Rendtorff remarks, "the surprising fact is that in all those texts that mention the *gēr* and the *'ezraḥ* together the point is not their difference or contrast but what they have in common."[20] At the core of what they have in common is their identity as part of the covenant people of Yahweh.[21]

In the explanation of the *Lex Talionis* in Lev 24:17–23, the law states clearly that there is no difference between the *gēr* and the native:

Lev 24:22 (MT)
מִשְׁפַּט אֶחָד יִהְיֶה לָכֶם כַּגֵּר כָּאֶזְרָח יִהְיֶה כִּי אֲנִי יְהוָה אֱלֹהֵיכֶם׃

Lev 24:22 (NRSV)
You shall have one law for the alien and for the citizen: for I am the LORD your God.[22]

In a more literal sense, the phrase can be translated as, "there exists one (same) judgment to you (pl.), no matter if you are *gēr* or natives, for I am Yahweh, your God." Both *gēr* and native Israelite are included in reference to the second person personal pronoun לָכֶם, "to you," here. The reason both *gēr* and native are under the same law is כִּי אֲנִי יְהוָה אֱלֹהֵיכֶם ("because Yahweh is your [pl.] God"). The title "Yahweh," as it is often argued, is used in the context of covenantal relationship between God and Israel.[23] Yet all of these regulations (or stipulations) are applied equally to the *gēr* because the *gēr* participates in the covenantal relationship with God, as does the native.

Although there is no difference between *gēr* and *'ezraḥ* in their theological identity, low social status or poverty seems to be a dominant attribute of the *gēr*. Leviticus pairs the poor and the *gēr* (לֶעָנִי וְלַגֵּר) as the objects of social welfare in Lev 19:10 and 23:22. In these verses, both the *gēr* and the poor together are designated beneficiaries of the generosity of those who harvest.[24] A similar image is also found

---

[20] Rendtorff, "Ger in the Priestly Laws," 81–82.
[21] Concerning this theological prescription of *gēr* and *'ezraḥ* in Priestly source, a more proper understanding of the set expression of *'ezraḥ* and *gēr* in the priestly source would be the "native born Israelites (the covenant people of Yahweh)" and "non-native Israelites (the covenant people of Yahweh)."
[22] NRSV's translation of גֵּר ("alien") and אֶזְרָח ("citizen") is problematic. Concerning the present discussion, ESV's "sojourner" and "native (or native born)" is preferable although even "sojourner" seems not properly reflect the usage of the term *gēr* in the Priestly source.
[23] Waltke, *Genesis*, 25.
[24] This idea, however, is not always the case. Leviticus 25:47 depicts a case where the *gēr* (sojourner) or *toshav* (stranger) among the Israelites becomes rich enough to buy an Israelite as a hired worker to probably functions as a servant or a slave.

in Deuteronomy. With the orphan and widow, the *gēr* completes the Deuteronomic triad: וְהַגֵּר וְהַיָּתוֹם וְהָאַלְמָנָה (*gēr*–orphan–widow). Deuteronomy 24 prevents perverting justice against the *gēr* or the orphan, or taking a widow's garment in pledge (Deut 24:14, 17) and instructs the Israelite to be generous to them in their harvest by purposely leaving behind uncollected grains (v. 19) or olives and grapes (vv. 20–21). In these verses, *gēr* describes the underprivileged along with the orphan and widow, and their vulnerability and neediness are the reason for Israel's material kindness to them.

However, a close look reveals a more fundamental reason for giving financial help to the *gēr*. In Deut 14:22–29, the third-year tithe is to be saved for and provided to Levites, *gērim*, orphans, and widows (Deut 14:28–29). The passage reveals that the Levite is listed here "because he has no portion or inheritance with you" (כִּי אֵין־לוֹ חֵלֶק וְנַחֲלָה עִמָּךְ; v. 29). Grammatically, this phrase is linked only to the Levites. Yet contextually, this phrase gives a good reason why orphans, widows, and the *gēr* should needfully be provided for by Israel. For various reasons peculiar to each, they lack inherited land by which they might feed themselves.

This idea is expressed more clearly later in Deut 26, where the text describes how one is to celebrate the harvest in the promised land. The whole passage is framed with the land that Yahweh gives to Israel for an inheritance (Deut 26:1). In v. 11, the Levites and *gēr* are explicitly mentioned, and it is not hard to speculate why the two groups are mentioned together here:

Deut 26:11 (MT)
וְשָׂמַחְתָּ בְכָל־הַטּוֹב אֲשֶׁר נָתַן־לְךָ יְהוָה אֱלֹהֶיךָ וּלְבֵיתֶךָ אַתָּה וְהַלֵּוִי וְהַגֵּר אֲשֶׁר בְּקִרְבֶּךָ: ס

Deut 26:11 (NRSV)
Then you, together with the Levites and the *gēr* who reside among you, shall celebrate with all the bounty that the LORD your God has given to you and to your house.

The common factor that the Levites and *gēr* share is that they do not have an allotment of land for an inheritance. The lack of inherited land seems a part of what defines the *gēr* in the context of Israelite community. If a *gēr* is not counted as a legitimate member of the covenant community, the reference to the *gēr* here in this verse (Deut 26:11) would not be necessary. The implicit subject of the verb, וְשָׂמַחְתָּ ("shall celebrate"), appears at the end of the sentence where וְהַלֵּוִי (the Levites) and וְהַגֵּר (the *gēr*) are included to the preceding second-person nominative pronoun, אַתָּה (you).

In the following verses (Deut 26:12–13) the Levites, the *gēr*, the orphan, and the widow are listed together as the beneficiaries for the third-year tithe of the Israelites' produce. And again, conceptually it is because first they are part of the Israelite community, and secondly, they are without an inheritance of land by which they might produce their own food rather than just because they are poor. The literal translation of יָתוֹם ("orphan") is "fatherless." The term seems to imply not only the loss of one's father as a person, but also being stripped of the inheritance which is related to one's father. The "fatherless" and the "widow" seem to lose their "father" or "husband," which commonly implies the loss of the link to their inheritance.[25]

Based on this argument, the usage of the term *gēr* in the Torah can be summarized as follows; ethnically, the *gēr* is a non-Israelite or half-Israelite. Yet the *gērim*, especially וְהַגֵּר אֲשֶׁר בְּקִרְבְּךָ (*gēr* who is among you), are considered an integral part of the society (the covenant people of Yahweh), joining in the covenant between Yahweh and Israel and so obligated to follow the covenantal laws and stipulations. The only difference between the *gēr* and other Israelites is the lack of allotted land for an inheritance. For this reason, the *gēr* is grouped with Levites, orphans, and widows in Deuteronomy and the Deuteronomistic history, and is counted an underprivileged group who is in need of social support because of lack of inherited land for food production.

3. Disorientation of *gēr*

The reality of the life of the *gēr* or the later understanding of the life of the *gēr* is described differently from what is prescribed in the regulations in Deuteronomy. Chronicles and prophetic texts report how *gērim* among Israelites are mistreated, which evokes the memory of the Israelites' being forced to labour in Egypt.

3.1. Chronicles

Three instances of the term *gēr* are found in the books of Chronicles (1 Chr 22:2; 2 Chr 2:17–18; 30:25). The first two instances are especially worth noting. 1 Chronicles 22 describes David's preparation for the construction of the Jerusalem Temple. The narrative depicts David's mobilization of the *gērim* as a labour force. King David summoned the *gērim* and made them cut the stones for the Temple construction (1 Chr 22:2). The purpose of gathering the *gērim* specifically is not explicitly mentioned in this verse, whether it is for them or against them. However, the *gēr*-exclusive mobilization is obviously distinctive from כַּגֵּר כָּאֶזְרָח ("as *gēr* as the native-born"; Lev 24:22) which commonly appears in the priestly sources.

2 Chronicles 2 narrates the mobilization of the *gēr* more clearly. According to the passage, King Solomon counted the *gērim* which were 153,600 altogether. Basically, all of them were allocated to the Temple construction; 3,600 were assigned as overseers to make the other 150,000 work (2 Chr 2:16–17 [MT]; vv. 17–18 [NRSV]). This type of forced servitude of the *gērim* for building construction is reminiscent of Pharaoh's treatment of the Hebrews in Egypt. Although it is not clearly mentioned whether

---

[25] This idea is not explicit in the Old Testament/Hebrew Bible. However, in the concept of Hebrew terms, בֵּית אָב (*Bêt-ʾāb*; "Father's House"), מִשְׁפָּחָה (*Mišpāḥâ*; "clan"), and גֹּאֵל (*gōʾēl*; kinsman-redeemer), we may have a glimpse of the financial role of a father or extended father(s) in Israel, especially in relation to the inherited land. The orphan ("fatherless") and the widow seem not only to lose their father or husband but also to be separated from their inheritance or the inheritance recovery system. See C. J. H. Wright, "Family," *ABD* 2:761–69, esp. 761–64.

the action was executed for the benefit of the *gēr* or for the exploitation of them, it is understood as forced labor by many scholars.²⁶ The *gēr*-exclusive servitude in Chronicles hardly seems consonant with Deuteronomistic prescriptions.

The *gēr*-exclusive servitude may actually be the Chronicler's idea,²⁷ expressing a discriminatory view toward the *gēr* congruent with the post-exilic returned Jews' attitude. The days of Ezra and Nehemiah were characterized by strong anti-alien sentiment borne of being under constant threat.²⁸ The negative view of the *gēr* in the narrative is a deaf ear to the covenantal stipulations in Deuteronomy and Priestly laws and is justly criticized by the prophets.

3.2. Prophets

Twelve instances of the term *gēr* are attested in the prophetic literature.²⁹ Many of them appear in the context of God's rebuke of the Israelites for their mistreatment of the vulnerable people of the covenant community—*viz.*, the orphan, the widow, and the *gēr*. It is part of the "unrighteousness" that brought down the covenantal curses of losing the land and going into exile. In Ezek 22:7 and 29, the people of the land (עַם הָאָרֶץ; Ezek 22:29) are accused of extorting from the *gēr* without a thought of justice. The passage (Ezek 22:1–16) lists "all the detestable" (כָּל־תּוֹעֲבוֹתֶיהָ; Ezek 22:2), on account of which God's judgment will come (Ezek 22:4–5). Oppression of the *gēr* is decried as a significant reason for Israel's exile (Ezek 22:15–16).

Jeremiah 22:3 reinforces this idea. Jeremiah 21 and 22 is an oracle from the time of King Zedekiah (21:1). This oracle predicts the fall of Jerusalem to Nebuchadnezzar (21:2–6), God's judgment against the house of the king of Judah (21:11), and God's commandment to the palace of the king of Judah (22:1). The oracle makes clear that God will punish the royal house of Judah and their palace according to their deeds (21:13; 22:4–5). The only concern in this passage is about executing justice (דִּינוּ לַבֹּקֶר מִשְׁפָּט; 21:12), including doing no wrong or violence to the *gēr*, orphan, and widow

---

²⁶ Edward L. Curtis, *A Critical and Exegetical Commentary on the Books of Chronicles*, ICC (Edinburgh: T&T Clark, 1910), 322–23; Raymond B. Dillard, *2 Chronicles*, WBC 15 (Waco, TX: Word Books, 1987), 21–22; J. A. Thompson, *1, 2 Chronicles*, NAC 9 (Nashville, TN: Broadman & Holman, 1994), 212–13.

²⁷ Rendtorff views the Chronicler's discourse as "an invention by the Chronicler to avoid the idea that Israelites had been forced to labor." See Rendtorff, "*Ger* in the Priestly Laws," 78. The theory is based on the paralleled Deuteronomistic history (1 Kgs 9:15, 20–22). 1 Kings 5:27–32 (5:13–18 in NRSV) implies that Israelites too were pressed into Solomon's building program. See Raymond Dillard, *2 Chronicles*, 61–63.

²⁸ Jonathan Dyck provides a helpful discussion on the scale of the identity of Israelites, the similarities and differences between the Chronicler's viewpoint and Ezra-Nehemiah's perspective. Consult Jonathan E. Dyck, "The Ideology of Identity in Chronicles," in Brett, ed., *Ethnicity and the Bible*, 89–116, esp. 90–96. A different perspective from the first two instances of the *gēr* is detected in 2 Chr 30:25. The more positive stance toward the *gēr* reinforces the arguments of Japhet or Williamson who hold that the Chronicler as an idealist without political agenda, so that the concept of Israel in Chronicles is more inclusive. See Jonathan Dyck, "The Ideology of Identity in Chronicles," 93–94; H. G. M. Williamson, *Israel in the Books of Chronicles* (Cambridge: Cambridge University Press, 1977); Sara Japhet, *The Ideology of the Book of Chronicles and its Place in Biblical Thought* (Winona Lake, IN: Eisenbrauns, 2009).

²⁹ Isaiah 5:17; 14:1; Jer 7:6; 14:8; 22:3; Ezek 14:7; 22:3, 29; 47:22, 23; Zech 7:10; Mal 3:5.

(22:3). These misbehaviours can even be equated with breaking the covenant and idol worship (22:9). The oracle in Jeremiah 21–22 clearly states that mistreatment of the *gēr*, orphan, and widow, and failing to practice justice (or fair judgment) are the decisive reason for the Babylonian exile.

A similar, even stronger oracle is found in Zech 7:9–10 addressed to the returned community (Zech 7:1). The larger passage (Zech 7:8–14) explains that Israel's oppression of the widow, orphan, *gēr*, and the poor is counted as one of the most significant reasons for the exile to Babylon and the desolation of the land (Zech 7:14). In Malachi 3, the oracle announces God's intention to put Israel on trial (Mal 3:5a) for thrusting aside the *gēr* (those who deprive the *gēr* of justice; 3:5b) and bring her to judgment (3:5a). Malachi is generally agreed to be post-exilic on account of the use of the Persian word פֶּחָה ("governor"; 1:8) and the presumed existence of the (second) temple.[30] The oracle seems to reflect a fragmented picture of post-exilic society, where justice and fair judgment for the weaker members of the community, including the *gēr*, were not in place.[31]

4. Reorientation of *gēr*

Prophets like Ezekiel, Jeremiah, Zechariah, and Malachi, alongside Ezra-Nehemiah and Chronicles, reflect the sad reality of the *gēr* in the pre-exilic and post-exilic periods or at least show the complexity of various attitudes toward the *gēr* in the Israelite community. The ideal of the inclusion of the *gēr* among Israel, which is prescribed in Torah and Deuteronomistic history, however, seems to have been well-understood by Ezekiel and is significantly reflected in Ezekiel's vision of the new temple and the new land.

The last part of Ezekiel (chs. 40–48) is a vision of the new temple, new torah, new land, and new city.[32] The oracle envisions a new temple and gives instructions for its personnel, festivals, and rulers. In Ezek 47:13–48:29, the passage draws the ideal boundaries and divisions of the new land. The new land is divided to the twelve tribes of Israel as their inheritance (תִּתְנַחֲלוּ, Ezek 47:13–23). The appearance of the term *gēr* in the middle of the land division passage is significant (Ezek 47:22). In Ezek 47:21–23, both *gēr* and Israelites are to be allotted land as inheritance (47:22, 24). As earlier demonstrated, inherited land is almost the only thing that distinguishes the Israelite from the *gēr*, aside from ethnic background. However, in Ezekiel's vision of the new land, both restored Israel (or Israel in the eschaton) *and* the children of the *gēr* are counted as native-born children of Israel (כְּאֶזְרָח בִּבְנֵי יִשְׂרָאֵל, v. 22) and consequently are assigned land as their inheritance (בְּנַחֲלָה, v. 23).

---

[30] Ralph L. Smith, *Micah-Malachi*, WBC 32 (Waco TX: Word Books, 1984) 298. See also Pieter A. Verhoef, *The Books of Haggai and Malachi*, NICOT (Grand Rapids, MI: Eerdmans, 1987), 156–60.

[31] However, at the same time, Zechariah and Malachi's stance towards the *gēr*, which is opposite to Chroniclers and Ezra-Nehemiah's view, might raise controversial discussions concerning the date of the compositions or the existence of contradictory voices about the *gēr* in the post-exilic period.

[32] The division is from Daniel I. Block, *The Book of Ezekiel: Chapters 25–48*, NICOT (Grand Rapids, MI: Eerdmans, 1998), viii.

Daniel Block comments: "recognizing the theological significance of landholding in Israel, Ezekiel insists that in the new order, all distinctions between *gērim* and ethnic Israelites (*'ezraḥ*) will be eliminated."[33] This vision of the "new order," a "re-orientation" toward the ideal identity of the covenant community, is presumptive of the theology of the year of Jubilee. The land ultimately belongs to Yahweh and Israelites, just as much as the *gēr* among them, are identified as *gēr* (*gērim*) in the eyes of Yahweh (Lev 25:23). Although it is mentioned only once in Leviticus, the statement there essentially explains all the *gēr* regulations so well. It is the theological foundation and centerpiece. The historical identity of the Israelites is "sons of Israel" (Lev 25:55). However, their theological and conceptual identity is *gēr* (or *gērim*; Lev 25:23) before Yahweh. Therefore, theologically, Israel and the *gēr* are without distinction. Ezekiel seems to make a re-orientation of the identity of the *gēr* toward what it meant to be in the theological identity of the covenant community by allotting land to the *gēr* as inheritance. According to Ezek 48:35, the city is named *Yahweh Shammah* (the LORD is there; יְהוָה שָׁמָּה). The *gēr* is to participate in the allotment of the land with other Israelites in the presence of the ultimate owner.

5. Conclusion

I have argued that covenant and land-inheritance are two significant elements of the theological conceptualization of the term *gēr* in the Old Testament/Hebrew Bible. With them, Ezekiel seems to close the significant gap between the *gēr* and native-born Israelites by legislating allotment of land to the *gēr* as an inheritance in its vision of the restored or eschatological land.

The glimpse of the Jewish community of the post-exilic period in Malachi and Ezra-Nehemiah seems far from the accomplishment of Ezekiel's vision. But then, as an oracle reaching toward the future, Ezekiel too attests to unsolved problems in the returned present community.

The presumptive portrait of the *gēr* in the post-exilic returned community continues to be a rather gloomy one at the close of the OT period with some shining points of light here and there. From that point, it would be a fruitful next step to plot the orientation, dis-orientation, and re-orientation arc and explore advances or regressions in how the *gēr* fares in Israel to the beginning of the common era. Beyond that, what can be said concerning the place of the *gēr* in the ministry and teaching of Jesus and in the mission and life of the apostolic church?

Bibliography

Awabdy, Mark A. *Immigrants and Innovative Law: Deuteronomy's Theological and Social Vision for the* גר. FAT 2/67. Tübingen: Mohr Siebeck, 2014.

Benzinger, P. "Fremdlinge bei den Habräern." *Realencyklopädie für protestantische Theologie und Kirche* 6 (1899): 262–65.

---

[33] Block, *Book of Ezekiel: Chapters 25–48*, 718.

Block, Daniel I. *The Book of Ezekiel: Chapters 25–48*. NICOT. Grand Rapids, MI: Eerdmans, 1998.

Botterweck G. J., and H. Ringgren, eds. *Theological Dictionary of the Old Testament*. Translated by J. T. Willis, G. W. Bromiley, and D. E. Green. 8 vols. Grand Rapids: Eerdmans, 1974–.

Brett, Mark G., ed. *Ethnicity and the Bible*. Leiden: Brill, 2002.

Broshi, B. "The Expansion of Jerusalem in the reigns of Hezekiah and Manasseh." *Israel Exploration Journal* 24 (1974): 21–26.

Brueggemann, Walter. *The Message of the Psalms: A Theological Commentary*. Minneapolis, MN: Fortress Press, 1984.

Bultmann, Christoph. *Der Fremde im antiken Juda*. FRLANT 153. Göttingen: Vandenhoeck & Ruprecht, 1992.

Chong, Joong-Ho. "A Study on *Gēr* in Ancient Israelite Society." *Korean Journal of Social Science* 23 (2004): 511–25.

Cohen, Shaye J. D. "Crossing the Boundary and Becoming a Jew." *Harvard Theological Review* 82 (1989): 13–33.

Curtis, Edward L. *A Critical and Exegetical Commentary on the Books of Chronicles*. ICC. Edinburgh: T&T Clark, 1910.

Dillard, Raymond B. *2 Chronicles*. WBC 15. Waco, TX: Word Books, 1987.

Dyck, Jonathan E. "The Ideology of Identity in Chronicles." Pages 89–116 in *Ethnicity and the Bible*. Edited by Mark G. Brett. Leiden: Brill, 2002.

Ha, Kyung-Taek. "Understanding the Multicultural Society from the Perspective of the Old Testament: Focusing on the Problem of the Immigrants (*gēr* and *nokri*)." *Korea Presbyterian Journal of Theology* 39 (2010): 61–88.

Japhet, Sara. *The Ideology of the Book of Chronicles and its Place in Biblical Thought*. Winona Lake, IN: Eisenbrauns, 2009.

Krauss, Stuart. "The Word '*gēr*' in the Bible and Its Implications." *Jewish Bible Quarterly* 34 (2006): 264–70.

Meek, T. "The Translation of *GER* in the Hexateuch and Its Bearing on the Documentary Hypothesis." *JBL* 49 (1930): 172–80.

Milgrom, Jacob, *Numbers*. The JPS Torah Commentary. Philadelphia, PA: The Jewish Publication Society, 1990.

Palmer, Carmen. *Converts in the Dead Sea Scrolls: The Gēr and Mutable Ethnicity*. Studies on the Texts of the Desert of Judah 126. Leiden: Brill, 2018.

Ra, Dong Kwang. "Theological Basis of a Sojourner." *Korean Journal of Christian Studies* 20 (2001): 187–209.

Ramírez Kidd, Jose E. *Alterity and Identity in Israel: The גר in the Old Testament*. BZAW 283. Berlin: Walter de Gruyter, 1999.

Rendtorff, Rolf. "The *gēr* in the Priestly Laws of the Pentateuch." Pages 77–87 in *Ethnicity and the Bible*. Edited by Mark G. Brett. Leiden: Brill, 2002.

Sarna, Nahum M. *Exodus*. The JPS Torah Commentary. Philadelphia, PA: The Jewish Publication Society, 1991.

Smith, Ralph L. *Micah–Malachi*. WBC 32. Waco, TX: Word Books, 1984.

Spencer, John R. "Sojourner." Pages 103–104 in vol. 6 of *Anchor Yale Bible Dictionary*. Edited by D. N. Freedman. 6 vols. New York: Doubleday, 1992.

Thiessen, Matthew. "Revisiting the Προσέλθτος in 'the LXX.'" *JBL* 132 (2013): 333–50.

Thompson, J. A. *1, 2 Chronicles*. The New American Commentary 9. Nashville, TN: Broadman & Holman, 1994.

Tigay, Jeffrey H. *Deuteronomy*. The JPS Torah Commentary. Philadelphia, PA: The Jewish Publication Society, 1996.
van Houten, Christiana. *The Alien in Israelite Law*. JSOTSup 107. Sheffield: Sheffield Academic Press, 1991.
Verhoef, Pieter A. *The Books of Haggai and Malachi*. The New International Commentary on the Old Testament. Grand Rapids, MI: Eerdmans, 1987.
Vink, J. G. *The Date and Origin of the Priestly Code in the Old Testament*. Oudtestamentische Studiën 15. Leiden: Brill, 1969.
Waltke, Bruce. *Genesis: A Commentary*. Grand Rapids, MI: Zondervan, 2001.
Wenham, Gordon. *Genesis 16–50*. WBC 2. Dallas, TX: Word Books, 1994.
Williamson, H. G. M. *Israel in the Books of Chronicles*. Cambridge: Cambridge University Press, 1977.
Woudstra Marten H. *The Book of Joshua*. The New International Commentary on the Old Testament. Grand Rapids, MI: Eerdmans, 1981.
Wright, C. J. H. "Family." Pages 761–69 in vol. 2 of *Anchor Yale Bible Dictionary*. Edited by D. N. Freedman. 6 vols. New York: Doubleday, 1992.

PART III
EXODUS IN THE SECOND TEMPLE JEWISH LITERATURE

Chapter 10

The Text of Exodus in the Qumran Corpus

Martin G. Abegg, Jr.

1. Introduction

This Exodus study—in honor of my colleague and friend, Larry Perkins—represents the initial steps of what might well become a much lengthier journey. So to keep the report of these steps within the limitations of a *Festschrift* but yet provide a resource for those who might want to follow and linger longer at certain points along the way, I have focused my attention on the evidence in the Qumran corpus for the canonical text of Exodus. These are recorded in Table 10.1.

Following the table, I have included four short studies concerning matters that I noticed alongside the path as I travelled through the quotation list. I offer these as inklings of the book that a fuller study might produce. First, I present two brief studies to help the reader interpret the regular variances between the Masoretic Text and that of the Qumran manuscripts. These variances reflect the common written form of the Hebrew language expressed by the scribes who copied the scrolls and should be ignored if the researcher is on the hunt for text-critical data. The first of these is a description of the ubiquitous orthographic and morphological variables. This is followed by an excursus on variations which evidence the devolution of the Hebrew verbal system. The third study concerns the use of the tetragrammaton (יהוה) in the non-biblical Qumran Scrolls. Finally, the fourth offers one example of the many interpretive issues which the scrolls preserve from among the debates of antiquity, here the half-shekel Temple tax. I have then appended a list of the occurrences of Exodus in manuscripts that have been called variously "Biblical Paraphrase," "Rewritten Scripture," or "Reworked Pentateuch." I have not included these in the quotation list as they are currently understood as simply more highly variable Hebrew Bible manuscripts.

2. The table

Table 10.1 presents the heart of this study and should prove useful as a reference for a wide variety of Exodus studies. Building on the work of Armin Lange and Matthias Weigold's 2011 publication, *Biblical Quotations and Allusions in Second Temple Jewish Literature*,[1] I have added numerous entries from my own years of research in the corpus of Qumran manuscripts. For this table I have given the Exodus reference (column 1); the Qumran reference to the quotation (column 2); an admittedly heuristic determination as to whether the Exodus citation is an actual quotation (a), an allusion (b), or simply a word or phrase adopted by the ancient writers that might well have had an origin in the book of Exodus (c) (column 3); and lastly the Masoretic Text of the passage (column 4).

Table 10.1. DSS quotations and allusions to Exodus

1:14[2]	4Q461 1 3	b	בעבדה קשה
3:8	4Q377 1 i 9	c	ארץ טובה ורחבה
4:14	CD 3:8 (‖ 4Q269 2 3)	c	ויחר אף יהוה
4:22	4Q504 1–2 iii 6	a	בני בכרי
6:12, 30	1QH^a 10:9, 20	c	ערל שפתים
7:1	4Q374 2 ii 6	b	נתתיך אלהים לפרעה
12:14[3]	11Q19 17:3–4; 27:4–5	c	היה היום הזה לכם לזכרון... לדרתיכם חקת עולם
12:16	11Q19 14:10–11	a	אך אשר יאכל לכל נפש הוא לבדו יעשה לכם
12:20[4]	11Q19 17:4; 21:9 (‖ 11Q20 5:12); 27:9	c	בכל מושבתיכם
13:21, 22	4Q470 3 5	b	בעמוד אש
14:24	4Q504 6 10	a	בעמוד אש וענן
15:3	4Q299 3a ii–b 12	c	יהוה שמו
15:4	1QM 11:9–10	b	מרכבת פרעה...שלשיו...בים סוף
15:10	1QH^a 16:20	c	כעופרת במים אדירים
15:11	1QM 10:8; 13:13; 1QH^a 15:31; 4Q431 1 4[5] (‖ 4Q427 7 i 8)	b	מי כמכה

---

[1] Armin Lange and Matthias Weigold, *Biblical Quotations and Allusions in Second Temple Jewish Literature*, JAJS 5 (Oakville, CT: Vandenhoeck & Ruprecht, 2011).

[2] Also Deut 26:6.

[3] Exodus 12:14 is in the context of the Passover but is incorporated by the Temple Scroll for the ordination ceremony for the priests (11Q19 17:3-4) and for the Day of Atonement (11Q19 27:4-5).

[4] See also Exod 35:3; Lev 3:17; 7:26; 23:3, 14, 21, 31; Num 35:29; Ezek 6:6, 14. But the relationship to Exod 12:20 is likely given the pairing with Exod 12:14 and the language of the Passover celebration.

[5] This manuscript was also published as 4Q471a (DJD XXXVI, 446–49) but is now correctly understood as 4Q431 (4QH^e) a Cave 4 manuscript of the Hodayot (1QHa).

10 The Text of Exodus in the Qumran Corpus

15:17–18	4Q174 1–2 i 3	a	מקדש אדני כוננו...יהוה ימלך לעלם ועד
16:29	CD 11:7–8 (|| 4Q270 6 v 13; 4Q271 5 i 4); 4Q251 1–2 4–5; 4Q265 6 4–5	b	אל יצא (בשבת)
18:16	4Q377 1 i 6	c	ושפטתי בין איש ובין רעהו
18:21	4Q275 2 3; 11Q19 57:8	b	אנשי חיל יראי אלהים אנשי אמת שנאי בצע
18:21, 25[6]	CD 13:1–2; 1QS 2:21–22; 1QSa 1:14–15; 2:1–29:1; 4Q491 1–3 10; 11Q19 57:4–5	b	שרי אלפים...ושרי עשרת
19:4	4Q504 6 6–7	a	ואשא אתכם על כנפי נשרים ואבא אתכם אלי
19:5	4Q299 60 3	c	סגלה מכל העמים
19:6	4Q504 4 10	a	ממלכת כהנים וגוי קדוש
20:6[7]	CD 20:21–22	a	ועשה חסד לאלפים לאהבי ולשמרי מצוותי
20:12	4Q416 2 iii 15–16, 19 (|| 4Q418 9+9a–c 17; 10a–b 2)	b	כבד את אביך ואת אמך
20:18	4Q377 2 ii 10	b	ויעמדו מרחק
20:18 (SP)[8]	4Q175 1:1–8	a	וידבר יהוה אל משה...אנכי אדרש מעמו
20:25	4Q547 8 3	b	מזבח אבנים
21:18–20	4Q251 4–7 I 2–5	a	וכי יריבן אנשים...את אמתו בשבט
21:26–30	4Q251 8 1–6	b	וכי יכה איש את עין...ככל אשר יושת עליו
22:28	4Q251 9 2–3	b	ודמעך לא תאחר
22:30	4Q251 12 3–4	b	טרפה לא תאכלו
23:7	1QS 5:15	a	דבר שקר תרחק
23:25–26	4Q285 8 8 (|| 11Q14 1 ii 11–12)	b	והסרתי מחלה...לא תהיה משכלה
24:10	4Q377 1 i 2	c	עצם השמים
24:12	4Q216 1:5–7	a	ויאמר יהוה אל משה...כתבתי להורתם
24:15, 16	4Q377 2 ii 10–11	b	ויכס הענן
24:18	4Q377 2 ii 10	b	ויבא משה בתוך הענן
25:3[9]	1QM 5:5, 8	b	זהב וכסף ונחשת
25:4[10]	11Q19 3:2	b	ותכלת וארגמן ותולעת שני
25:17	11Q19 3:9	b	כפרת זהב טהור

[6] Also Deut 1:15.
[7] Also Deut 5:10. These passages are conflated with Deut 7:9 (לאלף דור).
[8] See 4Q158 6 4–9 in the references to Rewritten Scripture in §4.
[9] Also Exod 35:5.
[10] The furnishings of the Temple are the topic. Cf. Exod 35:6, 23.

32:52	11Q18 8 2	b	ואמה רחבו
25:23–24	11Q19 8:5–7	a	ועשית שלחן עצי שטים...זר זהב סביב
25:26	11Q18 8 1	b	ארבע רגליו
25:30	11Q18 8 3	b	על השלחן לחם פנים
25:31–34	11Q19 9:1–5	a	ועשית מנרת זהב טהור...כפתריה ופרחיה
25:39[11]	11Q19 3:8	b	זהב טהור יעשה אתה את כל הכלים
26:31	11Q19 7:13	b	ועשית פרכת
27:21	1Q22 1 iv 4; 11Q19 8:13; 21:9 (‖ 11Q20 5:12); 22:14 (‖ 11Q20 6:6–7); 24:8–9; 25:8	c	חקת עולם לדרתם
27:21[12]	11Q19 9:14	b	יערך (נר)...חקת עולם לדרתם
28:42[13]	1QM 7:10	b	מכנסי בד
29:13[14]	11Q19 15:6–7 (‖ 11Q20 1:15)	a	ואת שתי הכלית ואת החלב אשר עליהן
	11Q19 16:7–8 (‖ 11Q20 2:6–7)	a	
29:14	11Q19 16:10–11 (‖ 11Q20 2:9)	a	ואת בשר הפר...תשרף...מחוץ למחנה
29:18, 25, 41[15]	1QS 8:9; 1QSb 3:1; 4Q220 1 5, 9; 4Q265 7 9; 11Q18 29 6; 33 1; 11Q19 20:8; 24:6; 27:012; 28:2, 6; 34:14; PAM 43.698 21 1	c	ריח ניחוח
29:20	11Q19 16:2–3 (‖ 11Q20 2:2–3)	b	ועל תנוך אזן...ועל בהן ידם הימנית
29:22[16]	11Q19 15:6–7 (‖ 11Q20 1:15)	a	ואת שתי הכלית ואת החלב אשר עלהן
	11Q19 16:7–8 (‖ 11Q20 2:6–7)	a	
29:24, 26	11Q19 20:16–21:01 (‖ 11Q20 5:1)	a	והנפת אתם תנופה לפני יהוה
29:34	11Q19 43:11–12	b	ושרפת את הנותר באש לא יאכל כי קדש
30:12–13	4Q159 1 ii 6–7	a	נתנו איש כפר נפשו...עשרים גרה השקל
30:12–13	11Q19 39:8–10	b	נתנו איש כפר נפשו...עשרים גרה השקל

[11] Also Exod 37:24.
[12] Cf. Lev 24:3.
[13] Also Lev 6:3; 16:4.
[14] Also 29:22.
[15] These are the first occurrences of this common Biblical Hebrew syntagm. It is also found at Lev 1:9, et al.; Num 15:3, et al.; Ezek 6:13, et al. I have not included the cases in the Temple Scroll (11Q19) where Lev 1:13 is clearly quoted: 11Q19 15:12-13 (//11Q20 1:19); and 16:10.
[16] Also 29:13.

10 The Text of Exodus in the Qumran Corpus

30:14	CD 10:1–2 (‖ 4Q270 6 iv 14); 15:6; 4Q271 2 13	c	עבר על הפקדים
33:7	4Q159 5 4–5	b	משה יקח את האהל...יצא אל אהל
33:11	4Q377 2 ii 6–7	b	פנים אל פנים כאשר ידבר איש אל רעהו
	4Q504 3 ii 17 (‖ 4Q506 125+127 2)	b	פנים אל פנים
34:6	1QHa 8:34; 4Q511 52+54–5+57–9 1	b	אל רחום וחנון ארך אפים ורב חסד ואמת
34:7	1QHa 4:24; 8:34	b	נשא עון ופשע וחטאה
34:7	4Q504 6 14	b	ונקה לא ינקה
34:9[17]	4Q504 4 7 (‖ 4Q506 131–132 14)	b	וסלחת לעוננו ולחטאתנו
34:10–13	11Q19 2:1–7	a	כי נורא הוא...ואת אשריו תכרתון
34:14–16	11Q19 2:11–15	a	כי לא תשתחוה לאל אחר... אחרי אלהיהן
34:27	CD 16:1 (‖ 4Q271 4 ii 3)	a	על פי הדברים...כרתי אתך ברית וא ישראל
35:1	1Q22 1 ii 11	a	אלה הדברים אשר צוה יהוה לעשת אתם
35:2	4Q218 1 2–3	b	כל העשׂה בו מלאכה יומת
35:5[18]	1QM 5:5, 8	b	זהב וכסף ונחשת
37:18	11Q19 9:3–4	b	ששה קנים יצאים מצדיה...קני מנרה מצדה השני
37:24[19]	11Q19 3:8	b	זהב טהור יעשה אתה את כל הכלים
39:28	1QM 7:11	b	פארי המגבעת
39:29[20]	1QM 7:10–11	b	אבנט שש משזר ותכלת וארגמן ותולעת שני

3. Excursus

1. The most striking challenges encountered by readers during their initial exposure to the Hebrew of the Qumran corpus are spelling variations (orthography) and changes in how various aspects of words are formed (morphology). There are at least 42 species of variation that occur in both the Qumran biblical and non-biblical manuscripts.[21] It is of special note that manuscripts that show the greatest variance vis-à-vis Classical Biblical Hebrew do not exhibit a symmetrical increase among these 42 elements.

---

[17] Also Jer 36:3.
[18] Also Exod 25:3.
[19] Also Exod 25:39.
[20] Priestly garments are the topic.
[21] Martin G. Abegg, Jr., "Scribal Practice and the Pony in the Manure Pile," in *Reading the Bible in Ancient Traditions and Modern Editions: Studies in Memory of Peter W. Flint*, ed. Andrew B. Perrin, Kyung S. Baek, and Daniel K Falk (Atlanta: SBL, 2017), 71–73.

Instead, there is a smaller group of elements that actuate this greater variance.[22] It is this variance that Emanuel Tov, the final Editor-in-Chief of Oxford Press' Dead Sea Scroll publication project, began examining in a series of articles beginning in 1986,[23] culminating as part of his book-length study entitled, *Scribal Practices and Approaches Reflected in the Texts Found in the Judean Desert*.[24] Tov has called the writing characterized by this smaller group of elements, Qumran Scribal Practice (QSP). He has posited that manuscripts that exhibit QSP also express the sectarian philosophy of the corpus.[25] My own research has determined that there are 17 orthographic/morphological elements that can be used to define QSP.[26] Although manuscripts that exhibit QSP are much more prevalent among non-biblical scrolls (70% of the manuscripts) than biblical scrolls (30%), for this current study it should be emphasized that biblical quotations in non-biblical manuscripts echo the scribal patterns of the manuscripts in which they occur. Thus these differences will be encountered throughout the Exodus quotations which are documented in Table 10.1.[27] At least 9 of the 17 elements that characterize QSP are found among the Exodus quotations listed in the table.[28]

Table 10.2. Qumran scribal practice in DSS's Exodus quotations

1. Full orthography: כול	Exod 12:20 (11Q19 17:4); 19:5 (4Q299 60 3); 20:18 (SP) (4Q175 1:2, 3, 4, 6); 25:39 (11Q19 3:8)
2. Full orthography: לוא	Exod 20:18 (SP) (4Q175 1:7); 29:34 (11Q19 43:11); 34:7 (4Q504 6 14); 34:14 (11Q19 2:11)
3. Full orthography: מושה	Exod 20:18 (SP) (4Q175 1:1); 33:7 (4Q159 5 4–5)
4. "Pausal" Qal imperfect: יקטולו	Exod 20:18 (4Q377 2 ii 10); 29:14 (11Q19 16:11); 34:13 (11Q19 2:7)
5. Long 2ms perfect: קטלתה	Exod 26:31 (11Q19 7:13)
6. Long 3ms pronoun: הואה	Exod 15:3 (4Q299 3a ii–b 12)
7. Long 2ms suffix: -כה	Exod 15:11 (1QM 10:8; 13:13; 1QHᵃ 15:31); 15:17 (4Q174 1–2 i 3); 20:12 (4Q416 2 iii 15, 16, 19; 4Q418 9+9a–c 17; 10a–b 2); 20:18 (SP) (4Q175 1:2, 5); 34:12 (11Q19 2:4)
8. Long 2mp suffix: -כמה	Exod 12:16 (11Q19 14:10–11)

---

[22] This can be clearly seen in the graph on p. 74 of "Scribal Practice and the Pony in the Manure Pile."
[23] Emanuel Tov, "The Orthography and Language of the Hebrew Scrolls Found at Qumran and the Origin of These Scrolls," *Textus* 13 (1986): 31–57.
[24] Emanuel Tov, *Scribal Practices and Approaches Reflected in the Texts Found in the Judean Desert*, STDJ 54 (Leiden: Brill, 2004).
[25] E. Tov, "Scribal Practices and Approaches Revisited," *HeBAI* 3 (2014): 371.
[26] Martin G. Abegg, Jr., "Qumran Scribal Practice: Won Moor Thyme," in *Scribal Practice, Text and Canon in the Dead Sea Scrolls*, ed. John J. Collins and Ananda Geyser-Fouché (Leiden: Brill, 2019), 180–81.
[27] Only CD (Exod 16:29; 30:14), 4Q216 (Exod 24:12), 4Q270 (Exod 16:29; 30:14), and 4Q374 (Exod 7:1), among the manuscripts with Exodus quotations, are not written in QSP.
[28] The eight remaining QSP elements are: full orthography: זאות, כיא, כוה; long 2mp perfect: קטלתמה; long 3fs pronoun: היאה; long 2mp pronoun: אתמה; "adverbial" *he*: מאודה; and "pausal" Qal imperative: קטולו.

10 *The Text of Exodus in the Qumran Corpus*   165

9. Long 3mp suffix: ‑המה/‑מה   Exod 12:14 (11Q19 17:3; 11Q19 27:5); 12:20 (11Q19 17:4); 20:18 (SP) (4Q175 1:5, 6); 27:21 (11Q19 9:14; 21:9; 22:14; 11Q20 5:12; 6:7); 29:24 (11Q19 20:16); 34:13 (11Q19 2:6, 7); 34:16 (11Q19 2:15)

2. There is evidence for what T. Muraoka describes as the "disintegration and collapse of the classical BH system" regarding verbal tense, aspect, and mood.[29] The most common example of this devolution involves a shift from *waw*-consecutive with the perfect to conjunctive *waw* plus the imperfect. This alternation occurs at least 24 times among biblical quotations in the Qumran non-biblical corpus.[30] There are three examples of this change in the quotations of Exodus. As an ideal example of the shift note 11Q19 20:16, which quotes Exod 29:24:

ויניפו אותמה תנופה לפני יהוה
וְהֵנַפְתָּ אֹתָם תְּנוּפָה לִפְנֵי יְהוָה

He shall wave them as a wave offering before the LORD.

For the other examples see 4Q175 1:3 (ויהיה), which quotes the Samaritan Pentateuch of Exod 20:18 (והיה, see in the MT at Deut 5:29, וְהָיָה), and 4Q175 1:6 (וידבר) which quotes the Samaritan Pentateuch of Exod 20:18 (ודבר, see in the MT at Deut 18:18, וְדִבֶּר). It would be tempting to focus our attention only on the decline of the perfect consecutive (which is entirely missing by the time of the Mishnah) and miss the fact that *waw* plus the imperfect—relatively rare in Biblical Hebrew—quite often connotes a volitive rather than a simple future. Thus two quite useful constituents of the Biblical Hebrew verbal system—the perfect consecutive and the volitive use of *waw* plus the imperfect—were on the decline in the second half of the Second Temple period.

3. Carol Newsom is renowned in Qumran circles for the most creative article title to date: "'Sectually Explicit' Literature from Qumran."[31] This article is also of note as it contains a statement that has become gospel in Qumran studies: "Even if one cannot be certain that documents composed by members of the sect will contain a distinctive content, there may be some features that are clearly *incompatible* with sectarian authorship. In documents that are demonstrably of Qumran authorship the tetragrammaton is always avoided, *except in quotations from scripture*."[32] This informs the one occurrence of the tetragrammaton among the Exodus quotations: 4Q174 1-2 I 3 (Exod 15:18).

---

[29] Takamitsu Muraoka, *A Syntax of Qumran Hebrew* (Leuven: Peeters, 2020), 85–90.
[30] There are also 34 occurrences of this shift among the biblical manuscripts, 25 of which are found in the Great Isaiah Scroll (1QIsaᵃ).
[31] Carol A. Newsom, "'Sectually Explicit' Literature from Qumran," in *The Hebrew Bible and Its Interpreters*, ed. William Henry Propp et al. (Winona Lake: Eisenbrauns, 1990), 167–88.
[32] Newsom, "Sectually Explicit," 177 (emphasis added).

In order to test Newsom's statement, I first searched יהוה in all the documents that Emanuel Tov designated as "sectarian" in Appendix 1b of *Scribal Practices and Approaches*.³³ This produced 54 occurrences, all of which are in biblical quotations except for 4QCommunal Confession (4Q393) 3 6 and 4QHodayot^c (4Q429) 6 2. In Daniel Falk's edition of Communal Confession he offers: "There are no concrete indications of sectarian origin, and its use of the Tetragrammaton would be surprising if the text had been composed at Qumran…"³⁴ Regarding the occurrence in 4QHodayot^c Eileen Schuller writes, "The use of the tetragrammaton in line 2 (if this is the correct reading) precludes taking this as a Hodayot fragment."³⁵ The evidence of circular reasoning—that is, the tetragrammaton does not occur in sectarian manuscripts (apart from biblical quotations), therefore its "non-quotational" use means a manuscript is not sectarian—should warn a researcher to be a bit circumspect, but for our present purposes it is certainly accurate to state that the use of the tetragrammaton in biblical quotation is the norm in the sectarian texts from Qumran. So the case of the tetragrammaton among the Exodus quotations at 4Q174 1-2 i 3 is in accordance with this norm.³⁶

There are two cases among the Exodus quotations where a reverent scribe has chosen to use a replacement for the tetragrammaton. At 4Q175 1:1, a quotation of Exod 20:18 from the Samaritan Pentateuch (a reworking of Deut 5:28: וידבר יהוה אל משה, "and the LORD spoke to Moses"), the tetragrammaton is replaced with 4 dots, termed "tetrapuncta." The use of tetrapuncta follows the same pattern as the tetragrammaton—that is, in sectarian texts this replacement for the divine name only occurs in biblical quotations.³⁷ The tetrapuncta replacement was thus treated with the same reverence as the tetragrammaton itself. The second case is somewhat less certain. I have included the quotation of Exod 15:3 at 4Q299 3a ii-b 12 following the judgment of L. H. Schiffman, who posits that the pronoun הואה (literally, "he") in this manuscript replaces the tetragrammaton so that שמו הואה should be translated "the LORD is his name."³⁸

4. The Qumran manuscripts occasionally record a new voice which evidences an unknown aspect of the exegetical debates which were present among the Jews of antiquity. As an example, the command in Exod 30:12-16 concerning the half-shekel offering that every adult must pay as a "ransom for his life" (כֹּפֶר נַפְשׁוֹ)—the so-called Temple Tax—led to a debate between the rabbinic sages and the Sadducees. The sages ruled that the half-shekel donation should be collected yearly and its proceeds used to purchase animals for the daily burnt offering. In contrast, the Sadducees opposed

---

³³ Tov, *Scribal Practices*, 281–85.
³⁴ Daniel K. Falk, "4QCommunal Confession," in *Qumran Cave 4.XX: Poetical and Liturgical Texts, Part 2*, DJD 29, ed. Esther Chazon et al. (Oxford: Clarendon Press, 1999), 48.
³⁵ Hartmut Stegemann and Eileen Schuller, *Qumran Cave 1.iii: 1QHodayot^a with Incorporation of 1QHodayot^b and 4QHodayot^a-f*, DJD 40 (Oxford: Clarendon, 2008), 194.
³⁶ For further discussion see Tov, *Scribal Practices*, 218-19.
³⁷ For further discussion see Tov, *Scribal Practices*, 238-46.
³⁸ Lawrence H. Schiffman, "4QMysteries^a," in *Qumran Cave 4.XV: Sapiential Texts, Part 1*, DJD 20, ed. Torleif Elgvin et al. (Oxford: Clarendon Press, 1997), 43. This might also be the case at CD 9:5 and its parallel at 4Q270 6 iii 19 (a quote of Nah 1:2), as well as 1QS 8:13 (a quote of Isa 40:3).

the use of the half-shekel donation for public offerings and determined that the offerings should be provided by individual donations.³⁹ The Qumran corpus reveals an additional aspect of this ancient debate which had been lost before the discovery of the Qumran Scrolls.

The New Testament reflection of the Exodus 30 passage in Matt 17:24–27 clearly expresses the interpretation that the tax was paid more than once in a person's life. When the tax collectors approached Peter and asked him if his teacher kept the commandment by paying the Temple tax, the verb—τελεῖ—is in the present tense. Peter responded, "Yes" (ναί), that is, my teacher pays the half-shekel being levied on each Jew (at every census). This interpretation was likely that of the rabbinic sages as well, thus providing sufficient funds to purchase animals for the daily burnt offering. But two passages from the Scrolls which quote Exod 30:12-13 reveal that there was another interpretation of the edict. Ordinancesᵃ (4Q159) comments, "He shall give it only o[nce] in his life" (4Q159 1 ii 7). The Temple Scroll (11Q19) expands the comment to include the age when a youth becomes a member of the adult congregation and is thus required to pay: "A woman may not enter there (the Temple), nor a boy until the day when he completes the period of [his] yo[uth; then he shall give] his own [redempti]on to the Lord, a half-shekel…" (11Q19 39:7–8). Clearly the phrase in Exod 30:13, "All who cross over to those counted," was interpreted by the Qumran writers in light of the same expression in v. 14 which is followed by "those twenty years old." So instead of being those counted in each census, the Exodus command was understood by the writers of the Qumran documents to refer to those who reach twenty years of age, that is "when he completes the period of [his] yo[uth" (11Q19 39:8). It is possible that the Sadducees also held this view, resulting in a smaller collection that would have required the public offerings to be funded by personal donation instead of the half-shekel tax.

4. Rewritten Scripture

The following verses from Exodus are found in five Qumran works⁴⁰ that were originally published as non-biblical manuscripts and called variously "Biblical Paraphrase," "Rewritten Scripture," "Reworked Pentateuch," or "Apocryphal Pentateuch." They are more often now considered to be biblical manuscripts which evidence a higher frequency of exegetical and theological opinions not present in previously known versions of the Pentateuch.⁴¹

---

³⁹ Yoram Erder, "הפולמוס הכיתתי בימי הבית השני על אודות מחצית השקל לאור ההלכה הקראית הקדומה" ("Second Temple Period Sectarian Polemic Concerning the Half-Shekel Commandment in Light of Early Karaite Halakhah"), *Meghillot* 8-9 (2010): 3–28.

⁴⁰ 4QReworkedPentateuchᵃ (4Q158), 4QReworkedPentateuchᵇ (4Q364), 4QReworkedPentateuchᶜ (4Q365), 4QReworkedPentateuchᵈ (4Q366), and 4QApocryphalPentateuch A (4Q368).

⁴¹ A convenient list of biblical manuscripts which contain the book of Exodus is found in James VanderKam and Peter Flint, *The Meaning of the Dead Sea Scrolls: Their Significance for Understanding the Bible, Judaism, Jesus, and Christianity* (San Francisco: HarperSanFrancisco, 2002), 408–409.

Table 10.3. Exodus in "rewritten Scripture"

3:12	4Q158 1-2 16	4Q Reworked Pentateuch[a]
	4Q158 4 1-2	4Q Reworked Pentateuch[a]
4:27	4Q158 1-2 13-14	4Q Reworked Pentateuch[a]
4:28	4Q158 1-2 14-15	4Q Reworked Pentateuch[a]
8:13	4Q365 2 2-3	4Q Reworked Pentateuch[c]
8:14	4Q365 2 3-4	4Q Reworked Pentateuch[c]
8:15	4Q365 2 4-5	4Q Reworked Pentateuch[c]
8:16	4Q365 2 6-7	4Q Reworked Pentateuch[c]
8:17	4Q365 2 7-9	4Q Reworked Pentateuch[c]
8:18	4Q365 2 9-11	4Q Reworked Pentateuch[c]
8:19	4Q365 2 11	4Q Reworked Pentateuch[c]
9:9	4Q365 3 1-2	4Q Reworked Pentateuch[c]
9:10	4Q365 3 2	4Q Reworked Pentateuch[c]
9:11	4Q365 3 2-3	4Q Reworked Pentateuch[c]
9:12	4Q365 3 3-4	4Q Reworked Pentateuch[c]
10:19	4Q365 4 1	4Q Reworked Pentateuch[c]
10:20	4Q365 4 1-2	4Q Reworked Pentateuch[c]
14:7	4Q365 5 2	4Q Reworked Pentateuch[c]
14:10	4Q365 5 1	4Q Reworked Pentateuch[c]
14:12	4Q365 6a i 1	4Q Reworked Pentateuch[c]
14:13	4Q365 6a i 1-3	4Q Reworked Pentateuch[c]
14:14	4Q365 6a i 3-4	4Q Reworked Pentateuch[c]
14:15	4Q365 6a i 4-5	4Q Reworked Pentateuch[c]
14:16	4Q365 6a i 5-6	4Q Reworked Pentateuch[c]
14:17	4Q365 6a i 6-7	4Q Reworked Pentateuch[c]
14:18	4Q365 6a i 7-8	4Q Reworked Pentateuch[c]
14:19	4Q365 6a i 8-10	4Q Reworked Pentateuch[c]
14:20	4Q365 6a i 11-12	4Q Reworked Pentateuch[c]
14:21	4Q365 6a i 12-13	4Q Reworked Pentateuch[c]
15:16	4Q365 6b 1	4Q Reworked Pentateuch[c]
15:17	4Q365 6b 1-2	4Q Reworked Pentateuch[c]
15:18	4Q365 6b 3	4Q Reworked Pentateuch[c]
15:19	4Q365 6b 3-5	4Q Reworked Pentateuch[c]
15:20	4Q365 6b 5-6	4Q Reworked Pentateuch[c]
15:21	4Q365 6b 6	4Q Reworked Pentateuch[c]
15:22	4Q365 6aii+6c 8	4Q Reworked Pentateuch[c]
15:23	4Q365 6aii+6c 9	4Q Reworked Pentateuch[c]
15:24	4Q365 6aii+6c 10	4Q Reworked Pentateuch[c]
15:25	4Q365 6aii+6c 10-11	4Q Reworked Pentateuch[c]
15:26	4Q365 6aii+6c 11-14	4Q Reworked Pentateuch[c]
17:3	4Q365 7 i 2	4Q Reworked Pentateuch[c]
17:4	4Q365 7 i 3	4Q Reworked Pentateuch[c]
17:5	4Q365 7 i 4	4Q Reworked Pentateuch[c]

18:13	4Q365 7 ii 1	4Q Reworked Pentateuch[c]
18:14	4Q365 7 ii 1-3	4Q Reworked Pentateuch[c]
18:15	4Q365 7 ii 4	4Q Reworked Pentateuch[c]
18:16	4Q365 7 ii 4	4Q Reworked Pentateuch[c]
19:17	4Q158 5 1-2	4Q Reworked Pentateuch[a]
	4Q364 14 1-2[42]	4Q Reworked Pentateuch[b]
19:19	4Q158 5 2-3	4Q Reworked Pentateuch[a]
19:21	4Q158 5 3-4	4Q Reworked Pentateuch[a]
19:22	4Q158 5 4-5	4Q Reworked Pentateuch[a]
19:23	4Q158 5 5	4Q Reworked Pentateuch[a]
20:12	4Q158 7-8 1	4Q Reworked Pentateuch[a]
20:16 (SP)	4Q158 6 1-2	4Q Reworked Pentateuch[a]
20:16	4Q158 7-8 1-2	4Q Reworked Pentateuch[a]
20:17 (SP)	4Q158 6 3	4Q Reworked Pentateuch[a]
20:17	4Q158 7-8 2	4Q Reworked Pentateuch[a]
20:18 (SP)	4Q158 6 4-9	4Q Reworked Pentateuch[a]
20:18	4Q158 7-8 3-4	4Q Reworked Pentateuch[a]
20:22	4Q158 7-8 5-6	4Q Reworked Pentateuch[a]
20:23	4Q158 7-8 6	4Q Reworked Pentateuch[a]
20:24	4Q158 7-8 6-7	4Q Reworked Pentateuch[a]
20:25	4Q158 7-8 7-8	4Q Reworked Pentateuch[a]
20:26	4Q158 7-8 8-9	4Q Reworked Pentateuch[a]
21:1	4Q158 7-8 9	4Q Reworked Pentateuch[a]
21:3	4Q158 7-8 10	4Q Reworked Pentateuch[a]
21:4	4Q158 7-8 11	4Q Reworked Pentateuch[a]
21:6	4Q158 7-8 12-13	4Q Reworked Pentateuch[a]
21:8	4Q158 7-8 13-14	4Q Reworked Pentateuch[a]
21:10	4Q158 7-8 14-15	4Q Reworked Pentateuch[a]
21:13	4Q364 13a-b 1-2	4Q Reworked Pentateuch[b]
21:14	4Q364 13a-b 2-3	4Q Reworked Pentateuch[b]
21:15	4Q158 9 1	4Q Reworked Pentateuch[a]
	4Q364 13a-b 6	4Q Reworked Pentateuch[b]
21:16	4Q158 9 1	4Q Reworked Pentateuch[a]
21:18	4Q158 9 2	4Q Reworked Pentateuch[a]
	4Q364 13a-b 5-6	4Q Reworked Pentateuch[b]
21:19	4Q364 13a-b 6-7	4Q Reworked Pentateuch[b]
21:20	4Q158 9 3	4Q Reworked Pentateuch[a]
	4Q364 13a-b 7-8	4Q Reworked Pentateuch[b]
21:21	4Q364 13a-b 8-9	4Q Reworked Pentateuch[b]
21:22	4Q158 9 4-5	4Q Reworked Pentateuch[a]
	4Q364 13a-b 9	4Q Reworked Pentateuch[b]
21:25	4Q158 9 6	4Q Reworked Pentateuch[a]
21:32	4Q158 10-12 1	4Q Reworked Pentateuch[a]

---

[42] Or perhaps an addition to Exod 24:11.

21:34	4Q158 10-12 2	4Q Reworked Pentateuch^a
21:35	4Q158 10-12 3	4Q Reworked Pentateuch^a
	4Q366 1 1-2	4Q Reworked Pentateuch^d
21:36	4Q158 10-12 3	4Q Reworked Pentateuch^a
	4Q366 1 2-3	4Q Reworked Pentateuch^d
21:37	4Q158 10-12 4	4Q Reworked Pentateuch^a
	4Q366 1 4-5	4Q Reworked Pentateuch^d
22:1	4Q158 10-12 5	4Q Reworked Pentateuch^a
	4Q366 1 5-6	4Q Reworked Pentateuch^d
22:2	4Q158 10-12 5	4Q Reworked Pentateuch^a
	4Q366 1 6-7	4Q Reworked Pentateuch^d
22:3	4Q158 10-12 6	4Q Reworked Pentateuch^a
	4Q366 1 7-8	4Q Reworked Pentateuch^d
22:4	4Q158 10-12 6-7	4Q Reworked Pentateuch^a
	4Q366 1 9-11	4Q Reworked Pentateuch^d
22:5	4Q158 10-12 8	4Q Reworked Pentateuch^a
	4Q366 1 12	4Q Reworked Pentateuch^d
22:6	4Q158 10-12 8	4Q Reworked Pentateuch^a
22:7	4Q158 10-12 9	4Q Reworked Pentateuch^a
22:8	4Q158 10-12 10	4Q Reworked Pentateuch^a
22:9	4Q158 10-12 11	4Q Reworked Pentateuch^a
22:10	4Q158 10-12 12	4Q Reworked Pentateuch^a
22:11	4Q158 10-12 12	4Q Reworked Pentateuch^a
22:13	4Q158 10-12 13	4Q Reworked Pentateuch^a
24:4	4Q158 4 2-3	4Q Reworked Pentateuch^a
24:5	4Q158 4 4	4Q Reworked Pentateuch^a
24:6	4Q158 4 4-5	4Q Reworked Pentateuch^a
24:12	4Q364 14 3-4	4Q Reworked Pentateuch^b
24:13	4Q364 14 4-5	4Q Reworked Pentateuch^b
24:14	4Q364 14 5-6	4Q Reworked Pentateuch^b
24:18	4Q364 15 1-3	4Q Reworked Pentateuch^b
25:1	4Q364 15 5	4Q Reworked Pentateuch^b
25:2	4Q364 15 5	4Q Reworked Pentateuch^b
26:1	4Q364 16 1-2	4Q Reworked Pentateuch^b
26:33	4Q364 17 1-2	4Q Reworked Pentateuch^b
26:34	4Q364 17 2-3	4Q Reworked Pentateuch^b
	4Q365 8a-b 1	4Q Reworked Pentateuch^c
26:35	4Q364 17 3-5	4Q Reworked Pentateuch^b
	4Q365 8a-b 1-2	4Q Reworked Pentateuch^c
26:36	4Q365 8a-b 2-3	4Q Reworked Pentateuch^c
26:37	4Q365 8a-b 3	4Q Reworked Pentateuch^c
28:16	4Q365 9a-b i 2	4Q Reworked Pentateuch^c
28:17	4Q365 9a-b i 2-3	4Q Reworked Pentateuch^c
28:18	4Q365 9a-b i 3	4Q Reworked Pentateuch^c
28:19	4Q365 9a-b i 3-4	4Q Reworked Pentateuch^c

10 The Text of Exodus in the Qumran Corpus

28:20	4Q365 9a-b i 4	4Q Reworked Pentateuch^c
29:20	4Q365 9b ii 1, 3-4	4Q Reworked Pentateuch^c
29:21	4Q365 9b ii 1-3	4Q Reworked Pentateuch^c
29:22	4Q365 9b ii 4	4Q Reworked Pentateuch^c
30:32	4Q158 13 2-3	4Q Reworked Pentateuch^a
30:34	4Q158 13 3	4Q Reworked Pentateuch^a
30:37	4Q365 10 1	4Q Reworked Pentateuch^c
30:38	4Q365 10 1-2	4Q Reworked Pentateuch^c
31:1	4Q365 10 3	4Q Reworked Pentateuch^c
31:2	4Q365 10 3-4	4Q Reworked Pentateuch^c
31:3	4Q365 10 4	4Q Reworked Pentateuch^c
33:11	4Q368 1 3-4	4Q Apocryphal Pentateuch A
33:12	4Q368 1 4-6	4Q Apocryphal Pentateuch A
33:13	4Q368 1 6-7	4Q Apocryphal Pentateuch A
34:11	4Q368 2 2-3	4Q Apocryphal Pentateuch A
34:12	4Q368 2 3-4	4Q Apocryphal Pentateuch A
34:13	4Q368 2 5-6	4Q Apocryphal Pentateuch A
34:14	4Q368 2 6-7	4Q Apocryphal Pentateuch A
34:15	4Q368 2 7-8	4Q Apocryphal Pentateuch A
34:16	4Q368 2 8	4Q Apocryphal Pentateuch A
34:17	4Q368 2 9	4Q Apocryphal Pentateuch A
34:18	4Q368 2 9-10	4Q Apocryphal Pentateuch A
34:19	4Q368 2 11	4Q Apocryphal Pentateuch A
34:20	4Q368 2 11-13	4Q Apocryphal Pentateuch A
34:21	4Q368 2 13-14	4Q Apocryphal Pentateuch A
34:22	4Q368 2 14-15	4Q Apocryphal Pentateuch A
34:23	4Q368 2 15-16	4Q Apocryphal Pentateuch A
34:24	4Q368 2 16	4Q Apocryphal Pentateuch A
35:2	4Q365 11 i 1	4Q Reworked Pentateuch^c
35:3	4Q365 11 i 1	4Q Reworked Pentateuch^c
35:4	4Q365 11 i 2-3	4Q Reworked Pentateuch^c
35:5	4Q365 11 i 3	4Q Reworked Pentateuch^c
36:32	4Q365 12a i 1	4Q Reworked Pentateuch^c
36:33	4Q365 12a i 1-2	4Q Reworked Pentateuch^c
36:34	4Q365 12a i 2-3	4Q Reworked Pentateuch^c
36:35	4Q365 12a i 4-5	4Q Reworked Pentateuch^c
36:36	4Q365 12a i 5-6	4Q Reworked Pentateuch^c
36:37	4Q365 12a i 6-7	4Q Reworked Pentateuch^c
36:38	4Q365 12a i 7-8	4Q Reworked Pentateuch^c
37:29	4Q365 12a-b ii 6	4Q Reworked Pentateuch^c
38:1	4Q365 12a-b ii 7-8	4Q Reworked Pentateuch^c
38:2	4Q365 12a-b ii 8-9	4Q Reworked Pentateuch^c
38:3	4Q365 12a-b ii 9-11	4Q Reworked Pentateuch^c
38:4	4Q365 12a-b ii 11-12	4Q Reworked Pentateuch^c
38:5	4Q365 12a-b ii 12-13	4Q Reworked Pentateuch^c

38:6	4Q365 12a-b ii 13-14	4Q Reworked Pentateuch^c
38:7	4Q365 12a-b ii 14	4Q Reworked Pentateuch^c
39:1	4Q365 12b iii 1-2	4Q Reworked Pentateuch^c
39:2	4Q365 12b iii 3	4Q Reworked Pentateuch^c
39:3	4Q365 12b iii 3-5	4Q Reworked Pentateuch^c
39:4	4Q365 12b iii 5	4Q Reworked Pentateuch^c
39:5	4Q365 12b iii 5-7	4Q Reworked Pentateuch^c
39:8	4Q365 12b iii 7-8	4Q Reworked Pentateuch^c
39:9	4Q365 12b iii 8-9	4Q Reworked Pentateuch^c
39:10	4Q365 12b iii 9-10	4Q Reworked Pentateuch^c
39:11	4Q365 12b iii 10	4Q Reworked Pentateuch^c
39:12	4Q365 12b iii 10-11	4Q Reworked Pentateuch^c
39:13	4Q365 12b iii 11-12	4Q Reworked Pentateuch^c
39:14	4Q365 12b iii 12-13	4Q Reworked Pentateuch^c
39:15	4Q365 12b iii 13-14	4Q Reworked Pentateuch^c
39:16	4Q365 12b iii 14	4Q Reworked Pentateuch^c
39:17	4Q365 13 1	4Q Reworked Pentateuch^c
39:18	4Q365 13 1-2	4Q Reworked Pentateuch^c
39:19	4Q365 13 2	4Q Reworked Pentateuch^c

Bibliography

Abegg, Jr., Martin G. "Qumran Scribal Practice: Won Moor Thyme." Pages 175–204 in *Scribal Practice, Text and Canon in the Dead Sea Scrolls*. Edited by John J. Collins and Ananda Geyser-Fouché. Leiden: Brill, 2019.

Abegg, Jr., Martin G. "Scribal Practice and the Pony in the Manure Pile." Pages 65–88 in *Reading the Bible in Ancient Traditions and Modern Editions: Studies in Memory of Peter W. Flint*. Edited by Andrew B. Perrin, Kyung S. Baek, and Daniel K. Falk. Atlanta: SBL, 2017.

Erder, Yoram. "הפולמוס הכיתתי בימי הבית השני על אודות מחצית השקל לאור ההלכה הקראית הקדומה" ("Second Temple Period Sectarian Polemic Concerning the Half-Shekel Commandment in Light of Early Karaite Halakhah"). *Meghillot* 8-9 (2010): 3–28.

Falk, Daniel K. "4QCommunal Confession." Pages 45–61 in *Qumran Cave 4.XX: Poetical and Liturgical Texts, Part 2*. DJD 29. Edited by Esther Chazon et al. Oxford: Clarendon Press, 1999.

Lange, Armin, and Matthias Weigold. *Biblical Quotations and Allusions in Second Temple Jewish Literature*. JAJS 5. Oakville, CT: Vandenhoeck & Ruprecht, 2011.

Muraoka, Takamitsu. *A Syntax of Qumran Hebrew*. Leuven: Peeters, 2020.

Newsom, Carol A. "'Sectually Explicit' Literature from Qumran." Pages 167–87 in *The Hebrew Bible and Its Interpreters*. Edited by William Henry Propp et al. Winona Lake: Eisenbrauns, 1990.

Stegemann, Hartmut, and Eileen Schuller. *Qumran Cave 1.iii: 1QHodayot^a with Incorporation of 1QHodayot^b and 4QHodayot^{a-f}*. DJD 40. Oxford: Clarendon Press, 2008.

Schiffman, Lawrence H. "4QMysteries^a." Pages 33–97 in *Qumran Cave 4.XV: Sapiential Texts, Part 1*. DJD 20. Edited by Torleif Elgvin et al. Oxford: Clarendon Press, 1997.

Tov, Emanuel. *Scribal Practices and Approaches Reflected in the Texts Found in the Judean Desert*. STDJ 54. Brill: Leiden, 2004.
Tov, Emanuel. "Scribal Practices and Approaches Revisited." *HeBAI* 3 (2014): 363–74.
Tov, Emanuel. "The Orthography and Language of the Hebrew Scrolls Found at Qumran and the Origin of These Scrolls." *Textus* 13 (1986): 31–57.
VanderKam, James and Peter Flint. *The Meaning of the Dead Sea Scrolls: Their Significance for Understanding the Bible, Judaism, Jesus, and Christianity*. San Francisco: HarperSanFrancisco, 2002.

Chapter 11

Prayer and Peace in 3 Maccabees 2:2–20: Trusting Precedent for Deliverance or Uttering Threats against the King?*

Jonathan Numada

1. Introduction

The Maccabean martyr traditions provide important background to understanding the crucifixion of Jesus and some of the logical foundations for the New Testament doctrine of the atonement.[1] Grouped together with 1, 2 and 4 Maccabees, 3 Maccabees resembles its companions only in its general sentiment: it lacks the heroic martyrdoms of 2 and 4 Maccabees or the anti-Gentile militancy found in 1 Maccabees. 3 Maccabees' limited reception means it appears to have lacked the theological influence of the other Maccabean books throughout history, but in recent decades it has come to be valued as a source for social history. As a source for historical and cultural information about the environment from which the deuterocanonical and New Testament writings emerged, 3 Maccabees can help fill important *lacunae* for understanding the types of choices faced daily by the Greek-speaking Egyptian Jewish community and Diaspora communities in general.

The present study argues that 3 Maccabees attempts to redirect nationalist sentiment towards non-violent forms of resistance against non-Jews by valorizing prayer as a more acceptable expression of religious devotion than intergroup violence.

---

* This essay is a revised version of a paper first delivered to the Canadian-American Theological Association when it met at the Associated Canadian Theological Schools in Langley, BC, on October 16, 2016. I am grateful for the opportunity to present this paper for publication in honor of Dr. Larry J. Perkins. As a former student and now colleague of Larry, I can say that he has played a pivotal role in my career. I have benefited personally from his instruction in the classroom, the guidance he gave as the second reader for my master's thesis, and the mentorship and leadership he provided as my former supervisor at Northwest Seminary and College.

[1] Jan Willem van Henten, *The Maccabean Martyrs as Saviours of the Jewish People: A Study of 2 and 4 Maccabees* (Leiden: Brill, 1997); Jarvis J. Williams, *Maccabean Martyr Traditions in Paul's Theology of Atonement* (Eugene, OR: Wipf & Stock, 2010).

While echoing the strong consciousness of ethnic and religious identity exhibited in other literature categorized as "Maccabean," 3 Maccabees presents prayer as an effective strategy for Jews that locates power to enact positive change in the God of their history. This allows 3 Maccabees, on the one hand, to present a more outwardly socially and theologically conservative vision than that found in the *Letter of Aristeas* while, on the other hand, still embracing *Aristeas*' socially integrationist ethic. In so doing, it also acknowledges the sentiments behind the more militarist visions of 1 or 2 Maccabees while working to prevent their outward expression, at least when dealing with non-Jews.[2] As such, 3 Maccabees endorses the Jewish cultural tradition of an assertive religious and social identity but advocates for a strategy that allows for continued coexistence among Gentiles in the Diaspora.

2. Survey of previous scholarship

Recent scholarship has been divided over whether the author of 3 Maccabees would have endorsed integration into Hellenistic Egyptian culture.[3] Many observe that 3 Maccabees shares much in common with 2 Maccabees, which as Daniel R. Schwartz notes, points out that Jews and Gentiles are equally fallible.[4] Meanwhile it is often noted that 3 Maccabees is written in highly stylized Greek[5] and uses intertextual allusions and features shared with other genres,[6] which can make it difficult to define

---

[2] Jews in the narrative later use violence against members of their community who had compromised themselves, but this was authorized by the state (3 Macc 7:12).

[3] Religion, ethnicity, civic identity, and culture were spheres that were deeply intertwined in this period, and it should be kept in mind that not everyone at the time would have drawn such distinctions. However, distinguishing between religion, ethnicity, civic identity, and culture remains useful because it can help identify the types of accommodation strategies that were advocated.

[4] Daniel R. Schwartz, *2 Maccabees* (Berlin: Walter de Gruyter, 2008), 48–54. See also Anne Gardner, who argues that 3 Maccabees develops many of the same elements as 2 Maccabees: both have important characters named Eleazar, have prominent prayers elevating the greatness of God, locate citizenship in Jerusalem (2 Macc 4:9, 19; 5:23 and 3 Macc 2:30; 3:21–23), and, she argues, neither holds to polarized views of Gentiles or their rulers. See Anne Gardner, "III Maccabees—A Reflection on the Maccabean Crisis," in *Proceedings of the Ninth World Congress of Jewish Studies* (Jerusalem: World Union of Jewish Studies, 1985), 2–4. See also C. W. Emmet, *The Third Book of Maccabees* (London: SPCK, 1918), viii–ix; Jeremy Corley, "Divine Sovereignty and Power in the High-Priestly Prayer of 3 Macc 2.1–10," in *Prayer from Tobit to Qumran*, ed. R. Egger-Wenzel and J. Corley (Berlin: Walter de Gruyter, 2004), 362–63. Potential challenges to dating 3 Maccabees to the late Ptolemaic period are the negative characterization of King Ptolemy Philopator and the use of λαογραφία in 2:28, which may suggest composition in the early Roman period.

[5] 3 Maccabees' style evokes commentary from many scholars. For example, "florid" as per Judith Newman, "God Condemns the Arrogance of Power: the Prayer in 3 Maccabees 6:2–15," in *Prayer from Alexander to Constantine: A Critical Anthology*, ed. Mark Kiley, et al. (London: Routledge, 1997), 49; "bombastic" as per Cameron Boyd-Taylor, "3 Maccabees: To the Reader," in *A New English Translation of the Septuagint*, ed. Albert Pietersma and Benjamin G. Wright (Oxford: Oxford University Press, 2007), 522; "[a] lack of sophistication and...overblown rhetoric," Loveday Alexander and Philip Alexander, "The Image of the Oriental Monarch in the Third Book of Maccabees," in *Jewish Perspectives on Hellenistic Rulers*, ed. Tessa Rajak, Sarah Pearce, James Aitken, and Jennifer Dines (Berkeley, CA: University of California Press, 2007), 94; "a specimen of the worst kind of pseudo-classicism," Emmet, *Third Book of Maccabees*, xii–xiii.

[6] J. R. C. Cousland, "Dionysius Theomachos? Echoes of the Bacchae in 3 Maccabees," *Biblica* 82 (2001): 539–48; Moses Hadas, "III Maccabees and the Tradition of Patriotic Romance," *Chronique d'Egypte* 24.47 (1949): 102–104; idem, "Third Maccabees and Greek Romance," *Review of Religion* 13 (1948–49): 155–62.

3 Maccabees' attitude towards Gentiles. Part of the issue is balancing the book's penchant for overstatement, in this case the positive and negative portrayals of non-Jewish characters. John M. G. Barclay suggests that positive comments made about some Gentile characters, particularly those Greeks willing to aid Jews as they face persecution, are obligatory and insincere. For Barclay, 3 Maccabees is ethnocentric and at odds with its host culture.[7] N. Clayton Croy, who likewise views 3 Maccabees as somewhat "anti-Gentile," agrees with Barclay.[8] John J. Collins and Sara Raup Johnson, on the other hand, view 3 Maccabees as trying to limit out-group hostility and encourage participation in broader Ptolemaic society while continuing in faithfulness to Jewish culture.[9]

Much 3 Maccabees scholarship has helped shed further light on this question. D. S. Williams argues that 3 Maccabees is an apology dating to the late Ptolemaic period on behalf of Diaspora Judaism to Palestinian Jews.[10] This proposal has been met with skepticism by some,[11] though his point that 3 Maccabees wants to promote a connection between Palestine and the Diaspora is supported by others.[12] Moses Hadas argues that, though its author is embedded in Greek culture, 3 Maccabees is an example of cultural resistance.[13] This proposal has gained more acceptance, and Hadas' ideas are developed further by J. R. C. Cousland[14] in his research on 3 Maccabees' genre and its possible social functions. For both Cousland and Hadas, 3 Maccabees employs Greek literary techniques to ensure the strength and unity of the Egyptian Jewish community while helping it to accommodate itself to Greek-dominated culture.

Scholars have also explored similar trends in 3 Maccabees' anti-Dionysiac polemic, often noting its satirical elements.[15] Cameron Boyd-Taylor argues that 3 Maccabees is

---

[7] Barclay, *Jews in the Mediterranean Diaspora*, 197.
[8] Clayton N. Croy, *3 Maccabees* (Leiden: Brill, 2006), xviii; John M. G. Barclay holds a similar opinion (*Jews in the Mediterranean Diaspora: From Alexander to Trajan [323 BCE–117 CE]* [Edinburgh: T&T Clark, 1996]), 197–201.
[9] Sara Raup Johnson, *Historical Fictions in Hellenistic Jewish Identity: Third Maccabees in its Cultural Context* (Los Angeles, CA: University of California Press, 2004), 180–81, 216–20; John J. Collins, *Between Athens and Jerusalem: Jewish Identity in the Hellenistic Diaspora* (2nd ed; Grand Rapids: Eerdmans, 2000), 126–29; also Alexander and Alexander, "Oriental Monarch," 104.
[10] D. S. Williams, "3 Maccabees: A Defense of Diaspora Judaism?" *JSP* 13 (1995): 14–29.
[11] J. R. C. Cousland, "Reversal, Recidivism and Reward in 3 Maccabees: Structure and Purpose," *JSJ* 34 (2003): 40.
[12] Johannes Magliano Tromp, "The Relations Between Egyptian Judaism and Jerusalem in Light of 3 Maccabees and the Greek Book of Esther," in *Feasts and Festivals*, ed. Christopher M. Tuckett (Leuven: Peeters, 2009), 70–76.
[13] Hadas, "III Maccabees and the Tradition of Patriotic Romance," 98–99; idem, "Aspects of Nationalist Survival under Hellenistic and Roman Imperialism," *Journal of the History of Ideas* 11 (1950): 131–39. Stefan Rebenich suggests that Atticism, a style 3 Maccabees imitates, would in part emerge as a response to Roman imperialism. See "Historical Prose," in *Handbook of Classical Rhetoric in the Hellenistic Period, 330 B.C.–A.D. 400*, ed. Stanley E. Porter (Leiden: Brill, 1997), 293–94.
[14] Cousland, "Reversal, Recidivism and Reward in 3 Maccabees," 39–51.
[15] Cousland, "Echoes of the Bacchae in 3 Maccabees," 539–48; Alexander and Alexander, "Oriental Monarch," 95–98; Cameron Boyd-Taylor, "Robbers, Pirates, and Licentious Women: Echoes of an Anti-Dionysiac Polemic in the Septuagint," in *Die Septuaginta: Texte, Kontexte, Lebenswelten* (Tübingen: Mohr Siebeck, 2008), 559–71; Noah Hacham, "3 Maccabees: An Anti-Dionysiac Polemic," in *Ancient Fiction: The Matrix of Early Christian and Jewish Narrative*, ed. Jo-Ann A. Brant (Atlanta, GA: SBL, 2005), 167–83.

"fashioning a politics of identity for the Diaspora,"[16] and that the importance of the cult of Dionysius in the broader culture may have impacted translation choices in some Septuagint passages as Jews attempted to respond to its influence.[17] Cousland draws connections between King Philopator as a historical individual, the cult of Dionysius, and Euripides' *Bacchae* that are detected in 3 Maccabees. He argues that the book seeks to demonstrate God's superiority over Dionysius,[18] while Noah Hacham follows Cousland in arguing that 3 Maccabees ridicules the Dionysian cult to present Judaism as offering superior benefits.[19] Loveday and Philip Alexander also explore the importance of alcohol consumption in the Dionysian cult, stating that 3 Maccabees draws on this motif to underscore the king's impulsiveness. According to Alexander and Alexander, 3 Maccabees is participating in a critique of absolute monarchy that was shared with some Greek thinkers, though it differs in its advocacy for passivist responses to tyranny grounded by faith in God.[20] A common thread is that recent scholarship on 3 Maccabees identifies a number of points of antagonism but also dialogue between the Egyptian Jewish Diaspora and the dominant culture in an effort to respond to contextual circumstances.

3. Methodology

I will apply select elements Self-Categorization Theory to interpret the characterization of Philopator and his party as antagonists who are representative of previous examples from salvation history. I will show that 3 Maccabees presents Philopator as an antagonist on par with the Giants, Sodomites, and the Pharaoh of the Exodus in order to highlight the daily struggles to remain faithful that were faced by its audience. In this environment, Simon's prayer in 3 Macc 2:2–20 attempts to model prayer as an acceptable form of cultural resistance because it allows for continued cultural engagement and its potential benefits.

Self-Categorization Theory (SCT) is a development from Social Identity theory (SIT). As the name of the paradigm suggests, people classify themselves and others into groups based on perceived similarity or difference.[21] What makes the same collection of people similar or different in one situation may be irrelevant in another.[22] Likewise, an abstract categorization (e.g., human being) tends to be more inclusive and encompass a broader range of individuals than less abstract categorizations (e.g., plumber), depending on what level of identity is relevant in a given context. In one

---

[16] Boyd-Taylor, "Robbers, Pirates, and Licentious Women," 539.
[17] Boyd-Taylor, "Robbers, Pirates, and Licentious Women," 559–71.
[18] Cousland, "Echoes of the Bacchae in 3 Maccabees," 539–48.
[19] Hacham, "An Anti-Dionysiac Polemic," 167–83.
[20] Alexander and Alexander, "Oriental Monarch," 92–110.
[21] S. Alexander Haslam, *Psychology in Organizations: The Social Identity Approach* (London: SAGE, 2002), 45–46.
[22] Michael A. Hogg, "Social Categorization, Depersonalization, and Group Behavior," in *Blackwell Handbook of Social Psychology: Group Processes*, ed. Michael A. Hogg and Scott Tindale (Hoboken, NJ: Wiley-Blackwell, 2002), 62.

instance people may choose to emphasize their common membership in a broad category (e.g., "humanity" or a nationality). Sometimes relatively minor differences such as a profession, heritage, or beliefs may be sufficient cause for a collection of individuals to cleave into smaller groups. Polarization between groups can result when a certain set of categorizations are given paramount importance.[23]

Another key element in SCT is the establishment of examples who are prototypical of a group, or the selection of an individual who best serves as a representative who embodies shared similarities that a group perceives as marking them as different from others.[24] Similarly, stereotyping is when an individual is no longer treated as an individual but is categorized according to perceptions about the group to which they belong. Stereotyping is predicated upon depersonalization, such as when people self-stereotype and set aside their individual identity to situate themselves with an ingroup or apply the same process to stereotype other people and associate them with an outgroup in spite of the fact that they are individuals.[25] Stereotyping, be it of oneself or others, is situational and contingent upon what is deemed relevant for perceiving similarity or difference at the time.[26]

3 Maccabees does not practice economy of language in its descriptions of characters or events, meaning it provides plenty of data that helps us better understand the social categorizations presented in the book and possibly also to glean information about the context in which it was written. In this study we will examine 3 Maccabees' treatment of Philopator and his party, and compare the social categorizations attributed to Philopator with those of others in the prayer. We will then attempt to determine if 3 Maccabees demonstrates polarization towards Greek culture and what sort of stance 3 Maccabees would have its audience adopt when dealing with conflict.

4. Simon's prayer[27]

Following the account of the battle of Raphia (1:1–5), Philopator and his circle visit nearby cities in celebration of their victory. When he visits Jerusalem, the king is greeted by the city's leadership and offers sacrifices in the temple (vv. 6–9). Philopator then attempts to enter the Jerusalem temple in the face of Jewish verbal opposition. News of this spreads through Jerusalem, prompting its inhabitants in various states of dress and dignity to gather to pray for the temple's deliverance from profanation. While this seems to echo the Heliodorus episode in 2 Macc 3:13–40, Philopator's attempted profanation is actually motivated by admiration for the temple's beauty, his inability to accept that he does not enjoy the necessary privileges for entry (1:9b–10),

---

[23] Blackwell, "Social Categorization, Depersonalization, and Group Behavior," 64.
[24] Haslam, *Psychology in Organizations*, 67–69.
[25] Haslam, *Psychology in Organizations*, 44.
[26] Haslam, *Psychology in Organizations*, 46–47.
[27] Some manuscripts include 2:1, which attributes the prayer to the high priest Simon as a representative character, while others do not (Emmet, *Third Book of Maccabees*, 19; Corley, "Divine Sovereignty and Power," 361). We will refer to 2:2–20 as "Simon's prayer," though the following analysis is not dependent upon this attribution.

and refusal to heed the Mosaic Law or instructions from the priests (1:10–15). This prompts the entire city to petition the Lord to prevent Philopator from entering the Temple in 1:16–29, and the high priest Simon specifically in 3 Macc 2:2–20. No characters, Jewish or Greek, engage in the use of force.

N. Clayton Croy notes there are contrasts between God and Philopator in the prayer, such as the differences in God's power vis-à-vis Philopator and their respective domains.[28] Closer examination of the vocabulary and antithetical parallelism suggests that 3 Maccabees considers prayer to be a form of resistance. Prayer is not a sign of desperation or powerlessness since in 2:1 it occurs at the temple, which is symbolic of God as the ultimate power. The high priest, on his knees, remains composed when he stretches out his hands in a deliberate, calculated, and controlled prayer in strong contrast to Philopator's impulsiveness. Close attention to the vocabulary used in Simon's prayer demonstrates that its program is outlined in 2:3:

σὺ γὰρ ὁ κτίσας τὰ πάντα καὶ τῶν ὅλων ἐπικρατῶν δυνάστης δίκαιος εἶ καὶ τοὺς ὕβρει καὶ ἀγερωχίᾳ τι πράσσοντας κρίνεις.

For you, the creator of all things and the governor of all, are a just ruler, and you judge those whose deeds are marked by pride and arrogance (NETS).

The prayer itself opens by labeling God as (1) creator (ὁ κτίσας τὰ πάντα), (2) governor of all (τῶν ὅλων ἐπικρατῶν), and (3) a just ruler (δυνάστης δίκαιος). These functional roles elaborate further upon four descriptions of God's status as outlined in 2:2 that ascribes kingly titles to God alone: "King of Heaven" (βασιλεῦ τῶν οὐρανῶν), "master of all creation" (δέσποτα πάσης κτίσεως), "sole ruler" (μόναρχε), and "almighty" (παντοκράτωρ).[29] This establishes God as the prototype for those categorized as leaders in the narrative, and serves as the criteria through which Simon's prayer offers its appraisal of Philopator.

The result is that Philopator is portrayed as yet another adversary on par with antagonists from biblical history, and it does not evaluate Philopator according to political criteria or power language befitting his role as a monarch.[30] Instead, the vocabulary demonstrates that Simon identifies Philopator with the same kinds of characteristics as exhibited by the Nephilim (Giants), the Sodomites, and the Pharaoh of the Exodus, which are primarily forms of moral evil. God stands alone in his power and status as a just judge and ruler.

---

[28] Croy, *3 Maccabees*, 51–53.

[29] Croy, *3 Maccabees*, 51.

[30] 3 Maccabees 1:6–7 would initially seem to suggest Philopator was trying to be a good king in terms of being a generous patron, at least before his character deteriorates in the narrative. Polybius describes Philopator's rule as subject to many problems on account of his instability and poor decision making (*Histories* 5.34). Bryan R. Dyer notes several connections made between Philopator and traditions that remember Phalaris as a brutal sadist (mentioned in 3 Macc 5:20, 42). See Dyer, "'Like Phalaris in Every Way': 3 Maccabees and Its Portrait of Tyranny," *JSJ* 50 (2019): 371–82; Moses Hadas, *The Third and Fourth Books of Maccabees* (New York: Harper & Brothers, 1953), 43.

5. Arrogant and prone to violence

On account of the episode taking place in Jerusalem, God's status as the prototypical king reigning from his earthly (and heavenly) temple is made salient. The premise for Philopator being categorized as arrogant is his mistreatment of the true king's temple and his subjects. In the prayer Philopator is frequently identified only indirectly through use of anarthrous nouns and adjectives, often vices, acting as substantives.[31] Together with other forms of encoding,[32] this has the effect of depersonalizing and deindividuating Philopator to reinforce negative stereotyping.

Alexander and Alexander observe that "the most common direct charge…against the king is "arrogance."[33] From the perspective of SCT, this accusation functions as a social categorization that makes Philopator of a kind with biblical antagonists by using overlapping semantic domains. 3 Maccabees 2:4 describes Philopator as similar to the Giants/Nephilim from Gen 6:4 in their arrogance.[34] Just as as Philopator is "grown insolent with presumption and power" (θράσει καὶ σθένει πεφρυαγμένου) in 2:2, so the giants "trusted in their might and courage" (ῥώμῃ καὶ θράσει πεποιθότες) in 2:4 (NETS). Both passages use τό θράσος[35] to describe Philopator's attitude, while they use the synonyms τό σθένος and τό ῥώμη to note that the cause is overconfidence in their strength and power.

3 Maccabees 2:5 uses similar phrasing regarding the Sodomites in their traditional role of exemplifying evil to make a similar point about the Greek king. In 2:17 the party led by the king "rejoice in the arrogance of their speech" (ἀγαλλιάσωνται ἐν ὑπερηφανίᾳ γλώσσης αὐτῶν). This is similar to the Sodomites, who are of a kind with the king but also exemplars "who practiced arrogance" (τό παράδειγμα…τοὺς ὑπερηφανίαν ἐργαζομένους Σοδομίτας).[36] As the king speaks, so the people of Sodom put into practice.

In the final example, 3 Maccabees establishes similarity between Philopator and Pharaoh in its use of θρασύς,[37] labelling the former as a "presumptuous man" (ὁ θρασὺς…οὗτος) in 2:14 and similar to "bold Pharaoh" (τὸν θρασὺν Φαραω) in 2:6. However, 3 Maccabees is not content merely to liken the Greek king to antagonists from biblical history. To Philopator are attributed a number of other terms associated with arrogance such as ὕβρει καὶ ἀγερωχίᾳ in 2:3. In 2:17–18 Philopator's party is described as being arrogant on account of possibly habitual profanation of pagan temples.

---

[31] Of the group: τοῖς ἐχθροῖς (2:13), οἱ παράνομοι (2:17). Of Philopator himself: ὑπὸ ἀνοσίου καὶ βεβήλου θράσει καὶ σθένει πεφρυαγμένου (3 Macc 2:2b). The connection is reflected in Boyd-Taylor's NETS translation.

[32] The near demonstrative τούτων, personal pronoun αὐτῶν. In verbs and verb phrases communicating similar information Καυχήσωνται; ἀγαλλιάσωνται ἐν ὑπερηφανίᾳ γλώσσης (2:17).

[33] Alexander and Alexander, "Oriental Monarch," 96.

[34] The portrayal of the giants as arrogant is in keeping with other traditions, such as Wis 14:6 and Sir 16:7. See Judith H. Newman, *Praying by the Book: The Scripturalization of Prayer in Second Temple Judaism* (Atlanta: Scholars, 1999), 172–79. She notes this is consistent with their reception history (196).

[35] "Audacity" in *GELS*, 331; MGS, 949.B. In a negative sense as "insolence" (LSJ).

[36] Newman, *Praying by the Book*, 180.

[37] Negatively, "arrogant" (LSJ); "excessively bold" (GELS, 331); "overconfident" (MGS, 950.B).

In a similar vein, and even though the Greek king had not yet exerted physical violence upon Jerusalem, 3 Maccabees categorizes Philopator as one prone to violence. This marks another point of similarity with the giants from Gen 6:4. 3 Maccabees describes the giants as strong (γίγαντες ἦσαν ῥώμῃ), suggesting they trust in their ability to use force even though at this point it remains a possibility on the part of the Greeks.[38] Furthermore, 3 Maccabees' reference to the Sodomites in 2:5 lacks explicit details concerning their propensity for violence, but this is central to the account of the deliverance of Lot and his family in Gen 19:4–11 and would have been known by the audience. In the case of Pharaoh (2:6–7), the use of violence is implicit in the enslavement of the Israelites and is resorted to on a number of occasions in Exodus. Simon's prayer does not concede to Pharaoh any descriptions of physical strength, inasmuch as these are solely attributed to God (δύναμις; κράτος) on account of his deeds during the deliverance of Israel from Egypt. The recounting of the Red Sea episode emphasizes God's power in drowning the Egyptians and his rulership over creation.

Meanwhile, the categorization of Philopator and his party as prone to violence is much more direct and receives more emphasis than these biblical examples. He is noted to boast in anger in 2:17 (ἐν θυμῷ)[39] and mistreat others.[40] His ability to oppress is mentioned twice (2:2, 13), as well as his ability to deprive others of power (παρείμεθα ἐν ἀδυναμίαις; 2:13). The ability to use force is probably what is meant by noting Philopator's strength in 2:2 (σθένος). In 2:3 the nature of God's rule is contrasted with Philopator's in God being "governor of all" (τῶν ὅλων ἐπικρατῶν) and a "just ruler" (δυνάστης δίκαιος). Meanwhile, Philopator lacks these traits in his insolence (ὕβρει) and arrogance (ἀγερωχία). Again, like 2:2, there is an implicit suggestion that in terms of what God has, Philopator only thinks he has.

3 Maccabees categorizes Philopator as similar to the Giants, Sodomites, and the Pharaoh of the Exodus in terms of their arrogance and willingness to resort to violence. The examples from biblical history are treated briefly, probably to keep the focus on the king as the main antagonist. Connections between the arrogance of Philopator and his party on the one hand, and the examples from history on the other, are made explicit in the text through vocabulary choices. A more diverse range of synonyms is attributed to Philopator and is used to highlight the grievous posture he is taking against his subjects, and to evoke the audience's sympathy for their plight.

6. Impious

3 Maccabees uses a similar approach to present Philopator as the foremost representative of the impious. The impiety of the Giants and the Sodomites are presented indirectly: 3 Maccabees offers a generalized description of the giants working injustice in 2:4, albeit this is in the sight of God and therefore reflects irreligiosity (σὺ τοὺς

---

[38] An apparent allusion to Hebrew Genesis, which describes the Nephilim as renowned warriors (Gen 6:4).
[39] Possibly also the use of φρυάσσω in 2:2. See LN 88.185.
[40] Καθυβρίζω (2:14); καταπατέω (2:18).

ἔμπροσθεν ἀδικίαν ποιήσαντας). For their part, the Sodomites in 2:5 are labelled as a notorious example of wickedness (διαδήλους ταῖς κακίαις γενομένους) who are subject to God's punishment.

The description of the Pharaoh of the Exodus in 2:6-7 follows a similar strategy of attributing him qualities similar to those of Philopator. The Israelites are labeled "[God's] holy people Israel" (τὸν λαόν σου τὸν ἅγιον Ισραηλ), making Pharaoh's enslavement of the Israelites an affront to God and an impious act. The plagues demonstrate God's judgment upon Egypt (ποικίλαις καὶ πολλαῖς δοκιμάσας τιμωρίαις), yet Pharaoh further demonstrates his impiety by resisting God's self-revelation (ἐγνώρισας τὴν σὴν δύναμιν ἐφ' οἷς ἐγνώρισας τὸ μέγα σου κράτος) as the ruler of all creation (σοὶ τῷ τῆς ἁπάσης κτίσεως δυναστεύοντι).

3 Maccabees repeatedly categorizes Philopator and his party as impious. Their identification as "the lawless" (οἱ παράνομοι) in 2:17 corresponds to other negative descriptions such as "impurity" (ἀνόσιος in 2:2; ἡ ἀκαθαρσία in 2:17) or the threefold designation of this group as people who engage in irreverent acts.[41] Simon also notes that in addition to violating the temple, Philopator follows the example of Pharaoh in affronting God by oppressing his people. However, 3 Maccabees uses a broader range of vocabulary to describe the misdeeds of the Greeks at the temple than Pharaoh.[42] This is consistent with 3 Maccabees' categorization of Philopator and his party as arrogant, and it appears to be an example of overspecification for the sake of emphasis.[43] The point is further highlighted when we consider that mention of Philopator and his party is interspersed throughout the prayer, which serves to keep them the focus of the audience's attention. While the biblical examples set historical precedent for the wrongdoing that takes place in the narrative, they also provide positive examples of how God has intervened in the past under similar circumstances.

In Simon's prayer, the author of 3 Maccabees is attempting to persuade his audience, presumably Alexandrian or Egyptian Jews, to persevere when facing persecution or oppression. Many Egyptian Jews likely experienced dissonance between a desire for social or economic integration and the religious and ethnic imperative to avoid assimilation. 3 Maccabees addresses this conundrum in the context of a discussion of the types of problems that result from maintaining such religious and ethnic distinctiveness as a minority in a majority-Gentile culture. Presenting Ptolemy Philopator as the most representative in a line of impious characters stretching back to biblical history directly associates the contemporary context of 3 Maccabees with these previous examples and highlights the importance of remaining faithful, even when facing the more mundane struggles likely experienced by the book's first readers. This association also ascribes to the humiliation and persecution of Jews living in Greek society—be it perceived or real, relatively minor or to the degree

---

[41] Seen in the use of a substantival adjective in a prepositional phrase indicating agency in 2:2 (ὑπὸ... βεβήλου); with a demonstrative pronoun in 2:14 ("this vile man"; βέβηλος οὗτος), and the use of ἡ βεβήλσις to describe their action in 2:17.

[42] Καταπονέω (2:2, 13); ὑπετάγημεν τοῖς ἐχθροῖς ἡμῶν (2:13); παρείμεθα ἐν ἀδυναμίαις (2:13); ἡ καταπτώσις (2:14).

[43] Steven E. Runge, *Discourse Grammar of the Greek New Testament: A Practical Introduction for Teaching and Exegesis* (Bellingham, WA: Lexham Press, 2010), 315, 321-22.

depicted in 3 Maccabees—a significance similar to Pharaoh's enslavement of Israel or Antiochus IV's profanation of the temple. However, 3 Maccabees also proposes a proactive response by presenting prayer as an effective means for soliciting help when facing such circumstances. This obviates the need for violence and portrays personal and corporate piety as providing tools that are fully adequate for facing intergroup conflict.

7. Does the prayer demonstrate a polarized attitude toward Greek culture?

At first glance the presentation of Philopator as the foremost antagonist in a line of biblical figures who oppose God would suggest that 3 Maccabees demonstrates a polarized attitude to Greek culture and its leaders, but is this really the case? As noted, while polarization is usually thought of as a group phenomenon, its causes may originate in specific issues or individuals. In the case of 3 Maccabees, the polarization in the narrative centers on things pertaining to God. This is premised upon the belief that it is possible for Gentiles to demonstrate piety, or at least an appropriate level of respect, towards the God of Israel and his people. This is something that Philopator initially does in 1:9 and returns to doing at the conclusion of the narrative.

This is further indicated in the contrast between God and Philopator in Simon's prayer. As noted previously, Philopator is denied the title of king. Meanwhile, 2:2–3 ascribes to God alone eight terms that are related to his status as ruler,[44] and these are further applied in 2:8–9 and 2:13.[45] Likewise, each of the historical examples that are used in the prayer describe God's power and mention his transcendence. While Philopator is clearly described as being an impure individual, the prayer emphasizes God's holiness, and similar categorizations are secondarily applied to the temple and Jews. While much of the prayer gives attention to the dishonor that Philopator's attempted violation of the temple brings upon Jews, this is because of the relationship between Jews and God. Israel is conceived in terms of its idealized cultural memory: a theocratic society centered on the worship of its God, and the references to adversity remind the reader of God's discipline upon Israel for its sin. Likewise, the temple derives its honor from its religious functions. 3 Maccabees does not present an approach to theodicy along the lines of a *2 Baruch* or *4 Ezra*, where God is in complete control of the violation of his own earthly temple, damage to which is reframed as of little consequence in light of the true Heavenly temple.

Simon's prayer functions as an exposition of the theological reasons for the conflict in the narrative. The Greek king does not revere God even though God is known through his glory and the teachings of Moses. Philopator therefore oversteps his bounds and disrespects God through mistreatment of the temple and his people, which results in the polarization seen in the narrative. Since the conflict in

---

[44] The titles include ὁ βασιλεύς; ὁ δεσπότης; ὁ δυνάστης; ὁ ἐπικρατῶν; ὁ κύριος; ὁ μόναρχος, and ὁ παντοκράτωρ, as well as being described as one who judges (σὺ...κρίνεις).
[45] A second use of ὁ παντοκράτωρ and a second and third use of ὁ βασιλεύς.

3 Maccabees does not have cultural origins and it is indeed possible for non-Jews to behave in a manner its author thinks appropriate, it is logical for 3 Maccabees to twice present prayer as a template for non-violent response to the types of conflict that Jews could expect to encounter as part of their life in the diaspora.

8. Conclusion

The prayer in 3 Macc 2:2–20 categorizes Philopator as a villain who is of a kind with those found in biblical history, but also presented as their most representative example. The Giants, Sodomites, and Pharaoh are all cited as examples who are subjected to God's retribution, but Philopator's evil is emphasized beyond these. Since they all faced retribution, this establishes a hope-giving precedent for non-violence when facing oppression in cases where there is a significant power differential. The prayers in the narrative place the prerogative for violent resistance against Greek rulers solely with God himself.

The categorizations found in the prayer reveal a polarized relationship that originates in conflict over theological convictions. 3 Maccabees does not take issue with Greek culture or rulers in terms of their being Greek *per se*, but in what it considers inappropriate behavior such as Philopator's attempted profanation of the temple and being in conflict over issues such as ἰσοπολίτης (2:30) that involve unacceptable theological compromise through participation in Greek civic cults. This is seen further when in 3 Macc 3:24 the narrator shifts blame to Philopator's courtiers to protect the king's legitimacy, in 6:25 when Jews are restored on account of their earlier faithful service as Ptolemaic soldiers, or when Jewish service to the government is described as exceptional in 3 Macc 6:26 and 6:28. These all appear to be sources of pride for the author of 3 Maccabees. However, the author also believes that the core elements of what it means to be Jewish, such as monotheism or obedience to the Law and ancestral customs, is not open to negotiation while a shared Greek civic identity is sufficiently flexible to accommodate groups such as Jews.[46] 3 Maccabees still follows *Aristeas* in envisioning a "non-Exodus" future for its audience of sojourners, with the greater threat to faithfulness to the Law of Moses actually originating from within the Jewish community among those willing to compromise.[47]

The prominent role of the prayers in 3 Maccabees 2 and 6 seem to acknowledge a possible cultural trend of high identification with Jewish nationalism following the Maccabean revolt but tries to channel this enthusiasm towards non-violent forms of expression towards non-Jews while still permitting it for enforcing conformity among their own community as allowed by the government. As a social strategy, theology

---

[46] Cousland notes that the reversal in the narrative allows for vindication of the Jewish characters and the promotion of orthopraxy among a Jewish audience while promoting Jewish loyalty to the local Gentile government. See Cousland, "Reversal, Recidivism and Reward," 50.

[47] Note that part of the rationale for violent retribution against Jews who had been unfaithful to the Law was that unfaithful Jews would also prove to be unfaithful subjects of the Greek king (3 Macc 7:11–12). On the "non-Exodus" motif, see Schmitz, "Pharao und Philopator," 176–77; Sylvie Honigman, *The Septuagint and Homeric Scholarship in Alexandria* (London: Routledge, 2003), 56.

becomes autonomy, prayer becomes a form of resistance for preserving a way of life, and restoration to peaceful intergroup relations and service to a foreign monarch is framed as a victory.

Bibliography

Alexander, Loveday, and Philip Alexander. "The Image of the Oriental Monarch in the Third Book of Maccabees." Pages 92–109 in *Jewish Perspectives on Hellenistic Rulers*. Edited by Tessa Rajak, Sarah Pearce, James Aitken, and Jennifer Dines. Berkeley, CA: University of California Press, 2007.

Barclay, John M. G. *Jews in the Mediterranean Diaspora: From Alexander to Trajan [323 BCE–117 CE]*. Edinburgh: T&T Clark, 1996.

Boyd-Taylor, Cameron. "Robbers, Pirates, and Licentious Women: Echoes of an Anti-Dionysiac Polemic in the Septuagint." Pages 559–71 in *Die Septuaginta: Texte, Kontexte, Lebenswelten*. Edited by Martin Karrer, Wolfgang Kraus, and Martin Meiser. Tübingen: Mohr Siebeck, 2008.

Boyd-Taylor, Cameron. "3 Maccabees: To the Reader." Pages 521–22 in *A New English Translation of the Septuagint*. Edited by Albert Pietersma and Benjamin G. Wright, Oxford: Oxford University Press, 2007.

Collins, John J. *Between Athens and Jerusalem: Jewish Identity in the Hellenistic Diaspora*. 2nd ed. Grand Rapids: Eerdmans, 2000.

Corley, Jeremy. "Divine Sovereignty and Power in the High-Priestly Prayer of 3 Macc 2.1–10." Pages 359–86 in *Prayer from Tobit to Qumran*. Edited by R. Egger-Wenzel and J. Corley. Berlin: Walter de Gruyter, 2004.

Cousland, J. R. C. "Reversal, Recidivism and Reward in 3 Maccabees: Structure and Purpose." *JSJ* 34 (2003): 39–51.

Cousland, J. R. C. "Dionysius Theomachos? Echoes of the Bacchae in 3 Maccabees." *Biblica* 82 (2001): 539–48.

Croy, Clayton N. *3 Maccabees*. Leiden: Brill, 2006.

Dyer, Bryan R. "'Like Phalaris in Every Way': 3 Maccabees and Its Portrait of Tyranny." *JSJ* 50 (2019): 371–82.

Emmet, C. W. *The Third Book of Maccabees*. London: SPCK, 1918.

Gardner, Anne Elizabeth. "III Maccabees—A Reflection on the Maccabean Crisis." Pages 1–6 in *Proceedings of the Ninth World Congress of Jewish Studies: The History of the Jewish People from the Second Temple Period until the Middle Ages*. Jerusalem: World Union of Jewish Studies, 1985.

Hadas, Moses. "III Maccabees and the Tradition of Patriotic Romance." *Chronique d'Egypte* 24.47 (1949): 97–104.

Hadas, Moses. *The Third and Fourth Books of Maccabees*. New York: Harper & Brothers, 1953.

Hadas, Moses. "Aspects of Nationalist Survival under Hellenistic and Roman Imperialism." *Journal of the History of Ideas* 11 (1950): 131–39.

Hadas, Moses. "Third Maccabees and Greek Romance." *Review of Religion* 13 (1948–49): 155–62.

Hacham, Noah. "3 Maccabees: An Anti-Dionysiac Polemic." Pages 167–83 in *Ancient Fiction: The Matrix of Early Christian and Jewish Narrative*. Edited by Jo-Ann A. Brant. Atlanta, GA: SBL, 2005.

Haslam, S. Alexander. *Psychology in Organizations: The Social Identity Approach*. London: SAGE, 2002.

Henten, Jan Willem. *The Maccabean Martyrs as Saviours of the Jewish People: A Study of 2 and 4 Maccabees*. Leiden: Brill, 1997.

Hogg, Michael A. "Social Categorization, Depersonalization, and Group Behavior." Pages 56–85 in *Blackwell Handbook of Social Psychology: Group Processes*. Edited by Michael A. Hogg and Scott Tindale. Hoboken, NJ: Wiley-Blackwell, 2002.

Honigman, Sylvie. *The Septuagint and Homeric Scholarship in Alexandria*. London: Routledge, 2003.

Newman, Judith H. *Praying by the Book: The Scripturalization of Prayer in Second Temple Judaism*. Atlanta: Scholars, 1999.

Newman, Judith H. "God Condemns the Arrogance of Power: The Prayer in 3 Maccabees 6:2–15." Pages 48–52 in *Prayer from Alexander to Constantine: A Critical Anthology*. Edited by Mark Kiley. London: Routledge, 1997.

Raup Johnson, Sara. *Historical Fictions in Hellenistic Jewish Identity: Third Maccabees in its Cultural Context*. Los Angeles, CA: University of California Press, 2004.

Rebenich, Stefan. "Historical Prose." Pages 265–337 in *Handbook of Classical Rhetoric in the Hellenistic Period, 330 B.C.–A.D. 400*. Edited by Stanley E. Porter. Leiden: Brill, 1997.

Runge, Steven E. *Discourse Grammar of the Greek New Testament: A Practical Introduction for Teaching and Exegesis*. Bellingham, WA: Lexham Press, 2010.

Schmitz, Barbara. "Pharao und Philopator. Exodusrezeption im Dritten Makkabäerbuch als Deutung des Lebens in der Diaspora." Pages 162–90 in *Exodus: Interpretation durch Rezeption*. Edited by Matthias Ederer and Barbara Schmitz. Stuttgart: Katholisches Bibelwerk, 2017.

Schwartz, Daniel R. *2 Maccabees*. Berlin: Walter de Gruyter, 2008.

Tromp, Johannes Magliano. "The Relations Between Egyptian Judaism and Jerusalem in Light of 3 Maccabees and the Greek Book of Esther." Pages 57–76 in *Feasts and Festivals*. Edited by Christopher M. Tuckett. Leuven: Peeters, 2009.

Williams, D. S. "3 Maccabees: A Defense of Diaspora Judaism?" *JSP* 13 (1995): 14–29.

Williams, Jarvis J. *Maccabean Martyr Traditions in Paul's Theology of Atonement*. Eugene, OR: Wipf & Stock, 2010.

PART IV

EXODUS IN THE NEW TESTAMENT AND CHRISTIANITY

Chapter 12

Mark's Incipit in Early Amulets and the Question of Its Original Reading

Craig A. Evans

One of the most disputed textual uncertainties in the Gospel of Mark concerns the words υἱοῦ (τοῦ) θεοῦ, "Son of God," at the end of its first verse, or incipit (Mark 1:1). The traditional reading is the long version, in which the words υἱοῦ θεοῦ are retained, so that the incipit reads, ἀρχὴ τοῦ εὐαγγελίου Ἰησοῦ Χριστοῦ υἱοῦ θεοῦ, "The beginning of the gospel of Jesus Christ, the Son of God" (so KJV, RSV, NRSV, and others). With the discovery of older texts, however, in which shorter versions are attested, the original reading is now very much an open question.

In a perceptive study Larry Perkins showed how the Markan evangelist drew upon the text of the prophet Jeremiah to explain Israel's obdurate response to Jesus and his message.[1] Others have drawn attention to the important role that the book of Isaiah plays in Mark's understanding of the good news that Jesus proclaims. I have myself suggested that Mark's incipit theologically subverts the Roman imperial cult with Isaiah's prophecy of redemption.[2] Every word of the incipit echoes the language of the cult. In light of this, the originality of the last two words, υἱοῦ θεοῦ, is a matter of great importance.

1. Mark 1:1 in continuous text manuscripts

The long version of Mark's incipit is old and widely attested. It is found in ℵ^c B D L W 2427 and its equivalent in many Latin and Syriac mss. (*See Figure 12.1.*) These authorities lack the definite article before θεοῦ, whose presence or absence is inconsequential.

---

[1] Larry Perkins, "The Markan Narrative's Use of the Old Greek Text of Jeremiah to Explain Israel's Obduracy," *TynBul* 60 (2009): 217–38. I salute Professor Perkins on his long and distinguished career.

[2] Craig A. Evans, "Mark's Incipit and the Priene Calendar Inscription: From Jewish Gospel to Greco-Roman Gospel," *JGRChJ* 1 (2000): 67–81. For Mark, Isaiah provides the true meaning of εὐαγγέλιον.

Of course, A K M U Γ Δ Π f¹ f¹³ 2 33 69 579 𝔐, along with most Coptic mss,[3] do have the definite article; so they read …'Ἰησοῦ Χριστοῦ υἱοῦ τοῦ θεοῦ. (*See Figure 12.2.*) At least one ms reads υἱοῦ τοῦ κυρίου, "Son of the Lord" (1241).

Figure 12.1. The beginning of Mark in Codex Vaticanus (B).

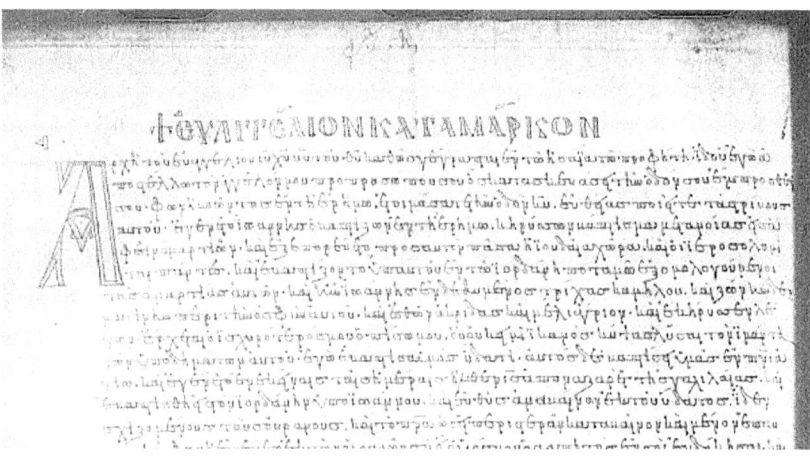

Figure 12.2. The beginning of Mark in miniscule 33 (the "queen of the miniscules").

---

[3] The Coptic usually makes use of Greek loan words (αρχη and ευαγγελιον, as well as the personal names ιησους and χριστος) and prefixes χριστός with the Coptic definite article πε, thus reading "Jesus the Christ."

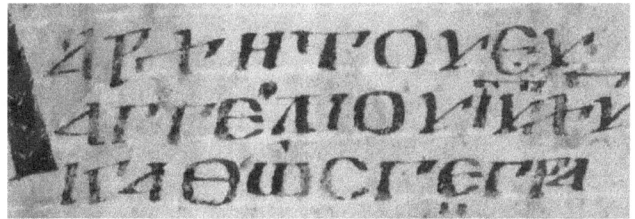

Figure 12.3. The beginning of Mark in Codex Koridethi (Θ).

Figure 12.4. The beginning of Mark in Codex 28.

The short version, that is, the version that ends with Ἰησοῦ Χριστοῦ, is witnessed in ninth-century Θ,[4] eleventh-century 28,[5] and, supposedly, ℵ*, among others.[6] I say "supposedly" because the two inserted words, υ(ἱο)ῦ θ(εο)ῦ (written as the *nomina sacra* ΥΥ ΘΥ), above the letters κα of καθώς, appear to be written in the hand of the scribe who penned the Gospel of Mark. (*See Figure 12.5.*) If so, the scribe has corrected his own work, which implies that the longer reading was present in his

---

[4] Ninth-century Codex Koridethi (Θ) reads αρχηγτουευ|αγγελιουιυχυ|καθωςγεγρα (left col., lines 1–3). (*See fig. 3.*)
[5] Ms 28, housed in the Bibliothèque Nationale de France as grec 0379 (also known as Colbertinus 4705), witnesses the short version of Mark 1:1 in two ways: 28* reads ἀρχὴ τοῦ εὐαγγελίου Ἰησοῦ; 28ᶜ reads ἀρχὴ τοῦ εὐαγγελίου Ἰησοῦ Χριστοῦ. The non-appearance of Χριστοῦ in 28* should be viewed as an omission on the part of the scribe who penned 28, probably due to homoioteleuton. It has been described as carelessly written. (*See fig. 4.*)
[6] Other witnesses to the absence of υἱοῦ θεοῦ include 530 582* 820* 1021 1436 1555* 1692 *et al*. These minuscules are all Medieval, ranging in date from the eleventh to fourteenth centuries. The absence of υἱοῦ (τοῦ) θεοῦ in these mss was in most cases likely accidental, due to homoioteleuton.

exemplar and was what he intended to write in the first place. The omission of the words υ(ἰο)ῦ θ(εο)ῦ was accidental and was probably due to homoioteleuton. Indeed, in Sinaiticus the final two letters of Mark's εὐαγγελίου carry over to the beginning of the second line, which means the scribe was looking at a string of words, including *nomina sacra*, ending with Υ. Before writing καθώς, "just as," the scribe was looking at either ΟΥΙΥΧΥ or, more likely, ΟΥΙΥΧΥΥΥΘΥ.[7] It is no surprise that the scribe's eye skipped over ΥΥΘΥ ("Son of God") in his exemplar. If this is correct, then there really is no early Greek evidence for the absence of υἱοῦ θεοῦ, at least not in continuous texts.

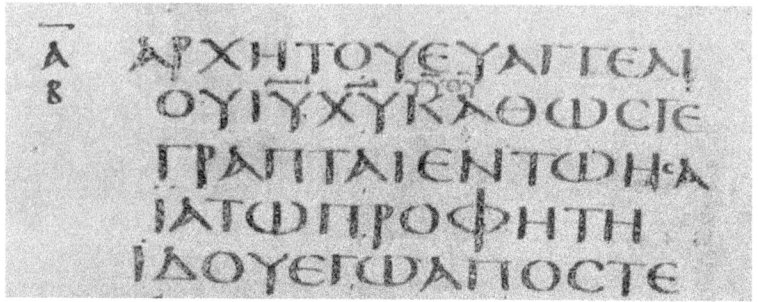

Figure 12.5. The beginning of Mark in Codex Sinaiticus (ℵ).

As already mentioned, the early versions support the "Son of God" reading in Mark 1:1. Jerome's Latin translation, which became known as the *editio vulgata* or Vulgate, was completed sometime in the late fourth century. Most of Jerome's Greek mss likely dated to the fourth century, although a few may have dated to the third. This means that the Vulgate is an important witness to the form of Greek text before the Byzantine text-type had become dominant in the Christian world. The Latin tradition overwhelmingly supports the longer version of the Markan incipit. As an example, Codex Sangallensis (n), one of the oldest surviving Latin mss in which Mark 1:1 is extant, reads, *Initium euuangelii ihū xpī filii dī*, "The beginning of the gospel of Jesus Christ, Son of God."[8] (*See Figure 12.6.*)

---

[7] That is, ου ι(ησο)υ χ(ριστο)υ υ(ιο)υ θ(εο)υ. The same applies to several mss (055 752 858 1337 1506) that omit υἱοῦ and so read ἀρχὴ τοῦ εὐαγγελίου Ἰησοῦ Χριστοῦ τοῦ θεοῦ. The scribes' eyes skipped over υἱοῦ in their respective exemplars, thus reading "The beginning of the gospel of Jesus Christ of God."

[8] The ms is Sangallensis (or St. Gall MS 1395), which dates to ca. 500 CE, or about one century after Jerome completed his work. See C. H. Turner, *The Oldest Manuscript of the Vulgate Gospels* (Oxford: Clarendon Press, 1931), 74. For other early editions of the Vulgate, see Walahfrid Strabo, Nicholas of Lyra, et al., *Bibliorum Sacrorum cum glossa ordinaria*, Tomus Quintus (Venice: Franciscan Fathers, 1603), cols. 481–82: *Initium Euangelii Jesu Christi filij Dei*; Pierre Sabatier, ed., *Bibliorum Sacrorum Latinae Versiones Antiquae*, Tomus Tertius (Paris: Franciscum Didot, 1749; repr. 1751), 187: *Initium Evangelii Jesu Christi, Filii Dei*; a reprint of a 1642 Cambridge edition Beza's Latin translation (c. 1565) in Roger Daniels, ed., *Jesu Christi Domini Nostri Novum Testamentum. Ex interpretatione Theodori Bezae* (Berlin: Societatis Bibliophilorum, 1898), 77: *Principium evangelii Jesu Christi, Filii Dei*; Edgar S. Buchanan, *The Four Gospels from the Codex Corbeiensis*, Old Latin Biblical Texts 5 (Oxford: Clarendon Press, 1907), 78: *Initium evangelii ihū xrī fili dī*; and R. Weber, *Biblia Sacra iuxta Vulgatam Versionem*, 2 vols., 3rd ed. (Stuttgart: Deutsche Bibelgesellschaft, 1985), 2:1574: *Initium evangelii Iesu Christi Filii Dei*.

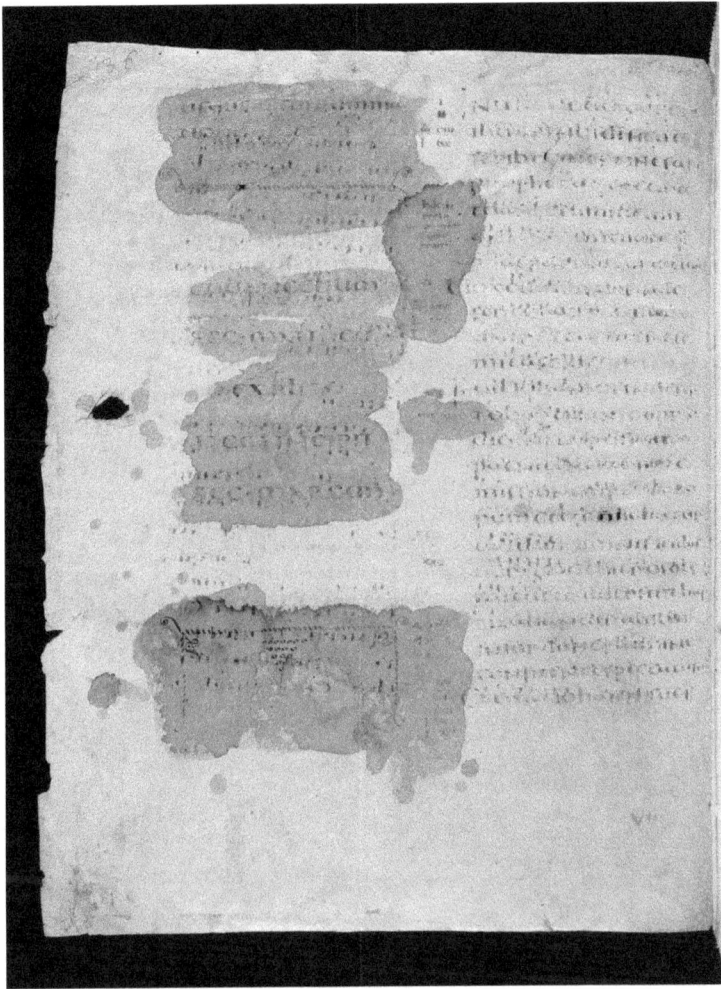

Figure 12.6. The beginning of Mark in Codex Sangallensis (n).

The Syriac tradition also overwhelmingly supports the longer version of Mark's incipit. The Peshitta reads: "The beginning of the gospel of Yešuʿ the Mešiyḥoʾ, the Son of God [ܒܪܗ ܕܐܠܗܐ, *bareh da-'loho*]."[9] The Philoxenian and Harklean versions of the Syriac text likewise witness the longer version.[10] (*See Figure 12.7.*)

[9] See Philip Edward Pusey and George Henry Gwilliam, eds., *Tetraeuangelium sanctum juxta simplicem Syrorum versionem ad fidem codicum, Massorae, editionem denuo recognitum* (Oxford: Clarendon Press, 1901), 198–99 (Syriac text and English translation on facing pages); Jeffrey W. Childers and George A. Kiraz, eds., *The Gospel of Mark according to the Syriac Peshitta Version with English Translation* (Piscataway, NJ: Gorgias Press, 2012), 2–3 (Syriac text and English translation on facing pages).

[10] See Joseph White, *Sacrorum Evangeliorum versio Syriaca Philoxeniana ex Codd. MSS. Ridleaianus*, Tomus primus (Oxford: Clarendon Press, 1778), 159. The title of White's work is misleading; it is

194   *Themes and Texts, Exodus and Beyond*

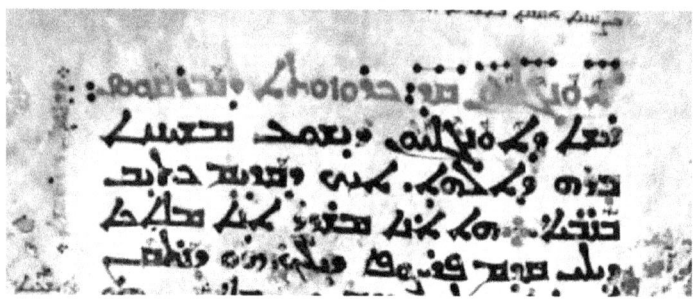

Figure 12.7. The beginning of Mark in Peshitta Yohanna MS C.

Figure 12.8. The beginning of Mark in an illustrated Coptic ms.

We find the same in the Coptic versions of the New Testament. Mark 1:1 in the Coptic reads: "The beginning [αρχη] of the gospel [ευαγγελιον] of Jesus [Ιη(σου)ς] the Christ [πεχ(ριστο)ς], the Son of God [ⲡϣⲏⲣⲉ ⲙ̄ⲫϯ ⁄ ⲡϣⲏⲣⲉ ⲙ̄ⲡⲛⲟⲩⲧⲉ]."[11] Very few

---

    not the Philoxenian Syriac version (which was translated from the Greek in 508 for Bishop Philoxenus) that he presents, but rather the Harklean *revision* of the Philoxenian version made by Thomas of Harkel in 616. (White adequately explains all this in his *Praefatio*.)

[11] Note the presence of the Greek loanwords. The words "Son of God" are in Coptic. For text and apparatus, see George William Horner, *The Coptic Version of the New Testament in the Northern Dialect*, vol. 1: *The Gospels of S. Matthew and S. Mark* (Oxford: Clarendon Press, 1898), 282; idem, *The Coptic Version of the New Testament in the Southern Dialect*, vol. 1: *The Gospels of S. Matthew and S. Mark* (Oxford: Clarendon Press, 1911), 354. By "northern dialect" Horner refers to Memphitic and Bohairic, and by "southern dialect" he refers to Sahidic and Thebaic.

Coptic witnesses lack the words "the Son of God," which usually appear in Coptic (Northern dialects: ⲡϣⲏⲣⲉ ⲙ̄ⲫ̄ϯ̄; Southern dialects: ⲡϣⲏⲣⲉ ⲙ̄ⲡⲛⲟⲩⲧⲉ), rather than in Greek. It should also be noted again that "Christ" is definite, with the addition of the Coptic prefix pe. (*See Figure 12.8.*) This will also be seen in the Coptic amulets that will be considered later in the chapter.

Figure 12.9. The beginning of Mark in *Novum Instrumentum omne* (1516). Courtesy of the Dunham Bible Museum, Houston Baptist University.

Desiderius Erasmus (1469–1536) retained the words in his 1516 *Novum Instrumentum omne*, both in Greek (υἱοῦ τοῦ θεοῦ) and in Latin (*filium dei*), and in subsequent editions that appeared under the more conventional title *Novum Testamentum omne*.[12] (*See Figure 12.9.*) The words are retained in subsequent editions of

---

[12] See Desiderius Erasmus, ed., *Novum Instrumentum omne* (Basel: Johann Froben, 1516), 73; idem, ed., *Novum Testamentum omne* (Basel: Johann Froben, 1519), 71; etc.

the Greek New Testamentum (for example, in the text of Stephanus), most of which closely follow one edition of Erasmus or another. The words are retained by John Mill (1645–1707) in his edition of Η ΚΑΙΝΗ ΔΙΑΘΗΚΗ, a work that pioneered what would become the modern textual apparatus.[13] The words are also retained by the influential editions produced by Johann Jakob Griesbach (1745–1812)[14] and Karl Lachmann (1793–1851).[15]

Early translations intended for the general public presupposed the longer version of Mark 1:1, as we see in the following examples: John Wycliffe (1382), "the sone of god"; William Tyndale (1526), "the sonne off God"; the so-called Matthew's Bible (1537), "the sonne of God"; the Geneva Bible (1560), "the Sonne of God"; the Bishops' Bible (1568), "the sonne of God"; and, of course, the King James Version (1611), "the Sonne of God," though today modernized as "the Son of God." Martin Luther's *Das Neue Testament* (1524) read (and still reads) "dem Sohn Gottes." Likewise Jacques Lefèvre d'Étaples' *Le Nouveau Testament* (1523) also retains the words, "le Fils de Dieu."

The discovery of fourth-century Codex Sinaiticus, known by the siglum א, changed everything. The interesting and disputed story of Constantine Tischendorf's acquisition and publication of Codex Sinaiticus need not detain us,[16] but his observation that the words υἱοῦ θεοῦ were not in the "original" text of the great codex was enough for him to omit them in his edition of the New Testament.[17] The words υἱοῦ θεοῦ do not appear in the text produced in 1881 by Westcott and Hort.[18] However, Samuel Tregelles (1813–1875) bucked the new trend by retaining the words;[19] so did Franz Delitzsch (1813–1890) in his 1877 Hebrew translation of the New Testament.[20]

---

[13] John Mill, ed., Η ΚΑΙΝΗ ΔΙΑΘΗΚΗ. *Novum Testamentum* (Oxford: E Theatro Sheldoniano, 1707), 83; repr. (Oxford: Clarendon Press, 1813), *ad loc*.

[14] Johann Jakob Griesbach, ed., *Novum Testamentum graece*, vol. I. *IV. Evangelia*, 2nd ed., (London: H. Saxon, 1796), 144; cf. Η ΚΑΙΝΗ ΔΙΑΘΗΚΗ: *Griesbach's Text, with various readings of Mill and Scholz, marginal references to parallels, and a critical introduction*, 4th ed., (London: Bell & Daldy, 1870), 74.

[15] Karl Lachmann, *Novum Testamentum graece* (Berlin: G. Reimer, 1831), 6.

[16] For accounts, see David Parker, *Codex Sinaiticus: The Story of the World's Oldest Bible* (London: The British Library; Peabody, MA: Hendrickson, 2010), 127–47; and Stanley E. Porter, *Constantine Tischendorf: The Life and Work of a 19th Century Bible Hunter* (London/New York: Bloomsbury, 2015), 24–54.

[17] Constantine Tischendorf, *Novum Testamentum Graeca* (Leipzig: Bernhard Tauchnitz, 1896), 57. In Tischendorf's apparatus only אᶜ is cited as retaining the two words!

[18] Brooke Foss Westcott and Fenton John Anthony Hort, *The New Testament in the Original Greek: Introduction and Appendix* (New York: Harper & Brothers, 1882), 72.

[19] Samuel Prideaux Tregelles, *The Greek New Testament, Edited from Ancient Authorities, with their Various Readings in Full, and the Latin Version of Jerome*, Part 1: *Matthew and Mark* (London: Bagster, 1857), 119. It is important to note that Tregelles did not retain υἱοῦ θεοῦ out of loyalty to the Textus Receptus, for he strongly believed that the Majority Text was faulty and that older and better authorities needed to be taken more fully into account.

[20] Delitzsch's Hebrew translation of Mark 1:1 reads: תְּחִלַּת בְּשׂוֹרַת יֵשׁוּעַ הַמָּשִׁיחַ בֶּן־הָאֱלֹהִים, "The beginning of the good news of Yeshua' the Messiah, Son of God." See ספרי הברית החדשה [= *Books of the New Covenant*] (London: Lowe & Brydone, 1960), 61; and ספר הבריתות [= *Book of the Covenants*] (Jerusalem: The Bible Society in Israel, 2010), 1034.

The Nestle-Aland²⁸ and UBSGNT⁴ᶜᵒʳ place the disputed words, υἱοῦ θεοῦ, in square brackets, indicating uncertainty as to their originality and at the same time a reluctance to omit them. Both editions supply an apparatus that cites the major authorities, though not always accurately. More recent editions, however, are breaking away from the hegemony of Nestle-Aland and UBSGNT. The SBL edition of the Greek New Testament omits the words altogether;²¹ but the new edition of the Byzantine text retains the words without brackets,²² as does the recently published Tyndale House Greek New Testament.²³

The conflicted opinions are well explained by the premier textual critic, the late Bruce Metzger, in his commentary on the decisions reached in the UBSGNT. He writes:

> The absence of υἱοῦ θεοῦ in ℵ* Θ 28ᶜ *al* may be due to an oversight in copying, occasioned by the similarity of the endings of the *nomina sacra*. On the other hand, however, there was always a temptation (to which copyists often succumbed) to expand titles and quasi-titles of books. Since the combination of B D W *al* in support of υἱοῦ θεοῦ is extremely strong, it was not thought advisable to omit the words altogether, yet because of the antiquity of the shorter reading and the possibility of scribal expansion, it was decided to enclose the words within square brackets.²⁴

How ancient the shorter reading truly is depends in large part on one's assessment of the "correction" in ℵ. In my view it offers no support to the shorter reading. Moreover, other evidence cited in support of the shorter reading has been misstated. In a lengthy and perceptive study of the variant readings related to Mark 1:1, Tommy Wasserman has reviewed the evidence mentioned here and much else besides.²⁵ He

---

[21] Michael W. Holmes, ed., *The Greek New Testament SBL Edition* (Atlanta: Society of Biblical Literature, 2010), 67. The apparatus, in keeping with the editor's comments, is quite simple and makes use of the Westcott-Hort text as the point of departure.

[22] Maurice A. Robinson and William G. Pierpont, eds., *The New Testament in the Original Greek: Byzantine Textform* (Southborough, MA: Chilton, 2005), 69. The definite article τοῦ before θεοῦ is also retained.

[23] Dirk Jongkind et al., eds., *The Greek New Testament, Produced at Tyndale House Cambridge* (Cambridge: Cambridge University Press; Wheaton: Crossway, 2017), 67. In the apparatus it is noted that the last two words are omitted in two authorities (i.e., ℵ* Θ).

[24] Bruce M. Metzger, *A Textual Commentary on the Greek New Testament* (London/New York: United Bible Societies, 1975 [corrected edition]), 73. Metzger's student Bart Ehrman (*The Orthodox Corruption of Scripture: The Effect of Early Christological Controversies on the Text of the New Testament* [New York/Oxford: Oxford University Press, 1993], 75) adds: "Scribes would have had little reason to delete the phrase 'the Son of God' from Mark 1:1, but they would have had reasons to add it." Similar reasoning is expressed by Heinrich Greeven in Heinrich Greeven and Eberhard Güting, eds., *Textkritik des Markusevangeliums*, Theologie: Forschung und Wissenschaft 11 (Münster: Lit Verlag, 2005), 41–43: "...eine Streichung der Apposition im ganzen als schwerer vorstellbar erschien als eine Einfügung" (43). We can agree with this reasoning, if the discrepant readings are interpreted as *intentional*. But the evidence for *unintentional* omission is very strong.

[25] Tommy Wasserman, "The 'Son of God' was in the Beginning (Mark 1:1)," *JTS* 62 (2011): 20–50. Some of the same arguments will be found in Alexander Globe, "The Caesarean Omission of the Phrase 'Son of God' in Mark 1:1," *HTR* 75 (1982): 209–18. Wasserman's lengthier study makes a much stronger case.

very helpfully clarifies the true nature of the versional and patristic evidence, which is sometimes misleadingly presented in the Nestle-Aland[28] and UBSGNT[4cor] editions.[26]

One telling example is found in Irenaeus (late second century) who appeals to Mark 1:1-2 to underscore the prophetic nature of the gospel. He says: τὸ δὲ κατὰ Μάρκον ἀπὸ τοῦ προφητικοῦ πνεύματος, τοῦ ἐξ ὕψους ἐπιόντος τοῖς ἀνθρώποις, τὴν ἀρχὴν ἐποιήσατο, λέγων· ἀρχὴ τοῦ εὐαγγελίου, ὡς γέγραπται ἐν Ἡσαΐᾳ τῷ προφήτῃ, "The (Gospel) according to Mark (which is) from the prophetic Spirit, when he spoke from on high to people, begins, saying, 'The beginning of the gospel, as it is written in Isaiah the prophet'" (*Haer.* 3.11.8). Here, Irenaeus isn't supporting the short version (as some critics mistakenly claim); he has omitted half of the verse (that is, Ἰησοῦ Χριστοῦ υἱοῦ θεοῦ, not just υἱοῦ θεοῦ), so that he can directly link "beginning of the gospel" with the prophetic witness cited in Mark 1:2.[27]

Elsewhere Irenaeus attests the long form of Mark 1:1. In one place the influential Father says: "Therefore also Mark, the interpreter and follower of Peter, does thus commence his Gospel narrative: "The beginning of the Gospel of Jesus Christ, the Son of God [*initium evangelii Iesu Christi filii Dei*]; as it is written…" (*Haer.* 3.10.5); and in another place: "…the Son of God being made the Son of man [*filius Dei hominis filius factus*], that through him we may receive the adoption—humanity sustaining, and receiving, and embracing the Son of God. Therefore Mark also says: 'The beginning of the Gospel of Jesus Christ, the Son of God [*initium evangelii Iesu Christi filii Dei*]; as it is written in the prophets.' Knowing one and the same Son of God, Jesus Christ, who was announced by the prophets" (*Haer.* 3.16.3). Although these passages are preserved in Latin translation and not in the original Greek, the nature of their arguments makes it clear that "Son of God" (υἱοῦ θεοῦ) was in the quotation of Mark 1:1 in the original Greek version of *Adversus haereses*, not just in the subsequent Latin translation. On good evidence Wasserman concludes that "Irenaeus, being the earliest Father who cites the verse, definitely knew the long reading, whereas there is no secure evidence that he had access to the short reading."[28]

Wasserman finds that the early Fathers knew both the short and the long readings of Mark 1:1. He also notes that "there is a marked tendency on the part of some Fathers to abbreviate the text for certain purposes." He suspects that in some of the

---

[26] He also criticizes Bart Ehrman's mishandling of some of the evidence. See Tommy Wasserman, "Misquoting Manuscripts? The Orthodox Corruption of Scripture Revisited," in Samuel Byrskog and Magnus Zetterhold, eds., *The Making of Christianity: Conflicts, Contacts, and Constructions. Essays in Honor of Bengt Holmberg* (Winona Lake, IN: Eisenbrauns, 2012), 325–50; Wasserman, "The 'Son of God,'" 41. I should note too that Peter Head's statement that "υἱοῦ θεοῦ or in some cases υἱοῦ τοῦ θεοῦ was added by the vast majority of manuscripts" is potentially misleading. The vast majority of copyists did not *add* υἱοῦ θεοῦ or υἱοῦ τοῦ θεοῦ to the text; they found the words in their exemplars and simply copied them. The quotation is from Peter M. Head, "Christology and Textual Transmission: Reverential Alterations in the Synoptic Gospels," *NovT* 35 (1993): 105–29 (115). For his argument in support of the short form of Mark 1:1, see Peter M. Head, "A Text-Critical Study of Mark 1.1: 'The Beginning of the Gospel of Jesus Christ,'" *NTS* 37 (1991): 621–29.

[27] Wasserman ("The 'Son of God,'" 26 and nn. 23–24) rightly notes that the words Ἰησοῦ Χριστοῦ are not found in the newer critical edition of *Adversus haereses*. He faults those who have used older editions of *Adversus haereses* or faulty and/or misleading older texts of the New Testament. Irenaeus at *Haer.* 3.11.8 offers no support to either the short or long versions of Mark 1:1.

[28] Wasserman, "The 'Son of God,'" 27.

cases where the short reading appears to be attested, the words υἱοῦ θεοῦ may have been intentionally omitted.²⁹ We shall find that this is often the case in non-continuous texts and quotations.

Wasserman also reviews the versions. He finds, consistent with what has already been said, that "the versional evidence on the whole is clearly in favour of the long reading, but at the same time confirms the impression that both readings are widespread."³⁰ His review of the Greek manuscripts of the Gospel of Mark, the Fathers, and the versions shows—when this evidence is cited accurately and in context—that the long reading enjoys much stronger support. The internal evidence suggests the same. Careful consideration of the literary and theological purpose and argument of Mark itself confirms that the long reading was very probably the original form of Mark 1:1.³¹

Wasserman also briefly comments on the recently published Oxyrhynchus amulet that quotes the short form of Mark's incipit.³² Three major studies have since been published that are quite relevant, two of which examine several amulets that contain Gospel incipits.³³ In my view, careful study of these amulets supports Wasserman's conclusion that in all probability the long version of Mark 1:1 was original. The balance of the present study will review the relevant Greek and Coptic amulets from late antiquity.³⁴

---

[29] Wasserman, "The 'Son of God,'" 34.
[30] Wasserman, "The 'Son of God,'" 39.
[31] Wasserman, "The 'Son of God,'" 50: "In conclusion, the balance of probabilities favours the long reading in Mark 1:1—the 'Son of God' was indeed in the beginning." A number of commentators have concluded that the long version of Mark 1:1 was original: Joachim Gnilka, *Das Evangelium nach Markus* 2 vols., EKKNT 2.1-2 (Zurich: Benziger; Neukirchen-Vluyn: Neukirchener Verlag, 1978), 1:43; Robert A. Guelich, *Mark 1–8:26*, WBC 34A (Dallas: Word, 1989), 6; M. Eugene Boring, *Mark: A Commentary*, NTL (Louisville: Westminster John Knox Press, 2006), 30; among others.
[32] Wasserman, "The 'Son of God,'" 23–24. He refers to the amulet P.Oxy. LXXVI 5073.
[33] Joseph E. Sanzo, *Scriptural Incipits on Amulets from Late Antique Egypt: Text, Typology, and Theory*, STAC 84 (Tübingen: Mohr Siebeck, 2014); Brice C. Jones, *New Testament Texts on Greek Amulets from Late Antiquity*, LNTS 554 (London/New York: Bloomsbury T&T Clark, 2016); Theodore de Bruyn, *Making Amulets Christian: Artefacts, Scribes, and Contexts* (Oxford: Oxford University Press, 2017). Interest in the presence and function of Gospel incipits in amulets was stimulated two decades ago by a paper by Paul Mirecki, "Evangelion-Incipits Amulets in Greek and Coptic: Towards a Typology," in J. J. Johnson Leese, ed., *Proceedings of the Central States Regional Meeting of the Society of Biblical Literature and the American Schools of Oriental Research* 4 (Kirkwood, MO: Central States Society of Biblical Literature, 2001): 143–53.
[34] An amulet is a sacred object that is believed to provide the wearer (or house, i.e., the whole family) protection from illness, evil spirits, curses, or bad luck. The earliest references to the word *amulētum* are found in Pliny the Elder: "They call it an amulet [*amulētum vocant*]" (*Nat. hist.* 25.115). The Latin word *amulētum* is a transliteration of the Arabic word *hamalet*, which refers to something "suspended." Greek equivalents include περίαμμα, περίαπτον, and φυλακτήριον. A few examples include: "it is a protective amulet [φυλακτήριον] of the Lord" (*T. Job* 47:11); "they also make suitable coverings and phylacteries [φυλακτήρια] for souls which are devoted to virtue" (Philo, *Migr.* 215); and "write the phylactery [φυλακτήριον] on a little sheet of tin" (*PGM* IV.3014–3015). Of particular relevance for the present study is the comment of Chrysostom who says "women and little children suspend Gospels from their necks as a powerful amulet, and carry them about in all places wherever they go" (*Stat.* 19.14; cf. PG 58:669). Wasserman ("The 'Son of God,'" 24 n. 15) is probably correct in suggesting that these suspended "Gospels" comprise no more than Gospel titles and incipits, not whole books.

2. Mark 1:1 in Late Antique Greek amulets

I begin with the Greek amulets. All derive from Egypt. I present them in an approximate chronological order, though admittedly the dates are far from certain. The first one created a lot of excitement when it was published a decade ago.

P.Oxy. LXXVI 5073
ἀνάγνωτι τὴν ἀρχὴν τοῦ εὐαγ'γελίου καὶ ἴδε
ἀρχὴ τοῦ εὐαγ'γελίου Ἰη(σο)ῦ τοῦ Χρ(ιστο)ῦ
ὡς γέγραπται ἐν τῷ Ἠσαΐᾳ τῷ προφήτῃ
ἰδοὺ ἀποστελῶ τὸν ἄγ'γελόν μου
πρὸ προσώπου σου ὃς κατασκευάσει[35] (lines 1–5)

Read the beginning of the Gos'pel and see:

> "The beginning of the gos'pel of Jesus the Christ,
> as it is written in Isaiah the prophet,
> 'Behold! I will send my an'gel
> before your face who will prepare'" (*See Figure 12.10.*)

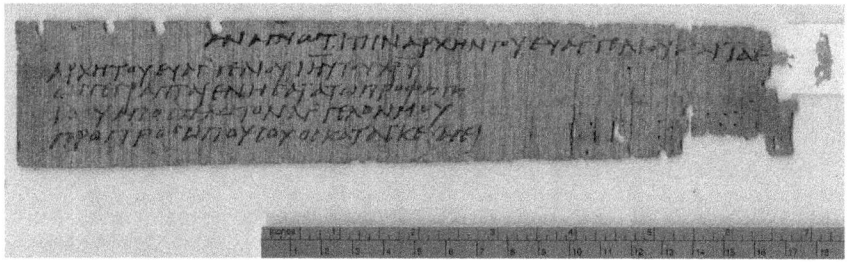

Figure 12.10. P.Oxy. LXXVI 5073. Courtesy of the Egypt Exploration Society and Imaging Papyri Project, Oxford.

Comment: The editors of the *editio princeps* date this amulet to the late third or early fourth century.[36] P.Oxy. III 560 (third century), P.Oxy. VII 1015 (third century), and P.Herm. Rees 4 (fourth century) are cited as comparanda that support the third-/fourth-century date of P.Oxy. LXXVI 5073. Nevertheless, Joseph Sanzo wonders if this date is too early. He notes that Mark's incipit is not found in the earliest extant amulets.[37] Another possible indicator of lateness is the presence of the definite article

---

[35] Geoffrey S. Smith and Andrew E. Bernhard, "5073," in Daniela Colomo and Juan Chapa, eds., *The Oxyrhynchus Papyri*. LXXVI (Nos. 5072–5100), Graeco-Roman Memoirs 97 (London: The Egypt Exploration Society, 2011), 19–23. Smith and Bernhard date the amulet to the late third / fourth century.

[36] Jones (*New Testament Texts on Greek Amulet*, 131) remarks that the "hand is a beautiful specimen of the type of sloping majuscule common in the third and fourth centuries."

[37] Sanzo, *Scriptural Incipits on Amulets*, 98 n. 91.

in Ἰη(σο)ῦ τοῦ Χρ(ιστο)ῦ, "Jesus the Christ." This is common in Coptic amulets that date to the fifth century and later (e.g., P.Lond. Copt. 317; P.Mich. Copt. 1559; P.Mosc. Copt. 36). One more possible indicator of lateness is the appearance of ὡς, rather than καθώς. The former is often found in later witnesses to Mark (e.g., A D 𝔐). The latter is in the oldest (א B). In any case, Sanzo finds the early date surprising and recommends further study.

For our purposes the most important feature of the amulet is the appearance of the short form of Mark 1:1, "The beginning of the Gospel of Jesus the Christ." Should this reading be viewed as evidence in support of the short form of Mark's incipit? Perhaps. But it is also important to note that Mark 1:2 is similarly abbreviated in this amulet, for the quotation ends with ὃς κατασκευάσει, "who will prepare." The ending is deliberate. Abrupt endings mid-sentence are not unusual in amulets.[38]

Another important feature is found in the amulet's quotation of Mark 1:2a, which in turn has quoted Exod 23:20,[39] ἀποστελῶ τὸν ἄγγελόν μου πρὸ προσώπου σου, "I will send my angel." B D and most mss read the present ἀποστέλλω, "I am sending" (or "I send"), in agreement with LXX Exod 23:20.[40] But our amulet, in agreement with א and Θ, reads the future ἀποστελῶ, "I will send," which intensifies the scriptural promise of sending help. Of course, this help is not a prophet who will speak, as would be expected in the parallel Mal 3:1, or in the message of Isa 40:3, part of which is also quoted in Mark 1:3, but a literal angel (τὸν ἄγγελόν μου, "my angel"), whose task is to protect the wearer of the amulet.[41] The shift from Mark's original ἀποστέλλω to ἀποστελῶ in the amulet was intentional. I might add that the composer of the amulet is quoting Mark, not Exodus. He probably had no idea that Mark had quoted Exodus. Had the composer of the amulet had in mind Exod 23:20, then we would have expected ὃς φυλάξει, "who will guard," rather than ὃς κατασκευάσει, "who will prepare."

A distinctive feature of our amulet is found in its opening exhortation, ἀνάγνωτι τὴν ἀρχὴν τοῦ εὐαγγελίου καὶ ἴδε, "Read the beginning of the Gospel and see." Wasserman calls our attention to a similar exhortation in Origen's apologetical response to the skeptic Celsus: "Let him read the gospel and see [ἀναγνώτω τὸ εὐαγγέλιον καὶ ὁράτω] that 'the centurion and those with him guarding Jesus seeing the earthquake and the things that were happening were exceedingly afraid, saying, 'This one was a son of God [θεοῦ υἱὸς ἦν οὗτος]'" (*Cels.* 2.36). Origen has cited Matt 27:54, including and

---

[38] As is rightly noted by Jones (*New Testament Texts on Greek Amulet*, 134) and others. The significance of P.Oxy. LXXVI 5073 for textual criticism is overstated in Peter M. Head, "Additional Greek Witnesses to the New Testament (Ostraca, Amulets, Inscriptions, and Other Sources)," in Bart D. Ehrman and Michael W. Holmes, eds., *The Text of the New Testament in Contemporary Research: Essays on the Status Quaestionis*, 2nd ed., NTTSD 42 (Leiden: Brill, 2012), 429–60, when he says that the amulet "clearly reflects a form of the text lacking the words 'Son of God'" in Mark 1:1 (442). Would we say that the amulet clearly reflects a form of the text that lacks the final words of Mark 1:2? What we will find in our survey is that amulets frequently abbreviate and paraphrase Scripture.

[39] The quotation in Mark 1:2–3 is a loose amalgam of Exod 23:20; Mal 3:1; and Isa 40:3. What the amulet quotes from Mark 1:2 is mostly taken from LXX Exod 23:20. See A. Suhl, *Die Funktion der alttestamentlichen Zitate und Anspielungen im Markusevangelium* (Gütersloh: Mohn, 1965), 135.

[40] A few authorities read ἀποστελῶ at Exod 23:20, as noted in John William Wevers, *Notes on the Greek Text of Exodus*, SBLSCS 30 (Atlanta: Scholars Press, 1990), 369.

[41] The same idea could be in view in P.Mich. inv. 4944b. See Brice C. Jones, "A Greek Papyrus Fragment with a Citation of Matthew 1:20," *JBL* 137 (2018): 169–74.

especially the centurion's confession, ἀληθῶς θεοῦ υἱὸς ἦν οὗτος, which could be woodenly rendered, "Truly a son of God was this one." Origen appeals to this passage as offering proof that even in his death the divinity of Jesus was revealed, as seen in what the centurion said.

The amulet's exhortation, "Read the beginning of the Gospel and see," is similar in a general sense.[42] But the amulet's exhortation has a more specific purpose. It implies that the amulet can protect the wearer because of what is said at the beginning of the Gospel of Mark, namely, that God "will send his angel." We probably should infer from the exhortation to read that the wearer of the amulet is to read *aloud* the words of Mark 1:1–2 and the promised angel will then provide the needed protection from illness, or more likely, from demonic threats.[43]

P.Oxy. VIII 1151

† ἐν ἀρχῇ ἦν ὁ λόγος, καὶ ὁ λόγος ἦν πρὸς τὸν θ(εό)ν, καὶ θ(εὸ)ς ἦν ὁ λόγος. πάντα δι' αὐτοῦ ἐγένετο, κ(αὶ) χωρεὶς αὐτοῦ ἐγένετο οὐδὲ ἕν ὃ γέγονεν. (lines 15–22)

† In the beginning was the Word, and the Word was with God, and the Word was God. All things came into existence through him and without him not one thing came into existence.

Comment: The amulet, which probably dates to the fifth century, is an incantation and prayer for healing on behalf of one Joannia, daughter of Euphemia.[44] The incantation begins with the formulaic command to flee: "Flee, hateful spirit! Christ pursues you" (lines 1–3).[45] The Synoptic incipits do not appear in this amulet, but it is worth observing that it quotes John 1:1, then 1:3, having omitted v. 2. Note the spelling of χωρεὶς, "without," instead of χωρίς. The amulet goes on to petition, "† Lord Christ, Son and Word of the living God [τοῦ θ(εο)ῦ τοῦ ζόντος]…" (with ζόντος, instead of ζῶντος). The reference to "living God" will appear often in the Coptic amulets.[46]

---

[42] Wasserman, "The 'Son of God,'" 24 n. 16; that is, in that these texts have an apologetical purpose.

[43] Smith and Bernhard, "5073," 20. For further details, see Sanzo, *Scriptural* Incipits *on Amulets*, 98–99; Jones, *New Testament Texts on Greek Amulets*, 130–34 + plate 15; de Bruyn, *Making Amulets Christian*, 147–49; and Robert Matthew Calhoun, "The Gospel(-Amulet) as God's Power for Salvation," *Early Christianity* 10 (2019): 21–55, esp. 50–52. Calhoun argues that the amulet is not appealing to angelic protection but to the power of the Gospel story itself, signified by the quotation of the Markan incipit.

[44] For the *editio princeps*, see Arthur S. Hunt, "1151. Christian Amulet," in idem, ed., *The Oxyrhynchus Papyri*, Part VIII (London: Egypt Exploration Society, 1911), 251–53.

[45] Warnings to flee directed against evil spirits or illnesses not only occur in amulets; popular Judeo-Christian literature speaks of fleeing evil spirits (e.g., *T. Dan* 5:11, "Beliar may flee from you"; *T. Benj.* 5:2, "the unclean spirits will flee from you"; James 4:7, "Resist the devil and he will flee from you").

[46] For further discussion, see Anne Luijendijk, "A Gospel Amulet for Joannia (P.Oxy. VIII 1151)," in Kimberly B. Stratton and Dayna S. Kalleres, eds., *Daughters of Hecate: Women and Magic in the Ancient World* (Oxford: Oxford University Press, 2014), 418–43; Sanzo, *Scriptural* Incipits *on Amulets*, 97–98; Jones, *New Testament Texts on Greek Amulets*, 134–40; de Bruyn, *Making Amulets Christian*, 107–109.

PSI VI 719

† Χ(ριστ)έ, [Σ](ῶτ)ερ. ἐν ἀρχῇ ἦν ὁ λόγος, καὶ ὁ λόγος ἦν πρὸς τὸν θεόν, καὶ θεὸς ἦν ὁ λόγος. βίβλος γενέσεως Ἰησοῦ Χριστοῦ υἱοῦ Δαυέτ υἱοῦ Ἀβραάμ. καθὼ[ς ε]ἶπεν Ἡσαιας ὁ προφήτης, [ἀρχὴ τοῦ εὐα]γγελίου Ἰησοῦ Χριστοῦ υἱοῦ θεοῦ υἱοῦ Ἀβραάμ. ἐπε[ιδ]ήπερ πολλοὶ ἐπιχείρησαν ἀν[ατάξα]σθαι δ[ι]ήγησιν περὶ τῶν πεπληροφορημένον ἐν ἡμῖ[ν π]ραγμάτων.⁴⁷ (lines 1–4)

† Christ, Savior! "In the beginning was the Word, and the Word was with God, and the Word was God." "Book of the geneaology of Jesus Christ, son of David, son of Abraham." "Just as Isaiah the prophet said: 'The beginning of the gospel of Jesus Christ, Son of God, son of Abraham.'" "Inasmuch as many have undertaken to arrange an account of the things that have been accomplished among us."

Comment: The amulet cites the incipits of all four Gospels in the order of John, Matthew, Mark, and Luke. David is spelled Δαυέτ, instead of Δαυίδ (UBSGNT) or Δαυείδ (B W). It is not certain, but the amulet's καθὼς εἶπεν Ἡσαΐας ὁ προφήτης, "just as Isaiah the prophet said," probably is a paraphrase of Mark 1:2, καθὼς γέγραπται ἐν τῷ Ἡσαΐᾳ τῷ προφήτῃ, "just as it is written in Isaiah the prophet." The amulet provides the long version of Mark's incipit, but extends it with the addition of υἱοῦ Ἀβραάμ, "son of Abraham," which has been taken from Matthew's incipit. This is odd, for the writer of the amulet obviously knows that υἱοῦ Ἀβραάμ is part of Matt 1:1. In the Lukan incipit note the spellings ἐπιχείρησαν for ἐπεχείρησαν, and πεπληροφορημένον for πεπληροφορημένων.

Girolamo Vitelli dated this amulet to the fourth or fifth century.⁴⁸ Uncertain of its provenance, he suggested Oxyrhynchus.⁴⁹ Although most scholars initially accepted Vitelli's early dating, Rosario Pintaudi has suggested a sixth-century date after observing certain overlooked Byzantine features on the backside of the amulet. His later date has been followed by other papyrologists.⁵⁰

---

⁴⁷ For early publications of PSI VI 719, see Girolamo Vitelli, *Pubblicazioni della Società Italiana per la ricerca dei Papiri greci e latini in Egitto: Papiri greci et latini*, vol. 6 (Florence: Pubblicazioni della Società Italiana, 1920), 151–52; Carl Wessely, "Les plus anciens monuments du christianisme écrits sur papyrus II. textes grecs," in *Patrologia Orientalis*, Tomus decimus octavus (Paris: Firmin-Didot, 1924), 412–13; K. Preisendanz, ed., *Papyri Graecae Magicae: Die Griechischen Zauberpapyri*, 2 vols. (Leipzig: B. G. Teubner, 1928–31; rev. ed., 1973; repr. Munich/Leipzig: K. G. Saur, 2001), 2:227–28 (no. 19).

⁴⁸ Followed by Wessely, "Les plus anciens monuments," 413; Preisendanz, ed., *Papyri Graecae Magicae*, 227; and M. Naldini, *Documenti dell'antichità cristiana: Papiri e pergamene greco-egizie della Raccolta Fiorentina* (Florence: Le Monnier, 1965), 32.

⁴⁹ Vitelli, *Pubblicazioni della Società Italiana*, 151.

⁵⁰ Rosario Pintaudi, "Per la datazione di PSI VI 719," *AnPap* 2 (1990): 27–28; Csaba A. Là'da and Amphilochios Papathomas, "A Greek Papyrus Amulet from the Duke Collection with Biblical Excerpts," *BASP* 41 (2004): 93–113 (109, 112). Sanzo (*Scriptural Incipits on Amulets*, 86 n. 53) seems to lean toward the later date. For further discussion, see Jones, *New Testament Texts on Greek Amulets*, 77–80 + plate. Jones also accepts the later date.

P.Berol. 6096 (BKT VI 7.1)

† ἐν ἀρχῇ ἦν ὁ λόγος καὶ ὁ λόγος ἦν πρ<ὸς> τὸν <θεόν> κ(αὶ) θ(εὸ)ς ἦν ὁ λόγος. οὗτος ἦν ἐν ἀρχῇ πρὸς τὸν θ(εό)ν. † βίβλος γεννέσευς Ἰ(ησο)ῦ Χ(ριστο)ῦ υ(ἱο)ῦ Δα(υὶ)δ υ(ἱο)ῦ Ἀβρ(αάμ). † ἀρχὴ τοῦ εὐαγγελίου Υἱσοῦ Χ(ριστο)ῦ υ(ἱο)ῦ θ(εο)ῦ. † ἐπειδήπερ πολλοὶ ἐπεχείρισαν ἀνατάξασθαι διήγισιν.[51] (lines 4–10)

† "In the beginning was the Word, and the Word was with God, and the Word was God. This one was in the beginning with God." † "The book of the Genealogy of Jesus Christ, son of David, son of Abraham." † "The beginning of the gospel of Jesus Christ, son of God." † "Inasmuch as many have undertaken to arrange a narrative."

Comment: Sanzo and de Bruyn date the amulet to the sixth or seventh century, while Jones dates it to the fifth or sixth.[52] As is typical with artifacts of this kind, idiosyncratic spelling is common, which sometimes complicates deciphering a text, such as P.Berol. 6096, which is very difficult to read in places. Note the spelling γεννέσευς,[53] instead of γενέσεως. Spelling variation is common, especially in texts of this nature.[54] Note also the spelling Υἱσοῦ, "of Jesus," rather than the more common Ἰησοῦ. The name Ἰησοῦς is spelled several different ways in Greek sources. Spelling variations in personal names are not unusual.[55] Note also the spelling of ἐπεχείρισαν, instead of ἐπεχείρησαν. In line 5 the scribe inadvertently omitted θεόν.

In line 10 we find ἀναδεξάσθαι, instead of the expected ἀνατάξασθαι. Rather than a spelling variation, we probably have a misquotation or perhaps a conscious reinterpretation. That is, instead of reading, "Inasmuch as many have undertaken to put in order a narrative," the amulet reads "Inasmuch as many have undertaken to *receive* a narrative" (note the reinterpretation of Luke 1 in the next example). Finally, note also the spelling διήγισιν, instead of διήγησιν. The idiosyncratic spellings of Υἱσοῦ, ἐπεχείρισαν, and διήγισιν probably reflect pronunciation distinctives. The important point in the present amulet is the attestation of the longer form of Mark's incipit.[56]

---

[51] For the *editio princeps*, see Fritz Krebs, "Altchristliche Texte im Berliner Museum," in *Nachrichten von der Königl. Gesellschaft der Wissenschaften und der Georg-Augusts-Universität zu Göttingen* (Göttingen: Dieterichsche Verlags-Buchhandlung, 1892): 114–20 (118–20) (no. IV). See also Carl Schmidt and Wilhelm Schubart, eds., *Altchristliche Texte*, BKT 6 (Berlin: Weidmann, 1910), 129–30 (no. VII.1); and Wessely, "Les plus anciens monuments," 412–13. For a more recent edition of the text, see Alfred Rahlfs and Detlef Fraenkel, *Verzeichnis der griechischen Handschriften des Alten Testaments*. Vol. 1.1: *Die Überlieferung bis zum VIII. Jahrhundert* (Göttingen: Vandenhoeck & Ruprecht, 2004), 21 (no. 2131).

[52] Sanzo, *Scriptural* Incipits *on Amulets*, 80; Jones, *New Testament Texts on Greek Amulets*, 65; de Bruyn, *Making Amulets Christian*, 144. (NB: Sanzo mistakenly cross-lists the amulet as P.Berol. 6069; it is 6096.)

[53] The faded letters are very hard to decipher. Krebs ("Altchristliche Texte," 119) reads γενέσεως. Sanzo (*Scriptural* Incipits *on Amulets*, 81) reads γεννέσευς, which I follow. Jones (*New Testament Texts on Greek Amulets*, 65) reads γεννέσεσενς. He also provides a good-quality color image (67 pl. 2).

[54] A number of other examples appear in portions of the amulet that have not been cited.

[55] This is well evidenced in Tal Ilan, *Lexicon of Jewish Names in Late Antiquity. Part I: Palestine 330 BCE–200 CE*, TSAJ 91 (Tübingen: Mohr Siebeck, 2002).

[56] For further discussion of this amulet, see Donatella Limongi, "La diffusione dei Vangeli in Egitto (secc. I–VIII): Osservazioni sul *Vangelo secondo Marco*," *AnPap* 7 (1995): 49–62 (57–58); Sanzo,

P.Berol. 954 (*BGU* III 954)

ἐν ἀρχῇ ἦν [ὁ λόγο]ς. βίβλος κε[νέσεως Ἰ(ησο)ῦ Χ(ριστο)ῦ υἱο[ῦ Δαυὶδ υἱοῦ Ἀβραάμ].[57] (lines 24–25)

In the beginning was the Word. Book of the genealogy of Jesus Christ, son of David, son of Abraham.

Comment: The amulet is dated to the sixth century. The Markan and Lukan incipits do not appear; however, it is worth noting that the Johannine incipit appears in abbreviated form, with only the first clause quoted; the Matthean incipit is in full form, though with restorations and a curious spelling of "geneaology" (κενέσεως, instead of γενέσεως).[58]

P.Vindob. G 348

[βίβλος] γενέσεως Ἰη(σο)ῦ Χρ(ιστο)[ῦ. ἀ]ρχὴ τοῦ εὐαν[γελίου]. ἐπειδήπερ πολλοὶ ἐπεχείρησαν [ἀνατά]ξασθαι διήγησιν. ἐν ἀρχῇ ἦν ὁ λόγος, καὶ [ὁ λόγο]ς ἦν πρὸς τὸν θ(εό)ν, καὶ θ(εὸ)ς ἦν ὁ λόγος. (lines 1–4)

"Book of the genealogy of Jesus Christ." "The beginning of the gospel." "Inasmuch as many have undertaken to arrange a narrative." "In the beginning was the Word, and the Word was with God, and the Word was God."[59]

Comment: The amulet is dated to the sixth or seventh century. The amulet quotes portions of the incipits of all four New Testament Gospels. The phrases, "son of David" and "son of Abraham" are omitted from Matthew's incipit. The phrases "of Jesus Christ" and "Son of God" are omitted from Mark's incipit. With respect to Luke, only the first half of v. 1 is quoted. All of the first verse of John is quoted. The spelling εὐανγελίου in Mark's incipit reflects later Byzantine spelling.[60]

P.Rainier 1 (P. graec. 337)

[ὁρκίζω ὑμᾶς κατὰ τῶν τεσσάρων εὐαγγ]ελίων τοῦ υἱο[ῦ θ(εο)ῦ... (lines 1–2)

"I adjure you by the four Gospels of the Son ..." (with restorations).[61]

Scriptural Incipits *on Amulets*, 80–81; Jones, *New Testament Texts on Greek Amulets*, 65–71; de Bruyn, *Making Amulets Christian*, 144–46.

[57] For the *editio princeps*, see Ulrich Wilken, "Heidnisches und Christliches aus Ägypten," *APF* 1 (1901): 396–436 (431–36); reissued in *Ägyptische Urkunden aus den Königlichen Museen zu Berlin: Griechischen Urkunden*, Dritter Band (Berlin: Weidman, 1903), 278–79 (no. 954); and re-edited (in better form) in Wessely, "Les plus anciens monuments," 420–22.

[58] For further discussion, see Sanzo, Scriptural Incipits *on Amulets*, 91–92; Jones, *New Testament Texts on Greek Amulets*, 107–12.

[59] For the *editio princeps*, see R. W. Daniel, "A Christian Amulet on Papyrus," *VC* 37 (1983): 400–404.

[60] For notes on restorations and spelling, see Daniel, "A Christian Amulet on Papyrus," 403–404; Sanzo, *Scriptural* Incipits *on Amulets*, 89.

[61] For text and discussion, see Preisendanz, ed., *Papyri Graecae Magicae*, 2:218 (no. 10); T. Wasserman, "𝔓⁷⁸ (*P.Oxy.* XXXIV 2684): The Epistle of Jude on an Amulet?" in Thomas J. Kraus and Tobias Nicklas, eds., *New Testament Manuscripts: Their Texts and Their World*, TENTS 2 (Leiden: Brill,

Comment: The amulet is dated to the sixth century. The amulet does not refer to the Gospel incipits, or even to the names of the Gospels. Rather, the adjuration is simply "by the four Gospels." The restoration υἱοῦ, "son," is virtually certain, but its meaning is not. I understand it as a reference to Jesus, the "Son of God" (or simply the "Son"), in the sense that the four Gospels tell his story, a story that features healing and exorcism. That it is the Gospel story that is in view is supported by the amulet's later adjuration "by the Gospel of the Lord [τὸ εὐαγγέλιον τοῦ κυρίου], who suffered on account of us humans" (lines 33–35). The purpose of the amulet is to drive away fever.

P.Oxy. XVI 1928

κατὰ Ἰωάννης καιτὰ Λουκᾶ κατὰ Μᾶρκος κατὰ Μαθθέας[(line 16)

according to John, according to Luke, according to Mark, according to Matthew…

Comment: The first fifteen lines of the amulet comprise a quotation of LXX Psalm 90, a favorite in amulets and exorcistic incantations. The last line of the amulet, as seen already, refers to the titles of the four New Testament Gospels, but in reverse order. It is interesting that three of Gospel names (Ἰωάννης, Μᾶρκος, and Μαθθέας) are in the nominative case, rather than in the expected accusative case. Λουκᾶ could be considered accusative but the more conventional accusative form is Λουκᾶν.[62] (The author of the amulet may have thought of Λουκᾶ as nominative.) So far as I know, the spelling Μαθθέας is otherwise unattested[63] (*secundum Mattheum* is found in some Latin mss).

Thebaid Grotto Chapel Walls

ἐπειδήπερ πολλοὶ ἐπεχείρησαν ἀνατάξασθαι διήγησιν περὶ τῶν πεπληροφο-ρημένων ἐν ἡμῖν πραγμάτων, ² καθὼς παρέδωσαν ἡμῖν οἱ ἀπ' ἀρχῆς αὐτόπται καὶ ὑπηρέται γενόμενοι τοῦ λόγου, ³ ἔδοξεν κ[ἀ]μοὶ παρηκολουθηκότι ἄνωθεν πᾶσιν ἀκριβῶς καθεξῆς σοι γράψαι, κράτιστε Θεόφι[λε. Ἐν ἀρχῇ ἦν ὁ λόγος, καὶ ὁ λόγος ἦν πρὸς τὸν θ(εό)ν, καὶ θ(εὸ)ς ἦν ὁ λόγος. ² οὗτος ἦν ἐν ἀρχῇ πρὸς τὸν θεόν. ³ πάντα δι' αὐτοῦ ἐγένετο, καὶ χωρὶς αὐτοῦ ἐγένετο οὐδὲ ἕν. ὃ γέγονεν ⁴ ἐν αὐτῷ] ζωὴ ἦν, καὶ ἡ ζωὴ ἦν τὸ φῶς τῶν ἀν(θρώπ)ων· ⁵ καὶ τὸ φῶς ἐν τῇ σκοτίᾳ φαίνει, καὶ ἡ σκοτία αὐτὸ ο[ὐ] κατέλαβεν. βίβλος γενέσεως Ἰ(ησο)ῦ Χ(ριστο)ῦ υἱοῦ Δα(υὶ)δ υἱοῦ Ἀβραάμ. Ἀβραὰμ ἐγέννησεν τὸν Ἰσαά[κ, Ἰσα]ὰκ δὲ ἐγέννησεν τὸν Ἰακώβ, Ἰακὼβ δὲ ἐγέννησεν τὸν Ἰούδαν καὶ τοὺς ἀδελφοὺς

2006), 137–60 (150 n. 44); Sanzo, *Scriptural* Incipits *on Amulets*, 5–6, 38–39. Sanzo is right to express the need for caution with respect to the extent of the restoration of the opening words of this amulet.

[62] For *editio princeps* and discussion, see Bernard Grenfell, Arthur Hunt, and Idris Bell, "Amulet (Psalm XC): Protocol," in *The Oxyrhynchus Papyri*, Part XVI (London: Egypt Exploration Society, 1924), 208–11; Paul Collart, "Un papyrus Reinach inédit: Psaume 140 sur une amulette," *Aegyptus* 13 (1933): 208–12 (on blending Gospel elements with LXX Ps 90); Sanzo, *Scriptural* Incipits *on Amulets*, 85; Rahlfs and Fraenkel, *Verzeichnis der griechischen Handschriften*, 301–302 (no. 2106).

[63] No example of Μαθθέας is listed in Ilan, *Lexicon of Jewish Names in Late Antiquity*, 191–96.

αὐτοῦ, ³ Ἰούδας δὲ ἐγέννησεν τὸν Φάρες καὶ τὸν Ζάρα ἐκ τῆς Θαμά[ρ. Ἀρχὴ τοῦ] εὐαγ[γε]λίου [Ἰ{ησο}ῦ Χ(ριστο)ῦ υ(ἱο)ῦ τοῦ θ(εο)ῦ. καθὼς γέ]γραπται ἐν [τῷ Ἠσαΐᾳ τῷ προφήτῃ· ἰδοὺ ἀποστέλλω τὸν ἄγγελόν μου πρὸ προσώπου σου, ὃς] κατασκευάσει τὴν ὁδόν σου.[64]

"Inasmuch as many have undertaken to arrange a narrative concerning the things that have been accomplished among us, just as those who were from the beginning were eyewitnesses and officers of the word passed on to us, it seemed good to me also, having followed everything carefully from the top, to write to you, most excellent Theophi[lus." "In the beginning was the Word, and the Word was with God, and the Word was God. This one was in the beginning with God; all things through him came into existence, and without him nothing came into existence. What came into existence in him] was life, and the life was the light of humans; and the light shines in the darkness, and the darkness has not overcome it." "The book of the geneaology of Jesus Christ, son of David, son of Abraham. Abraham sired Isaac, and Isaac sired Jacob, and Jacob sired Judah and his brothers, and Judah sired Phares and Zarah from Tamar." "The beginning of the gospel of Jesus Christ, the Son of God. Just as it is written in Isaiah the prophet: 'Behold, I send my angel before your face, who will prepare your way.'"

Comments: The inscriptions on the Thebaid Grotto Chapel walls, near the ancient site of Antinoöpolis, are dated to the eighth century. S. Kent Brown describes the site as follows: "At the base of the cliff, one meets the remains of a chapel built inside a large rock quarry. On the inner walls of this small chapel appear two lines of text that run around the entire circumference of the room."[65] The Gospel incipits are placed (starting north and moving clockwise) as follows: Luke 1:1–3 (north wall), John 1:1–5 (east wall), Matt 1:1–3 (south wall), and Mark 1:1–2 (west wall), with selections from LXX Psalms 118 (north, left), 127 (north, right), 31 (south, left), 40 (south, right), and 111 (west) interleaved, each of which begins with "blessed" (either plural μακάριοι or singular μακάριος).[66] The restoration from the end of Luke 1:3 to John 1:4a seems reasonable. It should be noted that the chapel's text of the Gospels and the Psalms agrees with Codex Alexandrinus (A). The names of the prophets Jeremiah, Isaiah, Nahum (?), Zechariah, and Malachi are also present.

The long form of Mark's incipit is restored in part, but given the spacing it seems required. This means reading υ(ἱο)ῦ τοῦ θ(εο)ῦ. The restoration includes the article τοῦ with θεοῦ, which, given the late date of the inscription and the widespread

---

[64] For *editio princeps*, see M. Gustave Lefebvre, "Égypte Chrétienne III," *Annales du Service des Antiquités de l'Égypte*, vol. 10 (Cairo: L'Institut Français d'Archéologie Orientale, 1910), 260–84 (260–71). For convenience I have added the verse numbers for the Gospel incipits.

[65] S. Kent Brown, "Coptic and Greek Inscriptions from Christian Egypt: A Brief Review," in Birger A. Pearson and James E. Goehring, eds., *The Roots of Egyptian Christianity*, Studies in Antiquity & Christianity (Philadelphia: Fortress Press, 1987), 26–41 (33).

[66] Lefebvre ("Égypte Chrétienne III," 264) provides a bird's eye diagram of the chapel indicating on which walls which quotations of Scripture appear. No psalm quotation appears on the east wall.

representation of the article in mss of Mark in this period, seems justified. Of course, the agreement with Codex Alexandrinus, which also reads υ(ἰο)ῦ τοῦ θ(εο)ῦ at Mark 1:1, lends further support to the restoration. The use of *nomina sacra* is also assumed.[67]

I now turn to the Coptic amulets that contain Gospel incipits.

3. Mark 1:1 in Late Antique Coptic amulets

The Coptic amulets with Gospel incipits are quite similar to their Greek counterparts. In fact, several of the Coptic amulets borrow Greek words (as Coptic in late antiquity in general did). One distinctive feature is that in the Coptic amulets Jesus is sometimes called "Jesus the Christ," rather than "Jesus Christ."

> **P. Anastasy 9 (Leiden ms AMS 9)**
> This is the order of the opening of the four Gospels. Matthew's Gospel: "The book of the generation of Jesus Christ, the son of David, the son of Abraham." The Gospel according to Mark: "The beginning of the gospel of Jesus the Christ [ⲡⲉⲭ(ⲣⲓⲥⲧⲟ)ⲥ], the son of the living God [ⲡϣⲏⲣⲉ ⲙ̄ⲡⲛⲟⲩⲧⲉ ⲉⲧⲟⲛϩ], as it is written in Isaiah the prophet." The Gospel according to Luke: "Inasmuch as many have undertaken to write the stories about the deeds that have been agreed to among us." The Gospel according to John: "In the beginning was the Word, and the Word was with God, and the Word was God."[68]

Comment: The amulet dates to the sixth century, though it could be later. I have only quoted part of this relatively lengthy charm. Here we not only have the long form of Mark's incipit, where the Greek loan words and names αρχη, ευαγγελιον, ιη, and χς appear, we also have the modifier "living" (ⲉⲧⲟⲛϩ), which qualifies God (and this language is found several other times in the charm). It reminds us of Peter's confession in the Matthean form, "You are the Messiah, the son of the living God [ὁ χριστὸς ὁ υἱὸς τοῦ θεοῦ τοῦ ζῶντος]" (Matt 16:16), as well as the opening words of the Coptic *Gospel of Thomas*, "These are the secret words that the living [ⲉⲧⲟⲛϩ] Jesus spoke..." (Prologue). The epithet "living God" is found frequently in the Old Testament (e.g., Deut 5:26; Josh 3:10; 1 Sam 17:26; Ps 42:2; etc.).

The first part of Mark 1:2 is also cited, "as it is written in Isaiah the prophet." After the quotation of John 1:1 the opening verse of LXX Psalm 90 is quoted.[69] In P. Rylands

---

[67] For further notes, see Sanzo, *Scriptural* Incipits *on Amulets*, 90–91.
[68] For *editio princeps*, see Willem Pleyte and Pieter Adrian Art Boeser, *Manuscrits coptes du Musée d'antiquités des Pays-Bas à Leide* (Leiden: Brill, 1897), 441–79 (477–78). I have used the translation provided in Marvin W. Meyer and Richard Smith, eds., *Ancient Christian Magic: Coptic Texts of Ritual Power* (Princeton NJ: Princeton University Press, 1999), 322 (slightly modified).
[69] For further notes, see Sanzo, *Scriptural* Incipits *on Amulets*, 82–83. De Bruyn (*Making Amulets Christian*, 87 n. 119) calls our attention to Ján Alexander Szirmai, *The Archaeology of Medieval Bookbinding* (Aldershot: Ashgate, 1999), 43 n. 6, who dates P. Anastasy 9 to the seventh–eighth century. The Anastasy papyrus gets its name from Greek dealer in antiquities Giovanni Anastasi (1765–1860).

101 Coptic, all of Mark 1:2 is cited, "As it is written in Isaiah the prophet, 'Behold, I send my angel [αγγελος] before your face, who will prepare your way.'" Mark 1:1 is not cited. Mark 1:2, with minor variations compared to the major witnesses of the Coptic Gospels, appears on the recto and a partial list of the Forty Martyrs of Sebaste appears on the verso.[70]

P.Berol. 22 235
"The book of the genealogy of Jesus the Christ." "The beginning of the gospel of Jesus Christ." "Inasmuch as many have undertaken." "In the beginning was the Word." "The book of the genealogy of Jesus the Christ."[71]

Comment: The date of this unpublished amulet is uncertain and its provenance is unknown. Sanzo suggests a range of third to sixth century. Note how the incipits of all four Gospels have been truncated (and Matthew's incipit appears twice).[72]

P.Lond. Copt. 317 (Brit. Lib. Or. 4919(2))
"The copy of the letter of Jesus the Christ, the Son of the living God." "The book of the genealogy of Jesus the Christ." "Inasmuch as many have undertaken." "In the beginning was the Word." "The beginning of the gospel of Jesus the Christ."[73]

Comment: Sanzo dates the amulet to the sixth to seventh century. The provenance is unknown. The last line, "of Jesus the Christ," is damaged, but the restoration seems reasonable. This amulet begins with incipit of the *Epistula Abgari* (the most popular tradition outside scripture itself), which is then followed by the incipits of Matthew, Luke, John, and Mark. The incipits of all four New Testament Gospels are truncated (the incipit of the apocryphal letter to Abgar is also truncated).[74]

Bodleian Coptic Limestone Inscription 426
"The book of the genealogy of Jesus the Christ, the son of David, the son of Abraham." "The beginning of the Gospel of Jesus the Christ, just as Isaiah the prophet spoke." "Inasmuch as many have undertaken to write the words concerning the things which were received by us." "In the beginning was the Word, and the Word was with God, and the Word was God." The four beginnings of the gospel, which is holy: the Gospel according to Matthew,

---

[70] Sanzo, *Scriptural* Incipits *on Amulets*, 99; de Bruyn, *Making Amulets Christian*, 218–20.
[71] Coptic text provided by Sanzo, *Scriptural* Incipits *on Amulets*, 84; my translation.
[72] Sanzo, *Scriptural* Incipits *on Amulets*, 83–84.
[73] For *editio princeps*, see Joseph E. Sanzo, "Brit. Lib. Or. 4919(2): An Unpublished Coptic Amulet in the British Library," ZPE 183 (2012): 98–100; cf. idem, *Scriptural* Incipits *on Amulets*, 81–82.
[74] On the popularity of the *Epistula Abgari* in amulets, see Sanzo, *Scriptural* Incipits *on Amulets*, 154. In n. 13 Sanzo cites several amulets that quote material from the Abgar correspondence (usually its incipit). These include P.Oxy. LXV 4469, P.Mich. inv. 6213, P. Got. 21, and P. Heid. G. 110. See also de Bruyn, *Making Amulets Christian*, 153–57. De Bruyn also discusses P.Vindob. inv. K 8636, written on behalf of one Christodora, daughter of Gabriel, quotes the *Epistula Abgari* and petitions that she be healed quickly.

the Gospel according to Mark, the Gospel according to Luke, the Gospel according to John. Mary bore Christ! Jesus, the Son of God, forever! †††
(Side A)[75]

Comment: The Bodleian limestone inscription is dated mid-seventh century. Its provenance is unknown, but Thebes has been suggested.[76] Matthew's incipit is given in full. The Markan incipit does not include "Son of God," but at the end of side A, Jesus is called "Son of God." Mirecki wonders if this shows an awareness of the longer form of the incipit.[77] He is probably correct. The wording of Mark 1:2 is slightly altered. So is the wording of Luke's incipit. The naming of the twelve apostles (cf. Luke 6:14–16) is found on side B of the stone.

P.Mich. 1559

The Gospel according to Matthew: "The book of the genealogy of Jesus the Christ, the son of David." The Gospel according to Mark: "The beginning of the gospel of Jesus the Christ." The Gospel according to Luke: "Inasmuch as many have undertaken to narrate." The Gospel according to John: "In the beginning was the Word, and the Word was with God."[78]

Comment: The amulet is dated to the seventh or eighth century. Its provenance is unknown. The incipits of all four Gospels, in their "canonical" order, are truncated and they are accompanied by unknown ritual symbols.[79]

Anchorite's Grotto in Nubia

The Gospel according to Matthew [μαθθευ<ιος>]: "Jesus was born in Bethlehem of Judea in the days of Herod the king." The Gospel according to Mark: "The beginning of the good news of Jesus the Christ, Son of God, as it says in Isaiah the prophet." The Gospel according to Luke: "Inasmuch as many have taken in hand to write." The Gospel according to John: "In the beginning was the Word, and the Word was with God, and the Word was God."[80]

Comment: The plaster inscription on the back wall of an anchorite's grotto could date to the year 739, but there is some uncertainty.[81] In place of Matthew's incipit

---

[75] For *editio princeps*, see Paul Mirecki, "A Seventh-Century Coptic Limestone in the Ashmolean Museum, Oxford (Bodl. Copt. Inscr. 426)," in Paul Mirecki and Marvin W. Meyer, eds., *Magic and Ritual in the Ancient World*, RGRW 141 (Leiden: Brill, 2002), 47–69. The translation is from Mirecki (57), slightly modified.

[76] Mirecki, "A Seventh-Century Coptic Limestone," 62 n. 31; Sanzo, *Scriptural* Incipits *on Amulets*, 78.

[77] Mirecki, "A Seventh-Century Coptic Limestone," 61.

[78] For *editio princeps*, see Gerald Browne, *Michigan Coptic Texts*, Papyrologica Castroctaviana (Barcelona: Castroctavian and Loyola University Press, 1979), 43–44.

[79] For additional notes, see Sanzo, *Scriptural* Incipits *on Amulets*, 2, 84.

[80] For *editio princeps*, see Francis Llewellyn Griffith, "Oxford Excavations in Nubia," *Liverpool Annals of Archaeology and Anthropology* 14 (1927): 57–116 (81–91 + plate LXIV [photo] and LXX [facsimile]). I have followed Sanzo's transcription (*Scriptural* Incipits *on Amulets*, 78), but I have also viewed Griffith's plates.

[81] On the date, see Archibald Henry Sayce, "Gleanings from the Land of Egypt," *Recueil de travaux relatifs à la philologie et à archéologie égyptiennes et assyriennes* 20 (1898): 169–76 (174): An

(i.e., Matt 1:1) the inscription quotes just over half of Matt 2:1. On the spelling of μαθθευ<ιος>, see P.Oxy. XVI 1928 (discussed already), where we have μαθθέας. The incipits of Mark and John are written out fully; the incipit of Luke is in the shorter form already observed.[82]

P.Mosc. Copt. 36
"The book of the genealogy of Jesus Christ, son of David." "The beginning of the gospel of Jesus the Christ, Son of God." "Inasmuch as many have undertaken to narrate the things accomplished among them." "In the beginning was the Word, and the Word was with God, and the Word was God."[83]

Comment: The Moscow amulet (also called the Pushkin Museum Coptic Amulet), written on parchment and of unknown date, provides the long version of Mark's incipit. Matthew's "son of Abraham" has been omitted. Note the third person at the end of the quotation of Luke 1:1, that is, "among them," instead of the expected "among us" (as noted by Sanzo). Otherwise Luke's shortened incipit reads as we usually find it. The whole of John's incipit has been written out.[84]

Robert Nahman Coptic Amulet
"Book of the genealogy of Jesus the Christ, son of David, son of Abraham." "In the beginning was the Word, and the Word was with God." "Inasmuch as many have undertaken." "The beginning of the gospel of Jesus the Christ."

Comments: The date of the Robert Nahman Coptic amulet is uncertain, ranging from as early as the fifth century to as late as the tenth century. It is possible that it originated in Oxyrhynchus (which then would support an earlier dating), but even that is only a guess.[85] The order of incipits is interesting: Matthew, John, Luke, and Mark. Of the four incipits only Matthew's is written out in full.

4. Concluding remarks

What I think this survey shows is that there was a tendency to abbreviate Gospel incipits, and to abbreviate them in a variety of ways. Sometimes all or some of the incipits are written out fully, but just as often all or some are abbreviated. In some

---

inscription on the south wall of the grotto "seems to give the date A. D. 739." Griffith ("Oxford Excavations in Nubia," 88) remarks on this possible date, but admits to uncertainty, given the restoration. The inscription in question seems to read: "Month of Choiach 8, of the 7th indiction year 45[5] of Diocletian."

[82] For further notes, see Sanzo, *Scriptural* Incipits *on Amulets*, 77–78.

[83] The *editio princeps* was published in Russian by B. A. Turaev in *Christianskye Vostok* [= *Christian East*] 1 (1912): 203–206. I have translated the text as transcribed in Sanzo, *Scriptural* Incipits *on Amulets*, 88.

[84] For more details, including Russian bibliography, see Sanzo, *Scriptural* Incipits *on Amulets*, 88.

[85] The date and provenance of the Robert Nahman Coptic amulet is discussed in James Drescher, "A Coptic Amulet," in Thomas Whittemore, ed., *Coptic Studies in Honor of Walter Ewing Crum* (Boston: The Byzantine Institute, 1950), 265–70. For comments on this amulet, including the problem of its date, see Sanzo, *Scriptural* Incipits *on Amulets*, 89–90.

cases there is simply a listing of the names of the four Gospels, or even a mere reference to "the four Gospels" (as in P.Rainier). We see something similar in the Fathers, whose quotations are more often than not according to the argument at hand, which can sometimes result in a change in wording or, as in the case of many amulets, abbreviation.

After his survey of New Testament texts in Greek amulets Brice Jones remarks that "these widely divergent citations must be studied only in terms of what they tell us about the reception of scripture and not for their text-critical value."[86] I agree; and we should view the Coptic amulets the same way. I believe that the evidence of the use of the Gospel incipits in the Greek and Coptic amulets supports the conclusion reached by Wasserman that "Son of God" was in the original version of Mark.

Bibliography

Ägyptische Urkunden aus den Königlichen Museen zu Berlin: Griechischen Urkunden. Dritter Band. Berlin: Weidman, 1903.
Boring, M. Eugene. *Mark: A Commentary.* Louisville: Westminster John Knox Press, 2006.
Brown, S. Kent. "Coptic and Greek Inscriptions from Christian Egypt: A Brief Review." Pages 26–41 *The Roots of Egyptian Christianity.* Edited by Birger A. Pearson and James E. Goehring. Studies in Antiquity & Christianity. Philadelphia: Fortress Press, 1986.
Browne, Gerald. *Michigan Coptic Texts.* Papyrologica Castroctaviana. Barcelona: Castroctavian and Loyola University Press, 1979.
Buchanan, Edgar S. *The Four Gospels from the Codex Corbeiensis.* Old Latin Biblical Texts 5. Oxford: Clarendon Press, 1907.
Calhoun, Robert Matthew. "The Gospel(-Amulet) as God's Power for Salvation." *Early Christianity* 10 (2019): 21–55.
Childers, Jeffrey W., and George A. Kiraz, eds. *The Gospel of Mark according to the Syriac Peshitta Version with English Translation.* Piscataway, NJ: Gorgias Press, 2012.
Collart, Paul. "Un papyrus Reinach inédit: Psaume 140 sur une amulette." *Aegyptus* 13 (1933): 208–12.
Daniel, R. W. "A Christian Amulet on Papyrus." *VC* 37 (1983): 400–404.
de Bruyn, Theodore. *Making Amulets Christian: Artefacts, Scribes, and Contexts.* Oxford: Oxford University Press, 2017.
Drescher, James. "A Coptic Amulet." Pages 265–70 in *Coptic Studies in Honor of Walter Ewing Crum.* Edited by Thomas Whittemore. Boston: The Byzantine Institute, 1950.
Ehrman, Bart. *The Orthodox Corruption of Scripture: The Effect of Early Christological Controversies on the Text of the New Testament.* Oxford: Oxford University Press, 1993.
Erasmus, Desiderius, ed. *Novum Instrumentum omne.* Basel: Johann Froben, 1516.
Evans, Craig A. "Mark's Incipit and the Priene Calendar Inscription: From Jewish Gospel to Greco-Roman Gospel." *JGRChJ* 1 (2000): 67–81.
Gnilka, Joachim. *Das Evangelium nach Markus.* 2 vols. EKKNT 2.1–2. Zurich: Benziger; Neukirchen-Vluyn: Neukirchener Verlag, 1978.

---

[86] Jones, *New Testament Texts on Greek Amulets,* 187. Jones nevertheless goes on to remark that some of the citations in Amulets could be helpful in sorting out variant readings. With regard to P.Oxy. LXXVI 5073, de Bruyn remarks that the "scribe could have written more of the opening verses of Mark, including the last few words of v. 2, but evidently did not think it necessary to do so" (*Making Amulets Christian,* 147).

Greeven, Heinrich, and Eberhard Güting, eds. *Textkritik des Markusevangeliums*. Theologie: Forschung und Wissenschaft 11. Münster: Lit Verlag, 2005.
Grenfell, Bernard, Arthur Hunt, and Idris Bell. "Amulet (Psalm XC): Protocol." Pages 208–11 in *The Oxyrhynchus Papyri*, Part XVI. London: Egypt Exploration Society, 1924.
Griesbach, Johann Jakob, ed. *Novum Testamentum graece*. Vol. I. *IV. Evangelia*. 2nd ed. London: H. Saxon, 1796.
Griffith, Francis Llewellyn. "Oxford Excavations in Nubia." *Liverpool Annals of Archaeology and Anthropology* 14. Liverpool: University of Liverpool, 1927.
Guelich, Robert A. *Mark 1–8:26*. WBC 34A. Dallas: Word, 1989.
Head, Peter M. "A Text-Critical Study of Mark 1.1: 'The Beginning of the Gospel of Jesus Christ.'" *NTS* 37 (1991): 621–29.
Head, Peter M. "Additional Greek Witnesses to the New Testament (Ostraca, Amulets, Inscriptions, and Other Sources)." Pages 429–60 in *The Text of the New Testament in Contemporary Research: Essays on the* Status Quaestionis, 2nd ed. Edited by Bart D. Ehrman and Michael W. Holmes. NTTSD 42. Leiden: Brill, 2013.
Head, Peter M. "Christology and Textual Transmission: Reverential Alterations in the Synoptic Gospels." *NovT* 35 (1993): 105–29.
Holmes, Michael W., ed. *The Greek New Testament SBL Edition*. Atlanta: Society of Biblical Literature, 2010.
Horner, George William. *The Coptic Version of the New Testament in the Northern Dialect*. Vol. 1: *The Gospels of S. Matthew and S. Mark*. Oxford: Clarendon Press, 1898.
Horner, George William. *The Coptic Version of the New Testament in the Southern Dialect*. Vol. 1: *The Gospels of S. Matthew and S. Mark*. Oxford: Clarendon Press, 1911.
Hunt, Arthur S. "1151. Christian Amulet." Pages 251–53 in *The Oxyrhynchus* Papyri, Part VIII. Edited by Arthur S. Hunt. London: Egypt Exploration Society, 1911.
Ilan, Tal. *Lexicon of Jewish Names in Late Antiquity. Part I: Palestine 330 BCE–200 CE*. TSAJ 91. Tübingen: Mohr Siebeck, 2002.
Initium Euangelij Jesu Christi, Filij Dei. Pierre Sabatier, ed. *Bibliorum Sacrorum Latinae Versiones Antiquae*. Tomus Tertius. Paris: Franciscum Didot, 1749; Repr., 1751.
Initium evangelii ihū xrī fili dī; and R. Weber, *Biblia Sacra iuxta Vulgatam Versionem*. 2 vols. 3rd ed. Stuttgart: Deutsche Bibelgesellschaft, 1985.
Initium Evangelii Jesu Christi, Filii Dei. A reprint of a 1642 Cambridge edition Beza's Latin translation (c. 1565) in Roger Daniels, ed. *Jesu Christi Domini Nostri Novum Testamentum. Ex interpretatione Theodori Bezae*. Berlin: Societatis Bibliophilorum, 1898.
Jones, Brice C. "A Greek Papyrus Fragment with a Citation of Matthew 1:20." *JBL* 137 (2018): 169–74.
Jones, Brice C. *New Testament Texts on Greek Amulets from Late Antiquity*. LNTS 554. New York: Bloomsbury T&T Clark, 2016.
Jongkind, Dirk et al., eds. *The Greek New Testament, Produced at Tyndale House Cambridge*. Cambridge: Cambridge University Press, 2017.
Krebs, Fritz. "Altchristliche Texte im Berliner Museum." Pages 114–20 in *Nachrichten von der Königl. Gesellschaft der Wissenschaften und der Georg-Augusts-Universität zu Göttingen*. Göttingen: Dieterichsche Verlags-Buchhandlung, 1892.
La'da, Csaba A., and Amphilochios Papathomas. "A Greek Papyrus Amulet from the Duke Collection with Biblical Excerpts." *BASP* 41 (2004): 93–113.
Lachmann, Karl. *Novum Testamentum graece*. Berlin: G. Reimer, 1831.
Lefebvre, M. Gustave. "Égypte Chrétienne III." Pages 50–65 in *Annales du Service des Antiquités de l'Égypte*. Vol. 10. Cairo: L'Institut Français d'Archéologie Orientale, 1910.

Limongi, Donatella. "La diffusione dei Vangeli in Egitto (secc. I–VIII): Osservazioni sul *Vangelo secondo Marco*." *AnPap* 7 (1995): 57–58.

Luijendijk, Anne. "A Gospel Amulet for Joannia (P.Oxy. VIII 1151)." Pages 418–44 in *Daughters of Hecate: Women and Magic in the Ancient World*. Edited by Kimberly B. Stratton and Dayna S. Kalleres. Oxford: Oxford University Press, 2014.

Metzger, Bruce M. *A Textual Commentary on the Greek New Testament*. New York: United Bible Societies, 1975.

Meyer, Marvin W., and Richard Smith, eds. *Ancient Christian Magic: Coptic Texts of Ritual Power*. Princeton NJ: Princeton University Press, 1999.

Mill, John, J. Martin Augustin Scholz, and Johann Jakob Griesbach, eds. *Griesbach's Text with the Various Readings of Mill and Scholz, Marginal References to Parallels, and Critical Introduction*. 4th ed. London: Bell & Daldy, 1870.

Mill, John, ed. Η ΚΑΙΝΗ ΔΙΑΘΗΚΗ. *Novum Testamentum*. Oxford: E Theatro Sheldoniano, 1707. Repr., Oxford: Clarendon Press, 1813.

Mirecki, Paul. "A Seventh-Century Coptic Limestone in the Ashmolean Museum. Oxford. Bodl. Copt. Inscr. 426." Pages 47–69 in *Magic and Ritual in the Ancient World*. Edited by Paul Mirecki and Marvin W. Meyer. RGRW 141. Leiden: Brill, 2002.

Mirecki, Paul. "Evangelion-Incipits Amulets in Greek and Coptic: Towards a Typology." Pages 143–53 in *Proceedings of the Central States Regional Meeting of the Society of Biblical Literature and the American Schools of Oriental Research* 4. Edited by J. J. Johnson Leese. Kirkwood, MO: Central States Society of Biblical Literature, 2001.

Naldini, M. *Documenti dell'antichità cristiana: Papiri e pergamene greco-egizie della Raccolta Fiorentina*. Florence: Le Monnier, 1965.

Parker, David. *Codex Sinaiticus: The Story of the World's Oldest Bible*. London: The British Library; Peabody, MA: Hendrickson, 2010.

Perkins, Larry. "The Markan Narrative's Use of the Old Greek Text of Jeremiah to Explain Israel's Obduracy." *TynBul* 60 (2009): 217–38.

Pintaudi, Rosario. "Per la datazione di PSI VI 719." *AnPap* 2 (1990): 27–28.

Pleyte, Willem, and Pieter Adrian Art Boeser. *Manuscrits coptes du Musée d'antiquités des Pays-Bas à Leide*. Leiden: Brill, 1897.

Porter, Stanley E. *Constantine Tischendorf: The Life and Work of a 19th Century Bible Hunter*. London/New York: Bloomsbury, 2015.

Preisendanz, K., ed. *Papyri Graecae Magicae: Die Griechischen Zauberpapyri*. 2 vols. Leipzig: B. G. Teubner. 1928–31. Rev. ed., 1973. Repr., Munich and Leipzig: K. G. Saur. 2001.

Pusey, Philip Edward, and George Henry Gwilliam, eds. *Tetraeuangelium sanctum juxta simplicem Syrorum versionem ad fidem codicum, Massorae, editionem denuo recognitum*. Oxford: Clarendon Press, 1901.

Rahlfs, Alfred, and Detlef Fraenkel. *Verzeichnis der griechischen Handschriften des Alten Testaments*. Vol. 1.1: *Die Überlieferung bis zum VIII. Jahrhundert*. Göttingen: Vandenhoeck & Ruprecht, 2004.

Robinson, Maurice A., and William G. Pierpont, eds. *The New Testament in the Original Greek: Byzantine Textform*. Southborough, MA: Chilton, 2005.

Sanzo, Joseph E. "Brit. Lib. Or. 4919(2): An Unpublished Coptic Amulet in the British Library." *ZPE* 183 (2012): 98–100.

Sanzo, Joseph E. *Scriptural Incipits on Amulets from Late Antique Egypt: Text, Typology, and Theory*. STAC 84. Tübingen: Mohr Siebeck, 2014.

Sayce, Archibald Henry. "Gleanings from the Land of Egypt." *Recueil de travaux relatifs à la philologie et à archéologie égyptiennes et assyriennes* 20 (1898): 62–67.

Schmidt, Carl, and Wilhelm Schubart, eds. *Altchristliche Texte*. BKT 6. Berlin: Weidmann, 1910.
Smith, Geoffrey S., and Andrew E. Bernhard. "5073." *The Oxyrhynchus Papyri*. LXXVI. Nos. 5072–5100. Edited by Daniela Colomo and Juan Chapa. Graeco-Roman Memoirs 97. London: The Egypt Exploration Society, 2011.
Strabo, Walahfrid. Nicholas of Lyra, et al. *Bibliorum Sacrorum cum glossa ordinaria*. Tomus Quintus. Venice: Franciscan Fathers, 1603.
Suhl, A. *Die Funktion der alttestamentlichen Zitate und Anspielungen im Markusevangelium*. Gütersloh: Mohn, 1965.
Szirmai, Ján Alexander. *The Archaeology of Medieval Bookbinding*. Aldershot: Ashgate, 1999.
Tischendorf, Constantine. *Novum Testamentum Graeca*. Leipzig: Bernhard Tauchnitz, 1896.
Tregelles, Samuel Prideaux. *The Greek New Testament, Edited from Ancient Authorities, with their Various Readings in Full, and the Latin Version of Jerome*, Part 1: *Matthew and Mark*. London: Bagster, 1857.
Turaev, B. A. *Christianskye Vostok* [= *Christian East*] 1 (1912): 203–206.
Turner, C. H. *The Oldest Manuscript of the Vulgate Gospels*. Oxford: Clarendon Press, 1931.
Vitelli, Girolamo. *Pubblicazioni della Società Italiana per la ricerca dei Papiri greci e latini in Egitto: Papiri greci et latini*. Vol. 6. Florence: Pubblicazioni della Società Italiana, 1920.
Wasserman, Tommy. "Misquoting Manuscripts? The Orthodox Corruption of Scripture Revisited." Pages 325–50 in *The Making of Christianity: Conflicts, Contacts, and Constructions. Essays in Honor of Bengt Holmberg*. Edited by Samuel Byrskog and Magnus Zetterhold. Winona Lake, IN: Eisenbrauns, 2012.
Wasserman, Tommy. "$\mathfrak{P}^{78}$ (*P.Oxy.* XXXIV 2684): The Epistle of Jude on an Amulet?" Pages 137–60 in *New Testament Manuscripts: Their Texts and Their World*. Edited by Thomas J. Kraus and Tobias Nicklas. TENTS 2. Leiden: Brill, 2006.
Wasserman, Tommy. "The 'Son of God' was in the Beginning (Mark 1:1)." *JTS* 62 (2011): 20–50.
Wessely, Carl. "Les plus anciens monuments du christianisme écrits sur papyrus II. textes grecs." *Patrologia Orientalis*. Tomus decimus octavus. Paris: Firmin-Didot, 1924.
Westcott, Brooke Foss and Fenton John Anthony Hort. *The New Testament in the Original Greek: Introduction and Appendix*. New York: Harper & Brothers, 1882.
Wevers, John William. *Notes on the Greek Text of Exodus*. SBLSCS 30. Atlanta: Scholars Press, 1990.
White, Joseph. *Sacrorum Evangeliorum versio Syriaca Philoxeniana ex Codd. MSS. Ridleaianus*. Tomus primus. Oxford: Clarendon Press, 1778.
Wilken, Ulrich. "Heidnisches und Christliches aus Ägypten." APF 1 (1901): 396–436.
ספר הבריתות [= *Book of the Covenants*]. Jerusalem: The Bible Society in Israel, 2010.
ספרי הברית החדשה [= *Books of the New Covenant*]. London: Lowe & Brydone, 1960.

Chapter 13

Combined Themes of a Composite Citation: Exodus and Wilderness in Mark 1:1–3*

Marie J. Fortin

Wilderness is where the soul wanders, as it wonders about the way to its destiny.

(Unknown author)

It is well established that authors from the New Testament had access to pre-existing literature and used it in a variety of ways in their own texts. Nonetheless, readers sometimes fail to appreciate how much authors used tradition to underline the significance of their message.[1] By referring to the Old Testament, New Testament authors could draw on the rich history and content of the texts from their past to weave themes and theological motifs into their compositions.[2] Mark uses this type of historical evocation in Mark 1:1–15 where he takes up the theme of the wilderness, the setting for Israel's rebellion as recounted in the book of Exodus, in order to teach the concept of the way to repentance. In this essay, I intend to demonstrate that, by appealing to an audience's memory, NT authors can evoke a theological concept or bring to mind a hard-learned lesson from the past. They effectuate this with citations from the Jewish Scriptures, and also with allusions woven into the surrounding narrative. This allows authors to underline the importance of a theme and to invite listeners or readers to accept this

---

* It has been my privilege to be one of Dr. Larry Perkins' protégés. I hope that the present volume succeeds in highlighting his precious contribution to the training of so many. Thank you, Dr. Perkins, for helping us in the wandering to our destiny, and through the wonderful book that is the Bible.

[1] For an introduction to the subject of the use of the OT in the NT, see G. K. Beale and D. A. Carson, eds., *Commentary on the New Testament Use of the Old Testament* (Grand Rapids, MI: Baker Academic, 2007).

[2] I realize that the Old Testament canon was not closed in the first century. For the sake of this discussion, I use the expression OT to refer to what would have been considered Jewish Scriptures during the first century.

message by stirring up their memories and imaginations.³ Mark reminds his audience of Israel's experiences in the desert by the means of a quotation. In doing so, he brings into play themes of wilderness and exodus to stress the urgency of repentance and a believing response to Jesus' message of good news.

In this discussion of Mark 1:1–15, I will focus on the composite citation of Mark 1:1–3 in order to examine the author's employment of the themes of wilderness and repentance.⁴ Composite citations (or conflated citations) result from the merging of texts from the OT (by the same or a different author). These texts are combined in such a way that the resulting citation is often not recognized as such by those who are unfamiliar with previous tradition since it appears as if it came from a single text.⁵ Given that the themes used by the author come from his understanding of the Jewish Scriptures, I will also briefly consider the co-text (the surrounding literary context) of the three segments from the Jewish Scriptures used by the originator⁶ of the composite citation of Mark 1:1–3, namely Exod 23:20, Mal 3:1, and Isa 40:3. This will be followed by a succinct overview of the larger discourse of Mark 1:1-15 and discussion of the so-called problem of the composite citation attributed to Isaiah. A subsequent investigation of the Markan integration of citations and motifs in this narrative will demonstrate how the author integrated citations and motifs in this narrative in order to convince his audience to accept the idea of the fulfillment of OT prophecies.

---

³ I regard the terms *motif* and *theme* to be synonymous. In his first composite citation, the Markan author also alludes to the ideas of Messiah and divinity, and to the notion of preparing the way by means of proclamation. I mention them briefly in this essay, but my focus is on the influence of the book of Exodus on the Markan introduction.

⁴ For the sake of the discussion, I accept the tradition that the author of this Gospel is Mark, Peter's companion, but the identification of the author has no real bearing on my conclusions. The Markan author, whether he is Mark or someone else, has demonstrated a particular skill in the use of citations and motifs, as I intend to demonstrate.

⁵ Most twenty-first-century readers are not familiar enough with the OT to know from where quotaations have been taken, or even that composite citations are combinations of more than one text. A first-century Jewish audience would likely have been able to recognize some well-known expressions, whereas a Gentile audience would have had more difficulty in doing so. However, it must be recognized that a public reader could easily have explained more obscure references. I will discuss this in more detail in §5. For a thorough discussion on composite citations, see Sean A. Adams and Seth M. Ehorn, eds., *Composite Citations in Antiquity: Jewish, Graeco-Roman, and Early Christian Uses*, LNTS 525 (London: T&T Clark, 2016), as well as their *Composite Citations in Antiquity: New Testament Uses*, LNTS 593 (London: T&T Clark, 2016).

⁶ I use the expression *originator* to differentiate Mark from the author of the composite citation, since there is no way of knowing whether Mark used a composite citation made by someone else or whether he created it himself. The constraints of this essay make it impossible to include a thorough discussion on the possible identity of the originator of the composite citation. Nevertheless, it should be noted that this composite citation may have been constructed by the Markan author, since Matthew and Luke use the same combination of Exodus and Malachi in one location (Matt 11:10; Luke 7:27) and Isa 40:3 elsewhere (Matt 3:3; Luke 3:4). In this case, either Mark followed them and combined their citations (their composite citation with a citation from Isaiah), or Luke and Matthew chose to separate the quotations that are combined in Mark 1:1–3. It is also possible that Jesus created the combination, since many composite citations in Mark are attributed to him (e.g., Mark 11:17; 13:24–26; 14:62). In this case, Jesus would have been the influence for the NT authors. Nevertheless, the composite citation could also be the creation of John the Baptist, Mark, or some unknown author.

1. Consideration for Citations

Citations are produced by the act of quoting from a text. They are often used to establish authority, but for that to take place, author and audience need to have a shared confidence in the authority of the tradition to which an appeal is made.[7] Nathalie Piégay-Gros proposes that a citation can also bring to mind a larger text—acting almost as a character in a narrative, inviting the audience to become the author's allies in interpreting the significance of the quotation.[8] In biblical interpretation, this implies that the co-text of the OT citation is included in the hermeneutical process of a NT author, who uses a citation to evoke the theological concept of the whole passage from which the quotation comes. In Mark 1:1–15, the Gospel writer illustrates this by his thoughtful integration of citations and specific vocabulary to cause the audience to recognize the connection between the wilderness motif and repentance.

Mark 1:1–3[9]

The beginning of the gospel of Jesus Christ, the Son of God. As it is written in Isaiah the prophet, "Behold, I send my messenger before your face, who will prepare your way, the voice of one crying in the wilderness: 'Prepare the way of the Lord, make his paths straight.'"

2. Investigation of the Old Testament tradition

Exodus 23:20

Behold, I send an angel before you to guard you on the way and to bring you to the place that I have prepared.[10]

Exodus 23:20 introduces a section (23:20–33) that brings the so-called Covenant Code (Exod 20:22–23:33) to a conclusion.[11] The writer reiterates the covenant promise from God (Exod 3:15–20) using the first-person pronoun in 23:20 to indicate that YHWH

---

[7] It is "equal with the performing of an act of authority" (Gillian Lane-Mercier, "Quotation as a Discursive Strategy," *Kodikas* 14 [1991]: 201). Christopher D. Stanley nuances the notion of authority by adding that "neither literacy nor familiarity with the original context is required for people to be moved by a quotation from a text deemed authoritative by a religious group" (*Arguing with Scripture: The Rhetoric of Quotations in the Letters of Paul* [New York: Bloomsbury T&T Clark, 2004], 52).I would agree with Stanley, but only in cases where there is a previously established trust between audience and author, or confidence in a group advocating for an authoritative source.
[8] Nathalie Piégay-Gros, *Introduction à l'intertextualité* (Paris: Dunod, 1996), 22–23. C. H. Dodd had already proposed that a reference could refer to a larger narrative context by the use of a citation even if he does not go as far as Piégay-Gros in his description. See C. H. Dodd, *According to the Scriptures: The Sub-Structure of New Testament Theology* (London: Fontana, 1965), 275.
[9] Unless stated otherwise, all English citations come from the ESV.
[10] Hebrew: הִנֵּה אָנֹכִי שֹׁלֵחַ מַלְאָךְ לְפָנֶיךָ לִשְׁמָרְךָ בַּדָּרֶךְ וְלַהֲבִיאֲךָ אֶל־הַמָּקוֹם אֲשֶׁר הֲכִנֹתִי.
[11] Geoffrey Williams Bromiley, "Covenant Code," in *The International Standard Bible Encyclopedia* (Grand Rapids, MI: Eerdmans, 1988), 1:793. The Covenant Code is also called the Book of the Covenant since this name occurs in Exod 24:7. It is usually accepted that it runs from Exod 20:22–23:33.

himself will send a messenger before his people. In context, the way is being prepared to go from the wilderness and into "the place/land" (מָקוֹם), namely the promised land, Canaan.[12] The people of Israel are required to obey the angel (23:21) and to "pay careful attention to him" (הִשָּׁמֶר מִפָּנָיו).[13] The command is followed by an instruction to conquer the various peoples of the land. God then makes additional promises related to their situation in the land, combined with warnings: his people will be prosperous *if* they serve God. The text is filled with covenant theology; there is a mixture of intolerance for sin (particularly idolatry) and of promises of blessings.

The term מַלְאָךְ, rendered angel, also means messenger,[14] but in this context the reference is to an angel, or perhaps to God's presence. מַלְאָךְ could also refer to the column of fire leading Israel, representing a spiritual being or God himself (Exod 13:21).[15] In this small section of Exodus 23, God is clearly the provider of the blessing to his people since he is the one who guides them in their exodus on the *way* out of the wilderness and into the promised land, fulfilling his covenant promises.

Malachi 3:1

Behold, I send my messenger, and he will prepare the way before me.[16]

In the book of Malachi, the prophet addresses the subject of the people's disillusionment following the return of Israel from exile and the rebuilding of the temple.[17] Malachi 2:17–3:5 explains that the sins of Israel are responsible for the delay of God's arrival. This is followed by a call to repentance. In Mal 2:17, the people ask how they have wearied God and receive the answer: "By saying 'Everyone who does evil is good in the sight of the Lord, and he delights in them' or by asking 'Where is the God of justice?'" To this last question, the speaker—God, who is not named but implied—responds that his messenger will lead the way (Mal 3:1); this answer is used in the Markan composite citation.

The rest of the prophecy speaks of God who is coming like a refiner's fire (3:2). He is described as the One who does not change and who comes to punish (3:3–15).

---

[12] "The word 'place' is probably to be taken in a general sense, not in its frequent sense of 'holy place', as though God were leading Israel to his sanctuary at Shiloh or elsewhere. Christ may be alluding to this verse in John 14:2, 3" (R. Alan Cole, *Exodus: An Introduction and Commentary*, TOTC 2 [Downers Grove, IL: InterVarsity Press, 1973], 189).

[13] The second person singular seems to address the people as individuals. Exodus 21:1 states, "Now these are the rules that you shall set before them." This introduces a set of rules given by God to Moses. Either Moses is repeating what YHWH has told him, or he is repeating commands in a way that is personal for each listener.

[14] The LXX adds the possessive pronoun, making the messenger "God's messenger."

[15] The angel of God or of YHWH (Gen 21:17; 31:11; Exod 3:2) sometimes appears as a messenger from God or as God himself. Consider the narrative in Exod 3:1–6, see *HALOT*, "מַלְאָךְ."

[16] Hebrew: הִנְנִי שֹׁלֵחַ מַלְאָכִי וּפִנָּה־דֶרֶךְ לְפָנָי.

[17] The words of Malachi reveal the discouragement of the people: "But you say, 'How have we despised your name?'" (1:6); "You cover the LORD's altar with tears, with weeping and groaning because he no longer regards the offering or accepts it with favour from your hand. But you say 'Why does he not?'" (2:13–14a). They also ask: "Where is the God of justice?" (2:17). The promises of 3:1 "suggest that there was continuing disappointment with the second temple, despite the encouragement of Haggai and Zechariah" (Joyce Baldwin, *Haggai, Zechariah and Malachi: An Introduction and Commentary* [Downers Grove, IL: Intervarsity, 1972], 264).

However, he will remember those who feared him (3:16).[18] The identity of the messenger is not revealed in Mal 3:1, but Elijah is mentioned in Mal 4:5 (3:23 MT) as the one coming before the Day of the Lord; the repetition of the verb שָׁלַח (send) indicates that the messenger is likely Elijah.[19] If John the Baptist is, according to Mark, the new Elijah coming to announce judgment, the direct implication is that judgment is now coming on Israel with the beginning of Jesus' ministry. While Malachi does not refer to the wilderness, the notion of judgment in the absence of repentance is made clear.

Isaiah 40:3

A voice cries: "In the wilderness prepare the way of the LORD; make straight in the desert a highway for our God."[20]

Isaiah 40:3 is found in a larger section (Isa 38–55) where the prophet's message is said to have been revealed "from the beginning" (40:21). Isaiah prophesies destruction to the kingdom of Judah in Isa 39:5-8. Those words are immediately followed by words of consolation for God's people. Three "voices" are to proclaim three different messages: that a way needs to be prepared for the LORD (40:3-5), that the word of God will stand forever (40:6-8), and that the Lord GOD comes with might (40:9-10).[21] In Isaiah, God is portrayed as the one leading the way (35:8; 42:16; 48:17-21; 55:12). In 40:3—cited in Mark's composite citation—the people are instructed to prepare a way (ὁδός[22]) for their Lord.[23]

Exodus 23, Malachi 3, and Isaiah 40 have something in common: they reveal that God is coming, and they promise blessings or, as a response to disobedience, judgment. Furthermore, Malachi 3 and Isaiah 40 call for preparation for a new *way*. In Mark's composite citation, the theme of the wilderness mentioned in the books of Exodus and Isaiah is associated with the motif of preparation for the way of the Lord. Additionally, Malachi claims that the Lord will come to his temple and expresses the same need for preparation. These common themes allow the author to do two things:

---

[18] The same expression is used in Joel 2:31 to refer to a coming judgment that could be understood both as Israel's destruction, but also as an 'already-but-not-yet' prophecy of the coming judgment at the end of the age when "everyone who calls on the name of the Lord shall be saved" (Joel 2:32). Malachi announces a day of judgment that follows the exile, a day when "all evildoers will be stubble" (4:1), but also says that for "you who fear my name, the sun of righteousness shall rise with healing in its wings" (4:2).

[19] Rikki E. Watts, *Isaiah's New Exodus in Mark* (Grand Rapids, MI: Baker Academic, 2001), 71.

[20] Hebrew: קוֹל קוֹרֵא בַּמִּדְבָּר פַּנּוּ דֶּרֶךְ יהוה יַשְּׁרוּ בָּעֲרָבָה מְסִלָּה לֵאלֹהֵינוּ.

[21] John N. Oswalt, *The Book of Isaiah, Chapters 40–66*, NICOT (Grand Rapids, MI: Eerdmans, 1998), 53. The voices seem to refer to different respondents, though they might refer to the same individual, presumably God or one of his messenger/angels (Isa 40:3, 6, 9). The first voice announces God's arrival (40:3) and this declaration is used in the composite citation of Mark 1:2-3.

[22] The two Greek terms used in the composite citation—ὁδός (way) and τρίβος (path)—appear in parallel lines and are the counterparts to דֶּרֶךְ and מְסִלָּה, respectively, in Isa 40:3; ὁδός metaphorically can denote a "course of behavior" in the NT (see *BDAG*, "ὁδός").

[23] The fact that the setting is the wilderness would imply a way that is rarely if ever used and is in need of preparation. The wilderness could also imply a location for spiritual preparation, away from the temptation offered by civilization. It could also refer to Israel's first exodus through the wilderness. More likely, it refers to all three.

to combine text from the Jewish Scriptures in a clever amalgam in Mark 1:2–3 and to skilfully weave the themes into the narrative of Mark 1:1–15.

The Markan author has demonstrated an ability to join OT texts with verbal and thematic similarities, but he has also shown a deliberate attention to the theological content of each OT text. Following this demonstration, the composite citation is investigated in its NT literary context, including the distinctive use of the Greek version from the LXX and the author's minor modifications.

3. Investigation of the New Testament citation

Mark's first composite citation, which appears at the very beginning of his book, is Mark's only explicit composite citation found within a narrative framework. All his other composite citations occur in dialogues.[24] Many commentators understand the prologue to consist of vv. 1–13.[25] Because of the interesting *inclusio* concerning the good news (1:1 and 1:14) and the reference to the fulfilment of a time of preparation as announced by Isaiah (1:2 and 1:15), it makes sense to see the pericope ending at v. 15.[26] Mark 1:14–15 concludes the initial section and transitions to a new subject by repeating the key points of the prologue. This arrangement of material creates a move from the prelude of Jesus' ministry to its more public beginning. This section considers Mark's use of Greek vocabulary before a closer look at the modifications he made to the LXX version.

3.1. Mark 1:1–2a

Ἀρχὴ τοῦ εὐαγγελίου Ἰησοῦ Χριστοῦ [υἱοῦ θεοῦ]. Καθὼς γέγραπται ἐν τῷ Ἠσαΐᾳ τῷ προφήτῃ·

Mark's first sentence leads off with an anarthrous noun which is the subject of a verbless clause: "The beginning of the Gospel of Jesus Christ, the Son of God."[27] Following

---

[24] "Composite Citations in the Gospel of Mark," in Adams and Ehorn, eds., *Composite Citations in Antiquity*, 16–33. The other Markan composite citations are attributed to Jesus (Mark 11:17; 13:24–26; 14:62) or to the Sadducees (12:19). Their classification will differ depending on one's definition of a citation vs. an allusion, or one's understanding of the nature of composite citations. For example, Steve Moyise considers 11:17 to be two citations and not a composite one, but he recognizes the other composite citations mentioned here even if 12:19 could also be catalogued as a composite allusion.

[25] William L. Lane, *The Gospel of Mark*, 2nd ed. (Grand Rapids, MI: Eerdmans, 1974), 39; James R. Edwards, *The Gospel According to Mark* (Grand Rapids, MI: Eerdmans, 2001), 23; R. Alan Cole, *Mark*, (Downers Grove, IL: Intervarsity, 1989), 103; Morna Hooker, *The Gospel According to Saint Mark*, (London: Continuum, 1991), 32; Mark L. Strauss, *Mark*, ed. Clinton E. Arnold (Grand Rapids, MI: Zondervan, 2014), 57.

[26] Robert A. Guelich, "'The Beginning of the Gospel': Mark 1:1–15," *BR* 27 (1982): 7–8. The notion of fulfillment is implied in Mark 1:2 by the introduction "as it is written," and in Mark 1:15 by "the time is fulfilled." Robert A. Guelich demonstrates how the phrase πεπλήρωται ὁ καιρός (Mark 1:15) is used by Mark to signify the fulfillment of Isaiah's prophecy. It is part of the first statement that Mark attributes to Jesus in his narrative. It summarizes Mark 1:1-13, but also announces what is to come by linking Jesus' words with Isaiah's prophecy.

[27] Unless Mark intends to communicate an implied verb "to be," which would render the translation: "It is the beginning…"

this first small pericope, the composite citation is introduced by a puzzling expression which seemingly attributes the full citation to Isaiah (Mark 1:2a).[28] What follows is a composite citation drawn from Exod 23:20 and Mal 3:1 in Mark 1:2b, combined with a citation from Isa 40:3 in Mark 1:3. Beginning with the conjunction καθώς—marking a comparison—Mark 1:2 indicates that the following words should be understood as the continuation of the statement made in Mark 1:1. This means that the first phrase is not a title or an independent clause, but is a main clause followed by a subordinate one.[29] Accordingly, the phrase "as it is written in Isaiah the prophet" acts as a transition; it comments on the preceding text and introduces the following one. With a small modification to the punctuation of the NA[28], the translation should thus be rendered as: "The origin/beginning of the gospel of Jesus Christ, [son of God] *is* as it is written in Isaiah: 'Behold, I send...'"[30]

Incidentally, Isaiah could easily be considered as a prophet of the gospel—YHWH's *good news*—in the Jewish Scriptures since the notion of good news is addressed in various ways in the book of Isaiah.[31] In Mark 1, the composite citation acts as an announcement of John the Baptist's role, with Malachi and Exodus used as a support for Isaiah's message. It is reasonable to assume that the author intended the word *gospel* to be understood both in the Greco-Roman sense of good news of victory associated with a powerful benefactor or divinity, and the Jewish sense of good news which is sent by YHWH to his people.[32]

---

[28] Some manuscripts do not include the name of Isaiah and instead include τοις προφηταις, "the prophets," probably the result of scribes desiring to correct the fact that the citation is composite and has references other OT writings (A K P W Γ *f* 13 28. 579. 1424. 2542 𝔐 vg^ms sy^h [bo^mss]; Ir^lat [from NA[28] Apparatus]).

[29] The clausal relationship proposed by NA[28] should be revised since v. 1 is not a separate independent sentence. The same phrase καθὼς γέγραπται (1:2a) appears in the NT in Luke 2:23; Acts 7:42; 15:15; Rom 1:17; 2:24; 3:4, 10, 4:17, and many more. Mark also uses καθὼς γέγραπται in 9:13 and 14:21 to refer to the preceding (9:13 concludes the sentence). Mark also uses a similar expression, καθὼς εἶπεν in 11:6 and 16:7 where, in the same manner, the expression refers to the preceding. The expression is sometimes used to introduce an OT citation, but never at the beginning of a new sentence. "When καθώς occurs in a formula with γέγραπται, it always refers to the preceding rather than to the succeeding material" (Robert A. Guelich, *Mark 1–8:26*, WBC 34A [Grand Rapids, MI: Zondervan Academic, 2018], 7). Καθὼς never begins a new sentence in Mark (or the rest of the NT).

[30] Understood this way, the beginning of the Gospel should not be viewed as a "title" added later by a different editor. The repetition of the word *gospel* in 1:14 concluding this section points to an orchestrated *inclusio*, as noted already.

[31] "The fact that Mark claimed that the beginning of the gospel was 'as it is written in the prophet Isaiah' suggests that he was well aware that the prophet had proclaimed 'good news'" (Morna D. Hooker, "Isaiah in Mark's Gospel," in *Isaiah in the New Testament*, ed. Steve Moyise and Maarten J. J. Menkel [London: T&T Clark, 2005], 37). See also Frederick J. Gaiser, "The Gospel According to Isaiah," *Word & World* 38, (2018): 239–51, where Frederick Gaiser presents a good overview of Isaiah's different uses of בְּשֵׂר and other texts presenting the hope to come. Six important verses are 40:9; 41:27; 52:5; 60:6; 61:1 (and 41:27 with a variant translation in the LXX). In the last section of the book of Isaiah (especially chs. 40–61), many prophecies speak of deliverance and God's blessings.

[32] "εὐαγγελίζομαι, εὐαγγέλιον, εὐαγγελιστής" in Ceslas Spicq, *Theological Lexicon of the New Testament*, trans. James D. Ernest (Peabody, MA: Hendrickson, 1994), 2:83–84. The term *gospel* or *good news* was an expression used in the LXX in the sense of *good tidings*, usually with God as its subject and human as objects of blessings; it became a religious, cultic, and messianic term. In the LXX, the word εὐαγγέλιον is found in 2 Kgdms (2 Sam) 4:10 and εὐαγγέλια in 2 Kgdms 18:22,25 and 4 Kgdms (2 Kgs) 7:9. The verb εὐαγγελίζω (or εὐαγγελίζομαι) is more commonly used in the OT to refer to good news in a religious sense, as good news from God (Pss 40:9; 96:2, Isa 40:9; 52:7; 61:1). In the

Mark's opening is impactful because it introduces the coming of one bringing the good news—Jesus Christ—and implies his divinity with the expression *Son of God*.[33] The following composite citation picks up these motifs, expands on them, and shows that this event is aligned with YHWH's program as revealed in the Jewish Scriptures.

3.2. Mark 1:2b–3

Καθὼς γέγραπται ἐν τῷ Ἠσαΐᾳ τῷ προφήτῃ·
ἰδοὺ ἀποστέλλω τὸν ἄγγελόν μου πρὸ προσώπου σου,
ὃς κατασκευάσει τὴν ὁδόν σου·
φωνὴ βοῶντος ἐν τῇ ἐρήμῳ·
ἑτοιμάσατε τὴν ὁδὸν κυρίου,
εὐθείας ποιεῖτε τὰς τρίβους αὐτοῦ

The composite citation begins with the demonstrative or presentative particle ἰδού, which, not unlike the Hebrew הִנֵּה, draws the listener's/reader's attention to what will follow. The context leads the audience to consider God as the first speaker in 1:2b because a prophet (i.e., Isaiah) introduces his speech. Interestingly, the composite citation, given the close association between Jesus and the Lord, makes the audience naturally infer that Jesus' way is being prepared. The originator of the composite citation in Mark purposefully linked Jesus' arrival with a prophecy for *God*'s arrival. Since Israel's way is being announced in Exodus 23, it is plausible that the originator applied to Jesus what the text in Exodus associates with Israel. The amalgam of Exod 23:20 with Mal 3:1 and Isa 40:3 declares the Christology of the originator of the composite citation. Effectively, the composite citation announces that since God's way is being prepared and Jesus is coming on that way, they must be one and the same. Furthermore, by pairing this first half (the combination of Mal 3:1 and Exod 23:20) with Isa 40:3, the originator of the composite citation applies the title κύριος to Jesus; Jesus becomes the Lord, the one coming in the way.[34]

---

imperial cult, emperors were to be like gods (or sons of gods) and their action would be considered εὐαγγέλια. See also Gerhard Kittel and Gerhard Friedrich, eds., *Theological Dictionary of the New Testament*, trans. Geoffrey W. Bromiley; 10 vols. (Grand Rapids, MI: Eerdmans, 1996), 2:722–25. The OT precedes the Greco-Romans' sense of the word, but it was also used by the Greco-Romans as good news of significance or *news of victory* in a military, political, or national sense. It is also possible that Mark had in mind Isaiah's use of the expression in 52:7 where the verb εὐαγγελίζω is used.

[33] Since the title "Son of God" was used in different ways, one cannot declare this to be a definitive title of divinity even if Mark certainly implies it. Moreover, it is an important narratological expression in Mark and it appears at key moments. It is used eight times in Mark (1:11; 3:11; 5:7; 9:7; 12:6; 13:32, 61; 15:39), either in God's words, in the mouth of demons, in a priest's question or in the direct speech of some Gentiles. Maybe Mark was intentionally underlining the Gentiles' reception of the Messiah in his gospel, and how they succeeded in recognizing Jesus' divinity where the Jews seem to fail to understand. This would be very ironic as some of those occurrences in the narrative come from demons (3:11 and 5:7) who, in the narrator's mind, obviously have no problem recognizing the divinity of the Son of God even if they did not use the title as part of any adoration.

[34] Attentive members of the audience could recognize Mark's implication, especially as they moved along Mark's narrative, even if it is not clearly stated in the introduction.

The preparation of the way suggests the idea of making the path "straight" (εὐθύς),[35] and the two terms path and way (ὁδός and τρίβος) are used in synonymous parallelism (κατασκευάσει τὴν **ὁδόν** and εὐθείας ποιεῖτε τὰς **τρίβους**). They appear three times in the composite citation (ὁδός twice) and are presented as one of its main points even if it is not repeated in the co-text of Mark 1:1–15. Already in Mark 1:9, 12, 14, Jesus is described as moving from one place to another; he is on his way.[36] The concept of ὁδός can be linked back to the *way* followed during the exodus and the Deuteronomic motif of eschatological entrance into the land.[37] In the same way, the entrance into the Kingdom is possible through the way.[38] Mark's narrative clarifies that the preparation for the *way* is not literal but serves as a metaphor for repentance and salvation.

In the larger section (1:1–15), the author incorporates the theme of wilderness by creating a link between the citation's substantival participle "the one crying in the wilderness" (φωνὴ βοῶντος ἐν τῇ ἐρήμῳ) and John (1:4–8) as someone who is located in the wilderness.[39] This theme was already introduced in the composite citation because of the word ἔρημος with its general sense of an uninhabited region, desert or wilderness;[40] it is now underlined in the co-text through his use of vocabulary evoking the wilderness.

3.3. Mark 1:4–15

The narrative opens in v. 4 by stating that John appeared (from the verb γίνομαι) and continues with a description of his activities and his physical appearance. Placed immediately after the composite citation, the writer's mention of John the Baptist expresses a consequence of this prophetic word in Mark 1:2–3. Mark describes John's apparel as being made of camel's hair with a leather belt, and John's diet consisting of locusts and wild honey (1:6). Both descriptions fit the wilderness theme of the passage because they correspond to some accounts made of prophets in the OT who could be considered "desert prophets" like Elijah,[41] and locusts and wild honey would have

---

[35] "Being in a straight or direct line, *straight*." See *BDAG*, "εὐθύς."
[36] Mark uses the concept of the *way* in his narrative (especially 8:27; 9:33–34; 10:17, 32, 46, 52) with some revelation made at key moments: for example, Jesus is revealed to be the Christ (8:27–30) and reveals his future suffering (8:31; 9:31; 10:32–33). The transfiguration occurs on the way (9:2–13), and Bartimaeus follows Jesus "on the way" (10:52). The concept of the *way* is also used metaphorically as a reference to Messianic movement by Luke in Acts (9:2; 19:9, 23; 22:4; 24:14, 22) and Peter (1 Pet 2:2, 21).
[37] For a longer discussion on the concept of the *way* as understood in the OT, see Joel Marcus, *The Way of the Lord: Christological Exegesis of the Old Testament in the Gospel of Mark* (London: T&T Clark, 2004), 31–33.
[38] "The old Exodus–Conquest route, the way through the wilderness, becomes at the same time the pilgrimage way to Zion" (Frank Moore Cross, *Canaanite Myth and Hebrew Epic: Essays in the History of the Religion of Israel* [Cambridge, MA: Harvard University Press, 1973], 108).
[39] Mark 1:3–6 "Wilderness…clothed with camel's hair and wore a leather belt around his waists… locusts and wild honey."
[40] "In contrast to cultivated and inhabited country." See *BDAG*, "ἐρήμῳ."
[41] Hooker, *The Gospel According to Saint Mark*, 37. Zechariah 13:4 refers to the hairy cloak of a prophet, and 2 Kgs 1:8 describes Elijah's garment as made of hair with a leather belt. Some prophets, especially Elijah, preached from the wilderness. It does not imply that prophets were all dressed this way, or that Elijah always wore such garments, but it is likely that a Jewish audience would have recognized the description.

been consistent "with someone living off the land."⁴² Wilderness as a theme continues since it is mentioned as the location for Jesus' temptation in Mark 1:12.⁴³ Mark also repeats the theme of baptism in the larger pericope (1:4, 8–11). Even though baptism is not mentioned in the composite citation, it is a rite of purification which follows repentance. In the narrative, it is linked to the preparation of the way for YHWH in the wilderness.⁴⁴ The repetition of the theme of wilderness in relation to repentance links the composite citation to the narrative and underlines its importance.

It is noteworthy that the narrative in v. 4 first introduces John's ministry of baptizing and proclaiming. In the narrative, John's physical appearance (v. 6) is only described after the report about his activities of proclamation (vv. 4-5). The focus on John's actions highlights John's undertaking of preparing God's *way*, making the baptism and the message of repentance the essence of the preparation itself. Baptizing and repentance become necessary for the announcement of the gospel, but it is John's presence that acts as the catalyst. Mark presents John the Baptist as the one who first calls people to repentance; his role in the Gospel may be small, but it is vital.

An investigation of the co-text of the OT citation and the NT narrative has demonstrated that Mark does not simply copy some words from the OT to incorporate into his text, he also uses the theological theme of each citation. However, to create the meaningful citation used in Mark 1:1–3, the originator had to incorporate different extracts and alter their wording slightly. As discussed, this first-century literary skill demonstrates a desire to weave in messages from the past into a cohesive citation.

4. Investigation of the Markan modifications

To integrate his motif of wilderness and his message of repentance, the originator of the composite citation did not hesitate to customize the original citations to adapt them to their new literary context. It has sometimes been proposed that composite citations result from imperfect recall, the outcome of lists of citations called "testimonies" or the consequence of a Jewish method of interpretation sometimes called "midrash."⁴⁵

---

⁴² Strauss, *Mark*, 65.
⁴³ This does not imply that the episode is fictive. The Markan author chooses the details included in his narration. It must be noted that Jesus goes through a form of preparation by baptism (1:9-11) and temptation (1:12-13), but the narrative never implies the necessity of repentance for him. Mark mentions again the wilderness in his later narrative as an isolated place (1:35; 45; 6:31-35), but he does not re-examine the link between wilderness and preparation/repentance apart from Mark 1:1-15.
⁴⁴ Βαπτίζω meaning to wash for purification, or for the renewal of relationship with God, or to experience an initiatory water-rite. See *BDAG*, "βαπτίζω."
⁴⁵ It is difficult to discuss such a complex subject in only a few sentences, but the usual responses to those theories are summarized in Sean A. Adams and Seth M. Ehorn, eds., *Composite Citations in Antiquity: Jewish, Graeco-Roman, and Early Christian Uses*. In one of the earliest discussions on the subject, Johnson demonstrates how the NT authors usually quote the OT with precision, making imperfect recall improbable (Franklin Johnson, *The Quotations of the New Testament from the Old, Considered in the Light of General Literature* [Philadelphia: American Baptist Publication Society, 1896]). Concerning circulating lists of citations, Sundberg demonstrates that one single *testimony* in circulation during the first century is quite unlikely because composite citations vary in the NT (Albert C. Sundberg, "On Testimonies," *NovT* 3 [1959]: 268–81). Since composite citations appear very rarely in Jewish writings, but are much more frequent in Greco-Roman writings, their

However, since first-century Hellenistic literature includes many composite citations adapting previous texts, it is reasonable to consider composite citations to be the result of intentional editing.[46]

This section observes how the author used and adapted tradition from the Jewish Scriptures and incorporated it in his narrative. The following chart compares Mark 1:2b with the LXX[47] and the MT from Exod 23:20 and Mal 3:1. Since the second half of the composite citation from Isa 40:3 is almost the LXX verbatim, it is not included in this table.[48]

Table 13.1. Comparison between Mark 1:2b and the LXX and MT versions of Exodus 23:20 and Malachi 3:1[49]

Mark 1:2b
Ἰδοὺ ἀποστέλλω τὸν ἄγγελόν μου πρὸ προσώπου σου ὃς κατασκευάσει τὴν ὁδόν σου **Behold I send my messenger before your face** who will prepare your **way**
Exodus 23:20 LXX
Καὶ **ἰδοὺ** ἐγὼ **ἀποστέλλω τὸν ἄγγελόν μου πρὸ προσώπου σου**, ἵνα φυλάξῃ σε ἐν **τῇ ὁδῷ**, ὅπως εἰσαγάγῃ σε εἰς τὴν γῆν, ἣν ἡτοίμασά σοι. **Behold, I send an angel before you** to guard you on **the way** and to bring you into the land that I have prepared.

appearance due to a Jewish influence is improbable. This does not imply that the various theories are wrong, but rather that they cannot reasonably explain all composite citations; each must be examined *in situ*.

[46] It is impractical to cover this subject appropriately given the constraints of this essay. Nonetheless, while it is impossible to prove that composite citations are not the result of great flexibility of interpretation or imperfect recall, Mark's first composite citation is so well adapted to its literary setting that it is difficult to consider it as something other than an intentional combination. In this case, it appears as if the Markan author artfully integrated a composite citation (created by himself, or possibly from another originator like Jesus) in his narrative.

[47] This analysis assumes that the Greek text available to the originator of the composite citation was the same as the LXX as it came down to us; it is entirely possible that some of the differences observed are caused by different sources.

[48] The only notable difference between the LXX and Mark's version is the substitution of τοῦ θεοῦ ἡμῶν for αὐτοῦ, probably for Christological reasons. In Hebrew, בַּמִּדְבָּר is located at the end of the discourse clause and marks the wilderness as the location for the way. In the rest of his narrative, the Markan author does not make the wilderness Jesus' location for his ministry (beside his temptation in 1:12–13). By following the LXX instead of the MT, Mark is saying that the wilderness is the location *of the one crying*; but changes in punctuation could explain the difference between the reading of the LXX and the MT.

[49] The NT Greek text is from the NA[28] and its English translation from the ESV. The LXX Greek texts are from Joseph Ziegler, ed., *Septuaginta Vetus Testamentum Graecum Autoritate Academiae Scientiarum Göttingensis Editum XIV: Isaias* (Göttingen: Vandenhoeck & Ruprecht, 1983); Joseph Ziegler, ed., *Septuaginta Vetus Testamentum Graecum Autoritate Academiae Scientiarum Göttingensis Editum XIII: Duodecim Prophetae* (Göttingen: Vandenhoeck & Ruprecht, 1984); John William Wevers and Quast Udo, eds., *Septuaginta Vetus Testamentum Graecum Autoritate Academiae Scientiarum Göttingensis Editum II: Exodus* (Göttingen: Vandenhoeck & Ruprecht, 1991). The English translation of the LXX comes from Albert Pietersma and Benjamin G. Wright, eds., *A New English Translation of the Septuagint (Primary Texts)* (New York: Oxford University Press, 2007). The Hebrew text is from Francis I. Andersen and A. Dean Forbes, *The Hebrew Bible: Andersen-Forbes Analyzed Text* (Bellingham, WA: Lexham Press, 2008); its English translation comes from the NRSV.

13 Combined Themes of a Composite Citation

Malachi 3:1 LXX / MT[50]
Ἰδοὺ ἐγὼ **ἐξαποστέλλω τὸν ἄγγελόν μου**, καὶ ἐπιβλέψεται **ὁδὸν πρὸ προσώπου** μου... **Behold, I send my messenger**, and he will prepare the **way** before me...
הִנְנִי שֹׁלֵחַ מַלְאָכִי וּפִנָּה־דֶרֶךְ לְפָנָי **See, I am sending my messenger to prepare the way** before me...

Mark's text follows the LXX version of Exod 23:20 closely with the introduction phrase "behold, I am sending my messenger."[51] The presence of πρὸ προσώπου σου ("before your face"), which comes after τὸν ἄγγελόν μου ("my angel/messenger") instead of being placed at the end of the citation, corresponds to the LXX version of Exodus text more exactly than the version of Malachi. While from the Malachi citation there are the associations of the messenger with Elijah, and of the way with YHWH, the motif of exodus and wilderness are from the book of Exodus.[52] Interestingly, the originator appears to have chosen κατασκευάζω ("to prepare or build a structure") to reflect the Piel of פנה in the MT of Malachi, instead of ἐπιβλέπω ("to look intently, pay attention or look attentively") which is found in the LXX.[53]

The shift to the second person (τὴν ὁδόν **σου** / **your** way) is another modification made by the originator, suggesting a desire to underline the Christology of the passage by making it appear as the way *of Jesus*, the Lord. This also parallels the previous πρὸ προσώπου σου.[54] The originator also put πρὸ προσώπου σου before τὴν ὁδόν σου, inverting Malachi's order. He did so probably to create a better parallel with the citation from Isa 40:3, or to follow Exod 23:20.[55] Consequently, this first half of Mark 1:2–3 as a composite citation is a good example of stylistic and grammatical rearrangements which conserve the main points of the previous tradition but combine texts to suit a specific goal.[56]

---

[50] Since the MT of Mal 3:1 differs slightly from its LXX version, I have included both.

[51] Watts, *Isaiah's New Exodus in Mark*, 62. Watts believes that Mark used Mal 3:1 and adapted it with Exod 23:20. Mark's preference for Exodus' use of ἀποστέλλω, instead of Malachi's ἐξαποστέλλω, could be explained by stylistic preference because ἐξαποστέλλω is used almost exclusively by Luke, and never by Mark.

[52] The distinction between the two texts may not be quite as distinct if Malachi used Exod 23:20. In this case, the motif of exodus could belong to both, even if it appears clearer in the book of Exodus. The association of John the Baptist with Elijah most likely comes from Malachi (Mal 4:5). Malachi 3:1 refers to a *way* for YHWH while Exodus has Israel's way in view.

[53] See *BDAG*, "κατασκευάζω" and "ἐπιβλέπω." פנה has the sense of turning aside in a particular direction, to turn to someone, but in its Piel form, it takes the sense of clearing away or tidying up, see *HALOT*, "פנה." Mark's choice certainly suits his composite citation better than the LXX version available today. While some scholars like Watts (*Exodus in Mark*, 61) believe that Mark used the MT, it is also possible that Mark used a different Greek translation (written or oral); this latter explanation is more likely since Mark follows the LXX at other times and does not demonstrate a knowledge of Hebrew elsewhere.

[54] Watts, *Isaiah's New Exodus in Mark*, 61–62. While the text itself does not declare Jesus as the Lord, it implies it.

[55] Isaiah 40:3: φωνὴ βοῶντος ἐν τῇ ἐρήμῳ· ἑτοιμάσατε τὴν ὁδὸν κυρίου, where ὁδόν appears at the end of the pericope.

[56] The originator of the composite citation does not hesitate to use a mixture from the LXX and the MT or a different Greek translation.

In the minds of some Jews from the first century, the wilderness was a location for the preparation of God's way and/or of repentance.[57] Philo sees the wilderness as the proper place for God to give Israel his commandments.[58] Josephus alludes to the Judean desert as a place of preparation[59] and ancient rabbis believed the Messiah would replicate the life of Moses.[60] Since it is possible to understand the original text of Isa 40:3 in Hebrew as "the voice of one crying: '*in the wilderness* prepare the way of the Lord,'" this may have influenced some groups to move to desert areas to prepare for YHWH's arrival. The wilderness is also the place of the establishment of the covenant with Israel, the presentation of Israel's election, and the place of rebellion. One could say that "the premises of Israel's cult are established in the desert,"[61] as well as her identity. Thus wilderness, repentance and the exodus from Egypt would be a natural association for many Jews.

The originator of the composite citation adjusted the text for its new literary context, following the citation conventions from the first century CE. In doing so, he demonstrates an understanding of the co-text the OT citations and a purposeful application of their theological lesson to the NT text. Mark incorporates the composite citation to fit his rhetorical intent; he draws upon the OT text and themes to convince his audience to accept his message.

The reception of this message needs to be investigated since it remains to be seen if the first Markan audience—most likely a mixed audience of Jewish and Gentiles believers—would have understood his three citations and their implied themes.[62] Was it more effective rhetorically to express it as a composite citation than as three separate and independent citations quoted distinctly?

5. Investigation of the audience's comprehension

In the larger pericope of Mark 1:1–15, the composite citation functions as an anchor for the text by introducing many elements that will be important to the Markan narrative. A Jewish audience would have been more prepared to understand all the nuances of the composite citation of Mark 1:2–3 since they would more likely have recognized the OT text. The origin of the citations would likely have been recognized with its notion of exodus and of the return of YHWH by those who were familiar

---

[57] It is noteworthy that the term wilderness, ἔρημος, should be understood in the sense of "a state of isolation," and not as the stereotypical desert of the far west or the modern images of the Sahara. The presence of the Jordan, or the implied food and clothing of the wilderness, does not negate the sense of wilderness.

[58] In his writing, he explains that God chose to prepare his people for the reception of the law because of the "unspeakable evils" found in cities (*Decal.* I.2).

[59] *Jewish Wars* 2.264; 6.351; 7.438.

[60] Mauser discusses Josephus' accusation against some groups who were preparing for the eschatological Messiah in the wilderness, but who also disturbed social order, as seen in *War* 2.258–260; 261–263. For more details, see Ulrich W. Mauser, *Christ in the Wilderness: The Wilderness Theme in the Second Gospel and Its Basis in the Biblical Tradition* (Eugene, OR: Wipf & Stock, 2009), 55–57.

[61] Mauser, *Christ in the Wilderness*, 25.

[62] Even if one admits to an audience consisting of Jewish and Gentile disciples of Jesus, their backkground and knowledge would have varied. It is also likely that non-believers were invited to public readings.

with the Jewish Scriptures. They would also have been better prepared to discern the implication of John the Baptist as the last messenger to appear before the coming of the Lord.

A Gentile audience not previously exposed to the message of the Gospel would probably have been interested in the pairing of the expression "Son of God" with a herald announcing a powerful leader, a king, or an emperor. Non-believing Gentiles presumably would not have recognized the implication of the wilderness but because of their prevalent Greco-Roman culture, they would likely have understood the importance of a divine king announced by prophecy. Paul and the author of the book of Hebrews use the theme of wilderness in association with repentance as well as Jesus' titles of Messiah and Son of God. Therefore, the early Church should have noticed the connections. It thus seems quite plausible that Jews and Christians would have appreciated that the gospel was initiated by God for covenant purposes, and many could have understood that this signalled the next phase of human salvation.[63] An audience from the early Church, especially if guided by a teacher, should not have had difficulties recognizing all the implications of Mark's composite citation. Since biblical texts such as Mark were usually read in public and not written for private reading, a public reader or any informed member of the community could have explained difficult texts.

6. Conclusion

The Gospel's introduction stands as the interpretative frame for the section—and the whole book—since it presents the author's principal subject: the necessity for repentance following the arrival of the kingdom of the Lord Jesus and his gospel. Mark's composite citation in 1:2–3 is intentionally woven into the fabric of his introductory discourse. It explains the following narrative, and the following narrative develops and elucidates the composite citation. By using vocabulary from the same semantic field as the wilderness, the author effectively links the OT theme of exodus with John's arrival and the beginning of Jesus' ministry.

Woven into the narrative, the composite citation announces someone that is to come which is accomplished with John's *appearance* in v. 4. By incorporating OT texts, the author of the composite citation combines two elements in the prophecy: the coming last messenger, and the coming Lord. Moreover, two messages are communicated through the composite citation: one of coming judgment and one of coming blessing. It is probably the combination of themes and theology that is the most remarkable in Mark's first composite citation. In a very few lines, the originator of the composite citation was able to introduce motifs of the wilderness and preparation of the *way* (the *exodus*) that find echoes in John's description and in Jesus' temptation in

---

[63] Mark may very well have used the term "Gospel" also in its military sense since God's coming represents victory over Israel's enemies, especially in light of Isa 40 and its implication of a military victory associated with a new exodus. Mark does not use the motif of military victory in his introduction. However, a first-century audience might have linked the notion of victory with the good news, even if this would not be as natural for a twenty-first-century audience.

Mark 1:4–15.[64] By alluding to the same motif of wilderness in the narrative, the author highlights its importance.

The theme of wilderness woven into the narrative implies a meeting with God where judgment and promises of blessing intertwine. All those concepts would have been recognized by a Jewish audience since the wilderness (whether it was taken literally, metaphorically, or both) was considered a place of repentance and preparation which preceded a future blessing of the land and its people. It is likely that the early Church would also have recognized this motif based on Jewish Scriptures.[65] Exodus 23:20 announces a Promised Land, but injects warnings stating that if the children of Israel rebel against the leading messenger, they will not be pardoned "for my [God's] name is in him" (Exod 23:21). By reminding his audience of Israel's wandering and the need for repentance as the people were on the way, the author effectually evokes the sins of Israel and God's blessings. Furthermore, the originator of the composite citation links the notion of repentance with the preparation from Mal 3:1 which points to the *necessity* of repentance as the only way to turn away from rebellion.[66] Thus, Mark provides a good example of the rhetorical power of a composite citation. The Markan audience is invited to consider the voices of the past with the author and agree with him: a new exodus is coming, and repentance is required.

Mark demonstrates literary skill by using prophecies of accomplishment to interpret their co-texts and dramatize the citations.[67] Removing superfluous material[68] gave the author the possibility of emphasizing more efficiently the desired message, making the composite citation a compelling rhetorical tool which is more effective than the employment of three separate citations. It is a compelling rhetorical message for the ones who recognize the original texts, but even without such foreknowledge, it still carries a powerful message because of the common themes that are developed in the continuing narrative. In essence, Mark's thoughtfully written introduction offers an invitation—now is the time for souls to stop going their own way and turn around to follow Jesus on his way.

---

[64] He also introduces motifs of divinity/Messiah, and prophecy/proclamations announcing John's role, but a discussion of those themes goes beyond the limits of this essay.

[65] Paul used the theme of the wilderness when he wrote to the Corinthians in 1 Cor 10:1–13 in his warning against idolatry, Stephen used similar vocabulary when he exposed Israel's disobedience in Acts 7, and the writer of Heb 3:7–11 alludes to a "voice," the Holy Spirit, and the wilderness in his warning against rebellion.

[66] Μετάνοια should be understood as a "change of mind" or the act of taking a new direction, see BDAG, "μετάνοια."

[67] Anna Wierzbicka, "The Semantics of Direct and Indirect Discourse," *Papers in Linguistic* 7 (1974): 267–307. Anna Wierzbicka believes that citations transfer to the audience the power of interpretation. This allows audiences to discover by themselves what the author has discovered.

[68] For example, if the originator of the composite citation had cited Mal 3:1, he would have added, "And the Lord whom you seek will suddenly come to his temple; and the messenger of the covenant in whom you delight, behold, he is coming, says the Lord of hosts." However, that more complete citation would have complicated the discussion with its mention of the temple as a location. The same principle applies to Exod 23:20, "and to bring you to the place that I have prepared." Exodus refers to a new land, while Mark's first composite citation discusses the coming of the one bringing the gospel. Composite citations allow authors to remove material that distracts from the key point and to focus attention on specific elements only.

Bibliography

Adams, Sean A., and Seth M. Ehorn, eds. *Composite Citations in Antiquity: Jewish, Graeco-Roman, and Early Christian Uses*. LNTS 525. London: T&T Clark, 2016.

Adams, Sean A., and Seth M. Ehorn, eds. *Composite Citations in Antiquity: New Testament Uses*. LNTS 593. London: T&T Clark, 2018.

Andersen, Francis I., and A. Dean Forbes. *The Hebrew Bible: Andersen-Forbes Analyzed Text*. Bellingham, WA: Lexham Press, 2008.

Baldwin, Joyce. *Haggai, Zechariah and Malachi: An Introduction and Commentary*. TOTC 28. Downers Grove, IL: Intervarsity, 1972.

Bauer, Walter. *A Greek–English Lexicon of the New Testament and Other Early Christian Literature*. Edited by Frederick William Danker. Chicago: University of Chicago Press, 2001.

Beale, G. K., and D. A. Carson, eds. *Commentary on the New Testament Use of the Old Testament*. Grand Rapids, MI: Baker Academic, 2007.

Bromiley, Geoffrey Williams. *The International Standard Bible Encyclopedia*. Grand Rapids, MI: Eerdmans, 1988.

Cole, R. Alan. *Exodus: An Introduction and Commentary*. TOTC 2. Downers Grove, IL: InterVarsity, 1973.

Cole, R. Alan. *Mark*. Downers Grove, IL: Intervarsity, 1989.

Cross, Frank Moore. *Canaanite Myth and Hebrew Epic: Essays in the History of the Religion of Israel*. Cambridge, MA: Harvard University Press, 1973.

Dodd, C. H. *According to the Scriptures: The Sub-Structure of New Testament Theology*. London: Fontana, 1965.

Edwards, James R. *The Gospel According to Mark*. Grand Rapids, MI: Eerdmans, 2001.

Gaiser, Frederick J. "The Gospel According to Isaiah." *Word & World* 38 (2018): 239–51.

Guelich, Robert A. "'The Beginning of the Gospel': Mark 1:1–15." *BR* 27 (1982): 5–15.

Guelich, Robert A. *Mark 1–8:26*. WBC 34A. Grand Rapids, MI: Zondervan Academic, 2018.

Hooker, Morna D. "Isaiah in Mark's Gospel." Pages 35–49 in *Isaiah in the New Testament*. Edited by Steve Moyise and Maarten J. J. Menkel. London: T&T Clark, 2005.

Hooker, Morna D. *The Gospel According to Saint Mark*. London: Continuum, 1991.

Johnson, Franklin. *The Quotations of the New Testament from the Old, Considered in the Light of General Literature*. Philadelphia: American Baptist Publication Society, 1896.

Kittel, Gerhard, and Gerhard Friedrich, eds. *Theological Dictionary of the New Testament*. Translated by Geoffrey W. Bromiley. 10 vols. Grand Rapids, MI: Eerdmans, 1996.

Koehler, Ludwig, et al. *The Hebrew and Aramaic Lexicon of the Old Testament*. Leiden: Brill, 1994.

Lane-Mercier, Gillian. "Quotation as a Discursive Strategy." *Kodikas* 14 (1991): 199–214.

Lane, William L. *The Gospel of Mark*. 2nd ed. Grand Rapids, MI: Eerdmans, 1974.

Marcus, Joel. *The Way of the Lord: Christological Exegesis of the Old Testament in the Gospel of Mark*. London: T&T Clark, 2004.

Mauser, Ulrich W. *Christ in the Wilderness: The Wilderness Theme in the Second Gospel and its Basis in the Biblical Tradition*. Eugene, OR: Wipf & Stock, 2009.

Oswalt, John N. *The Book of Isaiah. Chapters 40–66*. Grand Rapids, MI: Eerdmans, 1998.

Piégay-Gros, Nathalie. *Introduction à l'intertextualité*. Paris: Dunod, 1996.

Pietersma, Albert, and Benjamin G. Wright, eds. *A New English Translation of the Septuagint*. London: Oxford University Press, 2007.

Spicq, Ceslas. *Theological Lexicon of the New Testament.* Translated by James D. Ernest. 2 vols. Peabody, MA: Hendrickson, 1994.
Stanley, Christopher D. *Arguing with Scripture: The Rhetoric of Quotations in the Letters of Paul.* New York: T&T Clark, 2004.
Strauss, Mark L. *Mark.* Edited by Clinton E. Arnold. Grand Rapids, MI: Zondervan, 2014.
Sundberg, Albert C. "On Testimonies." *NovT* 3 (1959): 268–81.
Watts, Rikki E. *Isaiah's New Exodus in Mark.* Grand Rapids, MI: Baker Academic, 2001.
Wevers, John William, and Udo Quast, eds. *Septuaginta: Vetus Testamentum Graecum Auctoritate Academiae Scientiarum Gottingensis editum II.1: Exodus.* Vestus Testamentum Graecum. Göttingen: Vandenhoeck & Ruprecht, 1991.
Wierzbicka, Anna. "The Semantics of Direct and Indirect Discourse." *Papers in Linguistics* 7 (1974): 267–307.
Ziegler, Joseph, ed. *Septuaginta: Vetus Testamentum Graecum Auctoritate Academiae Scientiarum Gottingensis editum XIII: Duodecim prophetae.* Göttingen: Vandenhoeck & Ruprecht, 1967.
Ziegler, Joseph, ed. *Septuaginta: Vetus Testamentum Graecum Auctoritate Academiae Scientiarum Gottingensis editum XIV: Isaias.* Göttingen: Vandenhoeck & Ruprecht, 1967.

Chapter 14

Jesus' Performative Utterances and the Construction of the Future Anterior

James M. Scott

1. Introduction

What relationship, if any, exists between Jesus' proclamation of the Kingdom of God and his crucifixion? And what relationship, if any, exists between Jesus' proclamation and the self-perpetuating movement that he set in motion? The answer given to these questions focuses in the first instance on the character of Jesus' proclamation itself: Jesus proclaimed a message of the Kingdom of God that was performative, and, as such, it was understood as characteristic of a royal pretender (albeit a nonviolent one, in this case). Once the character of Jesus' proclamation is understood, the reason that the Jesus movement was able to perpetuate itself also becomes clear. For Jesus' message of the Kingdom called forth participation in a revolutionary process of transformation—the prefigurative construction of the people to come and the world to come in the shell of the old.

2. The performative utterances of Jesus as royal pretender

This section focuses on the presentation of Jesus in Mark's Gospel, particularly why both sympathizers and critics perceived he aspired to kingship and why he therefore ended up crucified as a royal pretender, "the King of the Jews."[1] The following discussion consists of three parts: (1) a brief review of the evidence that, according to Mark's Gospel, Jesus was crucified as a royal pretender; (2) a survey of the performative utterances of Hellenistic kings and royal pretenders; and (3) an examination of Jesus' performative utterances as recorded in Mark.

---

[1] For a fuller examination of the evidence in this section, see James M. Scott, "The Speech-Acts of a Royal Pretender: Jesus' Performative Utterances in Mark's Gospel," *JSHJ* 20 (2021): 1–37.

3. Jesus as royal pretender

Mark's Gospel presents Jesus as having been crucified as a royal pretender.[2] According to Mark 15:26, "The inscription of the charge against him read, 'The King of the Jews.'"[3] Dale C. Allison writes,

> My contention about Jesus' self-conception [i.e., that he sees himself as the end-time king of restored Israel] can appeal to a second likely fact: he was crucified as "king of the Jews." The circumstance, according to John Collins, suggests that Jesus "was viewed as a messianic pretender and that the kingdom he proclaimed was understood, at least by his followers, as a messianic kingdom." This makes sense. If Rome executed Jesus for making himself out to be a king, then in all probability some people, including presumably some sympathizers, or maybe even Jesus himself, hoped him to be such.[4]

If Mark presents Jesus as having been crucified as a royal pretender, "The King of the Jews," the question becomes how anyone could have come to this conclusion on the basis of what Jesus had said and done. For Allison, the imminent eschatological expectation in the Jesus tradition is what "makes sense of why the Roman authorities executed him as a messianic pretender."[5] At another point, Allison offers a different approach: "Yet perhaps the strongest argument for Jesus having been in fact crucified as 'king of the Jews' is the lack of a better suggestion regarding his alleged crime."[6] I would like to add to these reasons for Jesus' crucifixion as a royal pretender a new

---

[2] The term "pretender" is used here in the sense of a person who claims or aspires to a title or position, especially a claimant to a throne (often when considered to have no just title). Mark's Gospel is sensitive to the possibility that there may be rival claimants to the Jewish throne in the future: "And if someone says to you at that time, 'Look! Here is the Messiah!' or 'Look! There he is!'—do not believe it" (Mark 13:21; cf. Matt 24:23–24). This strongly implies that Jesus, who speaks of the prophecy of false messiahs, is the true Messiah.

[3] All four Gospels coincide: Jesus was sentenced and crucified as an alleged "king of the Jews," and the charge against him was stated on a placard, which, according to Matt 27:37 and John 19:19, was placed at the top of the cross. On the execution of Jesus as "King of the Jews," see Dale C. Allison, *Constructing Jesus: Memory, Imagination, and History* (Grand Rapid, MI: Baker Academic, 2010), 233–40. As Allison (234–35) argues convincingly, "The formulation 'King of the Jews' stems neither from proof from prophecy nor from the Christology of the community. In general early Christians hesitated to use the title 'King' for Jesus. Would the formulation of the inscription, with its decidedly political ring, really rest on a historicization of a dogmatic motif? This is not very plausible." In an interesting thought experiment, Allison (392–423) examines what we can know about the death of Jesus based solely on the testimony of Paul's letters. Although the apostle does not say why Jesus was crucified, he nevertheless gives enough clues about Jesus' perceived identity that we would be able to surmise, even without the Gospels, that the Romans executed Jesus "because they perceived him to be a royal pretender" (398).

[4] Allison, *Constructing Jesus*, 233–34, citing John J. Collins, *The Apocalyptic Imagination: An Introduction to Jewish Apocalyptic Literature*, 2nd ed. (Grand Rapids, MI: Eerdmans, 1998), 257. Note that, with one major exception, Allison (231) declines to attempt showing that any story or event happened as told in the Gospels. That exception is the sentencing of Jesus by Pilate for the crime of being "king of the Jews."

[5] Allison, *Constructing Jesus*, 137.

[6] Allison, *Constructing Jesus*, 235.

approach: Jesus' performative utterances, understood as pleas for recognition, gave credence to the case against him.

4. Performative utterances of Hellenistic kings and royal pretenders

The British analytical philosopher J. L. Austin wrote the signally important book, *How to Do Things with Words*, which describes speech-acts called "performative utterances."[7] A performative utterance performs an action in and by words that change the state of the world (e.g., I grant, I decide, I release [from taxation], I appoint, I decree, I promise, I curse).[8] Unlike statements of fact, such speech-acts are neither true nor false,[9] but rather either "felicitous" or "infelicitous," that is, they are either effective or they are not. Speech-acts are effective when they meet conventional expectations and are validated by the intended audience. A performative utterance is a sociopolitical act that depends on the institutional context in which it is performed, the manner in which it is performed, and the recognition with which it is received. The status-changing performative, "I now pronounce you husband and wife," must be said by the right person, in the right context, and be accepted by the intended audience in order to effect a marriage between two people, with all the rights and responsibilities attending to it.

For historians of the ancient world, speech-act theory provides a powerful tool for exploring, in a nuanced way, the meaning of words in context on multiple levels. Austin's seminal insight allows the historian to see the relationship between a speech-act, its accordance with a set of cultural conventions and expectations, and its (intended or actual) transformative effect on the world. Thus, speech-act theory helps the historian read textual evidence and provides a useful and powerful means for interpreting historical documents, enabling a thick description of how words affect the world by showing the relationship between power, language, and context. The result is more satisfying and complex readings of the textual evidence in its historical context.[10] These readings are also quite generative insofar as they allow us to perceive relationships between texts that might otherwise remain hidden.

John Ma uses speech-act theory in order to investigate the interaction between the ruler and the ruled in the Hellenistic world, employing the interplay between the Seleucid empire and the Jewish *ethnos* in Maccabean Judea (175–129 BCE) as a case study.[11] Ma argues that performative speech-acts (I give, I grant) were the language of

---

[7] J. L. Austin, *How to Do Things with Words*, 2nd ed. (Cambridge, MA: Harvard University Press, 1975).
[8] The exact form of the performative utterance is not at issue. A declaration, for instance, can be performative, if it actually enacts the event it proclaims (e.g., "You're fired!" or "All of you are one in Christ Jesus" [Gal 3:28]).
[9] This is indeed one of the chief values of speech-act theory: it goes beyond the narrow confines of propositional truth and formal logic, exploring instead the realm of language effecting action.
[10] For a primer of speech-act theory for historians, see John Ma, "Seleukids and Speech-Acts: Performative Utterances, Legitimacy and Negotiation in the World of the Maccabees," *Scripta Classica Israelica* 19 (2000): 71–112 (75–85).
[11] For statements of the goals of his study, see Ma, "Seleukids and Speech-Acts," 72, 105.

imperial power, the Hellenistic king's main medium for vertical communication with his subjects.[12] The post-conquest situation confronted the affected populace with a clearly defined institution of kingship, which entailed the authority to make performative utterances and the recognized conventions to ensure their acceptance. The form of the speech-act assumes not only its felicity, but also its efficacy and success. Yet, this seemingly top-down, one-way flow of words autocratically effecting transformative actions on the ground—what Pierre Bourdieu[13] called "social magic" (*magie sociale*)— was actually much more complicated and unstable than it would at first appear: The subjects themselves not only initiated the interaction in many cases but also played a major role in determining the outcome of the interaction, for their consent and approval were crucial to the establishment and maintenance of the power structure.[14] Thus, the interaction between ruler and ruled reveals the contractual nature of power, which is more akin to a negotiation (or "euergetical dialogue")[15] than a simple, unilateral pronouncement, even though the conventionalized, published language of the king's performative utterance tends to mask the transactional, *do ut des* nature of the interaction and the behind-the-scenes political wrangling for concessions.[16] In a

---

[12] Ma, "Seleukids and Speech-Acts," 108. Cf. idem, "Hellenistic Empires," in *The Oxford Handbook of the State in the Ancient Near East and Mediterranean*, ed. Peter Fibiger Bang and Walter Scheidel (Oxford: Oxford University Press, 2013), 324–57 (345): "[T]he state, by its control of performativeness (namely the legitimacy of speech with practical effects, such as orders or edicts), and its position as the ultimate holder of means of violence to enforce its will, found itself providing a whole range of services to the ruled, in terms of regulation, arbitration, and enforcement."

[13] Pierre Bourdieu, *Ce que parler veut dire. L'économie des échanges linguistiques* (Paris: Fayard, 1982), 125–26. Cf. Ma, "Seleukids and Speech-Acts," 89–90, 107–108: "Power imagines its transactions as simple Austinian illocutions: the speech-act is uttered, fulfils conditions, is accepted, and therein has effect on people and on things. To go further, it presents the unilateral efficiency of its utterances as a natural, unquestioned fact dependent on some god-like quality inherent to the uttering entity, rather than on acceptance by an audience. Unsurprisingly, it assumes that illocutionary uptake for its orders involves not only acknowledging the speech-act, but actually obeying the order. In contrast, the Maccabean example, characterized by transactions made ambiguous by the flux in the political situation, serves as a reminder that the magical, god-like effect of performative utterances depends on conditions outside and before the utterances: the effect is an eminently social construct, arbitrary and open to challenge or resistance—a fact which ideologies of domination try to obnubilate, by positing that arbitrary, historically determined systems of 'social magic' belong to the order of things." For more on "social magic" and performative utterances, see idem, "Epigraphy and the Display of Authority," in *Epigraphy and the Historical Sciences*, ed. John Davies and John Wilkes, Proceedings of the British Academy 177 (Oxford: Oxford University Press, 2012), 133–58.

[14] Cf. John Ma, "Paradigms and Paradoxes in the Hellenistic World," *Studi Ellenistici* 20 (2008): 371–86 (374): "[T]he central medium for the expression of royal power, the 'performative utterance', is also disturbingly open to weakness—a phenomenon C. Préaux termed 'la faiblesse du droit', the odd powerlessness of the central authority: the very appearance of absolute authority, expressed in centrally issued diktats, means that local practice must be integrated by *post-eventum* pronouncements in which initiative is often local." See further idem, *Antiochos III and the Cities of Western Asia Minor* (Oxford: Oxford University Press, 2000), 384; idem, "Seleukids and Speech-Acts," 107–108.

[15] For the term "euergetical dialogue," see, e.g., Ma, *Antiochos III*, 79, 186, 187, 191, 204, 208, 235, 239.

[16] Cf. Ma, "Seleukids and Speech-Acts," 85, 105: "The later Seleukids uttered formally correct speech-acts, as they made offers in the hope of securing support for their attempts on the throne or as they granted privileges which they had no power to refuse; but because of the ambiguous political situation and the lack of a clearly defined, stable power, their intended audience—the Maccabees—had considerable latitude in matters of choice, giving or refusing illocutionary uptake only on conditions that suited them. The situation could be analysed in the terms developed by Austin: the illocutionary acts ('I grant') also had a perlocutionary force ('I bargain')—except that this

time of political instability caused, for example, by an external threat or and internal challenge to the throne, the subjects had even more ability to negotiate favorable terms from their ruler, because the ruler was motivated to pacify the populace and keep them within the fold.[17] Royal pretenders, however, could up the ante by using performative language to promise even more favorable terms for the subjects if they would accept his rule instead of the current regime's. As Ma shows, the Maccabees were skillful in repeatedly playing off Seleucid king against royal pretender and vice versa, negotiating a better and better deal for themselves in the process. As a result, the Seleucids had to relinquish ever more political control and tax revenue, in what became for them a race to the bottom and an eventual path to complete independence for the Jewish people. In the end, "the Seleukids had nothing more to offer but infelicitous speech-acts: these no longer had the context of authority and conventions that ensured uptake, and they were predicated on 'facts' (such as the existence of Seleukid power) that were manifestly untrue. Josephus tells us (AJ 13.274) the poignant end of the story which had started with the long, confident, imperial, letter of Antiochos III concerning the Jews: a century later, Hyrkanos simply responded with contempt for both Seleukid kings [i.e., Antiochos VIII Grypos and Antiochos IX Kyzikenos], ἀμφοτέρων κατεφρόνησεν."[18]

The Seleucid letters embedded in 1 Maccabees can be viewed as efforts by successive Seleucid pretenders, then rulers, to integrate and constrain Maccabean Judea within imperial institutions, by congenial grants and privileges. As Ma observes, "When a pretender to the Seleukid throne writes a letter to Jonathan or Simon, he is formally uttering performative speech ('I confirm...I grant...I exempt from taxes...I renounce'), from a position reserved for a king. Nonetheless, he is not yet king: he will become so, if the subjects acknowledge his speech-act as performative, according it uptake to recognise its illocutionary force, then generally acknowledging or constituting his authority. *The pretender's proclamations are thus themselves attempts to seize the position of authority which will validate his utterances—including the initial one.*"[19]

Royal pretenders had to fulfill several conditions in order to pull off this attempt at self-legitimization,[20] but for our purposes, the most important one is this: the pretender's performative speech-acts needed to be accepted, despite their problematic, self-fulfilling nature. Ma calls them "'pseudo-performative' grants."[21] "The letters of

---

perlocutionary dimension was radically at odds with the appearance of power and authority which the illocutionary acts implied: these appear a mere veil for the 'real' bargaining going on. At any rate, awareness of the 'real,' perlocutionary transactions only makes the more remarkable the fact that the Seleukids and the Jews maintained the appearance of authoritative utterer and receptive subject, in a comedy of power played by each party for different reasons." See also Ma, "Seleukids and Speech-Acts," 108: "The concepts of speech-act theory, when applied to the Maccabean material, reveal that power rests not only on the exercise or the threat of violence, but also on some basic, invisible, contract between the rulers, whose speech-acts need acceptance but to be translated into reality, and the ruled, whose consent ultimately decides on the felicity of the rulers' utterances."

[17] Cf., e.g., Ma, "Seleukids and Speech-Acts," 94–95. The issue of royal pretenders is set in a broader context in Boris Chrubasik, *Kings and Usurpers in the Seleucid Empire: The Men Who Would Be King* (Oxford: Oxford University Press, 2016).
[18] Ma, "Seleukids and Speech-Acts," 104.
[19] Ma, "Seleukids and Speech-Acts," 100–101 (emphasis mine).
[20] Cf. Ma, "Seleukids and Speech-Acts," 101.
[21] Ma, "Seleukids and Speech-Acts," 103.

pretenders may look like 'normal' performatives: in fact, they are *pleas for recognition, offers in a negotiating situation, or rather a kind of illocutionary market by auction, where the interlocutors at the receiving end of the royal performatives can make a choice*. The capacity to work 'social magic,' this time, lies with the subjects: it is their choice which will make a king out of an adventurer writing to Jews on his landing in Syria and his attempt on the Seleukid throne."[22] Successive Seleucid royal pretenders used performative utterances "*to create the appearance of power and authority out of weakness.*"[23] In reality, however, the construction of power was thoroughly contractual in nature—an eminently social construct.

5. Jesus' performative utterances

If, as previously discussed, Jesus was crucified as a royal pretender, and if, as Ma shows, the Seleucid royal pretenders made performative utterances in an attempt to seize the position of authority that will validate their utterances in the first place, then reading Mark's presentation of Jesus may be enriched by an examination of Jesus' performative utterances. What speech-act theory allows us to do is to analyze the form of the exchanges and the tensions or ambiguities they carried. In the process, we will notice connections between parts of Mark's Gospel that have been partially hidden before. Examining Jesus' performative utterances will help us see that from the very inception of his proclamation in Galilee, Jesus is presented as asserting his kingship in a self-legitimizing move.[24] In fact, Jesus' performative utterances were pleas for recognition, offers in a negotiating situation, or rather a kind of illocutionary market by auction, where the interlocutors at the receiving end of the royal performatives can make a choice. It is their choice that will make a king out of Jesus. This is a more satisfying way to study the exchanges in the Gospel of Mark than merely paraphrasing them seriatim.

Austin's insights lead to a richer interpretation, and greater sensitivity to multi-layered interaction. These should be the contributions of any theory, when applied to historical material: allowing the historian to see more things and offer more sophisticated descriptions of socio-political transactions. Speech-act theory helps us understand how kingdom is created by royal pronouncement—that is, royal power as discourse. From this perspective, we can see that Jesus' numerous performative utterances as presented in Mark's Gospel were understood as Jesus' bid to claim the kingship.[25]

Jesus' first performative utterance in Mark's Gospel occurs in Mark 1:14–15, the summary of Jesus' proclamation in Galilee: "Now after John was handed over, Jesus

---

[22] Ma, "Seleukids and Speech-Acts," 101 (emphasis mine); cf. also 105.
[23] Ma, "Seleukids and Speech-Acts," 108 (emphasis mine).
[24] Most Hellenistic kings of the third and second centuries BCE were peripatetic; they spent the majority of their reign in constant motion on campaign. Cf. Angelos Chaniotis, *War in the Hellenistic World: A Social and Cultural History* (Oxford: Blackwell, 2005), 61. Similarly, Jesus was peripatetic.
[25] Some preliminary work on performative utterances in Mark's Gospel was done by James Maxey, "The Power of Words in Mark: Their Potential and Their Limits," *Currents in Theology and Mission* 37 (2010): 296–303. However, his study does not consider the thesis that we are developing in the present study.

went into Galilee, proclaiming the good news of God and saying, 'The time is fulfilled and the kingdom of God has come near/is at hand; repent and trust in the good news.'" Allison has made the case that "[w]hen the evangelists generalize in their editorial comments..., these are, notwithstanding the redactional agendas, the most reliable statements of all."[26] In that case, the précis of Jesus' message in Mark 1:14–15, which is surely redactional, should not be discarded for that reason. Jesus' proclamation as summarized here is not simply an impartation of information or a statement of fact; it is arguably a performative utterance—or rather, the "'pseudo-performative' grant" of the royal pretender—insofar as it seeks actually to effect the inauguration of the Kingdom of God that it announces,[27] a kingdom that will be consummated only in the future.[28] In the rest of Mark's Gospel, Jesus' speech-acts entail the unfolding of this inaugural performative in concrete words and deeds.[29] From the perspective of Mark's Gospel, Jesus set about to create the kingdom of God by royal pronouncement. It was a matter of royal power as discourse, on the model of the Hellenistic kings.

Several aspects of Jesus' proclamation are illuminated by comparison with the interactions between the Seleucid empire and the Jewish nation. First, by saying that "the time is fulfilled," Jesus announces the beginning of a new "era," just as the reign of Simon Maccabeus established a new era of Jewish independence from Seleucid rule in 142 BCE (cf. 1 Macc 13:41–42) and just as, before that, the reign of Seleucus I established a new era of his independent power in 311 BCE.[30]

---

[26] Allison, *Constructing Jesus*, 19.
[27] On the presence of the kingdom, see Allison, *Constructing Jesus*, 98–116 (116): "The upshot of the preceding pages is this: there is no reason to tear asunder what the tradition holds together. If Jesus sometimes, as so many are convinced, proclaimed the presence of God's kingdom, this is insufficient reason to urge that he did not also proclaim its future, apocalyptic revelation."
[28] On the futurity of the kingdom of God in the Jesus tradition, see Allison, *Constructing Jesus*, 36–39, 41, 164–204. That this expectation was a *Naherwartung*, see pp. 44–48, 54–55, 65–66, 97. Luke 19:11, for example, reports that when Jesus neared Jerusalem, his disciples "supposed that the kingdom of God was to appear immediately (παραχρῆμα)."
[29] Cf. Scott, "The Speech-Acts of a Royal Pretender," 25–32. Mark 1:14–15 has a possible parallel in Matt 11:2–4//Luke 7:18–23 (Q). In answer to John the Baptist's question about whether Jesus is the "coming one," Jesus responds: "Go and tell John what you have seen *and heard*: the blind receive their sight, the lame walk, the lepers are cleansed, the deaf hear, the dead are raised, the poor have good news brought to them." Jesus thereby alludes to Isa 61:1–2, along with several other Isaianic prophecies. Cf. Dale C. Allison, *The Intertextual Jesus: Scripture in Q* (Harrisburg, PA: Trinity Press International, 2000), 109–14. This raises the question of whether Jesus' proclamation of the "good news" is related to the deeds of power that are listed. Certainty cannot be had, but 4Q521 (4QMessianic Apocalypse) foretells that "[the hea]vens and the earth will listen to his [sc. God's] Messiah" (משיחו) and possibly ascribes to this messianic figure a list of miracles very reminiscent of Matt 11:2–4//Luke 7:22–23 (Q), concluding with a citation of Isa 61:1: "He will heal the wounded, and revive the dead, and bring good news to the poor." Cf. Allison, *Constructing Jesus*, 266; Adela Yarbro Collins and John J. Collins, *King and Messiah as Son of God: Divine, Human, and Angelic Messianic Figures in Biblical and Related Literature* (Grand Rapids, MI: Eerdmans, 2008), 171. Does this messianic figure perform these deeds of power by the word of his mouth? Cf. Isa 11:1–12.
[30] On the Seleucid era, see Paul J. Kosmin, "A Short Introduction to the Seleucid Era," *Center for Hellenic Studies Research Bulletin* 4/2 (2016): http://nrs.harvard.edu/urn-3:hlnc.essay:KosminP.Introduction_to_the_Seleucid_Era.2016. See further idem, *Time and Its Adversaries in the Seleucid Empire* (Cambridge, MA: Harvard University Press, 2018); Ma, "Hellenistic Empires," 324–25. On the creation of a "royal timespace," combining vivid involvement in the present and the local with broader scales and perspectives, which was "the very exercise of kingship and its deepest, most essential pleasure," see idem, "Kings," in *A Companion to the Hellenistic World*, ed. Andrew Erskine (Oxford: Blackwell, 2003), 177–95 (193–94).

Second, Jesus' announcement of the "kingdom of God" clearly shows that his intention is to establish an empire to usurp the current one(s).[31] The fact that this kingdom is "at hand" suggests that its coming is imminent; indeed, in and through Jesus' performative words, the kingdom was already beginning to dawn.

Third, Jesus' call for the people to "repent" has clear parallels to the Seleucid regime, which acknowledged repentance on the part of people who had rebelled against the empire and who were subsequently forgiven.[32] Jesus is saying that the people should desist from their former rebellion and side with him against his opponents, whoever they may be.

Fourth, Jesus exhorts the people to "trust in the good news." From the perspective we are developing here, this exhortation is analogous to a royal pretender making a performative utterance—ostensibly a bona fide royal grant—that is actually a plea for recognition.[33] Jesus is not a king—far from it! He often shows signs of profound weakness.[34] Yet, if the people acknowledge his speech-act as performative (i.e., they

---

[31] That Jesus was the central actor and main object of the "kingdom of God" is discussed in Allison, *Constructing Jesus*, 221–304 (231): "From my point of view, all the texts that I have cited are closely related; they constitute a family of traditions that requires explanation. All of them, whether they use a formal title or not, are united in one particular: when they look into the future, they see Jesus, and indeed Jesus front and center"; and 303: "[T]here is no good reason to reject the main thesis of this chapter, which is that he [sc. Jesus] was the center of his own eschatological scenario… Jesus did not envisage a 'brokerless kingdom.' Nor did he proclaim a 'kingless kingdom.' Rather, when he looked into the future, he saw thrones, including one for himself. What caused him to hold such a conviction is not subject to analysis. We can know only the fact, not the why."

[32] Cf., e.g., Chaniotis, *War in the Hellenistic World*, 69: "Its [sc. Amlada's] inhabitants, part Greek, part native, had taken advantage of the Pergamene involvement during the Third Macedonian War and of a Galatian invasion in 168 BC, and had overthrown the Pergamene garrison. When their revolt was subdued, they had to provide hostages and pay substantial sums for reparations. A few years later (160 BC?) Amlada was in a desperate financial situation. When the city appealed to the king's benevolence, Attalos, acting on behalf of his brother Eumenes II, explained why he accepted their request, released the hostages and reduced the tribute (*RC* 54): 'because I saw that you have repented of your former offences [θεωρῶν οὖν ὑμᾶς μετανενοηκότας τε ἐπὶ τοῖς προημαρτημένοις] and that you zealously carry out our orders.' Through the publication of this letter on stone, the principle of *do ut des* became an example for future generations."

[33] Even the language of belief and trust belongs in this context. When a city is conquered by a Hellenistic king (or capitulates preemptively), the people must "entrust" (πιστεύσαντες) themselves to their conqueror. Thus, the letter of Zeuxis (the viceroy of Antiochus III) to Amyzon (*RC* 38), written in the immediate aftermath of the conquest of the city (203 BCE), is framed in the wider context of "all those who have entrusted and handed themselves over to us" (α]ὐτοὺς πιστεύσαντες ἡμῖν ἐνεχείρισαν). Cf. Ma, *Antiochos III*, 179, 292–94 (no. 5, line 2). See also the Letter of the Scipio brothers to the Herakleians: "As for us, we happen to be well disposed towards all the Greeks, and we will try, since you have come over to our [faith] (παραγεγονότων ὑμῶν εἰς τὴν ἡμέτεραμ [πίστιμ]), to show solicitude as much as possible, always trying to be responsible for some advantage. We grant you your liberty, just as to other cities which have entrusted themselves to us, with the right to see all your own affairs conducted by yourselves according to your laws, and in all other matters we will try to assist you and always be responsible for some advantage." Cf. pp. 366–67 (no. 45, lines 7–14). Attalus I treated the Smyrnians well, because they had "preserved to the greatest extent their faith towards him (διὰ τὸ μάλιστα τούτους τετηρηκέναι τὴν πρὸς αὐτὸν πίστιν)" (Polybius 5.77.6). Cf. p. 55 n. 11.

[34] Cf., e.g., Mark 6:5–6: "And he could do no deed of power there [i.e., in his own hometown of Nazareth], except that he laid hands on a few sick people and cured them. And he was amazed at their unbelief" (6:5–6). As Ma observes, the Hellenistic empires were large and supralocal political structures of control and extraction, headed by a monarch and his power elite, sustained by violence, negotiation, and legitimacy ("Hellenistic Empires," 324). Jesus' kingdom was hardly large and

accord it uptake by recognizing its illocutionary force), that would reinforce Jesus' authority, his original offer of the kingdom would then have a basis for being enacted, and he would indeed become their king.³⁵ What was true of Seleucid royal pretenders is true of Jesus as well: "The pretender's proclamations are thus themselves attempts to seize the position of authority which will validate his utterances—including the original one."³⁶ As we can see throughout Mark's Gospel, however, Jesus' performative utterances cannot succeed unless people believe.³⁷ The reason for this inability is not immediately obvious in the text, so the nexus between belief in Jesus' performative utterance and the efficacy or inefficacy of that utterance can appear to be a kind of "magic." However, on the basis of our comparison with royal pretenders, we can see that this magic is actually "social magic": believing in Jesus' performative utterance reflects the reality that its enactment requires the acceptance by the audience.

6. Jesus' performative message and the construction of the future anterior

Performative speech-acts were used by successive Seleucid pretenders and kings to create the appearance of power and authority out of weakness.³⁸ As we have seen on the basis of Mark's Gospel, Jesus used performative utterances in a similar way, and, for that reason, he was recognized as a royal pretender by both sympathizers

---

supralocal (although, according to Mark, it was expanding into contiguous areas); its leaders were a motley bunch and anything but a power elite; and even the legitimacy of Jesus' birth was called into question (cf. Mark 6:3, where Jesus is referred to as "the son of Mary" rather than the normal patronymic). If Judas was thinking about kingdom in its usual terms, then he might have imagined a Hellenistic state run by and for the ruling elite, which controlled and extracted rent, tribute, and tax (cf. Ma, "Hellenistic Empires," 340, 343–44, 346–47; idem, "Kings," 183–84). Having finally perceived that Jesus' brand of "kingdom" would end badly, Judas opted for Plan B—to cash out. Cf. Ma, "Hellenistic Empires," 350 (emphasis mine): "[T]he presence of competing states that can often make *alternative offers, ideological or material, to local actors*... The institutional context of royal ownership and patronage further affected the individual powerholders within the state—the military colonists, officials, and high-ranking courtiers that constituted the state's apparatus were also bound to the state by *incentives*, namely the distribution of property and revenue extracted from below or generated by state activities such as warfare. *When these incentives were not fulfilled, the state's men could defect.*"

³⁵ The kind of reception that Jesus hoped for is exemplified in part in the so-called triumphal entry. When, in Mark 11:9–10, Jesus enters Jerusalem, the crowd hails him as a royal savior: "Hosanna! Blessed is the one who comes in the name of the Lord! Blessed is the coming kingdom of our ancestor David." In the immediately preceding context, blind Bartimaeus cries out to "Jesus, Son of David" (10:46–52). The fact that Jesus enters Jerusalem on a donkey implicitly fulfills Zech 9:9: "your king comes to you...humble and riding on a donkey" (cf. Matt 21:5; John 12:15). See further Anthony Le Donne, *Historical Jesus: What Can We Know and How Can We Know It?* (Grand Rapids, MI: Eerdmans, 2011), 121. On Jesus' entry into Jerusalem, see also David R. Catchpole, "The 'Triumphal' Entry," in *Jesus and the Politics of His Day*, ed. Ernst Bammel and C. F. D. Moule (Cambridge: Cambridge University Press, 1984), 319–34, who argues that the "triumphal" entry matches Peter's confession of Jesus as Messiah and has to do with the disclosure of Jesus' identity and status.

³⁶ Ma, "Seleukids and Speech-Acts," 100–101 (emphasis mine).

³⁷ Cf. Mark 2:5; 5:34, 36; 6:5–6; 9:23–24 (the plaintiff cry of the father whose son was possessed by an evil spirit: πιστεύω· βοήθει μου τῇ ἀπιστίᾳ), 42; 10:52; 11:22–24, 31; 15:31–32.

³⁸ Ma, "Seleukids and Speech-Acts," 108.

and critics alike. From the perspective of Mark's Gospel, Jesus set about to create the kingdom of God by royal pronouncement. It was a matter of royal power as discourse. The sympathizers, although growing in number, could not match the countervailing power of the ruling elites who found fault with him precisely because he was gaining a significant following and he had royal pretensions. In the end, therefore, Jesus was crucified as a royal pretender at the hands of the Romans. Speech-acts are effective when they meet conventional expectations and are validated by the intended audience. Jesus was crucified as a royal pretender precisely because he *did* meet conventional expectations for kingship, but his bid was not adequately validated by his intended audience. To the leaders of Jesus' day, both Jewish and Roman alike, Jesus represented, as a royal pretender, the presence of a competing state that can make alternative offers, ideological and material, to local actors, thus threatening a shift in popular support from the current regime to that of the pretender.

Jesus' performative utterances, understood as pleas for recognition, gave credence to the case against him as a royal pretender. Jesus' performative declaration that the Kingdom of God was at hand and the admonition to repent and believe the good news (Mark 1:14–15) inaugurated the building of a new world within and alongside the old. However, his performative language projected that which "will have been" as an unfolding, nonviolent revolutionary event. As yet, it had no objective status, only a conditional and experimental one: If, despite "factual" evidence to the contrary, you believe that Jesus is ushering in the Kingdom (i.e., that it *will have been* a revolutionary event), then that belief (and its attendant actions) functions in the future anterior.[39] If, however, because of the counterfactual evidence, you do not believe Jesus' proclamation, then the Jesus movement is an inconsequential moment to be either co-opted or crushed.

Judas, one of the intimate followers of Jesus, was co-opted, and Jesus himself was crucified as a royal pretender. But the Jesus revolution was not thereby extinguished. Instead, the Jesus revolution continued unabated, because it was a nonviolent revolution and therefore did not affect Jesus' followers.[40] As Josephus observed in the so-called *Testimonium Flavianum*:

---

[39] Previously in this chapter we referred to "social magic" to describe belief in Jesus' message.
[40] In a paper presented at the Annual Meeting of Biblical Meeting of the Society of Biblical Literature in 2020, "Josephus and Nonviolent Resistance to Romanization: The Immediate Jewish Matrix of Jesus of Nazareth," John Dominic Crossan argued that the Romans dealt with violent and nonviolent resistance differently: "For *violent* resistance Rome crucified the leader together with many of his major supporters. In 4 BCE at Jerusalem, for example, the Syrian legate captured 'the authors of the insurrection…the most culpable, in number about two hundred, he crucified' (*JW* 2:75 = *JA* 17.295). For *nonviolent* resistance, Rome crucified only the leader on the presumption that his followers would scatter and the movement would disappear. In the early 200s, for example, the famous Roman jurist, Julius Paulus, nicknamed Prudentissimus by his contemporary emperor, made a compilation of the *opinions*—in the juridical sense—of Roman law. Under 'Title XXII: Concerning Seditious Persons' he gave this legal precedent: 'The authors of sedition and tumult, or those who stir up the people, shall, according to their rank, either be crucified, thrown to wild beasts, or deported to an island' (*The Opinions of Julius Paulus Addressed to His Son*, Book V, Title 22.1)…- My second conclusion from Josephus alone is that Jesus was crucified for founding a *nonviolent* movement of resistance to Romanization."

At this time there appeared Jesus, a wise man, if indeed one should call him a man. For he was a doer of startling deeds, a teacher of people who receive the truth with pleasure. And he gained a following both among many Jews and among many of Greek origin. He was the Messiah. And when Pilate, because of an accusation made by the leading men among us, condemned him to the cross, those who had loved him previously did not cease to do so. For he appeared to them on the third day, living again, just as the divine prophets had spoken of these and countless other wondrous things about him. And up to this very day the tribe of Christians, named after him, has not died out. (*Ant.* 18.63–64)

Scholars have had doubts about some parts of this statement, arguing that the original composition was redacted by a later Christian scribe in order to make Josephus a witness to the divinity, messiahship, and resurrection of Jesus.[41] There is little doubt, however, that Josephus himself referred to Jesus generically as a "wise man."[42] But that could hardly have been the reason for the "accusation made by the leading men among us [sc. Jewish people/Judeans]." You don't have someone executed simply because he is wise or popular. There must have been more to the story. And that something more seems to be wrapped up with the short statement that Jesus was the Messiah, the end-time king of Israel. Even if Josephus did not say precisely, "He was the Messiah," he may well have said something similar. For example, in a parallel passage, the authenticity of which has not been questioned, Josephus refers to "the brother of Jesus who is *called* Messiah, James by name" (*Ant.* 20.200). Hence, Josephus may have originally written that Jesus was "the *so-called* Messiah," thus distancing himself from the claim. It would have been easy for a later Christian scribe to simply delete an attributive participle in the original *Testimonium Flavianum*. In that case, Josephus can be correlated with the Gospels that Jesus was executed as a royal/messianic pretender, but his nonviolent revolution was carried on by his followers after his death. And why, despite their leader's death, did "the tribe of Christians" not simply die out as a movement? Was it because they continued to live in the "future anterior"?[43] And were they able to do so because, as the Gospels (and Josephus?) attest, Jesus himself was believed to have been resurrected?

In this section, we argue that Jesus' inauguration of the Kingdom through his performative utterances entails the construction of the prefigurative future anterior—*that which will have been*. Jesus' message of the Kingdom of God has significant lines of continuity with the message of other revolutionary Jewish apocalyptic movements.[44]

---

[41] For the details of this controversy, see John P. Meier, *A Marginal Jew: Rethinking the Historical Jesus, Vol. 1: The Roots of the Problem and the Person*, ABRL (New York: Doubleday, 1991), 56–88.

[42] Cf. Meier, *A Marginal Jew,* 61–62.

[43] Cf. Allison, *Constructing Jesus,* 64: "The end of Jesus, to state the obvious, was neither the end of the present world order nor the beginning of its end. Why, then, did early Christians speak as though it was?"

[44] Cf. Anathea E. Portier-Young, *Apocalypse Against Empire: Theologies of Resistance in Early Judaism* (Grand Rapids, MI: Eerdmans, 2011), who makes a distinction between "resistance" and "revolution" (3–45). There can, of course, be a spectrum of responses to domination, but we are using the term "revolution" in a Deleuzian sense to refer primarily to nonviolent strategies. Cf. Thomas Nail,

We may briefly summarize their apocalyptic worldview as follows: although God created a good world, it has subsequently descended into chaos and wickedness. A day is coming, however, when God will restore the broken creation to its pristine state. In the meantime, these Jewish movements sought to anticipate God's full and final redemption by actualizing the expected revolution (transformation) in the future anterior, as *that which will have been* the beginning of a new form of life in the world to come. This entails the *prefigurative* construction of a new people and a new world in the shell of the old.[45]

Jesus easily fits within such a worldview.[46] Jesus was not looking for the end of the world per se, but rather for the restoration of a broken, topsy-turvy world. Moreover, he called upon his followers to anticipate that future renewed world by living in the prefigurative future anterior (that which will have been).[47] By believing that Jesus' performative proclamation of the Kingdom is an event, that belief functions in the future anterior. But this belief also entails concomitant action. In the words of Dale C. Allison, "Jesus wants some things even now to be the way they were in the beginning because that is how they are going to be in the kingdom of God."[48] Let us examine two examples of this principle from Mark's Gospel. Here, we will illustrate the *Urzeit-Endzeit* correlation and the construction of the future anterior in light of Mark 2:27 and 10:2–12.[49]

7. Mark 10:2–12

According to Mark 10:2–12, some Pharisees sought to "test" Jesus by asking him whether it is lawful for a man to divorce his wife (v. 2).[50] Jesus, however, answers their

---

"Deleuze, Occupy, and the Actuality of Revolution," *Theory & Event* 16 (2013). https:muse.jhu.edu/article/501858/. For example, Nail writes (author's emphasis): "Absolute positive deterritorialization [i.e., revolutionary transformation] is a kind of transformation that not only escapes the dominant political order, but also connects up to an increasing number of other escaped or freed elements whose ultimate collective aim is the transformation of the dominant political order… It accomplishes this through the *prefigurative* construction of a new world…"

[45] On the construction of the people to come and the world to come from a Deleuzian perspective, see further Ronald Bogue, "Deleuze and Guattari and the Future of Politics: Science Fiction, Protocols and the People to Come," *Deleuze Studies* 5 (2011): 77–97.

[46] Jesus did not originate the concept of the future anterior. Pious Jews who were apocalyptically oriented had already understood themselves to be living in the time of God's proleptic establishment of control over evil which anticipates his ultimate triumph at the end. Cf. Loren T. Stuckenbruck, "Overlapping Ages at Qumran and 'Apocalyptic' in Pauline Theology," in *The Dead Sea Scrolls and Pauline Literature*, ed. Jean-Sébastien Rey, Studies on the Texts of the Desert of Judah 102 (Leiden: Brill, 2014), 309–26.

[47] Cf. Allison, *Constructing Jesus*, 32 n. 7: "I maintain that Jesus was looking not for the literal 'end of the world' but instead for the restoration of a world in disrepair…"

[48] Dale C. Allison, *Jesus of Nazareth: Millenarian Prophet* (Minneapolis, MN: Fortress Press, 1998), 210.

[49] See further Lutz Doering, "Urzeit–Endzeit Correlation in the Dead Sea Scrolls and Pseudepigrapha," in *Eschatologie—Eschatology: The Sixth Durham-Tübingen Research Symposium. Eschatology in the Old Testament, Ancient Judaism and Early Christianity*, ed. H.-J. Eckstein et al., WUNT 272 (Tübingen: Mohr Siebeck, 2011), 19–58.

[50] See further Lutz Doering, "Marriage and Creation in Mark 10 and CD 4–6," in *Echoes from the Caves: Qumran and the New Testament*, ed. Florentino García Martínez, STDJ 85 (Leiden: Brill, 2009), 133–63.

question with another question: "What did Moses command you?" (v. 3). When the Pharisees answer, in accordance with Deut 24:1–2, that Moses allowed a man to write a certificate of dismissal and to divorce his wife (v. 4), Jesus responds by appealing to the Genesis creation accounts:

> Because of your hardness of heart he [sc. Moses] wrote this commandment for you. But from the beginning of creation, "God made them male and female" (Gen 1:27). "For this reason a man shall leave his father and mother and be joined to his wife, and the two shall become one flesh" (Gen 2:24). So they are no longer two, but one flesh. Therefore what God has joined together, let no one separate. (Mark 10:5–9)

Thus, Jesus' prohibition of divorce is a reaffirmation of the originally intended will of God for creation with respect to the institution of marriage. The assumption seems to be that since the Kingdom of God is at hand, and the renewal of the world has been inaugurated through Jesus' performative word (Mark 1:14–15), the people to come (i.e., those who accept Jesus' message) are to live now in the future anterior, which entails a process of constructing the prefigurative future in the present in anticipation of the full and final repristination. In other words, since God originally created the marital bond to be permanent, the later Mosaic concession to human hardheartedness (i.e., divorce) is now superseded. As Matt 19:8 puts it, "But from the beginning it was not so."

8. Mark 2:27

In Mark 2:1–3:6 comprises a collection of five controversy stories that reveal Jesus' authority. The fourth story (2:23–28) commences with the Pharisees asking reproachfully, "Look, why are they [sc. Jesus' disciples] doing what is not lawful on the Sabbath?" (v. 24), and it culminates with Jesus' authoritative pronouncement: "The Sabbath was made for humankind, and not humankind for the Sabbath; so the Son of Man is Lord (κύριος) even of the Sabbath" (vv. 27–28).[51] For our purposes, the first part of Jesus' authoritative pronouncement (v. 27) is of particular interest, for it evokes the creation account of Gen 1:1–2:3, which culminates in the sabbath rest on the final day of creation:

> And on the seventh day God finished the work that he had done, and he rested on the seventh day from all the work that he had done. So God blessed the seventh day and declared it holy, because on it God rested from all the work that he had done in creation. (Gen 2:2–3)

---

[51] On Mark 2:23–26, see further Lutz Doering, *Schabbat: Sabbathalacha und -praxis im antiken Judentum und Urchristentum*, TSAJ 78 (Tübingen: Mohr Siebeck, 1999), 409–16; idem, "'Much Ado about Nothing?' Jesus' Sabbath Healings and Their Halakic Implications Revisited," in *Judaistik und Neutestamentliche Wissenschaft: Standorte—Grenzen—Beziehungen*, ed. Lutz Doering et al., FRLANT 226 (Göttingen: Vandenhoeck & Ruprecht, 2008), 213–41, esp. 236–41.

In Gen 1:28, God had blessed humankind, and now he blesses the seventh day; that the two are brought together is clear from Exod 20:8–11, in which the commandment to keep the Sabbath is based on God's resting from his labors on the seventh day: "For in six days the Lord (κύριος) made heaven and earth, the sea, and all that is in them, but rested the seventh day; therefore the Lord (κύριος) blessed the sabbath day and consecrated it" (v. 11).[52]

It seems likely, then, that Mark 2:27 reflects a recovery of God's original intention in creation.[53] The idea that "the Sabbath was made for humankind" sends one back to the creation story in Genesis 1–2. The implicit logic seems to be this: when God's original purpose in establishing the Sabbath is rightly understood, it can override the prohibition of "work" on the seventh day if it is done for humanitarian purposes. The analogy with Mark 10:6 is clear, for there, too, Jesus trumps a Mosaic commandment by appealing to the originally intended will of God in creation.

9. Conclusion

We began the present study with a twofold question: what relationship, if any, exists between Jesus' proclamation of the Kingdom of God and his crucifixion? And what relationship, if any, exists between Jesus' proclamation and the self-perpetuating movement that he set in motion? The answer that we have pursued here is that Jesus' performative proclamation of the Kingdom was understood as having revolutionary implications that threatened the stability of the currently established world order.

The process of revolutionary intervention that Jesus set in motion brought into existence a new world of the present, not as a consequence of the past, nor merely as the *potential* for a new future "to come," but through the actual construction of a new present in a future anterior that "will have been." This strategy of prefiguration not only provided an alternative to the transformative methods engendered by opposition and insurrection, but it also aligned with God's originally intended will for creation.

Bibliography

Allison, Dale C. *Constructing Jesus: Memory, Imagination, and History*. Grand Rapids, MI: Baker Academic, 2010.

Allison, Dale C. *Jesus of Nazareth: Millenarian Prophet*. Minneapolis, MN: Fortress Press, 1998.

Allison, Dale C. *The Intertextual Jesus: Scripture in Q*. Harrisburg, PA: Trinity Press International, 2000.

---

[52] It would take us too far afield to explore whether the anarthrous use of κύριος in Mark 2:27 reflects that in Exod 20:11, for such a discussion would entail examining the rest of the Markan usage of the term. Suffice it to say that, in the context of Jesus' authoritative pronouncements in 2:1–3:6, the possibility of such a connection is at least intriguing.

[53] Cf. Joel Marcus, *Mark 1–8*, AB 27 (New York: Doubleday, 2000), 245, 246: "It may be that Mark thinks that Jesus restores the compassionate aspect of the original Sabbath, which in the interim has been effaced by a human hardheartedness that has transformed the good Sabbath into a source of destruction."

Austin, J. L. *How to Do Things with Words*. 2nd ed. Cambridge, MA: Harvard University Press, 1975.

Bogue, Ronald. "Deleuze and Guattari and the Future of Politics: Science Fiction, Protocols and the People to Come." *Deleuze Studies* 5 (2011): 77–97.

Bourdieu, Pierre. *Ce que parler veut dire. L'économie des échanges linquistiques*. Paris: Fayard, 1982.

Catchpole, David R. "The 'Triumphal' Entry." Pages 319–34 in *Jesus and the Politics of His Day*. Edited by Ernst Bammel and C. F. D. Moule. Cambridge: Cambridge University Press, 1984.

Chaniotis, Angelos. *War in the Hellenistic World: A Social and Cultural History*. Oxford: Blackwell, 2005.

Chrubasik, Boris. *Kings and Usurpers in the Seleucid Empire: The Men Who Would Be King*. Oxford: Oxford University Press, 2016.

Collins, Adela Yarbro, and John J. Collins, eds. *King and Messiah as Son of God: Divine, Human, and Angelic Messianic Figures in Biblical and Related Literature*. Grand Rapids, MI: Eerdmans, 2008.

Collins, John J. *The Apocalyptic Imagination: An Introduction to Jewish Apocalyptic Literature*. 2nd ed. Grand Rapids, MI: Eerdmans, 1998.

Doering, Lutz. *Schabbat: Sabbathalacha und praxis im antiken Judentum und Urchristentum*. TSAJ 78. Tübingen: Mohr Siebeck, 1999.

Doering, Lutz. "Urzeit–Endzeit Correlation in the Dead Sea Scrolls and Pseudepigrapha." Pages 19–58 in *Eschatologie—Eschatology: The Sixth Durham–Tübingen Research Symposium. Eschatology in the Old Testament, Ancient Judaism and Early Christianity (Tübingen, September 2009)*. Edited by Hans-Joachim Eckstein, Christof Landmesser, and Herman Lichtenberger. WUNT 272. Tübingen: Mohr Siebeck, 2011.

Doering, Lutz. "Marriage and Creation in Mark 10 and CD 4-6." Pages 133–63 in *Echoes from the Caves: Qumran and the New Testament*. Edited by Florentino García Martínez. STDJ 85. Leiden: Brill, 2009.

Doering, Lutz. "'Much Ado about Nothing?' Jesus' Sabbath Healings and Their Halakic Implications Revisited." Pages 213–41 in *Judaistik und Neutestamentliche Wissenschaft: Standorte—Grenzen—Beziehungen*. Edited by Lutz Doering, Hans Günther Waubke, and Florian Wilk. FRLANT 226. Göttingen: Vandenhoeck & Ruprecht, 2008.

Kosmin, Paul J. *Time and Its Adversaries in the Seleucid Empire*. Cambridge, MA: Harvard University Press, 2018.

Kosmin, Paul J. "A Short Introduction to the Seleucid Era." *Center for Hellenic Studies Research Bulletin* 4 (2016). http://nrs.harvard.edu/urn-3:hlnc.essay:KosminP.Introduction_to_the_Seleucid_Era.2016.

Le Donne, Anthony. *Historical Jesus: What Can We Know and How Can We Know It?* Grand Rapids, MI: Eerdmans, 2011.

Ma, John. "Hellenistic Empires." Pages 324–58 in *The Oxford Handbook of the State in the Ancient Near East and Mediterranean*. Edited by Peter Fibiger Bang and Walter Scheidel. Oxford: Oxford University Press, 2013.

Ma, John. "Epigraphy and the Display of Authority." Pages 133–58 in *Epigraphy and the Historical Sciences*. Edited by John Davies and John Wilkes. Proceedings of the British Academy 177. Oxford: Oxford University Press, 2012.

Ma, John. "Kings." Pages 175–95 in *A Companion to the Hellenistic World*. Edited by Andrew Erskine. Oxford: Blackwell, 2003.

Ma, John. *Antiochos III and the Cities of Western Asia Minor*. Oxford: Oxford University Press, 2000.

Ma, John. "Seleukids and Speech-Acts: Performative Utterances, Legitimacy and Negotiation in the World of the Maccabees." *Scripta Classica Israelica* 19 (2000): 71–112.
Marcus, Joel. *Mark 1–8*. AB 27. New York: Doubleday, 2000.
Maxey, James. "The Power of Words in Mark: Their Potential and Their Limits." *Currents in Theology and Mission* 37 (2010): 296–303.
Meier, John P. *A Marginal Jew: Rethinking the Historical Jesus. Vol. 1: The Roots of the Problem and the Person*. ABRL. New York: Doubleday, 1991.
Nail, Thomas. "Deleuze, Occupy, and the Actuality of Revolution." *Theory & Event* 16 (2013). muse.jhu.edu/article/501858/.
Portier-Young, Anathea E. *Apocalypse Against Empire: Theologies of Resistance in Early Judaism*. Grand Rapids, MI: Eerdmans, 2011.
Scott, James M. "The Speech-Acts of a Royal Pretender: Jesus' Performative Utterances in Mark's Gospel." *JSHJ* 20 (2021): 1–37.
Stuckenbruck, Loren T. "Overlapping Ages at Qumran and 'Apocalyptic' in Pauline Theology." Pages 309–26 in *The Dead Sea Scrolls and Pauline Literature*. Edited by Jean-Sébastien Rey. STDJ 102. Leiden: Brill, 2014.

Chapter 15

Matthew's Rewriting and Mosaic Discourse*

Kyung S. Baek

1. Introduction

As Hindy Najman has argued in her book entitled *Seconding Sinai* and as George J. Brooke has subsequently confirmed and expanded, the development of a textual constellation that has come to be called Mosaic Discourse and that became common in the era of Second Temple Judaism served four purposes: to confer authority, authenticity, immediacy, and continuity on a text. The Gospel of Matthew participates in this Second Temple Mosaic Discourse for these same reasons. On a structural level, Matthew rewrites the Gospel of Mark according to a Torah pattern, its five blocks of teaching corresponding to the five books of Moses, and he does this through a process of rewriting that intertwines authoritative traditions. On a narrative level, Matthew rewrites the Torah in the Sermon on the Mount (i.e., Jesus' Torah Discourse in Matt 5–7), a Torah Discourse that suggests a re-presentation of Moses at Sinai, wherein Jesus is the Mosaic figure bringing the Torah to the people. In the present essay, I first explain what is meant by Mosaic Discourse and rewriting and then go on to examine the Gospel of Matthew with a view to demonstrating how the paradigm of Second Temple Mosaic Discourse was employed for the purpose of ascribing authority, authenticity, immediacy, and continuity to the text.

2. Mosaic discourse and rewriting

In Second Temple Judaism, Moses' role and status, as well as texts associated with him, grew and became idealized as central and authoritative. A growing number of

---

* I am honored to dedicate this essay to Larry J. Perkins. Coincidentally, he was sitting in the audience on 2017 May 28 at the Canadian Society of Biblical Studies conference in Toronto, Ontario as I presented the present paper, which has now been substantially revised to become this contribution to his Festschrift.

compositions (i.e., Exodus, Deuteronomy, Jubilees, and the Temple Scroll) formed a corpus of Mosaic Discourse, which Hindy Najman characterizes as follows:

> The idea of a discourse tied to a founder provides, I want to suggest, a helpful way to think about the developing conceptions of the Mosaic Law and figure of Moses. On this understanding of a discourse tied to a founder, to rework an earlier text is to update, interpret and develop the content of that text in a way that one claims to be an authentic expression for the law already accepted as authoritatively Mosaic. Thus, what we might call a "new" law—perhaps even what we might regard as a significant "amendment" of older law—is characterized as the Law of Moses, this is not to imply that it is found within the actual words of an historical individual called Moses. It is rather to say that the implementation of the law in question would enable Israel to return to the authentic teaching associated with the prophetic status of Moses.[1]

Therefore, Mosaic Discourse is defined textually and thematically by a text's relationship to a chain or tradition of its predecessors.[2] Najman identifies four required features of Mosaic Discourse.[3]

1. The new text claims for itself the *authority* that already attaches to previous traditions by reworking and expanding them through interpretation.
2. The new text ascribes to itself the status of Torah. It may portray itself as having either a heavenly or an earthly origin, but in any event as an *authentic* expression of the Torah of Moses.
3. The new text is said to be a re-presentation of the revelation of Sinai. There is repeated emphasis on gaining access to revelation through a re-creation of the Sinai experience. This strategy emphasizes the presentness of Sinai—the *immediacy* of the event—even in the face of destruction and exile.
4. The new text is said to be associated with or derived from the founding figure, Moses. This claim serves to connect the new interpretations to established Torah, that they may be treated as divine revelation or dictation and as prophecy or inspired interpretation. The new text can thus be shown to have *continuity* with earlier ancestral discourse.

Accordingly, Jubilees and the Temple Scroll are examples par excellence: they identify themselves as Mosaic Discourses and so connect themselves with the previous Mosaic tradition, fashioning themselves as Torah and providing a re-presentation of Sinai so that they may be considered divine revelation. George J. Brooke distils Najman's

---

[1] Hindy Najman, *Seconding Sinai: The Development of Mosaic Discourse in Second Temple Judaism*, JSJSup 77 (Atlanta: SBL, 2003), 13.
[2] Jan Assmann, *Moses the Egyptian: The Memory of Egypt in Western Monotheism* (Cambridge, MA: Harvard University Press, 1997).
[3] Najman, *Seconding Sinai*, 16. If any of the four features are missing, then it must be compensated appropriately.

features into four purposes for rewriting: *authority* (claimed through interpretation), *authenticity* (attributed and ascribed status as the Torah or Moses), *immediacy* (re-presented as revelation at Sinai), and *continuity* (associated or produced by Moses as divine revelation).[4] This also occurs in the Gospel of Matthew: previous Mosaic traditions are interpreted to establish *authority*; the Gospel is identified with the Torah of Moses to establish *authenticity*; Moses at Sinai is re-presented through the figure of Christ to establish the *immediacy* of the revelation; and divine revelation is extended through the Mosaic figure to establish *continuity*.

Matthew's participation in Mosaic Discourse is executed through the process of rewriting.[5] For our purposes, George Brooke defines rewriting as, "any representation of an authoritative scriptural text that implicitly incorporates interpretive elements, large or small in the retelling itself."[6] This expands the concept of rewriting to include any representation of an authoritative scriptural text or tradition that implicitly incorporates interpretative elements in its retelling.[7] Thus, Matthew closely rewrites the Hebrew scriptures and Jewish authoritative traditions following its scriptural base texts while displaying editorial emendations. In other words, Matthew participates in Mosaic Discourse as he rewrites the Gospel of Mark by *blending* (conflating, emending, and rearranging) and supplementing Mark within a Torah structure (i.e., five blocks of Jesus' discourses). Additionally, in Jesus' Torah Discourse, usually known as the Sermon on the Mount (Matt 5–7), Matthew rewrites the Torah of Moses. This involvement in Mosaic Discourse through the process of rewriting ensures the Gospel of Matthew's authority, authenticity, immediacy, and continuity.[8]

---

[4] George J. Brooke, "Hypertextuality and the 'Parabiblical' Dead Sea Scrolls," in *In the Second Degree. Paratextual Literature in Ancient Near Eastern and Ancient Mediterranean Culture and Its Reflection in Medieval Literature*, ed. P. S. Alexander, A. Lange, and R. J. Pillinger (Leiden: Brill, 2010), 57–62.

[5] Evident in many Second Temple compositions, rewriting or "Rewritten Bible" was first coined by Geza Vermes and identified as a narrative composition that followed the Hebrew Bible and included a substantial amount of emendations and interpretative expansions (alterations, paraphrases, and comments). See Geza Vermes, *Les Manuscrits du désert de Juda* (Paris: Desclée de Brouwer, 1953), and *Scripture and Tradition in Judaism: Haggadic Studies*, 2nd ed.; StPB 4 (Leiden: Brill, 1973).

Currently, scholars use "Rewritten Scripture" in place of "Rewritten Bible." Scholarship on this topic can be generally divided into two groups: (1) viewing rewriting as a classification or genre; or (2) rewriting as a process that expands into other genres and categories. See Anders Klostergaard Petersen, "Textual Fidelity, Elaboration, Supersession or Encroachment? Typological Reflections on the Phenomenon of Rewritten Scripture," *Rewritten Bible after Fifty Years: Texts, Terms, or Technique? A Last Dialogue with Geza Vermes*, ed. József Zsengellér; JSJSup 166 (Leiden: Brill, 2014), 13–48.

[6] George J. Brooke, "Rewritten Bible," in *Encyclopedia of the Dead Sea Scrolls*, ed. L. H. Schiffman and J. C. VanderKam, 2 vols. (Oxford: Oxford University Press, 2000), 2:777–78.

[7] George J. Brooke, "Genre Theory, Rewritten Bible and Pesher," *DSD* 17 (2010): 361–86; Daniel J. Harrington, "Palestinian Adaptations of Biblical Narratives and Prophecies: The Bible Rewritten (Narratives)," in *Early Judaism and its Modern Interpreters*, ed. Robert A. Kraft and George W. E. Nickelsburg (Philadelphia, PA: Fortress Press, 1986), 239–47.

[8] George J. Brooke "Between Authority and Canon: The Significance of Reworking the Bible for Understanding the Canonical Process," in *Reworking the Bible: Apocryphal and Related Texts at Qumran: Proceedings of a Joint Symposium by the Orion Center for the Study of the Dead Sea Scrolls and Associated Literature and the Hebrew University Institute for Advanced Studies Research Group on Qumran, 15–17 January, 2002*, ed. E. G. Chazon, D. Dimant, and R. A. Clements; STDJ 53 (Leiden: Brill, 2005), 85–104.

3. Authority and interpretation

As a new Mosaic Discourse composition, the Gospel of Matthew claims for itself authority from previous traditions through interpretation of the Torah: "Do not think that I have come to abolish the law or the prophets; I have come not to abolish but to fulfill. For truly I tell you, until heaven and earth pass away, not one letter, not one stroke of a letter, will pass from the law until all is accomplished" (Matt 5:17-18). Beginning with a series of blessings, Jesus' Torah Discourse constitutes a rewriting and interpretation of previous authoritative traditions: the Decalogue (murder, adultery, stealing) and the Holiness Code (oaths, retaliation, and love of neighbours and enemies).[9] It includes core principles (5:3-20), key authoritative texts (5:21-48), and communal practices (6:1-7:27) and establishes its authority through the interpretation of the Torah of Moses.[10] Not only is Jesus' teaching authority confirmed by his sitting posture as a rabbi at the beginning and end of this discourse, but also by the crowd's astonishment by the authoritativeness of his words compared to those of the scribes and Pharisees who sit on the seat of Moses (5:1-2; 7:28-29; cf. 23:2). Matthew rewrites the Mosaic Torah depicting Jesus as Moses while emphasizing the giving of the Torah at Mount Sinai (cf. Exod 19-20).

Matthew rewrites and interprets the commandments through Jesus' words beginning with, "you have heard that it was said" (5:21, 27, 31, 33, 38, 43):[11] three interpret the Decalogue with murder, adultery and stealing (i.e., divorce and oaths);[12] and three interpret the Holiness Code concerning oaths, retribution, and love of neighbour (5:21-48).[13] Jesus' interpretation intensifies Torah practices and raises the qualifications for entering into the kingdom of heaven. Matthew radicalizes the Torah (cf. 19:8)[14]

---

[9] Jesus' Torah Discourse interprets the commandments on murder (5:21; Exod 20:13; Deut 5:17) and adultery (5:27; Exod 20:14; Deut 5:18), and actions concerning the taking of oaths (5:33; Lev 19:12; cf. Num 30:2), retaliation (5:38; Lev 24:20; cf. Exod 21:24), loving neighbours (5:43; Lev 19:18) and holiness (5:48; Lev 19:2). In Matthew, the order of the Decalogue (i.e., murder, adultery, and stealing) follows the MT, Josephus, Exod 20:13-15LXX (Manuscript A, F), and *Didache* 2:1-3 (Matt 15:19, 19:18; cf. Mark 10:19), in contrast to the order of adultery, murder, and stealing found in Mark 7:21, Luke 18:20, Rom 13:9, Jas 2:11, and Philo (*Dec.* 12; *Spec.* 3.2), and the Nash Papyrus. See Richard A. Freund. "The Decalogue in Early Judaism and Christianity," in *The Function of Scripture in Early Jewish and Christian Tradition*, ed. C. A. Evans and J. A. Sanders (Sheffield: Sheffield Academic Press, 1988), 60–100.

[10] By being directly written by God, the Decalogue could be viewed as the foundation of the Torah: the constitution of Israel that sets the ground rules for God's people (cf. Deut 5:22). See Patrick D. Miller, "The Place of the Decalogue in the Old Testament and Its Law," *Int* 43 (1989): 229–42.

[11] The Decalogue can be found in Exod 20:2-17 and Deut 5:6-30; it is reiterated in Exod 34:11-26 within the context of the rest of the Mosaic Torah (Exod 20:18-23:33; cf. Exod 34:1-35; 1Q2). The prophets also reference, reiterate and adapt the Decalogue (Hos 4:2; 12:10; 13:4 Jer 7:9; cf. Job 24:14-15, Pss 50:7; 81:10-11). The Holiness code is found in Lev 17-26 with Ezekiel adapting it (e.g., Ezek 22:10-11).

[12] For the Decalogue, this same order is found in Matthew's list of vices—murder, adultery, fornication, theft, bearing false witness, blasphemy (15:19; cf. Mark 7:21-22)—and commandments: murder, adultery, stealing, bearing false witness, honouring your father and mother, and loving one's neighbour as oneself (19:19; cf. Mark 10:19).

[13] Retribution (Exod 21:24; Lev 24:20; Deut 19:21), divorce (Deut 24:1-4), and love of neighbour (Lev 19:18).

[14] David Baker, "The Finger of God and the Forming of a Nation: The Origin and Purpose of the Decalogue," *TynBul* 56 (2005): 1–24.

and advocates for completely observing the Mosaic Torah in every detail and by the whole person (including one's feelings, thoughts, motivations, and actions). This is exemplified in Matt 5:48: "You will be perfect, therefore, as your heavenly Father is perfect."[15] This is a rewriting of Lev 19:18: "You will be holy, for I the LORD your God am holy." Not only does this verse summarize Matthew's rewriting of Mosaic Torah, but it introduces the ethical practices of almsgiving, prayer and fasting (6:1–18). Thus, in rewriting the Mosaic Torah, Matthew establishes a standard for the kingdom of heaven that exceeds the righteousness of the scribes and Pharisees.

Concerning Jesus and the Mosaic Law, scholars have said that Jesus opposed either some of it or ways of observing it.[16] However, it would be better said that for Matthew the Torah is to be perfectly performed, even as new demands are rewritten (5:17–22). E. P. Sanders argues that Jesus did not reject Jewish legalism but emphasized external and internal conformity to the Mosaic Torah that favoured piety through obedience.[17] Matthew does not set aside Mosaic Torah, but radically rewrites it as the standard for right motivation and behaviour affirming its validity.[18] Therefore, Matthew reframes Jesus and Mosaic Torah: (1) Jesus is pro-Torah as it is perfect and wise; (2) anti-Torah statements refer to Jewish legalism of the scribes and Pharisees, which is often only an external shell for public recognition; and (3) Jesus did not reduce Torah but emphasized its complete obedience as a demand from God.[19]

Correspondingly, Matthew puts mercy above cultic observances (9:13; 12:7).[20] In two controversies with the Pharisees, Jesus legitimates his own behaviour by radicalizing the Torah and quoting Hos 6:6. This characterizes "justice, mercy and faith" as the weightier matters of the Mosaic Torah while maintaining its practices in all its minutiae (23:23).[21] As Maarten Menken states:

> This point of view explains the antitheses with their quotations from Deuteronomy: the Old Testament laws remain valid, but Jesus interprets them in the light of the governing principle of love or mercy. Acting fully in accordance with this governing principle means that 'your righteousness exceeds that of the scribes and Pharisees' (5:20) and that one is 'perfect as your heavenly Father is perfect' (5:48; cf. 19:21).[22]

---

[15] I have translated ἔσεσθε as a second plural future indicative.
[16] See E. P. Sanders, *Paul and Palestinian Judaism: A Comparison of Patterns of Religion* (Philadelphia: Fortress Press, 1977), 1–29, and *Jesus and Judaism* (London: SCM Press, 1985), 1–58.
[17] E. P. Sanders. "When Is a Law a Law? The Case of Jesus and Paul," in *Religion and Law: Biblical-Judaic and Islamic Perspectives*, ed. E. B. Firmage, B. G. Weiss, and J. W. Welch (Winona Lake, IN: Eisenbrauns, 1990), 142, 139–58.
[18] Sanders, "When Is a Law a Law?" 147. See also Sanders, *Jesus and Judaism*, 256–60.
[19] Sanders, "When Is a Law a Law?" 141.
[20] Strict adherence in Matt 23:2–3 and 24:20 but more liberal in 19:19 and 22:34–40 (cf. Deut 6:5). See Maarten J. J. Menken, "Deuteronomy in Matthew's Gospel," in *Deuteronomy in the New Testament*, ed. S. Moyise and M. Menken, LNTS 358 (London: T&T Clark, 2007), 42–62.
[21] Both references to Hos 6:6 are missing in the Mark and Luke parallels (Matt 9:13; Mark 2:17; Luke 5:32; and Matt 12:7; Mark 2:26; Luke 6:4).
[22] Menken, "Deuteronomy in Matthew's Gospel," 52.

For Matthew's Jesus, the Mosaic Torah must be governed by love and mercy (5:38; cf. Deut 19:21). The Jesus' Torah Discourse statement that Jesus came to "not abolish but fulfil the Torah and the Prophets," affirms the legal, binding authority of the Mosaic Torah as a source for a "better righteousness" that exceeds that of the scribes and Pharisees as concerns kingdom entry and ethics (5:20; cf. 7:21; 10:34).

4. Authenticity and the Torah of Moses

All eight occurrences of νόμος in Matthew are associated with the Torah, but it should not be narrowly defined as just the Pentateuch: (1) the law and the prophets (5:17; 7:12; 22:40); (2) all the prophets and the law (11:13); and (3) the law (5:18; 12:5; 22:36; 23:23).[23] As George Brooke states: "The Torah can be conceptualized as more than the Pentateuch in a strict sense. From the evidence of the Dead Sea Scrolls, especially that from the eleven caves at or near Qumran, it is now widely acknowledged that Torah is something more than the five books of Moses in a pre- or proto-Masoretic form."[24] Therefore, the Torah (including νόμος in Matthew), for most Jews from the fifth century BCE to about the first century CE, had many textual forms with a common authoritative base.[25]

Furthermore, Matthew ascribes to itself the status of Torah by portraying itself as having a heavenly origin (i.e., the kingdom of heaven). It is therefore an authentic expression of the Torah of Moses.[26] On a structural level with Matthew's rewriting of Mark in a fivefold Torah pattern, Matthew claims authenticity as Mosaic Torah. Building on Bacon's fivefold discourse pattern with the end marker καὶ ἐγένετο ὅτε ἐτέλεσεν ὁ Ἰησοῦς ("now when Jesus had finished") and Green's chiastic structure, Matthew can be outlined as follows:[27]

---

[23] The Anchor Bible Dictionary defines the Torah as the Pentateuch. See Richard Elliott Friedman, "Torah (Pentateuch)," *ABD* 6:605–22. There is no entry for Torah.

[24] See George J. Brooke. "Torah, Rewritten Torah and the Letter of Jude," in *The Torah in the New Testament: Papers Delivered at the Manchester–Lausanne Seminar of June 2008*, ed. Michael Tait and Peter Oakes, LNTS 401 (London: T&T Clark), 180–93 (189).

[25] Johan Maier does not restrict the Torah to the legal contents of the Pentateuch or like texts but, by compiling numerous definitions from various Jewish groups in the Persian and Hellenistic periods, re-defines Torah as: "not a uniform unit but rather a conglomerate of different social, political, and religious tendencies, more or less organized as groups, all of them with their own concept of 'Torah' and authority, presupposing, of course, a common basis." See Brooke, "Torah, Rewritten Torah," 189.

[26] Torah can be both a reference to the canonical Pentateuch or have a wider meaning as discussed here. In Matthew, both understandings of Torah seem to be present (5:17–18). The combination of the Law and Prophets (ὁ νόμος καὶ οἱ προφῆται) seems to be a reference to the Jewish scriptures (5:17; 7:12; 11:13), but the law in 5:18 seems to encompass more (cf. 12:5; 23:23). For example, the word תורה can be found in many of the Dead Sea Scrolls with the broader understanding of a general idea of instruction or law often involving ethics (cf. CD 15:2, 9, 12; 1QS 5:8; 8:22).

[27] B. W. Bacon, "The Five Books of Matthew against the Jews," *The Expositor* 15 (1918): 56–66.

Prologue: Title and Introduction: Coming of the King (1:1–4:25)
    Discourse 1: Jesus' Torah Discourse (5:1–7:29; cf. 4:25–5:2)[28]
Narrative 1: Work of the King (8:1–9:34)
    Discourse 2: Jesus' Mission Discourse (10:1–11:1; cf. 9:36–37)
Narrative 2: Work of the King (11:2–12:49)
    Discourse 3: Jesus' Parables Discourse (13:1–53; cf. 13:1–3)
Narrative 3: Work of the King (13:54–17:27)
    Discourse 4: Jesus' Community Discourse (18:1–19:1; cf. 18:1, 3)
Narrative 4: Work of the King (19:2–22:46)
    Discourse 5: Jesus' Eschatological Discourse (23:1–26:1; cf. 24:3)
Narrative 5: Work of the King (26:2–27:66)
Epilogue: Conclusion and Commission: Going of the King (28:1–20)

Matthew's distinct discourse-narrative structure rewrites the Gospel of Mark in a Torah pattern.[29]

Correspondingly, Philip S. Alexander's list of seven features for rewriting narratives can be slightly re-adjusted for Matthew to highlight its identity and purpose within Mosaic Discourse.[30] First, Matthew generally follows the narrative and chronological sequence of Mark in a framework of the account of events concerning Jesus' life and can be broadly described as a history. Matthew rewrites Mark by primarily keeping its order and weaving Jesus' teaching (Q and M) and the Jewish scriptures into its narrative framework. Matthew follows its source text, Mark, and usually keeps its chronological sequence and narrative structure. This includes almost all of Mark's 661 verses, except for 55 verses, and uses 8,555 of Mark's 11,078 words.[31]

Second, although rewriting often replicates the form of its source, Matthew is an independent composition integrating his sources (Mark, Q, M, and the Jewish scriptures) into a coherent reworking of authoritative traditions in alternating narrative and discourse sections (Matt 1–4; 5–7; 8–9; 10; 11–12; 13; 14–17; 18; 19–22; 23–25; 26–28).[32] Third, Matthew does not intend to replace or supersede Mark (or

---

[28] See Keegan, "Introductory Formulae," 415–30.
[29] Bauer (*Structure of Matthew's Gospel*, 42) correctly accesses the fivefold pattern: "We contend that Matthew draws attention to the five great discourses, but that he also incorporates these discourses into the flow of the narrative. The function of these five discourses within the narrative framework is to point to Jesus' activity of instructing his community, with special reference to the post-Easter existence of the church."
[30] Philip S. Alexander, "Retelling the Old Testament," in *It is Written: Scripture: Essays in Honour of Barnabas Lindars, SSF*, ed. D. A. Carson and H. G. M. Williamson (Cambridge: Cambridge University Press, 1988), 99–121, esp. 116–18.
[31] W. Kümmel, *Introduction to the New Testament* (London: SCM Press, 1975), 57 n. 32.
[32] Even the material that is unique to Matthew (*Sondergut*) and not included in Mark is blended together into a coherent narrative: Jesus' birth narrative (Matt 1–2); two miracle accounts (9:2–34); trained scribes and parables (13:51–52); temple taxes (17:24–27); death of Judas (27:3–10); earthquake and appearance of dead (27:51–53); Jesus' final commission (28:16–20); Jesus' parables (13:44–50; 21:28–31; 25:1–13, 31–40); and discourse (15:13; 24:10–12, 26). See J. Andrew Doodle, *What was Mark for Matthew? An Examination of Matthew's Relationship and Attitude to his Primary Source*, WUNT 344 (Tübingen: Mohr Siebeck, 2013), 33.

the Jewish scriptures),[33] but as with many Second Temple Jewish rewritings, it functions as a companion to the underlying authoritative texts by offering a fuller and smoother composition that coherently interprets and contemporizes its sources for his audience.[34]

Fourth, although rewriting generally incorporates and follows the order of its source, Matthew improves upon Mark as he abbreviates, omits, and expands upon its text, often making it appear more moral, theological, or didactic in nature.[35] Fifth, Matthew intends to produce an interpretative reading of Mark and the Jewish scriptures by offering a fuller, smoother, and theologically advanced composition. Matthew's implicit and explicit interpretations of the Jewish scriptures are not a loose connection of traditions but blended together with narrative additions functioning as implicit scriptural exegesis: filling gaps, solving problems and explaining connections. For example, the addition of Isa 53:4 in Matt 8:17 presents Jesus' miracles as carrying out God's purposes as Jesus has been given God's power and authority over diseases, nature, demons and sin (8:1–9:1).[36]

Sixth, as rewriting pays close attention to its sources, Matthew notes obscurities, inconsistencies, and narrative lacunae, attempting to solve them within his composition.[37] Seventh, rewriting makes use of "non-biblical" traditions and sources (Mark, Q and M), fusing them to "biblical" material (Jewish scriptures), which form a synthesis

---

[33] See Harry Y. Gamble, *Books and Readers in the Early Church: A History of Early Christian Texts* (New Haven: Yale University Press, 1995), 102; and Adela Y. Collins, *Mark* (Minneapolis, MN: Fortress Press, 2007), 103–25. Around the late second century, Mark begins to appear with Matthew, Luke, and John in some manuscripts (P⁴, P⁶⁴ and P⁶⁷). Furthermore, as Doodle (*Mark for Matthew*, 21) states, "However, unlike Q, Mark survived the test of time: a collection of logia could not compete with this attribute of the written gospel, the storyline format lending credibility to the account and ensuring its triumph over the more flexible yet less stable oral traditions. Therefore, regardless of the genre we might ascribe to Mark today. Matthew clearly saw Mark as a 'life' of Jesus, or rather, as a 'death' of Jesus, *the* historical account of events in the months leading up to the crucifixion."

[34] Contrary to David C. Sim, "Matthew's Use of Mark: Did Matthew Intend to Supplement or to Replace His Primary Source?" *NTS* 57 (2011): 176–92. Deuteronomy, Chronicles, and Jubilees are examples of rewritten literary works that do not seem to replace their previous sources but re-contextualize them for their contemporary situation.

[35] See Warren Carter, *Matthew: Storyteller, Interpreter, Evangelist* (revised ed.; Grand Rapids: Baker Academic, 2004), 55.

[36] Daniel J. Harrington, *The Gospel of Matthew*, Sacra Pagina 1 (Collegeville, MN: Liturgical Press, 2007), 112–18; H. J. Held, "Matthew as Interpreter of the Miracle Stories," in *Tradition and Interpretation*, 165–299; W. G. Thompson, "Reflections on the Composition of Matt 8:1–9:34," *CBQ* 33 (1971): 365–88; J. D. Kingsbury, "Observations on the 'Miracle Chapters' of Matthew 8–9," *CBQ* 40 (1978): 559–73.

[37] Warren Carter (*Matthew*, 49–51) observes a number of omissions by Matthew that may deal with obscurities and inconsistencies in a diminished portrayal of Jesus or the disciples: (1) omission of Jesus' limitations (Matt 13:58//Mark 6:5; Matt 14:25//Mark 6:48); (2) omission of limiting Jesus' knowledge (Matt 9:21–22//Mark 5:30; Matt 16:4//Mark 8:12); and (3) omission of disciples' failings (Matt 13:18//Mark 4:13; cf. Matt 13:16–17; Matt 17:9//Mark 9:6; Matt 20:20–21//Mark 10:35–37). Matthew 8:26 identifies Jesus' disciples as having "little faith" rather than "no faith" (Mark 4:40; cf. Matt 14:31//Mark 6:50–51; Matt 16:8//Mark 8:17). Moreover, Matthew includes large additions to Mark that fill the narrative lacunae of Jesus' life and teachings: (1) Jesus' birth narrative (Matt 1–2); (2) five major sections of Jesus' teaching (Matt 5–7, 10, 13, 18, 23–25; cf. Mark 4 and 13) and (3) Jesus' resurrection appearances and commission (Matt 28). See Carter, *Matthew*, 53–54. Davies and Allison note Matthew's language gives evidence of the importance of Christology, eschatology, ethics, ecclesiology, and the role of the Hebrew Bible (*Saint Matthew*, 1:79–80; cf. Luz, *Matthew 1–7*, 73–74). Furthermore, Matt 24–25 expands Mark 13 by adding parables with many coming from Q (Matt 24:37–44, 45–51; 25:1–13, 14–30, 31–41).

of the whole tradition. Thus, Matthew unifies Jesus traditions onto a Torah base, blending text and interpretation as well as contextualizing these traditions.[38]

A final aspect of the Torah of Moses is Matthew's prologue and epilogue as they allude to a Genesis beginning (Matt 1:1–17) and a Deuteronomic ending (Matt 28:16–20). Indicators point to Matthew's Genesis beginning. (1) Matthew begins with the book of Genesis (βίβλος γενέσεως) as its incipit. (2) Βίβλος γενέσεως is found in Gen 2:4 and 5:1 LXX, a translation of אלה תולדות, a formula that runs throughout Genesis. (3) Matthew, with Jesus' identification as "son of Abraham" and his genealogy immediately following, seems to be suggesting a type of beginning or origins, especially as Abraham is the forefather to the nation of Israel. (4) In Jesus' genealogy, Matthew deliberately recollects and emphasizes three key phrases of Israelite history: beginning with Abraham, running through David and the Babylonian exile, and culminating in Jesus (1:17; cf. 1:2–17; Gen 12:2–3). Consequently, Matthew closes with a Deuteronomic ending with Jesus' commission of his disciples on a mountain is reminiscent of Moses' speeches in Deuteronomy and especially his farewell speech.

5. Immediacy and Mount Sinai

Matthew re-presents the revelation at Sinai through Jesus' mountain pericopes: Jesus' temptation (4:8), Jesus' Torah Discourse (5:1; 8:1), Jesus' walking on water (14:23), Jesus' healings (15:29), Jesus' transfiguration (17:1, 9), Jesus' Eschatological Discourse (24:3; 26:30), and Jesus' commission to his disciples (28:16).[39] Recreating the Sinai experience by using mountains as chain-links or catchwords, Matthew associates and brings immediacy to Jesus' teaching for the Matthean community. This strategy of repeatedly emphasizing mountains provides access to divine revelation through a re-creation of the Sinai experience by signalling the immediacy of Jesus' teaching and ministry (3:2; 4:17; cf. 11:7–15).[40] Moreover, this presentness of Sinai coincides with Matthew's use of the *Last Days* (i.e., as scriptural texts and prophecies are fulfilled in Jesus).[41]

---

[38] See Stanton, *Gospel for a New People*, 328–33; Doodle, *Mark for Matthew*, 43. For example, Matthew, in continuity with the Jewish scriptures, adds scriptural citations throughout his narrative as additions to Mark: (1) Isa 9:1 added to Jesus' ministry from Capernaum (4:12–17//Mark 1:1–14); (2) Isa 53:4 added to Jesus' healing miracles (8:16–17//Mark 1:32–34); (3) Hos 6:6 added to Jesus' appeal to God's mercy (9:9–13//Mark 2:13–17); (4) Hos 6:6 added to Jesus' appeal to God's mercy again (12:1–8//Mark 2:23–28); (5) Isa 42:1–4 added to Jesus' hope to the Gentiles (12:16–21//Mark 3:12); (6) Ps 78:2 added to Jesus' teaching in Parables (13:34–35//Mark 4:33–34).

[39] Matthew 4:8; 5:1; 8:1; 17:1, 9, 20; 21:21; 24:16; 28:16 are occurrences of mountains that seem to echo various aspects of Mount Sinai and the Exodus.

[40] In addition, Jesus' Eschatological Discourse can be connected to Jesus' Torah Discourse: (1) same group of people—the crowds and the disciples—are found at the beginning of the two discourses (5:1; 23:1; cf. 13:36; 14:15, 19, 22; 15:32–33, 36); (2) setting of a mountain acts as an *inclusio* bracketing both discourses (5:1; 8:1; 24:16; 26:30); (3) combination of blessings and curses links the two discourses with Matt 5–7 beginning with blessings and 23–25 starting with woes (cf. Luke 6:20–26 has blessings and curses together); (4) wisdom material with metaphors of two ways, parables of warning and judgment join both discourses; and (5) both discourses are larger blocks of Jesus' teaching and roughly the same size.

[41] For Matthew as apologetic, see Lindars, *New Testament Apologetic*. For occurrences of Jesus quoting or alluding to prophetic texts of the Hebrew Bible see Dale C. Allison Jr., *Constructing Jesus: Memory, Imagination, and History*, reprint (Grand Rapids: Baker Academic, 2010), 79–82.

Similarly, the Qumran community believed they represented the embodiment of biblical Israel and therefore possessed the true meaning of the revelation at Sinai and all subsequent revelations to Moses.[42] One way that the community bridged this gap was to envision its legislative activity as the most recent stage in the progressive revelation of law (1QS 5:7–13):

> The community believed that Moses received an initial one-time revelation of the Torah on Sinai. The interpretation of the Torah and the formulation of post-biblical law were disclosed to successive generations through a series of later revelations. The community viewed itself as the current beneficiary of this revelation. Its leaders, most notably the Teacher of Righteousness, were regarded as inspired individuals who interpreted the Torah and formulated law based on their status as recipients of legislative revelation. The Qumran rule books represent the record of the legislative activity of these inspired individuals during nightly study sessions. For the Qumran community, revelation serves as the source of all law. The members regarded Moses as both a lawgiver and a prophet and considered his lawgiving role to be directly related to his prophetic status as God's intermediary. Indeed, the vast majority of Jews in the Second Temple period shared this view of Moses.[43]

Correspondingly, Matthew connects Moses, Sinai, and Torah with Jesus—his discourses and mountain experiences—as the most recent period in the progressive revelation of Torah and participation in Mosaic Discourse (cf. 5:17–19). Along this on-going process, Matthew rewrites Mosaic Torah with Jesus sitting on a mountain and instructing his community and context about communal practices of legislation, ethics, and worship (Matt 5–7; 8:1).[44]

In addition, Torah is blended with wisdom. When the Mosaic Torah was not a sufficient guide for ordinary life, it was rewritten and blended with wisdom traditions. This can be seen in Baruch 4 and Sirach 24 (cf. Wis 18).[45]

Bar 4:1

She [Wisdom] is the book of the commandments of God, and the law that endures forever. All who hold her fast will live, and those who forsake her will die.

---

[42] Alex P. Jassen, "The Presentation of the Ancient Prophets as Lawgivers at Qumran," *JBL* 127 (2008): 307–37 (307 n. 1).
[43] Jassen, "Ancient Prophets," 307–308.
[44] Ethics and communal practices are emphasized through almsgiving, prayer, and fasting with various features of wisdom: judging, searching, and the golden rule, as well as two ways (gates, roads, trees and fruit, and building; cf. Prov 9:1–18).
[45] Ben Sira is a rewriting of Torah with Wisdom. See E. Earle Ellis, "The Old Testament Canon in the Early Church," in *Mikra: Text, Translation, Reading and Interpretation of the Hebrew Bible in Ancient Judaism and Early Christianity*, ed. M. Jan Mulder (Philadelphia: Fortress Press, 1988), 653–90, esp. 687–88.

Sir 24:23

All this [Wisdom] is the book of the covenant of the Most High God, the law which Moses commanded us as an inheritance of the congregations of Jacob.

Beginning Jesus' Torah Discourse are nine beatitudes (μακάριος) that express God's favour and reward. They are not only implicit imperatives but are also identity markers for those who are in the kingdom of heaven indicating an eschatological reversal and a transformation of the present situation (cf. 11:2-6). Also, they exhort behaviour in accordance to God's justice (cf. Isa 61; Ps 37), revealing the way of wisdom that observes the Torah (Pss 1:1-2; 33:12; 119:1-2; 144:15) with the several choices between life or death: (1) two gates and two roads, (2) two trees and two fruits, and (3) two builders with one being wise and another being foolish. Therefore, Jesus' Torah Discourse directs the Matthean community to the way of wisdom that leads to life rather than the way of folly that leads to death (Prov 8; cf. Matt 7:13, 19). Furthermore, the beatitudes, in comparing them with Jewish authoritative traditions, have immediacy as their four characteristics imply: (1) they are declarative statements; (2) they function in ritual; (3) they are eschatologically orientated as well as in the present; and (4) they are connected with ethics.[46]

In sum, Matthew rewrites Mosaic Torah with wisdom traditions (blessings, two ways and parables) to bring Torah into the present and into Matthew's context (re-presenting Sinai): beatitudes (5:3-11), the two gates and two ways (7:13-14), the two trees (7:17-20), and the parable of the wise and foolish builders (7:24-27).

6. Continuity and divine revelation

Associating Jesus with the figure of Moses and with Torah, Matthew as part of the Mosaic Discourse in Second Temple Judaism provides continuity with past Jewish traditions. Although Moses is only explicitly mentioned seven times (8:4; 17:3, 4; 19:7, 8; 22:24; 23:2), Matthew contains many Mosaic elements and allusions woven throughout its narrative to direct our attention unmistakably to the figure of Moses.[47] Dale Allison lists seven Mosaic typologies in Matthew; however, three more can be added for a total of ten.[48]

1. infancy narrative (Matt 1–2; Exod 1:1–2:10)
2. crossing of water (Matt 3:13–17; Exod 14:10–31)
3. wilderness temptation (Matt 4:1–11; Exod 16:1–17:7)
4. mountain of lawgiving (Matt 5–7; Exod 19:1–23:33)

---

[46] *Joseph and Aseneth* 16:7-8; Sir 48; Tob 12:6; *2 En.* 42:6-14; 4Q525 has 8 or 10 beatitudes in a 3×3 or 2×4+1 construction.
[47] Dale C. Allison Jr., *The New Moses* (Philadelphia, PA: Fortress Press, 1993), 137–270.
[48] Allision (*The New Moses*, 268) also adds the possibilities of feeding stories (14:13–22; 15:29–39), the entry to Jerusalem (21:1–17), and the last supper (26:17–25).

5. reciprocal knowledge of God (Matt 11:25–30; Exod 33:1–23)
6. transfiguration (Matt 17:1–9; Exod 34:29–35)
7. commission of successor (Matt 28:16–20; Deut 31:7–9; Josh 1:1–9)

Eight, the ten plagues and the exodus from Egypt seems to be a type for Jesus performing ten miracles (especially the herd of swine [legion] drowning in water) (8:2–9:34): (1) Jesus cleanses a leper (8:1–4); (2) Jesus heals a centurion's servant (8:5–13); (3) Jesus heals Peter's mother-in-law and others (8:14–17); (4) Jesus calms wind and sea (8:23–27): (5) Jesus heals the Gadarene demoniacs (8:28–34); (6) Jesus heals a paralytic (9:2–8); (7) Jesus heals a woman suffering from haemorrhaging (9:20–22); (8) Jesus raises girl from dead (9:18–19; 23–26); (9) Jesus heals two blind men (9:27–31); and (10) Jesus heals a demoniac who was mute (9:32–34).[49] Nine, Jesus discusses Moses' significance and authority with "the seat of Moses" (23:2–3) and his condemnation of the scribes and Pharisees. Ten, Moses at Mount Sinai is alluded to in Jesus' many mountain appearances when he is in a sitting posture. This alludes to the giving of the Torah and forming God's covenant people (5:1 [8:1]; 15:29; 24:3; 28:16; cf. 4:8; 14:23; 17:1, 9). Jesus' Torah Discourse is a rewriting of Torah providing instructions and legislations.

In Matthew, Jesus' association with Moses serves to authorize Jesus' teaching as divine revelation (inspired interpretation) in continuity with previous revelations (23:1–12; 28:18; cf. 7:29; 9:8; 21:23–27). Both Jesus' Torah Discourse and Eschatological Discourse including his parables of judgment (Matt 24) suggests continuity and the ongoing progressive revelation of Torah.

Moreover, this continuity coincides with Matthew's use of the *Last Days* (i.e., as scriptural texts and prophecies are fulfilled in Jesus). Likewise in the Dead Sea Scrolls, Alex Jassen lists Dead Sea Scrolls that combine the Torah with this aspect of prophetic and progressive revelation.[50] Therefore, the community's legislative program—system of lawgiving—was a continuation of the prophetic word from the ancient prophets. The prophets rewrite the Torah.[51] Prophetic instruction, grounded

---

[49] See Allison, *The New Moses*, 208–13. Cf. B. W. Bacon, *Studies in Matthew* (New York: Henry Holt, 1930), 187–89.

[50] Jassen ("Ancient Prophets," 310) states: "Qumran documents the ancient prophet's juridical responsibilities within the framework of the community's model for the formation and development of postbiblical law. Prophets in the Hebrew Bible rarely appear as lawgivers. In contrast, the Qumran texts routinely represent the ancient prophets as mediators of divinely revealed law, sometimes in cooperation with Moses and sometimes independent of Moses." (1) 1QS begins with an exhortation to members of the community to do what is good and right as God commanded through Moses and through all his servants the prophets (1QS 1:2–3). The language of doing what is good and right is from Deuteronomy and often refers to observing the Torah (6:18; 12:28; 13:19; cf. 11Q19 59:16–17; 4QMMT C31). (2) 1QS 8:15–16 introduces the prophets and their role of illuminating the performance of the Torah and providing instructions on how to properly observe it. The prophets, in sectarian writings, appear with great regularity as the mediators of divine law (1QS 8:15–16). Moses and the classical prophets are the first two stages in the revelation of law to Israel. The passage begins by introducing the Torah of Moses. (3) CD 5:21–6:1 and 4Q166 2:1–6 identify the prophets as the mediators of God's commandments. (4) 4Q390 2 i 4–5 and 4Q375 lines 1–4, non-sectarian documents, have the prophets mediating God's commandments. (5) 4Q380–381, non-canonical Psalms, specifically 4Q381 69:4, illustrate the prophetic role of instruction and teaching.

[51] See John R. Levison, *The Spirit in First-Century Judaism*, AGJU 29 (Leiden: Brill, 1997).

in the interpretation of the Torah itself, complements Moses' initial formation of the Torah (4Q381; cf. Neh 8:8; 13; 9:20).[52] Therefore, as Eileen Schuller indicates, the prophets are Torah instructors (ללמד) with the root למד ("to teach") being a common Deuteronomic term associated with Moses (Deut 4:1, 5, 14, 5:28, 6:1).[53] Through revelatory experiences, the prophets continue the task of prophetic lawgiving begun with Moses at Sinai, making the Torah intelligible and applicable in the present setting.

Correspondingly, a unique and characteristic feature in Matthew is its explicit fulfillment quotations from the Hebrew Scriptures.[54] Eleven fulfillment quotations illustrate the continuity of Matthew to previous Jewish authoritative traditions.[55] Consequently, although Matthew's quotations are not pesher-like and should be classified differently due to their form, they do function like Qumran *pesharim* as they both contemporize prophetic texts.[56] Furthermore, alongside dream-vision interpretation, Matthew's fulfillment quotations are divine revelation.[57]

In Matthew, Jesus as a figure of Moses instructs and interprets the Mosaic Torah for the Matthean community (5:17–19; Isa 2:3; cf. 30:20–21).[58] This is not a new Torah but emphasizes Matthew's internalization and contextualization of the Mosaic Torah through rewriting to legislate and judge (11:13; cf. Luke 16:16).[59] Matthew portrays

---

[52] In 4Q390 line 5–6, God declares that he will speak with the returnees and send them commandments (line 6; cf. Deut 5:28). God entrusts Moses, the first lawgiver, with the responsibility of transmitting divine law to Israel.

[53] See Eileen Schuller, *Qumran Cave 4.VI: Poetical and Liturgical Texts Part I*, ed. Esther Eshel et al., DJD XI (Oxford: Clarendon, 1998), 151. In *HALOT* 1:531, למד refers to formal instruction in wisdom or in a skill, except for in Deuteronomy.

[54] Matthew 3:3 is not unique to Matthew (cf. Mark 1:3; Luke 3:4; John 1:23). These quotations have two features that distinguish them from other quotations in the New Testament: (1) they occur as narrative comments outside Jesus' story and (2) contain an introductory statement using the lexemes "fulfill" (πληρόω) and "prophet" (προφήτης). For example, Matt 1:23, Τοῦτο δὲ ὅλον γέγονεν ἵνα πληρωθῇ τὸ ῥηθὲν ὑπὸ κυρίου διὰ τοῦ προφήτου λέγοντος, and 4:14, ἵνα πληρωθῇ τὸ ῥηθὲν διὰ Ἡσαΐου τοῦ προφήτου λέγοντος, are typical for fulfillment quotations with minor changes.

[55] (1) Matthew 1:22–23 quotes Isa 7:14; (2) Matt 2:15b quotes Hos 11:1; (3) Matt 2:17–18 quotes Jer 31:15 (identifies the prophet Jeremiah); (4) Matt 2:23 quotes Judg 13:5 or Isa 11:1; (5) Matt 3:3 quotes Isa 40:3 (identifies the prophet Isaiah); (6) Matt 4:15–16 quotes Isa 8:23–9:1 (identifies the prophet Isaiah); (7) Matt 8:17 quotes Isa 53:4 (identifies the prophet Isaiah); (8) Matt 12:17–21 quotes Isa 42:1–4 (identifies the prophet Isaiah); (9) Matt 13:35 quotes Ps 78:2; (10) Matt 21:4–5 quotes Zech 9:9 (cf. Isa 62:11); (11) Matt 27:9–10 quotes Zech 11:12–13; cf. Jer 18:1–2; 32:6–9 (identifies the prophet Jeremiah; cf. Matt 26:15).

[56] *Peshar* can be understood as divine revelation that contemporizes an authoritative text for its intended audience (1QpHab 8:8–11; cf. Hab 2:5–6). See Daniel A. Machiela, "The Qumran Pesharim as Biblical Commentaries: Historical Context and Lines of Development," *DSD* 19 (2012): 313–62; Alex P. Jassen, "The Pesharim and the Rise of Commentary in Early Jewish Scriptural Interpretation," *DSD* 19 (2012): 363–98.

[57] See George J. Brooke, "Aspects of Matthew's Use of Scripture," in *Teacher for All Generations*, ed. Eric F. Mason et al., JSJSup 153 (Leiden: Brill, 2012), 2:821–38, and "Prophets and Prophecy in the Qumran Scrolls and the New Testament," in *Text, Thought, and Practice in Qumran and Early Christianity*, ed. Ruth A. Clements and Daniel R. Schwartz; STDJ 84 (Leiden: Brill, 2009), 47; Kyung S. Baek, "Prophecy and Divination in the Gospel of Matthew," in *Reading the Bible in Ancient Traditions and Modern Editions*, ed. Andrew B. Perrin, Kyung S. Baek, and Daniel K. Falk; SBLEJL 47 (Atlanta: SBL Press, 2017), 653–78 (672–74).

[58] Messianic figures and claimants copied the Torah of Moses (*J.W.* 2:258–60; *Ant.* 20:97–99). The messiah also employs it with his mouth to destroy his enemies (Isa 11; cf. *4 Ezra* 13:10; *Pss Sol* 17:36; *1 En* 51:3).

[59] See Alistair I. Wilson, *When Will These Things Happen? A Study of Jesus as Judge in Matthew 21–25* (Eugene, OR: Wipf & Stock, 2004).

Jesus as a Torah interpreter, who represents Mosaic authority and divine revelation as he sits on Moses' seat (21:9; cf. Deut 18:15; Matt 23:2–3). Furthermore, as Matthew rewrites Mosaic Torah with wisdom and prophetic traditions, he provides continuity from Mount Sinai to Jesus' Discourses on mountains (Matt 5–7; 23–25). Matthew's continuity is evident in Jesus' prophetic woes, eschatological signs, and parables of judgment.[60] Matthew saw himself in the on-going process of rewriting Mosaic Torah[61] in continuity with the prophets and their message about the *Last Days* as Jesus signals that the time is at hand in his teaching and ministry (3:2; 4:17; cf. 11:7–15). Matthew provides divine revelation and continuity from the past as it contextualizes past traditions (re-presenting Sinai).[62]

7. Conclusion

By identifying features of Mosaic Discourse and defining Matthew's rewriting process, this paper has attempted to firmly establish the Gospel of Matthew within the Mosaic Discourse of Second Temple Judaism. This placement confers to Matthew authority as Jesus interprets Mosaic Torah, authenticity as the Torah of Moses, immediacy as it re-presents Sinai, and continuity as God's divine revelation for a new community.

First, Matthew confers authority in rewriting the Mosaic Torah in Jesus' Torah Discourse (Matt 5–7). As authority is conferred from the older traditions of Moses and given to Jesus' interpretation, Matthew's rewriting gives authority on both old and new rewritten compositions. Second, Matthew is authenticated as the Torah of Moses with its five blocks of Jesus' teaching. By weaving together narrative and discourse, Matthew rewrites the Gospel of Mark within a Torah pattern from Genesis to Deuteronomy. This rewriting process intertwines ancient Jewish and newer Christian authoritative traditions together. Authenticity integrates truth-claims of Mosaic Torah for each successive generation.

Third, re-presenting Sinai brings immediacy to Matthew as it recontextualizes Moses at Sinai to his audience. Similarities between Jesus and Moses at Sinai postulate Matthew's place in Mosaic Discourse. Rewriting Torah and the making of God's people at Sinai contributes to the immediacy of the person and teachings of Jesus in Matthew. Fourth in continuity with ancient Jewish authoritative traditions, Matthew rewrites the Mosaic Torah as divine revelation. As Mosaic Discourse establishing

---

[60] This continuity is emphasized with not a letter or stroke will pass away, which refers to the actual text rather than the contents of the text in a general way. See Siam Bhayro, "Matthew 5:17–18 in the Light of Qumran Scribal Practice," in *Paratext and Megatext as Channels of Jewish and Christian Traditions: The Textual Markers of Contextualization*, ed. A. A. den Hollander, U. B. Schmid, and W. F. Smelik; Jewish and Christian Perspectives Series 6 (Leiden: Brill, 2003), 42–45.

[61] The general milieu of the times with its socio-historical factors contributed to Matthew's composition. The destruction of the Temple in 70 CE, and the increase in textualization and the promulgation of Torah (e.g. *4 Ezra* and *2 Baruch*). The Torah with the destruction of the temple may have gained added significance. In addition, the corruption of the temple may have placed added weight on the Torah written by scribes in the Second Temple period (CD 5:6–7; 1QS 8:1–10; *Pss. Sol.* 2:2–4; 8:11–13; *1 En* 12–16; 89:72–90:29; 91:11–13 and 93:8–10).

[62] See Brooke, "Hypertextuality," 43–64. Authority is conferred to the rewriting and to what is being rewritten.

Moses as the lawgiver and interpreter, Matthew identifies Jesus with the figure of Moses as lawgiver and interpreter of Torah.

In sum, Matthew participating in Mosaic Discourse rewrites ancient Jewish authoritative traditions for his current generation (authenticating and contextualizing past traditions) by blending text and traditions with contemporary interpretation and application. Therefore, as Matthew rewrites Mark within a Torah pattern, he writes both early Christian (Mark, Q and M) and ancient Jewish traditions (Torah) into a coherent composition procuring authority, authenticity, immediacy, and continuity.

Bibliography

Alexander, Philip S. "Retelling the Old Testament." Pages 99–121 in *It is Written: Scripture: Essays in Honour of Barnabas Lindars, SSF*. Edited by D. A. Carson and H. G. M. Williamson. Cambridge: Cambridge University Press, 1988.

Allison Jr., Dale C. *Constructing Jesus: Memory, Imagination, and History*. Reprint. Grand Rapids: Baker Academic, 2010.

Assmann, Jan. *Moses the Egyptian: The Memory of Egypt in Western Monotheism*. Cambridge, MA: Harvard University Press, 1997.

Bacon, B. W. "The Five Books of Matthew against the Jews." *The Expositor* 15 (1918): 67–97.

Baek, Kyung S. "Prophecy and Divination in the Gospel of Matthew." Pages 653–78 in *Reading the Bible in Ancient Traditions and Modern Editions*. Edited by Andrew B. Perrin, Kyung S. Baek, and Daniel K. Falk. SBLEJL 47. Atlanta: SBL Press, 2017.

Baker, David. "The Finger of God and the Forming of a Nation: The Origin and Purpose of the Decalogue." *TynBul* 56 (2005).

Bhayro, Siam. "Matthew 5:17–18 in the Light of Qumran Scribal Practice." Pages 37–48 in *Paratext and Megatext as Channels of Jewish and Christian Traditions: The Textual Markers of Contextualization*. Edited by August den Hollander, Ulrich Schmid, and Willem Smelik. Jewish and Christian Perspectives Series 6. Leiden: Brill, 2003.

Brooke, George J. "Aspects of Matthew's Use of Scripture." Pages 819–38 in *A Teacher for All Generations: Essays in Honor of James C. VanderKam*. Edited by Eric F. Mason, Samuel I. Thomas, Alison Schofield, and Eugene Ulrich. JSJSup 153. Leiden: Brill, 2012.

Brooke, George J. "Between Authority and Canon: The Significance of Reworking the Bible for Understanding the Canonical Process." Pages 85–104 in *Reworking the Bible: Apocryphal and Related Texts at Qumran: Proceedings of a Joint Symposium by the Orion Center for the study of the Dead Sea Scrolls and Associated Literature and the Hebrew University Institute for Advanced studies Research Group on Qumran, 15–17 January, 2002*. Edited By Esther G. Chazon, Devorah Dimant, and Ruth Clements. STDJ 53. Leiden: Brill, 2005.

Brooke, George J. "Genre Theory, Rewritten Bible and Pesher." *DSD* 17 (2010): 361–86.

Brooke, George J. "Hypertextuality and the 'Parabiblical' Dead Sea Scrolls." Pages 41–64 in *In the Second Degree: Paratextual Literature in Ancient Near Eastern and Ancient Mediterranean Culture and Its Reflection in Medieval Literature*. Edited by Philip Alexander, Armin Lange, and Renate Pillinger. Leiden: Brill, 2010.

Brooke, George J. "Prophets and Prophecy in the Qumran Scrolls and the New Testament." Pages 31–48 in *Text, Thought, and Practice in Qumran and Early Christianity*. Edited by Ruth Clements and Daniel R. Schwartz. STDJ 84. Leiden: Brill, 2009.

Brooke, George J. "Rewritten Bible." In *Encyclopedia of the Dead Sea Scrolls*. Edited by Lawrence H. Schiffman and James C. VanderKam. 2 vols. Oxford: Oxford University Press, 2000.

Brooke, George J. "Torah, Rewritten Torah and the Letter of Jude." Pages 180–93 in *The Torah in the New Testament: Papers Delivered at the Manchester-Lausanne Seminar of June 2008*. Edited by Michael Tait and Peter Oakes. LNTS 401. London: T&T Clark, 2019.

Carter, Warren. *Matthew: Storyteller, Interpreter, Evangelist*. Revised ed. Grand Rapids: Baker Academic, 2004.

Collins, Adela Y. *Mark*. Minneapolis, MN: Fortress Press, 2007.

Doodle, J. Andrew. *What was Mark for Matthew? An Examination of Matthew's Relationship and Attitude to his Primary Source*. WUNT 344. Tübingen: Mohr Siebeck, 2013.

Ellis, E. Earle. "The Old Testament Canon in the Early Church." Pages 653–90 in *Mikra: Text, Translation, Reading and Interpretation of the Hebrew Bible in Ancient Judaism and Early Christianity*. Edited by M. Jan Mulder. Philadelphia: Fortress Press, 1988.

Freund, Richard A. "The Decalogue in Early Judaism and Christianity." Pages 60–100 in *The Function of Scripture in Early Jewish and Christian Tradition*. Edited by C. A. Evans and J. A. Sanders. Sheffield: Sheffield Academic Press, 1988.

Friedman, Richard Elliott. "Torah (Pentateuch)." *ABD* 6:605–22.

Gamble, Harry Y. *Books and Readers in the Early Church: A History of Early Christian Texts*. New Haven: Yale University Press, 1995.

Harrington, Daniel J. "Palestinian Adaptations of Biblical Narratives and Prophecies: The Bible Rewritten (Narratives)." Pages 239–47 in *Early Judaism and its Modern Interpreters*. Edited by Robert A. Kraft and George W. E. Nickelsburg. Philadelphia, PA: Fortress Press, 1986.

Harrington, Daniel J. *The Gospel of Matthew*. Sacra Pagina 1. Collegeville, MN: Liturgical Press, 2007.

Jassen, Alex P. "The Pesharim and the Rise of commentary in Early Jewish Scriptural Interpretation." *DSD* 19 (2012): 363–98.

Jassen, Alex P. "The Presentation of the Ancient Prophets as Lawgivers at Qumran." *JBL* 127 (2008): 307–37.

Kümmel, W. Introduction to the New Testament. London: SCM Press, 1975.

Levison, John R. *The Spirit in First-Century Judaism*. AGJU 29; Leiden: Brill, 1997.

Machiela, Daniel A. "The Qumran Pesharim as Biblical Commentaries: Historical Context and Lines of Development." *DSD* 19 (2012): 313–62.

Mendenhall, G. E. "Ancient Oriental and Biblical Law." *BA* 17 (1954): 25–46.

Menken, Maarten J. J. "Deuteronomy in Matthew's Gospel." Pages 42–62 in *Deuteronomy in the New Testament*. Edited by Steve Moyise and Maarten J. J. Menken. LNTS 358. London: T&T Clark, 2007.

Miller, Patrick D. "The Place of the Decalogue in the Old Testament and Its Law." *Int* 43 (1989): 229–42.

Najman, Hindy. *Seconding Sinai: The Development of Mosaic Discourse in Second Temple Judaism*. Supplements to the Journal for the Study of Judaism 77. Atlanta: SBL, 2003.

Petersen, Anders Klostergaard. "Textual Fidelity, Elaboration, Supersession or Encroachment? Typological Reflections on the Phenomenon of Rewritten Scripture." Pages 11–48 in *Rewritten Bible after Fifty Years: Texts, Terms, or Technique? A Last Dialogue with Geza Vermes*. Edited by József Zsengellér. JSJSup 166. Leiden: Brill, 2014.

Sanders, E. P. "When Is a Law a Law? The Case of Jesus and Paul." Pages 139–58 in *Religion and Law: Biblical-Judaic and Islamic Perspectives*. Edited by Edwin B. Firmage, Bernard G. Weiss, and John W. Welch. Winona Lake, IN: Eisenbrauns, 1990.

Sanders, E. P. *Jesus and Judaism*. London: SCM Press, 1985.

Sanders, E. P. *Paul and Palestinian Judaism: A Comparison of Patterns of Religion*. Philadelphia: Fortress Press, 1977.

Schuller, Eileen. *Qumran Cave 4.VI: Poetical and Liturgical Texts Part I*. Edited by Esther Chazon et al. DJD XI. Oxford: Clarendon, 1998.

Sim, David C. "Matthew's Use of Mark: Did Matthew Intend to Supplement or to Replace His Primary Source?" *NTS* 57 (2011): 176–92.

Vermes, Geza. *Scripture and Tradition in Judaism: Haggadic Studies*. 2nd ed. StPB 4. Leiden: Brill, 1973.

Vermes, Geza. *Les Manuscrits du désert de Juda*. Paris: Desclée de Brouwer, 1953.

Wilson, Alistair I. *When Will These Things Happen? A Study of Jesus as Judge in Matthew 21–25*. Eugene, OR: Wipf & Stock, 2004.

Chapter 16

Deliverance into the Coming Kingdom of God: Exodus Motifs in 1 Thessalonians*

Stephen Anthony Cummins

1. Introduction

This essay explores ways in which 1 Thessalonians employs various exodus-related motifs as Paul provides apostolic oversight and pastoral guidance to the church in Thessalonica. It is argued that Paul locates the Thessalonian believers within an unfolding divine economy that includes Israel's exodus and exile, Messiah Jesus' redemptive death and resurrection, the Thessalonians' Spirit-guided continuing participation in the people of God, and ultimate ingathering at the eschatological coming of the kingdom of God. The most notable motifs entailed—such as evocative language and imagery, typological correspondences, and certain resonant themes—will be explored in relation to four substantive features of the letter: (1) the gospel of God and the Thessalonians' initial deliverance; (2) Paul's nurture of the Thessalonian community; (3) his exhortation to conduct themselves as holy covenant people fitted for God's glorious kingdom; and (4) Paul's response to concerns over their ultimate entrance into the eschatological kingdom of God, specifically the destiny of the dead in Christ and the arrival of the day of the Lord. Together this indicates that Paul includes this elect, emerging, and at times hard-pressed community within the unfolding Israel-specific and yet creation-wide purposes of God, from their first to final deliverance.

---

* This essay originated as a paper presented at the Canadian Society of Biblical Studies annual meeting (University of Saskatchewan, Saskatoon, 2007), now revisited, revised, and expanded, and offered in honor of my colleague Larry J. Perkins. Among ever-expanding studies on 1 Thessalonians, see the recent helpful discussion of its text, context, themes, and interpretation in Nijay K. Gupta, *1 & 2 Thessalonians*, Zondervan Critical Introductions to the New Testament 13 (Grand Rapids: Zondervan, 2019).

2. The gospel of God and the Thessalonians' initial deliverance

It is readily recognized that Paul variously interacts with the book of Exodus and exodus-related motifs in his writings, especially in Romans, 1 and 2 Corinthians, and Galatians.[1] Moreover Paul's modest but notable use of the Old Testament in 1 Thessalonians has also been well considered.[2] However, little attention has been given to certain embedded yet discernible exodus-related motifs in this important early letter. That such elements are operative can first be seen in Paul's initial prayerful and powerful thanksgiving at 1 Thess 1:2–10. Here the apostle recalls the Thessalonians' remarkable reception of the gospel, and their inclusion among the rescued, elect, and covenant people of the living and true God. In this way, and at times amid affliction, the Thessalonians are following their spiritual forebears, participating in a lineage that includes the prophets, Jesus, fellow believers in Judea, and Paul and his companions (cf. 1:6; 2:14–15). They are journeying onwards in faith, love, and steadfast hope (1:3). Like faithful Israel called to be wise and discerning among the nations (e.g., Deut 4:5–8), they provide a steadfast example (τύπον) to believers throughout Macedonia, Achaia, and beyond, and so exhibit the glory of God before a watching wider world (1:7–8).[3] And they await their full and final redemption with the return of the Lord Jesus, Messiah and Son of God (1:10).

The gospel of God that Paul proclaimed upon his "entrance, visit" (εἴσοδον, 1:9; cf. 2:1), and which the Thessalonians accepted as the "word of God," warrants further consideration.[4] From the opening salutation it is clear that fundamentally it concerns "God the Father and the Lord Jesus Christ" (1:1).[5] God as "Father" is a motif

---

[1] Among recent overviews, see David M. Westfall, "Exodus in the Pauline Letters," in *Exodus in the New Testament*, ed. Seth M. Ehorn, LNTS 633 (London: T&T Clark, 2021), 109–26; Bryan D. Estelle, *Echoes of Exodus: Tracing a Biblical Motif* (Downers Grove, IL: IVP Academic, 2018), 263–85; Daniel Lynwood Smith, "The Uses of 'New Exodus' in New Testament Scholarship: Preparing a Way through the Wilderness," *CurBR* 14 (2016): 207–43, especially 216–20; and Craig A. Evans, "Exodus in the New Testament: Patterns of Revelation and Redemption," in *The Book of Exodus: Composition, Reception, and Interpretation*, ed. Thomas Dozeman, Craig A. Evans, and Joel N. Lohr (Leiden: Brill, 2014), 440–64, especially 451–57. Notable recent monographs include Carla Swafford Works, *The Church in the Wilderness: Paul's Use of Exodus Traditions in 1 Corinthians*, WUNT 2/379 (Tübingen: Mohr Siebeck, 2014); Rodrigo J. Morales, *The Spirit and the Restoration of Israel: New Exodus and New Creation Motifs in Galatians*, WUNT 2/282 (Tübingen: Mohr Siebeck, 2010); and, earlier, Sylvia C. Keesmaat, *Paul and his Story: (Re)Interpreting the Exodus Tradition*, JSNTSup 181 (Sheffield: Sheffield Academic, 1999), on Rom 8:14–39 and Galatians.

[2] See, for example, E. Elizabeth Johnson, "Paul's Reliance on Scripture in 1 Thessalonians," in *Paul and Scripture: Continuing the Conversation*, ed. Christopher D. Stanley (Atlanta: SBL Press, 2012), 143–62; and Jeffrey A. D. Weima, "1–2 Thessalonians," in *Commentary on the New Testament Use of the Old Testament*, ed. G. K. Beale and D. A. Carson (Grand Rapids: Baker Academic, 2007), 871–89; and the many commentaries on 1 Thessalonians.

[3] 1 Thessalonians 1:7–8 may be read in relation to LXX Isa 66 and the redeemed righteous of Israel who declare God's glory among the nations; see Gary S. Shogren, *1 & 2 Thessalonians*, ZECNT 13 (Grand Rapids: Zondervan, 2012), 69.

[4] On "gospel" (εὐαγγέλιον), compare 1 Thess 1:5; 2:2, 4, 8, 9; 3:2, and the use of the cognate verb εὐαγγελίζω at Isa 40:9; 52:7; and 61:1, in connection with the announcement of the salvation of Jerusalem and Israel.

[5] Here the English translation of the biblical text typically follows that of the NRSV; on occasion, as indicated, also used is *A New Translation of the Septuagint* (NETS), ed. Albert Pietersma and Benjamin G. Wright (Oxford: Oxford University Press, 2007).

found rarely in the Old Testament, but notably in "contexts where the redemption-restoration of Israel was in view."[6] Perhaps most significant is Isa 63:15–16 (cf. 64:8), where "the 'Fatherhood' of God [is] defined in terms of making himself known as 'Redeemer,'" with the exodus as the paradigmatic reference point (Isa 63:7–14).[7] God's identity as "Lord [YHWH]" over all things and his covenant relationship with his people is inextricably related to his presence and activity in the exodus: "You shall not profane my holy name, that I may be sanctified among the people of Israel: I am the LORD; I sanctify you, I who brought you out of the land of Egypt to be your God; I am the LORD" (Lev 22:32–33). It is also at the exodus that God instructs Moses to inform Pharaoh that "Israel is my firstborn son" (Exod 4:22). In 1 Thessalonians Paul identifies Messiah Jesus as God's son and indeed as sharing in his Father's lordship, and as the one in whom the Thessalonians' deliverance, holy identity, and destiny lies.[8]

Paul's opening comments culminate by explicating the gospel with particular reference to the Thessalonians' initial deliverance. He remarks, "you turned (ἐπεστρέψατε) to God from idols, to serve a living and true God, and to wait (ἀναμένειν) for his Son from heaven, whom he raised from the dead—Jesus, who rescues (τὸν ῥυόμενον) us from the wrath that is coming" (1:9b–10). God is here essentially identified as the one who delivered Israel out of Egypt and before whom they are to have no other gods (Deut 5:6–7). Moreover, Paul's gospel confronts the widespread polytheism with a Jewish monotheism delineated in terms that include Jesus who is God's Son, and who—via his risen and returning lordship (cf. 1:1; 2:19; 3:11–13; 4:15–17)—delivers the Thessalonians from the wrath that is the counterpart to God's full and final redemption of his holy people (1:10; cf. 2:16; 5:9).

A number of illuminating correlations may be made here. First, Paul later writes of his new covenant ministry among the Corinthians (2 Cor 3), whom he regards as themselves a letter written "with the Spirit of the living God" (2 Cor 3:3), and notes that "when one turns (ἐπιστρέψῃ) to the Lord, the veil [of Moses] is removed" (2 Cor 3:16; cf. Exod 34:29–35).[9] The Corinthians may thus be transformed "from one degree of glory to another" (2 Cor 3:18). Second, that the Thessalonians have been "rescued" from the coming wrath evokes Paul's dramatic exclamation, "Wretched man that I am! Who will rescue me (τίς με ῥύσεται) from this body of death?" (Rom 7:24). This is a remarkable summary statement of the condition described in Romans 7, arguably a depiction of humanity's captivity to sin with particular reference to

---

[6] Todd A. Wilson, "Wilderness Apostasy and Paul's Portrayal of the Crisis in Galatians," NTS 50 (2004): 550–71 (554).
[7] Quotation from Wilson, "Wilderness Apostasy," 554 n. 18, who also notes Deut 32:5–20; Isa 1:2; 64:4–12; Jer 3:12–19; 31:9; Hos 11:1–2, 10–11, and other references.
[8] See, for example, 1 Thess 1:1, 10; 3:11–4:2; the lordship language at various points in 4:13–5:11 and 5:23–24. Moreover, Paul thus implicitly advises the Roman emperor—just as Moses did Pharaoh—against any rival claims to God's rule. Compare the account of Paul's initial Thessalonian mission in Acts 17:1–9, including charges that he acted "contrary to the decrees of the emperor, saying that there is another king named Jesus" (17:7).
[9] On the Exodus narrative (and Numbers) in 2 Cor 3, see Westfall, "Exodus in the Pauline Letters," 116–19, including a discussion of 2 Cor 3:16 and LXX Exod 34:34, 118–19.

Israel's struggles to be the Torah-obedient covenant faithful people of God.[10] The rescued Thessalonians can confidently await their ultimate redemption at the return of Jesus. Third, Paul's use of the verb "wait" (ἀναμένειν), a New Testament *hapax legomenon*, bears comparison to Judith's reproach of the elders of Bethulia who want to surrender to Holofernes (Jdt 7:23-27; cf. Exod 17:1-7), instructing them rather to call on God "while we wait for his deliverance" (ἀναμένοντες τὴν παρ' αὐτοῦ σωτηρίαν, Jdt 8:17). To do otherwise is to test God (Jdt 8:12-13), risk the capture of all Judea, enslavement, and disgrace among the nations (Jdt 8:21-23; cf. Exod 32:11-14). Paul, however, can commend the rescued and covenant faithful Thessalonians for remaining steadfast, even under duress, worthy witnesses to the wider world, as they await their full and final divine deliverance with the coming of God's Son, the Lord Jesus.

3. Paul's nurture of the Thessalonian community

Paul provides an extended recollection of his initial "entrance, visit" (εἴσοδον, 2:1; cf. 1:9) and early ministry among the Thessalonians (2:1-16). He asserts that his initial presence and appeal was without "deceit" (πλάνης), "impurity" (ἀκαθαρσίας), or "guile" (δόλῳ, 2:3). Here Paul locates himself in the Jewish prophetic tradition by using language which figures prominently in the LXX of Isaiah 40-55 in association with Israel's liberation from exile, though perhaps now recast in rhetorically persuasive terms which would also have resonated with his wider Greco-Roman audience.[11] As such, like Jeremiah he acted as one "tested/approved" (δοκιμάζω) by God (cf. Jer 11:20), and was entrusted with the gospel, which he proclaimed "not to please mortals, but to please God who tests our hearts" (2:4).

Paul insists that he and his companions did not seek human "praise/glory" (δόξαν, 2:6).[12] Indeed, while they might have exerted their status as apostles of Christ, they acted with self-giving humility (2:7-12). At this point Paul employs a collocation of

---

[10] The verb ῥύομαι is used in reference to the exodus only four times out of more than two hundred instances in the LXX, at Exod 5:23; 6:6; 14:30; and Ps 22:4; so Seth M. Ehorn, "Exodus in the Disputed Pauline Letters," in Ehorn, ed., *Exodus in the New Testament*, 127-45 (140), referencing Douglas J. Moo, *The Letters to the Colossians and to Philemon*, PNTC (Grand Rapids: Eerdmans, 2008), 103 n. 94. Ehorn (139-40) offers interesting comments on the language of Col 1:12-14 and Exod 6:6-8. In Rom 7 echoes of Israel's exodus experience include the giving of the decalogue and law (Rom 7:7; Exod 20:17; Deut 5:21); possibly the golden calf incident at Mt. Sinai (Rom 7:8-9; Exod 32); the issue of covenant life and its opposite, sin and death (Rom 7:10-11; Lev 18:5; Deut 30:15-20), with sin incurring God's wrath (e.g., Exod 32:7-14). That for Paul this is not the end of Israel's story is evident in his remarks at Rom 11:25-32, which includes a mixed quotation from Isa 59:20-21 and 27:9: "Out of Zion will come the Deliverer (ὁ ῥυόμενος)" (11:26c). On Exodus and the exodus in Romans, see Westfall, "Exodus in the New Testament," 120-25, and more extensively on Rom 8:14-39 in particular, see Keesmaat, *Paul and his Story*, 54-154.

[11] See William Horbury, "I Thessalonians ii.3 as Rebutting the Charge of False Prophecy," *JTS* 33 (1982): 492-508.

[12] Abraham Malherbe observes: "Mostly, *doxa* has to do with Paul's ministry (2 Cor 3:7-11, ...cf. 4:7), which he carries out for God's glory (1 Cor 10:31; cf. 2 Cor 1:20; 4:17; cf. 8:19; 2 Thess 1:12)," *The Letters to the Thessalonians: A New Translation with Introduction and Commentary*, AB 32B (New York: Doubleday, 2000), 143.

familial images—child, nurse, and father—which have been variously investigated,[13] but which may make more sense when viewed in relation to certain exodus-related motifs. On the first of these, a number of scholars have argued persuasively on both external and internal grounds in favor of "infants/children" (νήπιοι) over "gentle" (ἤπιοί, at 2:7b), with the reasonable suggestion that Paul uses this metaphor to indicate childlike innocence among the Thessalonians.[14] However, an even more substantive denotation may be considered. In the Synoptic Gospels the term refers to the righteous recipients of God's wisdom (Matt 11:25//Luke 10:21; Matt 21:16). In Wis 10:15-21 we are informed that wisdom "delivered" (ἐρρύσατο) a holy and blameless Israel out of Egypt (10:15), enabled "the righteous" to plunder the ungodly at the sea, "and made the tongues of infants (εἶπον) speak clearly" (10:20-21). Earlier the prophet Hosea recalls God's parental love for Israel at the time of the exodus and ensuing wilderness wanderings: "For Israel was an infant (νήπιων), and I loved him" (11:1, NETS). It is Israel's law which is "making infants wise" (σοφίζουσα νήπια, LXX Ps 18:9 [19:7], NETS; cf. Ps 118:130 [119:130]). Reading Paul's remark in relation to these thematically interrelated antecedents, he may be asserting that while he and his companions could have exerted their apostolic authority (1 Thess 2:6), they lawfully and faithfully conducted themselves among the rescued and righteous children of God in Thessalonica, just as he urges them to remain "holy" and "blameless" until the final coming and deliverance of the Lord Jesus (3:13).

Paul then employs the first of two parental metaphors (here technically similes): he and his coworkers cared for the Thessalonians "like a nurse (τροφὸς) tenderly caring for her own children" (2:7c).[15] While Abraham J. Malherbe has persuaded many that this nurse metaphor has a Cynic background,[16] some such as Beverly Roberts Gaventa have drawn attention to Numbers 11 as another resonant reference point.[17] This chapter begins an extended account of Israel's disobedience and rebellion, and records Moses' lament to God concerning the burdens of leadership (Num 11:10-15). This

---

[13] See, for example, the wide-ranging monographs by Trevor J. Burke, *Family Matters: A Socio-Historical Study of Kinship Metaphors in 1 Thessalonians*, JSNTSup 247 (London: T&T Clark, 2003), especially 130-62; and Jennifer Houston McNeel, *Paul as Infant and Nursing Mother: Metaphor, Rhetoric, and Identity in 1 Thessalonians 2:5-8*, ECL 12 (Atlanta: SBL Press, 2014). On Paul's use of maternal imagery in his letters, see also Beverly Roberts Gaventa, *Our Mother Saint Paul* (Louisville: Westminster John Knox Press, 2007).

[14] Compare Stephen Fowl, "A Metaphor in Distress: A Reading of ΝΗΠΙΟΙ in 1 Thessalonians 2.7," *NTS* 36 (1990): 469-73; Beverly Roberts Gaventa, "Apostles As Babes and Nurses in 1 Thessalonians 2:7," in *Faith and History: Essays in Honor of Paul W. Meyer*, ed. John T. Carroll, Charles H. Cosgrove, and E. Elizabeth Johnson (Atlanta: Scholars Press, 1990), 193-207 (194-98); and also her *Our Mother Saint Paul*, 18-20; Jeffrey A. D. Weima, "'But We Became Infants Among You': The Case for ΝΗΠΙΟΙ in 1 Thess 2.7," *NTS* 46 (2000): 547-64; and similarly his *1-2 Thessalonians*, BECNT (Grand Rapids: Baker Academic, 2014), 180-87; and McNeel, *Paul as Infant and Nursing Mother*, 30-43.

[15] Weima makes a strong case for repunctuating 2:7-8, so that the infant metaphor concludes at 2:7b, and the nursing mother metaphor then begins at 2:7c, carrying on into 2:8; see his "'But We Became Infants Among You,'" 554-56, and *1-2 Thessalonians*, 184-85; see also McNeel, *Paul as Infant and Nursing Mother*, 43-47.

[16] Abraham J. Malherbe, "'Gentle as a Nurse': The Cynic Background to 1 Thess. 2," *NovT* 12 (1970): 203-17.

[17] Gaventa, "Apostles As Babes and Nurses in 1 Thessalonians 2:7," 202; and *Our Mother Saint Paul*, 23-24. See also McNeel, *Paul as Infant and Nursing Mother*, 108-11.

includes his remarks: "Did I conceive all this people? Did I give birth to them, that you should say to me, 'Carry them in your bosom, as a nurse carries a suckling child,' to the land that you promised on oath to their ancestors?" (Num 11:12). Although the LXX uses τιθηνός rather than τροφός, and Moses is complaining to God while Paul is not, the correlation remains intriguing. Among the Thessalonians, Paul is like a burden-bearing Moses figure, maternally nursing his nascent congregation, as he labored night and day on their behalf (1 Thess 2:8–10).

His apostolic labor also entailed dealing with each of them "like a father with his children" who urges them to "lead (περιπατεῖν) a life worthy of God" (2:11–12). If, as argued earlier, God as heavenly "Father" evokes the exodus-related redemption and restoration of Israel, and God's "Fatherhood" is defined in terms of his making himself known as "Redeemer," then by analogy Paul's derivative earthly function as "father" may further evoke a divinely appointed Moses-like role. God guided and tested his people through their wilderness wanderings and beyond, "as a parent disciplines a child" (Deut 8:5). Paul is called by God to instruct and guide the Thessalonians. Notably Paul employs the father metaphor elsewhere in expressing his deep desire to send his "son" Timothy to support the Philippians (Phil 2:19–24)—just as he had done previously in the case of the Thessalonians (1 Thess 3:1–2)—mindful that they are to "do all things without murmuring and arguing, so that [they] may be blameless and innocent, children of God without blemish in the midst of a crooked and perverse generation..." (Phil 2:14–15; cf. Exod 17:1–7; Deut 32:5), and continue steadfast until "the day of Christ" (Phil 2:16).[18]

By way of further thanksgiving Paul emphatically acknowledges the Thessalonians' reception of the "word of God that you heard from us" (λόγον ἀκοῆς παρ' ἡμῶν τοῦ θεοῦ, 2:13b). This statement stresses his own important mediating role in communicating to them the truly divine—not merely human—word which now operates in their lives. He here stands in the tradition of Moses and other Old Testament prophets who faithfully rendered God's word to Israel (e.g., Exod 19:1–24:8), even when they did not always obey (e.g., Exod 32) or understand as they ought (e.g., Deut 29:2–4; cf. Isa 6:9–10; 53:1). Yet the exemplary Thessalonians have embodied God's word even under duress from their fellow countrymen, imitating the afflicted faithful in Judea and throughout Israel's past. At this point Paul is aligning himself and the Thessalonians with God's persecuted people, including the Old Testament prophets, the Lord Jesus, and the aforementioned Judean believers, and his own apostolic mission.[19] James M. Scott has shown how these highly charged and challenging remarks at 1 Thess 2:14–16 exhibit four features evident in the Old Testament in the form of a Deuteronomic historical pattern (e.g., Deut 32); namely, (1) the sin of God's people, ongoing to the present; (2) God's sending forth his prophets, here including Paul; (3) who have been rejected; (4) a situation over which stands God's wrath (2:16c).[20]

---

[18] See also Paul's notable use of the father metaphor in relation to the Corinthian community, to whom he also sent Timothy, at 1 Cor 4:14–17.
[19] On various critical and contested issues related to 1 Thess 2:13–16, see Gupta, *1 & 2 Thessalonians*, 114–123.
[20] James M. Scott, "Paul's Use of Deuteronomic Tradition," *JBL* 112 (1993): 645–65, esp. 647–57. Two other elements in the Deuteronomic pattern include: the opportunity to repent remains, at

4. Paul's exhortation: 1 Thessalonians as holy covenant people fitted for the kingdom of God

Paul is no longer present with the Thessalonians, having been forced to depart and since hindered by Satan from returning (2:17–18; cf. 2:15b), and he and his companions now carry a threefold burden. First, they "were made orphans" (ἀπορφανισθέντες, 2:17c), with Paul here using a verb not found elsewhere in the New Testament, one which evokes the earlier child–parent metaphors, and which conveys a sense of being separated from the parent body of the covenant people of God in Thessalonica.[21] Second, they now experience a deep but as yet unfulfilled desire to see them again "face to face" (2:17), an intimate image with a notable Old Testament antecedent in Moses' intercession with God on behalf of Israel.[22] Third, they are anxious that the Thessalonians continue onwards, steadfast until the coming of the Lord (2:19–20).

Unable to bear this situation any longer (3:1, 5a), and fearful the "tempter had tempted" (ἐπείρασεν ὑμᾶς ὁ πειράζων) them in some way (3:5b), they dispatched Timothy who had recently returned with the encouraging news of their continuing faith and love (3:2, 5–6). Regarding Paul's use of the verb "bear" (στέγω)—at 3:1, 5 and elsewhere only at 1 Cor 9:12[23] and 13:7—Jeffrey A. D. Weima compares Philo's remark on Moses as "unable to contain [μὴ στέγων, mē stegōn] a feeling of reciprocal love and affection for his people" (*Virtues* 69).[24] That such love can carry its own cost may be implicit in Paul's earlier use of the nurse metaphor—itself evoking Moses' burden-bearing leadership of Israel (Num 11:10–15)—to convey his commitment to the covenant community in Thessalonica. Like Israel in the wilderness, the Thessalonians are being tested and tempted. Among seven instances of the verb πειράζω in Paul, two occur at 1 Thess 3:5 and two others in his typological treatment of the exodus and wilderness experience to warn the Corinthian believers to avoid idolatry and immorality (1 Cor 10:1–3).[25] Satan seeks to set up a roadblock on the Thessalonians' path to redemption. Yet Timothy's report, with its good news of their ongoing faith and love, is a source of encouragement and thanksgiving for Paul and his companions amid their afflictions, as they continually pray that they may yet

---

which point God will restore Israel to the land and renew his covenant relationship with them. Scott follows Odil H. Steck, *Israel und das gewaltsame Geschick der Propheten: Untersuchungen zur Überlieferung des deuteronomistischen Geschichtsbildes im Alten Testament, Spätjudentum und Urchristentum*, WMANT 23 (Neukirchen-Vluyn: Neukirchener Verlag, 1967).

[21] See further the discussion in Burke, *Family Matters*, 157–60.
[22] For example, Exod 32:11–14, 30–34; 33:7–23; Num 12:6–8.
[23] In Corinth, while Paul could appeal to the law of Moses and exert his apostolic authority (so 1 Cor 9:8–12b; cf. Deut 25:4), he would rather "bear/endure" (στέγω) anything rather than impede the gospel of Christ (1 Cor 9:12cd).
[24] Weima, *1–2 Thessalonians*, 207.
[25] At 1 Cor 10:9, 13; also "test, temptation" (πειρασμός) twice at 10:13. See further Weima, *1–2 Thessalonians*, 216–18. He notes (217) that the only other instance of "the Tempter" (1 Thess 3:5) as a title in the New Testament is in Matthew's account of Jesus' temptation in the wilderness (Matt 4:3).

again see them face to face (1 Thess 3:6–10). All this precipitates a remarkable "wish-prayer" that "our God and Father himself and our Lord Jesus direct our way to you" (3:11); that the Lord may make their love for one another and for all abound (3:12; recalling 1:8–9a and perhaps anticipating 4:9–12 and 5:15); and that they be holy and blameless "before our God and Father at the coming of our Lord Jesus with all his saints" (3:13).[26]

Thus integral to this apostolic letter, and especially its exhortations, now notably concentrated in 4:1–12, is the fortification and advancement of the Thessalonians as the called, covenant, and holy people of God, fitted for the kingdom of God and its ultimate realization at the return of the Lord Jesus. It is generally recognized that in 4:1–12 Paul is drawing upon Old Testament holiness teachings, now reworked via Paul's "instructions…through the Lord Jesus" (4:2).[27] Indeed, it is being holy (ἅγιος) which above all else demarcates delivered Israel as God's covenant people vis-à-vis the nations (e.g., LXX Exod 19:5–6; cf. Lev 11:44–45; 19:2; 20:7; 22:31–33; Deut 7:6–11; 26:16–19).[28] Essentially, then, Paul urges the Thessalonians to live holy lives in a challenging environment and especially, as the exodus generation was urged, in relation to sexual immorality.[29] (Here again we might compare Paul's exodus-related remarks at 1 Cor 10:1–13, especially 10:8.) The Thessalonians are to differentiate themselves from the nations who do not know God (1 Thess 4:5);[30] to fulfil their calling (2:13; cf. 1:9); and not to reject God who provided them with his Holy Spirit (4:8).[31] Moreover, beyond this, they are also to exhibit exemplary self-sacrificial love for one another (4:9–12).

Especially noteworthy is Paul's curious identification of the Thessalonians as those "taught by God" (θεοδίδακτοί, 1 Thess 4:9), a biblical *hapax legomenon*. After surveying several scholarly proposals, Weima follows most commentators in suggesting that Paul is here alluding to LXX Isa 54:13, in an oracle on the restoration of Jerusalem and exiled Israel, announcing "And I will cause all your sons to be *taught of God [didaktous theou]*."[32] Paul, "in a manner analogous to the 'reverse

---

[26] On the "wish-prayer" at 3:11–13, see Timothy A. Brookins, *First and Second Thessalonians*, Paideia: Commentaries on the New Testament (Grand Rapids: Baker Academic, 2021), 76–78.

[27] Weima, *1–2 Thessalonians*, 248–49, offers six "factors [which] indicate the apostle's indebtedness to the Jewish moral tradition" at 4:1–12.

[28] See further Jeffery A. D. Weima, "'How You Must Walk to Please God': Holiness and Discipleship in 1 Thessalonians," in *Patterns of Discipleship in the New Testament*, ed. Richard N. Longenecker (Grand Rapids: Eerdmans, 1996), 98–119, especially 101–102; also his *1–2 Thessalonians*, 263–65. Earlier, Robert Hodgson Jr., "1 Thess 4:1–12 and the Holiness Tradition (HT)," *SBLSP 21*, ed. K. H. Richards (Chico: Scholars, 1982), 199–215.

[29] See the detailed discussion on issues and options in Weima, *1–2 Thessalonians*, 267–74.

[30] On Gentile idolatry and sexual immorality, see, for example, Wis 14:12, 22–26, located within a wider section on the worship of nature (13:1–15:17), immediately preceded by an account of Egypt's idolatry (12:23–27), which led it to stray on "paths of error" (τῶν πλάνης ὁδῶν) and involved being "deceived like foolish infants (νηπίων)" (12:24).

[31] Weima, *1–2 Thessalonians*, 281, notes that Paul's "rejection" language echoes that of Jesus (at Luke 10:16), itself evoking God's remarks regarding Israel's rejection (1 Sam 8:7), which extends "from the day I brought them up out of Egypt to this day, forsaking me and serving other gods" (1 Sam 8:8). Weima (282–83) also detects here echoes of LXX Ezek 37:6, 14, further evidence that Paul views the Thessalonians as "members of the renewed Israel, the covenant people of God" (283).

[32] As given in Weima, *1–2 Thessalonians*, 288. Note also Deut 5:22–33 (cf. Exod 19:7–25; 24:1–18).

and combine' pattern of LXX compound-word formation noted by [Emanuel] Tov," has created a neologism,[33] which contributes to the Thessalonians' identity as the redeemed, instructed, covenant-keeping, and holy people of God. Notably Isa 54:13 is also cited at John 6:45 in Jesus' bread of life discourse in which he variously invokes Israel's exodus experience—for example, "your ancestors ate manna in the wilderness, and they died" (6:49)—while claiming that the living Father has sent him down from heaven as living bread which, when consumed, brings eternal life now and will raise one up on the last day (6:54–63). Paul notes that integral to the Thessalonians' instruction and formation is the Holy Spirit (1 Thess 4:8; cf. 1 Cor 2:13, "taught by the Spirit" (ἐν διδακτοῖς πνεύματος; also Rom 8:14–17),[34] which allows them to live well together and "behave properly" (εὐσχημόνως) before outsiders (1 Thess 4:12).[35] As Israel was instructed to remember its exodus deliverance and provide for others (Lev 25:35–43), so the Thessalonians are to look after one another and be a witness to the watching wider world.

5. Paul's response: destiny of the dead in Christ and the coming day of the Lord

Since Paul's departure certain members of the Thessalonian congregation have died (cf. the verb κοιμάω at 4:13, 14, 15) and two interrelated and pressing matters have arisen: the destiny of the dead, including whether they would have a full share alongside the living at Jesus' coming (4:13–18), and when more precisely Jesus would return (5:1–11). The first of these may entail a scenario analogous to Israel's initial wilderness generation, in which the death and departure of certain key figures, most significantly Moses, precipitated various concerns about loss of leadership, idolatry, breaking the covenant, and the possibility of God forsaking Israel leading to terrible afflictions (LXX Deut 31:14–18).[36] Paul's Christological response to the Thessalonians at 4:13–17 is to reassure them that, as a result of Jesus' own death, resurrection, and parousia, as the Lord triumphantly descends from heaven—"with a cry of command, with the archangel's call and with the sound of God's trumpet" (4:16ab)[37]—those dead in Christ

---

[33] See Stephen E. Witmer, "θεοδίδακτοί in 1 Thessalonians 4.9: A Pauline Neologism," NTS 52 (2006): 239–50 (239); see Emanuel Tov, "Compound Words in the LXX Representing Two or More Hebrew Words," Bib 58 (1977): 189–212.

[34] See Weima, *1–2 Thessalonians*, 289. On the exodus tradition at Rom 8:14–17, see Keesmaat, *Paul and his Story*, 54–96.

[35] On εὐσχημόνως, compare Rom 13:13; and 1 Cor 14:40.

[36] See, for example, "The LORD said to Moses, 'Soon you will lie down (σὺ κοιμᾷ) with your ancestors" (LXX Deut 31:16). Cf. the deaths of Miriam (Num 20:1) and Aaron (Num 20:23–29), the LXX using the verbs τελευτάω and ἀποθνῄσκω respectively. Other notable deaths, employing κοιμάω in the LXX, include Jacob (Gen 47:30), David (2 Sam 7:12–16; 1 Kgs 2:10), and Solomon (1 Kgs 11:43). For further references, see Weima, *1–2 Thessalonians*, 309.

[37] The only other New Testament reference to an archangel is at Jude 9, and concerns the archangel Michael contending with the devil over the body of Moses. Weima, *1–2 Thessalonians*, 328, notes that in Judaism the trumpet can be seen "as a signal, marking in particular the visible appearance of God not only in the past (Exod. 19:13, 16, 19; 20:18) but also at the future 'day of the LORD' (Isa. 27:13; Joel 2:1; Zeph. 1:14–16; Zech. 9:14)."

will be first to rise and be brought with him (4:14b; cf. 3:13), and then be joined by those still left alive "who will caught up in the clouds together with them" to meet and live with the Lord forever (4:17).[38]

Much of this Paul declares "by the word of the Lord" (4:15a), which some see as an echo of Jesus' eschatological discourse at Matt 24:29-31 (//Mark 13:24-27//Luke 21:25-28),[39] with its depiction of the appearance of the Son of Man in heaven, and the mourning of the nations of the earth, who "will see 'the Son of Man coming on the clouds of heaven' with power and great glory'" (24:30; cf. Dan 7:13-14). Notably in Matthew this is immediately preceded by the darkening of the sun and moon and falling stars, a scenario evoking Ezek 32:7-8 and its cosmic judgment on Pharoah king of Egypt, which in turn recalls the plague of darkness in Egypt prior to the exodus (Exod 10:21-23), a motif evident elsewhere in the Old Testament in association with God's judgment upon tyrants who oppress Israel (e.g., Isa 13:10; Joel 2:10, 31; 3:15). Paul, in effect, is arguing that the at times afflicted but steadfast Thessalonians are being delivered from such wrath (1 Thess 1:9; 2:16; 5:9) and, whether now dead or still alive in Christ, they will ultimately be vindicated and share in the Lord's eschatological deliverance and kingdom. That being the case, unlike those who rebelled and lamented Israel's lot when tested and disciplined in the wilderness (e.g., Num 11:1-3), the Thessalonians are not to "grieve as others who have no hope" (4:13; cf. Wis 11:12[40]), but rather to "encourage one another with these words" (4:18).

Paul responds to the second concern as to when precisely the day of the Lord would finally arrive and fully deliver the Thessalonians, by reminding them of what they already know: that it will come "like a thief in the night" (5:2; cf. Matt 24:43-44//Luke 12:39-40).[41] There will be no way out for those wrongly claiming "peace and security"; instead, they will suddenly experience "destruction" (ὄλεθρος) which will appear like the onset of "labor pains" (1 Thess 5:3).[42] Such a destiny entails eschatological judgment (cf. 2 Thess 1:9) which, as Paul instructed the Corinthians concerning the "destruction" (ὄλεθρον) of the incestuous believer, is to be avoided by cleansing the holy community and ensuring that it emulates the self-sacrificial paschal lamb of God (see 1 Cor 5:5-8). This rich language and imagery might also variously evoke the fate of those who heeded false prophets and leaders at the time of the Babylonian invasion

---

[38] Weima, *1-2 Thessalonians*, 332-33, observes how often in the Old Testament clouds are involved in a theophany (e.g., Exod 13:21-22; 14:19, 20, 24; 16:10; 19:16-17; Lev 16:2; Num 9:15-22; 10:11-12, and others) and that this continues in the New Testament, in Paul notably at 1 Cor 10:1-2.

[39] Weima, *1-2 Thessalonians*, 321, thinks it most likely that Paul is here loosely citing Jesus' saying as evident in the Synoptic Gospels, with Matt 24:29-33, 40-41 as "the best candidate."

[40] Wisdom 11:1-14 recalls Israel's wilderness experience, and contrasts God's provision for his people—even as he also "tested them as a parent" (11:10)—with the fate of the Egyptians. The latter's punishment, and the benefit it brought to Israel, constituted "a twofold grief" (11:12).

[41] In Matt 24:36-44 (cf. Luke 17:26-27) an analogy is drawn between those "eating and drinking" in the days of Noah and those unprepared at the coming of the Son of Man. Moreover, the former scenario may evoke comparison with Israel's worship of the golden calf as "the people sat down to eat and drink, and rose up to revel" (Exod 32:6), a cautionary example applied by Paul to the Corinthian congregation (1 Cor 10:6-7).

[42] The labor pain image is frequently used in a range of ways in the Old Testament and Jewish intertestamental texts; see Weima, *1-2 Thessalonians*, 351-52.

and ensuing exile (Jer 6:13-16; Ezek 13:8-16; cf. Mic 3:5), rather than walking in the liberating way of the Lord.[43]

The delivered Thessalonians, however, are already living in the eschatological age as children of light and day (5:4-5). And, shifting sharply from this image to a military metaphor, Paul also urges that they remain fortified in faith, hope, and love, as they await their final salvation and eternal life with the Lord Jesus Christ (5:8-9).[44] Here the military imagery echoes Isa 59:17 and God as the divine warrior who redeems Zion. It may also be compared to Wis 5:17-18, in a context which evokes God's protection of his people, paradigmatically so in his dramatic use of creation during Israel's deliverance out of Egypt and through the sea (Wis 5:20-23). It is for salvation and not wrath that the Thessalonians are "destined" (1 Thess 5:9), a reminder of their election and calling as a holy people within the purposes of God (cf. 2:12; 4:7) "through our Lord Jesus Christ" (cf. 1:10; 2:15; 4:14).

In the interim, as they continue to walk in the way of the Lord, they must not replicate those instances of Israel's drunken and darkened disobedience during the exodus experience,[45] but rather remain awake and sober (1 Thess 5:6). In this way, whether dead or alive at the coming of the Lord Jesus Christ, together "they may live with him" (5:10). For Paul this is the ultimate life-giving outcome envisaged by Moses at God's giving of the commandments to Israel at Mount Sinai: "You must follow exactly the path that the LORD your God has commanded you, so that you may live, and that it may go well with you, and that you may live long in the land that you are to possess" (Deut 5:33; cf. 11:8-9; 30:6, 11-20; 32:44-47). In this way, just as Jeremiah promised that God would "build up" Israel, so Paul urges them to "encourage one another and build up each other" (5:11).[46]

6. Conclusion

Paul's apostolic and pastoral instructions in 1 Thessalonians are intended to equip the community to embody the gospel in Macedonia, Achaia, and indeed throughout the Mediterranean world (1:8). He recognizes that their ability to accomplish this task arises out of their proper theological and historical location within the unfolding

---

[43] Weima, *1-2 Thessalonians*, 348-51, notes certain considerations that may count against seeing Paul's phrase "peace and security" as echoing such Old Testament antecedents, and he offers a range of evidence for Roman propaganda as the source of this slogan or theme. Arguably, though, both of these influences could be included within the broad scope of the divine economy that Paul has in view.

[44] Paul makes a similar dramatic shift from a day/night to a military metaphor at Rom 13:12, in the midst of wider remarks which urge believers to love one another and their neighbor (cf. 1 Thess 4:9-12)—thereby fulfilling the ten commandments (Rom 13:8-10)—and which also anticipate the onset of the day of the Lord (Rom 13:11-14).

[45] See again, for example, the golden calf incident (Exod 32:6, 19, 25); also Moses' warning that Israel heed the ten commandments and remember their deliverance out of Egypt (Deut 4:9-20), including that they "watch [themselves] closely" (Deut 4:9, 15); and his instruction that Israel recollects its divine deliverance, and remain sober in the knowledge that "the LORD [is] your God" (Deut 29:6).

[46] On the verb "build up" (οἰκοδομέω) at 5:11, Weima, *1-2 Thessalonians*, 372, references LXX Jer 24:6; 38:4 [31:4 Eng.] 40:7 [33:7 Eng.]; 49:10 [42:10 Eng]; also Ps. 27:5 [28:5 Eng.]. On Jer 24:4-7, cf. Jer 31:33 and Exod 19:5-6.

Israel-specific yet creation-wide purposes of God. This includes situating this Thessalonian congregation within a redemptive economy which encompasses Israel's exodus and exile; Messiah Jesus' death and resurrection; and their steadfast Spirit-empowered involvement and ultimate ingathering within the elect and covenant people at the eschatological coming of the kingdom of God. With this in view, embedded throughout this rich and resonant letter are various evocative and instructive exodus-related elements. These motifs are especially in play in Paul's account of the gospel as received by the rescued Thessalonians; and in his remarks concerning his apostolic nurture of the community. They are also evident in his exhortations designed to fortify their status as holy and blameless covenant people of God; and as he envisages their ultimate inclusion—both the dead and those alive in Christ—into God's kingdom and glory on the day of the Lord. In the meantime, an absent and at times anxious apostle Paul remains confident that the one who has called the Thessalonians into the kingdom is faithful and will accomplish his purposes from their first to final deliverance (2:12; 5:24).

Bibliography

Brookins, Timothy A. *First and Second Thessalonians*. Paideia: Commentaries on the New Testament. Grand Rapids: Baker Academic, 2021.

Burke, Trevor J. *Family Matters: A Socio-Historical Study of Kinship Metaphors in 1 Thessalonians*. JSNTSup 247. London: T&T Clark, 2003.

Ehorn, Seth M. "Exodus in the Disputed Pauline Letters." Pages 127–45 in *Exodus in the New Testament*. Edited by Seth M. Ehorn. LNTS 633. London: T&T Clark, 2021.

Estelle, Bryan D. *Echoes of Exodus: Tracing a Biblical Motif*. Downers Grove, IL: IVP Academic, 2018.

Evans, Craig A. "Exodus in the New Testament: Patterns of Revelation and Redemption." Pages 440–64 in *The Book of Exodus: Composition, Reception, and Interpretation*. Edited by Thomas Dozeman, Craig A. Evans, and Joel N. Lohr. Leiden: Brill, 2014.

Fowl, Stephen. "A Metaphor in Distress. A Reading of NHΠIOI in 1 Thessalonians 2.7." *NTS* 36 (1990): 469–73.

Gaventa, Beverly Roberts. "Apostles As Babes and Nurses in 1 Thessalonians 2:7." Pages 193–207 in *Faith and History: Essays in Honor of Paul W. Meyer*. Edited by John T. Carroll, Charles H. Cosgrove, and E. Elizabeth Johnson. Atlanta: Scholars Press, 1990.

Gaventa, Beverly Roberts. *Our Mother Saint Paul*. Louisville: Westminster John Knox Press, 2007.

Gupta, Nijay K. *1 & 2 Thessalonians*. Zondervan Critical Introductions to the New Testament 13. Grand Rapids: Zondervan, 2019.

Hodgson, Robert, Jr. "1 Thess 4:1–12 and the Holiness Tradition (HT)." Pages 199–215 in *SBLSP* 21. Edited by K. H. Richards. Chico: Scholars, 1982.

Horbury, William. "I Thessalonians ii.3 as Rebutting the Charge of False Prophecy." *JTS* 33 (1982): 492–508.

Johnson, E. Elizabeth. "Paul's Reliance on Scripture in 1 Thessalonians." Pages 143–62 in *Paul and Scripture: Continuing the Conversation*. Edited by Christopher D. Stanley. Atlanta: SBL Press, 2012.

Keesmaat, Sylvia C. *Paul and his Story: (Re)Interpreting the Exodus Tradition*. JSNTSup 181. Sheffield: Sheffield Academic, 1999.

Malherbe, Abraham J. "'Gentle as a Nurse': The Cynic Background to 1 Thess. 2." *NovT* 12 (1970): 203–17.

Malherbe, Abraham J. *The Letters to the Thessalonians: A New Translation with Introduction and Commentary*. AB 32B. New York: Doubleday, 2000.

McNeel, Jennifer Houston. *Paul as Infant and Nursing Mother: Metaphor, Rhetoric, and Identity in 1 Thessalonians 2:5–8*. ECL 12. Atlanta: SBL Press, 2014.

Moo, Douglas J. *The Letters to the Colossians and to Philemon*. PNTC. Grand Rapids: Eerdmans, 2008.

Morales, Rodrigo J. *The Spirit and the Restoration of Israel: New Exodus and New Creation Motifs in Galatians*. WUNT 2/282. Tübingen: Mohr Siebeck, 2010.

Pietersma, Albert, and Benjamin G. Wright, eds. *A New Translation of the Septuagint*. Oxford: Oxford University Press, 2007.

Scott, James M. "Paul's Use of Deuteronomic Tradition." *JBL* 112 (1993): 645–65.

Shogren, Gary S. *1 & 2 Thessalonians*. ZECNT 13. Grand Rapids: Zondervan, 2012.

Smith, Daniel Lynwood. "The Uses of 'New Exodus' in New Testament Scholarship: Preparing a Way through the Wilderness." *CurBR* 14 (2016): 207–43.

Steck, Odil H. *Israel und das gewaltsame Geschick der Propheten: Untersuchungen zur Überlieferung des deuteronomistischen Geschichtsbildes im Alten Testament, Spätjudentum und Urchristentum*. WMANT 23. Neukirchen-Vluyn: Neukirchener Verlag, 1967.

Tov, Emanuel. "Compound Words in the LXX Representing Two or More Hebrew Words." *Bib* 58 (1977): 189–212.

Weima, Jeffery A. D. "'How You Must Walk to Please God': Holiness and Discipleship in 1 Thessalonians." Pages 98–119 in *Patterns of Discipleship in the New Testament*. Edited by Richard N. Longenecker. Grand Rapids: Eerdmans, 1996.

Weima, Jeffery A. D. "'But We Became Infants Among You': The Case for ΝΗΠΙΟΙ in 1 Thess 2.7." *NTS* 46 (2000): 547–64.

Weima, Jeffery A. D. "1–2 Thessalonians." Pages 871–89 in *Commentary on the New Testament Use of the Old Testament*. Edited by G. K. Beale and D. A. Carson. Grand Rapids: Baker Academic, 2007.

Weima, Jeffrey A. D. *1–2 Thessalonians*. BECNT. Grand Rapids: Baker Academic, 2014.

Westfall, David M. "Exodus in the Pauline Letters." Pages 109–26 in *Exodus in the New Testament*. Edited by Seth M. Ehorn. LNTS 633. London: T&T Clark, 2021.

Wilson, Todd A. "Wilderness Apostasy and Paul's Portrayal of the Crisis in Galatians." *NTS* 50 (2004): 550–71.

Witmer, Stephen E. "θεοδίδακτοί in 1 Thessalonians 4.9: A Pauline Neologism." *NTS* 52 (2006): 239–50.

Works, Carla Swafford. *The Church in the Wilderness: Paul's Use of Exodus Traditions in 1 Corinthians*. WUNT 2/379. Tübingen: Mohr Siebeck, 2014.

Chapter 17

On the Reception of Exodus 24 and 25 in the Epistle to the Hebrews*

Wolfgang Kraus

1. Data set: Exodus 24:8 and 25:(39,) 40 in Hebrews 8 and 9[1]

There are two explicit quotes from Exodus 24 and 25 in the Epistle to the Hebrews:[2]

1. Exodus 25:(39,)40 is used in Heb 8:5 in the context of the comparison between Jesus' ministry as high priest at the heavenly sanctuary and Aaron's

---

* Larry J. Perkins has published extensively on New Testament and Old Testament issues, especially on LXX Exodus. He provided the translation of LXX Exodus in the *New English Translation of the Septuagint*. More than once we met at IOSCS Meetings and at conferences held by Septuaginta-Deutsch in Wuppertal where he gave papers. It is a pleasure for me to greet him on the occasion of his 75th birthday with some reflections on LXX Exodus in the Epistle to the Hebrews.
  An earlier version of this paper appeared in German in M. Hopf, W. Oswald, and S. Seiler, eds., *Heiliger Raum. Exegese und Rezeption der Heiligtumstexte in Exod 24–40*, Theologische Akzente 8 (Stuttgart: Kohlhammer, 2016), 91–112. Here it has been reworked. All translations of German citations into English are by the author. I thank Dr. phil. Michael Eber, Berlin, for his help with the translation into English.

[1] Recent contributions on the matter, with extensive bibliographies, include: Jared C. Calaway, *The Sabbat and the Sanctuary. Access to God in the Letter to the Hebrews and its Priestly Context*, WUNT 2/349 (Tübingen: Mohr Siebeck, 2013); Georg Gäbel, *Die Kulttheologie des Hebräerbriefes*, WUNT 2/212 (Tübingen: Mohr Siebeck, 2006); Jonathan Klawans, *Purity, Sacrifice, and the Temple. Symbolism and Supersessionism in the Study of Ancient Judaism* (Oxford: Oxford University Press, 2006); Hermut Löhr, ",Umriß' und ,Schatten'. Bemerkungen zur Zitierung von Exod 25,40 in Heb 8," *ZNW* 84 (1993): 218–32; Hermut Löhr, "Thronversammlung und preisender Tempel. Beobachtungen am himmlischen Heiligtum im Hebräerbrief und in den Sabbatopferliedern aus Qumran," in *Königsherrschaft Gottes und himmlischer Kult*, ed. M. Hengel and A. M. Schwemer, WUNT 55 (Tübingen: Mohr Siebeck, 1991), 185–205; David M. Moffitt, *Atonement and Resurrection in the Epistle to the Hebrews*, NovTSup 141 (Leiden/Boston: Brill, 2011); Kenneth L. Schenck, *Cosmology and Eschatology in Hebrews: The Settings of the Sacrifice*, SNTSMS 143 (Cambridge: Cambridge University Press, 2007); Helmut Utzschneider, "Tabernacle," in *The Book of Exodus*, ed. Th. Dozeman, C. Evans, and J. Lohr, VTSup 164 (Leiden/Boston: Brill, 2014), 267–301. See also the work of Christian Lustig cited in n. 56.

[2] Here and in the following, I will specify the passages according to the chapter numeration of the Hebrew text in the Luther Bible, if not otherwise indicated.

at the earthly one, the image of the heavenly sanctuary. It is combined with the substance of Exod 25:8, 9, for 25:40 originally only refers to the lampstand.
2. Exodus 24:8, the rite involving the blood of the διαθήκη, is quoted in Heb 9:20 in the context of the statement that everything is consecrated or cleansed with blood. The covenant ritual, Exod 23:3–8, forms the background to Heb 9:18–22, though with some significant differences.

Beyond that, there are several allusions to other texts concerning the sanctuary from Exodus in Hebrews: Exod 25:16, 18, 21, 22, 30, 31 form the background to Heb 9:1–5, which deals with the furnishing of the tabernacle; Exod 26:31–37 to the remarks on the curtain in Hebrews 9 and 10.[3]

2. Hebrews 7:1(8:1)–10:18: position in the structure and line of thought

Before we can deal with the quotations in detail, we need to be clear about the position of Heb 7:1–10:18 within the structure of Hebrews and about the line of thought of this text. There is no consensus among scholars on the structure of Hebrews, but the major caesurae are recognized by most exegetes (although they draw different conclusions from them).[4] Hebrews is characterized by alternating doctrinal and paraenetic passages. In this, it differs from the Pauline Epistles. However, this should be understood as an indication of rhetorical ability, rather than as expression of ineptness.

The structure of the text hinges on the question of the position of Heb 4:14–16 and 10:19–23. Are they "two clear, linguistically and factually closely related caesurae" that function as "bridge sections,"[5] that is, does the second main section of Hebrews begin with 4:14,[6] or does Heb 4:14–6:20 still belong to the first main section, whose conclusion only takes place in 5:10 resp. 6:20?[7] It seems clear, at least, that 5:11–6:20 is a transitional section that lays the groundwork for further explanations of Jesus' high priesthood in 7:1–10:18.[8]

---

[3] Other passages from Exod 30:6; 37(38LXX):25–28 will be discussed later.
[4] Cf. the extensive discussion of different structural models of Hebrews in Martin Karrer, *Der Brief an die Hebräer Kap. 1,1–5,10 = Heb I*, ÖTK 20/1 (Gütersloh: Gütersloher Verlagshaus, 2002), 69–78.
[5] Knut Backhaus, *Der Hebräerbrief*, Regensburger Neues Testament (Regensburg: Pustet, 2009), 42.
[6] Thus, among others, Hans-Friedrich Weiss, *Der Brief an die Hebräer*, KEK 13 (Göttingen: Vandenhoeck & Ruprecht, 1991), 291; Karrer, *Heb I*, 233; cf. idem, *Der Brief an die Hebräer Kap. 5,11–13,20 = Heb II*, ÖTK 20/2 (Gütersloh: : Gütersloher Verlagshaus, 2008), 24–25; Backhaus, *Hebräerbrief*, 177. Harold Attridge counts five main sections after the exordium in 1:1–4: I, 1:5–2:18; II, 3:1–5:10; III, 5:11–10:25; IV, 10:26–12:13; V, 12:14–13:25. See Harold Attridge, *The Epistle to the Hebrews: A Commentary on the Epistle to the Hebrews*, Hermeneia (Philadelphia: Fortress Press, 1989), 19.
[7] Thus Erich Grässer, *An die Hebräer: Heb 1–6*, EKK XVII/1 (Neukirchen-Vluyn: Neukirchener Verlag, 1990).
[8] Gerd Schunack calls this section a "metacommunicative intermediate section." Gerd Schunack, *Der Hebräerbrief*, ZBK: NT 14 (Zurich: Theologischer Verlag Zürich, 2002), 74. Karrer, *Heb II*, 19, refers to it as a "call to attention," while Weiss, *Hebrews*, 327, sees it as a "preparation for the remarks to the 'perfects.'"

One could argue for a caesura after 6:20 given that the remarks in Heb 7:1–10:18 represent a self-contained argument. This is also made clear by the fact that 10:19 could follow 6:20 directly; one could pass from 6:20 directly to 10:19. The remarks in the following more than three chapters elaborate on the statement further in 6:20: "After a long run-up, the theme set up in 6:20 is now, by linking key words, finally made the main point of the teachings on perfection that begin here."[9]

However, a caesura after 4:13 could be supported even more, since, in regard to Jesus' high priesthood, which is part of the traditional confession relevant for Hebrews (first mentioned in 2:17), the text makes three innovations that are not part of the traditional confession. All three occur beginning with Heb 4:14: (1) Jesus as a sympathetic, sinless high priest (4:15; 5:7–8); (2) Jesus as high priest "forever, according to the order of Melchizedek" (5:6, 10); (3) Jesus as high priest in the heavenly sanctuary (4:14; 5:9).[10]

The conclusion of the second main section also needs to be discussed here: Does it end at Heb 10:18[11] or at 10:31?[12] The appellation "Therefore, my friends" in 10:19 seems to offer a clearer structuring signal than the call to "recall those earlier days" in 10:32.

Where, finally, does the third main section end: with 12:29,[13] 13:19,[14] 13:21[15] or 13:25?[16] Perhaps the problem of the structure of Hebrews is also related to the fact that the author loves "smooth transitions."[17]

The most probable end of the third main section seems to be Heb 12:29. Here the author takes up what he said at the beginning of the tractate: God is again speaking. Hebrews 13 has not been part of the original speech of the author but has to be looked upon as an epistolary appendix.[18]

---

[9] Erich Grässer, *An die Hebräer, Heb 7,1–10,18*, EKK XVII/2 (Neukirchen-Vluyn: Neukirchener 1993), 7.

[10] Cf. Wolfgang Kraus, "Zur Aufnahme und Funktion von Gen 14,18–20 und Ps 109 LXX im Hebräerbrief," in *Text-Textgeschichte-Textwirkung Text-Textgeschichte-Textwirkung: Festschrift zum 65. Geburtstag von Siegfried Kreuzer*, ed. T. Wagner, F. Ueberschaer, and J. Robker, AOAT 419 (Münster: Ugarit-Verlag, 2014), 459–74.

[11] Thus, among others, Weiss, *Hebrews*, 291, 518; Backhaus, *Hebrews*, 177.355; Erich Grässer, *An die Hebräer Heb 10,19–13,25*, EKK XVII/3 (Neukirchen-Vluyn: Neukirchener, 1997), 9.

[12] Thus, among others, Karrer, *Heb II*, 213, 242; Franz-Josef Schierse, *Verheißung und Heilsvollendung. Zur theologischen Grundfrage des Hebräerbriefes*, Münchener Theologische Studien 9 (Munich: Zink, 1955), 200–203.

[13] Backhaus, *Hebrews*, 450, 458. Backhaus sees 13:1 as the beginning of "practical instructions," followed by a "final blessing" (13:20–21) and an "accompanying note" (13:22–25) (482, 488).

[14] In this case, Heb 13:20–21 would have to be seen as the final section of the *Logos Parakleseos* and 13:22–25 as an accompanying epistolary note.

[15] Grässer, *Heb III*, 9, 400, 409; Karrer, *Heb II*, 372, 377–79, 380.

[16] Weiss, *Hebrews*, 518. Weiss lets the epistolary conclusion begin at 13:18, though he counts it as part of the third main section (746).

[17] Karrer, *Heb II*, 213.

[18] Cf. on that Alexander Wedderburn, "The 'Letter' to the Hebrews and Its Thirteenth Chapter," *NTS* 50 (2004): 390–405; Wolfgang Kraus, "Zur Schriftverwendung in Hebräer 13. Zugleich ein Beitrag zur Frage nach dem Verhältnis von Heb 13 zu Heb 1–12," in *Die Schriftzitate im Hebräerbrief als Zeugen für die Überlieferung der Septuaginta*, ed. M. Sigismund and S. Kreuzer. WUNT 2/580 (Tübingen: Mohr Siebeck 2022), 177–92. Hebrews 13 has been added later on and makes the original tractate (1:1–12:29) to an epistle.

There is scholarly consensus on the fact that the situation of the addressees is characterized by internal and external problems.[19] From Heb 10:32–34 and 12:12–13, it becomes clear that their situation is marked by a fatigue of the faith and by social pressure. According to 12:4–5 and its context, though, there seem to have been no martyrs yet. So how did this state of affairs marked by pressure and fatigue of faith arise? Following David deSilva's research,[20] many see the ancient value system of "honour and shame" as the background and as an explanation for the fatigue. Social exclusion can certainly be oppressive. "Viewing Hebrews against the cultural background of a society that takes as its pivotal values honor and shame leads to a new insight into both the nature of the 'external pressure' and the cause of the 'waning commitment' to the Christian confession and involvement."[21]

However, this necessarily raises the question whether the external situation of the community can sufficiently explain the line of argument of the author of Hebrews: If the text is primarily about encouraging members of the community to persevere in the face of public pressure, what function would the extensive expositions on high priests, Yom ha-Kippurim, the blood of the covenants, the ash of the red heifer, new διαθήκη, and so on, serve? There necessarily has to have been a deeper *theological* problem,[22] and this would most probably have had to do with the *Christology of high priesthood*, since its sweeping treatment—comprising, after all, more than three chapters (Heb 7:1–10:18)—can best be understood as a response to this specific concern.[23]

Researchers also agree that, through the Christology of high priesthood, Hebrews wants to reinterpret the traditional confession of Jesus' humiliation and exaltation. The text does this by identifying Jesus as a high priest according to the order of Melchizedek, taking up Ps 109:4 LXX. The idea that Jesus is a high priest was probably already part of the traditional confession, as is evident from Heb 2:17 and 3:1. Already Paul spoke of Christ representing us to God (Rom 8:34). Here, the phrase which then becomes a *leitmotif* in Hebrews already appears: ἐν δεξιᾷ τοῦ θεοῦ. Hebrews refers to this several times (1:3, 13; 8:1; 10:12; 12:2).

As previously mentioned, Heb 7:1–10:18 represents a self-contained argument. In this argument, 7:1 links up directly with 6:20: Jesus as *prodromos* (forerunner, leader) went ahead behind the curtain and there acts as a high priest according to the order/quality of Melchizedek.[24] This "quality" of Jesus' high priesthood is described in detail in ch. 7 in interpretation of Genesis 14 and Ps 109:4 LXX. The oath from Ps 109:4 LXX and Abraham tithing to Melchizedek demonstrate the superiority of this priesthood over the Aaronic priesthood. At the end of this chapter, the author asserts that the

---

[19] In what follows, I take up considerations that I developed more fully in Wolfgang Kraus, "Zu Absicht und Zielsetzung des Hebräerbriefes," *KuD* 60 (2014): 250–71.
[20] David deSilva, *Despising Shame: Honor Discourse and Community Maintenance in the Epistle to the Hebrews*, SBLDS 195 (Atlanta: Scholars, 1995), and *Perseverance in Gratitude: A Socio-Rhetorical Commentary on the Epistle to the Hebrews* (Grand Rapids: Eerdmans, 2000).
[21] DeSilva, *Perseverance*, 18.
[22] Attridge, *Hebrews*, 22–23.
[23] The long introduction to this issue, as presented in Heb 5:11–6:20, also shows the centrality of the remarks beginning in ch. 7.
[24] The word "order," Greek τάξις, is difficult to translate. Elsewhere, the author says κατὰ τὴν ὁμοιότητα Μελχισέδεκ (7:15): lit. according to the "likeness"; I have rendered it as "quality." Going into this in more detail here, however, would lead too far away from the topic at hand.

swearing of this oath stood in opposition to the *nomos*: the oath, which came after the *nomos*, appoints the Son as a high priest who, unlike earthly priests, is not afflicted by weakness, but rather eternally perfected (7:28); in this respect, the stipulation of the *nomos* is voided, as is already stated in 7:12, 18.

Hebrews 8:1 begins with the rhetorical signal: κεφάλαιον δὲ ἐπὶ τοῖς λεγομένοις. Already in Heb 5:10-11, the author had advertised what his main concern would be: he wants to depict Jesus as the originator of eternal salvation, lauded by God as high priest according to the order of Melchizedek.[25] Κεφάλαιον δὲ marks the beginning of this section emphatically. Thereby, what follows is distinguished as decisive: now, the text will be concerned with its most crucial aspect. Ἐπὶ τοῖς λεγομένοις means: concerning the "current exposition."[26] Many exegetes agree that the decisive subject comes up in Heb 8:1-2, though there is disagreement over whether it is the decisive subject of 8:1-10:18[27] or of the entire tractate.[28] The continuation with ἐπὶ τοῖς λεγομένοις, however, cannot refer to what was said up to this point, or to the following chapters, but only to the entire exposition.[29] Georg Gäbel correctly speaks of the "*guiding consideration*, according to which the argument as a whole should be considered and understood and only through which everything else makes sense."[30] According to Knut Backhaus, κεφάλαιον can be taken as a *terminus technicus* of ancient rhetoric.[31] Following Gäbel, then, κεφάλαιον could be understood as marking the "punchline of the entire argument."[32]

This characterization is strengthened by the manifold contextual references: 8:1 again takes up the thesis from 4:14-16, as well as statements in 1:3, 2:17, and 3:1. The words "we have" go back directly to 7:26 (as well as 4:14: "he has"). Hebrews 10:19-21, in turn, takes up 8:1 and carries over "the statement on 'having a high priest'" into "the insight—which had been developed in the meantime—into the liberating and encouraging power of this certainty."[33]

This "guiding consideration" is characterized by three component parts: (1) we have τοιοῦτον ἀρχιερέα—a high priest "such as this," that is, characterized by certain particular attributes; (2) he has taken his seat (ἐκάθισεν) at the right hand of God's throne;[34] (3) this high priest serves at the (heavenly) sanctuary, at the true/real tabernacle. Georg Gäbel aptly summarized the meaning of the content of this statement:

---

[25] In what follows, I take up considerations that I developed more fully in my contribution in *KuD* 60 (2014).
[26] Herbert Braun, *An die Hebräer*, HNT 14 (Tübingen: Mohr Siebeck, 1984), 227.
[27] Karrer, *Heb II*, 101.
[28] Grässer, *Heb II*, 78: Heb 8:1-2 relates only to 8:1-10:18; Grässer, *Heb II*, 80: 8:1-2 mentions the main subject relating to the entire epistle.
[29] Friedrich Bleek, *Der Brief an die Hebräer, 2. Abteilung*, zweite Hälfte (Berlin: Dümmler, 1840), 418: since the participle (λεγομένοις) is given in present tense, it has to refer to "the entire discussion generally" (cited affirmatively in Gäbel, *Kulttheologie*, 240).
[30] Gäbel, *Kulttheologie*, 240 (italics original).
[31] Knut Backhaus, *Der Neue Bund und das Werden der Kirche: Die Diatheke-Deutung des Hebräerbriefs im Rahmen der frühchristlichen Theologiegeschichte*, NTAbh.NF 29 (Münster: Aschendorff 1996), 153; Backhaus, *Hebrews*, 288.
[32] Gäbel, *Kulttheologie*, 240.
[33] Backhaus, *Hebrews*, 289.
[34] This is not so much a *quotation* from Ps 109LXX, but rather an almost *verbatim resumption* of a sentence in 1:3. Both the word μεγαλοσύνη and the phrase ἐν δεξιᾷ are also repeated from 1:3—in

After Heb 7 had interpreted the swearing of the oath in Ψ 109:4, Heb 8 links the theme of high priesthood to the sessio ad dexteram according to Ψ 109:1. In 8:1–2, the two principal strands of the Christology of Hebrews (as well as both scriptural quotations undergirding it, i.e. Ψ 109:1, 4)—are joined together explicitly. Hebrews instructs the audience to see the heavenly high priest in Christ who, according to the traditional schema of humiliation and exaltation, is enthroned at God's right hand. Traditional Christology with its statements of exaltation is interpreted through the Christology of high priesthood.[35]

Hebrews' statements on cultic theology aim to develop the *current* soteriological significance of Jesus' actions and to strengthen the faith of the audience. Even if it is not currently visible that Jesus has already acquired salvation (Heb 2:8b), still there is no room to doubt the validity of this acquisition.

Jeremiah 38 LXX is quoted in order to prove that Jesus' investiture as high priest according to the order of Melchizedek was in accordance with Scripture. It provides scriptural grounding to demonstrate how, according to Scripture, it could even be possible for Jesus to be a high priest: it is possible because God had promised a new διαθήκη through Jeremiah which now is enacted in Jesus.

The concept of διαθήκη in Hebrews would warrant a more detailed exposition than I can give here.[36] For the purposes of this study, it only needs to be pointed out that translating διαθήκη in Hebrews as "covenant" is hardly appropriate. More accurate would be "decree," "statute," "order," "order of salvation," or, more specifically, "cultic order." Hebrews states: Jesus is μεσίτης of a superior διαθήκη. In 8:6, this is related to Jesus' more perfect ministry and confirmed by the statement that this superior διαθήκη had been enacted (νενομοθέτηται, cf. 7:11) through a more perfect promise. The use of the verb is a clear reference to 7:11–12, according to which a change in ministry would engender a change in *nomos*. The oft-repeated statement that Hebrews uses διαθήκη in the same sense as the LXX is of no real help here, since there is no *one* use of διαθήκη in the LXX (as evidenced, for example, by the varying uses of the term in Sirach).[37] When Hebrews speaks of the first/earlier (not *old!*) διαθήκη, this does not reference the Old Testament, nor Judaism, nor Israel either, but specifically the cultic order. Hebrews 8:13, this harsh statement on the "obsolescence" of "the old," therefore, does not mean that the Old Testament or the Old Testament people of God has become aged and therefore obsolete, but rather the old cultic order.

---

contrast to the phrasing of the psalm itself, where we read ἐκ δεξιῶν.
[35] Gäbel, *Kulttheologie*, 240. Cf. already Nikolaus Walter, "Christologie und irdischer Jesus," in idem, *Praeparatio Evangelica. Studien zur Umwelt, Exegese und Hermeneutik des Neuen Testaments*, ed. W. Kraus and F. Wilk, WUNT 98 (Tübingen: Mohr Siebeck, 1997), 151–69 (154).
[36] See Wolfgang Kraus, *Die Bedeutung von διαθήκη im Hebräerbrief*, in *The Reception of Septuagint Words*, ed. Eberhard Bons, Ralph Brucker, and Jan Joosten, WUNT 2/367 (Tübingen: Mohr Siebeck, 2014), 67–83; Wolfgang Kraus, "διαθήκη in Hebrews," in *Covenant—Concepts of Berit, Diatheke, and Testamentum: Proceedings of the Conference at the Lanier Theological Library in Houston, Texas November 2019*, ed. Christian Eberhart and Wolfgang Kraus in Collaboration with Richard Bautch, Matthias Henze, and Martin Rösel, WUNT 506 (Tübingen: Mohr-Siebeck, 2023), 503–19.
[37] On this, see Kraus, *Bedeutung*, 74–75.

Therefore, the new cultic order—this is precisely what the quotation of Jeremiah 38 LXX is supposed to demonstrate—was announced through Scripture itself. Jesus is the high priest at the heavenly sanctuary, the original, the true tabernacle (Heb 8:2), not at its image and shadow (Heb 8:5).[38] This is where the first of our two quotes from Exodus 25 appears. In Heb 9:1–10:18, the substance of Jesus' ministry as high priest, acting at God's right hand in favour of his own people, is explicated by evaluating other central biblical contexts (especially Lev 16; Exod 24; Num 19). Here, the quotation from Exodus 24 comes into play.

At the conclusion of his main argumentative section in Heb 10:12–18, the author again takes up both biblical contexts undergirding his argument, Psalm 109 LXX and Jeremiah 38 LXX, both enclosing, as it were, his conclusion: Heb 10:12–13 explicitly references Psalm 109 LXX and Heb 10:16–17 references Jeremiah 38 LXX. Thus, he has bent the arch of his argument all the way back to 8:1–2 and 8:8–13. With 10:18, he has reached his argumentative goal and can proceed from there to his third main section, which is essentially characterized by paraclesis.

This somewhat lengthy run-up was necessary in order to understand the context of the quotations from Exodus, since their meaning is not only determined by the wording, but also by their context. Let us know go over the individual quotes in detail.

3. The text of the quotations

3.1. Exodus 25:(39,) 40 in Hebrews 8:5

Exodus 25:39–40 (BHS and LXX-Gottingensis):
39 כִּכָּר זָהָב טָהוֹר יַעֲשֶׂה אֹתָהּ אֵת כָּל־הַכֵּלִים הָאֵלֶּה׃
40 וּרְאֵה וַעֲשֵׂה בְּתַבְנִיתָם אֲשֶׁר־אַתָּה מָרְאֶה בָּהָר׃

39 πάντα τὰ σκεύη ταῦτα τάλαντον χρυσίου καθαροῦ. 40 ὅρα ποιήσεις κατὰ τὸν τύπον τὸν δεδειγμένον σοι ἐν τῷ ὄρει.

39 All these vessels shall be a talent of pure gold. 40 See to it that you make it according to the pattern that has been shown to you on the mountain. (NETS, Perkins)

Hebrews 8:1–5 (NA[28] and NRSV):
1 Κεφάλαιον δὲ ἐπὶ τοῖς λεγομένοις, τοιοῦτον ἔχομεν ἀρχιερέα, ὃς ἐκάθισεν ἐν δεξιᾷ τοῦ θρόνου τῆς μεγαλωσύνης ἐν τοῖς οὐρανοῖς, 2 τῶν ἁγίων λειτουργὸς καὶ τῆς σκηνῆς τῆς ἀληθινῆς, ἣν ἔπηξεν ὁ κύριος, οὐκ ἄνθρωπος. 3 Πᾶς γὰρ ἀρχιερεὺς εἰς τὸ προσφέρειν δῶρά τε καὶ θυσίας καθίσταται· ὅθεν ἀναγκαῖον ἔχειν τι καὶ τοῦτον ὃ προσενέγκῃ. 4 εἰ μὲν οὖν ἦν ἐπὶ γῆς, οὐδ' ἂν ἦν ἱερεύς, ὄντων τῶν προσφερόντων κατὰ νόμον τὰ δῶρα· 5 οἵτινες ὑποδείγματι καὶ σκιᾷ

---

[38] On the question how the author of Hebrews himself imagines the heavenly sanctuary, see Otfried Hofius, *Der Vorhang vor dem Thron Gottes*, WUNT 14 (Tübingen: Mohr Siebeck, 1972), 55–73.

λατρεύουσιν τῶν ἐπουρανίων, καθὼς κεχρημάτισται Μωϋσῆς μέλλων ἐπιτελεῖν τὴν σκηνήν· ὅρα γάρ φησιν, ποιήσεις πάντα κατὰ τὸν τύπον τὸν δειχθέντα σοι ἐν τῷ ὄρει.

1 Now the main point in what we are saying is this: we have such a high priest, one who is seated at the right hand of the throne of the Majesty in the heavens, 2 a minister in the sanctuary and the true tent that the Lord, and not any mortal, has set up. 3 For every high priest is appointed to offer gifts and sacrifices; hence it is necessary for this priest also to have something to offer. 4 Now if he were on earth, he would not be a priest at all, since there are priests who offer gifts according to the law. 5 They offer worship in a sanctuary that is a sketch and shadow of the heavenly one; for Moses, when he was about to erect the tent, was warned, "See that you make everything according to the pattern that was shown you on the mountain."

Exodus 25:(39,) 40 is concerned with the creation of the golden lampstand and the associated utensils. Moses is to create everything according to the תבנית that was shown to him. תבנית can mean either "image," "likeness," "figure," or "model," "plan," "archetype."[39] This statement seems to presuppose implicitly that, on the mountain, Moses was shown a model of the sanctuary he was supposed to build.[40] However, this does not come up again later. Already Ibn Esra (796) discussed if this was to be understood as actual seeing or rather as prophetic vision.[41] According to C. Dohmen, though, Exodus 25 is not actually concerned with the question if and how Moses was shown anything; rather, "the references to 'seeing' and 'showing' as well as to the 'model'" are supposed to "indicate to the reader that the following instructions are only 'paraphrases' of an overall plan that Moses has 'in view.'"[42] The text in the LXX almost completely corresponds to the Hebrew. While the LXX usually translates תבנית as παράδειγμα (cf. Exod 25:9), in this instance, it is rendered as τύπος. The second person imperative of עשה is rendered in future tense in the LXX: ποιήσεις.[43]

Hebrews largely adopts the text of the LXX. The participle δεδειγμένον in the original LXX text is translated as δειχθέντα, which hardly makes a substantive difference. The author also adds a πάντα that is neither found in the Hebrew nor the Greek text. Interestingly, though, this πάντα is also found in the passage in question in Philo (Leg.All. III,33). Perhaps both go back to a strand of transmission that does

---

[39] Ges[18], 1424. Siegfried Wagner, "בנה," ThWAT 2:689–706, esp. 704–706. According to Wagner, Exod 25:9(bis), 40 uses it in the sense of "model," "design." According to him, P draws an abstraction from the temple in Jerusalem and transposes the model shown to Moses into the "theophanic-visionary events of Sinai"; this way, the word acquires the meaning of "archetype" or "model" (704). Wagner believes that the use of the term in Ps 144:12 and Josh 22:28 in the sense of "building" represents its primary and original meaning (704).
[40] Josef Schabert, Exodus, NEchtB 24 (Würzburg: Echter 1989), 104–105, rightly states: "Nowhere, however, are we told how JHWH exhibits this model to Moses."
[41] Mentioned in Christoph Dohmen, Exodus 19–40, HThKAT (Freiburg: Herder, 2004), 247.
[42] Dohmen, Exodus 19–40, 247.
[43] Friedrich Schröger, Der Verfasser des Hebräerbriefes als Schriftausleger, BU 4 (Regensburg: Pustet 1968), 160.

not agree with our version of the LXX; πάντα is also attested in some manuscripts for Exod 25:40 LXX. Another plausible explanation, though, is that Hebrews combined this statement, which only references the creation of the golden lampstand and its utensils in the original text, with another statement from Exod 25:8, 9. Here, we do find a πάντα.[44]

In the rabbinic tradition, the idea that Moses was shown a model of the sanctuary is used to underscore the dignity and permanence of the temple in Jerusalem. Philo interprets the passage in question in these terms: "For him, the original sanctuary is the incorporeal, spiritual creation, according to the model of which the visible creation came into being."[45] God dwells both in the cosmos and in the soul. "But the cosmos, too, is only the house of God that is perceptible to the senses, because that which is beautiful to the senses is an image of that which is spiritually beautiful."[46]

While we can probably assume that, in the Hebrew text of Exod 25:(9,) 40, תבנית is conceived of as an intelligible, transcendental model of the sanctuary, in early Jewish tradition (e.g., Sap.Sal 9:8) we increasingly encounter the idea that there was a "veritable heavenly sanctuary" that was shown to Moses.[47] Hebrews stands in this tradition. The τύπος shown to Moses *is* the heavenly sanctuary, that is, the same one that is described as ἐπουράνια earlier in the same verse. Therefore, it is no longer only an intelligible model, but the heavenly sanctuary itself. This also corresponds to the usage in Heb 9:23: the ὑποδείγματα refer to the earthly sanctuary, contrasted with τὰ ἐπουράνια—the heavenly sanctuary. Then, in Heb 9:24, it is stated that the earthly sanctuary is a "counter-image" (τὰ ἀντίτυπα) of the heavenly one. Having been created by hand (τὰ χειροποίητα), it is contrasted with the heavenly sanctuary created by God (Heb 8:2).[48] At the latter, Jesus serves his ministry. Georg Gäbel concisely summarized this: "It is characteristic for Hebrews that the relationship of the earthly sanctuary as being the image of the heavenly one—usually used to legitimize or valorise the earthly sanctuary—is here, quite contrarily, used to qualify [it]: The earthly sanctuary, too, possesses unique legitimacy based on divine revelation; but its character as an image also functions as its limitation, which scripture itself confirms."[49]

Excursus: Intermediate remarks on the History of Religion

At this point, I would like to take a short detour into the history of religion based on the terminology of Hebrews. It was and is often argued that Hebrews belongs to the tradition of Platonism, or Middle Platonism more specifically.[50] It cannot be denied that there are such influences in Hebrews. Interestingly, however, it entirely lacks

---

[44] Schröger, *Verfasser*, 160 n. 3. Cf. Gäbel, *Kulttheologie*, 243 n. 129.
[45] Schröger, *Verfasser*, 161.
[46] Schröger, *Verfasser*, 161.
[47] Gäbel, *Kulttheologie*, 243. On Exod 25:8–9, see Gäbel, *Kulttheologie*, 33.
[48] Gäbel, *Kulttheologie*, 243.
[49] Gäbel, *Kulttheologie*, 243–44.
[50] See especially Backhaus, *Hebrews 52–60*, and idem, *Der sprechende Gott: Gesammelte Studien zum Hebräerbrief*, WUNT 240 (Tübingen: Mohr Siebeck, 2009); Wilfried Eisele, *Ein unerschütterliches Reich: Die mittelplatonische Umformung des Parusiegedankens im Hebräerbrief*, BZNW 116 (Berlin: de Gruyter, 2003).

the epistemological vocabulary that would be expected in this case (ἰδέα, εἶδός, νοῦς, νοητός, αἴσθησις, αἰσθητός).⁵¹ The terminology of archetype/image in reference to the sanctuary in particular shows that the expected, specifically Middle Platonist terms are either absent or used differently. The contrast of παράδειγμα and μίμημα—which would have lent itself perfectly and plays a central role in Middle Platonism—is missing from Hebrews.⁵² Hebrews uses other terms than the Middle Platonist ones.⁵³ Therefore, it does not seem appropriate to assume a purely Middle Platonist background for Hebrews.

3.2. Exodus 24:8 in Hebrews 9:20

Exodus 24:8 (*BHS* and LXX-Gottingensis):
8 וַיִּקַּח מֹשֶׁה אֶת־הַדָּם וַיִּזְרֹק עַל־הָעָם וַיֹּאמֶר הִנֵּה דַם־הַבְּרִית אֲשֶׁר כָּרַת יְהוָה עִמָּכֶם עַל כָּל־הַדְּבָרִים הָאֵלֶּה

8 λαβὼν δὲ Μωυσῆς τὸ αἷμα κατεσκέδασεν τοῦ λαοῦ καὶ εἶπεν Ἰδοὺ τὸ αἷμα τῆς διαθήκης, ἧς διέθετο κύριος πρὸς ὑμᾶς περὶ πάντων τῶν λόγων τούτων.

8 Then Moyses taking the blood, scattered it over the people and said, "Look, the blood of the covenant that the Lord made with you concerning all these words." (NETS, Perkins)

Hebrews 9:18–22 (NA²⁸ and NRSV):
18 ὅθεν οὐδὲ ἡ πρώτη χωρὶς αἵματος ἐγκεκαίνισται· 19 λαληθείσης γὰρ πάσης ἐντολῆς κατὰ °τὸν νόμον ὑπὸ Μωϋσέως παντὶ τῷ λαῷ, λαβὼν τὸ αἷμα τῶν μόσχων [καὶ τῶν τράγων] μετὰ ὕδατος καὶ ἐρίου κοκκίνου καὶ ὑσσώπου αὐτό τε τὸ βιβλίον καὶ πάντα τὸν λαὸν ἐρράντισεν 20 λέγων· τοῦτο τὸ αἷμα τῆς διαθήκης ἧς ἐνετείλατο πρὸς ὑμᾶς ὁ θεός. 21 καὶ τὴν σκηνὴν δὲ καὶ πάντα τὰ σκεύη τῆς λειτουργίας τῷ αἵματι ὁμοίως ἐρράντισεν. 22 καὶ σχεδὸν ἐν αἵματι πάντα καθαρίζεται κατὰ τὸν νόμον καὶ χωρὶς αἱματεκχυσίας οὐ γίνεται ἄφεσις.

18 Hence not even the first covenant was inaugurated without blood. 19 For when every commandment had been told to all the people by Moses in accordance with the law, he took the blood of calves and goats, with water and scarlet wool and hyssop, and sprinkled both the scroll itself and all the people, 20 saying, "This is the blood of the covenant that God has ordained for you." 21 And in the same way he sprinkled with the blood both the tent and all the vessels used in worship. 22 Indeed, under the law almost everything is purified with blood, and without the shedding of blood there is no forgiveness of sins.

In Heb 9:16–17, the author has just justified the necessity of the death of Jesus, the inaugurator of the διαθήκη, through a juridical argument. In v. 18, he passes on to the

---

⁵¹ Gäbel, *Kulttheologie*, 112.
⁵² Gäbel, *Kulttheologie*, 112.
⁵³ See the table in Gäbel, *Kulttheologie*, 113–14.

dedication of the first διαθήκη. The transition is harsh, for vv. 16–17 was about "death"; now it is about "blood." The author "returns to his typological approach."[54]

The author distinguishes three acts: (1) Moses reading the divine precepts (v. 19a); (2) the book and the people being sprinkled with blood (vv. 19b–20); (3) the tabernacle and the utensils also being sprinkled with blood (v. 21). The phrase "This is the blood of the διαθήκη that God has ordained for you" references Exod 24:8. Very roughly, what is said in Hebrews corresponds to the progression of the ritual described in Exod 24:3–8; when it comes to the details, however, there are serious differences. The LXX corresponds exactly to the Hebrew text.

Hebrews has διέθετο instead of the LXX's ἐνετείλατο. This could serve to underscore the compulsory character of the divine precept.[55] Κύριος in the LXX is replaced by ὁ θεός. This can be explained as an expression of the intention to avoid confusion between God and Christ. The LXX's ἰδού is substituted with τοῦτο.[56]

More important for our current considerations are the substantive differences to the account in Exodus. Exodus 24 speaks only of bulls as whole burnt offerings. Hebrews adds goats in v. 19. Presumably the author again has the Yom ha-Kippurim in mind here, which already formed the implicit background to v. 12. Nowhere in the Torah are goats used for whole burnt offerings, but only for sin offerings (Num 28:30). The mention of "water, scarlet wool, and hyssop" also goes beyond Exodus 24. Here, the purification rites from Lev 14:4–5 and Num 19:6 most probably form the background. The ash of the red heifer was already mentioned in Heb 9:13. The idea that Moses also sprinkled the book, the tabernacle, and the utensils with blood does not come from Exodus 24. In fact, according to the account of Exodus 24, the utensils do not even exist yet; they will only be ordered in Exodus 25–31 and created in Exodus 35–39 (some omissions in the LXX).

Again, early Jewish parallels are instructive: comparable combinations of cultic precepts from Exod 40:9–11 and Lev 8:10–12 can be found in Josephus (*Ant.* 3.204–207) and Philo (*Mos.* 2.146).[57] Thus, the author of Hebrews could have stood in a particular tradition that dictated the thematic connection of διαθήκη, purification, and sanctuary.[58] One might mention Ezra 36:10–30, 33 in this context, since there, also, the renewal of the covenant is coupled with a purification ritual.[59] Verse 22 indicates the aim of the argument: the author is concerned with the effect of the blood. The blood canon is also witnessed several times in the Talmud (e.g., *b. Yoma* 5a; *b. Zebaḥ.* 26b).[60]

Hebrews, therefore, understood the conclusion of the covenant in Exodus 24 as a ritual of purification or consecration and conjoined it with the dedication of the

---

[54] Weiss, *Hebrews*, 479.
[55] Schröger, *Verfasser*, 169, citing Riggenbach and Windisch.
[56] There has been some discussion whether or not this could be a reference to the words of institution at the last supper. Christian Lustig in his *Tod und Opfer Jesu im Hebräerbrief*, WUNT 2/589 (Tübingen: Mohr Siebeck, 2023), 201–40, has convincingly argued for a reference to the words of institution.
[57] For details, see Gäbel, *Kulttheologie*, 408—with notes on the differences as well!
[58] Gäbel, *Kulttheologie*, 408.
[59] Gäbel, *Kulttheologie*, 409.
[60] Further evidence in Weiss, *Hebrews*, 482 n. 30.

sanctuary in Exodus 40 to create "one single cultic act"[61] (even though Exod 40 talks of anointment with oil). "The ritual in Exod 24 is here [in Heb 9] completed, as it were, and through this acquires a general relevance concerning the character of the 'first order of salvation.'"[62] This can then be exploited for the dedication of the new διαθήκη by the author of Hebrews.

4. Peculiarities of the reception of Exodus texts in Hebrews

The quotes from Exodus in Hebrews have to be appreciated within the overall theological conception of the text. Already in Heb 7:1, it had been indicated that perfection would be unattainable through the Levitical priesthood, but not yet expounded why this should be the case. And already in 7:18, Jer 38 LXX comes into view but is not yet quoted explicitly: the earlier precept is nullified because of its weakness.

In Hebrews 7, the author is first concerned with the Melchizedekian priesthood, its justification and characteristics.

In Hebrews 8, the weakness of the Levitical cultic order is justified by, among other things, the fact that Aaron and the other priests only serve at the image of the true sanctuary. In 8:1–2, we encounter a thetic summary of the meaning of Jesus' priesthood. According to 8:3–5, Jesus could not be a high priest on earth, since there already is an earthly priesthood. Still, he can be a high priest and serve as such at the heavenly sanctuary because of the new *diatheke*, which is based on a more perfect promise.

Hebrews 9 first references the earthly sanctuary itself as well as its dedication, with Exodus 25 and 26 in the background. The first section, 9:1–5, explicitly closes with v. 5. Verse 6 passes on to the priests' daily ministry at the sanctuary, which is then, in v. 7, related to the fact that the high priest only serves his ministry once. This idea informs the following exposition.

> **Hebrews 9:1–6 (NA[28] and NRSV):**
> 1 Εἶχεν μὲν οὖν [καὶ] ἡ πρώτη δικαιώματα λατρείας τό τε ἅγιον κοσμικόν. 2 σκηνὴ γὰρ κατεσκευάσθη ἡ πρώτη ἐν ᾗ ἥ τε λυχνία καὶ ἡ τράπεζα καὶ ἡ πρόθεσις τῶν ἄρτων, ἥτις λέγεται Ἅγια· 3 μετὰ δὲ τὸ δεύτερον καταπέτασμα σκηνὴ ἡ λεγομένη Ἅγια Ἁγίων, 4 χρυσοῦν ἔχουσα θυμιατήριον καὶ τὴν κιβωτὸν τῆς διαθήκης περικεκαλυμμένην πάντοθεν χρυσίῳ, ἐν ᾗ στάμνος χρυσῆ ἔχουσα τὸ μάννα καὶ ἡ ῥάβδος Ἀαρὼν ἡ βλαστήσασα καὶ αἱ πλάκες τῆς διαθήκης, 5 ὑπεράνω δὲ αὐτῆς Χερουβὶν δόξης κατασκιάζοντα τὸ ἱλαστήριον· περὶ ὧν οὐκ ἔστιν νῦν λέγειν κατὰ μέρος. 6 Τούτων δὲ οὕτως κατεσκευασμένων εἰς μὲν τὴν πρώτην σκηνὴν διὰ παντὸς εἰσίασιν οἱ ἱερεῖς τὰς λατρείας ἐπιτελοῦντες, [...]

> 1 Now even the first covenant had regulations for worship and an earthly sanctuary. 2 For a tent was constructed, the first one, in which were the lampstand, the table, and the bread of the Presence; this is called the Holy Place. 3 Behind the second curtain was a tent called the Holy of Holies. 4 In

---

[61] Gäbel, *Kulttheologie*, 407.
[62] Weiss, *Hebrews*, 481.

it stood the golden altar of incense and the ark of the covenant overlaid on all sides with gold, in which there were a golden urn holding the manna, and Aaron's rod that budded, and the tablets of the covenant; 5 above it were the cherubim of glory overshadowing the mercy seat. Of these things we cannot speak now in detail. 6 Such preparations having been made, the priests go continually into the first tent to carry out their ritual duties [...]

The enumeration of the furnishings of the first and second tent exhibits some peculiarities: there are twice three devices mentioned for the first and second tent. The triad corresponds to the biblical tradition (Exod 25:22-29, 30-40 LXX; 39:16-17; 3 Reg 7:34-35 LXX; 1 Macc 4:50-51; cf. Philo, *Her.* 266). Contrary to the original text in Exodus, however, the bread table and the table with gold overlays are distinguished. The order beginning with the lampstand, also contradicting Exodus 25, is attested elsewhere in early Jewish tradition (Philo, *Her.* 66 and Josephus, *B.J.* 388).

In the arc, there are a golden urn, Aaron's rod and the tablets. This is not written in Exodus. Weiss supposes that the author extrapolated this "as a scripturally learned conclusion from Exod 16:33-34 and Num 17:18, 25," possibly with the intention to get to the "triad of furnishings."[63] The placement of the altar of incense is of particular note:[64] It is localized within the Holy of Holies. Exegetes struggle to explain this.[65] The explanation could be rather simple, however: in Exod 30:6 LXX, the placement of the altar of incense is left ambiguous: ἀπέναντι τοῦ καταπετάσματος could mean "within" as well as "outside of" the curtain.[66] If this explanation holds water, one would have to assume that the author of Hebrews specified the position according to his scriptural learning, not according to his own visual examination. The description of the furnishings aims to emphasize the "(relative!) perfection and splendour of the earthly sanctuary."[67]

At 9:7, Hebrews passes on to Yom-ha-Kippurim, in order to combine this with the conclusion of the covenant in Exodus 24 and the ash of the red heifer in Numbers 19. The goal of the entire account up to v. 10 is—the splendour of the earthly sanctuary depicted in 9:1-5 notwithstanding—to emphasize its insufficiency in regards to the purification of the conscience, so that the author can then, starting at v. 11, interpret this typologically for the surpassing actions of Jesus he is interested in.

Verse 11 marks a new beginning. At the same time, Heb 9:11-15 represent the theological centre of meaning of the tractate. Jesus is μεσίτης or ἔγγυος of a superior διαθήκη. The fact that διαθήκη can truly not be translated as covenant, but rather as order (or the like) is further underscored by the progression of the argument.

---

[63] Weiss, *Hebrews*, 452.
[64] The author of Hebrews does not use θυσιαστήριον or θυσιαστήριον (τοῦ) θυμιάματος—as would usually be the case in the LXX (cf. Exod 27:1; 30:1, 27; Lev 4:7, 18; etc.), but rather θυμιατήριον; on this, see Wolfgang Kraus, *Der Tod Jesu als Heiligtumsweihe: Untersuchungen zum Umfeld der Sühnevorstellung in Röm 3,25-26a*, WMANT 66 (Neukirchen-Vluyn: Neukirchener 1991), 238 n. 22.
[65] Cf. the commentaries on this passage; see also Kraus, *Heiligtumsweihe*, 238 n. 22.
[66] Cf. Karrer, *Heb II*, 144, following Radu Gheorghita, *The Role of the Septuagint in Hebrews*, WUNT 2/160 (Tübingen: Mohr Siebeck, 2003). Aside from syrBar 6,7, there are no reliable parallels on the position of the altar of incense within the Holy of Holies in early Jewish literature (but cf. also Apoc. 8:3-4), cf. Weiss, *Hebrews*, 452 n. 15.
[67] Weiss, *Hebrews*, 451 (author's translation).

In order to explain that Jesus establishes a superior διαθήκη, the author provides a juridical argument: vv. 16–17. Here, διαθήκη seems to be—like in other Greek texts—a testamentary disposition, a last will and testament, which presupposes the testator's death in order to take effect.[68] In v. 18, we encounter a transition: from death to blood, and to the varying reception of the blood ritual from Exod 24:3–8. The author is preoccupied with blood, signifying consecration and purification.[69] The blood canon in v. 22 underscores the significance of blood as a medium of consecration. Verses 23–26 describe Jesus' entry into the heavenly Holy of Holies—on our behalf, once and for all.

Hebrews 10 continues the structure of this argument by now also incorporating *nomos*: just as the earthly sanctuary can only be an image and shadow of the heavenly one, so the *nomos* can only bring a shadow of the benefits yet to come, and not their true form. Therefore, previous remissions of sin can only refer to externalities; the consciousness of sin remains. This is demonstrated through scripture itself: the author uses critiques of sacrifice from Scripture to justify his own position. The first sacrifice is cancelled out by the second. With this, he can return to his fundamental textual basis, Jeremiah 38 LXX. Again, he quotes the statements on the promise he deems decisive and adds that sins are no longer remembered. Now, through the new διαθήκη, the nullification of sin becomes possible. Verse 18 finally emphasizes: every further sacrifice is superfluous.

What happens at this point in Hebrews? It is not simply a critique of sacrifices or of the cult. It is also not about bad-mouthing the Levitical cult in general. First of all, it should be said that, without the explicit ties to Old Testament precepts, the exposition contained in Hebrews would simply not be possible. Franz-Josef Schierse has demonstrated that the thought process of the author of Hebrews follows a three-step structure: similarity—difference—surpassing.[70] The peculiarity of the argument of Hebrews, however, is that everything that the author presents as "surpassing" has, according to his own view, already been announced in Scripture.

---

[68] The shift from "order" or "disposition" to "last will" is not so far. Cf. on διαθήκη in the LXX: Martin Rösel, "Exkurs: Zur Übersetzung von διαθήκη," in *Septuaginta Deutsch: Erläuterungen und Kommentare I*, ed. M. Karrer and W. Kraus (Stuttgart: Deutsche Bibelgesellschaft, 2011), 170; Adrian Schenker, "διαθήκη pour ברית: l'option de traduction de la LXX à la double lumière du droit successoral de l'Égypte ptolémaïque et du livre de la Genèse," in *Lectures et Relectures de la Bible: Festschrift P.-M. Bogaert*, ed. J.-M. Auwers and A. Wenin, BETL 144 (Leuven: Peeters, 1999), 125–31; Bernhard Kübler, "Testament," PRE V A/1:966–1010; Martin Rösel, "Is διαθήκη an Appropriate Translation for ברית? Covenant, Contract, and Testament in the Septuagint," in Eberhart and Kraus et al., eds., *Covenant—Concepts of Berit, Diatheke, and Testamentum*, 233–46.

[69] On blood as a medium of purification and dedication, see Christian Eberhart, *Studien zur Bedeutung der Opfer im Alten Testament. Die Signifikanz von Blut- und Verbrennungsriten im kultischen Rahmen*, WMANT 94 (Neukirchen-Vluyn: Neukirchener Verlag, 2002); Friedhelm Hartenstein, "Zur symbolischen Bedeutung des Blutes im Alten Testament," in *Deutungen des Todes Jesu im Neuen Testament*, ed. J. Frey and J. Schröter, WUNT 181 (Tübingen: Mohr Siebeck, 2005), 119–37; cf. also Kraus, *Heiligtumsweihe*, 45–69: "Die Blutapplikation als Weiheritus," and Kraus, "Der Erweis der Gerechtigkeit Gottes im Tod Jesu nach Röm 3,21–26," in *Judaistik und Neutestamentliche Wissenschaft*, ed. L. Doering, H.-G. Waubke, and F. Wilk, FRLANT 226 (Göttingen: Vandenhoeck & Ruprecht, 2008), 192–218, esp. 206–15.

[70] Schierse, *Verheißung und Heilsvollendung*. This schema was confirmed by Erich Grässer, "Mose und Jesus. Zur Auslegung von Heb 3,1–6," *ZNW* 75 (1984): 2–23, esp. 14 for Heb 3:1–6; however, it is not limited to Heb 3:1–6, but rather a continuous structural phenomenon of Hebrews; see Erich Grässer, "Der Hebräerbrief 1938–1963," *TRu* NF 30 (1964): 138–236, esp. 165.

Does he adequately interpret Scripture in doing so? No and yes; certainly not in our historical-critical sense. The starting point of his considerations is his conviction of the exaltation of Jesus according to Psalm 109 LXX. This is part of the confession handed down to him. But it seems to have become doubtful. Jesus has been exalted, but visible perfection has failed to appear; what has appeared is exclusion and suffering. In Heb 2:8, it is stated explicitly: we do not see yet that all foes are laid at his feet. Hebrews 10:37 alludes to the absence of perfection and stresses that ὁ ἐρχόμενος will come shortly and not be absent.

The exaltation of Jesus according to Ps 109:1 LXX is part of the traditional confession. Perfection is still outstanding. In order to counter the resulting fatigue of the faith, the author continues reading from Ps 109:1 to 109:4 LXX and integrates what he read into the traditional confession of the exalted one. Jesus acts on behalf of the believers ἐν δεξιᾷ τοῦ θεοῦ as a high priest according to the order of Melchizedek. Then, he finds a scriptural justification for this: the promise of a new διαθήκη according to Jeremiah 38 LXX.

The challenges facing the addressees of Hebrews resulted from their confession of the exaltation of Jesus, the expected visible enforcement of which had failed to arrive up to this point (Heb 2:8b; 10:13). The author of the tractate reacts to this with a sophisticated cultic theology; its subject is "the mediation between present-earthly life and eschatological-heavenly perfection of salvation."[71] The theological achievement of the author can be described as "having reinterpreted the traditional Christological kerygma in such a way that, through cultic theology, in becomes clear that and how the addressees *already in this moment* take part in the *present* perfection of salvation, even though their eschatological entry into this perfection of salvation is yet to come."[72]

5. Hermeneutic conclusions

First, the "biblical theology" of Hebrews is interpretation of Scripture. This interpretation is rhetorically sophisticated, very learned, and demands a lot from its hearers/readers. Biblical theology cannot simply take the Masoretic Text as its sole reference point.[73] The interpreter has to include the Septuagint.

Second, many things have changed between the first and the twenty-first century: Judaism and Christianity arose as children of one mother, but are now two distinguishable religions. Hebrews speaks to a different situation than ours. To simply quote it "biblically" would thus be inappropriate. Biblicism does not make theology. We need to conceive of and think with these texts continuing their directional meaning. In doing so, Hebrews can gain unexpected timeliness: the way it treats the challenges facing its audience could become exemplary. Through cultic theology, it made clear that and how the addressees already in their lifetime *through faith* take part in the

---

[71] Gäbel, *Kulttheologie*, 480.
[72] Gäbel, *Kulttheologie*, 482 (emphasis is mine).
[73] At the inception of the project Septuaginta Deutsch, Helmut Utzschneider wrote a programmatic article on the focus and orientation of the project: "Auf Augenhöhe mit dem Text," in *Im Brennpunkt: Die Septuaginta. Studien zur Entstehung und Bedeutung der Griechischen Bibel*, ed. Heinz-Josef Fabry et al., BWANT 153 (Stuttgart: Kohlhammer, 2001), 11–50.

present heavenly perfection of salvation. According to Heb 11:1, faith "is the reality of things hoped for, the proof of things unseen"[74] ("Εστιν δὲ πίστις ἐλπιζομένων ὑπόστασις, πραγμάτων ἔλεγχος οὐ βλεπομένων). With this conception, the author of Hebrews went a long way toward moving the focus away from the temporal expectation of the perfection of salvation and its related problems and moving the conversation along. He did not make temporal eschatology disappear completely by rhetorical sleight of hand, but rather shifted the focus away from it.[75]

Third, today, twenty centuries later, we are hardly justified to say: ἔτι γὰρ μικρὸν ὅσον ὅσον, ὁ ἐρχόμενος ἥξει καὶ οὐ χρονίσει· (Heb 10:37)—at least if we mean it in a concrete sense and the sentence is supposed to represent more than repetition of traditional statements. Rather, for theological reasons and also if we want to remain in academic conversation with current natural science, we have to speak about early Christian proximal eschatology differently; we have to understand creation itself as a dynamic, open process, and conceive of our own lives through the attainment of salvation that has already occurred through Christ in heaven.

Fourth, the direction that Hebrews points in could also be a signpost for us. For this is what the theology of Hebrews heads toward: Beyond temporal expectations, the true ministry of the believer consists in everyday actions since the heavenly high priest has already attained our salvation through his own ministry at the heavenly sanctuary. We do not have to add anything, but we can, Hebrews teaches us, take assured steps in the certainty that our life is securely anchored in the heavenly reality, in the confidence in God, and in the emulation of our *Prodromos* Jesus, as long as we lift up and strengthen the drooping hands and weak knees (Heb 12:12) of those in the community that take these steps together with us (12:13). Thus, high cultic theology in Hebrews has its enormous practical, real-life effects.

Bibliography

Attridge, Harold. *The Epistle to the Hebrews*. Hermeneia. Philadelphia: Fortress Press, 1989.

Backhaus, Knut. *Der Neue Bund und das Werden der Kirche. Die Diatheke-Deutung des Hebräerbriefs im Rahmen der frühchristlichen Theologiegeschichte*. NTAbh.NF 29. Münster: Aschendorff, 1996.

Backhaus, Knut. *Der Hebräerbrief*. Regensburger Neues Testament. Regensburg: Pustet, 2009.

Backhaus, Knut. *Der sprechende Gott. Gesammelte Studien zum Hebräerbrief*. WUNT 240. Tübingen: Mohr Siebeck, 2009.

Bleek, Friedrich. *Der Brief an die Hebräer*. Berlin: Dümmler, 1840.

Braun, Herbert. *An die Hebräer*. HNT 14. Tübingen: Mohr Siebeck, 1984.

Calaway, Jared C. *The Sabbath and the Sanctuary: Access to God in the Letter to the Hebrews and its Priestly Context*. WUNT 2/349. Tübingen: Mohr Siebeck, 2013.

---

[74] Translation according to Attridge, *Hebrews*, 305.
[75] On this, see Wolfgang Kraus, "Zur Aufnahme und Bedeutung von Ps 102 (101 LXX) im Hebräerbrief," in *Theologie und Textgeschichte. Septuaginta und Masoretischer Text als Äußerungen theologischer Reflexion*, ed. Frank Ueberschaer, Thomas Wagner, and Jonathan Miles Robker, WUNT 407 (Tübingen: Mohr Siebeck, 2018), 239–58.

DeSilva, David A. *Despising Shame: Honor Discourse and Community Maintenance in the Epistle to the Hebrews.* SBLDS 195. Atlanta: Scholars, 1995.
DeSilva, David A. *Perseverance in Gratitude: A Socio-Rhetorical Commentary on the Epistle to the Hebrews.* Grand Rapids: Eerdmans, 2000.
Dohmen, Christoph. *Exodus 19–40.* HThKAT. Freiburg: Herder, 2004.
Eberhart, Christian. *Studien zur Bedeutung der Opfer im Alten Testament. Die Signifikanz von Blut- und Verbrennungsriten im kultischen Rahmen.* WMANT 94. Neukirchen-Vluyn: Neukirchener Verlag, 2002.
Eisele, Wilfried. *Ein unerschütterliches Reich. Die mittelplatonische Umformung des Parusiegedankens im Hebräerbrief.* BZNW 116. Berlin: de Gruyter, 2003.
Gäbel, Georg. *Die Kulttheologie des Hebräerbriefes.* WUNT 2/212. Tübingen: Mohr Siebeck, 2006.
Gheorghita, Radu. *The Role of the Septuagint in Hebrews.* WUNT 2/160. Tübingen: Mohr Siebeck, 2003.
Grässer, Erich. "Der Hebräerbrief 1938–1963." *Theologische Rundschau Neue Folge* 30 (1964): 138–236.
Grässer, Erich. "Mose und Jesus. Zur Auslegung von Heb 3,1–6." *ZNW* 75 (1984): 2–23.
Grässer, Erich. *An die Hebräer.* 3 vols. Neukirchen-Vluyn: Neukirchener Verlag, 1990, 1993, 1997.
Hartenstein, Friedhelm. "Zur symbolischen Bedeutung des Blutes im Alten Testament. Pages 119–37 in *Deutungen des Todes Jesu im Neuen Testament.* Edited by Jörg Frey and Jens Schröter. WUNT 181. Tübingen: Mohr Siebeck, 2005.
Hofius, Otfried. *Der Vorhang vor dem Thron Gottes.* WUNT 14. Tübingen: Mohr Siebeck, 1972.
Karrer, Martin. *Der Brief an die Hebräer.* 2 vols. ÖTK 20. Gütersloh: Gütersloher Verlagshaus, 2002, 2008.
Klawans, Jonathan. *Purity, Sacrifice, and the Temple: Symbolism and Supersessionism in the Study of Ancient Judaism.* Oxford: Oxford University Press, 2006.
Kraus, Wolfgang. *Der Tod Jesu als Heiligtumsweihe. Untersuchungen zum Umfeld der Sühnevorstellung in Röm 3,25–26a.* WMANT 66. Neukirchen-Vluyn: Neukirchener Verlag, 1991.
Kraus, Wolfgang. "Der Erweis der Gerechtigkeit Gottes im Tod Jesu nach Röm 3,21–26." Pages 192–218 in *Judaistik und Neutestamentliche Wissenschaft.* Edited by Lutz Doering, Hans-Günther Waubke, and Florian Wilk. FRLANT 226. Göttingen: Vandenhoeck & Ruprecht, 2008.
Kraus, Wolfgang. "Die Rezeption von Jer 38,31–34 (LXX) in Hebräer 8–10 und dessen Funktion in der Argumentation des Hebräerbriefes." Pages 447–62 in *Text-Critical and Hermeneutical Studies in the Septuagint.* Edited by Johann Cook and Hermann-Josef Stipp. VTSup 157. Leiden: Brill, 2012.
Kraus, Wolfgang. "Zur Aufnahme und Funktion von Gen 14,18–20 und Ps 109 LXX im Hebräerbrief." Pages 459–74 in *Text—Textgeschichte—Textwirkung. Festschrift zum 65. Geburtstag von Siegfried Kreuzer.* Edited by Thomas Wagner, Jonathan Miles Robker, and Frank Ueberschaer. Münster: Ugarit-Verlag, 2014.
Kraus, Wolfgang. "Zu Absicht und Zielsetzung des Hebräerbriefes." *KuD* 60 (2014): 250–71.
Kraus, Wolfgang. "Die hermeneutische Relevanz der Septuaginta für eine Biblische Theologie." Pages 3–25 in *Die Septuaginta—Text, Wirkung, Rezeption.* Edited by Wolfgang Kraus, Siegfried Kreuzer, Martin Meiser, and Marcus Sigismund. WUNT 325. Tübingen: Mohr Siebeck, 2014.

Kraus, Wolfgang. "Die Bedeutung von *diatheke* im Hebräerbrief." Pages 67–83 in *The Reception of Septuagint Words*. Edited by Eberhard Bons, Ralph Brucker, and Jan Joosten. WUNT 2/367. Tübingen: Mohr Siebeck, 2014.

Kraus, Wolfgang. "Zur Aufnahme und Bedeutung von Ps 102 (101 LXX) im Hebräerbrief." Pages 239–58 in *Theologie und Textgeschichte. Septuaginta und Masoretischer Text als Äußerungen theologischer Reflexion*. Edited by Frank Ueberschaer, Thomas Wagner and Jonathan Miles Robker. WUNT 407. Tübingen: Mohr Siebeck, 2018.

Kraus, Wolfgang. "Zur Schriftverwendung in Hebräer 13. Zugleich ein Beitrag zur Frage nach dem Verhältnis von Heb 13 zu Heb 1–12." Pages 177–92 in *Die Schriftzitate im Hebräerbrief als Zeugen für die Überlieferung der Septuaginta*. Edited by M. Sigismund and S. Kreuzer. WUNT 2/580. Tübingen: Mohr Siebeck 2022.

Kraus, Wolfgang. "διαθήκη in Hebrews." Pages 503–19 in *Covenant—Concepts of Berit, Diatheke, and Testamentum: Proceedings of the Conference at the Lanier Theological Library in Houston, Texas November 2019*. Edited by Christian Eberhart and Wolfgang Kraus in Collaboration with Richard Bautch, Matthias Henze, and Martin Rösel. WUNT 506. Tübingen: Mohr-Siebeck, 2023.

Kübler, Bernhard. "Testament." *PRE* V A/1 (1934): 966–1010.

Löhr, Hermut. "'Umriß' und 'Schatten'. Bemerkungen zur Zitierung von Exod 25,40 in Heb 8." *ZNW* 84 (1993): 218–32.

Löhr, Hermut. "Thronversammlung und preisender Tempel. Beobachtungen am himmlischen Heiligtum im Hebräerbrief und in den Sabbatopferliedern aus Qumran." Pages 185–205 in *Königsherrschaft Gottes und himmlischer Kult*. Edited by Martin Hengel and Anna Maria Schwemer. WUNT 55. Tübingen: Mohr Siebeck, 1991.

Lustig, Christian. *Tod und Opfer Jesu im Hebräerbrief*. WUNT 2/589. Tübingen: Mohr Siebeck, 2023.

Moffitt, David M. *Atonement and Resurrection in the Epistle to the Hebrews*. NovTSup 141. Leiden: Brill, 2011.

Rösel, Martin. "Exkurs: Zur Übersetzung von διαθήκη." Page 170 in *Septuaginta Deutsch. Erläuterungen und Kommentare I*. Edited by Martin Karrer and Wolfgang Kraus. Stuttgart: Deutsche Bibelgesellschaft, 2011.

Rösel, Martin. "Is διαθήκη an Appropriate Translation for ברית? Covenant, Contract, and Testament in the Septuagint?" Pages 233–46 in *Covenant—Concepts of Berit, Diatheke, and Testamentum: Proceedings of the Conference at the Lanier Theological Library in Houston, Texas November 2019*. Edited by Christian Eberhart and Wolfgang Kraus in Collaboration with Richard Bautch, Matthias Henze, and Martin Rösel. WUNT 506. Tübingen: Mohr-Siebeck, 2023.

Scharbert, Josef. *Exodus*. Neue Echter-Bibel Kommentar Altes Testament 24. Würzburg: Echter, 1989.

Schenker, Adrian. "διαθήκη pour ברית: l'option de traduction de la LXX à la double lumière du droit successoral de l'Égypte ptolemaique et du livre de la Genèse." Pages 125–31 in *Lectures et Relectures de la Bible: Festschrift P.-M. Bogaert*. Edited by Jean-Marie Auwers and André Wenin. BETL 144. Leuven: Peeters, 1999.

Schenck, Kenneth L. *Cosmology and Eschatology in Hebrews. The Settings of the Sacrifice*. SNTSMS 143. Cambridge: Cambridge University Press, 2007.

Schierse, Franz-Josef. *Verheißung und Heilsvollendung. Zur theologischen Grundfrage des Hebräerbriefes*. Münchener Theologische Studien 9. Munich: Zink, 1955.

Schröger, Friedrich. *Der Verfasser des Hebräerbriefes als Schriftausleger*. Biblische Untersuchungen 4. Regensburg: Pustet, 1968.

Schunack, Gerd. *Der Hebräerbrief.* Zürich Bibelkommentare 14. Zurich: Theologischer Verlag Zürich, 2002.
Utzschneider, Helmut. "Tabernacle." Pages 267–301 in *The Book of Exodus. Composition, Reception, and Interpretation.* Edited by Thomas Dozeman, Craig A. Evans, and Joel N. Lohr. VTSup 164. Leiden: Brill, 2014.
Wagner, Siegfried. "בנה" *ThWAT* Bd. II (1973): 689–706.
Walter, Nikolaus. "Christologie und irdischer Jesus." Pages 151–69 in *Praeparatio Evangelica. Studien zur Umwelt, Exegese und Hermeneutik des Neuen Testaments.* Edited by W. Kraus and F. Wilk. WUNT 98. Tübingen: Mohr Siebeck, 1997.
Weiss, Hans-Friedrich. *Der Brief an die Hebräer.* Kritisch-exegetischer Kommentar über das Neue Testament 13. Göttingen: Vandenhoeck & Ruprecht, 1991.

Chapter 18

Exodus and *egressio*: Observations on Biblical Terminology in the Latin Language

Daniela Scialabba

1. Introduction

In a previous publication of mine, my concern was to investigate the Greek terminology and modes of expression that the texts of the Septuagint employ to express the concept bound up with the exodus of Israel from the land of Egypt.[1] That essay was devoted to the Greek term *exodos* and its semantic evolution. The intention was to show how the Greek word entered various modern languages—as *esodo* (in Italian), *exode* (in French), exodus (in English and German) and *éxodos* (in Spanish)—in a careful investigation of the process of migration of a collectivity and, more specifically, of a people, and to trace its most distant origins and its earliest uses precisely in the biblical texts written in Greek.

The aim of this present article is to investigate the Latin terminology in a parallel way. Even if not exhaustive, this study's objective is to complete the previous essay, answering two fundamental questions in particular. First, just when did the second book of the Pentateuch assume the Latin name of *liber exodi* or *exodus*? Second, how did the Latin versions of the Bible and the ancient Christian authors who wrote in Latin express the concept of migration with reference to Israel coming out of the land of Egypt—a fundamental stage in the history of the people of the covenant, a vantage point from which Israel was to begin to view the other events of its national story?[2]

To answer these questions, the first necessary step will be to go back over some elements relating to the language which the Septuagint uses in this regard. In this particular case, we must clarify the contexts which use terms like ἔξοδος or ἐξοδία to

---

[1] D. Scialabba, "L'uso specifico di 'Exodos' nei LXX: l'"Esodo' del popolo di Israele," in *Exodos. Storia di un vocabolo*, ed. E. Bons, A. Mambelli, and D. Scialabba (Bologna: Il Mulino, 2019), 87–102.
[2] Scialabba, "L'uso specifico di 'Exodos' nei LXX," especially on p. 91.

speak of the migration of the Israelites from Egypt. In fact, in order to have a better understanding of the Latin language relating to the "exodus," it will be necessary to know how the Latin-speaking authors were probably influenced by their Greek sources of reference. Following that, we shall present some select examples in which the use of the proper name *Exodus* appears to designate the second book of the Pentateuch. In the final part of this study, we shall seek to explain another linguistic evolutionary stage for the term *exodus* to gain a better understanding of how, and in what kind of contexts, the term became a substantive used to speak of the migration of the Israelites out of Egypt. Indeed, if such a study has already been carried out in Greek texts, to this day there is lacking a study that examines the beginnings of the reception of the Greek term in the Latin language.

The absence of detailed studies of this subject is confirmed also by the fact that a search of the dictionaries often does not lead to any result. In fact, as I shall show in this chapter, it is of note that, in the common Latin dictionaries, even the most respected ones, the lemma *exodus* is not even recorded, and, where it is mentioned, this is limited to reporting some information relating to the name of the book.

My study will make use of all those digital and printed resources that are currently available to anyone who wishes to carry out work on Christian texts in Latin. However, I do not claim that this is an exhaustive investigation due to the fact that some tools such as the corpora of the *Vetus Latina* are only partly available in critical editions published to date or else are unobtainable.[3]

2. The Greek background of the Latin use of the Term *Exodus*

The occurrences in the LXX where the term ἔξοδος assumes the sense of "migration" in relation to the departure of Israel from Egypt are far from numerous. In fact, in the LXX ἔξοδος has not yet become a technical term for identifying *de rigueur* the events recounted in the second book of the Pentateuch.[4] We find only five occurrences of such a use. In the corresponding Hebrew texts, in order to render the meaning of "departure" or "migration," rather than a substantive, it is always a verbal form that is used. The infinitive construct of the verb יצא, "to go out," within a stereotypical expression which indicates Israel's departure from Egypt, is different from what happens in the Greek text. Here, we find the word ἔξοδος with this specific function, once in Exod 19:1, once in Num 33:38, another time in 3 Kgdms 6:1, and twice in the book of Psalms (Pss 104[105]:38; 113[114]:1). In all the other historical books of the Old Testament, the substantive ἔξοδος never appears with this meaning. The same goes for the few other later texts of the Old Testament and the so-called deuterocanonical literature

---

[3] From this point of view, emphatic reference should be made here to the critical edition of P. Sabatier and B. Fischer, *Bibliorum Sacrorum Versionis Antiquate seu Vetus Italica. Additur Index Codicum Manuscriptorum quibus P. Sabatier usus est 1743*, 3 vols; reprint (Turnhout: Brepols, 1976), and the *Vetus Latina Database online* (http://apps.brepolis.net.eu1.proxy.openathens.net/vld/Default.aspx).

[4] As G. Leonardi has shown in "L'impiego di ἔξοδος nei Settanta: presentazione dei dati ed equivalenti ebraici," in Bons, Mambelli, and Scialabba, eds., *Exodos*, 67–85, the use of ἔξοδος in the LXX is quite varied since it is used with different meanings, including as the movement of departure or as the place of departure. In a transferred sense, it can be understood as "the end," that is, the term of something or as "origin, provenience," just as, also, "death."

which mention the exodus of Israel, as, for example, Sirach (cf. Sir 44:23–45:5: referring to Moses) and Jdt 5:10–15.

In two cases, rather than using the term in its masculine form, which is also the more common one, the LXX employs the same term but in its feminine form: ἐξοδία. These are the texts, Deut 16:3 and Mic 7:15, in which the formula is almost identical to the stereotype with the single difference that, here, it occurs in expressions that indicate the "day of the departure from the land of Egypt." In Deut 16:3, Israel is asked to remember "the day of your departure from the land of Egypt" (μνησθῆτε τὴν ἡμέραν τῆς ἐξοδίας ὑμῶν ἐκ γῆς Αἰγύπτου); in Mic 7:15, addressing his people, God will make them see wonders happening "as in the day of your departure from the land of Egypt" (κατὰ τὰς ἡμέρας ἐξοδίας σου ἐξ Αἰγύπτου).

If we prescind from the use of ἔξοδος to designate Israel's migration from Egypt, the term Ἔξοδος is already applied to designate the name of the second book of the Pentateuch in the Greek-speaking ecclesiastical tradition. According to what has been discovered by the scholars who have been occupied with this subject, including Professor Larry Perkins,[5] the first certain attestations in which Ἔξοδος is replacing the primigenial Hebrew name, šəmôṯ, for the book which tells of Israel's migration from Egypt can be ascribed to the Christian Church of the first centuries, more concretely, to the second half of the second century CE. In particular, these are Christian texts, and it is attested for the first time, around the middle of the second century CE in Justin Martyr's *Dialogue with Trypho* where it appears at various times and is almost always preceded by the substantive βίβλος, precisely to make clear that he is providing explanations on what is recorded in the book of Exodus. Along these lines we have *Dial.* 59.1, which contains the expression ἀπὸ τῆς βίβλου τῆς Ἐξόδου, "from the book of 'Exodus,'" and 59.2 where, with greater emphasis, it is explained that Justin is providing an interpretation of events which are recounted ἐν τῇ βίβλῳ ᾗ ἐπιγράφεται Ἔξοδος, "in the book which is entitled *Exodus*." However, these are not the only passages in Justin's works where the term designates the second book of the Pentateuch. In fact, he does not fail to make use of identical or similar expressions in other passages too, as in 75.1 (ἐν δὲ τῷ βιβλίῳ τῆς Ἐξόδου); in 126.2 (ἐν τῇ Ἐξόδῳ); and in 128.1 (ἀπὸ τῆς Ἐξόδου)[6].

After Justin, there are other authors who use the term in this sense, such as Melito of Sardis who, according to the testimony of Eusebius,[7] lists Ἔξοδος among the books of the Old Testament, and later Origen who cites it in various writings, not excluding, at least in one case, its citing alongside the name, Ἔξοδος, the traditional Hebrew name in Greek transliteration: Ἔξοδος, Ουελλεσμωθ, ὅπερ ἐστὶν 'ταῦτα τὰ ὀνόματα' (*Esodo, Ouellesmoth*, which means: "These are the names"). It is worth noting that Codex Vaticanus and Codex Alexandrinus both bear the Greek name for designating the second book of the Pentateuch.[8]

---

[5] Larry Perkins, "Ἐξαγωγή or Ἔξοδος: What Changed and Why," *BIOSCS* 39 (2006): 105–14. See also A. Mambelli, "ἔξοδος come titolo del secondo libro del Pentateuco," in Bons, Mambelli, and Scialabba, eds., *Exodos*, 167–77 (173–74).
[6] PTS 47.172; 200; 288; 292.
[7] *Storia ecclesiastica*, 4.26.14 (GCS 9/1,388).
[8] For further details, see Mambelli, "ἔξοδος come titolo del secondo libro del Pentateuco," 173–74.

3. The Latin title of the second book of the Pentateuch

Next, I shall focus on two authoritative voices of the ancient Latin Christian tradition, Tertullian and Jerome, who mention the word *Exodus* in connection with their references to the second book of the Pentateuch. In the light of these texts, we shall be able to note that the two authors reveal a certain familiarity with the name of the book deriving from Greek Christianity.[9]

3.1. Tertullian

For the use of the term *exodus*, a Latin transliteration of the Greek to indicate the homonymous book, we find the first attestations in Tertullian.[10] In his work, he refers to the second book of the Pentateuch, using spontaneously the nomenclature of the Greek tradition.[11] This involves several passages and several books out of his whole corpus. For example, in his work, *De ieiunio adversus psychicos* 10.9, speaking of the effectiveness of fasting as an instrument for the life of faith, he takes as an example an episode drawn from the book of Exodus, the battle of Moses against Abimelech (Exod 17:8–12) which the former sustained with prayer and fasting protracted until the evening. This attitude procured him the victory: *In Exodo habitus ille Moysis adversus Amalech orationibus proeliantis usque in occasum perseverans nonne statio fuit sera?*, "In Exodus, wasn't the conduct of Moses, who fought against Abimelech with prayers, persevering until sunset, perhaps, a prolonged *statio*?"[12]

It is also interesting to note that, in his *Adversus Marcionem*,[13] book IV.20.1, Tertullian makes use of the name *Exodus* with reference to the book that contains the miraculous episode of the opening up of the Sea of Reeds. In this connection, Tertullian wishes that Marcion would interpret correctly what is recounted there. In particular, in the passage in question, Tertullian sets in parallel what is recounted in Luke 8:22–25, where Jesus' stilling of the storm is recounted, and the miracle of the opening of the waters of the Red Sea performed by Moses in Exod 14:16–21. What is interesting is the comparison which Tertullian makes between Christ's power over the winds and waves and Moses' command of the waters of the Red Sea and the Jordan:[14]

---

[9] The Greek name as title of the book does not seem to be attested in other contemporary sources except for those of Christian provenance.

[10] Here, we have to point out that research is limited to the point where the present-day means of research enable us to explore the ancient biblical literature in Latin. In fact, as is well known, the texts of the *Vetus Latina* can be consulted in only a very partial way since they are still unpublished or not yet available in the data banks available today.

[11] R. Braun, *"Deus Christianorum": recherches sur le vocabulaire doctrinal de Tertullien* (Paris: Études Augustiniennes, 1977), does not deal with this subject. The term is not even present in W. Lechtner-Schmidt, *Wortindex der Lateinisch erhaltenen Pseudepigraphen zum Alten Testament* (Tubingen: A. Francke Verlag, 1990).

[12] "Statio" in the sense of "fast." In this connection, compare Quinto S. Tertulliano, "Il digiuno, contro gli psichici": introduzione, traduzione e note di S. Matteoli, in *Tertulliano. Opere Montaniste*, ed. A. Capone et al. (Rome: Città nuova, 2012), 211 n. 94.

[13] CSEL 47, p. 484. For a scientific edition, see the volume of C. Moreschini, ed., *Tertulliano. Opere Dottrinali. Contro Marcione* (Rome: Città Nuova, 2016).

[14] The story of the Exodus plays a very important role in the Fathers in relation to Christ and the Church. In this connection, see J. Daniélou, *From Shadow to Reality. Studies in the Biblical Typology*

> *Quis autem iste est qui ventis et mari imperat? [...] agnorant substantiae auctorem suum, quae famulis quoque eius obaudire consueverant. Inspice Exodum, Marcion, aspice mari rubro, vastiori supra omnia stagna Iudaeae, virgam Moysi imperantem, ut funditus proscissum et pari utrimque stupore discriminis fixum sicco populum pede intestino itinere transmitteret, rursus que sub eiusdem virgae nutu redeunte natura aegyptium exercitum undarum concordia obrueret, in quod opus et austri servierunt*

Who is this who commands the winds and the sea?[15] [...] The elements had recognised their Creator,[16] those elements that were accustomed to obey his servants too. Read Exodus, Marcion, look how the rod of Moses commands the Red Sea, vaster than all the lakes of Judaea, as it had been divided right at the beginning, and how Moses made the people to pass dry-shod through a path within it in the chaos caused by its being divided into two parts;[17] and how, again, by command of this same rod, the properties of nature returned and the sea swamped the Egyptians under the meeting of the waves:[18] in this deed, the winds of the south also took part.[19]

Finally, we can cite another example where Tertullian uses the term with reference to admonishments against idolatry, quoting Deuteronomy and the Decalogue recorded in the book of Exodus. In this connection, Tertullian employs the proper name of the book according to the Latinized wording of the Greek name also in the work, *Scorpiace* 2.2-3.[20] With regard to certain warnings about the unique nature of God, he cites the Decalogue just as it is found in the book of Exodus and some verses of Deuteronomy:[21]

> *"Ego sum," inquit, "Deus, Deus tuus, qui te eduxi de terra Aegypti. Non erunt tibi dii alii praeter me. Non facies tibi simulacrum eorum quae in caelo et quae in terra deorsum et quae in mari infra terram. Non adorabis ea, neque famulaberis eis. <Ego> enim dominus deus tuus."[22] Item in eadem Exodo: "ipsi vidistis, quod de caelo locutus ad vos sim. Non facietis vobis deos argenteos,*

---

of the Fathers (London: Burns & Oates, 1960), 154: "The Fathers have rightly insisted at all times that the types of the Exodus are fulfilled in the life of Christ and the Church, and in this they have but followed the teaching of the New Testament, which shows that these types are fulfilled in Christ."

[15] Luke 8:25.
[16] Luke 8:22-24.
[17] Compare Exod 14:22-29.
[18] Compare Exod 14:27.
[19] Compare Exod 14:21. "La traduzione [latina] di Tertulliano corrisponde a quella della Settanta, mentre la Vulgata ha *flante vento vehementi et urente* (Braun)," thus Quinto S. Tertulliano, *Opere Dottrinali. Contro Marcione*, ed. C. Moreschini (Rome: Città Nuova, 2016), 114.
[20] CSEL 20, p. 147.
[21] Compare Exod 20:3; Deut 6:4.
[22] Exodus 20:2-5.

*et deos aureos non facietis vobis."*²³ *Secundum haec et in Deuteronomio: "Audi Israel, dominus deus tuus unus est, et diliges dominum Deum tuum ex toto corde tuo et totis viribus tuis et ex tota anima tua"*²⁴

"I am God," he says, "your God who brought you out of the land of Egypt. You shall have no other gods but me. You shall not make for yourself the image of things which are in heaven or down on earth and in the sea under the earth. You shall not worship them and serve them. For I am the Lord, your God. The same again in Exodus: You have seen that I spoke to you from heaven. You shall not make gods of silver, and gods of gold you shall not make." Similarly, in Deuteronomy: "Hear, O Israel: the Lord your God is one alone. You shall love the Lord, your God, with all your heart and all your strength and all your mind."

It would not be difficult to find still other passages from the works of Tertullian where he does not hesitate to call the second book of the Pentateuch *Exodus*, following the proper name originating from the Greek tradition. This also means that the recipients of his works were familiar with this terminology which is clearly being used in a way that is spontaneous and habitual.

3.2. Jerome

In his Latin translation of the biblical texts, the so-called *Vulgate*, in order to designate the book in question, Jerome seems to adopt right from the beginning the name "Exodus," thus using the Greek wording according to the Latin diction.²⁵ In fact, in this Latin version, which he composes chiefly on the basis of the Hebrew texts, according to the adage, dear to him, of *hebraica veritas*,²⁶ he writes as title of the book: "Incipit liber *Ellescmoth* id est Exodus."²⁷ A similar explanation of the name is also found in his *Epistula* 32.1,²⁸ where, writing to Marcella, Jerome describes his work of comparing the texts of Aquila with the Hebrew scrolls and writes of having arrived at working on the book of Exodus and that he would quickly be passing on

---

²³ Exodus 20:22–23.
²⁴ Deuteronomy 6:4–5.
²⁵ Consulting the critical version of the *Vetus Latina* of P. Sabatier and B. Fischer, *Bibliorum Sacrorum Versionis Antiquate seu Vetus Italica*, the only one available for all the books of the Bible. As for the book of Exodus, it does not reveal any observation as to the explanation of or a possible reflection on the title of the second book of the Pentateuch. It is simply placed at the beginning with the words: "Liber Exodi."
²⁶ Hieronymus, *Sophronius Eusebius: Epistula* 106.2. Cited according to the following edition: *S. Eusebii Hieronymi Opera*, Sect. 1, Epistulae, P. 2, LXXI–CXX. Recensuit Isidorus Hilberg (Vienna: Tempsky, 1912); (CSEL 55, p. 239): *Sicut autem in novo testamento, si quando recurrimus ad fontem Graeci sermonis […], ita in veteri testamento, si quando inter Graecos Latinosque diversitas est, ad Hebraicam confugimus veritatem, ut, quicquid de fonte proficiscitur, hoc quaeramus in rivulis.*
²⁷ Compare *Biblia Sacra iuxta Vulgatam versionem*, ed. B. Weber and R. Gryson, 5th ed. (Stuttgart: Deutsche Bibelgesellschaft, 2007); Apparatus: *Exodus. Citantur GAOC et ΣΛΤΜΦ ac cr. Tit.* liber exodus hebraicae ueelle semoth c.
²⁸ CSEL 54, p. 252.

to Leviticus. In this sense, he states: *Exodum teneo, quem illi ele smoth vocant*, "I am now engaged on Exodus that they [= the Jews] call *Eleh šemôth*." We observe that if, on the one hand, Jerome takes note of the original Hebrew nomenclature of the book, on the other, he does not pass over but actually prefers to utilize the wording inherited from the Greek world. He will do the same thing in the other writings where he mentions the book. In fact, in his *Epistula* 53.8,[29] surveying the content of the biblical books which make up the Old Testament, Jerome mentions the second book of the Pentateuch by the name of *Exodus*, explaining that it contains not only the account of the plagues of Egypt but also the Decalogue and the other divine precepts: *videlicet manifestissima est Genesis, in qua de creatura mundi, de exordio generis humani, de divisione terrae, de confusione linguarum et de gente pergente usque ad Aegyptum scribitur hebraeorum. Patet Exodus cum decem plagis, cum decalogo, cum mysticis divinis que praeceptis*, "The book of Genesis is as clear as the sun, there is no doubt. There, there is an account of the creation of the world, of the origin of the human race, of the division of the earth, of the confusion of tongues and of the Jewish people until their entry into Egypt. Exodus does not bring difficulties when it speaks of the ten plagues, the Decalogue and the mystical precepts given by God."[30]

Moreover, the name of the book according to the Greek translation but in a Latinized form appears also in the *Commentarii in Isaiam* I.ii.8.2,[31] a passage where Jerome cites the Scriptures which exalt the power of God: it surpasses human power. In this connection, he cites some verses taken from two different psalms between which he interposes what is said in the so-called Moses' Song of the Sea (Exod 15:1–19). On this occasion, Jerome mentions the name of the book according to the Greek tradition: *unde et in psalmis dicitur: fallax equus in salutem*.[32] *Et in Exodo: equum et ascensorem deiecit in mare.*[33] *Et in alio psalmo: hi in curribus, et hi in equis; nos autem in nomine domini dei nostri invocabimus:*[34] "whence in the psalms it is also said: 'the horse is useless for salvation,' and in Exodus: 'he threw the horse and its rider into the sea.' And in another psalm: some [trust] in chariots, others in horses; but we will call upon the name of the Lord, our God."

3.3. Intermediate conclusion

From this brief examination of the texts available, we have observed that Tertullian and Jerome do not hesitate to use the name of *Exodus* with reference to the second book of the Pentateuch. Both often do so to support their arguments in favour of a correct interpretation of the texts and to reinforce the basis of their reasoning. In this sense, the natural way in which they employ the proper name of the book according

---

[29] CSEL 54, p. 454.
[30] San Girolamo, *Le Lettere. Translation and notes of S. Cola.* Vol. II: *Lettere LIII–LXXIX* (Rome: Città Nuova, 1962), 24.
[31] Cited according to the critical edition, Hieronymus, *"Commentariorum in Esaiam." Libri I–XI*, ed. M. Adriaen, CCSL 73 (Turnhout: Brepols, 1963), 32–33.
[32] Psalm 32:17.
[33] Exodus 15:1.
[34] Psalm 19:8.

to the nomenclature hailing from the Greek world leads us to think of a use of *Exodus* which had become rather consolidated in the Latin-speaking Christian world to designate the book in question. From this point of view, it is clear that the two authors do not hesitate to prolong the use of the name of Greek origin that had been inherited directly from the Christian tradition in the Greek world. Furthermore, it is surprising that, although Jerome is well known for his wish to translate his Latin version of the Bible, the so-called *Vulgate*, he nonetheless wished to keep the name of the book just as he had inherited it from the Greek tradition: a name which he was to retain also in his literary production in which it becomes clear that he had no need for further clarifications as to its meaning.

4. Latin technical terms used for the "exodus" understood as migration of the Israelites from Egypt to Canaan

While the use of *Exodus* as a proper name designating the second book of the Pentateuch is already attested in the works of Tertullian, the use of the term as a substantive referring to the events recounted in the book of Exodus is of a later period. This is probably due to the fact that the Latin-speaking Christians who did not also master the Greek language had difficulty understanding the term even when it had been Latinized for some time. In fact, if we take the case which is found in the works of Gaudentius of Brescia, a Christian author who lived in the fifth century (died around 411–412 AD), it is striking that he has to explain to his readers the meaning of *exodus* in connection with the departure of Israel from Egypt. At the same time, however, it is notable that Gaudentius takes for granted that the name of the book is understood by all and ascribed to the biblical book. In fact, in his *Tractatus I in Exodum* I.10, we read: *Sed iam tempus est, ut eorum in virtutem, quae in libro Exodi audivimus, disseramus. Exodus egressio appellatur; egressio autem fuit de captivitate Faraonis et Aegyptiorum, populi tunc Israhel, non nostri*, "But now is the time to discuss the power of those things which we have…in the book of Exodus. First of all, we know what 'the exodus' is. The departure is called 'Exodus'; but the departure was from the captivity of Pharaoh and the Egyptians, of the people of Israel at that time, not ours."[35]

Thus, the question arises spontaneously: how do the ancient Latin versions of the Bible express the concept of Israel's migration from the land of Egypt? We shall see from what follows that they clearly prefer other terms to *exodus*.

4.1. The evidence from the *Vetus Latina*

If we look at the texts of the *Vetus Latina*[36] which mention the migration of Israel from the land of Egypt, it is noticeable that the terms employed never coincide with the Latinization of the Greek term *Exodus*, not even where the corresponding Greek

---

[35] Gaudentius of Brescia, *X Tractatus Paschales. Tractatus I in Exodum*, I, 10 (CSEL 68, p. 20).
[36] For the *Vetus Latina* texts cited I have referred to the volumes *Bibliorum Sacrorum latinae versiones antiquae: seu, Vetus italica, et caeterae quaecunque in codicibus mss. & antiquorum libris reperiri potuerunt: quae cum Vulgata latina, & cum textu graeco comparantur*, Operâ & studio Petri Sabatier, vol. 3 in 6 (Reimis: Apud Reginaldum Florentain, 1743–49).

texts utilize the term ἔξοδος explicitly (e.g., Exod 19:1; Num 33:38; 3 Kgdms 6:1; Pss 104 [105]:38; 113[114]:1; Heb 11:22) or ἐξοδία (Deut 16:3 and Mic 7:15). In all these cases, the terminology of the passages in question coincides with what I shall describe in the following section with regard to the *Vulgate*. A single slight exception is found in Exod 19:1, where the *Vetus* uses the expression (in the genitive), *exitus filiorum Israel de Terra Aegypti*, rather than, as we shall see in this chapter: *egressionis Israël de terra Aegypti*.

4.2. The evidence from the Vulgate

If we look at the Latin translation in Jerome's *Vulgate*, we can observe that, in some of the texts examined so far, the Latin term used to translate the infinitive construct of יצא is *egressio*, "exit," "departure." In its turn, this recurs in a formula that is complete and almost identical in the three passages of Exod 19:1, Num 33:38, and 3 Kgdms 6:1: in the year or in the month *egressionis filiorum Israhel ex Aegypto/de terra Aegypti*. Something very similar happens in Deut 16:3 and Mic 7:15. Here, Jerome translates in a way that mirrors the Greek varying the formula, speaking of the "day of the departure from the land of Egypt" (Deut 16:3: *ut memineris diei egressionis tuae de Aegypto*; Mic 7:15: *Secundum dies egressionis tuae de terra Aegypti*). In the two psalms, on the other hand, by contrast with the *Septuagint*, where ἔξοδος appears in both cases, Jerome uses, respectively, two different words. In particular, in the Gallican Psalter (= *Psalterium iuxta Septuaginta*), where he translates the text of the *Septuagint's* Psalter[37] in Ps 104[105]:38, we find the term *profectio* in the formula, *in profectione eorum* ("in their departure"). In Ps 113[114]:1 Jerome again uses a substantive, this time in the expression *in exitu* ("in the exit/going out"), which here appears to be provided with the other elements that usually make up the formula: *in exitu Israhel de Aegypto* ("in Israel's departure from Egypt"). In the *Psalterium iuxta Hebraeos*, on the other hand, to render the infinitive construct יצא, Jerome prefers a translation with a verbal construction: *cum egrederentur* ("when they departed/went out"). In other words, in the case of the Gallican Psalter Jerome uses substantives in harmony with the Greek text of the two psalms in question, whereas in the case of the *Psalterium iuxta Hebraeos* he employs verbs which conform to the Hebrew text of the two quotations.

4.3. The evidence from the Latin Pseudepigrapha

With regard to the extra-biblical Latin texts, it is worth noting a passage taken from the *Liber antiquitatum Biblicarum* of Pseudo-Philo[38] where in XI.1 the author quotes Exod 19:1:

---

[37] For the translations of the Psalter which Jerome made, cf., for example, E. Schulz-Flügel, "Hieronymus, Feind und Überwinder der Septuaginta? Untersuchungen anhand der Arbeiten an den Psalmen," in *Der Septuaginta-Psalter und seine Tochterübersetzungen. Symposium in Göttingen 1997*, ed. A. Aejmelaeus and U. Quast (Göttingen: Vandenhoeck & Ruprecht, 2000), 33–50.

[38] As a critical edition with (French) translation, I have used, *Les Antiquités bibliques, Tome 1: Introduction et texte critique*, ed. Daniel J. Harrington; translated by Jacques Cazeaux, SC 229 (Paris: Les Éditions du Cerf, 1976), 118–19.

"Et in tertio profectionis filiorum Israel de terra Egipti, venerunt in heremum Syna et memoratus est Deus verborum suorum dicxit": *Dabo lumen mundo, et illuminabo inhabibitalia, et disponam testamentum meum cum filiis hominum, et glorificabo populum meum super omnes gentes, in quem eiciam excelsa sempiterna, que eis erunt in lumine, impiis vero in punitionem.*

In this case, even if we find the same tendency to avoid the transliteration of the Greek term, it is noticeable that the author of this work quotes Exod 19:1 using *profectio*. On the one hand, this word is well-known to the biblical tradition for expressing the concept of Israel's migration from the land of Egypt but, on the other hand, it does not correspond exactly to what is in the *Vetus Latina* as we have it, where we found *exitus*, or to the text of the *Vulgate* which reads *egressio*.

4.4. Does *exodus* mean the Exode?

As we mentioned at the beginning, if we search the Latin dictionaries we become aware that many of them do not know of the word *exodus*. In fact many, even the authoritative ones, do not register the word.[39] On the contrary, consistent with what we have seen in the previous sections, the dictionaries which concentrate more on the Latin vocabulary coming from Christian circles limit themselves to recording the meaning of *Exodus* as a book of the Bible.[40]

In fact, if we compare other texts in which Jerome refers to Israel's migration from the land of Egypt with those present in his Latin translations of the biblical texts, we note that he refers to the event in a way consistent with his mode of expressing himself in the texts cited. Thus, in his *Commentary on Isaiah* XII.14, where he quotes Isa 43:16–21 in a Latin translation,[41] he speaks of the event connected with the exodus of Israel from Egypt in terms of *egressio*: *sive qui dedit in mari rubro viam, ipse et in aquis torrentibus Iordanis fluvii reperit semitam, ut et egressio ex Aegypto, et introitus in terram repromissionis haberet miraculum...*,[42] "or else, the one who provided a path in the Red Sea, he himself also found a path in the waters of the torrents of the River Jordan so that both the departure from Egypt and the entry into the promised land might have a miracle..." In this passage, it is noteworthy that Jerome does not

---

[39] Compare, for example, Domino Du Cange, et al., *Glossarium mediæ et infimæ latinitatis* (Niort: L. Favre, 1883), 3:1184; P. G. W. Glare, *Oxford Latin Dictionary* (London: Oxford University Press/Clarendon Press, 1968).

[40] Thus in A. Blaise and H. Chirat, *Dictionnaire latin-français des auteurs chrétiens*, Réédition suivie d'addenda et de corrigenda (Paris: Librairie des Méridiens, 1954), 330. On the other hand, we note that I. Weitenauer, *Lexicon Biblicum in quo explicatur Vulgatae Vocabula et Phrases* (Turin: Marietti, 1866), 212, also registers the meaning with reference to the departure of Israel from Egypt as recorded in the book of Exodus: *Exodus. Graecum, exitus. Sicut inscribitur liber secundus Pentateuchi, seu quinque librorum Moysis: quia exitum Israëlitarum ex Aegypto narrat.*

[41] *Commentariorum in Esaiam* XII.14 (13.35); compare *S. Hieronymi Presbyteri Opera. Pars I. Opera Exegetica 2 A. Commentariorum in Esaiam. Libri XII–XVIII*, CCSL 73 (Turnhout: Brepols, 1963), 492.

[42] Here, Jerome makes a kind of paraphrase of Isa 43:16–17. In the *Vulgate*, the verse in question reads: *haec dicit Dominus qui dedit in mari viam et in aquis torrentibus semitam qui eduxit quadrigam et equum, agmen et robustum [...]*.

introduce in this context the Latin term *exodus* when he interprets the text of Isa 43:16 but remains faithful to his terminological choices as mentioned already, namely, utilizing a term derived from the verb *egredior*.

However, this is not the only way in which Jerome, like other Latin-speaking Christian authors, expresses himself in relation to the event of the migration of Israel from the land of Egypt. In fact, something slightly different from the passages seen previously happens in Jerome's *Commentary on Matthew*.[43] Jerome employs an expression very similar to that just observed, namely, the substantive *egressus* along with the usual substantive; however, what is striking is that he refers to "all the signs" that are contained in the "story of the Exodus": *quod que ex persona domini dicitur: aperiam in parabolis os meum; eructabo abscondita a constitutione mundi, considerandum attentius et inveniendum describi egressum Israhelis ex Aegypto et omnia signa narrari quae in Exodi continentur historia*, "And in everything that is said under the persona of the Lord: 'I will open my mouth in parables; I will utter things hidden since the foundation of the world' [= Ps 77[78]:2], one should attentively consider and discover that the departure of Israel from Egypt is being described and all the signs are being narrated that are contained in the history of Exodus."[44] Here, Jerome is alluding to vv. 12–16 of Psalm 77[78], which contain a brief summary of the story of the Exodus. This way of referring to the exodus as a "story" is a new element in the use of the term *exodus*. This use was to return in contemporary and later authors as, for example, in Cassiodorus and Augustine.

In his work, *Expositio psalmorum*, commenting on v. 31 of Psalm 77 (78),[45] which mentions the wrath of God towards the Israelites, Cassiodorus states that the psalmist is referring to the "history of the exodus" when, in Moses' absence, the people gave themselves to the idolatry of the Golden Calf: *Addidit et ira dei ascendit super eos. Et occidit plurimos eorum, et electos Israel impedivit. Hic illam exodi historiam tangit. Absente quippe Moyse, qui legem domini suscipiebat in monte, contra Aaron populus surrexit insanus, expetens deos sibi debere fieri, sicut omnis videbatur habere gentilitas*, "He added: *And the wrath of God came upon them. And he slew very many of them: and he hindered the chosen men of Israel*. Here, he touches upon the famous history of Exodus. In the absence of Moses, who was receiving the Law of the Lord on the mountain, the people in madness rose against Aaron, asking that gods should be accorded them, as all the Gentiles seemed to have."[46]

Augustine is on the same lines: in his *De utilitate credendi* III.8 he too speaks of "*exodi historia*." Giving over space for the methods of reading the Scriptures, in this passage, Augustine is concentrating on allegory in order to demonstrate that it is not necessary to interpret everything that is written to the letter. He explains that, just as

---

[43] *Commentariorum in Matthaeum*, II.948; compare *S. Hieronimy Presbyteri Commentariorum in Matthaeum libri IV*, ed. D. Hurst and M. Adrien, CCEL 77 (Turnhout: Brepols, 1969), 111.

[44] For this English translation, see *St. Jerome. Commentary on Matthew*, ed. Thomas P. Scheck (Washington, DC: Catholic University of America Press, 2008), 161.

[45] *Expositio psalmorum* LXXVII, 31,460; compare *Magni Aureli Cassiodori. Expositio Psalmorum LXXI–CL*, ed. M. Adriaen, CCSL 98 (Turnhout: Brepols, 1958), 720–21.

[46] For this English translation, I have used with slight modifications *Cassiodorus: Explanation of the Psalms*, translated and annotated by P. G. Walsh (New York: Paulist Press, 1990), 486.

in the Old Testament, allegory is present also in the New Testament. In this connection, he takes as an example what Paul says in 1 Cor 10:1-13. Here, referring to the facts of the Exodus, the Apostle declares that what happened for Israel must serve as an example for the Christian people. Thus, Augustine writes: *nam quid ego de apostolo paulo dicam, qui etiam ipsam exodi historiam futurae christianae plebis allegoriam fuisse significat ad corinthios epistula prima?* "What then shall I say of the Apostle Paul who, in the *First Letter to the Corinthians* [= 1 Corinthians 10:1-13], claims that the very story of the Exodus was an allegory of the future Christian people?"[47] It is interesting that Augustine refers to the Exodus as that collection of events which characterize its course, including the presence of the cloud, the crossing of the sea as well as the water springing from the rock. All these elements are reread by Paul in an allegorical key and considered by Augustine to be a single event like that of the exodus—rather, to be more precise, as a sequence of facts which make up a "story" that was linked to the Exodus of Israel, the memory of which must never be lost.

5. Conclusions

At the end of this brief investigation, it is possible to formulate three conclusions. First, the use of *exodus* as *story* marks a further passage in the way of referring to Israel's migration from Egypt because it designates not only the name of the book but the whole series of events which are recounted in the book of Exodus. Second, this term, as referring to the migration from Egypt, enters the Christian language slowly and does not suddenly replace terms like *egressio* or *egressus* and does not even coincide with *exitus* or *profectio* since all these terms are substantives known to a native Latin-speaker whereas *Exodus* is a Latin transliteration of a Greek term. However, third, the term still used today to refer to Israel's migration from the land of Egypt originates in the Greek, not the Latin, tradition. In fact, the Greek of the Septuagint, still more than the Latin versions, seems to have coined—albeit at an embryonic stage—a specific, almost technical, term to describe the epochal change which marked the history of Israel irremediably. Through its Latinization, this term entered into the vocabulary of our modern languages.

Bibliography

Adriaen, M. *Commentariorum in Esaiam. (Libri I-XI)*. CCSL 73A. Turnhout: Brepols, 1963.
Adriaen, M., and G. Morin, eds. *Commentariorum in Esaiam. (Libri XII-XVIII)*. CCSL 73. Turnhout: Brepols, 1963.
Adriaen, M., ed. *Cassiodori. Magni Aureli. Expositio Psalmorum LXXI-CL*. CCSL 98. Turnhout: Brepols, 1958.
Biblia Sacra iuxta Vulgatam versionem. Edited by Robert Weber and Roger Gryson. Quinta edizione. Stuttgart: Deutsche Bibelgesellschaft, 2007.

---

[47] Augustine, *De utilitate credendi* III.8 (CSEL 25, p. 11).

Blaise, A., and H. Chirat. *Dictionnaire latin–français des auteurs chrétiens*. Réédition suivie d'addenda et de corrigenda. Paris: Librairie des Méridiens, 1954.
Braun, R. *"Deus Christianorum": recherches sur le vocabulaire doctrinal de Tertullien*. Paris: Études Augustiniennes, 1977.
Capone, A., et al. (eds.), *"Il digiuno, contro gli psichici": introduzione, traduzione e note di S. Matteoli*, in *Tertulliano. Opere Montaniste 4/2*. Rome: Città nuova, 2012.
Daniélou, J. *From Shadows to Reality: Studies in the Biblical Typology of the Fathers*. New York: Bloomsbury, 2018.
Du Cange, D., et al., eds. *Glossarium mediæ et infimæ latinitatis*. Niort: L. Favre, 1883.
Glück, A., ed. *Gaudentius of Brescia. X Tractatus*. CSEL 68. Wien: Hoelder-Pichler-Tempsky, 1936.
Glare, P. G. W. *Oxford Latin Dictionary*. London: Oxford University Press/Clarendon Press, 1968.
Harrington, D. J., ed. *Pseudo-Philon: Les Antiquités bibliques*. Vol. 1. Translated by Jacques Cazeaux. SC 229. Paris: Les Éditions du Cerf, 1976.
Hieronymus. *Le Lettere. Traduzione e note di S. Cola*. Vol. II: *Lettere LIII–LXXIX*. Rome: Città Nuova, 1962.
Hilberg, I., ed. *Hieronymus. Sancti Eusebii Hieronymi Opera*. CCSL 55. Wien: Tempsky, 1912.
Hurst, D., and M. Adrien, eds. *S. Hieronimy Presbyteri Commentariorum in Matthaeum libri IV*. CCEL 77. Turnhout: Brepols, 1969.
Lechner-Schmidt, W. *Wortindex der Lateinisch erhaltenen Pseudepigraphen zum Alten Testament*. Tübingen: A. Francke Verlag, 1990.
Leonardi, G. "L'impiego di ἔξοδος nei Settanta: presentazione dei dati ed equivalenti ebraici." Pages 67–85 in *Exodos. Storia di un vocabolo*. Edited by Eberhard Bons, Anna Mambelli, and Daniela Scialabba. Bologna: Il Mulino, 2020.
Mambelli, A. "Le prime attestazioni di ἔξοδος come titolo del secondo libro del Pentateuco." Pages 167–77 in *Exodos. Storia di un vocabolo*. Edited by Eberhard Bons, Anna Mambelli, and Daniela Scialabba. Bologna: Il Mulino, 2020.
Moreschini, C., ed. *Tertulliano: Opere Dottrinali. Contro Marcione*. Rome: Città Nuova, 2016.
Perkins, Larry J. "Ἐξαγωγή or Ἔξοδος: What Changed and Why?" *BIOSCS* 39 (2006): 105–14.
Scheck, Thomas P., ed. *St. Jerome: Commentary on Matthew*. Washington, DC: Catholic University of America Press, 2008.
Schulz-Flügel, E. "Hieronymus, Feind und Überwinder der Septuaginta? Untersuchungen anhand der Arbeiten an den Psalmen." Pages 33–50 in *Der Septuaginta-Psalter und seine Tochterübersetzungen. Symposium in Göttingen 1997*. Edited by Anneli Aejmelaeus and Udo Quast. Göttingen: Vandenhoeck & Ruprecht, 2000.
Scialabba, Daniela. "L'uso specifico di 'Exodos' nei LXX: l' 'Esodo' del popolo di Israele." Pages 87–102 in *Exodos. Storia di un vocabolo*. Edited by Eberhard Bons, Anna Mambelli, and Daniela Scialabba. Bologna: Il Mulino, 2020.
Walsh, P. G., ed. *Cassiodorus: Explanation of the Psalms*. 3 vols. New York: Paulist Press, 1990.
Weitenauer, I. *Lexicon Biblicum in quo explicatur Vulgatae Vocabula et Phrases*. Turin: Marietti, 1866.

Bibliography of Larry J. Perkins

Current book projects

Preparing a Commentary on Greek Exodus for the series, *The Society of Biblical Literature Commentary on the Septuagint* (SBLCS). Sponsored by the International Organization for Septuagint and Cognate Studies (IOSCS).
Preparing a Monograph on Methodologies for Septuagint Exegesis.
Preparing a "Theology of Biblical Leadership" in collaboration with Dr. Don Chang.

Books and major segments of books

"VIII. People and Covenant." Pages 399–502 in *Handbuch zur Septuaginta LXX.H Band 5. Die Theologie der Septuaginta*. Edited by Hans Ausloos and Bénédicte Lemmelijn. Gütersloh: Gütersloher Verlagshaus, 2020.
The Art of Kubernēsis. Leading as the Church Board Chairperson. Eugene, OR: Wipf & Stock, 2019.
The Pastoral Letters. A Handbook on the Greek Text. Waco, TX: Baylor University Press, 2017.
"Exodus." In *A New English Translation of the Septuagint and the Other Greek Translations Traditionally Included under that Title*. Edited by Albert Pietersma and Benjamin Wright. New York/Oxford: Oxford University Press, 2007.
Being Church: Explorations in Christian Community, ed. by Larry Perkins, PhD Langley, BC: Northwest Baptist Seminary, 2007.

Articles and book chapters

"Divine Distinctiveness in Greek Exodus (With Special Focus on the Plague Narrative)." Pages 262–75 in *The Septuagint South of Alexandria. Essays on the Greek Translations and Other Ancient Versions by the Association for the Study of the Septuagint in South Africa (LXXSA)*, ed. by Johann Cook and Gideon R. Kotzé. VTSup 193. Leiden: Brill, 2022.
"Renderings of Paronymous Infinitive Constructions in OG Exodus and Implications for Defining the Character of the Translation." *HTS* 78 (2022): 1–8.
With Spencer Elliott. "The Use of οἰκία/οἶκος in Greek Exodus. An Attempt to Understand Principles of Lexical Variation in Greek Exodus." *JSCS* 54 (2021): 111–27.
"Discerning 'The Spirit' In Mark 2:8; 8:12 and 14:38." *NIMER* (June, 2021).
"ἀκούειν/εἰσακούειν (שמע) in Greek Exodus." *JSCS* 53 (2020): 43–65.
"'Drinking it New in the Kingdom of God' (Mark 14:25)—An Assertion of Ownership?" *NIMER* (November 2020).

"The Greek Translator(s')'s Rendering of אלהים." *CBQ* 82 (2020): 17–37.

"Yahweh's κατοικητήριον (Exod 15:13, 16–18): The Nature of Yahweh's Relationship to the Land of Canaan in Greek Exodus." Pages 315–27 in *Die Septuaginta—Themen, Manuskripte, Wirkungen 7. Internationale Fachtagung veranstaltet von Septuaginta Deutsch (LXX.D), Wuppertal 19–22. Juli 2018*. Edited by Eberhard Bons, Michaela Geiger, Frank Ueberschaer, Marcus Sigismund, and Martin Meiser. WUNT 444. Tübingen: Mohr Siebeck, 2020.

"New Testament Greek Terms and Mark's Gospel: Hermeneutical Inquiries." *NIMER* (2019).

"Mark 13:14—A Cryptic Prophecy of the Messiah's Death?" *NIMER* (2019).

"Observations on the Plague Narrative in Greek Exodus: Strategies Used by the Translator to Shape the Narrative." *JSCS* 52 (2019): 73–90.

"'Drawn from the Water': A Commentary on the Old Greek Text of Exodus 2:1–10." Pages 69–94 in *The SBL Commentary on the Septuagint. An Introduction*. Edited by Dirk Büchner. SBLSCS 67. Atlanta: SBL Press, 2017.

"The Greek Translator's Portrayal of Aaron in Exodus 32." *JSCS* 50 (2017): 134–54.

"Exodus Section 2.4.1.2: Septuagint." Pages 135–142 in the *Textual History of the Bible*. Edited by A. Lange and Emmanuel Tov. Leiden: Brill, 2017.

"Israel's Military Characterization in Greek Exodus." Pages 550–63 in *Die Septuaginta—Orte und Intentionen 5. Internationale Fachtagung veranstaltet von Septuaginta Deutsch (LXX.D), Wuppertal 24.–27. Juli 2014*. Edited by Siegfried Kreuzer, Martin Meiser and Marcus Sigismund. WUNT 361. Tübingen: Mohr Siebeck, 2016.

"Deuteronomy in Greek Translation." Pages 68–85 in *The Companion to the Septuagint*. Edited by James Aitken. New York: T&T Clark, 2015.

"The Translation of אהל מועד/משכן and שכן in Greek Exodus." *JSCS* 48 (2015): 8–26.

ἀθῷος-ἀθῳόω-ἀθῴωσις-ἀθῳότης. Entry in the *Historical and Theological Lexicon of the Septuagint*. Edited by Eberhard Bons. Tübingen: Mohr Siebeck, 2020.

"The Greek Translator of Exodus—Interpres (translator) and Expositor (interpreter)—His Treatment of Theophanies." *JSJ* 43 (2012): 1–41.

With Eric Fehr. "Mark's Use of the Verb Σκανδαλίζεσθαι and The Interpretation of Jesus' Visit to Nazareth." *Canadian Theological Review* 1 (2012): 23–36.

"The Order of Pronominal Clitics and Other Pronouns in Greek Exodus—An Indicator of the Translator's Intentionality." *JSCS* 45 (2012): 46–76.

"Faculty Vocation and Governance within A Consortium of Denominationally Accountable Seminaries." *Theological Education* 46 (2010): 79–86.

"'The Finger of God': Lukan Irony and Old Testament Allusion as Narrative Strategy (Luke 11:20 and Exodus 8:19)." Pages 148–60 in *Biblical Interpretation in Early Christianity Volume 3: The Gospel of Luke*. Edited by Thomas. R. Hatina. New York: T&T Clark, 2010.

"'Glory' in Greek Exodus: Lexical Choice in Translation and its Reflection in Secondary Translation." Pages 87–106 in *"Translation Is Required" The Septuagint in Retrospect and Prospect*. Edited by Robert J. V. Hiebert. Septuagint and Cognate Studies 56. Atlanta, GA: SBL, 2010.

"What's in a Name? Proper Names in Greek Exodus." *JSJ* 41 (2010): 447–71.

"Examples of Duality in Mark 16:9–20 and their Implications for The Markan Narrative." *Canadian Evangelical Review* 36–37 (Fall 2008–Spring 2009): 3–15.

"Greek Exodus and Greek Isaiah—Detection and Implications of Interdependence in Translation." *BIOSCS* 42 (2009): 18–33.

"The Markan Narrative's Use of the Old Greek Text of Jeremiah to Explain Israel's Obduracy." *TynBul* 60 (2009): 217–38.
"ΚΥΡΙΟΣ– Articulation and non-Articulation in Greek Exodus." *BIOSCS* 41 (2008): 17–33.
"'The Lord is a Warrior'—'The Lord Who Shatters Wars': Exodus 15:3 and Judith 9:7; 16:2." *BIOSCS* 40 (2007): 121–38.
"Ἐξαγωγής or Ἔξοδος—What Changed and Why?" *BIOSCS* 39 (2006): 105–14.
"Kingdom, Messianic Authority and the Re-Constituting of God's People –Tracing the Function of Exodus Material in Mark's Narrative." Pages 100–15 in *Biblical Interpretation in Early Christian Gospels. Volume 1: The Gospel of Mark*. Edited by Thomas Hatina. London: T&T Clark, 2006.
"'Let the Reader Understand'—A Contextual Reading of Mark 13:14." *BBR* 16 (2006): 95–104.
"Translating and Interpreting Mark 1:45." Pages 99–114 in *Acorns to Oaks. The Primacy and Practice of Biblical Theology*. Edited by Michael G. Haykin. Toronto: Joshua Press, 2003.
"Mark's Language of Religious Conflict as Rhetorical Device." *BBR* 11 (2001): 43–63.
"'Greater Than Solomon' (MT. 12:42)." *TJ* 19 (1998): 207–17.
"Bethany (Place)." In *Anchor Yale Bible Dictionary*. Edited by David Noel Freedman, et al. New York: Doubleday, 1992.
"Echatana (Place)." In *Anchor Yale Bible Dictionary*. Edited by David Noel Freedman, et al. New York: Doubleday, 1992.
With J. Kenneth Kuntz. "Uzziah (Person)." In *Anchor Yale Bible Dictionary*. Edited by David Noel Freedman, et al. New York: Doubleday, 1992.
"New Testament Texts Supporting a Congregational Form of Government." *Northwest Evangelical Baptist Journal* 1 (1991).
"The Septuagint of Jonah: Aspects of Literary Analysis Applied to Biblical Translation." *BIOSCS* 20 (1987): 43–53.
"The Place of SyH within the LXX Textual Tradition of Deuteronomy." Pages 223–32 in *De Septuaginta: Studies in Honor of John William Wevers on his Sixty-Fifth Birthday*. Edited by Alberta Pietersma and Claude E. Cox. Missisauga, ON: Benben, 1987.
"The So-Called 'L' Text of Psalms 72–82." *BIOSCS* 11 (1978): 44–63.

Reviews

Johann Cook and Martin Rösel, eds. *Toward a Theology of the Septuagint: Stellenbosch Congress on the Septuagint*. Atlanta: SBL, 2020. In *CBQ* 83 (2021): 530–34.
Lo Sardo, Domenico. *Post-Priestly Additions and Rewritings in Exodus 35–40*. FAT 2.119. Tübingen: Mohr Siebeck, 2020. Pp. 307. In *RBL*, May 2021.
Lee, John A. L. *The Greek of the Pentaeuch: Grinfield Lectures on the Septuagint 2011–12*. New York: Oxford University Press, 2019. In *CBQ* 82 (2020): 157–59.
Screnock, John. *Traductor Scriptor: The Old Greek Translation of Exodus 1–14 as Scribal Activity*. VTSup 174. Leiden: Brill, 2017. In *JHebS* 20 (2020).
Austin, Benjamin, M. *Plant Metaphors in the Old Greek of Isaiah*. SCS 69. Atlanta: SBL Press, 2019. In *RBL*, December 2019.
Jobes, Karen H., ed. *Discovering the Septuagint. A Guided Reader*. Grand Rapids, MN: Kregel, 2016. In *CBQ* 81 (2019): 521–22.
Ziegert, Carsten. *Diaspora als Wüstenzeit. Übersetzungswissenschaftliche und theologische Aspekte, griechischen Numeribuches*. Beihefte zur Zeitschrift für die alttestamentliche Wissenschaft 480. Berlin: De Gruyter 2015. In *JSCJ* (2019): 221–23.

Kraus, Wolfgang, Michaël N. van der Meer, and Martin Meiser, eds. *XV Congress of the International Organization for Septuagint and Cognate Studies, Munich 2013*. SBLSCS 64. Atlanta: SBL Press, 2016. In *CBQ* 80 (2018): 167–69.

Siegfried Kreuzer. *The Bible in Greek: Translation, Transmission and Theology of the Septuagint*. SBLSCS 63. Atlanta: SBL Press, 2015. In *CBQ* 79 (2017): 164–67.

Vorm-Croughs, Miriam. *The Old Greek of Isaiah: An Analysis of its Plusses and Minuses*. SBLSCS 61. Atlanta: SBL Press, 2014. In *CBQ* 78 (2016): 536–39.

Wilson de Angelo Cunha. *LXX Isaiah 24:1–26:6 as Interpretation and Translation: A Methodological Discussion*. SBLSCS 62. Atlanta: SBL Press, 2014. In *CBQ* 78 (2016): 345–47.

Black, David, ed. *Perspectives on the Ending of Mark: 4 Views*. Nashville, TN: Broadman & Holman Publishers, 2009. In *BBR* 20 (2010): 124–25.

Lemmelijn, Bénédicte. *A Plague of Texts? A Text-Critical Study of the So-Called 'Plagues Narrative' in Exodus 7:14–11:10*. Oudtestamentische Studiën 56. Leiden: Brill, 2009. In *BIOSCS* 42 (2009): 135–37.

Bock, Darrell L. *Blasphemy and Exaltation in Judaism. The Charge Against Jesus in Mark 14:53–65*. Grand Rapids, MA: Baker Books, 2000. In *BBR* 13 (2003): 143–45.

Hiebert, D. Edmond. *Second Peter and Jude. An Expositional Commentary*. Greenville, SC: Unusual Publications, 1989. In *JETS* 35 (1992): 544–45.

Clowney, Edmund. *The Message of 1 Peter: The Way of the Cross*. Downers Grove, IL: InterVarsity, 1988. In *JETS* 35 (1992): 542–44.

McGregor, Leslie John. *The Greek Text of Ezekiel: An Examination of Its Homogeneity*. Septuagint and Cognate Studies 18. Atlanta, GA: Scholars Press, 1985. In *TJ* 7 (1986): 111–15.

Conference papers

"Divine Distinctiveness in Greek Exodus (With Special Focus on the Plague Narrative)." Paper presented at the Annual Meeting of the *Society of Biblical Literature*, San Diego, CA, November 2019.

"The Use of οἰκία/οἶκος in Greek Exodus. An Attempt to Understand Principles of Lexical Variation in Greek Exodus." Paper presented at the Annual Meeting of the *Society of Biblical Literature*, San Diego, CA, November 2019.

"φάγομαι/ἔδομαι—Future Forms of ἐσθίω (אכל) in Greek Exodus." Paper presented at the SBL–SCS Workshop, San Diego, CA, November 2019.

"Observations on the Plague Narrative in Greek Exodus." Paper presented at the Annual Meeting of the *Society of Biblical Literature*, Denver, CO, November 2018.

"Yahweh's κατοικητήριον (Exodus 15:17–18): The Nature of Yahweh's Relationship to the Land of Canaan in Greek Exodus." Paper presented to the seventh *Internationale Fachtagung veranstaltet von Septuaginta Deutsch*, Wuppertal, Germany, July 19–22, 2018.

"The Greek Translator(s')'s Rendering of אלהים." Paper presented to the *Canadian Society of Biblical Studies*, Toronto, ON, May 2017.

"Response to A. van der Kooij's Proposal that Greek Exodus 'Testifies to the View of the Authorities of the Temple State in Judea." Paper presented at the Annual Meeting of the *Society of Biblical Literature*, Boston, MA, November 2017.

"ἐγώ εἰμι/ἐγώ Variation in Rendering Certain Hebrew Verbless Clauses in Greek Exodus." Paper presented to the *ISBL*, Seoul, Korea, July 2016.

"The Greek Translator's Portrayal of Aaron in Exodus 32." Paper presented at the Annual Meeting of the *Society of Biblical Literature*, San Diego, CA, November 2014.

"Israel's Military Characterization in Greek Exodus." Paper presented to the fifth *International Conference on the Septuagint "Die Septuaginta—Orte und Intentionen,"* Wuppertal, Germany, July 24–27, 2014.

"'Drawn from the Water': A Commentary on the Old Greek Text of Exodus 2:1–10." Paper presented to the *Canadian Society of Biblical Studies*, Victoria, B.C., May 2013.

"The Translation of מועד/אהל משכן and שכן in Greek Exodus." Paper presented at the Annual Meeting of the *Society of Biblical Literature*, Baltimore, MD, November 2013.

"Biblical Linguistics and Mark's Gospel: Hermeneutical Inquiries." Paper presented to the *CanIL/ACTS Conference*, Langley, B.C., 2012.

"The Order of Pronominal Clitics and Other Pronouns in Greek Exodus—An Indicator of the Translator's Intentionality." Paper presented to the *IOSCS* section of the Annual Meeting of the *Society of Biblical Literature*, Chicago, IL, November 2012.

"Deep Gospel must be Full Gospel—Reflections on Matthew's Vision of Gospel Reality in the light of Jim Belcher's call for 'Deep Gospel.'" Paper presented to *ReSourcing the Church* Conference, March 2011.

"The Greek Translator of Exodus—Interpres (translator) and Expositor (interpretor)—His Treatment of Theophanies." Paper presented to the *IOSCS* section of Annual Meeting of the *Society of Biblical Literature*, San Francisco, CA, November 2011.

"Narrative/Literary Dimension of Translation—Greek Exodus 19—A Brief Sortie." Paper presented to the *IOSCS* section of the Annual Meeting of the *Society of Biblical Literature*, Atlanta, GA, November 2010.

"Atonement in 1st Peter—Reflections on Isaiah 53." Paper presented to the *Baptist Identity Conference* at ACTS/TWU, Langley, B.C., March 2009.

"What's in a Name—Proper Names in Greek Exodus." Paper presented to the *IOSCS* section of the Annual Meeting of the *Society of Biblical Literature*, New Orleans, LA, November 2009.

"Greek Exodus and Greek Isaiah—Detection and Implications of Interdependency/Intertextuality in Translation." Paper presented to the *IOSCS* section of the Annual Meeting of the *Society of Biblical Literature*, Boston, MA, November 2008.

"KYRIOS—The Translation of Proper Names in Greek Exodus." Paper presented to the *IOSCS* section of the Annual Meeting of the *Society of Biblical Literature*, San Diego, CA, November 19, 2007.

"'Glory' in Greek Exodus: Lexical Choice in Translation and its Reflection in Secondary Translation." Paper presented to "Septuagint Translation(s): Retrospect and Prospect," a conference at Trinity Western University/ACTS, Langley, B.C. September 28, 2006.

"Reshaping the Story: Tracing the Translator's Hermeneutical Fingerprint in Exodus 19." Paper presented to "Septuagint Translation(s): Retrospect and Prospect," a conference at Trinity Western University/ACTS, Langley, B.C. September 28, 2006.

"'The Lord is a Warrior'—'The Lord Who Shatters Wars': Exodus 15:3 and Judith 9:7; 16:2." Paper read at the joint session of the Greek Bible and *IOSCS* section at the Annual Meeting of the *Society of Biblical Literature*, Washington, D.C., November 20, 2006.

"Papyrus Fouad 266 (Gottingen No 848). Is there Evidence of Secondary Revision toward the Hebrew Vorlage?" Paper presented to the *IOSCS*, November 1975.

Board governance

"A Ripple Effect. Fostering Skills in Seminary Governance Can Strengthen the Whole Church." *InTrust Magazine* (Spring 2012).
"Advice for the board chair: Avoid the Stockholm syndrome." *In Trust* (Summer, 2012).
"Governing in the Midst of Climate Change." *In Trust* (Autumn, 2012).

Exegetical and theological essays and posts

"The Significance of Aorist Indicative Passive of homoiō in Matthew's Gospel Passive Tense forms of homoiō in Matthew's Gospel." *Internet Moments with God's Word* (March 2022). Online: https://moments.nbseminary.com/archives/190-the-significance-of-aorist-indicative-passive-of-homoio-in-matthews-gospel/
"Analysis of the Greek Text with Brief Commentary on the Epistle of James." *Internet Moments with God's Word* (June 2021). Online: https://moments.nbseminary.com/archives/189-analysis-of-the-greek-text-with-brief-commentary-on-the-epistle-of-james/
"Who is tis in James 2:18–19?" *Internet Moments with God's Word* (May 2021). Online: https://moments.nbseminary.com/archives/188-who-is-tis-in-james-218-19/
"The Nature of True Religion thrēskia (James 1:26–27)." *Internet Moments with God's Word* (April 2021). Online: https://moments.nbseminary.com/archives/187-the-nature-of-true-religion-threskia-james-126-27/
"Hesitant, Doubting or Double-minded. dipsuchos in James 1:8; 4:8." *Internet Moments with God's Word* (February 2021). Online: https://moments.nbseminary.com/archives/186-hesitant-doubting-or-double-minded-dipsuchos-in-james-18-48/
"New Born Infants and 'Swaddling Clothes' (sparganoō in Luke 2:7, 12)." *Internet Moments with God's Word* (January 2021). Online: https://moments.nbseminary.com/archives/185-new-born-infants-and-swaddling-clothes-sparganoo-luke-27-12/
"The 'Dancing' Foetus in Luke 1:41, 44 (skirtaō)." *Internet Moments with God's Word* (December 2020). Online: https://moments.nbseminary.com/archives/184-the-dancing-foetus-in-luke-141-44-skirtao/
"God's 'Direction': (kateuthunō) in Paul's Ministry (2 Thessalonians 3:5)." *Internet Moments with God's Word* (December 2020). Online: https://moments.nbseminary.com/archives/183-gods-direction-kateuthuno-in-pauls-ministry-2-thessalonians-35/
"The Dance Is Not PERICHŌRĒSIS." *Internet Moments with God's Word* (December 2020). Online: https://moments.nbseminary.com/archives/182-the-dance-is-not-perichoresis/
"Hospitality—Demonstrating Transformational Change in the Messiah's Assembly—the Church." *Internet Moments with God's Word* (November 2020). Online: https://moments.nbseminary.com/archives/181-hospitality-a-spiritual-exercise-for-demonstrating-transformational-change-in-messiahs-assembly-the-church/
"New Analysis of the Greek Text of 1 Peter and Brief Commentary." *Internet Moments with God's Word* (November 2020). Online: https://moments.nbseminary.com/archives/180-new-analysis-of-the-greek-text-of-1-peter-and-brief-commentary/
"Paul as the leitourgos of the Messiah (Romans 15:16)." *Internet Moments with God's Word* (October 2020). Online: https://moments.nbseminary.com/archives/179-paul-as-the-leitourgos-of-the-messiah-romans-1516/

"What is the Function of an akrogōniaios Stone (1 Peter 2:6 = Isaiah 28:16)?" *Internet Moments with God's Word* (August 2020). Online: https://moments.nbseminary.com/archives/178-what-is-the-function-of-an-akrogoniaios-stone-1-peter-26-isaiah-2816/

"Peter's Critique of the 'Ancestral Lifestyle' (patroparadotos anastrophē in 1 Peter 1:18)." *Internet Moments with God's Word* (July 2020). Online: https://moments.nbseminary.com/archives/177-peters-critique-of-the-ancestral-lifestyle-patroparadotos-anastrophe-1-peter-118/

"'Made Firm/Strengthened' By God and Others (stērizō in 2 Thessalonians 2:17)." *Internet Moments with God's Word* (June 2020). Online: https://moments.nbseminary.com/archives/175-made-firm-strengthened-by-god-and-others-sterizo-2-thessalonians-217/

"A New Exegetical Resource on the Greek Text of Ephesians." *Internet Moments with God's Word* (May 2020). Online: https://moments.nbseminary.com/archives/175-a-new-exegetical-resource-on-the-greek-text-of-ephesians/

"When Paul Experienced No 'anesis' (2 Corinthians 2:13)." *Internet Moments with God's Word* (May 2020). Online: https://moments.nbseminary.com/archives/174-when-paul-experienced-no-anesis-2-corinthians-213/

"Who are the 'Elect' (eklektoi) in Mark 13:20?" *Internet Moments with God's Word* (May 2020). Online: https://moments.nbseminary.com/archives/173-who-are-the-elect-eklektoi-in-mark-1320/

"What Kind of thlipsis Is Jesus Talking About in Mark 13:19–-20?" *Internet Moments with God's Word* (April 2020). Online: https://moments.nbseminary.com/archives/172-what-kind-of-thlipsis-is-jesus-talking-about-in-mark-1319-20/

"The Gospel of Matthew's Eschatological Perspective (sunteleia in Matthew 13:39; 28:20)." *Internet Moments with God's Word* (March 2020). Online: https://moments.nbseminary.com/archives/171-the-gospel-of-matthews-eschatological-perspective-sunteleia-matthew-1339-2820/

"Busy with/Devoted to Spiritual Activity (proskartereō)." *Internet Moments with God's Word* (February 2020). Online: https://moments.nbseminary.com/archives/170-busy-with-devoted-to-spiritual-activity-proskartereo/

"The Function of a euaggelistēs (2 Timothy 4:5)." *Internet Moments with God's Word* (January 2020). Online: https://moments.nbseminary.com/archives/169-the-function-of-a-euaggelistes-2-timothy-45/

"Jesus' Response to the Pharisees' Testing (anastenazō in Mark 8:12)." *Internet Moments with God's Word* (January 2020). Online: https://moments.nbseminary.com/archives/168-jesus-response-to-the-pharisees-testing-mark-812-anastenazo/

"Who is the 'Scribe' (grammateus) in Matthew 13:52?" *Internet Moments with God's Word* (December 2019). Online: https://moments.nbseminary.com/archives/167-who-is-the-scribe-grammateus-in-matthew-1352/

"What is a proseuchē? (Acts 16:13,16)." *Internet Moments with God's Word* (December 2019). Online: https://moments.nbseminary.com/archives/what-is-a-proseuche-acts-161316/

"All things happen in parabolais (Mark 4:11)." *Internet Moments with God's Word* (September 2019). Online: https://moments.nbseminary.com/archives/165-all-things-happen-in-parabolais-mark-411/

"To What Do Believers Conform — the meaning of kanōn in Galatians 6:16." *Internet Moments with God's Word* (March 2019). Online: https://moments.nbseminary.com/archives/160-to-what-do-believers-conform-the-meaning-of-kanon-in-galatians-616/

"Commentary on the Greek Text of Colossians — A New Exegetical Resource." *Internet Moments with God's Word* (March 2019). Online: https://moments.nbseminary.com/archives/164-commentary-on-the-greek-text-of-colossians-a-new-exegetical-resource/

"New Exegetical Resources — Commentary on Greek Jonah." *Internet Moments with God's Word* (October 2018). Online: https://moments.nbseminary.com/archives/163-new-exegetical-resources-commentary-on-greek-jonah/

"Some New Exegetical Resources. Commentary on the Greek Text of Philippians." *Internet Moments with God's Word* (September 2018). Online: https://moments.nbseminary.com/archives/162-some-new-exegetical-resources/

"Conceited, Blinded or Deranged? What does tuphoomai mean in 1 Timothy 3:6; 6:4; 2 Timothy 3:4?" *Internet Moments with God's Word* (March 2018). Online: https://moments.nbseminary.com/archives/161-conceited-blinded-or-deranged-what-does-tuphoomai-mean-in-1-timothy-36-64-2-timothy-34/

"Where does the Power of God Establish its 'Living Quarters'? (episkēnoō) 2 Corinthians 12.9." *Internet Moments with God's Word* (December 2017). Online: https://moments.nbseminary.com/archives/159-where-does-the-power-of-god-establish-its-living-quarters-episkenoo-2-corinthians-12-9/

"The Concept of 'Reverence' (hieroprepēs) in Titus 2:3." *Internet Moments with God's Word* (November 2017). Online: https://moments.nbseminary.com/archives/158-the-concept-of-reverence-hieroprepes-in-titus-23/

"The Future of the Earth according to 2 Peter 3:10 heurethēsetai." *Internet Moments with God's Word* (March 2017). Online: https://moments.nbseminary.com/archives/157-the-future-of-the-earth-according-to-2-peter-310-heurethesetai/

"What does oikonomia mean? (Ephesians 3:2)." *Internet Moments with God's Word* (August 2016). Online: https://moments.nbseminary.com/archives/156-what-does-oikonomia-mean-ephesians-32/

"Paul's Role as 'Ambassador' (presbeuō; 2 Corinthians 5:20)." *Internet Moments with God's Word* (November 2015). Online: https://moments.nbseminary.com/archives/155-pauls-role-as-ambassador-presbeuo-2-corinthians-520/

"God's 'Primal Decision' (prothesis) for Human Salvation (2 Timothy 1:9)." *Internet Moments with God's Word* (November 2015). Online: https://moments.nbseminary.com/archives/154-gods-primal-decision-prothesis-for-human-salvation-2-timothy-19/

"Antilutron in 1 Timothy 2:6." *Internet Moments with God's Word* (August 2015). Online: https://moments.nbseminary.com/archives/153-antilutron-in-1-timothy-26/

"The Meaning of philostorgos in Romans 12:10." *Internet Moments with God's Word* (July 2015). Online: https://moments.nbseminary.com/archives/157-the-meaning-of-philostorgos-in-romans-1210/

"The Christian God — a God of Peace, not Confusion or Instability akatastasia." *Internet Moments with God's Word* (May 2015). Online: https://moments.nbseminary.com/archives/156-the-christian-god-a-god-of-peace-not-confusion-or-instability-akatastasia/

"Translating airō in John 15:2." *Internet Moments with God's Word* (May 2015). Online: https://moments.nbseminary.com/archives/155-translating-airo-in-john-152/

"'Imposters' or 'Cheats'—goēs in 2 Timothy 3:13." *Internet Moments with God's Word* (January 2015). Online: https://moments.nbseminary.com/archives/154-imposters-or-cheats-goes-in-2-timothy-313/

"Educating in an even-tempered manner 'those who oppose' (antidiatithēmi in 2 Timothy 2:25)." *Internet Moments with God's Word* (December 2014). Online: https://moments.nbseminary.com/archives/153-educating-in-an-even-tempered-manner-those-who-oppose-antidiatithemi-2-timothy-225/

"'Rekindling' a Spiritual Gift (anazōpureō in 2 Timothy 1:6)." *Internet Moments with God's Word* (September 2014). Online: https://moments.nbseminary.com/archives/152-rekindling-a-spiritual-gift-anazopureo-2-timothy-16/

"Paul's 'priestly' Ministry — hierourgeō in Romans 15:16." *Internet Moments with God's Word* (September 2014). Online: https://moments.nbseminary.com/archives/151-pauls-priestly-ministry-hierourgeo-in-romans-1516/

"The Gifts and Calling of God: ametamelētos in Romans 11:29." *Internet Moments with God's Word* (July 2014). Online: https://moments.nbseminary.com/archives/150-the-gifts-and-calling-of-god-ametameletos-in-romans-1129/

"A Disciple's 'Mindset' (phronēma in Romans 8:6, 7, 27)." *Internet Moments with God's Word* (July 2014). Online: https://moments.nbseminary.com/archives/149-a-disciples-mindset-phronema-romans-86727/

"Pursuing praupatheia — An Essential Virtue for Christian Leaders (1 Timothy 6:11)." *Internet Moments with God's Word* (June 2014). Online: https://moments.nbseminary.com/archives/148-pursuing-praupatheia-an-essential-virtue-for-christian-leaders-1-timothy-611/

"Conceited, Deluded, or Just Foolish — The Meaning of tuphoomai in the Pastoral Epistles." *Internet Moments with God's Word* (April 2014). Online: https://moments.nbseminary.com/archives/147-conceited-deluded-or-just-foolish-the-meaning-of-tuphoomai-in-the-pastoral-epistles/

"God Dwells in Unapproachable (aprositos) Light (1 Timothy 6:16)." *Internet Moments with God's Word* (February 2014). Online: https://moments.nbseminary.com/archives/146-god-dwells-in-unapproachable-aprositos-light-1-timothy-616/

"Is Godliness a 'means to financial gain'? The Wordplay in 1 Timothy 6:5–6 porismos." *Internet Moments with God's Word* (February 2014). Online: https://moments.nbseminary.com/archives/145-is-godliness-a-means-to-financial-gain-the-wordplay-in-1-timothy-65-6-porismos/

"Understanding Peter's Denial (aparneomai) in Mark 14:30–31, 72; 8:34." *Internet Moments with God's Word* (December 2013). Online: https://moments.nbseminary.com/archives/144-understanding-peters-denial-aparneomai-mark-1430-3172-834/

"The Reaction of the Rich Man to Jesus' Command (stugnazō) in Mark 10:22." *Internet Moments with God's Word* (December 2013). Online: https://moments.nbseminary.com/archives/144-the-reaction-of-the-rich-man-to-jesus-command-stugnazo-mark-1022/

"A People for Possession (peripoiēsis) in 1 Peter 2:9." *Internet Moments with God's Word* (October 2013). Online: https://moments.nbseminary.com/archives/142-a-people-for-possession-peripoiesis-1-peter-29/

"The Appropriate Recompense (amoibē) that Adult Children Owe to Parents (1 Timothy 5:4)." *Internet Moments with God's Word* (October 2013). Online: https://moments.nbseminary.com/archives/141-the-appropriate-recompense-amoibe-that-adult-children-owe-to-parents-1-timothy-54/

"Godly Exercise (gumnazō) in 1 Timothy 4:7–8." *Internet Moments with God's Word* (August 2013). Online: https://moments.nbseminary.com/archives/140-godly-exercise-gumnazo-1-timothy-47-8/

"Cauterized or Branded in One's Conscience (kekaustēriasmenōn) in 1 Timothy 4:2." *Internet Moments with God's Word* (July 2013). Online: https://moments.nbseminary.com/archives/139-cauterized-or-branded-in-ones-conscience-kekausterriasmenon-1-timothy-42/

"Epieikēs — Equity — A Key Quality of Christian Leaders (1 Timothy 3:3)." *Internet Moments with God's Word* (June 2013). Online: https://moments.nbseminary.com/archives/138-epeikes-equity-a-key-quality-of-christian-leaders-1-timothy-33/

"'Honourable Standing' as the Messiah's Agents (bathmos) in 1 Timothy 3:13." *Internet Moments with God's Word* (May 2013). Online: https://moments.nbseminary.com/archives/137-honourable-standing-as-the-messiahs-agents-bathmos-1-timothy-313/

"Thinking of others as 'Your own Superiors' (huperechōn in Phil. 2:3)." *Internet Moments with God's Word* (May 2013). Online: https://moments.nbseminary.com/archives/136-thinking-of-others-as-better-than-oneself-huperechon-phil-23/

"Shaking off the Dust (ektinazein in Matthew 10:14)." *Internet Moments with God's Word* (April 2013). Online: https://moments.nbseminary.com/archives/135-shaking-off-the-dust-ektinazein-matthew-1014/

"Experiencing Literal and Metaphorical Shipwreck (nauagein in 1 Timothy 1:19)." *Internet Moments with God's Word* (March 2013). Online: https://moments.nbseminary.com/archives/134-experiencing-literal-and-metaphorical-shipwreck-nauagein-1-timothy-119/

"Let the 'Messiah's Peace' rule or hold sway in your Heart brabeuein (Colossians 3:15)." *Internet Moments with God's Word* (February 2013). Online: https://moments.nbseminary.com/archives/133-let-the-messiahs-peace-rule-or-hold-sway-in-your-heart-brabeuein-colossians-315/

"To Go Astray, Deviate (astochein) in 1 Timothy 1:6." *Internet Moments with God's Word* (January 2013). Online: https://moments.nbseminary.com/archives/132-to-go-astray-deviate-astochein-in-1-timothy-16/

"Pastors as 'leaders' — the Use of hēgoumenos in Hebrews 13." *Internet Moments with God's Word* (December 2012). Online: https://moments.nbseminary.com/archives/131-pastors-as-leaders-the-use-of-hegoumenos-in-hebrews-13/

"The Scope of 'Pastoral' work poimēn (Ephesians 4:11)." *Internet Moments with God's Word* (November 2012). Online: https://moments.nbseminary.com/archives/130-the-scope-of-pastoral-work-ephesians-411/

"Submitting to the rules of the world (dogmatizesthai in Colossians 2:20)." *Internet Moments with God's Word* (October 2012). Online: https://moments.nbseminary.com/archives/129-submitting-to-the-rules-of-the-world-dogmatizesthai-in-colossians-220/

"Does 'allegorical' Mean 'Allegory?' (allēgoroumena in Galatians 4:24)." *Internet Moments with God's Word* (September 2012). Online: https://moments.nbseminary.com/archives/128-does-allegorical-mean-allegory-allegoroumena-galatians-424/

"Phragmos (Mt. 21:33; Mk. 12:1; Luke 14:23; Eph. 2:14)." *Internet Moments with God's Word* (August 2012). Online: https://moments.nbseminary.com/archives/127-phragmos-mt-2133-mk-121-luke-1423-eph-214/

"Black Eyes(?), Widows and Vindication (hupōpiazō in Luke 18:5)." *Internet Moments with God's Word* (July 2012). Online: https://moments.nbseminary.com/archives/126-black-eyes-widows-and-vindication-luke-185-hupopiazo/

"What was the Tax-Collector Asking God to do? (hilaskesthai in Luke 18:13)." *Internet Moments with God's Word* (May 2012). Online: https://moments.nbseminary.com/archives/125-what-was-the-tax-collector-asking-god-to-do-luke-1813-hilaskesthai/

"'Do not Defraud' — the Rich Man's Challenge (aposterein in Mark 10:19)." *Internet Moments with God's Word* (April 2012). Online: https://moments.nbseminary.com/ archives/124-do-not-defraud-the-rich-mans-challenge-aposterein-mark-1019/

"The Virtue of Spiritual Simplicity (haplotēs in Colossians 3:22; Ephesians 6:5)." *Internet Moments with God's Word* (March 2012). Online: https://moments.nbseminary.com/ archives/123-the-virtue-of-spiritual-simplicity-haplotes-colossians-322-ephesians-65/

"The Gift of 'Governance' (kubernēsis in 1 Corinthians 12:28)." *Internet Moments with God's Word* (February 2012). Online: https://moments.nbseminary.com/ archives/122-the-gift-of-governance-kubernesis-1-corinthians-1228/

"Redeeming the Cursed and Redeeming Time (exagorazein in Galatians 3:13; 4:5; Ephesians 5:16; Colossians 4:5)." *Internet Moments with God's Word* (January 2012). Online: https://moments.nbseminary.com/archives/121-redeeming-the-cursed-and-redeeming-time-exagorazein-galatians-313-45-ephesians-516-colossians-45/

"God's Instructions (chrēmatizein) Regarding His Son (Matthew 2:12, 26; Luke 2:26)." *Internet Moments with God's Word* (December 2011). Online: https://moments. nbseminary.com/archives/120-instructed-chrematizein/

"The Messiah's Triumph in the Cross (thriambeuō in 2 Cor. 2:14; Col.2:15)." *Internet Moments with God's Word* (October 2011). Online: https://moments.nbseminary.com/ archives/119-the-messiahs-triumph-in-the-cross-thriambeuo-2-cor-214-col-215/

"Reconciling (apokatallassein) all things to himself (Col. 1:20)." *Internet Moments with God's Word* (October 2011). Online: https://moments.nbseminary.com/ archives/118-reconciling-apokatallassein-all-things-to-himself-col-120/

"God's work that 'Makes us Qualified' (hikanoun) — Colossians 1:12." *Internet Moments with God's Word* (August 2011). Online: https://moments.nbseminary.com/ archives/117-gods-work-that-makes-us-qualified-hikanoun-colossians-112/

"Selecting and Appointing Church Leaders (cheirotonein) in the New Testament (Acts 14:23)." *Internet Moments with God's Word* (August 2011). Online: https://moments. nbseminary.com/archives/116-selecting-and-appointing-church-leaders-cheirotonein-in-the-new-testament-acts-1423/

"God at work–Paul's Concept of the Verb energein and Cognates (Philippians 2:12–13)." *Internet Moments with God's Word* (June 2011). Online: https://moments.nbseminary. com/archives/115-paul%e2%80%99s-concept-of-the-verb-energein-and-cognates-%e2%80%93-god-at-work-philippians-212-13/

"Punishment (kolasis, kolazein)—Eternal or Otherwise (Matthew 25:46; Acts 4:21; 2 Peter 2:9; 1 John 4:18)." *Internet Moments with God's Word* (May 2011). Online: https:// moments.nbseminary.com/archives/114-punishment-kolasis-kolazein-%e2%80%93-eternal-or-otherwise-matthew-2546-acts-421-2-peter-29-1-john-418/

"The Spirit is Willing (promuthos in Mark 14:38; Matthew 26:41)." *Internet Moments with God's Word* (May 2011). Online: https://moments.nbseminary.com/archives/113-the-spirit-is-willing-promuthos-mark-1438matthew-2641/

"Fathers, Anger, and Discipling Children (parorgizein in Ephesians 6:4 and erethizein in Colossians 3:21)." *Internet Moments with God's Word* (March 2011). Online: https:// moments.nbseminary.com/archives/112-fathers-anger-and-discipling-children-parorgizein-ephesians-64-and-erethizein-colossians-321/

"The Ministry of Patience (makrothumein in 1 Thessalonians 5:14)." *Internet Moments with God's Word* (March 2011). Online: https://moments.nbseminary.com/archives/ 111-the-ministry-of-patience-makrothumein-1-thessalonians-514/

"The Delicate Work of Spiritual Guidance (nouthetein in 1 Thessalonians 5:12–15)." *Internet Moments with God's Word* (February 2011). Online: https://moments.nbseminary.com/archives/110-the-delicate-work-of-spiritual-guidance-nouthetein-1-thessalonians-512-15/

"The Stone that Shatters (sunthlaomai) and Pulverizes (likmaō) in Matthew 21:44//Luke 20:18)." *Internet Moments with God's Word* (January 2011). Online: https://moments.nbseminary.com/archives/the-stone-that-shatters-sunthlaomai-and-pulverizes-likmaomatthew-2144-luke-2018/

"Mary's 'Interpretation' (sumballein) of the Shepherds' News (Luke 2:19)." *Internet Moments with God's Word* (November 2010). Online: https://moments.nbseminary.com/archives/108-marys-interpretation-sumballein-of-the-shepherds-news-luke-219/

"What's the Difference? Diastolē in Paul's Letters and Diastellō in Mark's Gospel." *Internet Moments with God's Word* (November 2010). Online: https://moments.nbseminary.com/archives/107-whats-the-difference-diastole-in-pauls-letters-and-diastello-in-marks-gospel/

"The Ministry of Encouragement (paramutheisthai in 1 Thessalonians 5:14)." *Internet Moments with God's Word* (September 2010). Online: https://moments.nbseminary.com/archives/106-the-ministry-of-encouragement-paramutheisthai-1-thessalonians-514/

"Describing 'Leadership' in the New Testament (proistēmi in 1 Thessalonians 5:12)." *Internet Moments with God's Word* (September 2010). Online: https://moments.nbseminary.com/archives/105-describing-leadership-in-the-new-testament-proistemi-1-thessalonians-512/

"'Appointing' Elders or 'Setting them in Order'? kathistēmi in Titus 1:5." *Internet Moments with God's Word* (August 2010). Online: https://moments.nbseminary.com/archives/appointing-elders-or-setting-them-in-orderkathist%e1%ba%bdmi-titus-15/

"'Lording it Over' (katakurieuō) in Mark 10:42 and 1 Peter 5:3." *Internet Moments with God's Word* (July 2010). Online: https://moments.nbseminary.com/archives/lording-it-over-katakurieuo-in-mark-1042-and-1-peter-53/

"Endangering one's life…for the work of the Messiah (paraboleusamenos in Philippians 2:30)." *Internet Moments with God's Word* (June 2010). Online: https://moments.nbseminary.com/archives/endangering-ones-life%e2%80%a6for-the-work-of-the-messiah-paraboleusamenos-philippians-230/

"Jesus' Sorrow in Gethsemane (Mark 14:33–36)." *Internet Moments with God's Word* (May 2010). Online: https://moments.nbseminary.com/archives/jesus-sorrow-in-gethsemane/

"The 'Spirit (pneuma) of Jesus' in Mark's Gospel (Mark 2:8; 8:12)." *Internet Moments with God's Word* (April 2010). Online: https://moments.nbseminary.com/archives/100-the-spirit-pneuma-of-jesus-in-marks-gospel-mark-28-812/

"The Wonder of Revelation (apokalupsis in Galatians 1:12; 2:2)." *Internet Moments with God's Word* (March 2010). Online: https://moments.nbseminary.com/archives/wonder-of-revelation/

"The Man of God (ho tou theou anthrōpos in 2 Timothy 3:16–17)." *Internet Moments with God's Word* (February 2010). Online: https://moments.nbseminary.com/archives/98-the-man-of-god-ho-tou-theou-anthropos-2-timothy-316-17/

"The Purpose of Paul's First Meeting with Peter (historēsai in Galatians 1:18)." *Internet Moments with God's Word* (January 2010). Online: https://moments.nbseminary.com/archives/the-purpose-of-pauls-first-meeting-with-peter/

"Having the Same Form (summorphizō) in Philippians 3:17." *Internet Moments with God's Word* (December 2009). Online: https://moments.nbseminary.com/archives/having-the-same-form/

"Contending (sunathlountes) … Not Being Intimidated (pturomenoi)." *Internet Moments with God's Word* (November 2009). Online: https://moments.nbseminary.com/archives/contending-not-being-intimidated/

"Guaranteeing the Gospel—bebaiōsis in Philippians 1:7." *Internet Moments with God's Word* (October 2009). Online: https://moments.nbseminary.com/archives/guaranteeing-the-gospel/

"'Astonishment' or 'Bewilderment'—ekstasis in Mark's Gospel (Mark 5:42; 16:8)." *Internet Moments with God's Word* (September 2009). Online: https://moments.nbseminary.com/archives/astonishment-or-bewilderment-in-mark/

"Reflecting and/or Contemplating Jesus' Glory (katoptrizomai in 2 Corinthians 3:18)." *Internet Moments with God's Word* (August 2009). Online: https://moments.nbseminary.com/archives/reflecting-or-contemplating-jesus-glory/

"Transformation—The Sense of metamorphoomai (Mark 9:12; Matthew 17:2)." *Internet Moments with God's Word* (July 2009). Online: https://moments.nbseminary.com/archives/transformation/

"'Moonstruck' in Matthew 4:24; 17:15 (selēniazomai)." *Internet Moments with God's Word* (June 2009). Online: https://moments.nbseminary.com/archives/moonstruck/

"How Witty Should Christians Be? (eutrapelia in Ephesians 5:4)." *Internet Moments with God's Word* (May 2009). Online: https://moments.nbseminary.com/archives/how-witty-should-christians-be/

"Knowing Christ (Philippians 3:10)." *Internet Moments with God's Word* (April 2009). Online: https://moments.nbseminary.com/archives/%e2%80%9cknowing-christ%e2%80%9d-philippians-310/

"'Searching the Word'—A Prophetic Task (eraunō/exeraunō in 1 Peter 1:10–11)." *Internet Moments with God's Word* (February 2009). Online: https://moments.nbseminary.com/archives/a-prophetic-task/

"Getting Access to God (prosagein in 1 Peter 3:18)." *Internet Moments with God's Word* (January 2009). Online: https://moments.nbseminary.com/archives/getting-access-to-god/

"The 'Coming of the Holy Spirit Upon You' (Luke 1:35 and Acts 1:8)." *Internet Moments with God's Word* (December 2008). Online: https://moments.nbseminary.com/archives/85-the-coming-of-the-holy-spirit-upon-youluke-135-and-acts-18/

"Discerning the Presence of God's Kingdom (meta paratērēseōs in Luke 17:20–21)." *Internet Moments with God's Word* (November 2008). Online: https://moments.nbseminary.com/archives/discerning-the-presence-of-gods-kingdom/

"Apekdusis—A Metaphor for Jesus' Work on the Cross and Our Personal Transformation in Christ (Colossians 2:11, 15; 3:9)." *Internet Moments with God's Word* (October 2008). Online: https://moments.nbseminary.com/archives/apekdusis-a-metaphor-for-jesus-work-on-the-cross-and-our-personal-transformation-in-christ-colossians-211-15-39/

"Warnings About 'Crafty Scheming' (methodeia in Ephesians 4:14; 6:11)." *Internet Moments with God's Word* (September 2008). Online: https://moments.nbseminary.com/archives/warnings-about-crafty-schemin/

"The 'innocent as doves'—A Disciple's Response to Jesus' Commission in Matthew 10:16 (akeraios)." *Internet Moments with God's Word* (August 2008). Online: https://moments.nbseminary.com/archives/innocent-as-doves/

"Protecting the Deposit (parathēkē in 2 Timothy 1:12, 14)." *Internet Moments with God's Word* (July 2008). Online: https://moments.nbseminary.com/archives/protecting-the-deposit/

"Casting Out Demons—A New Authority (ekballō in Mark 1:34)." *Internet Moments with God's Word* (June 2008). Online: https://moments.nbseminary.com/archives/casting-out-demons/

"Taught by God (theodidaktoi in 1 Thessalonians 4:9)." *Internet Moments with God's Word* (May 2008). Online: https://moments.nbseminary.com/archives/78_taught-by-god/

"Holding God in contempt—A Human Deception (muktērizō in Galatians 6:7)." *Internet Moments with God's Word* (April 2008). Online: https://moments.nbseminary.com/archives/77-holding-god-in-contempt/

"Being Imitators (mimētai) of God (Ephesians 5:1)." *Internet Moments with God's Word* (March 2008). Online: https://moments.nbseminary.com/archives/76-being-imitators-mimtai-of-god/

"Behave Respectably (euschēmonōs) to the Outsiders (1 Thessalonians 4:12)." *Internet Moments with God's Word* (February 2008). Online: https://moments.nbseminary.com/archives/behave-respectably-euschmons-to-the-outsiders1-thessalonians-412/

"Prayers for Moral and Spiritual Wholeness (holotelēs, holoklēros in 1 Thessalonians 5:23)." *Internet Moments with God's Word* (January 2008). Online: https://moments.nbseminary.com/archives/74-prayers-for-moral-and-spiritual-wholenessholoteles-holokleros-1-thessalonians-523/

"An Extraordinary Tenderness (homeiromai in 1 Thessalonians 2:8)." *Internet Moments with God's Word* (December 2007). Online: https://moments.nbseminary.com/archives/an-73-extraodinary-tenderness-1-thessalonians-28-homeiromai/

"Cultivating a Desire for Ministry Leadership—(oregesthai in 1 Timothy 3:1)." *Internet Moments with God's Word* (November 2007). Online: https://moments.nbseminary.com/archives/cultivating-a-72-desire-for-ministry-leadership-oregesthai-1-timothy-31/

"'So that we might die to sins'—the sense of apoginomai in 1 Peter 2:24." *Internet Moments with God's Word* (October 2007). Online: https://moments.nbseminary.com/archives/%e2%80%9cso-that-we-might-die-to-sins%e2%80%9d-%e2%80%93-the-sense-of-apoginomai/

"Spiritual 'Stumbling'." *Internet Moments with God's Word* (September 2007). Online: https://moments.nbseminary.com/archives/spiritual-stumbling/

"Fixing a Broken Faith—Ologopistos in Matthew's Gospel." *Internet Moments with God's Word* (August 2007). Online: https://moments.nbseminary.com/archives/fixing-a-broken-faithologopistos-in-matthews-gospel/

"God's Commissioning (anadeixis in Luke 1:80)." *Internet Moments with God's Word* (July 2007). Online: https://moments.nbseminary.com/archives/68-god%e2%80%99s-commissioning/

"Hearing God's Message (Luke 2:26)." *Internet Moments with God's Word* (June 2007). Online: https://moments.nbseminary.com/archives/67-hearing-gods-message-luke-226/

"The Promise of Matthew 24:14 (en holēi tēi oikoumenēi = in all the Roman Empire)." *Internet Moments with God's Word* (May 2007). Online: https://moments.nbseminary.com/archives/the-promise-of-matthew-2414-en-holei-tei-oikoumenei-in-all-the-roman-empire/

"Reactions to the News of Jesus' Resurrection." *Internet Moments with God's Word* (April 2007). Online: https://moments.nbseminary.com/archives/reactions-to-the-news-of-jesus%e2%80%99-resurrection/

"The Finger of God (Luke 11:20; Exodus 8:19)." *Internet Moments with God's Word* (March 2007). Online: https://moments.nbseminary.com/archives/65-the-finger-of-god-luke-1120-exodus-819/

"Holding fast to the Right Master (Matthew 6:24)." *Internet Moments with God's Word* (February 2007). Online: https://moments.nbseminary.com/archives/63-holding-fast-to-the-right-master-matthew-624/

"Worshipping, but Uncertain (Matthew 28:17)." *Internet Moments with God's Word* (January 2007). Online: https://moments.nbseminary.com/archives/62-worshipping-but-uncertain-matthew-2817/

"Praying, not Prattling (Matthew 6:7)." *Internet Moments with God's Word* (December 2006). Online: https://moments.nbseminary.com/archives/61-praying-not-prattling-matthew-67/

"Doubts and Disputes—Human Disposition (Matthew 15:19)." *Internet Moments with God's Word* (November 2006). Online: https://moments.nbseminary.com/archives/60-doubts-and-disputes-human-disposition-matthew-1519/

"Jesus Messiah, the 'Personal Tutor' (Matthew 23:10)." *Internet Moments with God's Word* (October 2006). Online: https://moments.nbseminary.com/archives/59-jesus-messiah-the-personal-tutor-matthew-2310/

"Learning the Messiah (Ephesians 4:20)." *Internet Moments with God's Word* (September 2006). Online: https://moments.nbseminary.com/archives/58-%e2%80%9clearning-the-messiah%e2%80%9d-ephesians-420/

"Renewal—paliggenesia (Matthew 19:28)." *Internet Moments with God's Word* (August 2006). Online: https://moments.nbseminary.com/archives/57-renewal-paliggenesia-matthew-1928/

"Matthew's View of Lost People (Matthew. 9:36)." *Internet Moments with God's Word* (July 2006). Online: https://moments.nbseminary.com/archives/56-matthew%e2%80%99s-view-of-lost-people-matthew-936/

"Our Identity as God's Servants (Romans 15:16)." *Internet Moments with God's Word* (May 2006). Online: https://moments.nbseminary.com/archives/55-our-identity-as-gods-servants-romans-1516/

"Motivation in Ministry (Galatians 6:9)." *Internet Moments with God's Word* (April 2006). Online: https://moments.nbseminary.com/archives/55-motivation-in-ministry-galatians-69/

"Vibrant Expectation—The Christian's Perspective (Galatians 5:5)." *Internet Moments with God's Word* (March 2006). Online: https://moments.nbseminary.com/archives/53-vibrant-expectation-%e2%80%93-the-christian%e2%80%99s-perspective-galatians-55/

"Paul—Slave of the Messiah (Galatians 1:10)." *Internet Moments with God's Word* (February 2006). Online: https://moments.nbseminary.com/archives/52-paul-%e2%80%93-slave-of-the-messiah-galatians-110/

"Finding Courage in the Midst of Difficulty (Philippians 2:19)." *Internet Moments with God's Word* (January 2006). Online: https://moments.nbseminary.com/archives/51-finding-courage-in-the-midst-of-difficulty-philippians-219/

"Jesus—A Sign Refused (Luke 2:34)." *Internet Moments with God's Word* (December 2005). Online: https://moments.nbseminary.com/archives/50-jesus-%e2%80%93-a-sign-refused-luke-234/

"Christian 'Body-Building' (Ephesians 4:16)." *Internet Moments with God's Word* (November 2005). Online: https://moments.nbseminary.com/archives/48-christian-%e2%80%98body-building%e2%80%99-ephesians-416/

"The Intercession of Jesus Christ and the Holy Spirit (Romans 8:27, 34; Hebrews 7:25)." *Internet Moments with God's Word* (October 2005). Online: https://moments.nbseminary.com/archives/48-the-intercession-of-jesus-christ-and-the-holy-spirit-romans-82734-hebrews-725/

"Ringing Out the Word of the Lord (1 Thessalonians 1:8)." *Internet Moments with God's Word* (September 2005). Online: https://moments.nbseminary.com/archives/47-%e2%80%9cringing-out-the-word-of-the-lord%e2%80%9d-1-thessalonians-18/

"Jesus our Guardian (episkopos in 1 Peter 2:25)." *Internet Moments with God's Word* (August 2005). Online: https://moments.nbseminary.com/archives/46-jesus-our-guardian-episkopos-1-peter-225/

"Where God's Glory and God's Spirit Rest (1 Peter 4:14)." *Internet Moments with God's Word* (July 2005). Online: https://moments.nbseminary.com/archives/45-where-god%e2%80%99s-glory-and-god%e2%80%99s-spirit-rest-1-peter-414/

"Compounding God's Mercy (1 Peter 1:3)." *Internet Moments with God's Word* (June 2005). Online: https://moments.nbseminary.com/archives/44-compounding-god%e2%80%99s-mercy-1-peter-13/

"This is my blood of the covenant poured out for many (Mark 14:24)." *Internet Moments with God's Word* (May 2005). Online: https://moments.nbseminary.com/archives/43-%e2%80%9cthis-is-my-blood-of-the-covenant-poured-out-for-many%e2%80%9d-mark-1424/

"Hemmed in With Apparently No Way Out (2 Corinthians 4:8)." *Internet Moments with God's Word* (April 2005). Online: https://moments.nbseminary.com/archives/42-%e2%80%9chemmed-in-with-apparently-no-way-out%e2%80%9d-2-corinthians-48/

"The Certainty of Faith—Giving God Glory (Romans 4:21)." *Internet Moments with God's Word* (March 2005). Online: https://moments.nbseminary.com/archives/41-the-certainty-of-faith-%e2%80%93-giving-god-glory-romans-421/

"God's Restraint (Romans 2:4; 3:26)." *Internet Moments with God's Word* (February 2005). Online: https://moments.nbseminary.com/archives/40-god%e2%80%99s-restraint-romans-24-326/

"Who is standing with you? (2 Timothy 4:17)." *Internet Moments with God's Word* (January 2005). Online: https://moments.nbseminary.com/archives/39-who-is-standing-with-you-2-timothy-417/

"Anna's Response to Jesus' Birth (Luke 2:38)." *Internet Moments with God's Word* (December 2004). Online: https://moments.nbseminary.com/archives/38-anna%e2%80%99s-response-to-jesus%e2%80%99-birth-luke-238/

"Not Just Equipped, but Completely Equipped (2 Timothy 3:16–17)." *Internet Moments with God's Word* (November 2004). Online: https://moments.nbseminary.com/archives/37-%e2%80%9cnot-just-equipped-but-completely-equipped%e2%80%9d-2-timothy-316-17/

"God's Crown Jewel—His People (Exodus 19:5; 1 Peter 2:9)." *Internet Moments with God's Word* (October 2004). Online: https://moments.nbseminary.com/archives/36-god%e2%80%99s-crown-jewel-%e2%80%93-his-people-exodus-195-1-peter-29/

"The Importance of a Comma! (Ephesians 4:12)." *Internet Moments with God's Word* (September 2004). Online: https://moments.nbseminary.com/archives/35-the-importance-of-a-comma-ephesians-412/

"Spilt Blood (Mark 14:24)." *Internet Moments with God's Word* (August 2004). Online: https://moments.nbseminary.com/archives/34-spilt-blood-mark-1424/

"'Elementary' Issues (Galatians 4:3, 9; 5:25; 6:16)." *Internet Moments with God's Word* (July 2004). Online: https://moments.nbseminary.com/archives/33-%e2%80%98elementary%e2%80%99-issues-galatians-439525616/

"A Christian's DNA (Galatians 6:15)." *Internet Moments with God's Word* (June 2004). Online: https://moments.nbseminary.com/archives/32-a-christian%e2%80%99s-dna-galatians-615/

"Military Language in the Service of the Gospel (Galatians 5:13)." *Internet Moments with God's Word* (May 2004). Online: https://moments.nbseminary.com/archives/31-military-language-in-the-service-of-the-gospel-galatians-513/

"The Messiah has made us free for freedom!... You were called for freedom! (Galatians 5:1, 13)." *Internet Moments with God's Word* (April 2004). Online: https://moments.nbseminary.com/archives/30-the-messiah-has-made-us-free-for-freedom-you-were-called-for-freedom-galatians-5113/

"Birthing the Messiah in Others the Work of Evangelism and Discipleship (Galatians 4:19)." *Internet Moments with God's Word* (March 2004). Online: https://moments.nbseminary.com/archives/29-birthing-the-messiah-in-others-the-work-of-evangelism-and-discipleship-galatians-419/

"Freedom and Slavery—The Context of Christian Living (Galatians 2:4)." *Internet Moments with God's Word* (February 2004). Online: https://moments.nbseminary.com/archives/28-freedom-and-slavery-%e2%80%93-the-context-of-christian-living-galatians-24/

"Rescued From Evil (Galatians 1:4)." *Internet Moments with God's Word* (January 2004). Online: https://moments.nbseminary.com/archives/27-rescued-from-evil-galatians-14/

"Peace and People Who Have God's Approval (Luke 2:14)." *Internet Moments with God's Word* (December 2003). Online: https://moments.nbseminary.com/archives/26-peace-and-people-who-have-gods-approval-luke-214/

"Global Positioning—Tracking with God (Philippians 3:20)." *Internet Moments with God's Word* (November 2003). Online: https://moments.nbseminary.com/archives/25-global-positioning-%e2%80%93-tracking-with-god-philippians-320/

"The Source of Paul's Spiritual Power (Philippians 4:13)." *Internet Moments with God's Word* (October 2003). Online: https://moments.nbseminary.com/archives/24-the-source-of-pauls-spiritual-power-philippians-413/

"The 'Form of God' (Philippians 2:6–7)." *Internet Moments with God's Word* (September 2003). Online: https://moments.nbseminary.com/archives/23-the-form-of-god-philippians-26-7/

"The Progress of the Gospel (Philippians 1:12, 25)." *Internet Moments with God's Word* (August 2003). Online: https://moments.nbseminary.com/archives/22-the-progress-of-the-gospel-philippians-11225/

"God's Mercy and Time (Mark 13:20)." *Internet Moments with God's Word* (July 2003). Online: https://moments.nbseminary.com/archives/21-gods-mercy-and-time-mark-1320/

"History in Parables: God's Questions (Mark 12:6)." *Internet Moments with God's Word* (June 2003). Online: https://moments.nbseminary.com/archives/20-history-in-parables-gods-questions-mark-126/

"People Jesus Loved (Mark 10:21)." *Internet Moments with God's Word* (May 2003). Online: https://moments.nbseminary.com/archives/19-people-jesus-loved-mark-1021/

"The Emotions of the Messiah." *Internet Moments with God's Word* (April 2003). Online: https://moments.nbseminary.com/archives/18-the-emotions-of-the-messiah/

"A Moment of Messianic Candour (Mark 9:19)." *Internet Moments with God's Word* (March 2003). Online: https://moments.nbseminary.com/archives/17-a-moment-of-messianic-candour-mark-919/

"Elijah's Restorative Ministry and the Son of Man's Suffering: Resolving a Scriptural Problem (Mark 9:12–13)." *Internet Moments with God's Word* (February 2003). Online: https://moments.nbseminary.com/archives/16elijahs-restorative-ministry-and-the-son-of-mans-suffering-resolving-a-scriptural-problem-mark-912-13/

"The Exchange Rate for a Soul (Mark 8:37)." *Internet Moments with God's Word* (January 2003). Online: https://moments.nbseminary.com/archives/14-the-exchange-rate-for-a-soul-mark-837/

"Taking Sides (Mark 8:33)." *Internet Moments with God's Word* (December 2002). Online: https://moments.nbseminary.com/archives/14-taking-sides-mark-833/

"Discipleship: The Challenge and Struggle to Understand (Mark 8:17, 21)." *Internet Moments with God's Word* (November 2002). Online: https://moments.nbseminary.com/archives/13-discipleship-the-challenge-and-struggle-to-understand-mark-81721/

"'Being Fully Satisfied'—Jesus' Special Gift (Mark 6:42)." *Internet Moments with God's Word* (September 2002). Online: https://moments.nbseminary.com/archives/%e2%80%9cbeing-fully-satisfied%e2%80%9d-%e2%80%93-jesus%e2%80%99-special-gift/

"Offended at Jesus (Mark 6:3)." *Internet Moments with God's Word* (August 2002). Online: https://moments.nbseminary.com/archives/offended-at-jesus-mark-63/

"Discerning the Positive in the Negative (Mark 5:3–4)." *Internet Moments with God's Word* (July 2002). Online: https://moments.nbseminary.com/archives/10-discerning-the-positive-in-the-negative-mark-53-4/

"The Mystery of the Kingdom of God (Mark 4:10–12)." *Internet Moments with God's Word* (June 2002). Online: https://moments.nbseminary.com/archives/9-the-mystery-of-the-kingdom-of-god-mark-410-12/

"Jesus is THE MAN (Mark 2:10)." *Internet Moments with God's Word* (May 2002). Online: https://moments.nbseminary.com/archives/8-jesus-is-the-man-mark-210/

"Filled With Compassion (Mark 1:41)." *Internet Moments with God's Word* (April 2002). Online: https://moments.nbseminary.com/archives/7-filled-with-compassion-mark-141/

"The Authority of Jesus (Mark 1:27)." *Internet Moments with God's Word* (March 2002). Online: https://moments.nbseminary.com/archives/6-the-authority-of-jesus-mark-127/

"Discerning God's Timing (Mark 1:15)." *Internet Moments with God's Word* (February 2002). Online: https://moments.nbseminary.com/archives/5-discerning-gods-timing-mark-115/

"Ruling With God Now." *Internet Moments with God's Word* (January 2002). Online: https://moments.nbseminary.com/archives/4-ruling-with-god-now/

"Surrendered—The Experience of Servant Leaders." *Internet Moments with God's Word* (December 2001). Online: https://moments.nbseminary.com/archives/3-surrendered-the-experience-of-servant-leaders/

"Split Skies and Ripped Curtains (schizein)." *Internet Moments with God's Word* (November 2001). Online: https://moments.nbseminary.com/archives/2-split-skies-and-ripped-curtains/

"Jesus: Messiah, Son of God, Yahweh." *Internet Moments with God's Word* (October 2001). Online: https://moments.nbseminary.com/archives/1-jesus-messiah-son-of-god-yahweh/

Index of References

OLD TESTAMENT/
HEBREW BIBLE
Genesis
1–2	246
1:1–2:3	245
1:22	97
1:27	245
1:28	97, 246
2:2–3	245
2:2	74
2:4	257
3:3	79
4:6	81
4:21	57, 58
5:1	257
6:4	180, 181
8:17	97
9:1	97
9:7	97
9:21	23
9:25	75
9:26	75
9:27	75
10:6	72
10:13	72
11–50	71
11:1	79
11:5	74
11:7	74
12	71
12:2–3	257
12:9	86
12:10–13:1	72
12:10	73, 74
12:13	79
12:14	72
12:16	75
12:17	78, 79
12:18	80
12:19	81
12:20	83
13	71
13:1–2	82
13:1	86
13:3	86
13:14	86
14	282
14:15	75
15	71, 82
15:11	74
15:12	74
15:13	73–75, 77, 78
15:14	73, 82
15:15	83, 85
15:16	73
16:1–6	72
16:1	72
16:6	78
16:9	78
16:15	72
18:3	74, 75
18:5	75
18:13	80
18:21	74
18:24	23
19:2	75
19:4–11	181
19:9	74
19:19	75
20:1	74, 86
20:6	79
20:8	75
20:14	75
21:17	219
21:21	72
21:23	74
21:25	75
21:34	74
23	145
23:4	85, 145
23:6	85
23:8	85
23:11	85
23:13	85
23:15	85
23:19	85
24:2	75
24:5	75
24:9	75
24:10	75
24:14	75
24:16	74
24:17	75
24:31	81
24:34	75
24:35	75
24:45	74
24:51	81
24:52	75
24:53	75
24:59	75
24:61	75
24:62	86
24:65	75
24:66	75
25:9	85
25:10	85
25:22	81
25:32	81
26	73, 74

26:1–3	72	37:5–11	72	44:4	80		
26:1	73	37:23–28	72	44:7	75, 81		
26:2	74	37:35	74	44:9	75		
26:3	74	37:36	72	44:10	75		
26:11	79	38:1	74	44:16	72, 75		
26:15	75	39:1–6	72	44:17	75		
26:19	75	39:1	72	44:18	75		
26:25	75	39:17	72, 75	44:19	75		
26:29	79	39:19–23	72	44:21	75		
26:32	75	39:19	72, 75	44:23	74, 75		
27:37	75	40:20	75	44:24	75		
27:46	81	41–47	73	44:26	74		
28:12	74, 79	41:10	75	44:27	75		
28:14	86	41:12	75	44:30	75		
29:25	81	41:17–45	72	44:31	75		
30:1	83	41:27	73	44:32	75		
30:38	54	41:30	73	44:33	75		
30:41	54	41:31	73	45:6	73		
30:43	75	41:36	73	45:7	74		
31:11	219	41:37	75	45:9	74		
31:26	81	41:38	75	46:3	74		
31:27	81	41:43	72	46:4	74		
31:30	81	41:50	73	46:34	75		
31:50	78	41:53	72	47:3	75		
32:4	74	41:54	73	47:4	73–75		
32:5	74, 75	41:56	73	47:13	73		
32:6	75	41:57	72, 73	47:15	81		
32:10	75	42–46	74	47:19	75		
32:11	75	42:1	81	47:20	73		
32:17	75	42:2	74	47:21	73		
32:19	75	42:3	74	47:25	75		
32:21	75	42:5	73	47:29–30	73		
32:25	79	42:6	72	47:30	274		
32:26	79	42:9	72, 86	48:7	85		
32:30	81	42:10	72, 75	49:29	85		
32:32	79	42:11	75	49:31	85		
32:33	79	42:13	75	50	83		
33:5	75	42:14	72, 86	50:2	75, 84		
33:14	75	42:33	82	50:5	83, 85		
33:15	81	42:38	74	50:6	83, 85		
34:2	78	43:1	73	50:7	75, 83, 85		
35:8	85	43:4	74	50:8	83		
35:11	97	43:5	74	50:12	85		
35:19	85	43:15	74	50:13	85		
35:27	74	43:18	75	50:14	85		
35:29	85	43:20	74	50:17	75		
35:30	85	43:28	75	50:18	75		

Genesis (cont:)		4:28	80, 168	9:30	76		
50:22	85	4:30	80	9:34	76		
50:24–25	60	5	76	10:1	76, 80		
50:24	73, 84	5:10–16	76	10:2	80		
50:25	73, 84	5:14	76	10:3	82		
50:26	85	5:15	76	10:6	76		
		5:16	76	10:7	76, 82		
Exodus		5:21	76	10:8	82		
1	96	5:23	269	10:9	82		
1:1–2:10	259	6:6–8	269	10:10	82, 83		
1:5	95	6:6	80, 269	10:19	168		
1:6	95	6:12	160	10:20	168		
1:7	95, 97	6:30	160	10:21–23	275		
1:8	78, 95	7:1	160, 164	10:24	82, 83		
1:9	95, 96	7:3	80	10:25–26	82		
1:10	97	7:4	80	11–12	50		
1:11	78, 97	7:9	76, 80	11:3	76		
1:12	78, 95, 97	7:10	76	11:4	60		
1:14	97, 160	7:20	76	11:8	76		
1:16	95, 97	7:28	76	11:9	80		
1:17–18	97	8:4	76, 82	11:10	80		
1:17	95	8:5	76	12:8–9	129, 130, 138		
1:18	95	8:7	76				
1:19	95, 97	8:8	82	12:8	130		
1:20	95, 96	8:9	76	12:9	129, 130		
1:22	95–97	8:11	76	12:12	80		
2:5	23	8:13	168	12:13	80		
2:8	96	8:14	168	12:14	160, 165		
2:21–27	145	8:15	168	12:16	131–33, 138, 160, 164		
2:22	146	8:16	168				
2:23–25	146	8:17	76, 168				
3:1–6	219	8:18	168	12:17	132, 133, 138		
3:2	219	8:19	168				
3:8	160	8:20	76	12:19	145, 147		
3:12	80, 168	8:21	76, 82	12:20	160, 164, 165		
3:20	80	8:23	80				
3:6b	99	8:24	76	12:22	79		
3:15–20	218	8:25	76, 82	12:30	76		
4:8	80	8:27	76	12:31	82		
4:9	80	8:29	76	12:32	82, 83		
4:10	76	8:31	76	12:35	83		
4:14	160	9:8	76	12:36	83		
4:17	80	9:9	168	13:6	130		
4:21	80	9:10	168	13:19	85		
4:22	160, 268	9:12	168	13:21–22	275		
4:24	99	9:14	76, 80	13:21	160, 219		
4:27	168	9:20	76	13:22	160		

14:5	76	17:3	168	20:17	136–38, 169, 269
14:7	168	17:4	168		
14:31	76	17:5	168	20:18–23:33	252
14:10–31	259	17:7	62	20:18	161, 164–66, 169, 274
14:10	168	17:8–12	301		
14:12	168	18:13	169		
14:13	168	18:14	169	20:22–23:33	143, 218
14:14	168	18:15	169	20:22–23	303
14:15	168	18:16	161, 169	20:22	169
14:16–21	301	18:21	161	20:23	5, 169
14:16	168	18:25	161	20:24	169
14:17	168	19–24	145	20:25	161, 169
14:18	168	19–20	252	20:26	169
14:19	168, 275	19	145	21–23	145
14:20	168, 275	19:1–24:8	271	21:1–23:19	37
14:21	168, 302	19:1–23:33	259	21:1–32	76
14:22–29	302	19:1	299, 306, 307	21:1	169, 219
14:24	160, 275			21:2–11	105
14:27	302	19:4	161	21:2–6	117
14:30	269	19:5–6	273, 276	21:3	169
15:1–19	304	19:5	161, 164	21:4	169
15:1	304	19:6	161	21:6	122, 138, 169
15:3	99, 100, 160, 164, 166	19:7–25	273		
		19:12	79	21:7–12	118
		19:13	79, 274	21:7–11	105, 117
15:4	160	19:16–17	275	21:7	4, 75, 104–106, 114, 115, 117–19
15:10	160	19:16	274		
15:11	160, 164	19:17	169		
15:16	168	19:19	169, 274		
15:17–18	161	19:21	169	21:8	132, 133, 138, 169
15:17	123, 164, 168	19:22	169		
		19:23	169	21:9	165
15:18	168	20	134, 145	21:10	169
15:19	168	20:2–17	252	21:11	118
15:20	168	20:2–5	302	21:13	169
15:21	168	20:3	134, 302	21:14	169
15:22	168	20:5	64	21:15	169
15:23	168	20:6	135, 138, 161	21:16	169
15:24	168			21:17	134
15:25	168	20:8–11	246	21:18–20	161
15:26	168	20:11	246	21:18	169
16:1–17:7	259	20:12	161, 164, 169	21:19	169
16:3	74			21:20	169
16:10	275	20:13–15	252	21:21	169
16:29	161, 164	20:13	252	21:22	169
16:33–34	291	20:14	252	21:24	252
17:1–7	269, 271	20:16	169	21:25	169

Exodus (cont:)		24:4	170	26:31–37	280		
21:26–30	161	24:5	170	26:31	162, 164		
21:26–27	107	24:6	170	26:33	170		
21:32	169	24:7	218	26:34	170		
21:34	170	24:8	6, 279,	26:35	170		
21:35	170		280, 288,	26:36	170		
21:36	170		289	26:37	170		
21:37	170	24:10	99, 161	27:1	291		
22:1	170	24:12	161, 164,	27:21	162, 165		
22:2	170		170	28:16	170		
22:3	170	24:13	170	28:17	170		
22:4	170	24:14	170	28:18	170		
22:5	170	24:15	161	28:19	170		
22:6	170	24:16	161	28:20	171		
22:7	170	24:18	161, 170	28:42	162		
22:8	170	25–31	289	29:13	162		
22:9	170	25	6, 279,	29:14	162, 164		
22:10	170		285, 286,	29:18	162		
22:11	170		290, 291	29:20	162, 171		
22:13	170	25:1	170	29:21	171		
22:14	165	25:2	170	29:22	162, 171		
22:15–31	146	25:3	161, 163	29:24	162, 165		
22:21–23	145	25:4	161	29:25	162		
22:21	146	25:8–9	287	29:26	162		
22:22	146	25:8	280, 287	29:34	162, 164		
22:27	36	25:9	280, 286,	29:37	79		
22:28	161		287	29:41	162		
22:30	161	25:16	280	30	167		
23	219, 220,	25:17	161	30:1	291		
	223	25:18	280	30:6	291		
23:3–8	280	25:21	280	30:12–16	166		
23:6–9	146	25:22–29	291	30:12–13	162, 167		
23:7	161	25:22	280	30:13	167		
23:9	146	25:23–24	162	30:14	163, 164,		
23:20–33	218	25:26	162		167		
23:20	201, 217,	25:30–40	291	30:27	291		
	218, 222,	25:30	162, 280	30:29	79		
	223, 226,	25:31–34	162	30:32	171		
	227, 230	25:31	280	30:34	171		
23:21	219, 230	25:39–40	6, 285	30:37	171		
23:25–26	161	25:39	162–64,	30:38	171		
23:29	125, 138		279, 285,	31:1	171		
24	6, 145,		286	31:2	171		
	279, 285,	25:40	279, 280,	31:3	171		
	289–91		285–87	32–34	128		
24:1–18	273	26	290	32	269, 271		
24:3–8	289, 292	26:1	170	32:6	275, 276		

32:7–14	269	34:30	98	39:17	172		
32:7	126–28, 138	34:34	268	39:18	172		
		34:35	98	39:19	172		
32:9	128	35–40	14	40	290		
32:11–14	269, 272	35:1	163	40:2	58		
32:13	128, 129, 138	35:2	163, 171	40:9–11	289		
		35:3	160, 171	40:17	58		
32:19	276	35:4	171				
32:25	276	35:5	161, 163, 171	Leviticus			
32:30–34	272			1:9	162		
32:52	162	35:6	161	1:13	162		
33	127, 128	35:23	161	3:17	160		
33:1–23	260	35:21	100	4:7	291		
33:3	127, 128, 138	35:36	100	4:18	291		
		36:2	100	5	29		
33:5	127, 128, 138	36:32	171	6:3	162		
		36:33	171	7:26	160		
33:7–23	272	36:34	171	8:10–12	289		
33:7	163, 164	36:35	171	9:3	36		
33:11	76, 163, 171	36:36	171	10	22		
		36:37	171	11:44–45	273		
33:13	171	36:38	171	14:4–5	289		
33:19	98	37:18	163	16	285		
34:1–35	252	37:24	162, 163	16:1	37		
34:6	163	37:28	163	16:2	37, 275		
34:7	163, 164	37:29	163, 171	16:4	162		
34:9	128, 163	38:1	171	16:13	37		
34:10–13	163	38:2	171	16:29	145, 147		
34:11–26	252	38:3	171	17–26	252		
34:11	171	38:4	171	17:8–9	147		
34:12	164, 171	38:5	171	18:5	269		
34:13	164, 165, 171	38:6	172	18:26	145, 148		
		38:7	172	19:2	252, 273		
34:14–16	163	39:1	172	19:8	36, 37		
34:14	164, 171	39:2	172	19:10	148		
34:15	171	39:3	172	19:12	252		
34:16	165, 171	39:4	172	19:18	252, 253		
34:17	171	39:5	172	19:20	113, 114		
34:18	171	39:8	172	19:34	146		
34:19	171	39:9	172	20	37		
34:20	171	39:10	172	20:2	148		
34:21	171	39:11	172	20:7	273		
34:22	171	39:12	172	20:17	36		
34:23	171	39:13	172	21:11	37		
34:24	171	39:14	172	22:9	37		
34:29–35	260, 268	39:15	172	22:18–19	148		
34:29	98	39:16	172	22:31–33	273		

Leviticus (cont:)		13:18	86	5:18	252		
22:32–33	268	13:21	87	5:21	136–38,		
23:3	160	13:22	86, 87		269		
23:14	160	13:23	86	5:22–33	273		
23:21	160	13:26	87	5:22	252		
23:22	148	13:27	87	5:26	208		
23:31	160	15:3	162	5:28	166, 261		
24	22	15:34	28	5:29	165		
24:3	162	17:18	291	5:33	276		
24:10–16	3, 22	17:25	291	6:1	261		
24:10–11	23	19	285, 291	6:4–5	303		
24:11	35–38	19:6	289	6:4	302		
24:12	25, 31–34,	20:13	62	6:5	253		
	38	20:15	74	6:12	126		
24:13–14	34	20:23–29	274	6:21	126, 129		
24:13	37, 38	21:1	86	6:22	126		
24:14	35, 37, 38	27:12–14	123	7:6–11	273		
24:15–16	35, 38	28:30	289	7:9	161		
24:15	24, 36	29:6	58	7:19	80		
24:16	25, 36,	30:2	252	7:22	125, 138		
	145, 148	33:38	306	8:5	271		
24:17–23	148	35:29	160	8:14	126		
24:20	252			9:6	127		
24:22	145, 148,	*Deuteronomy*		9:12	126, 128,		
	150	1:15	161		138		
24:23	35, 37	1:27	126	9:13	127, 128,		
25:23	146, 153	1:30	126		138		
25:35–43	274	4:1	261	9:26	126, 129		
25:44	75, 148	4:5–8	267	9:27	128, 129,		
25:55	153	4:5	261		138		
26:13	75	4:9–20	276	9:29	129		
		4:14	261	10	146		
Numbers		4:20	126	10:19	126		
9:15–22	275	4:34	80, 126	11:3	126		
10:2	59	4:37	126	11:8–9	276		
10:8	58	4:45	126	11:10	126		
10:11–12	275	4:46	126	11:32	135		
10:10	58	5	134	12–26	145		
11	270	5:6–30	252	12:1	135		
11:1–3	275	5:6–7	268	12:20	136		
11:10–15	270, 272	5:6	126	13:6	126		
11:12	271	5:7	134, 138	13:11	126		
12:6–8	272	5:10	135, 138,	14:22–29	149		
12:16	86		161	14:26	136		
13	86	5:14	137	14:28–29	149		
13:1	86	5:15	126, 129	14:29	149		
13:17	86	5:17	252	15:12–18	105		

15:15	126, 129	26:6	78, 160	8:35	144
15:17	122, 129, 138	26:8	126	15:21	86
		26:11	4, 149	22:28	286
16:1	126	26:12–13	149		
16:3	126, 300, 306	26:16–17	273	*Judges*	
		28	74	6:7–10	17
16:6	126	28:48	74	6:19	61
16:7	129–31, 138	29–30	147	13:5	261
		29	147		
16:8	130–32, 138	29:1	126, 129	*1 Samuel*	
		29:2–4	271	2	15
16:9	44	29:3	80	2:15	130
16:12	126, 129	29:6	276	8:7	273
18:15	262	29:15	126	8:8	273
18:18	165	29:21	50	17:26	208
19	146	29:24	126		
19:6	125	30:6	276	*2 Samuel*	
19:21	252, 254	30:11–20	276	1:13	144
20	82	30:15–20	269	4:10	222
20:1	126	31	147	7:12–16	274
20:7	82	31:1	147	18:22	222
21:14	132–34, 138	31:7–9	260	18:25	222
		31:9–13	147		
22:9	125	31:12	147	*1 Kings*	
23:1–3	74	31:14–18	274	2:10	274
23:2–4	74	31:16	274	5:13–18	151
23:5	126	32	271	5:27–32	151
23:7	74	32:5–20	268	6:1	299, 306
23:8	74	32:5	271	7:34–35	291
23:24	44	32:13	67	9:15	151
24	149	32:14	67	9:20–22	151
24:1–4	252	32:19	130	11:43	274
24:1–2	245	32:27	125	17:39	128
24:7	132, 133, 138	32:36	75		
		32:44–47	276	*2 Kings*	
24:9	126	32:49–51	123	1:8	224
24:14	149	34:1	129	7:9	222
24:17	149	34:3	86		
24:18	126, 129	34:5	129	*1 Chronicles*	
24:19	149	34:11	126	22	150
24:20–21	149			22:2	150
24:22	126, 129	*Joshua*		28:9	79
25:4	272	1:1–9	260	29:10–19	146
25:17	126	3:10	208	29:14	146
26	149	8	147	29:15	146
26:1	149	8:33	144, 145, 147	29:16	146
26:5	74			29:17	79

2 Chronicles		23:10	62	80:3	56–58
2	150	24:1	55	80:4–5	58
2:16–17	150	26:4	59	80:4	58
2:17–18	150	28:5 Eng:	276	80:5	62
30:25	150, 151	29:1	56	80:6	59, 60, 67
35:13	130	30:21	62	80:7–17	60
35:18	130	31	207	80:7–12	53
		31:6	59	80:7	60
Ezra		32:2	57	80:8	61, 62
6:2	44	32:17	304	80:9	63
10:16	79	33:12	259	80:10	63
36:10–30	289	35:17	100	80:11	60, 63
36:33	289	37	259	80:12	64, 65
		39	146	80:13–16	53
Nehemiah		39:12	146	80:13	64, 65, 67
8:8	261	40	44, 207	80:14–15	65
8:13	261	40:8	44, 66	80:14	65, 66
9:20	261	40:9	222	80:15	65
11	14	42:2	208	80:16	65–67
		43:1	54	80:17	53, 66, 67
Esther		43:21	63	81	58
2:23	79	45:12	62	81:10–11	252
		48:5	57	83	54
Job		49:1	55	83:1	54
24:14–15	252	50:7	252	87:1	61
30:3	99	53:5	63	91:4	57
30:14	99	54:10	62	94:1	57
32:11	79	55:10	61	96:2	222
36:23	79	56:9	57	97:5	56
37:23	79	58:13	66	97:6	58
38:27	99	65:3	66	101	294
		70:22	56, 57	101:3	61
Psalms		72:1–82:1	55	101:24	61
1:1–2	259	73:18	59	102	294
3:9	62	74:3	99	104:38	299, 306
7:9	79	77	308	105:32	62
7:10	79	77:12–16	308	105:38	299, 306
8	54	77:31	308	107:3	57
8:1	54	78	308	108:11	63
9:14	66	78:2	257, 261	108:27	59
17:44	62	78:12–16	308	109	283, 285, 293
17:45	66	78:31	308		
18:9	270	80	3, 52, 54, 58	109:1	293
19:7	270			109:4	282, 293
19:8	304	80:1	53, 67	111	207
22:4	269	80:2–6	53	113:1	299, 306
27:5	276	80:2	56	114:1	299, 306

Index of References

117:7	66	18:1–7	45, 46	62:11	261
117:23	59	18:1	45	63:1–6	47
118	207	18:5–6	45	63:7–14	268
118:42	61	18:5	44, 45	63:15–16	268
118:50	59	18:6	46	64:4–12	268
118:130	270	21:1	86	64:8	268
119:1–2	259	27:9	269	66:20	56
119:130	270	27:13	274		
125:46	54	30:6	86	*Jeremiah*	
127	207	30:20–21	261	3:12–19	268
131:6	59	35:8	220	6:13–16	276
137:3	61	38–55	220	7:6	151
138:23	79	39:5–8	220	7:9	252
139:23	79	40–61	222	11:20	269
143:9	57	40–55	269	14:8	151
144:12	286	40	220	17:10	79
144:15	259	40:3–5	220	18:1–2	261
146:1	57	40:3	5, 201, 217, 220, 222, 223, 226–28, 261	21–22	152
146:9	61			21	151
147:3	66, 67			21:1	151
149:3	57			21:2–6	151
150:3	57			21:11	151
151	55	40:6	220	21:12	151
151:1	57	40:9–10	220	21:13	151
151:3	55	40:9	220, 222	22	151
		40:21	220	22:3	151, 152
Proverbs		41:27	222	22:4–5	151
8	259	42:1–4	257, 261	22:9	152
9:1–18	258	42:16	220	24:4–7	276
30:23	113	43:16–21	307	24:6	276
		43:16–17	307	31:4 Eng:	276
Isaiah		43:16	308	31:9	268
1:2	268	47:11	99	31:15	261
2:3	261	48:17–21	220	31:33	276
2:4	44	52:5	222	32:6–9	261
5:17	151	52:7	222, 223	33:7 Eng:	276
6:9–10	271	53:1	271	36	44
7:14	261	53:4	256, 257, 261	36:2	44
8:23–9:1	261			36:3	163
9:1	257	54:13	273, 274	36:4	44
10:3	99	55:12	220	36:8–10	44
11	261	59:17	276	36:13–15	44
11:1–12	239	59:20–21	269	36:13	44
11:1	261	60:6	222	36:6:18	44
13:10	275	61	259	38	284, 290, 293
14:1	151	61:1–2	239		
18	45	61:1	222, 239	38:4	276

Jeremiah (cont:)		7:4	67	Zechariah	
40:7	276	11:1–2	268	5	3, 42, 44, 46, 47, 49
42:10 Eng:	276	11:1	261		
49:10	276	11:10–11	268	5:1–4	3, 41–43, 46, 49, 50
50:16	44	12:10	252		
		13:4	252	5:1–2	44
Lamentations				5:1	45
3:14	56, 57	Joel		5:2	44
3:40	79	2:1	274	5:3	46, 50
5:14	56, 57	2:10	275	5:14	41
		2:31	220, 275	6:14	56
Ezekiel		2:32	220	7:1	152
2	44	3	46	7:8–14	152
2:9–3:3	44	3:1–16	46	7:9–10	152
2:9	44	3:1–8	46	7:10	151
2:10	44	3:1–3	46	7:14	152
6:6	160	3:4	46	9:9	241, 261
6:13	162	3:5–6	46	9:14	274
6:14	160	3:9–16	46	11:12–13	261
13:8–16	276	3:9–12	46	13:4	224
14:7	151	3:10	44, 45		
22:1–16	151	3:11	47	Malachi	
22:2	151	3:12–13	47	1:6	219
22:3	151	3:12	46	1:8	152
22:4–5	151	3:13	44, 45, 47	2:13–14	219
22:7	151	3:15	275	2:17–3:5	219
22:15–16	151			2:17	219
22:29	151	Amos		3	152, 220
32:7–8	275	5:23	56	3:1	5, 201, 217, 219, 222, 223, 226, 227, 230
37:6	273				
37:14	273	Micah			
40–48	152	3:5	276		
47:13–48:29	152	4:3	44		
47:13–23	152	7:15	300, 306	3:2	219
47:21–23	152			3:3–15	219
47:22	151, 152	Nahum		3:5	151, 152
47:23	151, 152	1:2	166	3:16	220
47:24	152			3:23	220
48:35	153	Habakkuk		4:1	220
		2:5–6	261	4:2	220
Daniel		3:3	62	4:5	220, 227
2:19	59	3:9	62		
7:13–14	275	3:13	62	SEPTUAGINT	
				1 Kingdoms	
Hosea		Zephaniah		13:20–21	44
4:2	252	1:14–16	274	13:20	44
6:6	253, 257	1:15	99	13:21	44

Index of References

16:18	56	11:1	270	2:15	261
		11:10	275	2:17–18	261
2 Kingdoms		11:12	275	2:23	261
23:1	56	12:23–27	273	3:2	257, 262
		12:24	273	3:3	217, 261
2 Supplement		13:1–15:17	273	3:13–17	259
15:14	58	14:6	180	4:1–11	259
		14:12	273	4:3	272
Judith		14:22–26	273	4:8	257, 260
1:11	28	18	258	4:12–17	257
1:100	28			4:15–16	261
1:172	28	*Ecclesiasticus*		4:17	257, 262
		16:7	180	4:25–5:2	255
Job		24	258	5–7	249, 250,
21:12	56	24:23	259		255–59,
30:31	56	44:23–45:5	300		262
		48	259	5:1–7:29	255
Apocrypha/Deutero-		50:16	59	5:1–2	252
Canonical Books				5:1	257, 260
1 Esdras		*Baruch*		5:3–11	259
9:16	79	4	258	5:17–22	253
		4:1	258	5:17–19	258, 261
2 Esdras				5:17–18	252, 254
6:2	44	*1 Maccabees*		5:17	254
23:20	128	3:30	128	5:18	254
		4:50–51	291	5:20	253, 254
Tobit		13:41–42	239	5:21–48	252
12:6	259			5:21	252
		2 Maccabees		5:27	252
Judith		4:9	175	5:31	252
5:10–15	300	4:19	175	5:33	252
7:23–27	269	5:23	175	5:38	252, 254
8:12–13	269	7:37	79	5:43	252
8:17	269			5:48	253
8:21–23	269	New Testament		6:1–7:27	252
8:27	79	*Matthew*		6:1–18	253
9:7	100	1–4	255	6:3–20	252
16:1	57	1–2	255, 256,	6:18	260
			259	7:12	254
Wisdom of Solomon		1:1–4:25	255	7:13–14	259
5:17–18	276	1:1–17	257	7:13	259
5:20–23	276	1:1–3	207	7:17–20	259
9:8	287	1:1	203, 211	7:19	259
10:15–21	270	1:2–17	257	7:21	254
10:15	270	1:17	257	7:24–27	259
10:20–21	270	1:22–23	261	7:28–29	252
11:1–14	275	2:1	211	7:29	260

Matthew (cont.)		13:1–53	255	19:19	253
8–9	255	13:1–3	255	19:21	253
8:1–9:34	255	13:16–17	256	20:20–21	256
8:1–9:1	256	13:18	256	21:1–17	259
8:1–4	260	13:19	260	21:4–5	261
8:1	257, 258, 260	13:34–35	257	21:5	241
		13:35	261	21:9	262
8:2–9:34	260	13:36	257	21:16	270
8:4	259	13:44–50	255	21:21	257
8:5–13	260	13:51–52	255	21:23–27	260
8:16–17	257	13:54–17:27	255	21:28–31	255
8:17	256, 261	13:58	256	22:24	259
8:23–27	260	14–17	255	22:34–40	253
8:26	256	14:13–22	259	22:36	254
8:28–34	260	14:15	257	22:40	254
9:2–34	255	14:19	257	23–25	255–57, 262
9:2–8	260	14:22	257		
9:8	260	14:23	260	23:1–26:1	255
9:9–13	257	14:25	256	23:1–12	260
9:13	253	14:31	256	23:1	257
9:18–19	260	15:13	255	23:2–3	253, 260, 262
9:20–22	260	15:19	252		
9:21–22	256	15:29–39	259	23:2	252, 259
9:23–26	260	15:29	257, 260	23:23	253, 254
9:27–31	260	15:32–33	257	24–25	256
9:32–34	260	15:36	257	24	260
9:36–37	255	16:4	256	24:3	255, 257, 260
10	255, 256	16:8	256		
10:1–11:1	255	16:16	208	24:10–12	255
10:34	254	17:1–9	260	24:16	257
11–12	255	17:1	257, 260	24:20	253
11:2–12:49	255	17:3	259	24:23–24	234
11:2–6	259	17:4	259	24:26	255
11:2–4	239	17:9	256, 257, 260	24:29–33	275
11:7–15	257, 262			24:29–31	275
11:10	217	17:20	257	24:30	275
11:13	254, 261	17:24–27	167, 255	24:36–44	275
11:25–30	260	18	255, 256	24:37–44	256
11:25	270	18:1–19:1	255	24:40–41	275
12:1–8	257	18:1	255	24:43–44	275
12:5	254	18:3	255	24:45–51	256
12:7	253	19–22	255	25:1–13	255, 256
12:16–21	257	19:2–22:46	255	25:14–30	256
12:17–21	261	19:7	259	25:31–41	256
12:23	257	19:8	245, 252, 259	25:31–40	255
12:28	260			26–28	255
13	255, 256	19:18	252	26:2–27:66	255

26:15	261	1:8–11	225	9:6	256
26:17–25	259	1:9–11	225	9:7	223
26:30	257	1:9	224	9:13	222
27:3–10	255	1:11	223	9:23–24	241
27:9–10	261	1:12–13	225, 226	9:31	224
27:37	234	1:12	224, 225	9:33–34	224
27:51–53	255	1:14–15	221, 238,	9:42	241
27:54	201		239, 242,	10:2–12	244
28	256		245	10:2	244
28:1–20	255	1:14	221, 222,	10:3	245
28:16–20	255, 257,		224	10:4	245
	260	1:15	221	10:5–9	245
28:16	257, 260	1:32–34	257	10:6	246
28:18	260	1:35	225	10:17	224
		1:45	225	10:19	252
Mark		2:1–3:6	245, 246	10:32–33	224
1	222	2:5	241	10:32	224
1:1–15	216–18,	2:13–17	257	10:35–37	256
	221, 224,	2:17	253	10:46–52	241
	225, 228	2:23–28	245, 257	10:46	224
1:1–14	257	2:23–26	245	10:52	224, 241
1:1–13	221	2:24	245	11:6	222
1:1–3	5, 216–18,	2:26	253	11:9–10	241
	225	2:27–28	245	11:17	217, 221
1:1–2	198, 202,	2:27	244–46	11:22–24	241
	207, 221	3:11	223	11:31	241
1:1	5, 185,	3:12	257	12:6	223
	191, 192,	4	256	12:19	221
	194, 196–	4:13	256	13	256
	201, 208,	4:33–34	257	13:21	234
	209, 221,	4:40	256	13:24–27	275
	222	5:7	223	13:24–26	217, 221
1:2–3	201, 220,	5:34	241	13:32	223
	221, 223,	5:36	241	13:61	223
	224, 227–	6:3	241	14:21	222
	29	6:5–6	240, 241	14:62	217, 221
1:2	198, 201,	6:5	256	15:26	234
	203, 208,	6:31–35	225	15:31–32	241
	210, 221–	6:48	256	15:39	223
	23, 226	6:50–51	256	16:7	222
1:3–6	224	7:21–22	252		
1:3	222, 261	7:21	252	Luke	
1:4–15	224, 230	8:17	256	1	204
1:4–5	225	8:27–30	224	1:1–3	207
1:4	224, 225,	8:27	224	1:1	205, 211
	229	8:31	224	1:3	207
1:6	224, 225	9:2–13	224	2:23	222

Luke (cont.)

3:4	217, 261
5:32	253
6:4	253
6:14–16	210
6:20–26	257
7:18–23	239
7:22–23	239
7:27	217
8:22–25	301
8:22–24	302
8:25	302
10:16	273
10:21	270
12:39–40	275
16:16	261
17:26–27	275
18:20	252
21:25–28	275

John

1:1–5	207
1:1	202, 208
1:2	202
1:3	202
1:4–8	224
1:4	207
1:23	261
6:45	274
6:49	274
6:54–63	274
12:15	241
14:2	219
14:3	219
19:19	234

Acts

7	230
7:42	222
9:2	224
15:15	222
17:1–9	268
17:7	268
19:9	224
19:23	224
22:4	224
24:14	224

24:22	224

Romans

1:17	222
2:24	222
3:4	222
3:10	222
4:17	222
7	268, 269
7:7	269
7:8–9	269
7:10–11	269
7:24	268
8:14–39	267, 269
8:14–17	274
8:34	282
11:25–32	269
11:26	269
13:8–10	276
13:9	252
13:11–14	276
13:12	276
13:13	274

1 Corinthians

2:13	274
4:14–17	271
5:5–8	275
9:8–12	272
9:12	272
10:1–13	230, 273
10:1–3	272
10:1–2	275
10:6–7	275
10:9	272
10:1–13	309
10:13	272
10:31	269
13:7	272
14:40	274

2 Corinthians

1:20	269
3	268
3:3	268
3:7–11	269
3:16	268

3:18	268
4:17	269
8:19	269

Philippians

2:14–15	271
2:16	271
2:19–24	271

Colossians

1:12–14	269

1 Thessalonians

1:1	267, 268
1:2–10	267
1:3	267
1:5	267
1:6	267
1:7–8	267
1:8–9	273
1:8	276
1:9–10	268
1:9	267, 269, 273, 275
1:10	267, 268, 276
2:1–16	269
2:1	267, 269
2:2	267
2:3	269
2:4	267
2:6	270
2:7–12	269
2:7–8	270
2:7	270
2:8–10	271
2:8	267
2:9	267
2:11–12	271
2:12	276, 277
2:13–16	271
2:13	271, 273
2:14–16	271
2:14–15	267
2:15	272, 276
2:16	271, 275
2:17–18	272

2:17	272	*2 Thessalonians*		8:1–2	283, 284, 285, 290
2:19–20	272	1:9	275		
2:19	268	1:12	269	8:1	280, 282, 283
3:1–2	271				
3:1	272	*Hebrews*		8:2	285, 287
3:2	267, 272	1:1–12:29	281	8:3–5	290
3:5–6	272	1:1–4	280	8:5	279, 285
3:5	272	1:3	282, 283	8:6	284
3:6–10	273	1:5–2:18	280	8:8–13	285
3:11–4:2	268	1:13	282	8:13	284
3:11–13	268, 273	2:8	284, 293	9	6, 279, 280, 290
3:11	273	2:17	281–83		
3:12	273	3:1–5:10	280	9:1–10:18	285
3:13	270, 273, 275	3:1–6	292	9:1–6	290
		3:1	282, 283	9:1–5	280, 290, 291
4:1–12	273	3:7–11	230		
4:2	273	4:13	281	9:5	290
4:5	273	4:14–6:20	280	9:6	290
4:7	276	4:14–16	280, 283	9:7	290, 291
4:8	273, 274	4:14	280, 281, 283	9:10	291
4:9–12	273, 276			9:11–15	291
4:9	273	4:15	281	9:11	291
4:12	274	5:6	281	9:12	289
4:13–5:11	268	5:7–8	281	9:13	289
4:13–18	274	5:9	281	9:16–17	288, 289, 292
4:13–17	274	5:10–11	283		
4:13	274, 275	5:10	280, 281	9:18–22	280, 288
4:14	274–76	5:11–10:25	280	9:18	288, 292
4:15–17	268	5:11–6:20	282	9:19–20	289
4:15	274, 275	6:20	280, 281	9:19	289
4:16	274	7	282, 284, 290	9:20	280
4:17	275			9:20	288
4:18	275	7:1–10:18	6, 280–82	9:21	289
5:1–11	274	7:1	280, 282, 290	9:22	289, 292
5:2	275			9:23–26	292
5:3	275	7:11–12	284	9:23	287
5:4–5	276	7:11	284	9:24	287
5:6	276	7:12	283	10	280, 292
5:8–9	276	7:15	282	10:12–18	285
5:9	275, 276	7:18	283, 290	10:12	282
5:10	276	7:26	283	10:13	293
5:11	276	7:28	283	10:18	280, 281, 285
5:15	273	8	6, 279, 284, 290		
5:23–24	268			10:19–23	280
5:24	277	8:1–5	285	10:19–21	283
		8:1–10:18	283	10:19	281
				10:26–12:13	280

Hebrews (cont.)		1:9–10	178	15:3	57
10:31	281	1:9	183	17:36	261
10:32–34	282	1:10–15	179		
10:37	293, 294	1:16–29	179	Testament of Benjamin	
11:1	294	2	184	5:2	202
11:22	306	2:1	179		
12:2	282	2:2–20	5, 174, 177, 178, 184	Testament of Dan	
12:4–5	282			5:11	202
12:12–13	282				
12:12	294	2:2–10	179	Testament of Job	
12:13	294	2:2–3	183	47:11	199
12:14–13:25	280	2:2	179–82		
12:29	281	2:3	179–81	Qumran	
12:32	281	2:4	180, 181	1Q22	
13	281	2:5	180–82	1 ii 11	163
13:19	281	2:6–7	181, 182	1 iv 4	162
13:20–21	281	2:6	180		
13:21	281	2:8–9	183	1QHa	
13:22–25	281	2:13	181–83	4:24	163
13:25	281	2:14	180–82	8:34	163
		2:17–18	180	10:9	160
James		2:17	180–82	10:20	160
2:11	252	2:18	181	13:13	160
4:7	202	2:30	175, 184	15:31	160, 164
		3:13–40	178	16:20	160
1 Peter		3:21–23	175		
2:2	224	3:24	184	1QM	
2:21	224	5:20	179	5:5	161, 163
		5:42	179	5:8	161, 163
Jude		6	184	7:10–11	163
38	285	6:25	184	7:10	162
		6:26	184	7:11	163
Pseudepigrapha		6:28	184	10:8	160, 164
1 Enoch		6:35	57	11:9–10	160
12–16	262	7:11–12	184	13:13	164
51:3	261	7:12	175		
89:72–90:29	262			1QS	
91:11–13	262	4 Ezra		1:2-3	260
93:98–10	262	13:10	261	2:21-22	161
				5:7-13	258
2 Enoch		Joseph and Aseneth		5:8	254
42:6-14	259	16:7-8	259	5:15	161
				6:18	260
3 Maccabees		Psalms Solomon		8:1-10	262
1:1–5	178	2:2–4	262	8:9	162
1:6–9	178	3:2	57	8:13	166
1:6–7	179	8:11–13	262	8:15-16	260

8:22	254	9 6	169	12 3-4	161
12:28	260	10-12 9	170	4-7 I 2-5	161
13:19	260	10-12 8	170	8 1-6	161
		10-12 6-7	170	9 2-3	161
1QSa		10-12 6	170		
1:14-15	161	10-12 5	170	*4Q265*	
		10-12 4	170	6 4-5	161
1QSb		10-12 3	170		
3:1	162	10-12 2	170	*4Q269*	
		10-12 13	170	2 3	160
1QpHab		10-12 12	170		
8:8-11	261	10-12 11	170	*4Q270*	
4158 5 1-2	169	10-12 10	170	6 iii 19	166
		10-12 1	169	6 iv 14	163
4Q158		13 2-3	171	6 v 13	161
1-2 16	168	13 3	171		
1-2 14-15	168			*4Q271*	
1-2 13-14	168	*4Q159*		2 13	163
4 1-2	168	1 ii 6-7	162	4 ii 3	163
4 2-3	170	1 ii 7	167	5 i 4	161
4 4-5	170	5 4-5	163, 164		
4 4	170			*4Q275*	
5 2-3	169	*4Q166*		2 3	161
5 3-4	169	2:1-6	260		
5 4-5	169			*4Q285*	
5 5	169	*4Q174*		8 8	161
6 1-2	169	1-2 i 3	161, 164–		
6 3	169		66	*4Q299*	
6 4-9	161, 169			3a ii-b 12	160, 164,
7-8 9	169	*4Q175*			166
7-8 7-8	169	1:1	164, 166	60 3	161, 164
7-8 6-7	169	1:2	164		
7-8 6	169	1:3	164	*4Q364*	
7-8 5-6	169	1:4	164	13a-b 1-2	169
7-8 3-4	169	1:5	165	13a-b 2-3	169
7-8 2	169	1:6	164, 165	13a-b 5-6	169
7-8 14-15	169	1:7	164	13a-b 6-7	169
7-8 13-14	169	1:1-8	161	13a-b 6	169
7-8 12-13	169			13a-b 9	169
7-8 11	169	*4Q216*		14 1-2	169
7-8 10	169	1:5-7	161	14 3-4	170
7-8 1-2	169			14 4-5	170
7-8 1	169	*4Q218*		14 5-6	170
9 1	169	1 2-3	163	15 1-3	170
9 2	169			15 5	170
9 3	169	*4Q251*		16 1-2	170
9 4-5	169	1-2 4-5	161	17 2-3	170

4Q365		8a-b 3	170	4Q366	
2 11	168	9a-b i 2-3	170	1 1-2	170
2 2-3	168	9a-b i 2	170	1 12	170
2 3-4	168	9a-b i 3-4	170	1 5-6	170
2 4-5	168	9a-b i 3	170	1 7-8	170
2 6-7	168	10 1-2	171	1 9-11	170
2 7-9	168	10 1	171		
2 9-11	168	10 3-4	171	4Q368	
3 1-2	168	10 4	171	1 3-4	171
3 2-3	168	11 i 1	171	1 4-6	171
3 2	168	11 i 2-3	171	1 6-7	171
3 3-4	168	11 i 3	171	2 2-3	171
4 1-2	168	12a i 1-2	171	2 3-4	171
4 1	168	12a i 1	171	2 5-6	171
5 1	168	12a i 2-3	171	2 6-7	171
5 2	168	12a i 4-5	171	2 7-8	171
6a i 1-3	168	12a i 5-6	171	2 9-10	171
6a i 1	168	12a i 6-7	171	2 9	171
6a i 11-12	168	12a i 7-8	171	2 11-13	171
6a i 12-13	168	12a-b ii		2 11	171
6a i 3-4	168	11-12	171	2 13-14	171
6a i 4-5	168	12a-b ii		2 15-16	171
6a i 5-6	168	12-13	171	2 16	171
6a i 6-7	168	12a-b ii			
6a i 7-8	168	13-14	172	4Q374	
6a i 8-10	168	12a-b ii 14	172	2 ii 6	160
6aii+6c	168	12a-b ii 6	171		
6aii+6c		12a-b ii 7-8	171	4Q375	
10-11	168	12a-b ii 8-9	171	ll: 1-4	260
6aii+6c 10	168	12a-b ii 9-11	171		
6aii+6c		12b iii 1-2	172	4Q377	
11-14	168	12b iii 10-11	172	1 i 2	161
6aii+6c 8	168	12b iii 10	172	1 i 6	161
6aii+6c 9	168	12b iii 11-12	172	1 i 9	160
6b 1-2	168	12b iii 12-13	172	2 ii 6-7	163
6b 1	168	12b iii 13-14	172	2 ii 10-11	161
6b 3-5	168	12b iii 14	172	2 ii 10	161, 164
6b 3	168	12b iii 3-5	172		
6b 5-6	168	12b iii 3	172	4Q381	
6b 6	168	12b iii 5-7	172	69:4	260
7 i 2	168	12b iii 5	172		
7 i 3	168	12b iii 7-8	172	4Q390	
7 i 4	168	12b iii 8-9	172	l: 6	261
7 ii 1-3	169	13 1-2	172	ll: 5-6	261
7 ii 1	169	13 1	172	2 i 4-5	260
8a-b 1-2	170	13 2	172		
8a-b 2-3	170				

Index of References

4Q393		4QMMT		27:4-5	160
3 6	166	C31	260	27:5	165
				27:9	160
4Q416		11Q14		27:12	162
2 iii 15-16	161	1 ii 11-12	161	28:2	162
2 iii 15	164			28:6	162
2 iii 16	164	11Q18		39:7-8	167
2 iii 19	164	29 6	162	39:8-10	162
		33 1	162	39:8	167
4Q418		8 1	162	39:14	167
9+9a-c	161	8 2	162	43:11-12	162
9+9a-c 17	164	8 3	162	43:11	164
10a-b 2	161, 164			57:4-5	161
		11Q19		57:8	161
4Q427		2:1-7	163	59:16-17	260
7 i 8	160	2:4	164		
		2:6	165	11Q20	
4Q429		2:7	164, 165	1:15	162
6 2	166	2:11-15	163	2:2-3	162
		2:11	164	2:6-7	162
4Q431		2:15	165	2:9	162
i 45	160	3:2	161	5:1	162
		3:8	162, 163	5:12	160, 162, 165
4Q461		3:9	161		
1 3	160	7:13	162, 164	6:6-7	162
		8:5-7	162	6:7	165
4Q470		8:13	162	22:14	162
3 5	160	9:1-5	162	24:8-9	162
		9:3-4	163	25:8	162
4Q491		9:14	162, 165		
1–3	161	14:10-11	160, 164	CD	
		15:6-7	162	3:8	160
4Q504		16:2-3	162	5:6-7	262
1-2 iii 6	160	16:7-8	162	5:21–6:1	260
3 ii 17	163	16:10-11	162	9:5	166
4 7	163	16:11	164	10:1-2	163
4 10	161	17:3-4	160	11:7-8	161
6 6-7	161	17:3	165	13:1-2	161
6 10	160	17:4	160, 164, 165	15:2	254
6 14	163, 164			15:9	254
52+54-5+		20:8	162	15:12	254
57-9 1	163	20:15–21:1	162	16:1	163
125+127 2	163	20:16	165	20:21-22	161
131-132 14	163	21:9	160, 162, 165		
		22:14	165	MISHNAH	
4Q547				Sanhedrin	
8 3	161	24:6	162	7.5	2

Talmuds
b. Sanhedrin
56a	24
56a 15	36
56a.12	24

b. Yoma
5a	289

b. Zeb.
26b	289

Josephus
Antiquities
2.82.4	57
3.204-207	289
12.323.4	57
12.349.2	57
13.274	237
17.295	242
18.63-64	243
20.200	243
20.97-99	261

War
2.75	242
2.258-60	261
2.258-260	228
2.261-263	228
2.36	201
2.264	228
388	291
6.351	228
7.438	228

Philo
De decalogo
I.2	228
12	252

Legum Allegoriae
III,33	286

De migratione Abrahami
215	199

Quis rerum divanarum heres sit
266	291

De specialibus legibus
3.2	252

De vita Mosis
2.146	289

Other Jewish Sources
Sifra Emor
14	28
14.2–3	25

Christian Authors
Didache
2.1-3	252

Classical Works
Aeschylus
Seven against Thebes
1020–1024	85

Aristophanes
Wasps
764	28

Frogs TLG
5014.12	62

Aristotle
Conception of Equity
749	27

Nicomachean Ethics
1119a	28

Rhetoric
1375b	28

Augustine
De utiliate credendi
III.8	308, 309

Chrysostom
Stat
19.14	199

Diodorus Siculus
Library of History
31.17c	76

Euripides
Ion
190	49

Eusebius
224.20–21	55
224.21–22	55
417.32	56

Gaudentuis
Tract i in Exodum
I.10	305

Hesiod
Theogonia
147–149	48
160	48
175	48

Hippocrates
Epidemics
4.1.32	108
4.1.9	108

Homer
Iliad
21.322–323	85
24.664–667	85

Irenaeus
3.10.5	198
3.11.8	198
3.16.3	198

Isocrates
Archidemus (Or. 6)
45	84

Jerome
Commentariorum in Isaiam
I.ii.8.2 304
XII.14 307

Epistulae
32.1 303
53.8 304

Sophronius Eusebius: Epistula
106.2 303

Justin
Dialogue
59.1 300
59.2 300
75.1 300
126.2 300
128.1 300

Lycurgus
Against Leocrates
86 49

Origen
Contra Celsum
236 201

Plato
Cratylus
410d 79

Plato
Hippias minor
364c 28

Laws
834a 28
847b 27

Respublica
2.348a–b 28
2.376b 28

Pliny
Natural History
25.115 199

Polybius
The Histories
4.87.5 76
5.77.6 240
15.25.17 76

Simonides
Fragments
531.4–5 84

Sophocles
Fragments
866, 1 107

Tertullian
Scorpiace
2.2-3 302

Xenephon
Anabasis
6.1.22 27

Hellenica
5.2.10 27

Memorablia
1.1.9 27

OSTRACA, PAPYRI AND TABLETS
Archaiologikē Ephēmeris
l. 4 112
l. 10 112
l. 12 112
l. 20 112
ll. 30–31 112
ll. 45–46 112
1,303,C.
  10–11 112
110,59,V.
  29–30 112
155,400 112

155,401 112
155,403 112
166,405,A.
  7–20 112
188,418a 112

BGU
6 1465 27

Bodleian Coptic Inscription
426 209

FD
III 1:294, col. 1. 12 114

IG
IX,2 1257,
  1–3 113
IX,2 1282 112
XI,4 1247 33
XI,4 1299 33

IMT Kyz Kapu Dağ
1727 113

IsMetr
112 33

Malibu
83.AE.346 49

P.Amh.
2 33 29

P.Anastasy
9 208

P. Berol.
22 235 209
954 ll. 24-25 205

P.Bodmer
XXIV 55, 59

P.Cair.Zen		P.Mich.		P.Tebt.	
1 59021	30	1 57	30	3.772	27
1 59044	26	1 71	31		
2 59140	27	1 98	27	P.Vindob	
2 59236	32	1559	201, 210	G 348 ll. 1-4	205
3 59426	33	inv. 4944b	201		
5 59832	30	inv. 6213	209	P.Zen.Pestm.	
59034	33			49	30
		P.Mosc. Copt.			
P.Col.		36	201	PAM	
3 12	32			43.698 21 1	162
4 88	27	P.Oxy			
		III 560	200	PG	
P.Eleph.		VII 1015	200	58:669	199
12	26	VIII 1151	202		
		VIII 1151		PGM	
P.Eleph. DAIK		ll. 1-3	202	IV.3014–	
1	32	VIII 1151		3015	199
		ll. 15-22	202	XIII.637–	
P.Enteux.		XVI 1928		638	75
12	31	l. 16	206		
		LXV 4469	209	PSI	
P.Giss.		LXXVI 5073	200, 212	5 502	31
1 2 l. 13	116	LXXVI 5073		5 539	32
1 2 l. 20	116	ll. 1-5	200	VI 719	
				ll. 1-4	203
P.Got.		P.Petr.			
21	209	2 38 R (b)	30	SB	
		3 32	31	16 12519	29
P.Gurob.		(2) 1 13		18 13256	30
2	32	l. 1.11	115		
		(2) 1 13		SEG	
P.Hal.		ll. 1.8–10	115	26:72	114
1.188–189 l. 196				26:689. 2–5	112
		P.Rainier			
P.Heid. G.		1 ll. 1-2	205	TAM	
110	209			III,1	
		P.Ryl.		276	113
P.Hib.		1 54	49	429	113
1 34	32			483	113
		P.Sorb.		490	113
P.Lille	114	1.9	79	743	113
1 29,1. 29	114	3 107	27		
				TM	
P.Lond. Copt.		P.Tarich		60164	49
317	201	3 a 1–2	84		

UPZ
1 112   30
1 116   31
1 20   33
1 71   27

ZPE
152.191   30

Index of Authors

Abegg, M. G. ix, 2, 4, 5, 159, 163, 164, 172
Ackroyd, P. R. 11, 21, 105, 120
Adams, S. A. 217, 225, 231
Adriaen, M. 304, 308, 309
Aejmelaeus, A. 121, 122, 129, 132–34, 137–39, 142, 306, 310
Aitken, J. K. 17, 18, 47, 49, 135, 175, 185, 312
Albright, W. F. 16, 19
Alexander, L. 175–77, 180, 185
Alexander, P. S. 185, 251, 255, 263
Allison, D. C. 234, 239, 240, 243, 244, 246, 256, 257, 259, 260, 263
Altman, P. 127, 141
Andersen, F. I. 226, 231
Armoni, C. 84, 87, 88
Assmann, J. 250, 263
Attridge, H. 280, 282, 294
Ausloos, H. 17, 19, 67, 311
Austermann, F. 67
Austin, B. 313
Austin, J. L. 235, 236, 238, 247
Auwers, J. M. 292, 296
Awabdy, M. A. 144, 153

Baasten, M. F. J. 122, 139
Backhaus, K. 280, 281, 283, 287, 294
Backhuys, T. 84, 87
Bacon, B. W. 254, 260, 263
Baek, K. S. 1, 6, 163, 172, 249, 261, 263
Baethgen, D. F. 58, 67
Bagnall, R. S. 27, 39, 115, 116, 119
Baker, D. 252, 263
Baker, M. 91, 102
Baldwin, J. 219, 231
Barclay, J. M. G. 176, 185
Barr, J. 61, 67, 90, 102, 122, 124, 139
Barrick, W. B. 59, 67
Bauer, W. 231, 255

Baumgärtel, F. 121, 139
Bauschatz, J. F. 26, 32, 39
Bautch, R. 284, 296
Beale, G. K. 216, 231, 267, 278
Bell, I. 213
Ben-Dov, J. 127, 128, 140
Benjamin, W. 90–92, 96, 101–103
Benzinger, P. 143, 153
Berman, A. vi, 4, 89–96, 98–101, 103
Berman, I. 89–92, 94–96, 99, 102, 103
Bernhard, A. E. 200, 202, 215
Betz, H. D. 76, 87
Bhayro, S. 262, 263
Bienkowski, P. 19, 21
Blaise, A. 307, 310
Blavatskaja, T. V. 106, 120
Bleek, F. 283, 294
Block, D. I. 152–54
Boer, P. A. H. 59, 67
Boeser, P. A. A. 208, 214
Bogue, R. 244, 247
Bons, E. 67, 125, 141, 284, 296, 298–300, 310, 312
Boring, M. E. 199, 212
Botterweck G. J. 154
Le Boulluec, A. 105, 106, 120, 134, 136, 137, 140
Bourdieu, P. 236, 247
Boyd-Taylor, C. 67, 68, 89, 92, 93, 101–103, 175–77, 180, 185
Brant, J. A. A. 176, 185
Braun, H. 283, 294
Braun, R. 301, 302, 310
Bremmer, J. N. 49, 50
Brenner, D. A. 127, 141
Brett, M. G. 144, 151, 154
Briggs, C. A. 58, 67
Briggs, E. G. 58, 67
Bromiley, G. W. 154, 218, 223, 231

Brooke, G. J. 6, 249–51, 254, 261–64
Brookins, T. A. 273, 277
Broshi, B. 144, 154
Brown, D. 45, 51
Brown, S. K. 207, 212
Browne, G. 210, 212
Brownson, C. L. 27, 39
Brucker, R. 284, 296
Brueggemann, W. 144, 154
Bubelis, W. 34, 39
Buchanan, E. S. 192, 212
Büchner, D. ix, 2, 3, 22, 23, 39, 54, 68, 312
Bultmann, C. 144, 145, 154
Burke, T. J. 270, 272, 277
Burtt, J. O. 51
Byrskog, S. 198, 215

Cadell, H. 135, 140
Calaway, J. C. 279, 294
Calhoun, R. M. 202, 212
Campbell, D. A. 84, 88
Capone, A. 301, 310
Carroll, J. T. 270, 277
Carson, D. A. 2, 214, 231, 255, 263, 267, 278
Carter, W. 256, 264
Catchpole, D. R. 241, 247
Cazelles, H. 106, 119
Chaniotis, A. 238, 240, 247
Chapa, J. 200, 215
Chazon, E. G. 166, 172, 251, 263, 265
Cherniss, H. 107, 120
Childers, J. W. 193, 212
Chirat, H. 307, 310
Chong, J. H. 143, 154
Chrubasik, B. 237, 247
Clements, R. 251, 261, 263
Coggins, R. J. 46, 47, 50
Cohen, S. J. D. 144, 154
Cole, R. A. 219, 221, 231
Collart, P. 206, 212
Collins, A. Y. 239, 247, 256, 264
Collins, J. J. 164, 172, 176, 185, 234, 239, 247
Collins, N. L. 47, 50
Colomo, D. 200, 215
Colson, F. H. 68
Cook, J. 50, 295, 311, 313
Corley, J. 175, 178, 185
Cosgrove, C. H. 270, 277

Cousland, J. R. C. 175–77, 184, 185
Cox, C. E. 17, 19, 61, 67, 313
Cross, F. M. 15, 16, 20, 224, 231
Croy, C. N. 176, 179, 187
Curtis, E. L. 151, 154

Daniel, R. W. 192, 205, 212, 213
Daniel, S. 118, 119
Daniélou, J. 301, 310
Davies, G. I. 97, 102, 256
Davies, J. 236, 247
de Bruyn, T. 199, 202, 204, 205, 208, 209, 212
Deist, F. E. 16, 20
Delitzsch, F. 62, 68, 196
Dell'Acqua, A. P. 48, 135, 140
Derow, P. 27, 39, 115, 116, 119
DeSilva, D. A. 282, 295
Deutsch, R. R. 46, 51
Dillard, R. B. 151, 154
Dimant, D. 251, 263
Dines, J. M. 42, 43, 47, 48, 50, 124, 140, 175, 185
Dodd, C. H. 218, 231
Doering, L. 244, 245, 247, 292, 295
Dogniez, C. 122, 124, 129, 132, 140
Dohmen, C. 286, 295
Doodle, J. A. 255–57, 264
Dorival, G. 123, 135, 140
Dozeman, T. 267, 277, 279, 297
Drescher, J. 211, 212
Driesbach, J. K. 15, 20
Driver, S. R. 130, 140
Du Cange, D. 307, 310
Dyck, J. E. 151, 154
Dyer, B. R. 179, 185

Eberhart, C. 284, 292, 295, 296
Eckstein, H. J. 244, 247
Ederer, M. 186
Edgar, C. C. 29, 39
Edwards, J. R. 221, 231
Egger-Wenzel, R. 175, 185
Ehrman, B. 197, 198, 201, 212, 213
Ehorn, Seth M. 217, 221, 225, 231, 267, 269, 277, 278
Eisele, W. 287, 295
Elgvin, T. 166, 172
Ellis, E. E. 258, 264
Emmet, C. W. 175, 178, 185

Epp, Eldon J. 12, 20
Erder, Y. 167, 172
Erskine, A. 49, 50, 239, 247
Estelle, B. D. 267, 277
Evans, C. F. 11, 21, 105, 119
Evans, C. A. vii, x, 2, 5, 189, 212, 252, 264, 267, 277, 279, 297
Evans, T. V. 97, 101
Eynikel, E. 79, 88

Falk, D. K. 163, 166, 172, 261, 263
Fassa, E. 32, 33, 39
Fauseet, A. R. 51
Fernández Marcos, N. 92, 93, 101, 102
Flashar, M. 60, 61, 67
Flint, P. ix, 163, 167, 172, 173
Flotow, L. 91, 102
Fohrer, G. 16, 21
Forbes, A. D. 226, 231
Fowl, S. 270, 277
Fowler, H. N. 79, 88
Fox, M. V. 17, 18, 20, 125, 141
Fraenkel, D. 204, 206, 214
Frankel, Z. 105, 119, 123, 140
Freedman, D. N. 87, 154, 155, 313
Fresch, C. J. 17, 20
Freund, R. A. 252, 264
Friedman, R. E. 254, 264
Friedrich, G. 223, 231
Futato, M. D. 51

Gäbel, G. 279, 283, 284, 287–90, 293, 295
Gagos, T. 33, 39
Gaiser, F. J. 222, 231
Gamble, H. Y. 256, 264
Gardner, A. E. 175, 185
Gasparini, V. 32, 39
Gaventa, B. R. 270, 277
Geiger, A. 25, 39, 105, 119
Gerstenberger, E. 37, 39
Geyser-Fouché, A. 164, 172
Gheorghita, R. 291, 295
Glare, P. G. W. 307, 310
Glenny, W. E. 17, 20, 42, 51
Glück, A. 310
Gnilka, J. 199, 212
Godley, A. D. 87
Golubcova, E. S. 106, 120
Gorea, M. 17, 20
Grässer, E. 280, 281, 283, 292, 295

Green, D. E. 154
Greeven, H. 197, 213
Grenfell, B. 206, 213
Griesbach, J. J. 196, 213, 214
Griffith, F. L. 210, 211, 213
Gronewald, M. 55, 67
Gryson, R. 303, 309
Gschnitzer, F. 106, 107, 114, 119
Guelich, R. A. 199, 213, 221, 222, 231
Gupta, N. K. 266, 271, 277
Güting, E. 197, 213
Gwilliam, G. H. 193, 214

Ha, K. T. 144, 154
Habicht, C. 88
Hacham, N. 176, 177, 185
Hadas, M. 175, 176, 179, 185
Hallett, T. J. 51
Harlé, P. 23, 25, 39
Harrington, D. J. 251, 256, 264, 306, 310
Harrison, R. K. 45, 51
Hartenstein, F. 292, 295
Haslam, S. A. 177, 178, 186
Hauspie, K. 79, 88
Head, P. M. 198, 201, 213
Helmbold, W. C. 107, 120
Hendel, R. S. 16, 20
Hengel, M. 279, 296
Henten, J. W. 174, 186
Henze, M. 284, 296
Herrmann, J. 121, 139
Hertog, C. G. 122, 123, 126, 129, 134, 137, 140
Heyvaert, S. 95, 102
Hiebert, R. J. V. xi, 1–4, 71, 98, 100, 102, 312, 314
Hilberg, I. 303, 310
Himbaza, I. 134, 137, 140
Hinge, G. 49, 51
Hodgson, R. 273, 277
Hofius, O. 285, 295
Hogg, M. A. 177, 186
den Hollander, A. 262, 263
Holmes, M. W. 197, 213
Honigman, S. 184, 186
Hooker, M. D. 221, 222, 224, 231
Hopkinson, N. 110, 120
Horbury, W. 269, 277
Horner, G. W. 194, 213
Hort, F. J. A. 196, 197

Hossfeld, F. L. 54, 68
Houtman, C. 106, 117, 119
Howard, G. E. 41, 42, 51
Hubbard, D. A. 47, 51
Hubbard, R. L. 45, 51
Hunt, A. S. 29, 39, 202, 206, 213
Hurst, D. 308, 310

Ilan, T. 204, 206, 213

Jamieson, R. 45, 51
Japhet, S. 151, 154
Jassen, A. P. 258, 260, 261, 264
Jellicoe, S. 12, 20
Johnson, E. E. 267, 270, 277
Johnson, F. 225, 231
Jones, B. C. 199–205, 212, 213
Jones, R. N. 83, 84
Jongkind, D. 197, 213
Joosten, J. 67, 100, 102, 105–107, 113, 114, 115, 118, 119, 284, 296
Jouguet, P. 30, 39

Kalleres, D. S. 202, 214
Kamenszain, T. 91, 102
Karrer, M. 123, 135, 140, 141, 185, 280, 281, 283, 291, 292, 295, 296
Kasser, R. 68
Keel, O. 46, 51
Keesmaat, S. C. 267, 269, 274, 277
Keil, C. F. 62, 68
Kim, H. 121, 122, 124, 140
Kiraz, G. A. 193, 212
Kittel, G. 223, 231
Kittel, R. 16, 20
Klawans, J. 279, 295
Klein, R. W. 16, 20
Knibb, M. A. 42, 50
Knoppers, G. N. 18, 20
Koehler, L. 120, 231
Köhlmoos, M. 18, 20
Korytko, J. xi, 2, 4, 37, 39, 76, 77, 87, 102, 106, 117, 118, 120
Kosmin, P. J. 239, 247
Kotzé, G. 18, 20, 311
Kraft, R. A. 251, 264
Krasilnikoff, J. A. 49, 51
Kraus, H. J. 58, 60, 61, 64, 66, 68
Kraus, T. J. 205, 215

Kraus, W. xi, 105, 119, 185, 281, 282, 284, 291, 292, 294–96, 314
Krauss, S. 144, 154
Krebs, F. 204, 213
Kreuzer, S. 123, 127, 140, 141, 281, 295, 296, 312, 314
Kübler, B. 292, 296
Kümmel, W. 255, 264

La'da, C. A. 203, 213
Labahn, M. 123, 126, 129, 134, 137, 140
Lachmann, K. 196, 213
Landmesser, C. 247
Lane, W. L. 221, 231
Lane-Mercier, G. 218, 231
Lange, A. 12, 16, 19–21, 160, 172, 251, 263, 312
Langlois, M. 16, 21, 125, 127, 140–42
Le Boulluec, A. 105, 106, 120, 134, 136, 137, 140
Le Donne, A. 241, 247
Lechner-Schmidt, W. 301, 310
Lee, J. A. L. 53, 57, 68, 74, 88, 96, 102, 117, 120, 122, 140, 313
Leese, J. J. J. 199, 214
Lefebvre, M. G. 207, 213
Lemmelijn, B. 18, 20, 50, 95, 102, 311, 314
Leonardi, G. 299, 310
Lesch, J. P. 123, 140
Levine Gera, D. 98, 102
Levinson, B. M. 130, 141
Levison, J. R. 260, 264
Lewis, N. 31, 39
Lichtenberger, H. 247
Limongi, D. 204, 214
Löhr, H. 279, 296
Lohr, J. N. 267, 297
Longenecker, R. N. 273, 278
Luijendijk, A. 202, 214
Lust, J. 17, 79, 88, 124
Lustig, C. 279, 289, 296

Ma, J. 235, 236–41, 247, 248
Machiela, D. A. 261, 264
Maehler, H. 30, 39
Malherbe, A. J. 269, 270, 278
Maloney, L. M. 54, 68
Mambelli, A. 298–300, 310
Mandēlaras, V. G. 135, 140
Marcus, J. 224, 231, 246, 248

Marcus, R. 67
Martínez, F. G. 50, 124, 140, 244, 247
Mason, E. F. 261, 263
Maurais, J. xi, 2, 4, 123, 125, 141
Mauser, U. W. 228, 231
Maxey, J. 238, 248
Mayo, T. 111, 120
McCarthy, C. 126, 128–30, 133, 136, 141
McNeel, J. H. 270, 278
Meek, T. 143, 154
Meier, J. P. 243, 248
Meiser, M. 105, 119, 185, 295, 312, 314
Mendenhall, G. E. 264
Menken, M. J. J. 253, 264
Messing, G. M. 80, 88
Metzger, B. M. 197, 214
Meyer, M. W. 208, 210, 214
Milgrom, J. 25, 26, 29, 36–39, 154
Mill, J. 196, 214
Millard, A. 19, 21
Miller, P. D. 252, 264
Milligan, G. 68
Mirecki, P. 199, 210, 214
Modrzejewski, J. M. 77, 135, 141
Moffitt, D. M. 279, 296
Moo, D. J. 296, 278
Morales, R. J. 267, 278
Moreschini, C. 301, 302, 310
Morin, G. 309
Motyer, J. A. 45, 46, 51
Moulton J. H. 68
Moyise, S. 221, 222, 231, 253, 264
Munnich, O. 62, 68, 123, 135, 140
Muraoka, T. 26, 39, 62, 122, 139, 165, 172
Murray, A. T. 85, 87

Nail, T. 243, 244, 248
Najman, H. 6, 249, 250, 264
Naldini, M. 203, 214
Newman, J. H. 175, 180, 186
Newsom, C. A. 165, 166, 172
Nickelsburg, G. W. E. 251, 264
Nicklas, T. 205, 215
Norlin, G. 84, 87
Notley, R. S. 86, 88

O'Connell, K. G. 102, 120
O'Connor, M. P. 43, 50, 51, 81, 88
O'Neill, E. 50
Oakes, P. 254, 264

Oates, W. J. 50
Ogden, G. S. 46, 47, 51
Olofsson, S. 47, 51
Oswald, H. C. 58, 68, 279
Oswalt, J. N. 45, 51, 220, 231
Otto, E. 130, 132, 134, 141

Palmer, C. 143, 154
Papathomas, A. 203, 213
Parker, D. 196, 214
Paton, W. R. 88
Pavlovskaja, A. L. 106, 120
Pearce, S. 175, 185
Perkins, L. J. 1, 7, 13, 22, 24, 41, 52, 71, 89, 95, 98, 100, 102–104, 121, 124, 135, 141, 143, 159, 174, 189, 214, 249, 266, 279, 285, 288, 300, 310, 311–29
Perrin, A. B. 163, 172, 261, 263
Parry, D. W. 15, 20
Peters, M. K. H. 51, 67, 122, 141
Petersen, A. K. 251, 264
Piégay-Gros, N. 218, 231
Pierpont, W. G. 197, 214
Pietersma, A. xi, xii, 2, 3, 23, 39, 51, 52, 68, 89, 95, 101–103, 122, 141, 175, 185, 226, 231, 267, 278, 311, 313
Pillinger, R. J. 251, 263
Pintaudi, R. 203, 214
Pleyte, W. 208, 214
Pola, T. 123, 126, 129, 134, 137, 140
Porter, S. E. 2, 176, 186, 196, 214
Portier-Young, A. E. 243, 248
Potter, R. 50
Pralon, D. 23, 25, 39
Preisendanz, K. 75, 88, 203, 205, 214
Prior, D. 46, 47, 51
Propp, W. H. C. 105, 120, 165, 172
Pusey, P. E. 193, 214

Quast, U. 226, 232, 306, 310

Ra, D. K. 143, 154
Rahlfs, A. 68, 102, 204, 206, 214
Rainey, A. F. 86, 88
Rajak, T. 175, 185
Ramírez Kidd, J. E. 145–47, 154
Raup Johnson, S. 176, 186
Rebenich, S. 176, 186
Renberg, G. 32–34, 39
Rendtorff, R. 144, 148, 151, 154

Rey, J. S. 244, 248
Ringgren, H. 154
Robinson, M. A. 197, 214
Robker, J. M. 281, 294, 295, 296
Rösel, M. 25, 40, 54, 68, 93, 101, 103, 121, 123, 141, 284, 292, 296, 313
Runge, S. E. 2, 96, 103, 182, 186

Sailhamer, J. H. 68
Saley, R. 15, 20
Sanders, E. P. 253, 265
Sanders, J. A. 252, 264
Sandevoir, P. 105, 106, 120, 134, 136, 137, 140
Sanzo, J. E. 199–206, 208–11, 214
Sarna, N. M. 145, 154
Sarton, G. 49, 51
Sayce, A. H. 210, 214
Schäfer, R. 18, 21
Schaper, J. 135, 141
Scharbert, J. 296
Scheck, T. P. 308, 310
Schenck, K. L. 279, 296
Schenker, A. 292, 296
Schierse, F. J. 281, 292, 296
Schiffman, L. H. 166, 172, 251, 264
Schiødt, S. 84, 88
Schmid, U. 262, 263
Schmidt, C. 204, 215
Schmitz, B. 184, 186
Schofield, A. 263
Scholl, R. 115, 116, 120
Scholz, J. M. A. 196, 214
Schröger, F. 286, 287, 289, 296
Schubart, W. 204, 215
Schuller, E. 166, 172, 261, 265
Schulz-Flügel, E. 306, 310
Schunack, G. 280, 297
Schwagmeier, P. 127, 141
Schwartz, D. R. 175, 186, 261, 263
Schwemer, A. M. 279, 296
Schweppenhäuser, H. 92, 96, 102
Scialabba, D. xii, 6, 298–300, 310
Scott, J. M. 6, 233, 239, 248, 271, 272, 278
Segal, M. 127, 141
Sellin, E. 16, 21
Shogren, G. S. 267, 278
Sigismund, M. 281, 295, 296, 312
Sim, D. C. 256, 265
Smelik, W. 262, 263

Smith, D. L. 267, 278
Smith, G. S. 200, 202, 215
Smith, J. 54, 68
Smith, R. L. 152, 154
Smith, R. 208, 214
Smyth, H. W. 24, 80, 88, 95, 96, 103
Sommella, V. 90–92, 94–96, 99, 101, 102
Sommerstein, A. H. 85, 87
Spencer, J. R. 59, 67, 143, 144, 154
Spicq, C. 222, 232
Stanley, C. D. 218, 232, 267, 277
Stead, M. R. 50, 51
Steck, O. H. 272, 278
Stegemann, H. 166, 172
Steiner, D. 110, 120
Stipp, H.J. 295
Stratton, K. B. 202, 214
Straus, J. A. 77, 88, 115, 120
Strauss, M. L. 221, 225, 232
Stuckenbruck, L. T. 244, 248
Suhl, A. 201, 215
Sundberg, A. C. 225, 232
Szirmai, J. A. 208, 215

Tait, M. 254, 264
Talmon, S. 11, 12, 16, 20, 21
Talshir, Z. 18, 21
Tate, M. E. 58–60, 64, 68
Taylor, B. A. 76, 88, 93, 102, 118, 120, 123, 142
Testuz, M. 68
Thackeray, H. St. J. 57, 68
Theocharous, M. 123, 124, 139, 141
Thiessen, M. 144, 154
Thomas, S. I. 263
Thompson, J. A. 151, 154
Thompson, W. G. 256
Tiedemann, R. 92, 96, 102
Tigay, J. H. 125, 141, 145, 155
Tindale, S. 177, 186
Tischendorf, C. 196, 214, 215
Tooman, W. A. 17, 21
Tov, E. xii, 2, 3, 11–13, 15–21, 94, 99, 100, 103, 115, 121, 125, 127, 129, 131, 137, 139, 141, 142, 164, 166, 173, 274, 278, 312
Trapp, T. H. 45, 51
Tregelles, S. P. 196, 215
Tromp, J. M. 176, 186
Tuckett, C. M. 176, 186

Turaev, B. A. 211, 215
Turner, C. H. 192, 215

Ueberschaer, F. 281, 294–96, 312
Ulrich, E. 15, 20, 205, 215, 228, 231, 263
Utzschneider, H. 279, 293, 297

Vahrenhorst, M. 23–26, 40
van der Louw, T. A. W. 89, 90, 95, 102, 122, 142
van der Meer, M. N. 47, 50, 105, 119, 314
van Houten, C. 144, 145, 155
van Minnen, P. 84, 88
van Peursen, W. T. 122, 139
VanderKam, J. C. 167, 173, 251, 263, 264
Venuti, L. 90, 94, 102
Vergote, J. 84, 85, 88
Verhoef, P. A. 152, 155
Vermes, G. 105, 120, 251, 264, 265
Vervenne, M. 50, 124, 140
Veymiers, R. 32, 39
Vierros, M. 84, 88
Vink, J. G. 144, 155
Vitelli, G. 203, 215

Wade, M. L. 95, 103
Wagner, S. 286, 297
Wagner, T. 281, 294–96
Walbank, F. W. 88
Walsh, P. G. 308, 310
Walter, N. 284, 297
Waltke, B. K. 43, 50, 51, 81, 88, 146, 148, 155
Walton, F. R. 87
Wasserman, T. 197–99, 201, 202, 205, 212, 215
Watts, J. D. 51
Watts, R. E. 220, 227, 232
Waubke, H. G. 247, 292, 295
Weber, R. 192, 213, 303, 309
Weigold, M. 160, 172
Weima, J. A. D. 267, 270, 272–76, 278
Weingreen, J. 25, 40
Weiser, A. 58, 60, 61, 68
Weiss, H. F. 253, 265, 280, 281, 289–91, 297
Weitenauer, I. 307, 310

Wenham, G. J. 81, 84, 85, 88, 146, 155
Wenin, A. 292, 296
Wessely, C. 203–205, 215
West, M. L. 57, 58, 68
Westcott, B. F. 196, 197, 215
Westermann, W. L. 106, 107, 112, 114, 115, 118, 120
Westfall, D. M. 267–69, 278
Wevers, J. W. ix–xii, 1, 2, 23–26, 40, 78, 79, 81, 86, 88, 95, 97, 98, 103, 121, 123, 125–31, 133–36, 142, 201, 215, 226, 232, 313
Whitaker, G. H. 68
White, J. 31, 34, 40
White, J. 193, 194, 215
Wierzbicka, A. 230, 232
Wildberger, H. 45, 46, 51
Wilk, F. 247, 284, 292, 295, 297
Wilken, U. 205, 215
Wilkes, J. 236, 247
Williams, D. S. 176, 186
Williams, J. J. 174, 186
Williams, M. J. 125, 141
Williamson, H. G. M. 151, 155, 255, 263
Willis, J. T. 154
Wilson, A. I. 261, 265
Wilson, T. A. 268, 278
Wisemen, D. J. 51
Witmer, S. E. 274, 278
Works, C. S. 267, 278
Woudstra, M. H. 147
Wright, B. G. xii, 23, 39, 51, 75–77, 88, 89, 90, 95, 101–103, 118, 120, 122, 141, 175, 185, 226, 231, 267, 278, 311
Wright, C. J. H. 150, 155
Wright, C. 94, 103
Wyatt, W. F. 85, 87

Yardney, S. 122, 142

Zahn, M. M. 127, 142
Zenger, E. 54, 68
Zetterhold, M. 198, 215
Ziegler, J. 226, 232
Ziemer, B. 16, 21, 125, 142
Zsengellér, J. 251, 264

www.ingramcontent.com/pod-product-compliance
Lightning Source LLC
Chambersburg PA
CBHW071226230426
43668CB00011B/1318